THE LETTERS OF
WILLIAM AND DOROTHY
WORDSWORTH

VI. *THE LATER YEARS*

PART III
1835—1839

WORDSWORTH

from the wax medallion by Edward William Wyon, 1835

THE LETTERS OF WILLIAM AND DOROTHY WORDSWORTH

SECOND EDITION

VI

The Later Years

PART III

1835—1839

REVISED, ARRANGED,
AND EDITED BY

ALAN G. HILL

FROM THE FIRST EDITION
EDITED BY THE LATE
ERNEST DE SELINCOURT

CLARENDON PRESS. OXFORD

1982

Oxford University Press, Walton Street, Oxford OX2 6DP

London Glasgow New York Toronto
Delhi Bombay Calcutta Madras Karachi
Kuala Lumpur Singapore Hong Kong Tokyo
Nairobi Dar es Salaam Cape Town
Melbourne Auckland

and associate companies in
Beirut Berlin Ibadan Mexico City

Published in the United States by
Oxford University Press, New York

British Library Cataloguing in Publication Data

Wordsworth, William, 1770–1850
The letters of William and Dorothy Wordsworth.
—2nd ed.
6: The later years. Part 3: 1835–1839
1. Wordsworth, William, 1770–1850—Biography
2. Poets, English—19th century—Correspondence
3. Wordsworth, Dorothy—Biography
4. Authors, English—19th century—Correspondence
I. Title II. Wordsworth, Dorothy
III. De Selincourt, Ernest IV. Hill, Alan G.
821'.7 PR5881

ISBN 0–19–812483–X

Library of Congress Cataloging in Publication Data

Wordsworth, William, 1770–1850.
The letters of William and Dorothy Wordsworth

CONTENTS: 1. The early years, 1787–1805, revised
by Chester L. Shaver.—2. The middle years: pt. I
1806–1811, revised by Mary Moorman.—[etc.]—
6. The later years: pt. 3. 1835–1839, revised,
arranged, and edited by Alan G. Hill.
1. Wordsworth, William, 1770–1850—Correspondence.
2. Wordsworth, Dorothy, 1771–1855—Correspondence.
3. Poets, English—19th century—Correspondence.
I. Wordsworth, Dorothy, 1771–1855. II. De Selincourt, Ernest, 1870–1943, ed. III. Shaver,
Chester L. IV. Title.
PR5881. A48 1967   821'.7   67–89058   AACR1

Typeset by Macmillan India Ltd., Bangalore
and printed in Great Britain
at the University Press, Oxford
by Eric Buckley
Printer to the University

CONTENTS

LIST OF ILLUSTRATIONS

ABBREVIATIONS

PERSONAL INITIALS

W. W., D. W., M. W., R. W., C. W.: William, Dorothy, Mary, Richard, and Christopher Wordsworth.

S. H.: Sara Hutchinson. E. Q.: Edward Quillinan. S. T. C.: Samuel Taylor Coleridge. C. C.: Catherine Clarkson. H. C. R.: Henry Crabb Robinson. I. F.: Isabella Fenwick.

SOURCES

Broughton	*Some Letters of the Wordsworth Family*, edited by L. N. Broughton, Cornell University Press, 1942.
Cornell	Department of Rare Books, Cornell University Library, Ithaca, N.Y.
Cottle	*Early Recollections, chiefly relating to the Life of S. T. Coleridge*, by Joseph Cottle, 2 vols., 1837.
Curry	*New Letters of Robert Southey*, edited by Kenneth Curry, 2 vols., Columbia University Press, 1965.
DWJ	*The Journals of Dorothy Wordsworth*, edited by Ernest de Selincourt, 2 vols., 1941.
EY	*The Letters of William and Dorothy Wordsworth*, edited by the late Ernest de Selincourt, second edition, I, *The Early Years*, 1787–1805, revised by Chester L. Shaver, Oxford, 1967.
Griggs	*Collected Letters of Samuel Taylor Coleridge*, edited by Earl Leslie Griggs, 6 vols., Oxford, 1956–71.
Grosart	*The Prose Works of William Wordsworth*, edited by Alexander B. Grosart, 3 vols., 1876.
Hamilton	*The Life of Sir William Rowan Hamilton*, by R. P. Graves, 3 vols., 1882–9.
Haydon	*Correspondence and Table Talk of Benjamin Robert Haydon*, edited by his son, F. W. Haydon, 1876.
HCR	*Henry Crabb Robinson on Books and their Writers*, edited by Edith J. Morley, 3 vols., 1938.
Jordan	*De Quincey to Wordsworth, a Biography of a Relationship*, by J. E. Jordan, 1962.
K	*Letters of the Wordsworth Family*, edited by William Knight, 3 vols., 1907.

Lamb	*The Letters of Charles and Mary Lamb*, edited by E. V. Lucas, 3 vols., 1935.
LY	*The Letters of William and Dorothy Wordsworth, The Later Years*, edited by Ernest de Selincourt, 3 vols., Oxford, 1939.
Mem.	*Memoirs of William Wordsworth*, by Christopher Wordsworth, 2 vols., 1851.
MLN	*Modern Language Notes.*
MLR	*Modern Language Review.*
Moorman i, ii	*William Wordsworth, A Biography*, i, *The Early Years*, ii, *The Later Years*, by Mary Moorman, Oxford, 1957 and 1965.
Morley	*Correspondence of Henry Crabb Robinson with the Wordsworth Circle*, edited by Edith J. Morley, 2 vols., Oxford, 1927.
MP	*Modern Philology.*
MW	*The Letters of Mary Wordsworth*, edited by Mary E. Burton, Oxford, 1958.
MY	*The Letters of William and Dorothy Wordsworth*, edited by the late Ernest de Selincourt, second edition, II: *The Middle Years*: Part I, 1806–11, revised by Mary Moorman, Part II, 1812–20, revised by Mary Moorman and Alan G. Hill, Oxford, 1969–70.
NQ	*Notes and Queries.*
Pearson	*Papers, Letters and Journals of William Pearson*, edited by his widow. Printed for private circulation, 1863.
PMLA	*Publications of the Modern Language Association of America.*
Prel.	*Wordsworth's Prelude* edited by Ernest de Selincourt: second edition, revised by Helen Darbishire, Oxford, 1959.
Prose Works	*The Prose Works of William Wordsworth*, edited by W. J. B. Owen and Jane Worthington Smyser, 3 vols., Oxford, 1974.
PW	*The Poetical Works of William Wordsworth*, edited by Ernest de Selincourt and Helen Darbishire, 5 vols., Oxford, 1940–9, and revised issues, 1952–9.
RES	*The Review of English Studies.*
R.M. Cat.	*Catalogue of the Varied and Valuable Historical, Poetical, Theological, and Miscellaneous Library of the late*

Abbreviations

	venerated Poet-Laureate, William Wordsworth . . . Preston, 1859; reprinted in *Transactions of the Wordsworth Society*, Edinburgh, [1882−7].
RMVB	*Rydal Mount Visitors Book*, Wordsworth Library, Grasmere.
Rogers	*Rogers and his Contemporaries*, edited by P. W. Clayden, 2 vols., 1889.
Sadler	*Diary, Reminiscences and Correspondence of Henry Crabb Robinson*, edited by Thomas Sadler, 3 vols., 1869.
SH	*The Letters of Sara Hutchinson*, edited by Kathleen Coburn, 1954.
Southey	*Life and Correspondence of Robert Southey*, edited by C. C. Southey, 6 vols., 1849−50.
TLS	*Times Literary Supplement*.
Warter	*A Selection from the Letters of Robert Southey*, edited by John Wood Warter, 4 vols., 1856.
WL	The Wordsworth Library, Grasmere.

LIST OF LETTERS

PART VI

1835

List of Letters

xiii

List of Letters

List of Letters

List of Letters

xvii

List of Letters

List of Letters

List of Letters

856. W. W. to BASIL MONTAGU

Address: Basil Montagu Esqre, Lincoln's Inn, London.
Postmark: 3 Jan. 1835. *Stamp*: Kendal Penny Post.
MS. *Harvard University Library.*
LY ii. 720.

[*In M. W.'s hand*]

Rydal Mount
Jan^{ry} 1st 1835

My dear Montagu,

Your sheets have been read with much pleasure—they begin at the first chapter and end at page 336—inclusive—the Title page etc. and the remaining sheets being wanting. If you forward what you kindly design for me to Longman's it will reach me free of expence either to yourself or me—as I shall have two parcels coming down in succession—but send it as soon as you can, and I may perhaps have it by the former. I congratulate you sincerely on bringing to a close this important and laborious work.[1]

The baser part and it is to be feared much the larger of the Whigs having made common cause with the Enemies of the British Constitution, I concur with you that the prospect of the Gover^{nt}[2] and the Nation is indeed a sad one—All this was distinctly foreseen by the Internal part of the Community from the first broaching of the Reform bill. Good and discreet men must act cleaving to the Roman virtue of never despairing of the Country—this they must do for Conscience sake, whatever come of it.

Ever faithfully yours,
[*signed*] W Wordsworth

---

[1] Montagu's edition of Bacon. See also pt. ii, L. 846.

[2] The new Tory government under Sir Robert Peel, who was now preparing to fight a general election to gain a majority in Parliament. See Ls. 860 and 861 below.

857. W. W. to THOMAS NOON TALFOURD

Address: Sergeant Talfourd, Temple, London.
Postmark: 3 Jan. [?1835]. *Stamp*: Kendal Penny Post.
MS. Berg Collection, New York Public Library.
K (—). *LY ii. 720* (—).

[*In M. W.'s hand*]

Rydal Mount Jan^{ry} 1st, 1835

My dear Sir,

Your letter brought a great shock to us all. I had not heard from yourself when you were here that any thing was threatening Lamb's health, and Miss Hutchinson who saw him late in the Spring reported that he was looking wonderfully well, and appeared in excellent Spirits. He has followed poor Coleridge within six months.[1] It seems to us upon reflection that his Sister will bear the loss of him better than he could have borne that of her; and we are bound to believe so, as it has pleased God to take him first. There seems to be, with respect to his dear Sister, from your account, enough to provide her with all comforts which her melancholy situation will admit of— Should it however not be so, there can be no doubt that Lamb's surviving friends will be too happy to contribute whatever might be desired. I need scarcely have mentioned this, because L. tho' exceedingly generous, and charitable above measure— was also prudent and thoughtful. Do let us hear from you again on the subject by and bye; for our minds and hearts are full of the sad Event, and one cannot but be very anxious to know the state of poor Miss Lamb's mind—after she has been more tried by the loss she has sustained.

Since you left us my Sister has had a severe attack of bilious fever, which confined her to her bed for three weeks—She is recovering, but slowly, being not yet able to walk.

The complaint under which my Daughter was suffering while you were here[2] proved to be an affection of the Spine— and she has been nearly 10 weeks under a course of bleeding and

---

[1] Thomas Noon Talfourd (see pt. i, L. 4) had written on 29 Dec. 1834 to announce the death of Charles Lamb at Edmonton two days before after a fall in the street (*WL MSS.*). As Lamb's literary executor, he was now proceeding to settle his affairs. H. C. R. gives an affecting account of Mary Lamb at this time, *HCR* ii. 454–6.

[2] Talfourd called the previous September (*RMVB*).

2

blistering, and confined in a great measure to the Sofa. We hope that She may have strength of Constitution (having naturally an excellent one) to carry her thro' this painful and tedious complaint.

My little Vol.[1] is printed off all but the last sheet—A Copy will be sent to you and the one designed for our dear departed friend may go to Moxon's to be delivered by Mrs M. to Miss Lamb whenever it shall be thought proper. Upon most carefully reviewing all that concerned the political Poem,[2] which you and I agreed had better be withheld, I determined to publish it. I felt it due to myself to give this warning to my Countrymen, at this awful Crisis—utterly useless it may prove, but I should have suspected myself of cowardice or selfish caution, if I had suppressed what I had thought and felt, upon that momentous change. The Reform bill I have ever deemed from the night on which Ld J Russel brought forth his motion,[3] an unwise measure, which could not be carried but by unworthy means. We are now about to gather the fruits of it in sorrow and vain repentance. For Heaven's sake, whatever influence you have, let it be put forth to baffle the mad projects of those Whigs and Radicals who have now made common cause—to baffle I have [   ][4] that it is feared is impossible, for at [   ] your own conscience's sake [do] what you can.

The matter to which you direct my attention at the close of your letter,[5] presses closely on my mind—I should decide at once to do what you recommend, but there are many considerations that make me doubt and cause me a good deal of uneasiness—but you will hear again from me upon this subject, as I shall decide in a few days.

[1] The *Yarrow Revisited* volume.
[2] Probably *The Warning* (see pt. ii, L. 753).
[3] Lord John Russell's motion 'that the present state of representation of the people in Parliament requires the most serious consideration of the House' was brought forward on 25 Apr. 1822.
[4] *MS. torn.*
[5] Talfourd had written, 'May I be permitted to express my hope that you will not omit the opportunity afforded by the present political state of things to effect the arrangement you desire as to your office? I the rather urge it, as I think the continuance of the Ministry very uncertain, and you may not choose to receive even so trifling a favour from the *next* Administration.'

I cannot conclude without thanking you for your renewed invitation—be assured it will not be forgotten.

With every good wish which in old times might have been offered with more confidence than [at] present, to yourself and yours in which my family join, I remain my dear Sir

Your sincere friend
[*signed*] Wm Wordsworth

858. W. W. to MESSRS. LONGMAN AND CO.

Address: To Messrs. Longman, Pater noster Row.
Franked: Penrith January four 1835 Lowther.
Postmark: (1) 4 Jan. 1835 (2) 6 Jan. 1835.
Stamp: Penrith.
MS. Columbia University Library. Hitherto unpublished.

Jan^{ry} 4th 1835
Lowther Castle near Penrith

Dear Sirs,

If the sheets of my Volume[1] have not been sent off, as desired, pray let them be forwarded under cover to Lord Viscount Lowther, Lowther, Penrith, but not more than 50 pages under one cover—The Letter sent some time since mentioned, up to what page the Sheets had been received—I hope it has not been mislaid; but to the best of my recollection the last sheet received, closed with a Sonnet, beginning, On to Iona—[2]

I remain dear Sirs
faithfully yours
Wm Wordsworth

[1] *Yarrow Revisited, and Other Poems.*
[2] See *PW* iv. 42.

859. W. W. to HENRY TAYLOR

Address: H. Taylor Esqre.
MS. Bodleian Library.
K (—). LY ii. 721.

[*In M. W.'s hand*]

Rydal Mount, Jan^ry 6th. [? 1835]

My dear Sir,

Thank you for the King's Speech, which I have not yet read, having been employed all the morning in writing letters. Political knowledge is at a low ebb in the village of Rydal, nor will you think much of its political Sagacity when I tell you that a leading man among our humbler yeomanry refused to sign the Laity's declaration of attachment to the Church 'because the list of signatures would be sent up to London there to be kept in a safe place, till the Dissenters and Papists had got the uppermost, which they would soon do, and then, with the list in their hands, they would come and cut off the heads of all who had signed it' And, would you believe it, that this Person, in the concerns of daily life, is one of the shrewdest of our little yeomen. This caution reminds me of the prospective prudence of a Gentleman of rank and large Property, who resided in our neighbourhood some years, and would never attend the Parish Church, lest he should become the unwilling eye-witness of some misconduct of the Clergyman, and be consequently called upon to give evidence against him in some of the Courts. The Clergyman was in fact a graceless [   ][1] and the discretion came from Scotland. What other country could have given birth to it?

The Doctor[2] seems to take well. I am heartily glad of it.

One of the enclosed letters I have not directed, it is merely an acknowledgement for a couple of vols received yesterday—and the like for Mr Southey—which ought to have come to hand some months ago. I cannot defer my thanks till I have an opportunity of getting a frank here. Will you therefore *at your convenience* procure one for me, and forward the note? I shall not trouble you in this way again.

---

[1] *Word missing.*

[2] The first two vols. of Southey's *The Doctor* had been published the previous year.

5

We had pleasant accounts from Keswick yesterday—including good tidings of the Bride and Bridegroom,[1] who are at present at their Father's[2] house in Shropshire. My Sister, you will be glad to hear, has been in a comfortable state since we had the pleasure of seeing you here. And my eyes are well and would be useful to me for reading and writing if I could keep my mind quiet—but the worst part of my case is that mental labour, *if persisted in*, is always injurious to them; and, unfortunately for me, if I am not *possessed* by my employment, I cannot work at all.

I hope that Mrs Taylor,[3] as also our good friend Miss Fenwick,[4] have enjoyed their health throughout the late boisterous and rainy, tho' mild season. With the united good wishes of this household, believe me to be, my dear sir, very sincerely yours,

[*signed*] Wm Wordsworth

860. W. W. to EDWARD MOXON

Address: Edward Moxon Esq., 44 Dover Street, London.
Franked: Penrith January twelve 1835 Lowther.
Postmark: (1) 12 Jan. 1835 (2) 14 Jan. 1835. *Stamp*: Penrith.
MS. Henry E. Huntington Library.
K (—). *LY ii. 722.*

Lowther Castle
near Penrith
[*c.* 11 Jan. 1835]

My dear Sir,

Your letter of the 7th followed me to this place, and I sincerely thank you for it. The distressing intelligence of our lamented Friend's death[5] had been communicated by Mr Talfourd; and the disposal of his property had been mentioned also though less in detail than by you—As far as our fallible judgements are

---

[1] Edith Southey and her husband, the Revd. J. W. Warter.

[2] Henry de Grey Warter (1770–1853), of Cruck Meole, nr. Shrewsbury.

[3] Henry Taylor's stepmother.

[4] Isabella Fenwick (see pt. ii, L. 680), now well established as a good friend of the Wordsworths.

[5] The death of Charles Lamb on 27 Dec. (see L. 857 above).

entitled to decide upon such an event there appears to be cause for congratulation that it should have pleased God to remove the Brother before the Sister—We can all under my roof sympathize with your heavy loss and Mrs Moxon's. The shock to us was great, for we were not in the least prepared for it.—It is a great consolation that Miss Lamb has so judicious a Friend to take care of her.—You allude to his Letters. I agree with you they must be valuable. Unfortunately we possess very few; much the most interesting we ever received, unaccountably disappeared within a day after its arrival, and we never could make out what became of it; which, I assure you, is a subject of mortification to which we have not infrequently recurred.—

The proof of the Title page of my Poems[1] has just reached me here, and [it][2] gives me great pleasure to see your name there. Owing to the state of the times I have been very slack and indifferent about pushing it through the Press; and I care as little about its Publication, my mind being wholly engrossed by the wretched state of public affairs.[3]—I have been in the midst of one Revolution in France, and recoil with horror from the thought of a second, at home. The Radicals and foolish Whigs are driving the nation rapidly to that point—Soon, alas! it is likely to be found that power will pass from the audacious and wicked to the more audacious and wicked, and so to the still more and more, till military despotism comes in as a quietus; and then after a time the struggle for liberty will re-commence, and you, young as you are, should your life be prolonged to the 70 years of the psalmist, will not live to see her cause crowned with success.

Farewell—give my kindest regards to Mrs Moxon and believe me ever faithfully your much obliged friend

W Wordsworth

Mrs Moxon will be so kind as to paste the under written in a copy of my Poems which I shall order to be sent to her—Should you ever have a parcel of any kind to send me, pray enclose a Copy of Southey, Selections.[4] The 2nd Edition of my

---

[1] *Yarrow Revisited, and Other poems*, 1835.

[2] *Word dropped out.*

[3] W. W. was now at Lowther for the election campaign (see L. 856 above and next letters).

[4] *Selections from the Poems of Robert Southey . . . , chiefly for the use of Schools*, 1831.

Selections[1] is very neatly got up—Thank you for the Copy sent and also for the Trial of Wm Shakespear[2]—very clever.

861. W. W. to LORD LONSDALE

Address: The Earl of Lonsdale, Cottesmore, Stamford.
Postmark: 13 Jan. 1835. *Stamp*: Penrith.
MS. Lonsdale MSS. Hitherto unpublished.

Lowther Castle
Tuesday Jan[ry] 13th [1835]

My Lord,
   I have been here since Saturday before last, and should have written before had there been any particulars to mention, but such as you would hear from higher sources.

The strange and discreditable movement of Mr Wilson[3] has much strengthened our cause, both by shewing how little he could do against it, and by renewing the communication between the Members and the Constituency. Whether, if the stir in West[nd] had not been made, Major Aglionby[4] would have come forward, is uncertain; but there is some reason for believing that he, or someone else would, so that upon the whole it seems that a Contest was threatened in West[nd].

---

[1] i.e. the new edition of Hine's *Selections* (see pt. ii, L. 850).

[2] *Citation and Examination of William Shakespeare . . . touching Deer-stealing . . .* , by Walter Savage Landor, 1834.

[3] The behaviour of Col. George Wilson of Dallam Tower, whose intervention as an alternative to Lord Lowther in the Westmorland representation had been feared in previous elections (see pt. ii, L. 666), was exciting renewed comment now. Lord Lonsdale's birthday had been celebrated in Kendal on 29 Dec., and Wilson declined to attend, on the ground that the celebration had the character of a political meeting. He subsequently received an address of congratulation from 150 gentlemen of Kendal (see *Carlisle Patriot* for 2 Jan. 1835). But his efforts to undermine the two Lowther candidates were of no avail, and they were returned for Westmorland unopposed.

[4] Major Francis Aglionby (see also pt. i, L. 3) unsuccessfully contested West Cumberland for the Whigs in the by-election of 1833 and again in the General Election of 1835, but came out bottom of the poll. The sitting members, Samuel Irton (see pt. ii, L. 667) and Edward Stanley (see pt. ii, L. 700), were re-elected. Aglionby carried East Cumberland in 1837 against Sir James Graham, when the latter's desertion of the Reform Ministry made him no longer acceptable to the electors.

And now my Lord let me thank you for the kindness with which you noticed my application on behalf of my Son. At my request Dr Wordsworth mentioned his situation to Mr Goulburn,[1] who expressed much willingness to serve him, but said the patronage of the home-office was very limited, and unpromising for a person of 25 years of age, as he must begin at the bottom of the Ladder. Mr G. kindly offered to confer with Lord Lowther as to any means which might open for serving him, but, I own I have so little hope of such an event occurring, that I have turned to a thought which has frequently been in my mind, *viz* the transfer of my place as Distributor of Stamps, to my Son. Might I then request of your Lordship to interest yourself in the Matter, and to state to Sir Robert Peel that I am ready to give up the Office which I have held for nearly 22 years, in case he would have no objection to put my Son in my place; if you would be so kind as to do this with a request on my Son's behalf from your Lordship, it would be adding one more to the countless obligations which I am under to yourself and the family of Lowther. Lord Lowther has reviewed the matter with me, and I write with his sanction and entire approbation. I have also mentioned it to the Col:,[2] whose first observation was, no time must be lost, as no one can say what may become of the Ministry as soon as Parliament meets. Knowing your Lordship's ever ready inclination to meet a reasonable wish of mine, I have presumed to make this request, and to express a hope that in case the plan meet your approbation, you would extend to my Son the same support in the way of security for him, that you have done so long to myself; otherwise I fear the thing would fall to the ground. And now, my Lord, I leave the matter in your hands, with a renewal of my acknowledgements for all your kindness; and I can sincerely add that gratitude to you has been one of the happiest sensations that I have known through a large portion of my Life.—

Poor Mr Fleming,[3] as you will have heard, is no more: He was never a good Economist, so that it is to be feared that his affairs will be found embarrassed.

---

[1] Henry Goulburn, Home Secretary in Peel's first administration, and about to be re-elected for Cambridge University.

[2] Col. Lowther.

[3] John Fleming of Rayrigg had died on 11 Jan. See also L. 863 below.

I think of returning by Coach to night to Kendal and hope to be at home early to morrow

I remain my Lord ever your
much obliged Wm Wordsworth

Sir James Graham[1] appears to have been playing a slippery part upon the Hustings; and the whole country seems growing more radical. In the metropolitan Returns is exhibited the deformity of the Reform Bill, in a way which might startle the most unthinking. During the French Revolution as it advanced, the most atrocious characters were sent to the Legislature from Paris.

Pray offer my kindest remembrances to Lady Lonsdale.

862. W. W. to JOHN THORNTON[2]

MS. WL.
LY ii. 724.

Jany 13th [1835]
Lowther Castle near Penrith.

My dear Sir,

Bearing in mind your very kind attention to me and my interests, I venture to write to you upon a point in which I am at present much concerned. You will probably remember that when I had the pleasure of seeing you in Westmorland[3] I more than once mentioned the parental anxiety which I felt for my younger Son, having been, through an error of judgement, the cause of his losing his health, and greatly impairing his constitution, by sending him while yet too young for so great a

---

[1] Sir James Graham had resigned as first Lord of the Admiralty in Grey's government the previous summer (see pt. ii, L. 835) over a proposal to interfere with the revenues of the Church of Ireland. The following December, he was offered office by Sir Robert Peel, but refused. At the General Election he defended his conduct and was re-elected for East Cumberland, but in the course of the next Parliament he gradually moved towards the principles of the Conservative party and supported the Peel administration in crucial divisions.

[2] See pt. ii, L. 780.

[3] In the summer of 1833.

change, to the Charterhouse.—He was consequently turned out of the course of life, viz, the university, for which I designed him. He is now 25 years of age and has been acting more than three years as my Subdistributor, a situation that leads to nothing and is dependent on many contingencies. In the present Government I have more than one Friend who is desirous to serve him, but an opening might not occur till a change takes place; and I have therefore written to my honored Friend the Earl of Lonsdale expressing a wish to give up my office of Distributor of Stamps which I have held nearly 22 years, in case his Lordship through the present prime minister [1] could procure a transfer of it to my son. And now my dear Sir you will guess why I have troubled you with this Letter; which is to request that you would, upon this occasion, if the matter should come before you or the Board, do what you can consistently with your public Duty, to forward my views, which I am sure you as a Father will deem laudable. Should I be cut off, my Wife and Daughter would have little, though enough to support them in their humble way; but my Son would suffer exceedingly in mind were he to become in the least burthensome to them; indeed he would not endure it. I am myself nearly sixty five, and my Contemporaries are dropping fast around me—I need say no more—as I am sure you will enter into my feelings.

I sincerely hope that yourself Mrs Thornton and all your family have enjoyed good health since we had the pleasure of seeing you. My Sister still languishes, and alas! my only Daughter is confined to the couch, and has long been so, going through a course of bleeding and blistering on account of a spinal complaint.—My eyes, though tender, are very much better.

With kindest regards to yourself Mrs Thornton and my young friends of your family I remain my dear Sir

very faithfully your much obliged
Wm Wordsworth

I return to Rydal tomorrow.

[1] Sir Robert Peel.

863. W. W. to ROBERT PERCEVAL GRAVES

Address: Robert Graves Esqre, Trinity College, Dublin. [*readdressed to*] Post office, Chester.
Postmark: (1) 22 Jan. 1835 (2) 24 Jan. 1835.
Stamp: Kendal Penny Post.
MS. Cornell. Hitherto unpublished.

[*In S. H.'s hand*]

Rydal Mount
Jany 20th 1835

My dear Sir,

The Revd J. Fleming[1] Rector of Bootle and Curate of Bowness having died lately, during my absence, Mrs Wordsworth wrote instantly to Archdeacon Wrangham reminding him of your wish for a Curacy in this neighbourhood,[2] and bespeaking his good offices[3] in your behalf *in case none of the 2 Sons of Mr F.*[4] *should desire to succeed their Father in the Curacy*—being thought eligible for the office by the Bp. if the appointment rested with him.

In reply to M^rs W's Letter the Archdeacon says 'I have communicated with the Bp on the subject of the Curacy of B——, and his Ldp[5] thinking, with me, that from previous introductions, it will probably exactly suit M^r G's wishes has (I believe) written to him by last night's post to that purport'.

While we are disposed to give the Bp. credit for his wish to introduce you to this curacy, we cannot but have some fear that in his zeal he may have overlooked considerations, which you I am sure when made acquainted with particulars will deem important. Mr Fleming is supposed to have died in embarrassed circumstances—his Family were born and brought up at Rayrigg, their family Estate—within a mile of Bowness. There are two Sons—yet minors—one of whom[6] is just gone to

---

[1] W. W.'s school friend John Fleming had held the living of Bootle, on the Cumberland coast, but resided at Rayrigg and acted as Sir Richard le Fleming's curate at Bowness.   [2] See pt. ii, Ls. 782 and 783.

[3] Archdeacon Wrangham was a Prebendary of Chester, in which diocese the parish of Windermere was at this time included.

[4] W. W. is presumably referring to the two sons who were already ordained: Fletcher Fleming, the eldest, and Thomas Fleming (see pt. ii, L. 769), now a Fellow of Pembroke College, Cambridge.

[5] His Lordship.

[6] George Fleming (see pt. ii, L. 769), later a curate in Yorkshire.

College there to be maintained out of the fellowship of his Brother Thomas, at present Curate upon his father's Living at Bootle—his Father not having been able to meet that expence. The other is a Boy at School[1]—There are also 3 Sisters[2]—and 2 other Brothers[3] in the Church holding perpetual Curacies of about £100 per An. each. Now, as far as we know, the three already in the Church are persons of exemplary Life—and for our own Minister, the eldest of the Family, we can affirm that he is inferior to no one in the zealous and careful discharge of his pastoral duty—and now to the point.

We are of opinion that after having learnt these particulars, however much you might desire the situation of Curate at B—— you would be indisposed to accept it, should any of the three Brothers be anxious to succeed his Father. Had M[r] Wrangham's communication contained any conditions to this effect, there would have been no other motive for our writing to you now than for the purpose of congratulating you upon a prospect so agreeable to your wishes—and falling in so aptly with our own. The Family of Flemings are much respected in this neighbourhood and should you succeed their father, to the precluding of any one of them to whom it might be an important object, you would enter upon your ministry here under great disadvantages.

It is reported that the Incumbent Sir R. Fleming intends to resume his duty with an assistant Curate, who has been named in the same reports, a step which perhaps he has legally the power to take—but which, I doubt not, would be so offensive to the Parish that every possible remonstrance would be made against it, and great endeavours used to keep him away.

We have felt anxious to know what has occurred in your professional prospects since you left us. Pray remember us kindly to your Brother and to M[rs] Hemans—and believe me with the joint regards of this family—most sincerely and faithfully

Yours—

[*signed*] W[m] Wordsworth

---

[1] Herbert Fleming (1818–46), a pupil at Sedbergh. He later went out to Madras as a cadet in the East India Company and died of cholera.

[2] Two of the girls had in fact died in infancy.

[3] W. W. seems to mean Fletcher and Thomas Fleming—but his account of the family is somewhat confusing, and he may be referring to two other brothers (John Fleming had eight sons in all).

I have rec^d the P.S.[1] from the Printer, which you forwarded, and have detained it with a view to make some alterations.

Pray do not destroy this Letter—lest any of the Friends of the Family should charge us with having interfered in this matter without due consideration of their claims.

864. W. W. to LORD LONSDALE

MS. Lonsdale MSS. Hitherto unpublished.

Rydal Mount, Kendal
24th Jany 1835

My Lord,

Most heartily do I congratulate you upon the triumphant close of the vexatious contest for West Cumberland;[2] many of the particulars I have heard from my younger son, who is come from Keswick, where he voted, to make a short stay with us.

As far as one can judge, the returns upon the whole are much in our favor—a great deal more, so it should seem, than Lord Lowther apprehended during the earlier stages of the Elections. It is however deplorable to see how far the spirit of faction carries many men, who from their education and station in society, might be expected to think, feel and act differently. Dr Arnold, Master of Rugby, who is during the two half-yearly vacations our neighbour, went to Warwickshire, taking his servant who is a freeholder, along with him, to vote for a Radical Candidate.[3] Dr A. has declared over and over again,

---

[1] Perhaps some corrections for W. W.'s new volume *Yarrow Revisited*, which had been with the printer since the previous summer. But the possibility cannot be entirely ruled out that W. W. is referring here to an earlier draft of the *Postscript, 1835*, written *before* W. W. set out for London in February, but completely rewritten with the help of H. C. R. (see *HCR* ii. 459–60) during the London visit in March, when the controversies surrounding the Poor Law Amendment Act (1834) and the proposals of the Ecclesiastical Commission (see L. 865 below) were the subject of eager debate, and might have seemed to W. W. to deserve more extended treatment than he had first given them. But see *Prose Works*, iii. 231 ff., where it is assumed that the *Postscript, 1835* was drafted *after* W. W. came to London.

[2] See L. 861 above.

[3] In his reply of 2 Feb. Lord Lonsdale commented: 'Whatever may be Dr Arnold's real opinion, He shews but little of that Discretion which ought to distinguish an Instructor of youth by putting forth Sentiments such as you

that he would accept no measures, however good, from the present Ministers, but turn them out instantly without a trial—and yesterday, would you believe it? he said in my hearing, at Mr Hamilton's,[1] when the subject of conversation was—who would be chosen as Speaker[2]—that the choice might be a point of great consequence if the Parliament should be driven by the King to imitate the example of the Long Parliament in Charles the 1st's time; and vote itself not dissolveable but with its own consent. 'Nay, Dr Arnold,' I could not help replying, 'if it should come to that, Speakers and parliaments will be of little consequence; swords will have to settle the matter, and better one tyrant in the person of a 2nd Cromwell, than the hundreds which might make the majority of the wretched house that might remain'—but too much of this fanaticism!

With the approbation of L[d.] Lowther, I wrote to my friend Mr Thornton,[3] Deputy Chairman of the Board of Stamps and Taxes, to bespeak his good Offices in furthering my wish as to the transfer[4] which I requested your Lordship would be so kind as to endeavour to accomplish for me. The enclosed is Mr T's answer. I was previously aware of the case, which you will find adverted to in Mr Thornton's letter, and of the objection which the Duke of Wellington had to appoint Sons as successors to their Fathers; but that objection has not been placed by Mr Thornton exactly upon the same grounds in which it stood in the Duke's mind, as I learnt from Mr T. himself, when he was residing in this neighbourhood, the summer before last. The Duke was averse to such arrangements, because they narrowed the range of government patronage, by admitting an hereditary

---

allude to—but this is not the only occasion in which His bad Feeling has been accompanied by his bad Taste.' (*WL MSS.*)   [1] Capt. Thomas Hamilton.

[2] Charles Manners-Sutton (see pt. ii, L. 730) had wished to retire from the Speakership in 1832, but had been persuaded to carry on in the reformed Parliament, in spite of opposition from some radicals. At the General Election of 1835 he was again returned for Cambridge University: his re-election as Speaker was more strongly opposed, and his opponent James Abercromby, later 1st Baron Dunfermline (1776–1858), M.P. for Edinburgh, was elected on 19 Feb. by a majority of ten votes. The contest for the Speakership excited much public interest as a touchstone of party strength at a time when political alignments were uncertain and confused.

[3] See L. 862 above.

[4] i.e. the proposed transfer of W. W.'s Distributorship to his son Willy. See L. 862 above and L. 866 below.

claim, or pretension, which it would be impolitic to admit; the Patronage of Government having been at that time so far reduced. Presuming your Lordship to be inclined to forward my intention, I would observe, that however strongly supported the claims of Mr Brown[1] might be, it is scarcely possible that that support could be brought into comparison with what would be on the side of anyone honored with your Lordship's favour and patronage. It was not my desire to urge, in support of my application, an hereditary plea; nor did I allude to that principle in my letter to your Lordship. I would much rather, that it should rest upon the reasonableness of any wish being attended to, upon a matter of this sort, which your Lordship should express. I would further observe that it is for the interest of the Conservative cause that there should be placed in this Office a *young* person of character, brought up in conservative principles, in preference to one like myself near the close of his sixty-fifth year. I will conclude the subject with one remark, the justice of which will scarcely be questioned either by Sir Robert Peel or the Duke of Wellington; that I have myself some claim upon my country as a man who in the most disinterested way has devoted his life to the service of sound literature; and now, when the success with which this has been done, is generally acknowledged, and a pecuniary return might be expected to be made to my family, the Law respecting copyright steps in, and declares that the greatest part of my productions, shall be public property the moment I cease to breathe; it would be surely therefore hard, if under these circumstances, my wish to resign in favor of my son were not complied with.

Hoping you continue to enjoy good health and that Lady Lonsdale and the family at Cottesmore are all well,

I remain most faithfully
your Lordship's much obliged Ser^nt
Wm Wordsworth

[1] Unidentified.

865. W. W. to FRANCIS WRANGHAM

Address: The Venerable Archdeacon Wrangham.
MS. Henry E. Huntington Library.
Mem. K. LY ii. 725.

[*In M. W.'s hand*]

Rydal Mount
Feb^{ry} 2^d [1835]

My dear Wrangham,

Sincere thanks are due from me for the attention you paid to Mrs W.'s letter, written during my absence. You know the favourable opinion I entertain of Mr Graves, and I was under a promise to let him know if any vacancy occurred in this neighbourhood, and to do all I could, without infringing upon prior or stronger claims, to promote the attainment of his wishes. Mrs W. judiciously and properly stated in her letter that it was not her desire, and she trusted it was no one's else, to interfere with any claims which in the judgement of the Bp the Sons of our late friend[1] might have. Had she not made this proviso, I should have regretted she mixed at all in a business of so delicate a nature; but I will not conceal from you, that out of these well-intended, and right endeavours of hers, has arisen much uneasiness to herself—from the circumstance that Mr Thos Fleming who was his Father's Curate at Bootle, is now likely to be without employment. Of him *personally* we have but slight knowledge, but it redounds much to his honor that he had set aside before his Father's death, the proceeds of his Fellowship to maintain a younger Brother at College, his Father not being able to do it; he himself living upon his stipend as his Father's Curate. This fact was mentioned some little time ago to Mrs W. by a friend and benefactress of the family. It grieves me to add, that the Eldest Son,[2] our Minister,—a most excellent Person and a zealous Pastor,—has taken offence at what we have done in this business, the whole particulars of which were laid openly before him. This gives *me* no concern but on his own account. Because all that has been done by us, was done with deliberation, and from motives pure, and entirely disinterested. We were governed only by joint considerations of what was due to Mr G., to the Family of Fleming, and above all of what

[1] John Fleming of Rayrigg. See L. 863 above.
[2] Fletcher Fleming, who now succeeded to Rayrigg.

17

promised to be beneficial to the Parishioners; for without this last thought I should not have stirred in the affair for the sake of any Friend whatsoever.

And now my dear friend to a point which I have a good deal at heart. Could the situation of Mr T. F. [1] be suggested to the Bp in such a way as might tend to reconcile him to this disappointment, by placing him in some *other* eligible Curacy for which he might be fit.

The mind of every thinking man who is attached to the Ch: of England must at this time be especially turned to reflections upon all points of Ecclesiastical polity, [2] government, and management, which may tend to strengthen the Establishment in the affections of the People, and enlarge the sphere of its efficiency. It cannot then I feel be impertinent in me, tho' a Layman, to express upon this occasion my satisfaction, qualified as it is by what has been said above, in finding from this instance that our Diocesan is unwilling to station Clergymen in Cures with which they are locally connected. Some years ago, when the present Bp of London, [3] then of Chester, was residing in this neighbourhood, I took the liberty of strenuously recommending to him not to ordain young men to Curacies in places where they had been brought up, or in the midst of their own relatives. I had seen too much of the mischief of this, especially as affecting the functions and characters of ministers born and bred up in the lower classes of Society. It has been painful to me to observe the false position, as the French would call it, in which men so placed, are. Their habits, their manners, and their talk, their acquaintanceships, their friendships—and let me say their domestic affections, naturally, and properly draw them one way, while their professional obligations point out another; and accordingly, if they are sensible of both, they live in a perpetual

[1] Thomas Fleming.

[2] The Ecclesiastical Commission of 1832 (re-established in 1833 and 1834) to inquire into Church revenues and patronage was to produce its lengthy Report on 16 June. Sir Robert Peel was also about to set up (on 4 Feb.) a new Commission to inquire into the distribution of episcopal revenues and duties, to consider how cathedrals and collegiate churches might be made more efficient, and to look into the problems of pluralities and non-residence. Its first Report appeared on 17 Mar., while W. W. was in London. Some of these issues were discussed in the *Postscript* added to the *Yarrow Revisited* volume (see L. 863 above).

[3] C. J. Blomfield.

conflict; and are liable to be taxed with pride and ingratitude, as seeming to neglect their old friends when they only associate with them with that reserve and under those restraints which their sacred profession enjoins. If, on the other hand, they fall into unrestrained familiarity with the Associates of their earlier life and boyish days, how injurious to their Ministry such intercourse would be, must flash upon every Man's mind whose thoughts have turned for a moment to the subject. Allow me to add a word upon the all-important matter of Testimonials—the case of the Rector of Bowness and of Grasmere[1] presses it closely upon my mind. Had the Individuals who signed his been fitly impressed with the awfulness of the Act they were about to engage in, they could not have undertaken it. His character was at that time too notorious. Would it not be a good rule for Bishops to exclude Testimonials from Relatives and near Connections? It is painful to notice what a tendency there is in men's minds to allow even a slight call of private regard to outweigh a very strong claim of Duty to the Public, and not less in Sacred concerns than in civil.

Your hands,[2] my dear friend, have failed, as well as my eyes, so that we are neither of us in very flourishing trim for active correspondence—be assured however I participate [in] the feelings you express. Last year has robbed me of Coleridge, of Charles Lamb—James Losh[3]—Rudd[4] of Trinity—and Fleming just gone—and other Schoolfellows and Contemporaries. I cannot forget that Shakespear, who scarcely survived 50—(I am now near the close of my 65th year) wrote

> In me that time of life thou dost behold
> When yellow leaves, or few or none, do hang
> Upon the bough.

How much more reason have we to break out into such a strain? Let me hear from you from time to time. I shall feel a lively interest in all that concerns you.

I remain, faithfully yours
[*unsigned*]

[1] Sir Richard le Fleming had succeeded the Revd. William Barton (see *MY* ii. 468) as rector of Windermere in 1823.

[2] See pt. ii, L. 846.

[3] James Losh (see pt. i, L. 49) had died on 23 Sept. 1833.

[4] John Rudd (1771–1834) of Cockermouth, educated at Hawkshead Grammar School: Fellow of Trinity College, Cambridge, 1794; vicar of Blyth, Notts., 1813–30, and thereafter rector of Waltham, Lincs.

866. W. W. to SIR ROBERT PEEL

Endorsed: 5 Feby 1835. William Wordsworth.
MS. British Library.
Sir Robert Peel from his Private Papers, ed. Charles Stuart Parker, 3 vols., 1899,
ii. 305 (—).

Rydal Mount, Kendal
Feb^{ry} 5th 1835

Sir,

I have the honor to acknowledge the receipt of your Letter of the 3^d Inst^{nt}.[1] That, at a period of such national anxiety, with so heavy a pressure of public business as you must now be under, you should have made, I cannot say *found*, leisure to express yourself as you have done, concerning me and my writings, affords me a gratification inferior to none which during a pretty long literary life I have ever known. With these words inadequate as they are to my feelings, a consciousness of the value of your time, obliges me to content myself.

The best manner in which I can meet your kind request that I would tell you without reserve whether there be any thing which you can do to serve me, is to state explicitly the motives which induced me to apply for your Patronage thro' my honored Friend Lord Lonsdale, for the transfer to my Son of the office I have held for nearly twenty two years. He is now in his 25th year. I designed him for one of the English Universities; but, when a Boy, he lost his health through an error of judgement on my part; and consequently could not be put forward in that walk of life. He was afterwards placed in

---

[1] Peel had written on 3 Feb. regretting that 'on account of official impediments', he was unable to promote W. W.'s proposal that his Distributorship should be transferred to his son. 'But I assure you that no man recognises more fully than myself the Public claims which you possess on those who are entrusted with Power—claims to which I should have the greatest pride and personal satisfaction in doing justice. I have not the Honour of being known to you, but you must allow the sincerest Respect for your character, and admiration of those works which will secure you lasting Fame, to supply the place of personal acquaintance, and if you will tell me without reserve, whether there be any thing which I can do to gratify your present wishes, or relieve you from anxiety about the future, you will make your communication to one who will have as much pleasure, if he shall be enabled to accomplish your wishes, as you can have in finding them realized.' (*WL MSS.*)

Germany under a private Tutor, and subsequently he passed a short time at the University of Heidelberg, whence he returned upon an opening occurring at Carlisle, where, by acting as my Subdistributer for three years, he has been able merely to maintain himself. This is but a melancholy station in life for one of his years, and connections.

After consulting with my powerful Friends, and, through my Brother the Master of Trinity, with the Home Sec^ry,[1] I saw no prospect of effectually serving him, notwithstanding their zealous wishes, but by making, for his benefit, this, to me, important sacrifice of the place which I hold.—Under no other circumstances should I have desired the transfer. For the duties of this Off: I know him, from experience, to be fit; as I trust he may be for many others, where the confinement is not excessive, and the labor *severe*; as in that case I should fear for his health, which is now good.—He is a Youth of sound principles, and staid opinions, modest, though of lively and agreeable manners, prudent, assiduous, very active, and methodical. The duties of an employment rather ambulatory than sedentary, would suit him best. But I must check my pen, fearing that as a prime minister you may smile at the above, as a parental eulogy; it is nevertheless a report which every competent Judge in the City of Carlisle, however differing from him in politics, would readily confirm.—

Allow me to say in further explanation and justification of myself for having thus troubled my Friends, that the course of my life, though strictly economical, has not allowed me to lay up more than would be necessary for the comfortable maintenance, in the event of my decease, of my Widow and only Daughter. My elder Son who for the last twelve months has held the Living of Workington for his Brother in law will have to retire with his family in less than two years to a Benefice under £200 per ann: which he owes to the patronage of Lord Lonsdale. Such is the State of my small family. Had I followed Literature as a *Trade* it might, as to pecuniary circumstances, have been very different. In common with the worthier and nobler class of Authors, who write not with a view to instant profit, and immediate effect, but with a hope of being permanently benefical to mankind, I have to complain of injury proceeding from the laws of my own Country and the practices

---

[1] Henry Goulburn.

of a neighbouring one. During more than thirty years many of my productions have been before the Public. No one will deny that they had gradually wrought their way into estimation; and now when the Sale of them might considerably benefit such part of my family as may survive, the short time of Copy-right[1] allowed by law, would make these public property, some at my decease, and others soon after. In the meanwhile the Parisian Piracies, for *morally* such they are, inundate our Country, with Copies at a price under what can possibly be afforded, if the claim of the Author is to be regarded.—

Pray excuse this long Letter, which precludes me from giving vent to the expression of my heartfelt satisfaction in seeing one so distinguished for every Statesmanlike quality at the head of affairs. You and your Colleagues have the good wishes, I sincerely believe, of a vast majority of the educated portion of our Countrymen, and of the Friends to the Constitution. May the almighty disposer of events support and guide you through the trials that await you!

I have the honor to be
with sincere admiration, and grateful respect
most faithfully your obliged Ser[vnt]
W[m] Wordsworth

867. W. W. to HENRY TAYLOR

Address: H. Taylor Esq[re], Colonial Off.
MS. Bodleian Library.
LY ii. 728.

Saturday morn: [? Feb. 1835][2]

Your kind Letter has just been received—I wish you were stronger in body. Among my friends the yellow leaf has been falling and the green leaf swept off lately in an appalling way— So it appears to have been among yours.

---

[1] The Copyright Act of 1814 had extended the term of protection for an author's works from fourteen to twenty-eight years from the date of publication, or for the rest of the author's life, if he were still living. But at his death his works became public property, except that any posthumously published works continued to belong to his heirs for a further twenty-eight years.

[2] Undated, but probably written (as de Selincourt notes) about the same time as L. 865 above to Francis Wrangham.

Your view of the Case is quite correct and I repeat that I am sorry I mentioned it to you. Farewell. I have nothing to add to-day.

affectionately yours,
Wm Wordsworth

868. W. W. to ROBERT MONTGOMERY[1]

Address: R. Montgomery Esqre, Strand on the Green, Kew, London.
Postmark: 8 Feb. 1835. *Stamp*: Kendal Penny Post.
MS. Cornell.
Mem. (—). *K* (—). *LY ii. 730* (—).

[In M. W.'s hand]

[c. 7 Feb. 1835]

My dear Sir,

On my return home, after an absence of some length, I have had the pleasure of receiving your 2 volumes,[2] together with a copy, from the Editor, of your Selections.[3] As you are probably in communication with this Gentleman may I request that you would present to him my thanks for this mark of his attention.

You may not perhaps be aware that my eyes,—tho' answering well the ordinary purposes of seeing, except that they cannot bear strong sun-shine or candle-light striking full upon them,—have been for some time in a state that allows me little gratification either from reading or writing—Thro' the hands

---

[1] Robert Montgomery (1807–55), a popular religious versifier of no great gifts, whose work had been castigated by Macaulay in the *Edinburgh Review* for Apr. 1830. *The Omnipresence of the Deity* had appeared in 1828, with a dedication to Dr. William Howley, and Montgomery had sent a copy to W. W. with a covering note on 10 Mar. of that year (*WL MSS.*).

[2] The 13th edition of *The Omnipresence of the Deity* (1834), and one of Montgomery's other volumes: probably *The Messiah, A Poem*, 1832 (8th edn., 1842). In his covering letter of 6 Jan., Montgomery expressed his admiration for W. W. and the improvement in his taste that had been effected by study of his works: ' . . . When exaggeration, verbosity, and a mock intensity of feeling were the fashion of the day, you stood aloof in lofty singularity, and have never succumbed to debauch the intellect or deprave the affections . . .' (*WL MSS.*)

[3] *Selections from the Poetical Works of Robert Montgomery . . . With introductory remarks and appendix . . .* The editor's name is not recorded.

of another I must therefore thank you for your present, and I do it this speedily and before I have been able to read the Poem, from a dread of the recurrence of a mortification to which I have often lately been subject—a mortification occasioned by deferring my acknowledgements of favors of this kind, thro' a hope of making them more acceptable by being accompanied with some account of the impression which the works made upon me during perusal.

With your 'Omnipresence of the Deity' I was acquainted long ago, having read it and other parts of your writings with much pleasure, tho' with some abatements, such as you yourself seem sufficiently aware of, and which, in the works of so young a writer, were by me gently judged, and in many instances regarded, though in themselves faults, as indications of future excellence. In your letter, for which also I thank you, you allude to your Preface, and desire to know if my opinion concurs with yours on the subject of Sacred Poetry. [1] That Preface has been read to me, and I can answer in the affirmative; but at the same time allow me frankly to tell you that what *most* pleased me in that able composition is to be found in the few concluding paragraphs, beginning 'It is now seven years since.' [2]

---

[1] In his Preface to the 13th edition, Montgomery had defended his conception of religious poetry from his critics: ' . . . Taken in the full and philosophical meaning of the words, sacred poetry comprehends whatever is sublime in Religion, grand in Morals, holy in Man, or attractive in Nature . . .'

[2] 'It is nearly seven years since this poem was published; and how much he has been indebted to it, for the personal friendship and sympathy it has gained him in hearts and homes, where, but for its introduction, he had been a stranger,—can only be understood and appreciated by those who have had the same reasons to be grateful. But this recollection is not unmingled with melancholy: for in our retrospect of a few years, how much is there that the sigh of memory would in vain recall!—Many who greeted his first attempts have gone to their rest; and many a voice that counselled and cheered him in his onward path, has been hushed in the grave. Alas for our affections, if *this* life were all! . . . But the hope of Immortality makes the dawning heaven of our earth; and he who clings to this, will alone be enabled to speculate rightly on life and conduct, and on that which is to be revealed beyond the grave. . . . The appreciation of fame is laudable under certain moral limitations . . . But in the war of emulation the noble aims of mental exertion soon evaporate . . . Yet may the eye of the contemplatist repose on a more attractive scene; and behold in the varied ranks of learning, science, and taste, men who stand apart from the emulations around them,—silently building

Your message shall be delivered to Mr Southey—the note you allude to[1] I was not acquainted with till your letter pointed it out to my attention; my friend's indignant feelings are shared by me, to the full—I cannot conceive what possesses the hearts of men who write in this strain. Mrs Southey I am sorry to say makes but a slow progress towards recovery;[2] nor does her physician hold out hope of a speedy amendment.

I cannot conclude without one word of literary advice, which I hope you will deem my advanced age entitles me to give. Do not, my dear Sir, be anxious about any individual's opinion concerning your writings, however highly you may think of his genius or rate his judgment. Be a severe critic to yourself; and depend upon it no Person's decision upon the merit of your works, will bear comparison in point of value with your own. You must be conscious from what feeling they have flowed, and how far they may or may not be allowed to claim, on that account, permanent respect—and, above all, I would remind you, with a view to tranquillize and steady your mind, that no man takes the trouble of surveying and pondering another's writings with a hundredth part of the care which an author of sense and genius will have bestowed upon his own. Add to this reflection another, which I press upon you, as it has supported me thro' life, viz, that Posterity will settle all accounts justly, and that works which deserve to last will last; and if undeserving this fate, the sooner they perish the better.

Believe me to be faithfully,
Your much obliged,
[*signed*] Wm Wordsworth

their monument of fame; or, from time to time sending forth streams of thought that refresh and invigorate the world of truth . . .'

[1] Southey had defended Montgomery in the *Quarterly* against the malignity of recent attacks on Montgomery's early satires.

[2] For Mrs. Southey's mental breakdown the previous autumn, see pt. ii, L. 851.

869. W. W. to VISCOUNT LOWTHER

Address: Private—Viscount Lowther, M.P. etc. etc. etc.
MS. Harvard University Library.[1]
LY ii. 728.

[*In S. H.'s hand*]

Feb. 14th [1835]

My dear Lord Lowther,

It is my present intention to set off in a day or two for London as you recommend[2]—but, this season being trying to my eyes, I may be prevented, and therefore trespass upon your kindness by answering some of your questions by Letter, as briefly as I can— first thanking you sincerely for your zealous exertions.

My first object of anxiety is my younger Son, who is now in a dependant situation, which leads to nothing. He would be fit for such an Office as I hold, or any other connected with the revenue, or other department where the confinement is not excessive, or the labour *severe*. In which case his health, tho' now good, might break down—as he suffered so much from ill- health during 3 or 4 years of his Boyhood. He is prudent, methodical, observant, ingenious and in action very per- severing—his book attainments are not as extensive as I could wish, owing to that long sickness—but he has read a good deal, and knows and speaks the German Language.

Seeing how difficult it is to find an opening, I should have

---

[1] There is also a draft of this letter in M. W.'s hand in the *WL*.

[2] Lord Lowther wrote on 12 Feb. stating that he had seen Peel about the proposed transfer of W. W.'s Distributorship to his son (see Ls. 864 and 866 above), and that he was sympathetic to the plan, but that a recommendation of the late Government for uniting Cumberland and Westmorland with the Lancaster District made it difficult to accomplish. '. . . He is well disposed to act according to the Professions he has made, the want of means or rather opportunity prevent his carrying his wishes into effect . . .' He, and Peel, suggested as possible alternatives, placing M. W. on the Civil List, and appointing W. W. jnr. to some other office if a suitable one could be found. 'If it is not inconvenient or disagreeable, I think you had better get into the mail coach and come to London when *we* with other of your friends might decide the specific mode of serving yourself and family, that would be most agreeable to you. I should feel some difficulty and a responsibility I do not like in being put in the situation of deciding for you, my intentions are good but they might not entirely agree with yours—' (*WL MSS.*). Lord Lowther was now back in office as Treasurer of the Navy, and Vice-President of the Board of Trade.

been pleased to resign in his favour—but to this there was one great objection, the emolument of the place would not have allowed him to ensure his Life for my benefit in case he died before me—and *our common* income would have been reduced by giving up the Sub-distributorship of Carlisle—so that if anything respectable could be found for him in another quarter I should be well content to continue as I am—tho', as I told you, I have an ardent desire to be at liberty (now that the state of my eyes interferes so much with reading) to travel a little on the Continent—in Italy especially.

As to the civil pension List—under no circumstances would M[rs] Wordsworth, myself, or any of the family desire such a thing—rather let me say accept it. In fact it would not be necessary—my Wife and Daughter, in case of my death would be left in circumstances equal to their *very* moderate wishes. I have not laid up anything—my literary distinction, such as it is, having involved me in unavoidable expenses, without bringing in a pecuniary equivalent. I have however insured my Life for 2000£ and have not spent my own little patrimony, nor my Wife's—but during the life of M[rs] W. and my Daughter nothing could be spared for my Sons, which makes me so anxious on account of the younger *especially*.

I think the Lord Chancellor[1] would be disposed to serve me should anything under his patronage fall vacant, that there might be no professional obstacle to my younger Son's holding—but perhaps there is no such thing.

Odd things are done in party arrangements—and not the least odd is the scheme of the late Gov[t] for attaching the very large District to the very small one—the Breast of Veal (excuse the allusion) to the Sweet-bread[2]—and not the Sweet-bread to the Breast of Veal! I am an old man—Mr G.[3] a young one—that might put it into their heads—but I fear it was a stroke unfairly aimed at your Family.

I wish I could be in better heart than your Letter upon the returns[4] allows.—I certainly concur with you, in the way in which the present Gov[t] ought to behave. The Ship of the

---

[1] Lord Lyndhurst.

[2] *Written* Sweat-bread.

[3] Mr. B. P. Gregson, Distributor for Lancaster.

[4] i.e. the election returns. Though his party won about a hundred seats, Peel failed to secure the steady majority he was seeking. After repeated defeats he resigned on 8 Apr., and Lord Melbourne became Prime Minister again.

Constitution is in a storm and must sink if the men now at the helm are obliged to abandon her—therefore let them stick to their post to the last.

Again and again I thank you for the proof of cordial friendship which you have given me upon this and all other occasions—

and believe me, dear Lord Lowther,
ever faithfully—your most obliged
[*signed*] Wm Wordsworth

870. W. W. to ALEXANDER DYCE

Address: Revd Alexander Dyce, 9 Gray's Inn.
Postmark: 2 Mar. 1835. *Stamp*: Piccadilly.
MS. Victoria and Albert Museum.
LY ii. 732.

Monday morn^g March 2 [1835]
56 Jermyn Street[1]

My dear Sir,

Many sincere thanks for your elegant and valuable editions of *Akenside*, *Beattie*, and *Shakespear*,[2] from the perusal of which I promise myself much pleasure.

On Wednesday at half past six I shall be happy to take dinner with you.

Mr Southey's Book shall be conveyed to him—he leaves Town,[3] perhaps has already left it, this morning, but I will take care of the Book for him.

I remain my dear Sir
ever faithfully yours,
Wm Wordsworth

[1] W. W. and M. W. left for London on 17 Feb. (see *SH*, p. 439), and arrived in time to dine with Rogers, Wilkie, and Moore on the 20th (*Memoirs, Journal and Correspondence of Thomas Moore*, ed. Lord John Russell, vii. 69–73). H. C. R. first saw W. W. and M. W. in London on 3 Mar., when W. W. was sitting for a new portrait from Pickersgill (*HCR* ii. 457).

[2] Three contributions to the Aldine Press editions of the English poets, published by William Pickering (1796–1854).

[3] Southey had come south to accompany his son Cuthbert to the Warters' rectory in Sussex. On his return journey he brought his wife back to Keswick from the asylum in York where she had been confined for several months.

871. W. W. to W. W. JNR.

Address: Wᵐ Wordsworth Esqʳᵉ, Carlisle.
Franked: London March Nine 1835. R. H. Inglis.
Postmark: 9 Mar. 1835.
MS. WL. Hitherto unpublished.

[9 Mar. 1835]

My dear Wᵐ,

I have this moment received your Letter, and being able to procure a Frank, I sit down to say, that your interests have never been out of my thoughts since I came to Town and that I shall do all in my power, as I have done to promote them. But as you will know, opportunities and openings cannot be created.—We shall go down to Cambridge in about 10 days, and then shall be within easy call; as I agree with you, it is desirable to be upon the spot or near it as long as we can. Lord Lowther's engagements are too pressing and numerous to allow me to see much of him, but nothing can exceed his kindness. He is one of the best creatures existing. Yesterday your Uncle and I dined with Mr Goulburn.[1] Mr Southey will mention your case to Mr Herries.[2] I saw Mr Thornton immediately on my arrival, and he satisfied me that nothing will be done in the Stamp Off.—I have not seen the paragraph in the [? Sun][3] you allude, but I suspect that your words meant kindly are ironical. Both the Globe and Morning Post have mentioned my being in Town, but not in unfriendly terms. I left a Card with the Chancellor[4]—he told Lord Lowther that he might have a Living of 250 or so at his disposal for John, but it would not be worth John's while to move unless for some thing better.—I have named you to Mr Courtenay, Sir John [? Beckett],[5] and just now to Sir Robert Inglis, all with a view to procure information, and assistance if necessary. I left a card at Sir R. Peel's and he knows that I am in Town. We have been at the Archbishops.[6] We went on Friday to Hendon and your mother will return today when we shall take up our abode at Miss Fenwick's, Mr Henry Taylor's Cousin. But your

---

[1] Henry Goulburn, the Home Secretary.
[2] John Charles Herries (see also pt. i, L. 330), M.P. for Harwich, and Secretary at War under Peel.
[3] *Blot on MS.*
[4] The Lord Chancellor, Lord Lyndhurst.
[5] For Sir John Beckett, see *MY* ii. 515—but the reading here is uncertain.
[6] The Archbishop of Canterbury, Dr. William Howley.

Mother has written of all our movements at length, in [a] Letter which will be forwarded to you. Farewell.

Ever your affectionate Father
W W.

Mr Timms[1] called upon us, and I was truly sorry to hear of poor Papendick's[2] death. How glad am I that you got away from that place in Time.—

[*M. W. writes*]

Dearest Willy, I have just come in from Hendon, and have not a moment to write to save this frank—I was grieved to hear of y[r] friend Pap[ks] death—saw Timms—he called [as] we were just going out, but he had heard from Bremen—y[r] friend died very suddenly—All at Hendon[3] send a thousand loves to you. Mr Prince speaks of you with great regard—you may be sure no stone will be left unturned for y[r] advantage—but nothing yet has occurred so good as the place you hold—we heard *under the rose* of the changes to be made at the Stamps and Taxes, and this was one cause why it was not recommended to be turned over to you. It is most probable that y[r] Father will have to give up, with a remuneration—but this is conjecture. I have not seen y[r] uncle. Tell them to send my scrawls if you can read them, for I have not time to write to you also. God love you

M. Wordsworth

---

[1] A fellow student of W. W. jnr. at Bremen. He died later this year.

[2] W. W. jnr.'s host in Bremen from 1829 to 1831.

[3] i.e. Mrs. Gee, Miss Lockier, and Mr. and Mrs. Prince (see *MY* ii. 612). W. W. and M. W. also saw Julia Myers at Hendon, where she was now teaching, and the poet wrote in her autograph album (owned by the late Mrs. Jane Myers).

872. W. W. to ALEXANDER DYCE

Address: The Revd A. Dyce, Gray's Inn.
Postmark: 11 Mar. 1835. *Stamp*: Charles St.
MS. Victoria and Albert Museum.
LY ii. 732.

19 South Parade
Floodyer Street Gate
[11 Mar. 1835]

My dear Sir,
    Here we are.[1]
    I lent Mr Rogers your Akenside,[2] on returning it he writes
me: Akenside's life is very entertaining and I could not leave it
till I had done it. Many thanks for it. Tell Mr Mitford [3] that the
passage in King John is at the close of the 4th Act[4]—the words
these, or something like it—

> *Vast confusion waits as* doth a Raven *on*, etc.
> The imminent decay—

near the commencement of the fifth act you meet the word
Amazement[5]—all shewing that Gray when he wrote his Ode

---

[1] The Wordsworths were now staying near St. James Park with Henry
Taylor, who described the poet thus in a letter to a friend: 'This old
philosopher is one of the most extraordinary human phenomena that one
could have in the house. He has the simplicity and helplessness of a child in
regard to the little transactions of life; and whilst he is being directed and dealt
with in regard to them, he keeps tumbling out the highest and deepest
thoughts that the mind of man can reach, in a stream of discourse which is so
oddly broken by the little hitches and interruptions of common life that we
admire and laugh at him by turns. Everything that comes into his mind comes
out—weakness or strength, affections or vanities, so that, if ever an
opportunity was afforded of seeing a human being through and through, we
have it in the person of this "old man eloquent". He is very happy with us, and
very social with everybody, and we have a variety of people to meet him
every day at breakfast and dinner.' (*Correspondence of Henry Taylor*, ed.
Edward Dowden, 1888, p. 63.) The Wordsworths later moved on to stay
with Isabella Fenwick, before going on to Cambridge on 27 Mar.

[2] Dyce's new edition: see L. 870 above.

[3] John Mitford (1781–1859), editor of the *Gentleman's Magazine*,
1834–50. He had edited the *Poetical Works of Gray* in 1814, and the *Works* in
1816, and he produced a new five-volume edition, 1835–43.

[4] *King John*, IV. iii. 152–4.

[5] Ibid. v. i. 35. 'And wild amazement hurries up and down.'

was fresh from the perusal of these scenes. The parallel passages in the Ode are—

> Confusion on thy banners wait
> Amazement in his Van

And the acknowledged passage threatening the Air with colours idly spread—'banners'.[1] I hope we shall meet again before I leave London. I shall be here about 10 days.—

ever very sincerely yours
Wm Wordsworth

On the 18th I dine at the Rev[d] Mr Johnson's,[2] 107 Regent Street—to meet Mr Southey. Mr Johnson is a particular Friend of mine and it would give me great pleasure to introduce you to Mr Southey at his house if you would call in the evening.

873. W. W. to ALLAN CUNNINGHAM

Address: Allan Cunningham Esq[r], 27 Lower Belgrave Place [*In unidentified hand*]
Postmark: 19 Mar. 1835. *Stamp*: Piccadilly.
MS. Mr. W. Hugh Peal.
K (—). *LY ii. 733* (—).

Wednesday Morn
[18 Mar. 1835]

My dear Friend,

In extreme hurry I sit down to thank you for your life and edition of Burns,[3] received last night, and for your obliging Letter.

It would give me much pleasure to be of any use to you in your meditated Edition of the Poets; but I am not aware how I can, except by my opinion as to the Authors which it might be expedient to add to your Selection, or to exclude. This, after conference with Mr Southey, I should do with great pleasure. In the mean while I do sincerely regret that the multiplicity of my

---

[1] Ibid. v. i. 72, cited by Gray in a note to *The Bard*, l. 4.

[2] William Johnson, formerly schoolmaster in Grasmere, and now in charge of the Central School in London, which had moved from Baldwin Gardens to Regent St.

[3] *The Works of Robert Burns; with his Life*, 8 vols., 1834.

engagements prevents me from calling upon you again;[1] otherwise, by conversation something might have been done between us.

—I remain here till Tuesday next and if you could try your chance of finding me at home, which I can scarcely wish you should do however, and we should meet, it would give me great pleasure to discuss the matter. About half past one tomorrow I should be at home.

ever faithfully yours
Wm Wordsworth

873a. W. W. to JULIUS CHARLES HARE

Address: The Revd J. C. Hare, Herstmonceux, Battle, Sussex.
Postmark: [   ] 1835.
MS. Mr. R. L. Bayne-Powell. Hitherto unpublished.

[*c.* 20 Mar. 1835]

My dear Sir

This moment I have received your Letter, which I reply to in extreme haste. We think of going to Cambridge on Thursday but possibly may stay a day or two longer. —Therefore if I am to have the pleasure of seeing you which I much desire, you must be before that day. It would answer our common purpose much better, however, if you could stretch a point and come to Cambridge where we might walk and talk at leisure—If this be out of your power I should be happy to see you here, though I am overwhelmed with engagements, as all persons who come to London rarely and for a short time unavoidably are.—

We must take establishments for good and for bad,—and without either condemning or approving the refusal of the *Heads* to admit of a Coleridge Prize,[2] it may be maintained in

---

[1] W. W. and M. W. had visited Chantrey's studio in Pimlico the previous day by invitation (*WL MSS.*).

[2] Julius Hare had written to W. W. on 17 Mar. about a public memorial to S.T.C., either in the form of a prize essay, as suggested by John Sterling, or a bust by Chantrey in the Abbey: 'Surely something ought to be done to raise a memorial to that glorious old man eloquent, to show that the generations in which he lived are not utterly unmindful and unworthy of him. There is a striking and sad contrast between the activity of the Germans in raising memorials to the honour of Schleiermacher, and our own careless, mammon-ridden torpour with regard to Coleridge.' He had been hoping to see

defence of suspension of judgement that it is known that Mr Coleridge has left a large Body of metaphysical, theological MSS behind which is intended for publication. Now I am inclined to think that it would be best in any University connected as ours are with peculiar tenets in divinity, [not][1] to found such a prize, till it is ascertained what doctrines these MSS inculcate.

ever faithfully
yours W. Wordsworth

Pray excuse this vile penmanship—I have but a moment to write and a wretched Pen, which I cannot mend—

874. W. W. to ROBERT JONES

Address: The Rev^d. Robt Jones, Plas yn Llan, near Ruthin, N. W.
Postmark: (1) [?1] Apr. 1835 (2) 3 Apr. 1835.
MS. National Library of Wales.
Herbert G. Wright, 'Two Letters from Wordsworth to Robert Jones', RES xiii (1937), 39—45. LY ii. 734.

[*In M. W.'s hand*]

Trinity Lodge Mar 30 [1835]

My dear Friend

Your letter dated Feb 7th has remained far too long unanswered, a short time after the receipt of it, Mrs W. and I started for London and took the letter along with us, meaning to reply to it, from that place, where we knew we could procure franks with great ease,—but during a residence of 5 weeks in Town whither we had gone on business—we were so much hurried and fatigued, that we had neither time nor spirits to sit down and write, in the way we wished to write to you. We have been now 3 days here, where we are like ships in harbour after a storm. My B^r tho' much harrassed by business, and having survived a dangerous attack of cholera last Autumn, is very active—and looking well for him. Two of his Sons, who are

W. W. while he was in London: ' . . . Coleridge's death, which has been followed so soon by Charles Lamb's, is ever bringing the thought before me that too soon there may be no one left in England, whom I can revere.' (*WL MSS.*)

[1] *Word dropped out?*

fellows of this College, are also well, and we have the pleasure of seeing them at all hours when they are not elsewhere engaged. You remember Greenwood,[1] my old Schoolfellow—he is still here residing as Senior fellow—he looks pretty well, but complains of many infirmities. I called upon the Master of St John's[2] yesterday, but did not see him, he is said to wear well—I had a friend with me who took me thro' the Lodge and in the Combination room I saw my own Picture—which the Master and Fellows did me the honour of subscribing for—it looks well, but is of too large a size for the room and would be seen to much more advantage in the Hall. But had there been room for it there, there is an objection to that place—the charcoal smoke I am told, is ruinous to Pictures, and this which is really well done cost much money.

We were glad to hear of your good health, and it was kind in you, giving a particular account of my old Friends of your family—I hope your brother will continue to be as careful of himself as the state of his constitution seems to require—pray give my kind remembrances to him, and best wishes to your Sisters. My own Sister continues to languish—as she may do perhaps for a long time—during 8 months of the year, she can scarcely be said to quit the House—and is not for a much less time confined to her room—and during the severity of the winter, in a great measure to her bed. But her sufferings are upon the whole less than they used to be, and she endures her privations with resignation—and unless when she has a recurrence of a bilious attack, she reads a good deal, and is in mind active and cheerful.

We have another cause of sorrow in our house, which is the state of my poor Daughter's health—her appetite has gradually failed for several years—and a consequent weakness has superinduced a spinal complaint, which has subjected her to severe courses of bleeding and blistering, which, you will be grieved to hear, have not yet produced for us steady hopes of her recovery. During our stay in London, we have been in frequent consultation about her cure, with a kind medical friend D[r] Holland[3]—and we [hope] she will have as much benefit from

---

[1] For Robert Hodgson Greenwood, see *EY*, pp. 56–7 and T. W. Thompson, *Wordsworth's Hawkshead*, ed. R. S. Woof, 1970, pp. 78–81.

[2] Dr. James Wood (see *EY*, p. 427; *MY* ii. 653).

[3] Probably Dr. Henry Holland (see pt. i, L. 42).

the best advice as can be had without her being actually seen by the Persons consulted. If it should be in our power to have her brought to London, that will be done, but at present she cannot bear such a journey.—You will be much concerned to hear that our excellent friend Mr Southey and his family have been suffering from a severe domestic affliction. Symptoms of mental derangement appeared in Mrs S. last autumn.—She was removed to the Retreat at York—but there appears to be little hopes of her final recovery—and her husband is about to take her back to Keswick.

The business which brought me to London arose out of a hope of procuring some respectable situation for my Son W^m from Sir R^t Peel's Government—and in this I should have had no doubt of succeeding, if the present administration could have kept their ground.[1] But the Whigs have behaved more dishonorably than any great Party ever did. The consequence will be, the displacing of the only Men who are able to have deferred, at least for some time, a general convulsion. The Whig Lords will and must take the alarm, but it will be too late to save either themselves or their constitutional opponents.

A Copy of the MSS. of Coleridge which you possess, would be welcome to his Executor Mr Green,[2] I have no doubt; and with a view of having it conveyed to him, I request you would be so kind as to enclose it as follows—First a cover to—Green Esq, Surgeon, Lincolns Inn fields—to whom you will please to signify how it was given to you—and that I had requested you to forward it to him. This packet enclose to 'Henry Taylor Esqre and again enclose 'to The Under Secretary of State, Colonial Office, London'. The Book upon Mona[3] which you kindly offer I should be glad to receive. When you should have an opportunity to send it to Liverpool, if you direct it to John Bolton Esqre for Mr Wordsworth Rydal—it will not be long before it will reach me by some parcel of his to his residence on Windermere. I have ordered my forthcoming little volume[4] to

[1] The crucial four-day debate on Lord John Russell's motion on the application of the surplus revenues of the Church of Ireland opened on 30 Mar. On 2 Apr. Peel was defeated by an alliance of the Whigs and O'Connell, and after further defeats he resigned office on the 8th.

[2] Joseph Henry Green (see pt. ii, L. 844).

[3] Angharad Llwyd, *A History of the Island of Mona, or Anglesey*, 1833: it was in W. W.'s library at his death (see *R. M. Cat.*, no. 133).

[4] *Yarrow Revisited, and Other Poems.* The delay in publication had been

be sent to you through the Bookseller at Ruthen—it will be out in about a fortnight.

You will recollect Mr Fleming[1] of Rayrigg, formerly of St John's, he died suddenly about 3 months since, and not in good circumstances.

My Son John is still at Workington, where he holds the Living for his Brother in Law—but he will soon have to fall back upon his Vicarage at Brigham—he is building a house which will cost not much less than £1,000—£400 of which is contributed by the Patron and the Building Society. In the volume about to appear you will find a Sonnet beginning 'Pastor and Patriot'[2] upon the building of his house—I think he has had a Son born since you heard from us last—who, tho' an uncommonly fine Child when we saw him, at about a month or six weeks old, has since been a great sufferer, together with his Mother—from Influenza and Low fever—and the Child has been reduced to a state of weakness which has caused much anxiety to the Parents—he is however beginning, we hear, to gather strength. John seems to think that the situation of the Rectory at Workington is not favorable to health—being low and contiguous to marshy ground—so that we shall be glad of the change, when his family retire to the banks of the Derwent.

My wife joins me in every good wish to yourself and Sisters—Had I not now been so long absent, we had some of us meditated paying you a visit this Summer—as it is, we must hope to be spared to meet at some more distant time—unless you can muster courage—should you have leisure—to come to see us at Rydal.

Believe me my dear Friend to remain
faithfully and affectionately yours
[*signed*] Wm Wordsworth

I regret not having a frank—but I shall not wait for one thinking you would rather pay postage than that I sh^d do so.

---

caused by the preparation of the *Postscript* after W. W. arrived in London. See L. 863 above.

[1] See L. 861 above.
[2] See *PW* iv. 24.

875. W. W. to [?] HENRY THOMAS LIDDELL [1]

MS. untraced.
LY ii. 737.

Trinity Lodge, March 30th [1835]

My dear Sir,

I hope you have not thought me insensible to your kindness for having deferred so long my acknowledgements for your very kindly letter written upon a subject so interesting to me. Your letter followed me to London, but I was then in a course of frequent interviews with Dr Holland [2] relative to my Daughter's case—and her mother, who was with me was in correspondence with her on the subject: in order to Dr Holland's being put into possession of particulars with a view to lay them before Sir B. Brodie, [3] whose skill had restored your suffering Brother to health. I did hope that the result would have been, that I might have accompanied my thanks for your suggestions with an account that my daughter had been much relieved, and was in a fair way of recovery—on which account I deferred writing. It grieves me to say that for various causes with the statement of which you need not be troubled, Dr H. in the end did not think that any good would arise from consulting Sir B. B——— ; and accordingly it has not been done—and the same treatment which my daughter was under when we left home 6 weeks ago, continues to be used,—with some change in the mediums recommended by Dr H. to strengthen the digestive organs. I ought to have begun with mentioning that your letter was shown to Dr Holland, and taken by him into serious consideration. The sum of her case is, that she is relieved for a

---

[1] Henry Thomas Liddell (1797–1878), like W. W., educated at St. John's, Cambridge; successively Tory M.P. for Northumberland, Durham, and Liverpool, and like W. W. a strong opponent of the Reform Bill and the disestablishment of the Church of Ireland: author of *The Wizard of the North and other poems*, 1833 (*R. M. Cat.*, no. 569). W. W. sought his support in 1838 during his campaign for extending the period of Copyright. He succeeded his father as 2nd Baron Ravensworth in 1855, and he was created Earl of Ravensworth in 1874.

[2] Dr. Henry Holland.

[3] Sir Benjamin Collins Brodie, 1st Bart. (1783–1862), one of the most famous surgeons and doctors of his day: President of the Royal College of Surgeons, 1844, President of the Royal Society, 1858–61, first President of the General Medical Council, and a keen admirer of W. W.'s poems.

time by bleeding and blistering but after a week or so, the pains, and the disorder in the stomach recur—and the same course is repeated so that our anxiety cannot be said to be much less diminished on her account, and we long for the day when it shall be possible to bring her to Town in order that she may be seen both by Dr Holland and Sir Ben Brodie.

With persons who come to London so seldom as Mrs Wordsworth and I, and only for a short time—they are unavoidably much hurried, and glad to return to any quiet harbour, so is it with us—we are now guests with my Brother, the Master of Trin: Coll., Cambridge. This day, we are told, is to decide the fate of the Ministers,[1] and with them that of the Nation. Never having been hopeful, I am much less disturbed than is natural to one, who has so deep a feeling of the miseries that will be produced by those convulsions towards which we are rapidly advancing. Nevertheless the scenes that I witnessed during the earlier years of the French Revolution, when I was resident in France, come back on me with appalling violence— we are told that the King will send for Lord Grey,[2] does he hope that hoary-headed Magician, whose wand with Royal concurrence excited the storm, will be able to appease it. Alas, alas, for the shortsightedness of our nautical Sovereign!

Pray be so kind as to tell me how my little vol: of Poems[3] must be sent to you? It is printed, but my Publisher does not chuse to send it forth till the middle of April. You will find in it some political verses, which highflying critics will not allow to be poetry—enough for me, if they be admitted to be good rhetoric and enlightened patriotism, which the Whigs will, of course, be slow to consent to.

Pray present my kind respects to Mrs Liddell[4] and best wishes for her recovery, and believe me, with sincere thanks, my dear Sir,

Y^r much obliged
Wm Wordsworth

P.S. We shall remain here at least a fortnight.

---

[1] It was the opening day of the crucial debate on Lord John Russell's motion on the Irish Church. See previous letter.

[2] Lord Grey refused all overtures to resume the premiership, and on 11 Apr. the King sent for Lord Melbourne.

[3] *Yarrow Revisited, and Other Poems.*

[4] She was Isabella (d. 1856), eldest daughter of Lord George Seymour.

876. W. W. to JAMES WOOD

Address: The Master of St John's etc. etc, St John's Coll:—
MS. St. John's College, Cambridge. Hitherto unpublished.

[*In unidentified hand*]

April 1st [1835]
Trin: Lodge

Mr Wordsworth, with much pleasure, will do himself the honor of waiting upon the Master and Fellows of St John's to Dinner on Saturday next.—

877. W. W. to Mr B.[1]

MS. Private Collection. Hitherto unpublished.

Trin. Lodge
Wednesday Morn:
[? early Apr. 1835]

Mr Wordsworth is sorry that he did not recollect, yesterday, his having an engagement with Mr Worsley[2] between twelve and one, this day—If Mr B. could join him there, i.e. at Downing Coll: all might go together to the Pictures.[3] Or, could Mr B. call here a little before One?

[1] Unidentified: perhaps one of the Fellows of Trinity—or possibly William Boxall, the artist.
[2] The Revd. Thomas Worsley (1797–1885) had graduated at Trinity but transferred to Downing College, where he was Fellow and Tutor (1824–36), and then Master; and Vice-Chancellor of the University (1837–8). He was also rector of Scawton, Yorks., 1826–81. In 1842 he married Katharine, eldest daughter of Stansfeld Rawson of Wastdale Hall. D. W. mentions meeting him in her MS. Journal on 22 Feb. 1829 (*WL MSS.*), while she was visiting Cambridge from Whitwick (see pt. ii, L. 415). See also *R MVB* for 1843 and 1846.
[3] Probably the collection bequeathed to the University by Daniel Mesman. The pictures came into the possession of the University in 1834, and at first hung in a room in the Pitt Press, until they were transferred to the Fitzwilliam Museum in 1848.

878. W. W. to SAMUEL ROGERS

Endorsed: Not to be Published S.R.
MS. Sharpe Collection, University College, London.
Rogers. K (—). LY ii. 739.

[In M. W.'s hand]

Trinity Lodge April 5th [1835]

My dear Rogers,

The Papers announce the death of your, and let me add *my*, long-known and long-valued Friend, R^d Sharp;[1] sincerely do I condole with you and with his nearest connections upon this loss. How a thought of the presence of living friends brightens particular spots, and what a shade falls over them when those friends have passed away! This I have felt strongly in the course of the last twelve months in respect to London, vast as the place is. And even in regard to the Lakes, it makes me melancholy to think that Sharp will visit them no more. If you be in communication with Mrs Sharp[2] and Miss Kinnaird, pray assure them that Mrs W. and I sympathize sincerely with them in their bereavement.

The Papers also tell us that you have suffered a serious loss of Property by a robbery[3] committed in your house—the offender one of your own Servants. Was it the Footman? I remember being a good deal startled by your telling me that that Servant took the liberty of being absent as much as 4 hours at a time. I made some observation upon what you said, but not in such strong terms as would have been used had I not been in the habit of placing reliance upon your discretion. You expressed dissatisfaction and talked of dismissing him. After all, this may not be the man. Have any valuable pieces of virtu been taken? if not I shall be glad, and also to hear both that the value of the Property, viz £2,000, has been exaggerated, and part of it, at least, recovered.

[1] Richard Sharp had died at Dorchester on 30 Mar., on his way home from Torquay, where he had spent the winter.

[2] Richard Sharp's sister-in-law.

[3] *The Times* for 2 Apr. records that, on 31 Mar., Rogers's footman Sims, on being ordered to get ready for a breakfast party some plate which had not been in use for some time, absconded. It was then discovered that much valuable silver (including four dishes worth over £1,000) was missing, and it was conjectured that his thefts had extended over a considerable period. Rogers discussed the robbery in his reply to W. W. (*WL MSS.*).

Pray write to us at your early convenience. The great public unsettling[1] with which we are threatened unsettles my little plans also, causing me to doubt whether I shall return to London or not. Whatever may be shaken or altered, be you assured of my unchangeable attachment, and that I am, and ever shall be, firmly yours,

[*signed*] Wm Wordsworth

Kindest regards from Mrs W. and myself to your Sister.

879. W. W. to H. C. R.

Endorsed: Spring 1835, Wordsworth, Opinion of his own Works.
MS. Dr. Williams's Library.
K (—). *Morley, i. 271.*

[Rydal Mount]
[*c.* 27 Apr. 1835]

My dear Friend,

We arrived here on Friday last[2] an hour or two before sunset. We found our two invalids not worse than we feared. My Sister is indeed a good deal thinner, and continues to be troubled with squeamish sickness, but putting all things together, we have reason to hope that milder weather will benefit her. Poor Dora! occasions us much anxiety; she looks much worse than when we left her; and her stomach is deplorably deranged. For my own part I have no hope of any amendment, nor has her medical attendant, till the inflammation of the spine can be so far subdued, as to allow her of going Southward. So that you see nothing is left for us but patiently to wait God's will, using our best endeavours in the meanwhile, to forward the attainment of our wish, her removal for change of air etc.—

We found your Letter here, which removed a weight of anxiety from my mind. The thing may now be considered as settled, and my duty done[3]—In this matter as in a hundred

---

[1] The impending resignation of Peel's ministry.

[2] 24 Apr., which fixes the approximate date of this letter (see *MW*, p. 142).

[3] During his visit to London W. W. had been trying to arrange a final settlement with Caroline Baudouin, whereby the annuity of £30, which he had paid since her marriage in 1816, might be discontinued; and H. C. R. had been acting as his intermediary with her husband, who may have been making unreasonable demands. Under the new arrangement negotiated by H.C.R. and set out in his letter of 22 Apr. (which has not survived), W. W. settled a

others I feel deeply obliged to your ever-ready Friendship.—

We took three days to come down the weather being good, and I travelled on the outside, which gave me a sight of the Town of Coventry with its three spires gilded by a declining Sun.—Upon comparing notes at Birmingham with Mrs W—I found that she had known nothing of our having passed through Coventry, and, like other Insiders had seen little. I was pleased also with the Country about Trentham[1] the Duke of Sutherlands—near it is a valley prettily named the Vale of Springs—or Spring Vale—what a throng of poetic feelings does such a name prompt!—When I was at Hampstead[2] the accidental sight of the Words 'Goulders Hill' painted on a Board, as you see the names of streets, in London, stirred my mind agreeably in the same way, by recalling an Ode[3] of Akenside's written at that place, where, on recovery from a severe sickness, he visited his Friend Dyson,[4] who had been so generous to him in the earlier part of his life when the Poet started in London as a Physician.—The weather here is very sharp and today we have a blustering wind, tearing off the blossoms and twigs from the trees, with almost equal disregard.

—At Breakfast this morning we received from some unknown Friend the Examiner,[5] containing a friendly notice of my late Vol.—Is it discreditable to say that these things interest

final sum of £400 on Caroline. See *HCR* ii. 461–3; Moorman, ii. 333; and Edith C. Batho, *The Later Wordsworth*, 1933, pp. 390–5.

[1] Trentham Park, Staffs., seat of the Duke of Sutherland: now demolished.

[2] W. W. and M. W. had left Cambridge in the middle of April and spent a week with Mrs. Hoare in Hampstead, where there were more meetings with Rogers, H. C. R., and Henry Nelson Coleridge. They left for the north on the 22nd.

[3] *Odes on Several Subjects*, Book II, ode xii: *On Recovering from a Fit of Sickness; in the Country. 1758*. It begins:

Thy verdant scenes, O Goulder's hill,

Once more I seek, a languid guest.   (Morley's note.)

[4] Jeremiah Dyson (1722–76), Clerk to the House of Commons, and (later) M.P. and Lord of the Treasury: Akenside's patron, who had him appointed physician to the Queen in 1761. In 1772 he published an edition of Akenside's poems, with a Life.

[5] H. C. R. had sent *The Examiner*. 'I did not send it because I thought the article one of great sagacity, but because it was written in a spirit of honest love—The praise was not grudgingly given—Indeed it is pleasing to remark this everywhere . . . ' (Morley, i. 274). The author of the review was the literary editor of *The Examiner*, John Forster (see pt. ii, L. 659).

me little, but as they may tend to promote the sale; which with the prospects of unavoidable expense before me, is a greater object to me[1] much greater than it would otherwise have been.—The private testimonies which I receive very frequently of the effect of my writings upon the hearts and minds of men, are indeed very gratifying—because I am sure *they* must be written under *pure* influences—but it is not necessarily or even probably so with strictures intended for the public. The one are *effusions,* the other *compositions,* and liable in various degrees to inter-mixtures that take from their value—It is amusing to me to have proofs how Critics and Authors differ in judgement, both as to fundamentals and Incidentals.—As an instance of the latter—see the passage where I speak of Horace,[2]—quoted in the Examiner. The Critic marks in Italics for approbation, certain passages—but he takes no notice of three words, in delicacy of feeling worth in my estimation, all the rest—'he only listening'! Again what he observes in praise of my mode of dealing with Nature, as opposed to my treatment of human life, which as he says is not to be trusted, would be reversed as it has been by many who maintain that I run into excess in my pictures of the influence of natural objects, and assign to them an importance which they are not entitled to; while in my treatment of the intellectual instincts affections and passions of mankind, I am nobly distinguished by having drawn out into notice the points in which they resemble each other, in preference to dwelling, as dramatic Authors must do, upon those in which they differ. If my writings are to last, it will I myself believe, be mainly owing to this characteristic. They will please for the single cause, 'That we have all of us one human heart!'

farewell.

Do let us hear from you pretty often. And as you can get franks you can write as briefly as you like.

Ever affectionately yours
W W.

[*M. W. writes*]

My dear friend,

I must correct what W. says about Dora. The inflammation *is*

---

[1] *Three words deleted.*

[2] *See Liberty (PW* iv. 153), ll. 100 ff. The poem was first published in the *Yarrow Revisited* volume.

in a great measure subdued. But the stomach and power of digestion seem worse than ever—and my only hope is from change of air. How that is to be effected I do not see[1]—She is so bound to home! We have scarcely yet ventured on the subject.

God bless you.

aff^{ly} y^r obliged friend
M Wordsworth.

880. W. W. to EDWARD SIMMS[2]

Address: Edward Simms Esqre, Great Malvern, Worcestershire. [*In M. W.'s hand*]
Stamp: Kendal Penny Post.
MS. Exeter University Library. Hitherto unpublished.

Rydal Mount Apr. 27th [1835]

Dear Sir,

Upon my return from London two days ago[3] I found your letter of the 16th Inst^t, containing an elegant Sonnet addressed to myself, and a copy of Verses to the memory of Sir Walter Scott. For both these marks of regard I thank you, and not without regret that my absence from home prevented me do[ing][4] so earlier.—Your Letter affords a proof in addition to many of the same kind, of the injury which may be done by bad criticism; and this in case of my Writings is the more remarkable as their sale for the last 35 years has shown that notwithstanding every endeavour to impede their circulation they have been in constant and regular, though not in great demand. Take care, however, that the sense of injustice both to yourself and me, in having neglected, or rather disregarded them so long, does not by a natural reaction of the mind impel you now to overrate them.—

[1] The Wordsworths were at this stage hoping to return with Dora W. to London.

[2] Probably to be identified with the Revd. Edward Sims (b. 1803), author of the *Book of Psalms*, who graduated M.A. from Wadham College, Oxford, in 1829, and appears (very much later) as vicar of Escot, Devon (1870–7). The Exeter University archives preserve a letter addressed to him at George Street, Bath, from J. G. Lockhart, dated 6 Nov. 1832, thanking him for his verses to the memory of Scott, and promising to try and get them published; but nothing further is known about them.

[3] W. W. actually arrived home on the evening of the 24th.

[4] *Written* do.

27 April 1835

Your Verses to the memory of Sir Walter Scott are not unworthy of the Subject. The former part is especially tender and appropriate. But will you allow me to say as one practised in the *Art* of Composition, that the notice of Sir W.'s writings is a little too much in detail, to come after the pathetic introduction. From an opinion thus sincerely given you may fairly gather that I admire the poem upon the whole *very much.*

Believe me dear Sir
respectfully
Your obliged Ser^{vnt}
Wm Wordsworth

881. W. W. to MESSRS. BELL BROTHERS AND CO.

Address: Messrs Bell Brokers, 164 Aldersgate Street, London.
Postmark: (1) 2 May 1835 (2) 5 May 1835. *Stamp*: Kendal Penny Post.
Endorsed: Rydal Mount May 4th 183[5] Wm Wordsworth. Rec:^d — 5th. Ans.^d—
MS. Yale University Library. Hitherto unpublished.

[*In M. W.'s hand*] Rydal Mount May 4.th [1835]

To Messrs Bell etc—

Gent.

I have to request you will pay the proceeds of the demand as on the preceeding page—together with any other balance in hand, to Philip Courtenay Esqre, on my account—retaining the charges out of the money you may have received.

I am Gent. yours sincerely

[*signed*] Wm Wordsworth

46

882. W. W. to SAMUEL ROGERS

Address: Sam¹ Rogers Esqre, St James' Place. [*In M. W.'s hand*]
Endorsed: Not to be Published S. R.
MS. Sharpe Collection, University College, London.
Rogers. LY ii. 740.

4th May 1835
Rydal Mount

My dear Rogers,
      I enclose a line barely to say that after a journey of three days, having slept at Birmingham and Manchester, we reached this place in good health.
      My poor Sister is rather better; but every day and hour add to our anxiety for the removal of my Daughter to London for medical advice.
      I hope when we return we shall find you in London. It grieved me to come away without seeing you again. My Son W^m is now with us, and looking better than I have seen him do for some years. He bears his disappointment in being still without a better provision as well as could be expected. You would be pleased to see how sensible he is of your affectionate kindness towards him, and happy am I to see he is not unworthy of it. He is a great comfort to us all in our distress. Poor Mrs Southey appears to be but little, if at all, improved. Your Portrait¹ is much liked in this house—I own, elegant as it is, I could have wished for something with more strength. Love from everyone here to yourself and sister,

And believe [me], my dear Friend
most faithfully yours
Wm Wordsworth

¹ Probably one of the several engravings produced of Sir Thomas Lawrence's portrait of Rogers, published by Cadell and Davies in *Contemporary Portraits*, 1822. See also Rogers, i. 366.

882a. W. W. to MESSRS. HUDSON AND NICHOLSON [1]

Address: Messrs Hudson and Nicholson, Booksellers, Kendal. [*In M. W.'s hand*]
MS. Cornell. Hitherto unpublished.

Rydal Mount
7th May 1835

Sirs,

My Book upon the Lakes [2] is out of Print, and it has struck me that an arrangement might be made with you for its being printed and published at Kendal; and I should like to know, if you approve of the proposal, upon what terms you would undertake it, so as that the joint interests of Author and Publisher might be fairly and best promoted.—I am persuaded that this little Book would have a considerable sale, if any Publisher Resident in the Country would undertake to circulate it through the Lake district, and in the leading Towns of the North. Of course an arrangement would be expedient so that the Book might be had at Messrs Longmans and Moxon my Publishers in London, and any other Bookseller.

Let me have your answer as soon as you can, as I wish to go to press instantly in order to secure the advantage of the sale of the approaching season.—

If either of you Gentlemen should be coming this way I should be glad to settle the *terms* etc by conversation.

I am Gentlemen
Your obedient Ser^{vnt}
Wm Wordsworth

883. W. W. to THOMAS NOON TALFOURD

MS. Harvard University Library. Hitherto unpublished.

May 13th [1835]
Rydal Mount

My dear Sir,

I have taken the liberty of returning the Enclosed through you.—

[1] The Kendal publishers. See L. 935 below.

[2] i.e. 4th edition of 1823. For the new edition see Ls. 915 and 919 below.

I was very sorry to leave the South without seeing you and Mrs Talfourd; but [it][1] could not be helped.

We found my poor Sister much weaker and she continues to be so. My Daughter also is deplorably reduced in Flesh and we are most anxious to have her moved southwards as soon as her Doctor shall give us leave. We are of course suffering under much anxiety, but bear up as well as we can. I directed my new Vol[2] to be sent you.

> Believe me
> dear Mr Talfourd,
> ever faithfully yours
> W. Wordsworth

884. W. W. to EDWARD MOXON

Address: Ed. Moxon Esqre, Dover Street.
Postmark: 15 May 1835.
MS. Wellesley College.
LY ii. 741.

[*c*. 14 May 1835]

My dear Sir,

Thank you for the sonnets.[3] I am not at all disappointed in them. They are very pleasing; and we all like them much.— You need not apologize for dedicating them to me—for they aim at no rivalship with mine, being so different both in the unity of the subject, and in the metre and style of versification. Yours are of Elizabeth's and James's and the 1st Charles' time; mine rather after the model of Milton.

We reached home without mischance—but found little in either of our invalids to rejoice over—I am most anxious for my daughter's moving southward as soon as her Doctor shall give her leave. With kindest remembrances to yourself and Mrs M and your Br and sister, in which Mrs W and my family unite,

> I remain my dear Sir
> Your sincere friend
> Wm Wordsworth

[1] *Seal.*

[2] *Yarrow Revisited, and Other Poems.*

[3] The second volume of Edward Moxon's *Sonnets*, dedicated to W. W., was published in 1835.

885. D. W. and ISABELLA W. to C. W. JNR.

Address: Revd Christopher Wordsworth, Trinity College, Cambridge. [*In Dora W.'s hand*]
Stamp: Kendal Penny Post.
MS. British Library. Hitherto unpublished.

[*c.* 18 May 1835][1]

My good and dear Nephew,
      You would be more than recompensed for the sacrifice (from your apartment in Trinity College to my quiet prison-house) of the Virgin and her two lovely Babes if you could form a notion of the deep delight I have in looking upon the placid figure of the Mother, and the infantine grace of the Children. My first feeling when the Box was opened was chiefly my gratitude to you and a touch, I hope, of innocent pride in the possession of the love and thoughtful friendship of so many Nephews all removed far from me. The picture itself pleased me much, but compared with the feeling which I *now* always have in looking on your precious gift it was nothing; my admiration grows daily— It hangs opposite to the bottom of my Bed and when all the Family are gone to Rest is my soothing companion when lighted up by the temperate blaze of the fire; and my pleasure increases the more it is indulged. But I must cut short. Though I write lying on my back it wearies me—so in few words I will entreat you if possible to come to Rydal this summer—Mrs Hoare threw out a hint that you wished to come and perhaps *might*. It would be a great happiness to me to see you once again. I trust our poor Dora is really improved. The Back certainly *is* much relieved, and, though still very weak I believe her to be a little stronger; but she suffers grievously from her stomach. The shower bath agrees with her and I am hopeful that in a short time we may see a great change and that she may be strong enough to bear the journey to her kind and best of Friends Mrs and Miss Hoare. Isabella will write the letter,—for mine deserves not the name,—and will tell you about us all—but never can she tell you what delight I should have in seeing your dear Father and all of you. Your Uncle admonishes me to write

---

[1] This letter was written a few days after Isabella W. and her two children arrived at Rydal Mount on Wednesday 13 May (see *MW*, p. 145). S. H.'s letter to Mrs. Hutchinson which mentions the same event (*SH*, p. 445), should probably be dated a week earlier.

no more so Farewell! and may God bless and prosper you through life

Your loving Aunt
Dorothy Wordswoth.

The Mother will perhaps be too modest to praise her little Jane as she deserves—therefore I must tell you that she is a sweet lively child as ever was born and wins her way into all hearts.

[Isabella W. writes]

My dear Cousin,

Our dear Aunt has deputed me to finish her letter. She has given you an unworthy scribe, but a very willing one; so I hope the latter quality will a little compensate for the former. We arrived here on Wednesday evening: it is a year and nine months since I was last here: of course I see a great change, in poor Aunt Wordsworth, tho' she still looks better in the face than I expected, but she is dreadfully weak and languid, more so than usual, I understand, for the last few days. The beautiful print which you sent is a source of great delight to her; I think the patience with which she bears her sufferings is the very triumph of Christianity! It rejoices me to tell you that our dearest Sara,[1] appears by all accounts, to have gained ground the last week; indeed she is better, far better, than I dared to have expected. My Father[2] has lent her an old carriage of his, in which I hope when the weather becomes milder, she will consent to go, in the first instance to Workington, and afterwards to London. I am desired by Father[3] to say that when he sees Mother and Dora comfortably settled in some watering place, he will pay you a visit. A sofa bed he says will be all he shall require. Willy, probably, will be with him; and he will be equally easy as to his accommodation—but he hopes this intimation will not prevent your coming here; Aunt does so long to see you! and pray do not forget your friends at Workington; I hope you will stay with me as long as you possibly can: and I do not forget Cousin Charles's promise of visiting us this summer: pray tell him so, with my kind love. Willy returned to Carlisle today: We are loath to part with him: dear, merry fellow: my Husband has

---

[1] S. H. had been suffering from lumbago, which later turned to rheumatic fever, and proved fatal.

[2] Henry Curwen.

[3] i.e. W. W.

[gone] part of the way with him and probably will stay all night with Dr Jackson at Lowther. Father was much pleased by your letter; the Archbishop's comment[ary?][1] is a very touching one and truth itself: we are kept busy reading all the *proofs*: I have been reading Wilson's[2] in *Blackwood* to Aunt: it is extraordinary how he is puffed in all the Whig and Radical publications; and scarcely noticed in the Tory and Conservative Papers. John has to preach before the Bishop of Chester at his Visitation in the Summer and we shall have to entertain his Lordship and his suite, into the bargain. Is dear Cousin John at Cambridge now? I have wished to write to him for long: but really I have nothing to say worth his reading. I am pretty impudent in writing to you, I think: but dear Aunt must bear the blame. Our little girl meets with unbounded love and kindness. I am much disappointed at not introducing our sweet wee son; but he is a delicate plant, and not as yet able to bear transplanting, so I have left him under my Mother's care. I am charged with kind loves and wishes without end to yourself, Dr Wordsworth and Your Brother: Mother would have written to you, had she not done so to John just before.

> Believe me, ever dear Chris
> Your very affectionate Cousin
> Isabella C. Wordsworth

886. W. W. to UNKNOWN CORRESPONDENT

MS. National Library of Scotland. Hitherto unpublished.

> May 19th [? 1835] Rydal Mount
> near Ambleside

Dear Sir,

On my return home after an absence of two months I find your Vol: of Poems with several others waiting my arrival. For this mark of your attention I sincerely thank you, promising myself much pleasure from the perusal of your book at my early leisure.

> Believe me to be sincerely your much obliged
> Wm Wordsworth

[1] *MS. obscure.*

[2] John Wilson, 'Wordsworth's New Volume', *Blackwood's Magazine*, xxxvii (May 1835), 699–722, a notable survey of some of the later poetry.

887. W. W. to H. C. R.

Address: H. C. Robinson Esq., Temple.
Endorsed: May 1835, Wordsworth family matters.
MS. Dr. Williams's Library.
K (—). *Morley, i. 275.*

[late May *or* early June 1835]

My dear Friend

You will be surprized at not hearing from us; in fact we have been in sad distress. Miss Hutchinson has been dangerously ill in a severe rheumatic fever from which we *trust* she is recovering though slowly and somewhat doubtfully. My poor Sister grows weaker and weaker, more and more emaciated. The last month was very hard upon all our Invalids, Dora included, who in common with both her poor Aunts suffered grievously from Influenza, caused by the changeableness of the weather. She is however, God be thanked, better in a stomach which has been much injured by a preparation of steel recommended as a trial, by Dr Holland. Her restlessness and anxiety for her aunts have thrown her back, but upon the whole she is not so ill as when we arrived from Town.

Had not my family been in so distressing a state, I should have gone to London by Cambridge about the beginning of next month which probably would have allowed me the pleasure of seeing you before your departure for the Continent. At present I can entertain no such project, as it seems impossible that my beloved Sister can put on for any length of time. The extreme heat has been very unfavorable to all our invalids; the thermometer for these last three days has never been under 68 in my sisters room in any of the 24 hours, and often at 78— notwithstanding all our endeavours to moderate the heat. Will you pardon me when I mention that in the· midst of all this sorrow and anxiety I have not yet had the courage to look at the Italian Verses you sent me. They are however carefully preserved, and shall be studied as soon as I can command myself so as to take any interest in literature of that kind.—

Pray Do not fail to see Mr Courtenay before you go respecting any thing he may have to say, of my little temporalities, especially what relates to the Government Annuities and the disposal of any money which might become due from that quarter. I mention this point as I don't like to teaze him with Letters, and as in all probability he will be absent from

London during great part of the ensuing summer.—

Mes^{rs} Bell[1]

are my Brokers, and should you be passing that way, you might learn from them how the account stands, and when any thing is likely to be due. I am very unwilling to worry Mr Courtenay about this affair—Pray let us know how dear Miss Lamb is—and believe me with much regret that I am obliged to write in this sad strain

ever your affectionate Friend

Wm Wordsworth

888. W. W. to JOHN MACRONE[2]

Address: J. Macrone Esqre, 3 St James Square, London. [*In M. W.'s hand*]
Postmark: 11 June 1835. *Stamp*: Strand.
MS. Henry E. Huntington Library.
LY ii. 741.

Rydal Mount Ambleside
June 2nd [1835]

Sir,

Accept my thanks for the life of Milton which you have sent me, and my sincere acknowledgements of the honor done me by the Dedication[3] which is more acceptable as uniting my name with Mr Southey's. This mark of respect to us both will I trust meet with the approbation of our common Friend, the Author, who is well fitted to do justice to the arduous task which he has undertaken.

I remain
Sir
respectfully
your obliged Ser^{vnt}
Wm Wordsworth

This Letter would have been posted earlier but it was detained for the opportunity of a Frank.

---

[1] See L. 881 above.

[2] John Macrone (1809–37) set up as publisher on his own account at 3 St. James's Square in 1834. *The Poetical Works of John Milton*, ed. Sir Egerton Brydges, with illustrations by J. M. W. Turner, 6 vols., 1835, was his most ambitious venture to date.

[3] It ran: 'To William Wordsworth and Robert Southey these volumes are appropriately dedicated.'

889. W. W. to SAMUEL CARTER HALL

Address: C. Hall Esqre, 59 Upper Charlotte St, Fitzroy Square [*In M. W.'s hand*]
MS. Mr W. Hugh Peal. Hitherto unpublished.

Rydal Mount
near Kendal
5th June [? 1835][1]

Dear Sir,

Your obliging Letter through Mr Johnstone[2] has remained too long unanswered for which, sickness in my family and much consequent anxiety must be the cause.

I had always a strong aversion to have any thing to do with Annuals. Money tempted me into one, and if money were not to a Person in my situation a rational object, I should have been properly punished by the subsequent conduct of those Parties[3] for being seduced by such a consideration.

I am pleased with your frankness, and your sagacity has anticipated my answer. Poets, whatever Painters may do, seldom succeed when they work to order. I am not under that necessity having several Pieces by me which were Voluntaries, but a word will suffice between us, the best terms you can offer are below what I can bring my self to accept—You are perhaps aware that the Annuals with their ornaments, have destroyed the Sale of several Poems which—till that Invention of some evil Spirit (a German one I believe)[4] was transplanted to this Country—brought substantial profit to their Authors, [and][5]

---

[1] This letter is difficult to date with any certainty. It must have been written some time before 1837 when Hall gave up the editorship of *The Amulet*, but later than 1831, for in that year Hall was not yet resident in Upper Charlotte Street. The most likely year seems to be 1835. W. W. probably met Hall again during his recent visit to London, and this may have prompted Hall to renew his application for a contribution to *The Amulet*.

[2] Probably the Revd. William Johnson, whom W. W. had seen again in London on 18 Mar. (see L. 872 above).

[3] Charles Heath and F. Mansel Reynolds of *The Keepsake*. See pt. ii, L. 438.

[4] Rudolph Ackermann (1764–1834), the fine-art publisher, a German by origin, set up in 1817 a press for reproducing lithographic plates, after his earlier success with the *Microcosm of London*, 3 vols., 1808–11, and other collections; and in 1822 he introduced the illustrated annual from Germany. His *Forget-me-not*, edited by F. Shoberl, ran from 1825 till 1847.

[5] *MS. torn.*

were regarded as Standard works. You will regret this, I know, as much as any one, and your liberality would prompt you, I am sure to do your utmost, for the less wealthy part of that community—but what avails it?—Competition, the Idol of the Political economists, in fact ruins every thing.—Adieu, present my Comp^ts to Mrs Hall,[1] and believe me sincerely yours

Wm Wordsworth

890. W. W. to GEORGE DYER

Address: George Dyer Esq., Clifford's Inn.
Postmark: 11 July 1835. Stamp: Strand.
MS. Cornell. Hitherto unpublished.

Rydal Mount
Ambleside
June 6th 1835

My dear Mr Dyer,
    Your valuable Present of the Privileges of the University of Cambridge,[2] and the Academic Unity,[3] have duly been received; accept my sincere thanks for this token of your regard at so late a period of life, and under the pressure of your sad privation. These Volumes will have a place in my small library, by the side of your History of the University, for which I was indebted long ago to your kindness; and which I not unfrequently refer to with instruction and pleasure. The same I hope to derive from these Volumes which may be considered as a supplement to that work.
    Wishing you ease and consolation for the remainder of your days, and a quiet passage to a happy Immortality, I remain my dear Sir

very faithfully
your obliged Friend
Wm Wordsworth

[1] Anna Maria Hall (1800—81), author of *Sketches of Irish Character*, 3 vols., 1829 (2nd series, 1831), had married S. C. Hall in 1824. A prolific author and editor in her own right, she also published numerous volumes jointly with her husband.

[2] *Privileges of the University of Cambridge*, 1824.

[3] *Academic Unity*, 1827.

891. W. W. to BENJAMIN DOCKRAY

Address: Benjamin Dockray Esq, Lancaster.
Stamp: Kendal Penny Post.
MS. Cornell.
Broughton, p. 72.

Rydal Mount
June 7th (1835 B D)

My dear Friend

The affliction under which my family has been suffering for some time, no less than three of its members[1] being confined to the bed or couch by severe or dangerous illness, will I am sure be accepted as a more than sufficient apology for my not having sooner thanked you for your obliging Present. I have looked over your little treatise,[2] but my mind being so much troubled, I have not been able to bestow upon it the reflection which, in common with every thing from your pen, it deserves. All that I can now do is to thank you for this mark of your regard and to unite with you in a wish that Mutual Tolerance may spread wide as Christianity itself.

I remain
with much respect
Your obliged Friend
W[m] Wordsworth

892. W. W. to ROBERT SOUTHEY

MS. Henry E. Huntington Library.
LY ii. 742.

Sunday Morning
June 7 [1835]

My dear Southey,

We have been and are, in sad distress in this House. My Beloved Sister's days are drawing steadily to a close; She

---

[1] i.e. D. W., Dora W., and S. H.

[2] *On Mutual Tolerance, And on the Ultimate Test of Truth: Occasioned by a Recent Publication, Entitled 'A Beacon to the Society of Friends'*, 1835: a plea for the exercise of mutual charity in religious disputes, and a defence of traditional Quakerism against the strictures of Isaac Crewdson (1780–1844), who resigned from the Society of Friends, and sparked off a schism that drove many into Evangelical Christianity and permanently weakened the Society (see Elizabeth Isichei, *Victorian Quakers*, 1970).

grows obviously weaker and weaker every day; And dear Miss Hutchinson too is still suffering under her severe attack; lumbago, at first, then rheumatic fever, with frequent delirium, which is not yet quite gone. We hope however and trust that she is recovering; Mr Carr, who has been very anxious about her, tells us that it is chiefly weakness that causes the symptoms, which continue to make us uneasy. The changeable weather during the last month was very injurious to both these Invalids, and to Dora also; they were all attacked with severe Influenza; Dora's stomach is certainly improved but in other respects I fear she is but little better. The blistering that was suspended by the severity of her Influenza has been resumed, but the benefit has been greatly frustrated by her anxiety and restlessness on account of her two Aunts.—

I hope, my dear Friend, you have better accounts to give of your own family. God bless you, and may he in his goodness give us both strength to support our trials, and the same to all who suffer along with us. ever affectionately yours

W. Wordsworth

[*M. W. adds*]

My dear Girls,[1]

I cannot put up this scrawl to y[r] good father, without telling you that my beloved Sister in all her wanderings by night and by day, which have continued for at least a week, often turned her thoughts to you, with anxiety that you should be told *why* she was seeming to neglect you—'They never forget me, in their and my anxiety' has she often exclaimed—Sainted Miss W's pleasant and beneficent days on Earth will soon be closed— as far as human foresight may so say. God love and support us all—Aff[ly] yours   M. Wordsworth

Sunday 10, o'C mng
Pray send the enclosed to J. W.[2]

---

[1] Bertha and Kate Southey.
[2] Probably the Revd. John Warter.

893. W. W. to MRS. WILLIAMSON[1]

Address: The Rev^d—Williamson, Farnley, near Leeds.
Endorsed: For Mrs. W.
Stamp: Kendal Penny Post.
MS. Cornell. Hitherto unpublished.

Rydal Mount
7th June 183[5]

Dear Mrs Williamson,

Accept our thanks for the friendly communications made to us through your Letter to Mrs Fisher,[2] who put it into our hands yesterday. I have undertaken to answer to your kind proposal, the females in my house being all except Mrs W. unable to hold correspondence with their Friends. Poor Miss W. grows weaker and weaker; and Miss Hutchinson has been attacked by a most severe rheumatic fever, under which she was light-headed for many days. We trust however that she is now at last out of danger and doing well. Her medical attendant who has seen her this morning is in very good heart about her.—

Under these circumstances you will be aware that Mrs W. has no leisure to write; and we do not allow Dora to take that liberty with herself. She is certainly, upon the whole, better, particularly in the stomach which caused us all so much alarm. A preparation of steel advized by Dr Holland, disagreed most deplorably with her, and much increased the derangement in her digestive organs; indeed it acted like a sort of poison upon them. She has now recovered, I trust, from that mischief; and would I think have been much better in all points, but for the restlessness both of mind and body caused by the condition of her dear Aunts. The weather of last month was by the sharpness of its changes of temperatures very hurtful to our Invalids, and now the heat is most oppressive: but God is merciful, and my beloved Sister is also somewhat better than she was two or three days ago.

In answer to your proposal and invitation, of which we are all duly sensible, you will see that we can only at present return our cordial thanks. We are indeed most anxious for Dora's removal

---

[1] Wife of the Revd. William Williamson (1799–*c*. 1865), Fellow of Sidney Sussex College, Cambridge (1826–8), curate of Farnley, Leeds (1831–3), and perpetual curate of Headingley (1836–63): probably a friend of the Marshalls. See *RMVB*, 1831, etc. See also *MW*, p. 264.

[2] A local friend (see *SH*, p. 422).

southward, but at present it is out of the question to fulfil engagements previously made with your Southern Friends. We were grieved to learn that your Sister had been so poorly. Let us hope that Barden with its fine air, its beauty and quiet, along with due care on her part, will restore her to health and strength. The Country all about Barden as far as I have seen is delicious. Pray accept our kindest remembrances and present the same to Mr Williamson and your Sisters. Mrs Wordsworth has just come down from her Sister Sarah's room and reports that she is *much* better. So that I hope every thing will go on well with *her*, as to my own dear Sister, it is with her a mere question of time; as it seems, humanly speaking, impossible that she should rally in any effectual degree.

ever faithfully your much obliged

Wm Wordsworth

P.S. Mrs Fisher will send off the Boxes on Friday—and reply to y^r other questions—when aught is fixed regarding Mr Kingsley's[1] continuance at Grasmere—which is at present in suspence—the unworthy Rector[2] having returned to the Parsonage.

894. W. W. to JOHN WORDSWORTH[3]

Address: Mr Wordsworth, Keswick.
MS. WL.
LY ii. 743.

Sunday morning, June 7th [1835]

My dear John,

You will grieve to hear of the state of this House, which makes it quite impossible that we can see you here. Your poor Aunt is growing weaker and weaker every day and hour; and Miss Hutchinson lies suffering under a severe and still somewhat dangerous attack of Rheumatic fever, it began with lumbago, upon which was accumulated the Influenza, under which Dora suffered very much and which did not spare your Aunt Dorothy, so that we have a sad House of it. Mr Carr trusts that the worst is over with Miss Hutchinson, but she is light headed

---

[1] Apparently a temporary curate at Grasmere (see *RMVB*, Jan. 1833).
[2] Sir Richard le Fleming.
[3] R. W.'s son.

at this moment I am now writing, as she has been frequently, and for a length of time together. As soon as a decided change takes place in any of our patients I shall write again. Your poor Aunt Wordsworth is much harassed.

During the attack of Influenza Dora's blistering was stopped, it has been resumed but with less benefit on account of her anxiety and restlessness about her poor Aunt.

Pray give my kind regards to your Mother and comp^{ts} to Mr Lightfoot;[1] and believe me my dear John, with love from all, which I know they would send you, could I tell them that I was writing,

ever your affectionate Uncle
Wm Wordsworth

895. W. W. to JOSHUA WATSON

MS. WL.
LY ii. 744.

Rydal Mount Ambleside
16th June, 1835

My dear Sir,

Pray excuse my breaking in upon you with the old concern; viz—the interests of my younger Son into which you entered in so friendly a manner. The Papers announce that a new Church Commission[2] is formed; among the members are several of the present administration, who, I have no doubt, are well disposed to me *personally*, in particular the Marquis of Lansdown[3] and Spring Rice.[4]—Should the new appointments rest wholly with

---

[1] 'Keswick John's' stepfather, the attorney.

[2] See L. 865 above.

[3] Henry Petty-Fitzmaurice, 3rd Marquess of Lansdowne (1780–1863), was educated at Edinburgh University, where he was the friend of Brougham, Jeffrey, and Horner, and at Trinity College, Cambridge. At the age of 25 he became Chancellor of the Exchequer in Grenville's ministry of 'All the Talents' (1806), and was later a strong supporter of Catholic Emancipation and the Reform Bill. In 1830 he became President of the Council under Grey, and held the same post in both of Lord Melbourne's administrations. He was a moderate Whig much respected on both sides of the House, and (like W. W. himself) had a strong interest in national education.

[4] Thomas Spring Rice, M.P. for the borough of Cambridge, and now Chancellor of the Exchequer in Melbourne's second administration.

Lord Melbourne, Wm's prospect would I fear be unfavorable enough; as of him I know nothing. If the Archbishop of C—[1] could be satisfied as to my Son's fitness, I should be pretty sure of his support. Pray my dear Sir, could you do any thing for us in this emergency, or put me in the way of exerting myself with men now in power, without compromising my own independence as a Writer or in conversation. The Bp of London[2] also I think is one of my well wishers.

You will grieve to hear that our House has been greatly afflicted with sickness since Mrs W— and I reached home. My poor Sister has been gradually growing weaker if her state be measured by weeks, and now she cannot stand. My daughter continues to be confined to the Couch: My Wife's Sister who has passed three parts of the last 30 years under our roof, has been, and still is, suffering from a rheumatic fever, by which she is reduced to deplorable weakness, and lastly one of our two Maid Servants had been ten days confined to her bed by the same complaint. Through all these trials Mrs W bears up in an admirable manner, though attendant day and night upon one sickbed or another. Her Sister-in-Law[3] has come from Hereford to help us, and we wait patiently God's pleasure.

My Publisher tells me that upwards of nine hundred Copies of my late Vol. are disposed of, so that your little Paragraph[4] upon the *right* of the poor to public support, has had a chance of being pretty extensively read. Pray give my affectionate remembrances to Miss Watson in which, as well as in the like to yourself, Mrs W. unites—

ever faithfully your obliged friend

W. Wordsworth

[1] Dr. William Howley.
[2] C. J. Blomfield.
[3] Mrs. Mary Hutchinson from Brinsop.
[4] Probably the ninth paragraph of the *Postscript, 1835* (*Prose Works*, iii. 242), in which W. W. voiced his misgivings about the Poor Law Amendment Act. As Owen and Smyser point out, W. W. was here combating the views of such as Malthus, who denied that the poor have any 'right' to public support, and was advancing a novel argument of his own. Under the old Poor Laws, which went back to Reformation times, parish officers were obliged to relieve the poor; but the poor had no 'right' to relief.

MS. *Kenneth Spencer Research Library, University of Kansas.*
Hitherto unpublished.

Rydal Mount
16th June [1835]

My dear Mr Taylor,

We have heard of your severe illness through our excellent Friend, Miss Fenwick, but it is more than time that we should inquire of you, from yourself. Pray write, however short a notice, to let us know how you are; we hope completely recovered.

It seems also incumbent upon me to tell you that my family has been much afflicted with sickness since we came home. My Sister is so feeble that she cannot stand. My daughter, though something better, is confined still to the Sofa; Miss Hutchinson my wife's Sister, has been dangerously ill of rheumatic fever, which has reduced her deplorably, and lastly one of our two Maid-servants is confined to her bed by something of the same complaint. It rarely happens that so many are so ill at once in so small a family, without infection from which, thank God, we are free. Mrs W—— supports herself wonderfully through these trials.—

It is not without reluctance that I allude under these circumstances to worldly interests; though coming near me, they are not however my own, being those of my younger Son, whom I took so much trouble about as you know. My wish was to procure for him the appointment of one of the three new Commissioners recommended to be made in the Report upon that subject. The Papers announce that Lord Lansdown and Mr Spring Rice are both of the new Commission;[1] perhaps you might have an opportunity of mentioning to them my wishes in respect to my Son, and the exertions I made in his behalf. The Archbishop of Canterbury would, I know, were he satisfied of his Competence be well disposed to serve him. As to his fitness for business I can affirm that he has a good judgement, is most diligent and orderly, and as my Subdistributor in a situation of great responsibility has for several years acted entirely to my satisfaction.

But I must conclude with a thousand good wishes in which

---

[1] The Church Commission. See previous letter.

Mrs W. cordially unites, ever faithfully yours

Wm Wordsworth

[*M. W. adds*]

Are we to see you in the North.   M. W.

897. W. W. to UNKNOWN CORRESPONDENT

MS. Harvard University Library.
LY ii. 745.

Rydal Mount, Ambleside.
June 17th 1835.

Sir,

Accept my thanks for your valuable Pamphlet.[1] The subject is of high importance, and you have treated it in a convincing and masterly manner.

You have proved that the argument drawn from the supposed practice of antiquity is without foundation. As to the question of expediency one is surprized that men above the lowest vulgar should be unable to see that selection of Spiritual Teachers, as a general measure for the Mass of the people, is strictly *preposterous*: in as much as it presumes the preexistence of that state of judgement in religious matters, and those acquisitions of knowledge, which it is the office of a fit Minister to labour all he can to produce, and to communicate. Moreover, what cabals and factions and heart-burnings, and antichristian feelings and practices of all kinds does the popular mode of election excite and prolong?

I remain, Sir,
With thanks and sincere respect
your obliged Ser^{vnt}
Wm Wordsworth

[1] Unidentified; but probably a discussion of the Patronage question which, along with so many other issues, was agitating the Church of England at this time.

898. W. W. to H. C. R.

Address: H. C. Robinson Esqr, 2 Plowden's Buildings, Temple, London. [*In M. W.'s hand*]
Postmark: 26 June 1835. *Stamp*: Kendal Penny Post.
Endorsed: 24th June 1835, Wordsworth Death of Miss Hutchinson.
MS. Dr. Williams's Library.
K (—). Morley, i. 277.

Rydal Mount
Wednesday June 24th [1835]

My dear Friend,

I will not distress you with a detail of all that we have feared and hoped, and suffered during these last five weeks. One of our anxieties is over and not that which we thought would first cease. Dear Miss Hutchinson, was seized with illness five weeks ago, and expired yesterday. A sharp attack of Lumbago with which her illness began, was followed by rheumatic fever; that was subdued by medicine, but she never recovered her strength— on Monday she sunk alarmingly, yesterday at noon a change took place that left no hope of saving her life, and before seven all was over, leaving upon her face as heavenly an expression in the peace and silence of death as ever human Creature had. I write through tears, but they are not the tears of sorrow. Break this matter to dear Mr and Mrs Clarkson as well as you can. My poor Sister is very feeble but we are all in health much better than our friends could think possible—Mrs Thomas Hutchinson, tell Mrs Clarkson, has been here some time, and but for her, my Wife must have sunk under watching and over-exertion. Farewell—God bless you—

Most affectionately yours
Wm Wordsworth

Pray call at Henry Coleridges Chambers and tell him what has happened, and how we are; I hope we shall some of us be able to write to them soon—H. C. will be so good as to inform our good friend Mrs Hoare, and also Mrs Gillman; Mrs Hoare, or dear Sarah,[1] will be so good as to write to Mrs Gee. —And pray tell Miss Lamb.—

---

[1] i.e. Sara Coleridge.

899. W. W. to ROBERT SOUTHEY

MS. untraced.
K. LY ii. 747.

[24 June 1835][1]

My dear Southey,

My letter of yesterday must have prepared you. All was over before seven in the afternoon. She[2] had no acute suffering whatever, and within a very short time of her departure—when Dora asked Mr Carr if something could not be done to make her easier—she opened her eyes in strength, and with a strong and sweet voice, said, 'I am quite, I am perfectly comfortable'. Mr Carr supposed that her debility produced a suffusion on the brain, which was the immediate cause of her death. O, my dear Southey, we have lost a precious friend; of the strength of her attachment to you and yours, you can but imperfectly judge. It was deep in her heart. I saw her within an hour after her decease, in the silence and peace of death, with as heavenly an expression on her countenance as ever human creature had.[3] Surely there is food for faith in these appearances; for myself, I can say that I have passed a wakeful night, more in joy than sorrow, with that blessed face before my eyes perpetually, as I lay in bed. We are all much better than our friends could think possible. God Almighty bless you and yours! Your dear girls have had a loss to which time will never make them insensible; but God is good, as they will feel in all their sorrow. Farewell.

Ever most faithfully yours,
W. W.

¹ Misdated by Knight: S. H. died on 23 June.
² S. H.
³ Cf. W. W.'s sonnet *November, 1836*, beginning 'Even so for me a Vision sanctified' (*PW* iii. 17). Southey replied the following day: 'A sadder loss than yours or mine, could not easily be found. But in both we are supported; and you and I are of an age when, by God's mercy, it is more natural to look forward with hope, than backward with regret. A few short years at farthest will restore to us all that we have lost. I go about my work with the feeling and something like the alacrity of a man who is setting his house in order, before he departs for a long journey . . .' (*MS. Mr. Jonathan Wordsworth.*)

Address: The Revd Dr Wordsworth, Trinity College, Cambridge. [*In Dora W.'s hand*]
Stamp: Kendal Penny Post.
MS. British Library. Hitherto unpublished.

[24 June 1835]

My dear Brother,

You will be grieved and somewhat shocked to hear that dear Miss Hutchinson has departed this Life. She expired yesterday afternoon between six and seven. Five weeks ago she was suddenly seized with Lumbago; after that with severe influenza and rheumatic fever which was subdued; but she never recovered strength. On Monday she sank alarmingly, and at one o'clock yesterday afternoon no hope was left of saving her Life. She was to this House an inestimable Friend, disinterested, generous, noble-minded, a sincere and pious Christian, and we trust her Spirit will receive its reward. As she was in health and strength before her illness, I scarcely doubted of her recovery, till Monday—and her departure is something like a dream to us all. Our dear Sister is of course very feeble; she was sick yesterday with anxiety, but after all was over, became tranquil. Dora supports herself wonderfully, and *was* better, though obliged to be blistered again within a few days, and without the beneficial effects which Mr Carr expected, but the good was counteracted by unavoidable restlessness,—from the State of the House; for in addition to our other distresses and cares, our Maid-servant Anne who has lived with us twelve years has been and still is severely ill, though we trust not dangerously. We can never be sufficiently grateful that Mrs Thomas Hutchinson came to us some time ago. Mary must otherwise I think have sunk for want of sleep and over-exertion.

I have told you these melancholy particulars, being able to add that through God's mercy we are all far better than our Friends could think possible. At eleven yesterday my departed *Sister*, for such indeed she was, told me she was doing well; about twelve the change took place, and before seven I saw her in the silence of death, with as heavenly an expression on her face as ever human creature had. God bless you and my dear Nephews, for whom this Letter is in part designed.

Your affectionate and faithful Brother
Wm Wordsworth

67

901. W. W. to W. W. JNR.

MS. Mr. W. Hugh Peal.
LY ii. 746.

Wednesday morn:
half-past nine.—
[24 June 1835]

My dear Wm,

From the black seal of this Letter you will have concluded that your poor Aunt Wordsworth was no more—it is not so; dear Aunt Sara has gone before her. She never gained strength after the severe fever was subdued. On Monday she sank alarmingly, at noon yesterday we had not the slightest hope of her recovery, and it pleased God that she should depart this life before the day was closed.

She was an excellent woman, and we trust that she is among the blessed. Your Mother and Aunt Hutchinson[1] support themselves, as I have said in my letter to John, in a way becoming their characters and their faith in God's goodness. How this awful event will ultimately affect Aunt Wordsworth and Dora it is impossible to foretell. I have not seen either of them this morning, but shall see them before this Letter is closed, and if nothing be added you will conclude they are doing well at present.

Pray come to the funeral unless the Inspector's visit makes it impossible.

God bless you my dear Son. I give the love of all, or rather you must take it, for no one is in the room where I am writing. Farewell. Let us all be good to each other.

Your affectionate father
W. W.

If your Uncle Henry[2] should have passed pray forward to him this letter.

[*? In Mary Hutchinson's hand*]

The funeral will not be before tuesday.

---

[1] Mrs. Mary Hutchinson from Brinsop.
[2] Henry Hutchinson, who stayed at Rydal Mount this month, presumably for the funeral.

902. W. W. to WILLIAM MARSHALL[1]

Address: Wm Marshall Esq., M.P., London.
Postmark: 27 July 1835. *Stamp*: Kendal Penny Post.
MS. WL.
LY ii. 748.

Rydal Mount, Thursday [25 June 1835]

My dear Sir,

Read the enclosed, and send or take it to your Mother. Mrs W. Marshall I know will feel for us, as must all our friends. God bless you,

faithfully your friend
Wm Wordsworth

Be so good as send the enclosed for Mr Rogers to the two-penny Post.

903. W. W. to JANE MARSHALL

Address: Mrs Marshall.
MS. WL.
LY ii. 748.

Rydal Mount, Thursday [25 June 1835]

My dear Mrs Marshall,

We have been greatly afflicted for some time past in this House. Miss Hutchinson five weeks ago was seized with rheumatic fever, and I grieve to say, as you will grieve to hear, that she has departed this life. She expired on Tuesday, having never been able to recover strength after the fever was subdued. Mrs Hutchinson, Mrs W.'s Sister in Law has been with us during the last fortnight, otherwise I think my poor Wife must have sunk under watchings and unremitting anxieties; for in addition to what you know so well, our valuable servant Anne who has lived with us twelve years has been confined to her bed for some time by severe and alarming sickness. She is recovering.

Your beloved Friend, my poor Sister, survives. How this event will ultimately affect her and Dora cannot be foreseen.

---

[1] John Marshall's eldest son, now M.P. for Carlisle in place of William James (see pt. ii, L. 610).

We trust in God's Goodness. Farewell.
May the Almighty bless you and yours.—
Be so kind as to write to your Sisters.
    I have written many Letters, for the poor departed had many
and dear Friends. She suffered no acute pain after the fever was
subdued by medicine and passed away with gentleness as perfect
as could be wished

again farewell.
W. W.

904. W. W. to SAMUEL ROGERS

Address: Samuel Rogers, Esq., St. James's Place.
Postmark: 27 June 1835. *Stamp*: Park St.
Endorsed: not to be Published S.R.
MS. Sharpe Collection, University College, London.
Rogers. LY ii. 749.

Rydal Mount
Thursday—[25 June 1835]

My dear Rogers,
    I write merely to announce that one of the many anxieties
with which this house has been afflicted is over. Miss Hutchinson, after an illness of five weeks, expired on Tuesday Evening.
After the fever was subdued she suffered no acute pain, and
passed away as gently as her dearest Friends could wish. She will
be deeply lamented by many out of her own family.—
    According to your request I did not write after the melan-
choly tidings of your last; nor need you write now. We have in
this house more before us, which *must* be passed through
shortly, and much that may. Pray for us—my poor Wife bears
up wonderfully.
    Be assured, my dear Friend, that in pleasure and pain, in joy
and sorrow, you are often and often in my thoughts. Present our
united love to your Sister

affectionately yours
Wm Wordsworth

905. W. W. to ROBERT PERCEVAL GRAVES

Address: Rev^d. R. P. Graves, Bowness.
Stamp: Kendal Penny Post.
Endorsed: Mr Wordsworth about the funeral of his Sister-in-law Sarah
Hutchinson. June 183[5].¹
MS. Harvard University Library.
LY ii. 749.

Friday Morning.
[26 June 1835]

My dear Mr Graves,

We are grateful for your sympathizing Note; and take very kindly your proposal of testifying your respect by attendance on the funeral. According to her own wishes it will be quite private, no one *invited* but the Clergyman and Medical Attendant;² but of course our Friends are at liberty to yield to their feelings, and do as they think right—all will be taken well—

As you are so near a Neighbour I will not enter into particulars, further than to let you know that my family are supported under this affliction by God's goodness, and have not yet suffered much, (apparently at least) in their bodily health. The rest I will speak of when we meet.

farewell most affectionately yours
W. Wordsworth.

P.S. the funeral will take place at 12 o'clock on Tuesday.

906. W. W. to HENRY TAYLOR

MS. Bodleian Library.
LY ii. 750.

[*c.* 26 June 1835]

My dear Mr Taylor,

Little did we think when we hastened home upon the summons of Miss Hutchinson, who was then so anxious about my Sister's and Daughter's state, that she herself would be the first member of our household whose loss we should have to deplore. This inestimable Person, as I know you will grieve to hear, expired after an illness of five weeks' continuance. She

¹ Misdated 1836.
² The Revd. Fletcher Fleming and Mr. Carr.

71

suffered little or no acute pain after the Rheumatic fever that had seized her gave way to medicine, but she did not recover strength. Nevertheless we were not alarmed till within two days of her departure, as her weakness did not seem to encrease.—

Knowing that Mr Robinson had more leisure than any other of our most esteemed Friends in London I wrote to him the day after her decease, which took place on Tuesday, and expressed a wish that he would make it known among those who valued her or were likely to feel for us. Perhaps you would hear the tidings from him. I hope you did, and may I beg that you would mention the event to your Father.[1] Miss H. when she lived at Middleham Hall[2] used to see much of your Uncle[3] and Aunt, and had no common esteem for both them and your father. As this Letter could gain nothing by being put into the Post to-day, I hope to enclose one for dear Miss Fenwick.

Pray do not trouble about the business I mentioned in my[4] last. The Commission, I now understand, is of a character and composition that would not allow you to serve us, in connection with it. I am sorry I mentioned the matter at all.

I need only add a hope that your health is re-established, and an assurance that my poor Sister and Daughter bear this severe shock far better than could have been thought possible. My dear Wife supports herself as it becomes her to do under all our trials.

I remain with a world of good wishes
affectionately yours
Wm Wordsworth

I have heard from Mr Southey this morning. He loved Miss H. deeply, as did all his Daughters. Her fortune in this particular was remarkable that so many Persons influential for their genius and talents were so strongly and firmly attached to her. I may name Charles Lamb and Coleridge above all. Poor Mrs Southey[5] will not, I think, remain long in this world. Farewell.

[1] George Taylor.

[2] Near Durham, where S. H. kept house for her brother George from 1800 to 1802 (see *EY*, pp. 332, 345—6). George Taylor ran a farm at Bishop Middleham during his early married life, 1796—1800.

[3] George Taylor had two elder brothers: probably the reference here is to the eldest, William Taylor (1761—c. 1826) of Swinhoe, Northumberland, who graduated at Trinity College, Cambridge, in 1785, and thereafter entered the Middle Temple.

[4] *Written* your. For the 'business', see L. 896 above.

[5] Mrs. Southey lingered on until 16 Nov. 1837.

Address: Miss Fenwick.
MS. WL.
LY ii. 751.

[*c*. 26 June 1835]

My dear Miss Fenwick,

Mrs W. would have written in a way more agreeable to my wish than I am able; but at present she has not courage to touch the Pen. Dear Miss Hutchinson, her beloved Sister, and let me say, mine also, was seized with Rheumatic fever five weeks ago —the fever was subdued by medicine, but she did not recover her strength—nevertheless (she had been in such fine health before the attack) we had little fear about her, but an alarming change took place on Monday, and she departed this life on Tuesday evening. This has been a grievous shock, little did we apprehend when her anxiety for my sister and daughter hastened us home, that she herself would be the first called away. Upon the beauty of her character I will not dwell—she is we humbly trust among the blessed. We are comforted by this faith, and bear up as well as human infirmity allow. My poor Sister *must* soon follow her, she is calm and said to me only yesterday 'my tears are all to shed', and to another of the family she said, 'I do not feel that I have lost her, I am brought nearer to her'. Dora does not yet seem to have suffered in her health to the degree that we feared—and my Wife is wonderfully supported. She had her Sister-in-law with her, from Herefordshire, nearly three weeks; otherwise she must have sunk with anxiety and care and watching, for in addition to what you know, I must mention, that one of our two maid-servants who has lived with us twelve years has also been severely ill with something of the same complaint that carried off the one of our small household that we have lost.

It would have seemed unjust to our friendship for you, dear Miss Fenwick, if I had withheld these melancholy details—they will distress you, but the distress may do your spirit good. Pray for us, and do not forget how feelingly we love you. Farewell. May the Almighty bless you—

ever faithfully yours,
Wm Wordsworth

908. W. W. to EDWARD QUILLINAN

Address: Edwd Quillinan Esq, Oporto.
Stamp: Lisboa.
Endorsed: 1835. Mr Wordsworth, Rydal—Rec^d and Ans^d in July by the W. Faurelt Steamer which left Porto July 22—Death of dear Miss Hutchinson.
MS. WL.
LY ii. 752.

[*c.* 27 June 1835]

My dear Mr Quillinan,

Poor Miss H.—It is my sad duty to let you know that one of our anxieties, that for her, is over. How different an account am I to give from that you would receive from Dora. When the fever was subdued, we continued full of hope, though she did not recover strength, but we did not doubt, as she was so well and strong when first seized, that strength would return. Weeks passed and she did not seem to lose ground, so we were still without fear. But last Monday she sunk alarmingly and before seven the following day she expired.

I know not how she has escaped from us, but it was God's will that this excellent creature should quit the earth. My poor dear sister and Dora seem to bear up wonderfully— so does Mrs W. We have had Mrs Hutchinson with us for a fortnight—a great blessing. I know how you valued the dear departed, her loss [is]¹ irreparable to us all.—It is astounding to me that she should have gone before my beloved sister who is very feeble and suffers much at times—Her departed friend had little or no acute pain after the fever left—O—What a heavenly expression was on her face after the breath had left her body; it would have done your Soul good to see it.

I write through tears, but scarcely tears of sorrow—so has it been often and often since she left us—farewell—I know not where you are; perhaps on your way to England, perhaps landed. We have not yet written to your children.

Dora is not I think quite so well as when she wrote to you, the distress of the family with so many sick—Anne² has been perilously ill—has made her quit her couch oftener that she ought to have done.

[*cetera desunt*]

¹ *Word dropped out.*
² Servant at Rydal Mount.

74

909. W. W. to HENRY SOUTHEY[1]

Address: Dr Southey, 1 Harley S^t, London.
Postmark: 2 July 1835. *Stamp*: Kendal Penny Post.
MS. Cornell. Hitherto unpublished.

Rydal Mount
near Ambleside
June 30th [1835]

My dear Sir,

You will excuse I doubt not the liberty I am about to take in submitting to your consideration a particular respecting the family at Keswick; but before I enter upon that subject let me discharge the sad duty of informing you that Miss Hutchinson, my Sister in Law, whose home has been under our roof, for the most part during the last thirty years, has departed this Life. She expired this day week after an illness of five weeks, her complaint a rheumatic fever which gave way to medical treatment but She never recovered her strength; and languished away with little or no acute suffering. She was a Friend very dear to your Brother and his family and they heavily deplore her loss. Of our afflictions in other points I will not speak, but will transcribe a passage from a letter of Bertha received this morning which has determined [me][2] to write to you.

'My poor Mother fails fast, and latterly we have had heartbreaking work with her, at times she is very violent, and we are obliged to hold her down by main force. It is a hard thing to see her daily losing strength for want of taking medicine, and proper nourishment. We never get her out now, nor does she employ herself'.—In another part of the letter she adds 'I will not write more, my hand *shakes* much'—Marking the word *shakes* in Italics. She adds that her Sister and herself are 'wonderfully well; how much better than we should have once thought it possible to be under such distressing circumstances!'

Accounts like the above which our departed Friend and Dora have not unfrequently received, have caused us all to be of opinion that A Nurse or sort of Keeper should be provided by your Brother to relieve his Daughters in a task and care to the whole burthen of which, even assisted as they are by Betty,[3] it seems impossible that either their minds or bodies can be equal.

---

[1] Southey's younger brother, the London physician (see pt. ii, L. 522).
[2] *Word dropped out.*
[3] Servant at Greta Hall

If the state of my own family had allowed me to go over to Keswick, I would have endeavoured myself to break this proposition to your Brother in the course of conversation. But I cannot bring myself to name it by Letter. It would seem to be presuming too much upon my own judgement. Besides, I am not at present assured that particulars respecting Mrs Southey's state confidentially named in their Letters to my Daughter by Bertha and Kate are all known to their Father.—Now may I beg that if you think proper you would direct or advise the step to be taken which has so long to our judgement seemed urgently call [ed] for. Do not on any account let it be known that you have heard from me upon the subject, of which I need say no more, not doubting that I shall escape blame from you for the part my judgement and feelings have compelled me to take in this communication.

Miss H. is to be buried this day.[1] Farewell believe me my dear Sir

faithfully yours   W. Wordsworth

910. W. W. to THOMAS HAMILTON[2]

Address: Thomas Hamilton Esq.—[*delivered by hand*]
MS. Cornell. Hitherto unpublished.

[late June 1835]

My dear Sir,

Mrs Wordsworth thanks you affectionately as I do for your sympathizing Letter. We bear up against the pressure, but time moves with us sadly and slowly; the blow has been so sudden!

The enclosed were written some time ago—Mrs W. has misdirected one of the Letters. Will you be so kind as to rectify the mistake. Mr Wilson[3] will be so good as to take charge of them, and to remember [me][4] to his Father—

Ever faithfully yours
Wm Wordsworth

---

[1] In Grasmere churchyard. The inscription on her gravestone (see *Mem.* ii. 299) was probably composed by W. W.

[2] See pt. ii, L. 673.

[3] One of Professor Wilson's two sons, John or Blair (see pt. ii, L. 567).

[4] *Word dropped out.*

911. W. W. to MESSRS. JOHN WAKEFIELD AND SONS[1]

Address: Messrs J. Wakefield and Sons.
MS. Lord Wakefield of Kendal.
Sunday Times, 4 Jan. 1953. George Chandler, Four Centuries of Banking, 1964–8,
    ii. 44.

[*In unidentified hand*]

Rydal Mount 2nd July /35

Gentlemen,

The Revd Fletcher Fleming,[2] who has a Mortgage upon the property of my late Brother who's son will attain his Majority at the close of the present year,[3] has occasion for the money a week or ten days hence: I therefore beg to be informed whether you could supply the sum (£1,620) upon my placing the Deeds of the property in your Hands, should you require it

Waiting your reply

I am

Gentlemen

Your obd^t Ser^t

[*signed*]   Wm Wordsworth

912. W. W. to H. C. R.

Address: Henry Crabbe Robinson Esq., Temple, London.
Postmark: 8 July 1835.   *Stamp*: Kendal Penny Post.
Endorsed: 6th July 1835, Wordsworth.
MS. Dr. Williams's Library.
K (—). *Morley, i. 278.*

Monday 6th July—[1835]

My dear Friend

Gladly would I have replied instantly to your two last affectionate Letters, but I could not muster courage.

—It will be a week to-morrow since our dear Friend[4] was laid in Grasmere Churchyard, near two of her Sister's Children,[5] and where in all probability we shall all be laid one

---

[1] The Kendal bankers (see also *MY* ii. 428–9, 447; and pt. i, L. 108).
[2] Curate of Rydal.
[3] John Wordsworth, R. W.'s son, came of age on 29 Jan. 1836.
[4] S.H.
[5] Thomas and Catherine Wordsworth, who both died in 1812.

after another—When a beloved Friend departs in this way without any organic disease, it is difficult to carry about with one the habit of feeling that she will never be seen again on earth. But no more of this—You are anxious to hear how we are going on.

My Daughter has lost ground considerably—My sisters health of body seems to have suffered less than her mind. Her recollection is greatly impaired since the event, I mean her recollection of recent events. She complains of weakness and foolishness of mind which is sad to hear of—the bilious sickness and cough and expectoration which harrassed her and weakened her so much are gone; but no doubt will return. The sickness without catching cold and the coughing with it when change of weather comes. At present she complains of faintness and hollowness and has an incessant craving for some thing to support her. Such is her sad condition, nevertheless I should say that upon the whole her bodily health is better.—I return to my Daughter—she has lost ground considerably as I said—It would be utterly in vain to attempt getting her from here as long as her Aunt continues in this feeble way; therefore I have only to thank you for your most kind offer of service in connection with her supposed Journey to Leamington, where I wish with all my Soul, I had her. But at present I am sure she could not move—therefore pray consider yourself at Liberty to make any excursions which may tempt you—How I wish I could go along with you, as I stand much in need of change of scene, but that is impossible. My dear and excellent Wife supports herself admirably under all these trials—

Now for a few words of business—it is already July—I leave the disposal of the sum from the annuities to Mr Courtenays judgement, and yours if you think proper to suggest any thing.

Messrs Longman have paid 280 on my account into the Kendal Bank—but I know not what part of that sum could be added to the 300 from the Annuities, as my expenses, owing to so much sickness in the family have been very heavy, and money owing me for my annual expenses has not been paid.

I fear you cannot read this Letter. I feel my hand-shaking, I have had so much agitation to-day, in attempting to quiet my poor Sister, and from being under the necessity of refusing her things that would be improper for her. She has a great craving for oatmeal porridge principal [ly] for the sake of the butter that she eats along with it and butter is sure to bring on a fit of bile

78

sooner or later. Her memory is excellent, this morning I chanced to mutter a line from Dyers Grongar Hill—she immedia [tely][1] finished the passage—reciting the previous line and the two following—Speaking of her faculties she told me that Miss Hutchinson's vanishing had be [en] a sad *shattering* to them.

God bless you—Let me repeat my thanks for all your zealous and devoted acts of friendship. My Sister begged me to send you her tender love—again and again most Affectionately yours.—

I do not invite you to this House of mourning—you could not be of any use and it would only afflict you—

W. Wordsworth

913. W. W. to LADY FREDERICK BENTINCK

MS. untraced.
Mem. Grosart. K. LY ii. 753.

[Summer 1835][2]

. . . You were not mistaken in supposing that the state of public affairs has troubled me much. I cannot see how the government is to be carried on, but by such sacrifices to the democracy as will, sooner or later, upset everything. Whoever governs, it will be by out-bidding for popular favour those who went before them. Sir Robert Peel was obliged to give way in his government to the spirit of reform, as it is falsely called; these men are going beyond him; and if ever he shall come back, it will only, I fear, be to carry on the movement in a shape somewhat less objectionable than it will take from the Whigs. In the mean while the Radicals, or Republicans, are cunningly content to have this work done ostensibly by the Whigs, while

---

[1] *MS. torn.*
[2] This letter was written shortly after Peel had been replaced as Prime Minister by Lord Melbourne, and when the question of corporation reform was coming up for consideration. The Municipal Corporations Bill, based on the report of a commission appointed in 1833, was introduced in the Commons by Lord John Russell, the Home Secretary, on 5 June, and with the general support of Peel and the Opposition, it secured a 3rd reading on 20 July. It was, however, considerably altered by the Lords in Committee, and a confrontation between Lord and Commons was only narrowly averted, before the Bill was finally passed on 7 Sept.

in fact they themselves are the Whigs' masters, as the Whigs well know; but they hope to be preserved from destruction by throwing themselves back upon the Tories when measures shall be urged upon them by their masters which they may think too desperate. What I am most afraid of is alterations in the constituency and in the duration of Parliament, which will bring it more and more under the dominion of the lower and lowest classes. On this account I fear the proposed corporation reform, as a step towards household suffrage, vote by ballot, etc. As to a union of the Tories and Whigs in Parliament, I see no prospect of it whatever. To the great Whig lords may be truly applied the expression in *Macbeth,*

> They have eaten of the insane root
> That takes the reason prisoner. [1]

I ordered two copies of my new volume to be sent to Cottesmere. And now farewell; and believe me,

Dear Lady Frederick, ever faithfully yours,
W. Wordsworth

914. W. W. to JOHN ANSTER [2]

Address: John Anster, Esq, to the care of Messᵣˢ Longman and Co, Pater noster Row.
MS. Cornell. Hitherto unpublished.

Rydal Mount
Ambleside
July 21ˢᵗ [1835]

Sir,

It is some little time since I had the honour of receiving your Translation of Faustus; and though there is not a notice in the Book that it was your wish it should be sent me I presume so far as to thank you for a work from which I promise myself no inconsiderable gratification, when the burthen of affliction, under which I have been for some time suffering, shall be, (if it should please God), somewhat lightened. Three of my small

[1] See *Macbeth,* I. iii. 84–5.

[2] John Anster (1793–1867), poet and translator: Regius Professor of Civil Law at Trinity College, Dublin, from 1850. The volume referred to here was his translation of the first part of Goethe's *Faust.* Anster's translation of the second part was not published until 1864.

family, one of whom is dead, and another at the point of death, have occupied all my thoughts, so that books are to me as a dead Letter, and so must they be for some time. Pray excuse the abrupt brevity of this. I have the honour to be

sincerely
Your obliged Ser^{vnt}
Wm Wordsworth

915. W. W. to EDWARD MOXON

Address: Edward Moxon Esq^e, Dover S^t. [*In M. W.'s hand*]
MS. Henry E. Huntington Library.
LY ii. 754.

Rydal Mount
August 2nd—[1835]

Dear Mr Moxon,

I have been from home eight days or I should have written sooner, the Frank also was delayed by being sent round through Dublin.

If I had given way to my feelings I should have observed upon the beauty of many of the sonnets.[1]—

I have made a few verbal alterations which I hope you will think improvements.

Many thanks for your kind invitation. It will be borne gratefully in mind, but I know not when I shall move southwards; as I cannot venture to go more than a few days' journey from home, while my poor Sister is in this [?].[2]

My Daughter, thank God, is a little better.—I have been reprinting and republishing at Kendal my little Book on the lakes.[3] with some additions. I took the liberty of adding your

[1] Moxon's sonnets. See L. 884 above.
[2] *MS. illegible.*
[3] *A Guide through the District of the Lakes in the North of England, with a Description of the Scenery, etc. For the Use of Tourists and Residents. Fifth Edition, With Considerable Additions.* By William Wordsworth. Kendal: Published by Hudson and Nicholson, and in London by Longman and Co., Moxon, and Whittaker and Co., 1835. This was the third separate edition of the *Guide*, now so called for the first time, and the last to be revised by W.W. himself. The major additions included an expansion of 'Directions and Information for the Tourist' and the inclusion of two quotations from 'the Author's Miscellaneous Poems'. (See *Prose Works*, ii. 134.)

name to Longmans on the Title page; the Publishers, on their part, added their own London publisher, Whitaker.—I hope some Copies have been forwarded to you, as I requested they might.

Pray remember the English Dictionary, and keep Copies for me which I shall direct my Nephew to call for.—

My Yarrow[1] appears to have sold well and to be generally liked. Do not fail to remember me to Mrs Moxon and your Sister and Brother.

ever very sincerely and faithfully your friend
W Wordsworth

916. W. W. to BERTHA SOUTHEY

MS. Mr. Jonathan Wordsworth. Hitherto unpublished.

[early Aug. 1835]

My Dear Bertha,

I promised to let you know how our Invalids are.

I found my Sister no worse as to suffering, but her recollection of passing events somewhat more impaired. Dora, I would fain hope, through this perplexing mist of better and worse, is upon the whole improving—though certainly her looks are not what we would wish, and she is as thin almost as possible.

Anne is doing well. So much for our bulletin.

Ever affectionately yours
W. Wordsworth

Tell your father that the Doctor[2] pleases me exceedingly—as far as I have been able yet to become acquainted with him.

[1] *Yarrow Revisited, and Other Poems.*

[2] The first two volumes of Southey's *The Doctor* had appeared in 1834; the third came out in 1835.

917. W. W. to CATHERINE CLARKSON

Address: Mrs Clarkson, Playford Hall, Ipswich. [*In M. W.'s hand*]
Stamp: Kendal Penny Post.
MS. Cornell.
LY ii. 755.

Rydal Mount
August 6th 1835

My dear Mrs Clarkson,

Mrs W— has just come with her eyes full of tears begging I would write to you, for she, much as it has been upon her mind cannot, nor ever has been able to undertake the task, since our days have lately darkened so much upon us. Mr R.[1] as we requested would let you know how we were deprived of our beloved Sister Sarah—She is we trust among the blessed, but to us the loss is upon earth irreparable. My poor Sister languishes in her sick room and mostly upon her sick bed, how long she may yet have to struggle we cannot foresee—her weakness is deplorable, but of acute pain we hope she has not much to endure; I say hope for her mind since Sarah's departure has been so confused as to passing events, that we have no distinct knowledge of what she may actually have to support in the way of bodily pain. She remembers and recollects all but recent things perfectly, and her understanding is, as far as her strength will allow her to think, clear as ever it was.

The Complaint in Dora's spine has been a good deal subdued by bleeding and and blistering, but her digestive organs seem as weak and as liable to derangement as ever; but had we been less afflicted there is reason to think she might have been better by this time.—Our Cook, Anne, is also recovering steadily—Out of our small family, eight persons servants included, four were incapable of serving each other; and in a house small as ours it was a great addition to our distress, that the Invalids un-avoidably disturbed each other, so that Dora who stood so much in need of the refreshment of sleep often was kept all night, and unable to remain in bed from a hope of being useful in some degree to the others. This is a sad tale, but God tempers the wind to the shorn Lamb, blessed be his holy Name! Mrs Hutchinson came to us from Brinsop, otherwise my poor wife must have been quite worn out—She looks harrassed and aged, but makes no Complaint.

---

[1] H. C. R.

It is now time that I should inquire after you and dear Mr Clarkson—pray let us know how you both are. I do not like to conclude without filling up this page; but what to touch upon I know not—Perhaps a particular or two concerning your departed friend's illness may be acceptable. Her bodily sufferings were not we think very great after the violence of the first attack of fever was subdued. It left her legs much swollen, and though she made no progress towards recovery of strength, if she grew weaker at all it was slowly and to us insensibly, till within two or three days of her decease. Upon the morning of that event she told me that she was doing well, quite well, and only required time to bring back her strength, but between twelve and one at noon a change took place that left not a shadow of hope:—she died a little after six in the afternoon, with a heavenly expression left by death upon her beloved face.

God bless you my dear Friend—Remember us affectionately to Mr Clarkson—I could not write any more if my paper were not filled—

ever faithfully yours
W. Wordsworth

[*M. W. adds*]

O yes, Wm is mistaken—I have written two or three letters—but to *you*, dearest Mrs Clarkson, who loved her so well, and knew so well what you loved—I could not trust my own feelings—God bless you and good dear Mr C—

M. W.

918. W. W. to WILLIAM ROWAN HAMILTON

Address: Professor Hamilton, Observatory, Dublin.
Postmark: 8 Aug.   *Stamp*: (1) Kendal Penny Post (2) Dublin Penny Post.
MS. Cornell. Hitherto unpublished.

Thursday
Augst 6th 1835

[*In Dora W.'s hand*]

My dear Mr Hamilton,

I cannot let a post go by without thanking you for your very kind invitation[1] and expressing my sense of the flattering

---

[1] Hamilton was preparing for the meeting of the British Association in Dublin, 10–15 Aug., and had written on 3 Aug., inviting W. W. to be his

manner in which you enforce it. Besides there may be yet time
for some other of your friends to profit by an offer which I am
compelled to decline. You know what a grievous loss my
family has lately sustained in the decease of Mrs Wordsworth's
excellent Sister. My own Sister is so weak and emaciated that
she may be taken off any day, yet from the nature of her
complaint she may linger on for months. My Daughter also
though somewhat better in health is very far from well. Having
been told these particulars you will enter into my feelings and I
need say no more but that I hope we shall meet sometime or
other. This hope I cherish notwithstanding all the instabilities
and uncertainties of human life. Pray thank your good Sister for
her long and interesting letter to me and present my good
wishes to Mrs Hamilton—both for her now that her confinement is approaching[1] and at all times. Farewell! All here unite
with me in kind remembrances.

Believe me dear Mr Hamilton
Your faithful and much obliged
friend
[*signed*] Wm Wordsworth

[*W. W. writes*]

I regret that we have no Frankers in this neighbourhood, and
there is not time to send this Letter to a distance.—

guest during the proceedings (*Cornell MSS.*). On the last day of the meeting,
Hamilton was knighted by the Viceroy, the Earl of Mulgrave. See *Hamilton*, ii.
156—8.

[1] Hamilton's second child, another boy, was born on 4 Aug.

919. W. W. to MESSRS. HUDSON AND NICHOLSON[1]

Address: Messrs Hudson and Nicholson, Kendal.
MS. Cornell. Hitherto unpublished.

[*In M. W.'s hand*]

Wed 11th [Aug. 1835][2]

Dear Sirs,

I am surprized to find by a letter from Longmans this morn^g that they have not rec^d a Supply of the book of the Lakes—Pray, if you have not already done so lose no time in forwarding a parcel to that house, and also to Mr Moxon and—

I am truly y^{rs} etc

[*signed*] Wm Wordsworth

920. W. W. to ELIZABETH HUGHES[3]

MS. WL transcript. Hitherto unpublished.

Rydal Mount
August 16th [1835]

Dear Mrs Hughes,

Your letter containing so many sad particulars has remained too long unanswered; I deferred writing at first from a hope that I might be able to let you know that the Book which I am anxious to receive as a memorial of my departed Friend had reached me. Mr Bolton has been some time at his Residence in this neighbourhood, but it has not been sent to me yet. In a few days I shall go to his house when I will make inquiries after it.

Be assured, my dear Madam, that we truly sympathize with your second grievous recent loss, in the decease of your only surviving Brother. He was a man, I doubt not, esteemed wherever he was known, by me he will always be remembered with lively interest. The consolations of religion which you

---

[1] The Kendal publishers of the new edition of *A Guide through the District of the Lakes.* See L. 915 above and L. 924 below.

[2] Wednesday was the 12th. The only time after this that the 11th was a Wednesday was in November, which is rather late for this letter.

[3] Youngest sister (see *EY*, p. 51) of W.W.'s college friend Robert Jones, who had died on 3 Apr. 1835.

feelingly speak of are the only ones capable of supporting human nature under such afflictions as your family has had to endure in such near succession. We also in this family have been severely tried.

Mrs Wordsworth's Sister, who has lived with us during much the greater part of her life, died a few weeks ago under our roof, after an attack of rheumatic fever, from the effects of which she never recovered. My Sister, the only one I ever had, has been languishing for upwards of four years, and is confined to her room and almost to her bed, without the least prospect of recovery. My only Daughter has for some time been suffering from a spinal complaint which was preceded by much weakness and disorder in the digestive organs which still continue weak and liable to frequent derangement, though, thank God, the pains in the back and arms have been much alleviated by frequent bleeding and blistering.

In addition to these distresses a faithful servant who has lived with us twelve years has been very ill, she however, is recovering; so that out of a small Household of eight, four have been disabled from assisting the others. Under these circumstances we have felt not the less, but the more for the Friends who have been visited in a similar way, and especially for your family. Though your Brother Robert and I had not been in the way of much personal intercourse with each other for many years, the hope of meeting him again was always dear to me; we loved each other with a faithful affection, and that mutual respect which gives a strength to friendships formed in early life, which none of more recent origin can have. But I must not indulge in melancholy reflections; let me hope that your own health and spirits and those of your excellent sisters may improve; with a prayer that God may continue his blessings to you all, in which Mrs W. joins, as would my sister and Daughter if they knew that I was writing to you; I remain dear Mrs Hughes

yours very faithfully
Wm Wordsworth

920a. W. W. to GEORGE TICKNOR[1]

Address: George Ticknor Esq., Salutation Hotel, Ambleside.
MS. untraced.
LY iii. 1135.

Rydal Mount
Tuesday Morning [1 Sept. 1835]

My dear Sir,

It will give me much pleasure to see you and Mrs Ticknor at any time this afternoon which may suit you, the sooner the better as the days are become short. If you reach Ambleside too late for Rydal this evening pray come over to morrow to breakfast; our hour is a little after eight, but don't mind that, we can easily suit your convenience.

ever faithfully yours
Wm Wordsworth

---

[1] This letter was incorrectly dated by de Selincourt to summer 1842. But it clearly refers to George Ticknor's second visit to Rydal Mount, Tuesday, 1 Sept.—Thursday, 3 Sept. 1835. See *RMVB* and *Life, Letters, and Journals of George Ticknor*, 2 vols., Boston, 1876, i. 432–4. Ticknor noted W. W.'s political preoccupations at this time: 'He holds strongly and fondly, with an affectionate feeling of veneration, to the old and established in the institutions, usages, and peculiarities of his country, and he sees them all shaken by the progress of change. His moral sensibilities are offended; his old affections are wounded; his confidence in the future is disturbed. But though he talks about it as if it were a subject that oppresses him, he talks without bitterness, and with the large and flowing eloquence which marks his whole conversation. Indeed, he feels the whole matter so deeply and so tenderly, that it is not easy to avoid sympathizing with him, even when the strictness of his political system is most apparent. He was very curious, too, about our institutions in America, and their effect upon society and character, and made many shrewd as well as kind remarks about us; but is certainly not inclined to augur well of our destinies, for he goes upon the broad principle that the mass of any people cannot be trusted with the powers of government.' Ticknor had not seen W. W. since 1819 (see *MY* ii. 504). He and his wife were now engaged on an extended tour of Europe that lasted until 1838, when they called upon the poet again just before their return to America.

921. W. W. to JOHN DAVY[1]

Address: Dr Davy, Kean-ground.
MS. Lilly Library, Indiana University.
LY iii. 1377.

[Aug.—Sept. 1835]

My dear Sir,

Many thanks for your kind enquiries.

My Daughter is at Mr Parry's,[2] Grasmere, I saw her yesterday and thought her something better. Mr Parry however tells me that her breakfast this morning did not remain upon her stomach. Mrs Wordsworth is going to see her and will report to-day to Mr Carr.

I feel much obliged by your account of Mrs Curwen, and am truly thankful that she has had the benefit of your advice.—

My poor Sister is in a sad state when the action of the opium is not upon her. She takes it twice in the 24 hours. This morning of her own accord she refused to take her pills, and although she had moaned a good deal, I do not think that she has been at all worse than when the pill was taken, after the action of it was somewhat abated.—I should see Mr Carr this afternoon, and am not wholly without hope from this trial, by her own choice, that the quantity may be reduced.—Let me repeat my sincere thanks for your attentions to these Sufferers. It is most unlucky that my Horse has caught an ugly distemper, otherwise I should certainly have called at Keane Ground tomorrow. I was unable

---

[1] Dr. John Davy, F.R.S. (1790–1868), brother of Sir Humphry Davy, had been educated at Edinburgh, and travelled abroad in the army medical service, in Malta, and elsewhere, eventually becoming Inspector General of army hospitals. In 1830 he married Margaret, daughter of Mrs. Elizabeth Fletcher (1770–1858), later of Lancrigg, in Easedale, the widow of an Edinburgh lawyer, and friend of Brougham, Jeffrey, the Arnolds, and Mazzini. Dr. Davy and his family had been staying with Mrs. Fletcher, a regular visitor to the Lakes (see pt. ii, L. 759) at Keen Ground, a small house near Hawkshead, since mid-May (see MW, p. 145): in September he took up his appointment as chief medical officer at Fort Pitt, Chatham (see Autobiography of Mrs Fletcher, Edinburgh, 1875, p. 222). Dr Davy compiled the Memoirs of his brother (1836), and the collected edition of his Works (1839), and spent his retirement at Lesketh How, Ambleside.

[2] Mr. Parry, a retired lawyer from the Temple, had taken over Gell's Cottage on the death of Samuel Barber, his brother-in-law. Mr. and Mrs. Parry visited Rydal Mount in June 1832 (RMVB).

to go over the other day, nor was I at Coniston as you learned I believe from Mr Marshall.

With kindest regards to yourself, Mrs Davy, and all your Party

believe me my dear Sir
Your very much obliged
Wm Wordsworth

922. W. W. to JULIET SMITH[1]

MS. Mr. W. Hugh Peal. Hitherto unpublished.

Salutation Inn
Ambleside
Wednesday Evening [early Sept. 1835]

Dear Madam,

May I be allowed to request that Mr and Miss Watson[2] of Park Street Westminster, most particular friends of mine, and Mr and Mrs Norris,[3] without intruding upon you may be permitted to see the two charming views from the front of Tent Lodge.

I sincerely hope that [your][4] health may be if not improved, at least no worse than when I had last the pleasure of seeing you.

Pray excuse this liberty and believe me dear Mrs Smith with great respect

faithfully yours
Wm Wordsworth

[1] Of Tent Lodge, Coniston.
[2] Joshua Watson and his daughter were touring the Lakes on their return from Scotland.
[3] For the Revd. H. H. Norris, see pt. i, L. 135.
[4] *Word dropped out.*

923. W. W. to MESSRS. LONGMAN AND CO.

MS. *Royal Society of Tasmania. Hitherto unpublished.*

[*In M. W.'s hand*]

Rydal Mount
Sep^{tr} 17 [1835]

Dear Sirs,

Not having heard from you I am somewhat at a loss to know how you mean to proceed with the printing of the Yarrow etc.[1] The objection to go on as the printer had begun, seems to me utterly insurmountable, unless the Edition of 1832 should be quite, or nearly exhausted; in that case an Ed: uniform in all respects (inside and out) might be produced by taking some 60 pages or more from the 3 vols of miscellaneous poems, and uniting them to the Yarrow as printed in the Specimen you sent me. The whole work would then consist of 5 vols—4 Misc^l and the Excursion—But perhaps you have already acted upon a decision which makes this proposal impracticable, even if it were expedient from the present state of the Sale. The whole affair puzzles me not a little.

On the other page are add^l corrections for the Printer.

I am dear Sirs
yours very Sincerely
[*signed*] Wm Wordsworth

Page 314 At the end of the last line but three, substitute a note of interrogation for the Semicolon.

p. 330 from 2^d line inclusive—print thus to the end of the sentence, done with mutual understanding that the relief each is ready to bestow upon his still poorer neighbours will be granted to himself, or his relatives, should it hereafter be applied for.[2]

---

[1] The second edition of *Yarrow Revisited, and Other Poems*, which appeared in 1836.

[2] See *Prose Works*, iii. 245. This was the reading adopted in the *Postscript* in the editions of 1836 and 1839.

924. W. W. to MESSRS. SIMPKIN MARSHALL AND CO.

Address: Messrs. Simpkin Marshall and Co., Booksellers, London.
MS. Cornell. Hitherto unpublished.

Sept^{br} 24th [? 1835]

Gentlemen,

In answer to your Letter received some time ago, I have to say, that I have never had any thing to do with the Sale of my books—Some time since Messrs. Longman informed me that my Book on the Lakes was out of Print, and for the sake of interesting a local Publisher[1] in it, I put the work into his hands, leaving to him to fix the Price, without being in the least aware of the probability of any person being injured in any way by the change, or that any inconvenience could arize out of it to any one; and I cannot see what I can do in the case—

Sorry for your disappointment, which seems inevitable, in cases of this kind.

I remain Sirs
Your Obedient Servant
Wm Wordsworth

I deferred writing till I might have an opportunity of sending my Letter to London free of Postage.

925. W. W. to ROBERT SPENCE[2]

Address: R. Spence Esq, North Shields.
Franked: Penrith September twenty four 1835 H. C. Lowther.
Postmark: 24 Sept. 1835. *Stamp*: Penrith.
MS. Mrs. Spence Clepham. Hitherto unpublished.

Lowther Castle Sept^{br} [24, 1835]

Dear Sir,

The enclosed are from the Pens of Messers Coleridge and Southey.

I had not forgot my promise but I had great difficulty in procuring this of Mr Coleridge, and Mr Southey's un-

---

[1] Hudson and Nicholson. See Ls. 882a and 915 above.
[2] The banker at North Shields. See pt. ii, L. 485.

fortunately wants his signature, which he never gives in his
Letters to me.

I remain dear Sir
Thanking you for your very obliging Letter
Very sincerely yours
W Wordsworth

926. W. W. to EDWARD MOXON

Address: Mr Moxon.
MS. Harvard University Library
LY ii. 760.

Lowther Castle
near Penrith
[*c.* 25 Sept. 1835]

Dear Mr Moxon,

I thank you for the present of valuable Books which arrived
at Rydal since I left it.

You may depend upon having Lamb's Letters,[1] which I am
glad you mean to publish.

Don't give yourself the least trouble about pushing my Lake
Book[2]—it is a mere trifle, and I had your name put into the title
page solely out of regard to you.

I am in great difficulty about a new edition of my Poems, as I
know not how to contrive so that the last Vol. (Yarrow revisited) and the four others shall be out of print at or near the
same time. Longmans are going to press with another edition of
the Yarrow[3]—

If it were not for those vile french Piracies we should do well;
I am informed that an edition of my entire works, no doubt
including the Yarrow is just advertized in Paris, not by
G[alig]nani[4] who pirated the other Vols, but by another
publisher.[5] This will prove very injurious.

—Be so good as to pay the foreign postage of this Letter,[6] I

[1] See L. 940 below.
[2] The new (Kendal) edition of the *Guide to the Lakes*. See L. 915 above.
[3] i.e. the 2nd edition of *Yarrow Revisited*. See L. 923 above.
[4] *Hole in MS.*
[5] This French piracy was in fact a reissue of the Galignani edition of 1828.
[6] Probably a letter to W. W.'s daughter Madame Baudouin (see also L. 879 above).

enclose a shilling which I believe is the amount for that purpose, from London, it costs two from this place.—

Kind regards to Mrs M. your Sister and Brother and believe me my dear Mr Moxon faithfully

your much obliged
W Wordsworth

927. W. W. to HENRY ALFORD [1]

MS. The Robert H. Taylor Collection, Princeton, N. J.
Life, Journals and Letters of Henry Alford, D.D. Edited by His Widow, 1873, p. 104.

Lowther Castle near Penrith
Sept[br] 26th [1835]

My dear Sir,

A few days before I left home, I had the honor of receiving your two Vols The School of the Heart, and some time before, a letter from you, for both [of][2] which marks of your esteem I beg to return you my sincere thanks. Being at present in a house where Franks abound, and not purposing to return home immediately, I avail myself of this opportunity to say, that I was so much pleased with the *Lessons* which I read, that I have no doubt that the whole of the work will delight me, when I shall be able to peruse it at leisure. The strains of sentiment are such as I have been in the habit of cultivating, for my own great benefit (as I have lately had much cause to feel under severe domestic

---

[1] The Revd. Henry Alford, D.D. (1810–71), poet and hymn writer—author of the well-known harvest hymn 'Come, ye thankful people, come'—was elected Fellow of Trinity College, Cambridge (where he was the friend of C. W. jnr. and the Tennysons) in 1834: but he had now become vicar of Wymeswold, Leics., where he remained for eighteen years, working at his edition of the *Greek Testament* (1849–61). *The School of the Heart* appeared in 1835, *The Abbot of Muchelnaye* in 1841: later on, he became the first editor of the *Contemporary Review*. He was appointed Dean of Canterbury in 1857. Alford had written to W. W. on 7 Aug., sending his volumes of poems *The School of the Heart:* ' . . . I thought it but due to send some acknowledgment to you to whom I owe so very much. You will find in them . . . many trains of thought in which your own influence may be traced. May they prove to be (however crude) the legitimate fruits of your planting among us, for which the country owes you a debt only second to her obligations to Shakespeare.' (*WL MSS.*) See *Cornell Wordsworth Collection*, no. 2215.

[2] *Word dropped out.*

afflictions), and also with no little service, as you encourage me
to believe, to others. My right arm is suffering under a severe
sprain, which must be my excuse for not writing at greater
length; and so illegibly. Believe me to be, my dear sir,

very sincerely yours
Wm Wordsworth

928. W. W. to C. W.

Address: The Rev. the Master, Trinity College, Cambridge.
Franked: Penrith September twenty six 1835 Lonsdale.
Postmark: 26 Sept. 1835. *Stamp*: Penrith.
MS. Mr. Jonathan Wordsworth.
Charles Wordsworth, Annals of My Early life, 1806–1846, 1891, p. 171 (—).

Lowther Castle
Saturday (Sept. 26, 1835)[1]

My dear Brother,
    I have this moment received your letter forwarded from
Rydal, and should answer it at length but for a severe sprain in
my right arm which makes it painful and injurious for me to
write.—
    As dear Charles seemed so much set upon marrying, there
seems upon the whole good reason for congratulation that he
has obtained the appointment at Winchester;[2] but I cannot but
hold to the opinion that his abilities would have rendered him
useful, and eminently, so in [a] less restricted line of occupation.
Pray present him my best wishes and kind congratulations. I
would have written to him from this place but for the cause I
have mentioned.
    I know not whether thanks have been sent to Chris: for his
valuable present and the copies of his Ode,[3] which arrived just

    [1] Date added by C. W.
    [2] Charles Wordsworth had just been elected Second Master at Winchester,
a post never held before by anyone but a Wykehamist. His marriage followed
at the end of the year.
    [3] C. W. jnr.'s *Ode* performed in the Senate House, Cambridge, on 7 July
1835 at the first commencement after the Installation of Marquess Camden
(see pt. i, L. 44) as Chancellor. The setting was by Thomas Attwood
Walmisley (see pt. ii, L. 732), Professor of Music from 1836. '. . . the Music
was admired,' Romilly noted: 'parts of the Poetry was praised but I thought it
obscure and uninteresting.' (*Romilly's Cambridge Diary*, p. 83.)

95

before I left home; if not he must excuse his friends. Writing is injurious to Doro—and poor Mrs W. has so much to do, and is, besides, Secretary to the whole family. Pray present this apology to him with my best love, and also to John, thanking him for his Letter. Tell him also that I have altered the passages which he found obscure; all but the last, in *the power of Sound*. 'Even She'—that is obscure solely on account of the omission of a note of Interrogation immediately preceding the words, 'Even She', viz. the Power of sound, or, in this place, of harmony.[1]

The enclosed paper of Queries is from Dr Jackson[2]—one of your Sons will be so good as to answer it to Dr Jackson under cover to Lord Lonsdale. Lord L. had a sharp fit of illness on his arrival here a few weeks since, but he instantly recovered and is quite well—a wonderful man for his years.

Now for our Invalids. Doro is certainly a good deal better— having gained a four pounds and a half of flesh, from improved appetite and better digestion, but still I cannot but be anxious about her, and do not think that she will be cured without uninterrupted recumbency for a considerable time. When the pain in the vertibrae has been removed by bleeding, she cannot resist the temptation to move about. In vain Do we press upon her the necessity of self denial in this particular, yet it is not at all to be wondered at that she should stir about, when she feels no pain. A thousand thanks for your invitation—at present she is quite incapable of profiting by it, as the motion of a carriage would instantly bring back the inflammation of her spine.— Our dear Sister is in bodily health undoubtedly much better. We have been able without injury to reduce the opiates more than one half, and she is gathering flesh; but her mind received a shock upon the death of Miss Hutchinson from which it has never recovered. It is as sound as ever with regard to events past long ago, and also as to judgements and opinions, but her memory of passing events has greatly failed, and her judgements also in all that respects her disease, though not at all in other things. Indeed I think upon points of morals, character, literature, etc., she expresses herself as well or better than ever she did; but in regard to her own bodily powers, and to space and time as connected with these, she is almost childish. When, however, I consider her [?] that she is not yet 64 years of age, I cannot but hope that if her strength should return, and her health grow improved, her faculties of mind may be con-

---

[1] *On the power of Sound*, l. 76 (*PW* ii. 326).
[2] Rector of Lowther.

siderably restored. I have always thought that this weakening of the mind has been caused by the opium which was thought necessary on account of her great bodily sufferings—this has been—as I have said, much reduced and will I trust be still more [so], but there is yet no restoration of the mental powers of recollection etc.—

How glad am I my dear Brother, that your health did not suffer from the fatigues of the commencement.—My stay here has been prolonged by Sockbridge Johns business: it will be necessary to sell the greatest part of his Estate and I am making arrangements for that event, a sort of business for which I am little suited. He and your Nephew William are going to Herefordshire, to Mr Hutchinson, from which place John will proceed to resume his Studies in London. If the Residue of his property allows the means of his Education, that will be all, I fear it will not, and if the mother or rather her Husband[1] insists upon her annuity, I mean the whole of it, [he wi]ll not have a farthing. Mr Watson[2] will [tell you][3] about his visit to us, truly glad [were we] to see him and Miss W.—affectionately yours

W.W.

929. W. W. to SAMUEL ROGERS

MS. Sharpe Collection, University College, London.
Rogers. LY ii. 758.

Lowther Castle
Sept[r] 28th [1835]

I have long owed you an acknowledgment, my dear Friend, for an affectionate Letter,[4] which was very welcome, distressed as we were, had been, and alas! still are.

It is a week since I came to this hospitable mansion, which I leave today. The Country is most beautiful, the leaves in many places changed to the exact point of autumnal splendor and

[1] John Lightfoot, the Keswick attorney.
[2] Joshua Watson.
[3] *MS. torn.*
[4] Rogers had written on 17 Aug. about the death of S. H.: '. . . but there are some noble spirits in the house—some who were not aware of their strength till it was called for; and I make no doubt they have found it.' (*WL MSS.*)

variety. During my walks I missed you much, and also our Friend Sir George.[1] Lady Frederick is not here, she comes at the end of the week. Lord Lonsdale had a sharp attack of indisposition when he first came, but he threw it off in two or three days, and, to the great joy of his Friends, is as active and well as ever. Lady Lonsdale also, one of the best of Women, is quite well. Lady Anne[2] and Miss Thompson[3] are both here; so is Mrs O'Callaghan.[4]

You will be desirous, I am sure, to learn how our invalids are. My dear Sister, in bodily health, is decidedly better, though quite unable to stand. Her mind, however, is, I grieve to say, much shattered. The change showed itself upon the death of dear Miss Hutchinson, but probably was preparing before. Her case at present is very strange; her judgement, her memory, and all her faculties are perfect as ever, with exception of what relates to her own illness, and passing occurrences. If I ask her opinion upon any point of Literature, she answers with all her former acuteness; if I read Milton, or any favourite Author, and pause, she goes on with the passage from memory; but she forgets instantly the circumstances of the day. Considering that she is not 64 years of age, I cannot but hope that her mind may be restored, if her bodily health should go on improving.

My daughter is a good deal better, but very far from being strong and well.—

Lady Lonsdale is in the room and begs to be remembered to you.—

When shall we meet again? You know well how much I delight in your conversation and what a value I set upon your friendship. I am not likely to be soon in London, but when will you come again Northwards?

Miss Kinnaird, I am told, is about to be married to L. Drummond,[5] of calculating celebrity. Is he an amiable Man? I

---

[1] i.e. the late Sir George Beaumont.

[2] Lady Ann Beckett, Lady Lonsdale's younger daughter (see *MY* ii. 515).

[3] One of Lady Lonsdale's circle.

[4] Wife of the Hon. George O'Callaghan (see pt. i, L. 115).

[5] i.e. Lieut. Drummond. Thomas Drummond (see pt. i, L. 79) had made his name in the army as a mathematician and chemist, inventing the use of limelight (known as the 'Drummond light') and an improved heliostat. He had now taken up his post as Under-Secretary in Dublin, where he won over O'Connell, and secured a lasting reputation as a wise and just administrator, before his early death from over-work in 1840.

should like to know, for she is a great favourite with me and mine.—

Miss Rogers, I hope, is well. My poor Body is always getting into some scrape or other. Last year it was my foot, now it is my right arm which I have sprained so violently that I can scarcely guide my pen; and I much fear you will not think my letter worth the trouble of decyphering.

Southey, from whom I heard this morning, is upon the point of finishing his first Vol: of Cowper. His edition will have 101 original Letters of the poet. Pray write, at your early convenience, as I wish to know how you are and where spending the summer.

most affectionately yours
W. Wordsworth

930. W. W. to ROBERT SOUTHEY

Address: Robert Southey Esqre, Keswick.
Franked: Penrith September twenty eight 1835 Lonsdale.
Postmark: 28 Sept. 1835. *Stamp:* Penrith.
MS. Harvard University Library.
LY ii. 757.

Lowther Castle Monday 28th
[Sept. 1835]

My dear S.

Many thanks for two notes. I am glad you liked the Medallion; I was anxious for your opinion of it, and more particularly as it was not to be seen by my Friends and Family at Rydal.

Mr Wyon[1] seemed a person of agreeable and gentlemanly

---

[1] Edward William Wyon (1811–85), the sculptor, cousin of William Wyon, R. A. (1795–1851), chief engraver at the Mint, with whom he was confused by de Selincourt (see Blanchard, *Portraits of Wordsworth*, pp. 160–1). Southey describes the genesis of Wyon's medallion of W. W. in his letter to Grosvenor Bedford on 29 Sept.: 'Mr Wyon has killed two birds with one shot. Seeing how perfectly satisfied everybody here was with his medallion of me, he asked for an introduction to Wordsworth, which I was about to have offered him. Off he set in good spirits to Rydal, and not finding Wordsworth there, was advised to follow him to Lowther. To Lowther he went, and came back from thence delighted with his own success, and with the civilities of Lord and Lady Lonsdale, who desired that they might have both medallions. Nothing, I think, can be better than Wordsworth's and he is equally pleased

manners: In common with all here, I thought his likeness of you a very successful one, and I shall be glad *to hang* in such good company.

It gives me much pleasure to hear that your Cowper[1] is in such a state of forwardness. I see it advertised in the London papers, which announce the first Vol: will be out in October.

Your improved Wesley[2] will prove a most interesting Work, and will be well timed as through the force of factious passions, and presumptuous opinions, a great secession from the Society as established by its Founder, appears to be taking place.

My accounts from home respecting my Sister are pretty much such as you give of Mrs Southey. Her bodily health is decidedly improved, but the state of the mind, I fear, not at all. The change shewed itself soon after the death of dearest Miss H—, but must have been preparing before. For my own part, her age being not sixty four, I cannot but ascribe the failure of recollection of passing events, and her impaired judgement as to her bodily powers and in regard to time and space, these I cannot but ascribe to the great quantity of opium which it has been thought proper to give her. At present it is reduced considerably more than one half and we are going on reducing it, with the approbation of Mr Carr—Dora is upon the whole better.—

With affectionate wishes for an improvement in dear Mrs Southey, I remain

Most faithfully yours

W. W.

I quit this place to-day for Mr Marshall's and I shall be home on Thursday *at the latest.*

with mine.' (Southey, vi. 273.) A copy of Wyon's medallion is now in the National Portrait Gallery. See *Frontispiece.*

[1] *The Works of Cowper . . . With a Life of the Author,* vol. i, 1835; vols. ii—ix, 1836; vols. x—xv, 1837.

[2] *The Life of Wesley and the Rise and Progress of Methodism* was published in 1820. The 'improved edition' did not appear until 1846, edited by Cuthbert Southey, and included the MS. notes written in his own copy by Coleridge, and *Remarks on the Life and Character of John Wesley* by Alexander Knox (for whom see pt. ii, L. 740), an intimate friend of Wesley's.

931. D. W. to JAMES GREENWOOD [1]

MS. Brown University Library. Hitherto unpublished.

Rydal Mount Octob[r] 1835

My dear Sir,

Mary Fisher [2] tells me your wish for a Copy of some of my verses. Without further preface I begin,

To my good and faithful Friend

Thomas Carr.

Five years of sickness and of pain
This weary frame has travelled o'er
But God is kind, and now again
I rest upon a tranquil shore.

I rest in quietness of mind
Oh! may I thank my God
With heart that never shall forget
The perilous path I've trod.

They tell me of one fearful night
When thou, my faithful Friend,
Didst part from me in holy trust
That soon my earthly cares must end.

Dorothy Wordsworth

Copied by D W for Mr Greenwood.

932. W. W. to JOSEPH BENN [3]

Address: John Benn Esqre, Lowther.
Endorsed: 2 Octr. 1835. M[r] Wordsworth.
MS. Lonsdale MSS. Hitherto unpublished.

Ambleside October 2[d], 1835.

Dear Sir,

I have taken the liberty of forwarding to you my Son William Wordsworth's Deeds of the White Moss Estate; in

---

[1] Of the Wyke, Grasmere. See pt. ii, Ls. 686 and 721, and *Letters of Hartley Coleridge* (ed. Griggs), p. 280.

[2] The friend mentioned in L. 893 above.

[3] Lord Lonsdale's land agent. W. W. addressed the letter to 'John' Benn by mistake.

order that my other Son's Annuity, the Revd John Wordsworth, may duly be Registered by the Clerk of the Peace. Upon reference to the Deeds you will find the Annuity recognised and the property duly described. I have given you this trouble from an apprehension that the Annuity has not been duly registered by the Clerk of the Peace. Moreover the Annuity Deed which was executed at the same time that the property was transferred to my Son William is missing, which Mr Carter my Clerk suggests may have been sent to Mr Stephenson [1] the Clerk of the Peace for enrolment and may still be in Mr. Stephenson's possession. Will you have the goodness to make Inquiries about the Deed at Appleby at your convenience; and at all events do your best to make my Son's Vote valid. I am more anxious about this matter as my Son proposes to sell his other Westmorland Vote in order to purchase a Freehold to support the Conservative Cause in East Cumberland.—

Whatever expense may be incurred in this matter I will thank you to let me to know when the Deeds are returned thro' Mr Garnett. [2]

> I remain Dear Sir
> very Truly yours
> Wm Wordsworth

933. W. W. to JOSHUA WATSON

Address: Joshua Watson Esqre, 6 Park Street, Westminster [*readdressed to*] Rectory, Diggeswell, n^r Welwyn.
Postmark: 7 Oct. 1835. *Stamp*: Kendal Penny Post.
Endorsed: W. Wordsworth Esq. 5 Octr 1835 with lines sent to MSW. [3]
MS. Swarthmore College Library.
Memoir of Joshua Watson (—). *John Edwin Wells, 'Wordsworth and Church Building: Airey-Force Valley', MLR xxxv (1940), 350—4.*

[*In M. W.'s hand*]

Rydal Mount Octr 5th. [1835]

My dear Sir

What a pity after so pleasant and profitable a journey you should have been attacked with illness on the road—your letter

---

[1] Richard Stephenson, attorney at Appleby.
[2] Postmaster at Penrith.
[3] Mary Sikes Watson, Joshua Watson's daughter.

was forwarded to me by Lord Lonsdale, who says 'that if Mr
Watson returns to this country at any future time, tell him how
glad I should be to have an opportunity of making his
acquaintance'. Why did you give yourselves a moment's
trouble upon my having to walk 3 miles, and thro' so beautiful a
Country?—I was indeed disappointed in having an hour or two
less of your company, and not being able to shew you more of
the Lake; and especially the view from Mr Marshall's house and
ground. It would also have given me much pleasure to have
introduced you and Miss W. to that excellent family. You
know that they are dissenters and far-going Reformers; but,
John, the second Son, offered no less a sum than £2,800 towards
building and endowing a Church to stand in the Town of
Keswick—the Parish Ch:[1] as you know being at a distance, and
besides too small for the Population; Other Persons residing in
the neighbourhood and elsewhere felt the desireableness of
having a new Ch: or Chapel, and some were willing to
subscribe as much as £600 a piece—but only on condition that
each Person so subscribing, should be a Trustee having a voice
equivalent to Mr J. M. in the appointment of a Minister: To this
he objected, and more particularly as they were all of one
Party—commonly called 'the Saints'—he then proposed that
he should represent himself as a Trustee—disclaiming all wish to
appoint any Relative or Connection of his own—and that the
others on their part conjointly elect another—if that Trustee
and he could agree in the choice of the Minister, so much the
better—if not, they should name *their* man, and he his, and the
decision be left to the Bishop: This proposal they utterly
rejected, and yet these men, who are so afraid of the selection of
a Bp: under these circumstances, would be shocked if you were
to call them Dissenters. Our Ch: alas! swarms with such enemies
fostered in her own bosom, and it is to be feared the most
dangerous she has to contend with.

My son, the vicar of Brigham, will be absent from Workington for a fortnight, having been tempted, by the great
Protestant meeting which was to take place in Dublin yesterday
to go to that City, which he had never seen—his wife opened
the communication which contained your note, but the Papers
you allude to, were not in the Packet. Perhaps they may have

---

[1] At Crosthwaite. The new church of St. John at the opposite end of
Keswick, designed by Anthony Salvin, was not opened until 1838.

been sent to Mr Fawcett,[1] who, as Minister of the Ch: of Cockermouth, seems more strictly connected with the business, tho' the Town of C. is part of the Parish of Brigham. It was an agreeable surprize to me that you have moved in this business—thinking as I do, that when particulars are enquired into, it will be found that Cockermouth and its neigh[bour]hood including the large village of Papcastle, would be much benefitted by the erection of a Ch:[2] towards the lower end of that Town. The Earl of Lonsdale is Lay Rector of Brigham, and having occasion to write to him this morn[g] I mentioned the conversation you and I had had together, and the substance of your note to John, which has been forwarded to me by his wife.

When my Carpet Bag etc reached Hallsteads, I found that a Plaid belonging to some of your Party, had been left, thro' mistake, as mine—I fear you might miss it much—it shall be taken care of, till I have an opportunity of restoring it to you. My walk from Lyulph's Tower to Hallsteads was beguiled by throwing into blank verse a description of the Scene which struck Miss Watson and me at the same moment. Here it is

>   Not a breath of air
> Ruffles the bosom of this leafy glen,
> From the brook's margin wide around, the trees
> Are stedfast as the rocks; the brook itself
> Following, in patient solitude a course
> Old as the hills that feed it from afar,
> Doth rather deepen than disturb the calm
> Where all things else are still and motionless.
> And yet even now, a little breeze, perchance
> Escaped from boisterous winds that rage without,
> Has entered, by the sturdy oaks unfelt;
> But to its gentle touch, how sensitive
> Is the light ash, that pendant from the brow
> Of yon dim Cave, in seeming silence makes
> A soft eye-music of slow waving boughs
> Powerful almost as vocal harmony
> To stay the Wanderer's steps and soothe his thoughts.[3]

[1] The Revd. Edward Fawcett (1778–1864), educated at Heversham School and Magdalene College, Cambridge: rector of Fambridge, Essex, from 1802, and perpetual curate of Cockermouth from 1809.

[2] This is the first reference to the scheme to build a new church in W. W.'s native town, which occupied his energies throughout the following year, as later letters show.   [3] *Airey-Force Valley* (*PW* ii. 209).

I am sorry not to have been able to transcribe these lines for Miss
W. with my own hand—but my arm is become so much worse,
that I cannot even tie my own neck cloth.

Our Invalids are much as you left them. With our united kind
and affec regards to yourself and Miss W—begging also to be
remembered to Mr and Mrs Norris[1]—I remain my dear Sir,
very faithfully yours

[signed] Wm Wordsworth

934. W. W. to DAVID LAING[2]

Address: Mr D. Laing, Bookseller, Edinburgh.
Franked: Penrith October eight 1835 Lonsdale.
Postmark: (1) 8 Oct. 1835 (2) 9 Oct. 1835. *Stamp*: Penrith.
MS. Edinburgh University Library.
Geoffrey Bullough, 'The Wordsworth-Laing Letters', MLR xlvi (1951), 1–15 (—).

[*In M. W.'s hand*]

Rydal Mt Octr 7th [1835]

My dear Sir

You will wonder, and perhaps blame me, that your last very
friendly letter has remained so long unanswered. The cause has
been your request that I would transcribe certain lines as an
Autograph. This I have been unable to do, having had the
misfortune to sprain my right arm so severely, that no
penmanship that I could execute would resemble my natural
hand-writing. Furthermore it is both painful and injurious to
me to write at all.

This note is written in my name by Mrs W. to explain the
cause of the delay, and to thank you for y^r endeavours to
procure the Mss—and to request that when you shall have
procured the books, you will send them by the first *safe*
opportunity directed to "the care of Mr Wordsworth, Stamp
Off. Carlisle"—who will forward them to Rydal.

With kind regards to your Sister from this family, believe me
faithfully

Your much obliged
[signed] Wm Wordsworth

[1] See L. 922 above.

[2] David Laing had visited W. W. at Rydal Mount in August of this year
(*R MV B*).

935. W. W. to CORNELIUS NICHOLSON[1]

MS. Kendal Public Library. Hitherto unpublished.

[*In M. W.'s hand*]

Rydal Mount Octr 7th, 1835

Sir,

Having received this morning your letter; enclosing the Rules and Regulations of the Kendal Natural History, and Scientific Society,[2] with an intimation of my having been elected an Honorary Member thereof; I take leave to request that you would communicate to the Society my sense of the honor conferred upon me, and likewise my warmest wishes for the extension and success of an Institution, the objects of which are so interesting and important.

I am Sir your obedient S^t

[*signed*] Wm Wordsworth

To the Secretary of the 'Kendal Nat. His^{ry} and Scientific Society'.

---

[1] Cornelius Nicholson (1804–89), son of the postmaster at Ambleside, was apprenticed to Richard Lough, proprietor of the *Kendal Chronicle*, and from 1825 began his publishing and bookselling business in Kendal in partnership with John Hudson. The first edition of his *Annals of Kendal* appeared in 1832 (2nd edn. enlarged, 1861). In 1833 he married Mary (d. 1877), daughter of the Revd. John Hudson, vicar of Kendal (see pt. ii, L. 610). He was Mayor of Kendal, 1845–6, and an enthusiastic promoter of railways in the north-west. For a time he owned Haydon's portrait of *Wordsworth on Helvellyn*, now in the National Portrait Gallery.

[2] Founded by Cornelius Nicholson and Thomas Gough, the naturalist, on 20 Aug. 1835, under the presidency of Edward Wilson of Abbot Hall and Rigmaden Park. At the general meeting on 22 Sept., W. W. and Southey, along with Lord Brougham, John Dalton the physicist, Adam Sedgwick, and Professor Wilson, were elected Honorary Members. William Pearson took a prominent part in the activities of the Society, and later on, Hartley Coleridge lectured and gave poetry readings (1846–7). The Minute Books of the Society are preserved at the Kendal Public Library.

936. W. W. to C. W. JNR.

Address: The Revd Chris: Wordsworth, Trinity Coll: Cambridge. *Favoured by Mr Lodge.* [*In Dora W.'s hand*]
MS. British Library. *Hitherto unpublished.*

[*In M. W.'s hand*]
From Your Uncle

Rydal Mt Octr 23^d [1835]

My dear Chris:

Your very welcome letter to Dora reached us yesterday, and I have an opportunity of replying to it by Mr Lodge,[1] a young Man whom I met in Trinity Combination-room last Spring— he is of Hawkshead and going to Mag: Coll:—How delighted we were to hear that your Father was so well. Your Aunt W. as you see holds the pen for me (a beautiful one it is) my wrist being little better, and Dora not being allowed to write. She was obliged to have the leeches again last Monday—principally on account of a pain in her side—which Mr Carr is inclined to believe and hopes proceeds from what is still left of spinal injury. Her appetite however and digestion are certainly much improved, which we owe to that frightful poison the Prussic acid. It has cured Bertha Southey of stomach complaints to which she has been subject for many years.

The Wm Wordsworth whose Epitaph you give, is most probably of our family, and his connection with it could perhaps be made out by Mr Hunter,[2] to whose book, letters, and conversation I am indebted for most of what I know about our Ancestors. The word Anchoress[3] is no doubt a coinage— tho' I rather think not originally of mine—Anchoritess, the proper term, is unmanageable in that Place, and neither Hermitess nor Votaress, both allowable words, exactly suit my purpose. If you cannot stomach Anchoress take the latter. Going on with your letter I have to say, that we never hear a word—*any of us*—about the Wilberforcean warblings on

---

[1] Edmund (b. 1819) elder son of Richard Lodge, surgeon, of Hawkshead. He took his degree in 1841, but nothing further is known about him.

[2] For Joseph Hunter the antiquarian, see pt. ii, L. 648.

[3] 'Anchoress' is in fact the usual medieval form of the word, which survives in Latimer, Jewell, and Fairfax's Tasso. W.W. is probably referring to his use of the word in his sonnet *St. Catherine of Ledbury* (*PW* iii. 34), first published in the *Yarrow Revisited* volume.

Rydal, or any other lake. Something of the like enquiries had been made of us thro' the Marshalls—and were answered in the same way. The state of mind in the sorrowing relatives and friends of that good and able Man, reminds me strongly of the process by which Gods and demigods were made out of the departed, in the olden time. Can we wonder at this when we remember how the poor Man was famed in his life time. This piece of biography, [1] I have private reasons for believing, will prove a strange composition. Some of its intended iniquities, however, for such they were, iniquities caused by bigotry, have received a timely check.

We were in hopes to have seen some of you at Christmas—but the wedding, [2] which God prosper, will, we apprehend, prevent our wishes being gratified. Had it taken place during a *Summer* vacation, we might have hoped to see the Bride and Bridegroom here on a wedding excursion. Yet, happy as Charles must needs be, we cannot but think he might spare you or John. Hartley Coleridge has nothing to do with the Doctor. [3] He is going to publish another Vol: of Poems [4]—he writes a good deal. I am grateful for your dispositions to my young friend Henry Lowther [5]—the whole family are so kind to me, as I mentioned in my last—and Lady L. in particular so affectionate, that I would gladly repay them in any way in my power. Be assured that having so recently made this application to you I felt that the enclosed letter from Mr Stansfield Rawson [6] was most unluckily timed. The writer is a most excellent Man, both in public and private life; and I regret that his request could not be complied with. I told him in answer, that a direct introduction for his young Friend to the Master of Trinity would be an awkward and unprofitable thing for him as it

---

[1] William Wilberforce had died on 29 July 1833, and his sons Robert and Samuel (see also *MY* ii. 482) were now compiling his *Life*, which appeared in 5 vols. in 1838. The work stirred up a controversy in which both W.W. and H.C.R. were interested, by appearing to disparage Thomas Clarkson's contribution to the abolition of slavery.

[2] For Charles Wordsworth's wedding, see L. 968 below.

[3] Southey's work.

[4] They did not appear till 1851.

[5] Henry (1818—76), eldest son of Col. H. C. Lowther, and eventually 3rd Earl of Lonsdale (see also *MY* ii. 463). He had just entered Trinity College, Cambridge, from Westminster School. He later joined the Life Guards, and was M.P. for West Cumberland, 1847—72.   [6] See pt. ii, L. 704.

would be for any Undergraduate. Will you excuse me for having felt myself obliged to add, that all that I could do was to forward his letter to you, expressing my belief that you would not be indifferent towards a Person in whom he was so much interested; and if your engagements would allow you to serve him in any way, he might rely upon its being done. I have yet one more favor to ask of you, which is, when you fall in with Mr Hymers[1] you would beg, from me, that he would look with an eye of encouragement upon my Nephew Th^{os} Hutchinson of St. John's. Poor fellow! *he* has lost an invaluable friend by the death of his Aunt. She paid for his private Tutor—his Father *not* deeming it prudent, in the present distressed State of Agriculture, to furnish the money. Tom will now have to proceed without such assistance—which is to be regretted as he is wholly without literary ambition or enthusiasm—so that he would not have gone to Coll: at all, had there been an opening for him in any other quarter. In all moral points I believe him to be an excellent young Man—and a little countenance from Mr H. I know would not be lost upon him.

Your Cousin John, the *Stop-gap* of Workington, and I fear the good-natured Dupe of a skilful but dishonest Builder, at Brigham—has dear fellow just returned from a fortnight's ramble in Ireland. He heard O'Connell deliver his infamous Speech[2] to the Trades Union—staid 5 days in Dublin, went to Limerick, Killarney and Cork, and returned thro' Kilkenny and Clonmel, to Dublin. He gives deplorable accounts of the Romanists, and is any thing but satisfied with the Protestants— so many of the Ministers preaching [as far][3] as he could hear and learn, popery under other names. William who has been also absent, had a most narrow escape for his life in his return from Hereford towards Shrewsbury. The Mail Coach on the outside of which he was a Passenger—owing to the bad state of the lamps was overturned in crossing Ludlow bridge. W. by the first shock against the parapet of the Bridge, was cast into the air—but thro' God's mercy alighted on his feet, behind the Coach, without more injury than a bruised knee and a scraped [?][4] the back. I have begged that he would as a public duty state

---

[1] For John Hymers, see pt. ii, L. 562.

[2] Daniel O'Connell was now pressing for an extension of corporation reform to Ireland, and to Dublin in particular, as a means of breaking the Protestant ascendancy.

[3] *Words dropped out.*

[4] *MS. torn.*

the case to Sir F. Freeling. [1] The other Mail when they met it had no lamps lighted.

I have nothing to add, but that your poor Aunt D. is much as when I last wrote to your Father. We have this comfort however that her opium has been reduced to one quarter—and other stimulants in greater proportion—so that if we can keep off diarrhea we hope we shall do well. Your Aunt, who has returned from Workington, says that Isa and the children are quite well and thriving.

[*cetera desunt*]

937. W. W. to M. W.

MS. WL.
LY ii. 715.

Whitehaven Monday Morn.
[2 Nov. 1835]

My dearest Mary

Thanks for the good news of your Letter.—John was at St Bees when I arrived; did not see him till next morning. Found Isabella suffering from a cough and cramp, and both the Children pulled down somewhat by teething.—We had a nice chat all the evening. Next day John brought me here, [2] and dined one of a very large party—I shall follow the direction about bathing, meaning to go in at noon to day. The family here all wonderfully well; my arm is something better; my eyes are pretty well, but there is more tenderness and aching occasionally in the ball of the right eye than I used to have, and I am not sure that the pain in the jaw on that side of the face may have something to do with it, as it makes all that side of the face so sensible of cold. Isabella told me that her mother's face was very nervously affected in the same way when having got her new teeth, and they not fitting, she was obliged to masticate, as I have had for a long time, on one side of her jaw. She was very ill with it, the cold always flying to that side of the face.—I shall not write much from here; Lord L. being the only franker, and having so few covers to dispose of.

---

[1] For Sir Francis Freeling, Bart., Secretary of the G.P.O., see pt. i, L. 321.
[2] To Whitehaven Castle.

I send you without comment Miss Peabody's Letter, [1] which I found in the Parcel. I did not look at the book, so far even as to ascertain that it was hers.—John continues to look very well.—This morning I put the watch into Edgar's [2] hands, and called at the [?] [3]—the man not at home—was not [able] [4] to pay a bill.—I have nothing more to say except pray write. The family here stay till friday at least, perhaps saturday, but write me by tomorrow's post. Be particular about Dora also—remember me kindly to Mrs Ellwood, [5] if she depart before my return, which will not perhaps be before the middle of next week.

Ever most affectionately yours, with kindest love to Dora and Sister—

W. Wordsworth

938. M. W. to DAVID LAING [6]

Address: David Laing Esq[re], Bookseller, Old Town, Edinburgh. By favour of Allen Harding Esq[re].
MS. Edinburgh University Library.
The Wordsworth-Laing Letters (—).

[early Nov. 1835]

My dear Sir,

A Lady from Edinburgh who intends visiting this neighbourhood shortly will afford us a convenient opportunity of receiving the 2 little books (which you have kindly undertaken to procure from Prof: Wilson) safely. M[r] Allen Harden, [7] who is

---

1 Elizabeth Peabody (see pt. i, L. 312) had become assistant to Bronson Alcott (1799–1888) in his Temple School in Boston the previous year, and published her account of his educational methods in *Records of a School*, (anon.), 1835, which she sent to W. W. on 7 Sept. with a covering letter explaining how his poetry was being used to develop the innate ideas of the children. 'You would be pleased to find yourself made foster-father to young Spirits:—how I should like to know what you would say to the commentary of that young child on "Our birth is but a sleep and a forgetting!" How I wish you could have seen how like the breeze of Spring, the first stanzas of that Ode passed over the young blossoms of Life—the very sound of wakening Nature seemed to breathe from their lit-up faces . . .' (*WL MSS.*)

2 Robert Edgar, the Whitehaven watchmaker.

3 *MS. illegible.*

4 *Word dropped out.*

5 For Mrs. Ellwood, see pt. i, L. 9.   6 See also L. 934 above.

7 Son of John Harden, formerly of Brathay.

the Bearer of this, will I hope give you Mrs Rankin's[1] address and mention the time of her departure so that you may send the parcel whither he directs. Mr Wordsworth is gone to Whitehaven for a short time—intending while there, to have the benefit of a warm sea-bath, which I hope may cure his sprained arm and enable him to perform his promise to you, which he has hitherto regretted being unable to do.

Will you make our kind remembrances to your good Sister. We felt obliged to her for her intention to write to my Sister— but poor thing! she herself would only perhaps have a transitory pleasure in being told that Miss Laing thought of her. Her long illness has much impaired her Memory. Our comfort, in our attendance upon her, is in seeing her generally very happy.

My daughter, you will both be glad to hear, we think much better. She joins me in best regards and in thanks for your aid to have her little Packet restored to her—and believe me d^r Sir

to remain   your obliged
M Wordsworth

939. W. W. to W. W. JNR.

Address: Mr Wordsworth, Stamp Off., Carlisle.
MS. WL.
LY ii. 718.

[Whitehaven]
Saturday [7 Nov. 1835]

My dear Wm

Here I have been just a week, and shall stay till Monday or Tuesday. I have bathed in the warm sea-baths three times, with some benefit to my arm and shall take another bath on Monday. I shall stay 3 or 4 days with John,[2] and a day with Sir Francis Vane[3] (who is here) and then home.—The accounts I have from Rydal of our Invalids are good.—

What a frightful accident your's was;[4] I hope you will soon be clear of the necessity of poulticing.

[1] Perhaps wife of B. M. Rankin, an Edinburgh solicitor.
[2] At Workington Rectory.
[3] Sir Francis Fletcher-Vane, 3rd Bart. (1797–1842), of Hutton-in-the-Forest, nr. Penrith: Sheriff of Cumberland, 1837.
See L. 936 above.

Lord and Lady L. are wonderfully well; so is Lady Frederick who is here.—This note goes through a frank of Miss Grisdale's.[1]

Your ever affectionate Father
W. Wordsworth

I had a Letter from Isabella yesterday, the Children pretty well; John had had a bad cold. She does not mention her own health; but I was sorry to see when I was at Workington Hall that her cough had come back. My sprain leaves me little command of my finger, so you must excuse this bad writing.

940. W. W. to EDWARD MOXON

Address: Edward Moxon Esqre, 44 Dover Street, London. Single Sheet.
Postmark: 23 Nov. 1835. *Stamp*: Kendal Penny Post.
MS. Henry E. Huntington Library.
K (—). *LY ii. 760* (—).

[*In M. W.'s hand*]

Rydal Mount Novr. 20 1835

My dear Sir,

In a few days I hope to have an opportunity of sending through a private channel such a selection of Lamb's letters, to myself and this family, as appear to us not unfit for immediate publication. There are however in these, some parts which had better be kept back, but being fearful of using the pencil marks too freely we have left the decision to your discretion and that of our common friends—especially Mr Talfourd[2] and Mr Robinson—I need scarcely add, Mrs M.[3] and poor dear Miss L., if she be in a state of mind that allows of her attending to such a matter. I have kept back several letters—some because they relate merely to personal and domestic concerns, others, because they touch upon the character and manners of individuals who are now living, or too recently deceased to be brought under the public eye, without indelicacy.—I have also thought proper to suppress every word of criticism upon my own Poems—though the strictures are merely such, as might

---

[1] Lady Lonsdale's friend.

[2] Talfourd was to be the editor of *The Letters of Charles Lamb, With a sketch of his life*, 1837.

[3] Mrs. Moxon, Lamb's adopted daughter.

prove generally interesting—and occasionally lead to pleasing strains of sentiment, and descriptions which he has himself felt or observed. The suppressed letters shall not be destroyed.— Those relating to my works are withheld, partly because I shrink from the thought of assisting in any way to spread my own praises and still more, as being convinced that the opinions or judgements of friends given in this way are mostly of little value. On this point I have no more to say, than that I trust to your care for preventing the possibility of any suppressed portion of the letters sent, being copied by any one, from any motive whatever—and that the originals may be returned to me through safe hands after you have done with them.

On the other page you have the requested Epitaph,[1] it was composed yesterday—and, by sending it immediately, I have prepared the way, I believe, for a speedy repentance—as I dont know that I ever wrote so many lines without some retouching being afterwards necessary. If these verses should be wholly unsuitable to the end Miss L. had in view, I shall find no difficulty in reconciling myself to the thought of their not being made use of, tho' it would have given me great, *very* great pleasure to fulfil, in all points, her wishes.

The first objection that will strike you, and every one, is its extreme length, especially compared with epitaphs as they are now written—but this objection might in part be obviated by engraving the lines in double column, and not in capitals.

Chiabrera[2] has been here my model—tho' I am aware that Italian Churches, both on account of their size and the climate of Italy, are more favourable to long inscriptions than ours—His Epitaphs are characteristic and circumstantial—so have I endeavoured to make this of mine—but I have not ventured to touch upon the most striking feature of our departed friend's character and the most affecting circumstance of his life, viz, his faithful and intense love of his Sister. Had I been pouring out an Elegy or Monody, this would and must have been done. But for

[1] A first draft of the Epitaph on Charles Lamb, which was later expanded into the poem now entitled *Written after the Death of Charles Lamb* (*PW* iv. 272). In the event it proved unsuitable as an inscription for Lamb's memorial in Edmonton Church, but ll. 30, 31, and 38 of the final version of the poem were used.

[2] Gabriello Chiabrera (1552–1638). W. W. 's admiration for him is clear from the *Essay on Epitaphs* (see especially *Prose Works*, ii. 91), and from his nine translations from Chiabrera (*PW* iv. 248–53).

seeing and feeling the sanctity of that relation as it ought to be seen and felt, lights are required which could scarcely be furnished by an Epitaph, unless it were to touch on little or nothing else.—The omission, therefore, in my view of the case was unavoidable: and I regret it the less, you yourself having already treated in verse the subject with genuine tenderness and beauty.

Now for a few words of business. What is doing with the engraving of my Portrait?[1] of which I hear nothing. If I told you that my Yarrow was out of print, I said more than was true. Messrs L. only told me that it was so nearly out that it would be well to go to press with another Ed: which accordingly they set about[2]—but what progress has been made I do not know, never hearing from them. If you see Mr Talfourd tell him that we are all delighted with his drama[3]—and which may seem odd—*that* is the very reason why I have put off writing to him—as I wished to do more than merely let him know, with thanks, how much he has pleased us. If you should be in communication with Mr Trench[4]—say I beg, a few words for me to him which may be done with the utmost sincerity to the same effect. I had a sprain in my right arm, 3 months ago, and I am yet unable to write with my own hand. You know how much the only pen I can command must be occupied—but I will express my gratitude and admiration to both the Gentlemen as soon as I shall be able. I cannot conclude without adding that the Ep: if used at all, can only be placed *in* the church. It is much too long for an out-door stone, among our rains, damps, etc.

Dora is much better and my poor Sister easier in body tho' her mind has of late faded sadly.

[1] This proposal for an engraving of the Pickersgill portrait apparently came to nothing; but it was later engraved by W. H. Watt for the *Poetical Works* of 1836.

[2] See L. 923 above.

[3] *Ion* (1835). W. W. was present at the first performance in London the following May. Talfourd wrote on 28 Nov.: 'I need not tell you how proud I was to hear through Mr Harness that you were pleased with some parts of my little Drama which had been read to you. I was also glad to hear that you had not heard the whole, because I think I have made it rather less unworthy your attention in the new impression which I now send you. There are also . . . a few Sonnets, which can only be interesting as tributes to the unrivalled beauty of your's, which it was as impossible to know without attempting the same form of composition as really to imitate.' (*WL MSS.*)

[4] For Richard Chenevix Trench, see L. 949 below.

Kindest regards to y^rself and every one about you in which Mrs. W. unites.

I remain faithfully yours

[*signed*] W. W.

After an absence of 3 weeks I only returned home last Wednesday, else you should have heard from me sooner. Kindest remembrances to Mr Rogers if he be returned from Ramsgate.

[*In M. W.'s hand*]

EPITAPH

To the dear memory of a frail good Man
This Stone is sacred. Here he lies apart
From the great City, where he first drew breath,
Was rear'd and taught, and humbly earned his bread;
To the strict labours of the Merchant's desk
By duty chained. Not seldom did those tasks
Teaze, and the thought of time so spent depress,
His Spirit, but the recompence was high;
—Firm Independence, Bounty's rightful Sire:
Affections, warm as sunshine, free as air!
And, when the precious hours of leisure came,
Knowledge and wisdom, gained from converse sweet
With books, or while he ranged the crowded streets
With a keen eye, and overflowing heart:
Hence truths poured out in Works by thoughtful love
Inspired, — and potent over smiles and tears.
From the most gentle Creature nursed in fields
Had been derived the name he bore — a name,
Wherever Christian Altars have been raised,
Hallowed to meekness, and to innocence;
And if in him meekness at times gave way
Provoked out of herself by troubles strange,
Many and strange, that hung about his life;
Or suddenly dislodged by strong rebound
Of animal spirits that had sunk too low,
Or by impetuous fancy and quaint views
Of domineering humour, overcome—
And if too often, self-reproached he felt
That innocence belongs not to our Kind—
He had a constant friend in *Charity*;
Her who, among the multitude of Sins

That she can cover, left not *his* exposed
To an unforgiving judgment from just Heaven—
O, he was good; if e'er a good Man lived!

[*Then follow, in M. W.'s hand, Lamb's lines To Dora W. on being asked by her Father to write in her Album*[1]]

941. M. W. to H. C. R.

Address: H. C. Robinson Esqre, Plowdens Build^gs, Temple, London.
Postmark: 21 Nov. 1835. *Stamp:* Kendal Penny Post.
Endorsed: Nov 1835, Mrs Wordsworth — and W. W.
MS. Dr. Williams's Library.
K (—). Morley, i. 280.

[*c.* 20 Nov. 1835]

My dear Friend

We heard by a letter from Moxon dated the 9th of your arrival in England—and you should not have remained so long without welcome salutation from Rydal Mount, but that W^m was from home, and I forwarded the letter to him—and depended upon his writing a few lines of greeting to you from Whitehaven—however he is returned, not having done so— finding that writing was inconvenient to him, from a sprain he got some weeks ago in his right arm, and for which he has been using hot sea-baths, and is better—but yet it devolves upon me to send you a few hasty lines, which I readily do—hoping I may induce you to come at *your convenience* the sooner the better— and chear us by a detail of your adventures. It must be purely a work of charity—Your presence to W. would be inestimable— he wants such a friend to take him out of himself and to divert his thoughts from the melancholy state in which our poor Sister is *struggling* (to use her own word)—You will be surprized to hear that her *bodily health* is good—but her mind is, I may say in a state of childishness—From the *wonderful change* that has taken place in her constitution—our medical attendant has been induced to attempt to withdraw *gradually all* stimulants—and this has nearly been effected without bad consequences—and we look with somewhat of *hope*, to the time, when she is restored to the diet of a Person in health. Her memory for *passing* events, which at one period was quite gone, (tho' *retrospectively* it was perfect, and her mind *if it could be fixed* on

---

[1] *Works* (ed. Lucas), v. 73.

117

books or serious matters as vigorous as ever) is much re-covered—and this encourages us to trust that her intellect also may be restored—but alas at PRESENT her thoughts and manners are quite child-like. She has much wild pleasure in her sallies—yet almost at the same time bemoans her sufferings which it is difficult for us to understand. But this slight sketch must satisfy you—at present. Dora thank God is better—but still an invalid.

In a few days we shall have an opportunity to forward (which Moxon's letter asked us to do) *such portions* of Ch: Lamb's letters as W. chuses to part with—We should like your judgem^t to be exercised regarding any thing that should be withheld from the public—You know we are very delicate upon the point of publishing the letters of private friends—but we feel that in the case of dear Ch. L— the objections are not so forcible—The Essays he himself gave to the public are so much in the character of his letters.

Should you find it convenient to come to us, we shall expect and *insist* upon, your being an inmate during the day at R. M.— but it would neither be comfortable to you nor to ourselves, for you to lodge under this roof—I have no scruple in telling you this—knowing your habits, and that you like the liberty of a lodging of your own—and such are to be had as will exactly suit you at the foot of our hill—where you alight from the Coach— *observe* that one runs 3 times a week from Kendal and arrives here at 10 o.c. on the Monday and Wed: and Fridy Mg^s—Let us hear from you, and believe me with affec regards from all to be very sincerely but in haste

Yours
M. Wordsworth

Dora, upon asking what I have said about y^r coming to see us, suggests that—as I have put it upon Charity—your good nature may induce you to set off at y^r own inconvenience—but I do not mean you to do this on any account—and in fact y^r company would be to us more valuable a month hence when we shall lose a little niece[1] of mine who has been sojourning with us during the last melancholy twelvemonths—and who has been an interesting Companion to her Uncle on his Walks.

We have not heard from Mr Courtenay since you went away.

---

[1] Elizabeth (Ebba) Hutchinson from Brinsop, who had been at Rydal Mount since the previous January (see *SH*, p. 538).

942. W. W. to EDWARD MOXON

Address: Edwd Moxon Esqre, 44 Dover St, London.
Postmark: 25 Nov. 1835. *Stamp*: St. James's St.
MS. Henry E. Huntington Library.
LY ii. 763.

[*In M. W.'s hand*][1]

Rydal Mount Novr 23rd [1835]

My dear Mr Moxon

I have already written this morning rather more than agrees either with my hand or eyes, so you must excuse this short note from the pen of another and I have little scruple in sending it as it will reach London in a frank. It has been in respect to the Epitaph as I foretold; I have been tempted to retouch it, and beg that after the word 'overflowing heart'[2] you would read thus:

So Genius triumphed over seeming wrong,
And poured out truth in works by thoughtful love
Inspired—works potent over smiles and tears.

The composition is by this alteration a little inspirited, but at the cost of an add^l line—for which room may be made by striking out the two that follow, some lines below—viz

'Or suddenly disloged by strong rebound
Of animal spirits that had sunk too low'—[3]

and indeed these two lines may easily be spared. Again I cannot help expressing a wish that Miss L.'s purpose had been better carried into effect. Suppose Mr Talfourd or yourself were to try? I cannot *put* aside my regret in not having touched upon the affection of the Brother and Sister for each other

Ever faithfully yours
[*signed*] Wm Wordsworth

[1] But the opening of the letter was written by Dora W.
[2] l. 14 of the first draft in L. 940 above.
[3] ll. 24−5 of the first draft.

943. W. W. to EDWARD MOXON

Address: Edward Moxon Esqre, 44 Dover Street, London. *paid* Single [*In M. W.'s hand*]
Postmark: 26 Nov. 1835. *Stamp*: Kendal Penny Post.
MS. Henry E. Huntington Library.
K (—). *LY ii. 764* (—).

Tuesday [24 Nov. 1835]

My dear Mr Moxon

I have sent you the Epitaph again revized; yesterday I sent through a frank a few alterations, those which the present sheet contains being added, I send the whole repenned.

I hope the changes will be approved of, at all events, they better answer my purpose. The lines, as they now stand, preserve better the balance of delicate delineation, the weaknesses are not so prominent, and the virtues placed in a stronger light; and I hope nothing is said that is not characteristic. Of this you and Mrs Moxon will be more competent judges than myself, as I never saw my poor dear Friend, when his afflictions were lying most heavily upon him—written in extreme haste to save the Post

Affectionately yours,

W W

[*There follows*[1] *the 'Epitaph' ll. 1—38, as in PW iv. 272, except that in ll. 34—5 read 'He had a constant friend in Charity;/Her who, among the multitude of Sins'*]

[*W. W. adds*]

If the length makes the above utterly unsuitable, it may be printed with his Works as an effusion by the side of his grave; in this case, in some favorable moment, I might be enabled to add a few Lines upon the friendship of the Brother and Sister.[2]

---

[1] ll. 1—22 are in an unidentified hand (perhaps Ebba Hutchinson's): the rest was written by M. W.

[2] For the expansion of the poem, see next letters, and Alan G. Hill, 'Lamb and Wordsworth. The Story of a Remarkable Friendship', *The Charles Lamb Bulletin*, Jan. 1982.

944. W. W. to H. C. R.

Address: H. C. Robinson Esqre, 2 Plowdens Build^gs, Temple, London.
Endorsed: 25 Novr 1835, Wordsworth.
MS. Dr. Williams's Library.
K (—). *Morley, i. 283.*

Rydal Mount Novr 25th 1835

My dear friend

(I M. W. hold the pen for my Husband)

Your prompt acceptance of our united invitation[1] was nothing more than your long and often experienced kindness had led us to expect. We shall rejoice to see you, but upon one condition—that having been so long abroad lately, you do not on our account set aside the claims which your Relatives and friends in the South, particularly your Brother, have upon you—by putting off, or shortening your visits to them. And with respect to the ensuing three weeks, I think it right to let you know, that it would add to our distress if you should be a witness of the anxiety we are undergoing on account of the experiment now in progress, and drawing towards a conclusion—I allude to our dear Sister—You know I believe how much Opium has been thought necessary for her—We expect in the course of a fortnight to get rid of it altogether—and shall do so, if a diarrhea does not come on—but her present sufferings appear to be, from withdrawing this medicine so severe, that we would rather you were not conscious of them to the extent that would be unavoidable, if you were with us.

At the lodging where the Coach will set you down at the foot of our hill you can be accommodated also with a sitting room—and attendance. I have been to look at the house this morning—the rooms are well-sized, tho' low—for a single Person, and neatly furnished—the only objection to them is, that the situation is too low, and somewhat confined—but at this season of the year far less so than in summer, when the leaves are on the trees—the better sitting room, for you have a choice of two, looks directly up our hill, and commands, now that the trees are bare, rather a chearful view of Lady Fleming's Park. But the great advantage of this lodging lies in being so near us that our intercourse need not be at all dependent upon weather.

Before this reaches you you may probably have seen Moxon

---

[1] To Rydal Mount for Christmas. See L. 941 above.

121

or heard from him about our late communication with him.—
and have learnt our determination upon dear Lamb's letters and
our wishes respecting them—therefore I need not touch further
upon that point—As to the lines sent—the more I think of them,
the more do I feel that their number renders it little less than
impossible that they should be used as an Epitaph—so convinced am I of this, that I feel strongly impelled, as I hinted to
Moxon in my yesterday's letter, containing a revised copy of
the lines, to convert them into a Meditation supposed to be
uttered by his Graveside;[1] which would give me an opportunity
of endeavouring to do some little justice to a part of the subject,
which no one can treat *adequately*—viz—the sacred friendship
which bound the Brother and sister together, under circumstances so affecting. Entertaining this view, I have *hoped* rather
than expected that I might be able to put into ten or twelve
couplets, a thought or feeling which might not be wholly
unworthy of being inscribed upon a stone—consecrated to his
memory and placed near his remains. Having however thrown
off my first feeling already, in a shape so different—I wish that
some one else, Mr Talfourd, Mr Moxon, Mr Southey, or any
other of his friends accustomed to write verse would write the
Epitaph.—Miss L. herself, if the state of her mind did not
disqualify her for the undertaking.—*She* might probably do it
better than any of us.

Before you set off northwards pray call at Longmans and
enquire about my Poems—whether the Yarrow has been
reprinted and if it has, bring down a Copy—and if not finished
as many of the Sheets as are struck off—also learn if you can
what number of the 4 Vols are still on hand. See also Mr
Courtenay and ask Moxon if the engraving from my Portrait[2]
has been begun—It is often enquired after. You will *see* Mr
Moxon of course. My Nephew John Wordsworth[3]—now
lodges at 7 Howard St. Strand—pray drop him a line by the 2nd
Post, telling him *when* you set off—he may have something to
send.—We write these requests with a smile at what y[r] good
nature has brought upon you. My Sister lived some time in
Norfolk[4] when she was young, and fancies that she should like

---

[1] W. W. had now completed his epitaph on Charles Lamb in 38 lines, but
was already thinking of expanding it further. See Ls. 954 and 958 below.

[2] See L. 940 above.

[3] R. W.'s son.

[4] At Forncett, from 1788 till 1793.

some Norfolk Beefins,[1] and has often said she was sure if Mr Robinson knew how *she longed* for them, you would send her some—Could yould contrive to bring her a Box—all kinds of fruit are grateful to her—but none are left now, and oranges are not yet eatable.

With affec remembrances from all here, ever faithfully
Yours [*signed*] Wm Wordsworth

P.S. If it be not disagreeable, call and make enquiries in our name after Mr Rogers and his Sister—and thank him for his letter to me from Ramsgate, which I will answer as soon as I have anything comfortable to say—tell him I luckily escaped Willis[2]—as did, I believe, Southey—he has however reported some impertinences concerning us both—from the mouth as he affirms of Prof: Wilson. Upon which point if you have any pleasure in observing inconsistencies in character, I will amuse you when you come.

Poor dear Miss Lamb! We gather from both you and Moxon that she is better—but as neither of you have spoken definitely—we know not how to address ourselves to her—so leave it to your judgment to say every thing tender and affectionate at a fit opportunity for us—we do feel for and love her dearly.

---

[1] Morley cites the following definition: '*Biffin* written *beefin* in East Anglia. A kind of large rosy winter apple, preserved by being dried in baker's ovens and occasionally pressed till it becomes soft and flat.'

[2] Nathaniel Parker Willis (1806–67), American poet, journalist, and editor. He travelled in Europe, 1832–6, arriving in London in June 1834 (see *HCR* i. 443–4), where he was introduced to Lady Blessington and her circle. The observations on English life which he sent back to the *New York Mirror* were bitterly resented by the Tory press.

945. W. W. to ALARIC WATTS

Address: A. A. Watts Esqre, Torrington Square, London.
Postmark: 27 Nov. 1835.
MS. University of Iowa Library.
Alaric Watts (—).

[*In M. W.'s hand*]

Rydal Mount, Novr 25th 1835

My dear Sir,

I lose not a moment in replying to your letter, which on your own account, and still more on that of Mrs Watts, has given me the deepest concern. Heavy charges, you tell me (for I have not seen the Publication alluded to), have been made against you,[1] in which I am brought forward as one whom you, 'in return for obligations received, have cheated and ill-used.' Now, as to obligations, I have no hesitation in saying, that you never owed any to me—so that the imputation of ingratitude, involved in the charge, falls to the ground at once. The obligations were wholly on my side. Nor had I ever, during such times as we have been in communication with each other, the slightest cause to complain of your behaviour towards me in any respect whatever; and this declaration you are at liberty to make public.

You allude to my *silence* apparently with some uneasiness—be assured that the apprehensions you express are wholly groundless. I do not apologize for not writing to you, for I scarcely hold correspondence with any one, for several reasons, and particularly from the irritable state in which my eyes have long been: but in this case, it appears you do not know how the fact stands. A few years back I sent to your Souvenir a Sonnet on the departure of Sir W. S.[2] for Naples. I received no acknowledgment for this, neither did the book upon its

---

[1] In the notice of Watts in his popular 'Gallery of Literary Characters', William Maginn (1793–1842) had written as follows: 'There is not a man to whom he has been under an obligation, from Jerdan to Lockhart, from Theodore Hook to Westmacott . . . from Crofton Croker to Carter Hall, from Wordsworth to Byron, from Scott to Southey, from Landseer to Wilkie,—from the man who fed him from charity to the man who has from equal charity supported his literary repute, whom he has not in his poor way libelled.' (*Fraser's Magazine*, xi (June 1835), 652.) Watts's friends rallied to his defence, he commenced proceedings for libel, and was awarded damages.

[2] See pt. ii, L. 657.

publication, come to my hands—as I own I expected; but as a volume of that work, of a former year, which I knew you intended for me, did not reach me, I apprehended the same mistake had been made, and wrote either to Messrs Longman or yourself (I forget which) expressing a desire to have the volume, but to my disappointment I neither received it, nor an explanatory letter. I need scarcely add, that I cast no blame on any one, knowing well how often hurry prevents these little things being done at the time, or how easily they slip out of mind afterwards. No intercourse has passed between us since the transmission of that Sonnet; unless a number of the 'United Service Journal'[1] in which my Poems were noticed in a very friendly spirit, was sent by you—which I thought might be the fact, and which I took kindly.

I remain d^r Sir, with respect and the best of good wishes for the recovery of Mrs W's health and peace of mind very sincerely

Yours
[*signed*] Wm Wordsworth

P.S. The exertions you are making in the good cause are much to your honour.

946. W. W. to THOMAS NOON TALFOURD

MS. untraced.
K. LY ii. 817.

Rydal Mount, November 28 [1835]

My dear Mr Talfourd,

Yesterday brought me the second edition of your drama,[2] together with your very friendly note. Part of the play was read aloud last evening and I finished it this morning. . . . You have most ably fulfilled your own purpose, and your poem is a distinguished contribution to English literature. I reserve the sonnets as a *bonne bouche* for to-morrow. But I must tell you that Mrs Wordsworth read me the second preface, which is written with much elegance of style and a

---

[1] *The United Service Journal and Naval and Military Magazine* ran from 1829 to 1841.

[2] i.e. the second privately printed edition of *Ion*, 1835, which Talfourd had sent on 28 Oct. (see L. 940 above).

graceful modesty. I cannot help catching at the hope that, in the evening of life, you may realize those anticipations which you throw out.[1] Chaucer's and Milton's great works were composed when they were far advanced in life. So, in times nearer our own, were Dryden's and Cowper's; and mankind has ever been fond of cherishing the belief that Homer's thunder and lightning were kept up when he was an old man and blind. Nor is it unworthy of notice that the leading interest attached to the name of Ossian is connected with gray hairs, infirmity, and privation.

God bless you! I have not mentioned Lamb's epitaph, having said all I have to say on that subject to Mr Moxon and Mr Robinson. Let me, however, be excused for adding that I was sorry to see the italics at the close of the printed copy sent me down to-day. Mrs Wordsworth takes to them all,[2] except those in the last line. That upon the word 'her' is the only one I approve of, or wish to have retained.

Ever faithfully and affectionately your,

Wm Wordsworth

[1] The Preface to the second edition, dated Oct. 1835, held out the hope that Talfourd might return to dramatic composition 'in the evening of life', in a mood of repose, when his professional exertions were at an end. It replaced the first Preface, which contained a tribute to W. W. and his influence on the taste of the age.

[2] As de Selincourt notes, a word such as 'exception' has probably dropped out after 'takes'. W. W. is referring to the printed copy of the first version of the poem which Moxon had just struck off (see L. 958 below). Talfourd expressed his gratitude for the epitaph in his reply of 16 Dec. (*WL MSS.*), and took the occasion to defend his forthcoming publication of Lamb's letters, 'entirely concurring in your feeling as to the delicacy and reserve with which the letters of a friend so recently taken from us should be treated. . . . But I cannot scrutinize the treasures of fine observation and harmless pleasantry which Lamb's accumulated letters contain without thinking that, with proper reserves, they ought not to be withheld from his admirers.'

947. W. W. to JOHN HERNAMAN[1]

Address: John Hernaman Esqre, 69 Pilgrim Street, Newcastle, Tyne [*In M. W.'s hand*]
Stamp: Kendal Penny Post.
MS. Yale University Library. Hitherto unpublished.

[30 Nov. 1835]

Private

Dear Sir,

I send you these verses[2] on the other page—a parting tribute of my respect, for the manner in which your journal is conducted, and the great variety of solid information that it contains. My friend Captn Kelly,[3] I have reason to believe, has told you why I feel it proper to discontinue it, and assured you, I trust, that it was not in the least from dissatisfaction with your labours but merely as a matter of personal convenience. If you print the Verses, let them by all means appear in your *next* number, and *printed correctly,* which the haste unavoidable in the bringing out of newspapers often prevents being done.—

I remain, dear Sir
sincerely yours
Wm Wordsworth

[*There follow, in M.W.'s hand, the first seven stanzas of* Extempore Effusion, *upon reading in the Newcastle Journal, the notice of the death of the Poet, James Hogg, as in* PW *iv. 276, except that the first version of l. 13 reads 'And scarcely twice the year has measured', and in l. 26 read 'survive' for 'remain'. The lines are autographed by W. W. and dated Novr 1st, 1835*]

---

[1] Editor of the *Newcastle Journal* (founded 1832).

[2] The first draft of the *Extempore Effusion upon the Death of James Hogg* (*PW* iv. 276, 459). *Kilvert's Diary* (ed. William Plomer, 3 vols., 1938–40, i. 318) records Ebba Hutchinson's recollections of the genesis of the poem: '. . . Once when she was staying at the Wordsworths' the poet was much affected by reading in the newspaper the death of Hogg, the Ettrick Shepherd. Half an hour afterwards he came into the room where the ladies were sitting and asked Miss Hutchinson to write down some lines which he had just composed. She did so and these lines were the beautiful Poem called The Graves of the Poets.' Hogg had died on 21 Nov.: the poem was first published in the *Newcastle Journal* for 5 Dec. See also next letter and Ls. 950 and 956 below.

[3] Of Newcastle: apparently a fairly recent acquaintance (see *RMVB* for 1832 and 1834), and a friend of the Benson Harrisons (see *MW*, p. 160).

127

948. W. W. to JOHN HERNAMAN

Address: To the Editor of the Newcastle Journal, Newcastle, Tyne. *Post pd.*
Stamp: Kendal Penny Post.
MS. Yale University Library. Hitherto unpublished.

[*In M. W.'s hand*]

Rydal Mount Decr 1st [1835]
Private

Dear Sir,

By yesterday's post I forwarded to you a copy of Extempory
Verses (which thro' inadventure were dated Decr 1st instead of
Nov^{r}30th) and which I will beg you, if not too late, to correct—
as well as the word 'survive', in the 7th Stanza for which pray
substitute 'remain'. And add to the poem the following 3
Stanzas, which were *cast*, but unfinished yesterday; and I did not
wait, not knowing if I should turn to it again in time for your
next publication. If this alteration does not suit your convenience for this week, I should rather the Poem were kept back
till the week following—both for the fact above stated, and
because without the concluding Stanz: the verses scarcely do
justice to the occasion that called them forth.

I am Sir respectfully yours
[*signed*] Wm Wordsworth

[*There follow, in M. W.'s hand, the eighth, ninth, and eleventh
stanzas of the Extempore Effusion, as in PW iv. 277, except that in
ll. 34—5 read 'but why/O'er ripe fruit' and in l. 44 'And Ettrick
mourns with her their Shepherd dead.' The lines are autographed by
W. W. and dated 'Rydal Mount Novr 30th'*]

note. In the above is an expression borrowed from a Sonnet by
Mr G. Bell, the author of a small vol: of Poems[1] lately printed in
Penrith. Speaking of Skiddaw, he says—'yon dark cloud *rakes*
and shrouds its noble brow.' These Poems, tho' incorrect often
in expression and metre, do honour to their unpretending
Author; and may be added to the number of proofs, daily
occurring, that a finer perception of the appearances of Nature is
spreading thro' the humbler Classes of Society.—

[1] George Bell, *Descriptive and Other Miscellaneous Pieces, in Verse*. Penrith:
Printed for the Author by J. Brown, 1835.

[*In W. W.'s hand*]

I have written the last line over again below to prevent a mistake
And Ettrick mourns with her their Shepherd dead!

949. W. W. to RICHARD CHENEVIX TRENCH[1]

Address: The Rev^d. R. C. Trench, Curdridge, Hants.
Franked: Stamford December Fourteen 1835 H.C.Lowther.
Postmark: (1) 14 Dec. 1835 (2) 15 Dec. 1835
         (3) 16 Dec. 1835 (4) 18 Dec. 1835.
Stamp: (1) Stamford (2) Newbury (3) Winchester.
MS. Mr. W. Hugh Peal. Hitherto unpublished.

[early Dec. 1835]

Dear sir,
    It is some time since I received from Mr Moxon your Volume of Poems; I knew not that it was sent me at your desire—but that is of little consequence, I was so very much pleased with the Poems that I ought long ago to have expressed my gratitude. In fact, the admiration which I felt on perusing the Poems, was the cause why I did not take the liberty of writing to you sooner. I wished to enter somewhat into particulars, an undertaking to which, from many causes, and some of them very sad ones, I felt myself unequall. It is the same with me at present—and I must therefore content myself with saying that I was charmed with the dignity and beauty of the style, in a degree only inferior to the interest I took in the spiritual-mindedness which, more or less, pervades the Volume. If I should ever have the pleasure of an interview with you, we might talk these things over, and

---

[1] Richard Chenevix Trench (1807–86), friend of Tennyson, Hallam, Milnes, etc. at Trinity College, Cambridge, and one of the 'Apostles'. In 1833 he was curate to H. J. Rose and was present at the Hadleigh Conference: in 1835 he became perpetual curate of Curdridge, Hants., and published his first volume of verse, *The Story of Justin Martyr, and other poems*: in 1846 he was appointed Professor of Divinity at King's College, London, and ten years later Dean of Westminster; and finally in 1863 he became Archbishop of Dublin. He was well known for his Biblical studies, *Notes on the Parables of Our Lord*, 1841, and *Notes on the Miracles of Our Lord*, 1846, and also for a popular excursion into philology, *On the Study of Words*, 1851.

then I might be emboldened to turn to certain favorite passages, and also to point out where a closer attention to construction of phrase, and minutiae of expression, would have brought out the meaning instantaneously which now requires a little searching after.—

I remain dear Sir
with sincere thanks
your much obliged
Wm Wordsworth

I hope you will be able to decypher this wretched penmanship. My pen is vile, and the wrist of my right hand *sprained.*—

950. W. W. to EDWARD MOXON

MS. Henry E. Huntington Library.
K (—). LY ii. 768 (—).

[*In M. W.'s hand*]

Decr. 6th [1835]
Dear Mr Moxon,
I send you an Epitaph volunteered for Ch. Lamb by the Son of his old friend Charles Lloyd, to whom I had shewn my Verses observing that they were unfit on acc^t of their length. I did the same to Mr Hartley Coleridge and *asked* him to try his powers. Now as he is very ready, and has *great* powers, and retains a grateful affection for our deceased Friend, we expect something good and appropriate and suitable. Not that it is our wish that any thing from this quarter should take [the] place of what may be produced by Mr Talfourd, yourself, or any other London friend. Mr Owen Ll.'s verses are not without merit, and would be read with pleasure in many a church, or ch.yd, but they are scarcely good or characteristic for the Subject.
I forwarded by the Post to-day a Newcastle Journal, in which you would find some verses of mine, suggested by the death of the Ettrick Shepherd.[1] They were sent to you on account of the

---

[1] The earlier version of the *Extempore Effusion*, given in Ls. 947 and 948 above, was published in the *Newcastle Journal* for 5 Dec. and (through

mention of our departed friend and of Mr Coleridge.

There are two or three mistakes for which the printer is not answerable—the adjectives mortal and godlike are both correct; and for 'For ripe fruit' should be 'O'er ripe fruit'. It also might be a question for criticism whether the Stanza beginning 'Our haughty life' should not be separated from the foregoing either by asterisks or a break, as if it were the beginning of [a]2ᵈ Fit or Part of the same lyric effusion.

Should you see Mr Robinson [tell him][1] that we think our Sister going on so favorably that we shall be glad to see him at his convenience, and if he will *drop us* a line to say when his rooms are wanted, they shall be prepared for him.

We enclose a parcel which if Mr Q.[2] does not call and receive at your house *soon* (he is shortly expected in London) we shall thank you to send it to the address in Wyndham Place when perfectly convenient. Dear Love to Miss Lamb, if she is well enough to receive it, and with affec. remembrances to yʳ self and Mrs M. ever faithfully

Yours in haste
[*signed*] W Wordsworth

951. W. W. to PHILIP COURTENAY

MS. Brotherton Collection, University of Leeds Library.
Hitherto unpublished.

[*In M. W.'s hand*]

Rydal Mount
Decʳ 7ᵗʰ 1835

My dear Mr Courtenay

I enclose, with thanks for your continued kind attentions, the Deed of Transfer—witnessed by my Clerk.

I wish you had said a word where you passed last summer, as I

Moxon's initiative) in the *Athenaeum* for 12 Dec., and thereafter it was copied into several of the daily papers. Soon afterwards, the poem was completed by the addition of a stanza commemorating Mrs. Hemans (see L. 956 below).

[1] *Words dropped out.*
[2] Quillinan.

am always glad to hear of your relaxations and pleasures as well as of your business.

believe me to be faithfully yours
[*signed*] Wm Wordsworth

Mrs W. asks if you received a pair of Westmorland Hams 4 or 5 Months ago—and if they reached you in *good condition*.

952. W. W. to MARIA DRUMMOND

Address: Mrs Drummond, Park Lane, Corner of Grosvenor St.
    To be forwarded.
Postmark: Dec. 1835.
MS. WL transcript.[1]
LY ii. 769.

Rydal Mount
7th Decr 1835

My dear Miss Kinnaird, that *was*,

My dear Mrs Drummond, (as I learn from the Westmorland Gazette) that *is*,

In the name of all this family, and on my own part, I offer you most hearty congratulations upon the event which has just taken place.[2] May it prove as happy a union as you deserve!— ever faithfully yours

Wm Wordsworth

Dora offers her condolences to Mrs Sharp[3]—I wish I could say that D— had got rid of her Complaint. I have not the honor of knowing Mr Drummond, it cannot however be taking an unwarrantable liberty if I beg you to present to him my respects; my best wishes are of course included in what has been already said to you—farewell—

---

[1] By Mrs. Rawnsley.
[2] Her marriage to Thomas Drummond (see L. 929 above).
[3] Sister-in-law of the late Richard Sharp.

953. W. W. to BASIL MONTAGU

MS. untraced.
K (—). LY ii. 770.

Rydal Mount, December 10, 1835.

My dear Montagu,

. . . Under this roof we have indeed had our share of affliction, a great part of which continues to this hour; but it must be borne, and we trust for the ultimate benefit of all concerned. In answer to your very friendly offer, I can only say, with most sincere thanks, that it is quite out of our power to profit by it. If my daughter were well enough to go to London, she would be well enough to go anywhere, the seat of her complaint being in the spine; and as to my poor sister, there is no prospect of her being other than a prisoner in her bed or room for the remainder of her days.

I congratulate you heartily on your release from the labour of your profession, not doubting that your mind has resources which will prevent leisure from being a burden.

With kindest remembrances, believe me, my dear Montagu,

Faithfully yours,
Wm Wordsworth

954. W. W. to EDWARD MOXON

Address: Edward Moxon Esqre, 44 Dover Street.
Postmark: 14 Dec. 1835.
MS. Berg Collection, New York Public Library. Hitherto unpublished.

[In M. W.'s hand]

Rydal Mount Decr 10th 1835

My dear Mr Moxon

By this time I hope you have rec^d the packet of Lamb's letters—to speak frankly—I am scarcely at ease in my own mind at having given them up: it appears that L. destroyed all the letters that he rec^d from his friends, except one or two. If it may not be inferred from this, that he would not have been sorry if his own had met with the same fate, the fact if it be a fact, at least seems to imply, that he cared little or nothing about their being preserved. Nor am I at this moment satisfied, that he would have approved of the publication which you are preparing

133

In L's case I could not have got over the objection I feel to publishing private letters, had it not been the habit of *his* mind to throw itself off in an unpremeditated way. His letters may often be considered as the growth of the same tree that produced the Essays of Elia. For my own part, I do most earnestly wish that not a single letter I ever wrote should survive me: and I shall endeavour to make it known to all my correspondents, whether accidental or regular, that such is my wish: and farther that I sh^d deem a breach of the laws of social intercourse as I wish them to be maintained, between me and my friends and acquaintances, if either they do not destroy my letters, or send them to myself or representatives. Having spoken thus strongly, I seem still more to involve myself in condemnation for having parted with those of Lamb, which I fear I shall scarcely ever get rid of entirely.

As to the letters of Coleridge, it gives me great pain to learn that any such publication is so *speedily* intended:[1] the mischief which I am certain will in many ways accompany the work, will not be obviated, or even abated, by suppressing names. On the contrary, an additional zest will be given to the obnoxious passages by that reserve. The other day I heard Mr Hartley Coleridge speak in condemnation of his Coz and Brother-in law's practice[2] in this respect. '*Who* was the Person mentioned by the writer,' said he 'must unavoidably be known to many,' and *I* might add, were it known but to *one*, that would be quite sufficient in these little tattling days, for the spreading of it every where.

Of the notices which may occur in these letters respecting Mr S.[3] and myself in particular, I have no hesitation in saying, that little value can attach to any thing which poor C. would be likely to say of us, either for evil or good. He was subject to write or speak inconsiderately from the mere impression of the moment—the character of which was either more or less [?][4] by bodily feelings—or a state of spirits independent wholly of the Person or thing he was writing about. Presuming that you will throw this into the fire as soon as you have read it. I may say, that

---

[1] Coleridge's friend Thomas Allsop (1795–1880) was about to publish with Moxon his *Letters, Conversations, and Recollections of S. T. Coleridge*, 2 vols., 1836.

[2] Henry Nelson Coleridge had this year brought out his *Specimens of the Table Talk of the Late Samuel Taylor Coleridge*.

[3] Southey.   [4] *Illegible words written in above the line.*

there are causes lying far deeper which will prevent any judgement or opinion respecting Mr S. or myself being unbiassed to a degree which is indispensable for giving weight to such opinion or judgement, in the estimation of the discerning. Pray who is the Editor?

If you have lately seen Mr Robinson he has perhaps told you, that the more I have thought about the lines I sent you, the more I am convinced of their unfitness for an Epitaph—therefore say to dear Miss L., with my love, how much I am pleased that her determination coincides with my own.[1] My taking up the subject again will depend upon impulses concerning which I can only vaguely conjecture. I should like to know, however, what time your publication is likely to come out. The verses upon dear Lamb, threw my mind into that train of melancholy reflexion which produced several things in some respects of the same character, such as those lines upon Hogg[2] and some others brought forth with more reflexion and pains—for on turning over an old vol: of Mss, I met with some verses that expressed my feelings at the Grave of Burns[3] 32 years ago. These I was tempted to retouch, and not only added to them, but threw off another piece,[4] which is a record of what passed in my mind when I was in sight of his residence on the banks of the Nith, at the same period. So that I have to the best of my power done my duty to that great, but like many of his Brother Bards, unhappy man.

With best regards to Mrs M, and your brother and sister, I remain aff[ly] yours

W. Wordsworth

[1] According to Moxon's letter of 8 Dec., Mary Lamb had approved of the verses on Lamb, if they were to be taken as a poem written by the graveside, but they were too long for an epitaph. 'She has also an objection to the allusion to her brother's troubles, which she herself brought upon him, and which she would rather should not be inquired into by those who may visit his grave. But she would not object to the allusion in a distinct Poem. I am sorry that we have given you so much trouble, but the verses are too good to be wholly lost.' (*WL MSS.*)

[2] The *Extempore Effusion.*

[3] *At the Grave of Burns* (*PW* iii. 65).

[4] *Thoughts Suggested the Day Following, on the Banks of Nith, Near the Poet's Residence* (*PW* iii. 67). W. W. is referring to the first draft of the poem in 42 lines, quoted in the next letter. The text was revised and expanded, and a final stanza added, four years later, as W. W. explains in his letter to Henry Reed of 23 Dec. 1839 (L. 1359 below). The poem was not published until 1842.

955. W. W. to DAVID LAING

Address: David Laing Esqre [delivered by hand]
MS. Edinburgh University Library.
The Wordsworth-Laing Letters (—).

[In M. W.'s hand]

Rydal Mount
Decr 11th 1835

My dear Sir,

Finding that my wrist allowed me a greater command of my pen than I have had for some time I transcribed this morning the two Sonnets you requested to have; and as a small token of regard, I have added a Poem written only a few days ago, but a faithful record of my feelings, when in the Summer of 1803 I passed near Ellisland.[1] I have to request that you will not give a Copy of this Poem, having particular reasons for not wishing it to be made public. Perhaps also it is as well not to shew this piece to those who are in the habit of throwing off Verse to furnish Magazines etc.

The two Albums which were in the hands of Prof: Wilson have been received—he has been so kind as to write in them both. I have to thank you for the additions to my little Collection of first Editions—that of Armstrong,[2] was particularly acceptable, as I have always placed his Poem high in the Class to which he belongs. If you could fall in with the first Ed: of Falconer's Shipwreck,[3] I should be glad to have it; it is a Quarto. You are probably aware that the love story was afterwards interwoven, to the great injury, as Dr Anderson[4] has justly observed, to the dignity of the subject. The Rape of the Lock, I was very glad to see in its original shape.[5] I must correct what I have said above of Armstrong,—I am indebted to my friend Mr Dice[6] for that—I had confounded it with Beattie's Judgment of Paris.[7] Mr Dice has reprinted this Piece, in his late

---

[1] See also previous letter.

[2] For John Armstrong, author of *The Art of Preserving Health*, see pt. i, L. 201.

[3] William Falconer (1732—69): *The Shipwreck*, 1762.

[4] Dr. Robert Anderson (see *MY* ii. 151).

[5] Pope's *Rape of the Lock* appeared in 2 cantos in 1712, and was enlarged and published in 5 cantos in 1714.

[6] Alexander Dyce.

[7] Published 1765.

Ed: of Beattie's Poems;[1] tho' Beattie expressly tells you in an Advertisement to the Minstrel, that that Work and two or three small things added to it, are the only Poems which he wishes to be judged by, or to be considered as the Author of. This Plan of Mr Dice's is I think in this, and every other case of the kind unjustifiable; as I shall take the liberty to tell Mr D. the first communication I have with him. It may be said nescit vox missa reverti, and I am far from laying it down that writings which an Author may have excluded ought not to be in any shape reprinted, but I do think that no Editor can incorporate them with his Works, without disrespect to his memory, and probably in the end, without injury to the interests of literature.

You concur with me, I dare say, in condemning the raking together every thing that may have dropped from a distinguished Author's pen. Of this abuse we have had many instances lately; and it may be observed, by the bye, that these voluminous Ed[ns] are also an imposition upon the public: for tho' each Vol: is sold at the low price of 5/- the whole comes in very dear to the Purchaser. Not only has the public to pay for all that an Author may himself have written, but for the revival of no small portion of the forgotten trash that may have been written about him.

M[rs] W holds the pen for me, and when I add that the State of my eyes has not for many years allowed me to read by candle-light—and that I can only read a short time by day without injury, you will deem this privation a sufficient excuse for not paying the attention to the Poems of Dunbar[2] which I have long anxiously wished to give. When the days lengthen they will I hope allow me greater liberty for reading.

If you see M[r] and M[rs] Smith[3] —the bride and bridegroom you introduced to me, pray tell them that I have heard of the arrival of their present at Carlisle and I shall receive it very soon.

With kind remembrances to your family, in which M[rs] W joins, I remain, faithfully

your obliged
[*signed*] W[m] Wordsworth

[*There follow, in M. W.'s hand (autographed by W. W.), Fancy and Tradition, as in PW iii. 277; "There!" said a Stripling, pointing*

---

[1] Vol. xii (1830) of the Aldine Press edition of the British poets.
[2] See pt. ii, L. 829.
[3] Of Edinburgh: see *RMVB* for Oct. 1835.

with meet pride, as in PW iv. 44, and the following, Composed near
Ellisland Burn's Farm upon the Banks of the Nith.]

Too frail to keep the lofty vow
Made, doubtless, after his young brow
Was wreath'd (the *VISION* tells us how)
    With holly-spray,
He sank—he drifted to and fro,
    Then passed away.

But leaving each unquiet theme
Where gentlest judgements might misdeem,
And pleased to welcome every gleam
    Of good and fair,
Let us, beside this limpid Stream,
    Breathe hopeful air.

How oft, inspired, must he have trod
These pathways, yon far-stretching road;
There lurks his Home! in that Abode,
    With mirth elate,
Or, in his nobly-pensive mood,
    The Rustic sate.

No more of sorrow, wreck, or blight;
Think rather of a shining Light;
Think of those moments pure and bright,
    And not a few,
When Wisdom prosper'd in his sight,
    And Goodness too.

Through crowded street and lonely Glen
Is felt the magic of his Pen;
He rules mid winter-snows, and when
    Bees fill their hives;
Deep, deep within the hearts of men
    His power survives.

What need of Fields in some bright clime,
Where Sages, Heroes, Bards sublime,
And all that fetched the flowing rhyme
    From genuine Springs,
Shall dwell—sequester'd 'till old Time
    Folds up his wings?

Thee, Minstrel, to the gates of *Heaven*,
May Mercy lead:—thy sins forgiv'n,
The rueful conflict, the heart riv'n
    With vain endeavour,
And memory of earth's bitter leaven,
    Effaced for ever!—

Wm Wordsworth
Rydal Mount
12th Decr 1835

956. W. W. to ROBERT PERCEVAL GRAVES

Address: Revd R. P. Graves, Bowness.
Stamp: Kendal Penny Post.
MS. Harvard University Library.
LY ii. 770.

[mid-Dec. 1835]

My dear Sir,

To save you the trouble of hunting for the verses,[1] I have had them transcribed, with the stanza given to the memory of our lamented Friend.[2] We should be glad to hear that your Sisters have not been detained by the snow.

ever faithfully yours
Wm Wordsworth

[*There follows in Dora W.'s hand* Extempore Effusion on reading in a Newspaper the Notice of the death of the Poet James Hogg, *as in PW iv. 276, except that ll. 37—40 appear as ll. 29—32 and read*:

    She, too, a Muse whose holy spirit
    Was sweet as Spring as Ocean deep,
    She, e'er her Summer yet was faded,
    Has sunk into a breathless Sleep.]

[1] The *Extempore Effusion* had now been completed by the additon of the stanza on Mrs. Hemans. See also L. 950 above. The poem was included in the *Poetical Works* of 1837, and also in the 4th edition of Joseph Cottle's *Selection of Poems, Designed Chiefly for Schools and Young Persons*, which appeared the same year, or a little earlier.

[2] Mrs. Hemans had died in Dublin on 16 May 1835. Sara Coleridge wrote to Emily Trevenen on 12 July about Mrs. Hemans: 'Mr W. says it is a great thing to have said of her that she has given so much innocent pleasure—and that her verses may be more useful to the Americans—with whom she is a favourite—in their present state of intellectual culture, than more powerful productions.' (*Texas University MSS.*)

Address: Mrs Marshall, Heddingly, near Leeds.
Stamp: Kendal Penny Post.
Endorsed: Mrs Wordsworth and Dorothy. Miss Wordsworth's first Note.
MS. WL.
LY ii. 771 (—).

[mid–Dec. 1835]

My dear Friend,

From the specimen on the other page you are not to suppose that our dear Sister is not capable at times to guide a pen better—but she was 'too *lazy* to rise from her pillow' Dora says, who made a point that she should thank you *herself* for a present that had given her so much delight. And I was myself desirous to acknowledge the arrival of the Fowls—and the more so, knowing that you would, at this important period, be anxious to hear how we are going on. It is now 4 days that our poor Invalid has been quite without her treacherous support—and tho' I cannot say that we mark *no* change consequent upon it, (as regards bodily feelings—for she has complained a good deal of pain in her bowels, and to a certain extent we have proof that they *are* affected) yet hitherto nothing has occurred to alarm us. But *as yet* I cannot (I regret to add) gather much hope respecting any improvement in her mind. Her memory is less confused and I think gradually strengthens—but the same childishness governs her—and lately her passions have been *more* ungovernable. But we must attribute this to the great change that has been made—only I am here checked by the recollection, that before we began to reduce the Opium, she was (except that her memory was then gone) much as she is at present. This my dear friend is all that I can say beyond what you already know of her situation—So that I will spare you and myself further detail, till I can give you some more decisive report.

I wish you could but have seen the joy with which that countenance glistened at the sight of your never-to-be forgotten present. She was up and in her disturbed way, when I took them to her and held them before her, every sensation of irritation, or discomfort vanished, and she stroked and hugged the Turkey upon her knee like an overjoyed and happy child—exulting in, and blessing over and over again her dear, dearest friend—telling Jane, by whom I suppose she had fancied herself ill-used at the time 'You see, I *have* good friends who care for me, tho' you do not.'—Poor Jane gives hourly proof of her tender care and love of her, but this by the bye—The two beautiful lily white Chicken were next the object of her admiration, and when Dora said it was a pity that such lovely creatures should have been killed, she scouted the regret, saying 'What would they do for *her* alive, her friend knew best what she wanted—and she should eat them every bit herself.'

Indeed, indeed my kind friend, I cannot express what *I*, and we all feel towards you, for your considerate regard for us—but deeply must the impression rest with us. Your remembrance of Dora affected her greatly when she opened out the Parcel from Mr Garnett, and saw the *new* boots—the Treasures you had supplied her with last winter were mended a day or two before by her for the last time, with great perseverence,—and we had attempted to get proper worsted at Kendal—for me to try to imitate them—so that no arrival could have been more opportune, and I am to express her thanks most heartily. She has not been quite so well lately—but indeed, circumstanced as our household has been for the last 2 or 3 weeks, it is somewhat encouraging to find her no worse—for it is impossible to guard any one against the agitations that we are all subject to—and I am convinced till Dora can have perfect rest of body and mind, her amendment will be often retrograde. We must however keep up hope and heart, and trust that a few tranquil days may yet be in store for us.

I had a letter from Isabella this morning who tells me that her Mother is considerably better since her return to Workington—but that she remains in a state to require the greatest care. It is rather unfortunate at this time that her daughter Jane[1]—her only one that is of use, as an assistant to her Mother—is about to leave home for the benefit of instruction, which has already been too long delayed, and also that dear Isabella expects her confinement[2] at the end of this month. The children are quite well and thriving, and are a great pleasure to their Grandfather and Grandmother. Mrs. Ed. Stanley Curwen[3] has just been confined at Brussels with a 2ᵈ Son[4], and the confinement of their Son Henry's wife[5] is looked for shortly, at the Isle of Man,

---

[1] Isabella's youngest sister.

[2] She was about to give birth to her third child, William (1835–1917).

[3] See pt. ii, L. 748.

[4] Alfred Francis Curwen, later rector of Harrington.

[5] The Revd. Henry Curwen (see pt. ii, L. 482) had married Dora, daughter of General Goldie, of the Nunnery, Isle of Man.

where that couple at present reside with her Father Gen[1] Golding—This is the Son for whose benefit John holds the Living of Workington.

I shall feel very glad when our portion of that encreasing Family are snugly settled in their own Parish[1]—they are a very happy Pair, and when they are removed from many anxieties they are now subject to, I hope to see Isabella more healthy.

At length, for I have been so egotistical as to say all that I had to say of our own family, before I turned to yours, let me congratulate you upon your prosperous journey, and promise of domestic enjoyment. God grant you may be blest with health throughout the winter, and have good reports from y[r] absentees—To each of whom, especially to your Sisters give our tenderest regards—I shall be well content with your report of them—and it will be a *mutual* advantage our being spared writing individual letters. For indeed the duty of letter-writing falls rather heavily upon me, as you may suppose, having the work that used to be carried on by 5 pens upon my hands. Do not d[r] friend think that it is any thing but a *relief* to me to unburden myself to you. I should not have said the above had it been otherwise. God bless you and yours—

M. Wordsworth

[*D. W. writes*]

My dearest friend, risen from the bed of death I write to you with a thousand thousand blessings on y[r] dear head and on all your family.—May we meet again in this world.

Dorothy Wordsworth

Many many thanks for the Turkey etc—and love and thanks to dear Mr Marshall for using his own hand to direct them. Come to see me when you return to Hallsteads. Love to all and every one, Mr M etc

Ever your aff[ate] Friend D. W.

---

[1] i.e. Brigham.

958. W. W. to EDWARD MOXON

MS. Henry E. Huntington Library.
LY ii. 768.

[*In M. W.'s hand*]

[mid-Dec. 1835]

My dear Moxon,

Thanks for the printed Copy,[1] which, tho'a line longer than I supposed, *looks* at least a good deal shorter than in M.S.—The *italics* at the close must all be struck out except in the word *her*[2]—Mrs W accounts for the *if e'er*[3] being in italics, by the supposition of her having made a stroke to signify the lines were finished—The rest she marked designedly. The only thing I am *anxious* about is, that the lines should be approved of by Miss L. as a not unworthy tribute, as far as they go, to her dear Brother's memory.

ever faithfully yours

[*signed*] Wm Wordsworth

959. W. W. to H. C. R.

Address: H.C. Robinson Esqre, Plowdens Build^{gs}, Temple, London.
Postmark: (1)16 Dec. 1835 (2) 18 Dec. 1835 Stamp: Kendal.
Endorsed: 18(Decr 1835.), Mrs Wordsworth on publishing the letters of the deceased.
MS. Dr. Williams's Library.
K (—). Morley, i. 287.

[15 Dec. 1835]

My dear Friend (I write for William)

If you have seen Mr Moxon lately he will have told you that whenever it suits you to be here, we shall be glad to see you. Your letter of yesterday[4] was very welcome, and I prepare this to take with me to Kendal tomorrow, where I shall gain the best knowledge about Coaches—to enable me to give advice for

---

[1] Moxon had now run off a printed copy of the Epitaph on Charles Lamb in its first form (see *Cornell Wordsworth Collection*, no. 85).

[2] l. 35 of the version given in L. 940 above.

[3] l. 38, the closing line of the poem.

[4] The letter dated 8 Dec. (Morley, i. 286).

your journey—I may say however at present that in order to avoid the expence of a special conveyance—a Car or Chaise— you must contrive to be at Kendal—on the Tuesday, Thursday, or the Sunday even^g—so as to benefit by the Coach the next morn^g. But after all this might be no great object, as if you were to reach K. on the intermediate days, by the earlier coaches, some of which arrive at 2 or 3 oc—you might come on in a Gig or Car (stipulate as you have a right to do for 9d a mile, but they may attempt to make you pay 1/) which would not make your travelling expenses more than lodging at Kendal. Agnes Atkinson's is the house where you must stop. Thank you for the proposal about the Tamarinds. Our poor Sister smiled at the passage in your kind letter where you speak of your wish to bring her aught to '*stimulate* her appetite'—that alas! is keen enough, for she told me poor Creature this morn^g that 'she is never happy but when she is eating'. It would be wrong to conceal from you that the great experiment we have made— (tho' its effects upon the body have not disappointed us—or indeed made any material change, the *bodily* improvement had taken place before—or what has been done *could not* have been effected) has brought no comfort with respect to the *mind*—The recollection of passing objects is indeed greatly restored—but is more than counterbalanced by increasing irritability, which when her wishes are necessarily opposed amounts to rage and fury.

I have been very uneasy since I sent off the selection of Lamb's Letters, as by so doing I seem to sanction a practice, which I hold, for the most part, in utter detestation—viz—that of publishing the casual effusions (and most letters are nothing more) of men recently dead—I was much pleased to learn from the life of Mackintosh that Sir Ja^s Scarlet[1] destroyed all letters but those upon business, I wish this to be done towards myself and I would do it towards others, unless where I thought the Writer himself wished for their preservation. I earnestly desire you would get a sight of those of L., which I have sent to Mr M.[2]—and if they are to be used at all, after what I have said to you and Mr M., that you and He would strike out every passage

---

[1] Sir James Scarlett, now Lord Abinger (see pt. i, L.236) contributed a letter of reminiscences to *Memoirs of the Life of the Right Honourable Sir James Mackintosh*, ed. Robert James Mackintosh, 2 vols., 1835.

[2] Moxon.

which you think L. or his Sister would object to—above all, such as you think would give pain to any living individual[1]—or the Persons connections, after his death.

I rather grieve for what you report of Miss L's spice of vanity.[2] His submitting to that mechanical employment, placed him in fine moral contrast with other men of genius, his contemporaries, who in sacrificing personal independence, have made a wreck of morality and honour to a degree which it is painful to consider. To me this was a noble feature in Lamb's life and furnishes an admirable lesson by which thousands might profit.

Your critical objection[3] is valid—it is true that regret is in its nature a passive quality, and deep regret or deeply-seated regret would be a better expression, than *strong* regrets: but I used the word in connection with what follows to designate regret as spreading itself over a large portion of past time and including multifarious objects with an active and unsatisfied appetite. But this meaning is not sufficiently brought out Your parenthesis is so unimpassioned and awk[w]ard that the faulty passage had better [stand][4] as at present with a chance of being over-looked—besides I have no doubt that the sheet is struck off long since.—I should even prefer to your parenthesis, omitting regrets altogether, and leaving the passage thus weakened the line thus 'And our fond hopes, so eager in their grasp.'

---

[1] *Written* indivual.

[2] H. C. R. had written: 'Dear Mary with all her excellencies is not without a tinge of vanity. She does not take pleasure in seeing the *servile* state and humble life of her brother recorded and she shrinks naturally enough from all allusion to calamities or sufferings—'.

[3] H. C. R. had made some criticism of *Roman Antiquities* (*PW* iii. 278): 'In one of your finest sonnets, at least one of my favourites, you say

> Heaven out of sight, Our Wishes what are they?
> Or fond regrets impatient in their grasp?

Now it seems to me that however *impatient* and *grasping wishes* may be, these are inappropriate qualities when extended to *regrets*—The former are essentially active, the latter passive—Why not thus?

> Heaven out of sight, our wishes what are they,
> (Or fond regrets) impatient in their grasp?

[4] *Word dropped out.*

or read the whole thus

> Heaven out of sight—hopes, wishes, what are they?
> And what is knowledge with its eager grasp?
> The Sages theory? etc

Still better,

> Our hopes, our aims, so eager in their grasp,

The 'Red Rover' from Bull and Mouth London at ½ past 7 or eight in the evening arrives in Manchester at 4 following evening.

'Telegraph' leaves London at 5 in the Morning arrives in Manc^r at 11 same evening.

Coaches from Manchester to Kendal at 6 8 and ¼ before 12 A M from the Royal Hotel Swan and Commercial—the Mail at ½ past 3 P M arrives in Kendal ¼ before 12.—[1]

[unsigned]

960. W. W. to UNKNOWN CORRESPONDENT

MS. WL. Hitherto unpublished.

[late 1835]

. . . I shall see Mrs Curwen[2] in a few days, but I am sorry to say that the illness still hangs upon her. She intends to go to Cheltenham soon; and it will be a happy event if her health should there be restored; for her life is of the utmost importance to her family—She no sooner rallies from one attack of jaundice, than another follows.

My daughter is decidedly better . . .

[cetera desunt]

---

[1] The last lines of travelling instructions are in another hand—or possibly M. W. has changed her pen.

[2] Isabella W.'s mother, Mrs. Curwen senior.

961. W. W. to MISS MURRAY[1]

MS. untraced.
Bookseller's Catalogue.

Rydal Mount
New Year's day [1 Jan. 1836]

. . . [My sister] has disappointed us as to her improvement in health; her mind continues still so much affected by something of inflammatory affection in her head.

Dora has been tempted to take too much exercise and has a slight return of the spine complaint.

I hope Mr Bolton continues pretty well . . .

My son W^m sends me from Carlisle a sad account of the new municipality.

[cetera desunt]

962. W. W. to EDWARD MOXON

MS. Henry E. Huntington Library.
K (—). LY ii. 771.

[Jany 4th 1836][2]

My dear Sir,

Thanks for Lamb's Poems, and the Verses[3]—they are now quite correct and I have no wish to alter them further: the only thing which I find amiss in them is the position of the two words By God, in the beginning of a line which gives them the appearance of an oath, but I cannot alter it without weakening the passage.[4] Pray send a Copy to Mrs Marshall 41 upper

---

[1] A friend of John Bolton of Storrs. The Wordsworths had known her since at least 1830, when she called at Rydal Mount (RMVB).

[2] Date added in another hand.

[3] W. W. had now expanded the Epitaph on Charles Lamb written the previous November (see Ls. 940 and 954) into a poem of 131 lines, the later section being 'an elegy or monody' in which he paid tribute to Lamb's love for his sister; and Moxon continued to print off copies incorporating W. W.'s corrections until the final version was established early in February and the poem was ready for distribution among W. W.'s friends (see PW iv. 459 and Cornell Wordsworth Collection no. 95). The poem was read to H. C. R. on 3 Jan. (see HCR ii. 477).

[4] See l. 66. 'By' was later altered to 'Through'.

Grosvenor Street, another for Miss Fenwick 2 lower Seymour Street, Portman Square, and let Mr Robinson have one for Mr S. Cookson, a friend of mine.[1] And pray send 3 Copies enclosed to Joshua Watson Esq. No 6 Park Street Westminster.—

I have been much pleased with several things in Lamb's Poems that I had not sufficiently noticed before, particularly with the latter part of Lines upon the death of a newborn Infant.[2]—At Mr Southey's two days ago I had a peep at the two vols about Coleridge.[3] The Editor is a man without judgement, and therefore appears to be without feeling. His rule is to publish *all the truth* that he can scrape together about his departed Friend, not perceiving the difference between the real truth and what *appears to him* to be true. The maxim de mortuis nil nisi *verum* was never meant to imply that *all* truth was to be told, only nothing but what *is true*. This distinction also has escaped his sagacity and ever will escape those of far superior talents to Mr A. who care not what offence or pain they give to living persons provided they have come to a conclusion, however inconsiderately, that they are doing justice to the dead.

My prospect of getting to London this Spring is rather darkened.—

Messrs. Longman have proposed, if the Excursion is nearly out of print, to have it stereotyped as the Yarrow[4] has been, and to do the same with the other 3 Volumes. But I cannot give them an answer, as they have furnished me with no facts as to the Expense, or other particulars. Do favor me with some guidance for my judgement. There are left of the 4 volumes[5] 180, and they wish to begin printing. I wish much to correct [? yours] substantially with this Publication, but how is it to be done? and what would you advise, as to any ornaments such as

---

[1] Strickland Cookson, W. W.'s solicitor.

[2] *On an Infant Dying as soon as Born* (*Works*, ed. Lucas, v. 49), first published in *The Gem*, 1829, then under the editorship of Thomas Hood whose first-born inspired the poem.

[3] Thomas Allsop's *Letters, Conversations, and Recollections of S. T. Coleridge* (see L. 954 above). In his letter to W. W. of 22 Dec. 1835 (WL MSS.), Moxon had remarked of Allsop, 'He is a very amiable Man, but sadly deficient in tact as an Editor.' For Southey's view of the work see Warter, iv. 439. See also *Letters of Hartley Coleridge* (ed. Griggs), pp. 203—4.

[4] The 2nd edn. of *Yarrow Revisited*, published jointly by Longman and Moxon.

[5] Of the edition of 1832.

prefixed to Murray's Edit. of Crabbe and Boswell's Johnson.[1]
These were[2] strongly recommended to me by a spirited
Bookseller of Carlisle. The three Volumes also, if they are to be
uniform with the Yarrow in the inside ought to be spread over
4, one Sonnet only being on a page with correspondent
resemblance in other respects. Do you think that Poems which
have been so long before the public would bear this. The whole
would then consist of 6 Volumes, and certainly would have a
much better appearance. If you see Mr Robinson ask him about
this; he complains of the present Edition having a shabby
appearance from the crowded page.

    With kind regards from all to yourself and Mrs M. very
sincerely

Yours[3]
Wm Wordsworth

963. W. W. to [?] ALARIC WATTS

MS. Cornell. Hitherto unpublished.

Rydal Mount
Jan[y] 10th —36

My dear Sir,

    I felt much gratified by your valuable Present,[4] and the more
so as coming from One who interested me so long since both
upon his own account, and that of our ever to be lamented
Friend, Mrs Fletcher.[5]

    Your Collection as far as I am yet acquainted with it appears
to be judiciously made; I cannot but regret however that it does
not contain a single specimen from my old Friend Charlotte
Smith,[6] who was the first *Modern* distinguished in that

---

[1] Murray's edition of Crabbe (see pt. ii, L. 810) and the revised edition of
Croker's Boswell's Johnson (see pt. ii, L. 506), which appeared in 10 vols. in
1835, were both embellished with topographical engravings by Finden after
Clarkson Stanfield, R. A.

[2] *Written* was.

[3] These last words are in M. W.'s hand. She has also corrected the wording
in one or two places elsewhere in the letter.

[4] Apparently an anthology of sonnets, perhaps published anonymously.

[5] Formerly Maria Jewsbury, who had died in India in 1833.

[6] See *EY*, p. 68, and pt. ii, L. 529.

Composition; I also think you might have had some very pleasing Specimens from the Pen of my valued young Friend Mr Moxon the Bookseller. Having two Copies by me of the 2nd Series[1] I beg your acceptance of one. I sent the first Verses for your perusal, which you may return to Me at any time, when convenient.

You have properly animadverted upon the foolish remark of Sir E. B.[2]—that Sonnets—to become interesting—require the name of some distinguished Author. His own Sonnet, Echo and Silence,[3] would be enough to prove the contrary, though the first 5 lines ought to be rewritten. How absurd for any One to affirm that it is impossible to include within the compass of 14 lines, a noble thought, or affecting sentiment, so noble and affecting as to stand unpropped by any name, in solitary beauty or grandeur. Take for instance to the contrary the thirteen lines in the Par. lost which follow the words—'nor think tho' men were none'[4] etc., and Prefix a Word or two, like these, 'Think not beloved Eve though Men were none' etc., and you have, in blank verse, all the essentials of a Sonnet. Again expand Shakespeare's lines—

> Ah me of all that I could ever learn
> Could ever read in tale or history
> The course of true love never did run smooth[5]

into 14 which the subject would well bear, and you would have there also the essentials of an exquisite Sonnet—supposing the dialogue, which is a great disfigurement to the thought, to be omitted—farewell. Believe me, dear Sir, faithfully

Your most obliged
Wm Wordsworth

Pray do not omit calling at Rydal Mount if you ever come this Way.—

We value exceedingly the possession of the pencil sketch of Miss Jewsbury which you did so long ago.

[1] See L. 884 above.
[2] Sir Egerton Brydges.
[3] See pt. ii, L. 754.
[4] *Paradise Lost*, iv. 675.
[5] *A Midsummer Night's Dream*, I. i. 132—4.

964. W. W. to SIR WILLIAM ROWAN HAMILTON

Address: Sir William R. Hamilton, Observatory.
Postmark: (1) 11 Jan. 1836 (2) 12 Jan. 1836.
MS. Cornell.
Grosart (—). *Hamilton* (—). *K* (—). *LY ii. 773* (—).

[*In M. W.'s hand*]

[*c.* 11 Jan. 1836]

My dear Sir William,

With much pleasure I have received two letters lately from you through the hands of my Son, for both of which accept my cordial thanks. We took it very kindly that you were so particular in entering into the State of your family and your relatives. We often think with much interest of your Sister Eliza, and with a thousand good wishes that her bold adventure may turn out well.[1] If she find herself at liberty to move about, her sensitive imagination and thoughtful mind cannot but be profitably excited and substantially enriched by what she will see in that most interesting part of the world. How should I like, old as I am, to visit those classic shores, and the holy land, with all its remembrances, so sweet and solemn!

My Son speaks with pleasure of the brief interview he had with you lately, and we are all sensible of your kindness in taking so much trouble to have Mr C. Curwen[2] well placed— his future good conduct would prove of infinite importance to his Parents, above all to his poor Mother, who has been in rather an alarming State of health for some time, and disquietude of mind, is, from the nature of her complaint, especially injurious.

Do not you recollect a young Lady named Kinnaird, who was with us once when you were here. She is now residing in Phoenix Park, with her Husband, Mr Secretary Drummond[3] to whom she has been lately married. She tells Dora that she wishes you to be reminded of her, from which I infer that a call from you at your convenience would be taken well. She is very amiable and accomplished Person, has travelled a good deal, and resided abroad. She sings charmingly and is a great favourite in

---

[1] Eliza Hamilton had recently left on a year's tour of the Near East.
[2] John W.'s brother-in-law Charles, who died soon after this.
[3] See Ls. 929 and 952 above.

this house. Her fortune was large, and Mr. D. may be envied the possession of such a prize.

As Mrs. W. holds the pen for me, I barely advert to the irreparable loss our family suffered last Summer in the decease of her Sister Miss Hutchinson. My own Sister was then languishing and still continues much in the same State, not worse—perhaps better in *bodily* health, but then the mind has sunk and is generally weakened and when her will is opposed, much disturbed.[1] My daughter has recovered her appetite and digestive powers, but has still so much weakness hanging about her as disquiets us not a little. Mrs W. and myself are quite well, and my eyes less subject to irritation, and I trust somewhat strengthened.

Mrs W. and my daughter have just read the Bishop of Limerick's and Mr Knox's correspondence[2] with great interest. So should I have done, but the allowance of daylight is now so short; and I do not venture to read or write at all by candle-light; and this is the cause why Mrs W. now holds the pen for me. I never shall forget Mr Knox, to whom you introduced me,[3] nor his eloquent, and dignified conversation. I remember we diff[ered][4] upon one point, viz. the inward unchangea[bleness of] Romanism; the opinions which I find express[ed by him] about the year 1824 are much more in accor[dance with] what mine have always been than those wh[ich he ex]pressed during the interview I have alluded to. [I wish] I had seen more of him. His friend and correspondent [the] Bishop of L. as also the Editor of the Letters, Mr Foster,[5] I saw more than once at Clapham. The good Bp: was so obliging as to send his Carriage to London for me, and I passed a night at his house.

Surely I ought to have said before this, a word upon the honor[6] thrust upon you by the Lord Lieutenant, in his Majesty's name, and so I should, but the great Bully O'Connel[7] stood in my way, and the Protestant Established Ch: of Ireland, which I

[1] H. C. R., who was at this time staying at Rydal, gives a sad account of D. W. See *HCR* ii. 474.

[2] *Thirty Years Correspondence between J. Jebb . . . and A. Knox*. See pt. ii, L. 740.

[3] During the Irish tour of 1829.

[4] The MS. is badly damaged at this point and words have been written in in another hand.   [5] The Revd. Charles Forster.

[6] Hamilton's knighthood (see L. 918 above).

[7] Daniel O'Connell was now turning his attention to the question of

hold precious as my life, seemed to cry out to me, 'What honor
can come from men who are the Slaves of Bigots and Traitors
bent upon my destruction!' But whether Sir William, or plain
Mr Hamilton, be you assured of my affectionate admiration. I
must congratulate you however, upon your growing family,[1]
and your happiness as a married man. Pray present our united
regards to Lady H and give each of your young Philosophers,
perhaps they may prove Poets, a Kiss for my Sake. You are
growing rich as a Father, while I am keeping pace with you as a
Grandfather. Do let us hear of you, from time to time.

Ever aff[ly] yours,
[*signed*] W[m] Wordsworth

965. W. W. to JOHN LIGHTFOOT[2]

Address: W[m] Wordsworth Esq, Rydal [*readdressed to*] John Wordsworth Esq,
7 Howard St, Strand.
MS. WL.[3] *Hitherto unpublished.*

[*In John Carter's hand*]

11 Jany 1836

Dear Sir,
In answer to the question put to me in your letter of the 9th
Inst[nt], I regret that I have only this to say, that you must be
aware that until a portion of the real Estate of my late Brother
can be sold there will be no funds to discharge even any of the
subsisting specialty debts against that Estate; of course none of
the claims arising out of the Will.
As the Estate in fact now belongs to my Nephew (subject to
the outstanding claims) no Sale can be effected but by him; and I
have no doubt of his concurrence with the Trustees, in carrying
into effect the Sales that may be found necessary or deemed

municipal reform in Ireland, and in Jan. 1836 addressed huge crowds in
Liverpool and Birmingham.
[1] Hamilton now had two sons.
[2] The Keswick attorney, who married R. W.'s widow.
[3] This is a copy (unsigned by W. W.) of the letter sent, written on the back
of Lightfoot's letter about the settlement of the remaining debts on R. W.'s
estate, and sent on to R. W.'s son with a covering note (see next letter)

exped[t] for that purpose; and I shall write to him immed[y] on this business.

I am dear Sir

Yours respectf[y],

W W.

966. W. W. to JOHN WORDSWORTH [1]

MS. WL. Hitherto unpublished.

[*In M. W.'s hand*]

Rydal Mount Jan[ry] 12th 1836

My dear John,

We congratulate you most cordially upon being now out of your minority, with every wish for your health and happiness and an earnest prayer that you may live in the love and fear of God through all your days, be the allowance long or short.— You will learn from the above[2] that the Trustees can act no longer without your concurrence as to the Sale of any part of the lands[3]—All that has yet been done has been confined to having new plans made where there was none before and the whole estate surveyed and valued by Mr Studholme of Carlisle,[4] the account of which I am looking for every day. Thinking it next to impossible you should be able to determine satisfactorily to yourself what portion of the land should be sold, I feel it indispensible to request, that with whatever interruption of your studies it might occasion, you should come down immediately if a Sale is to take place forthwith: but, if the lands could be let upon tolerable terms for the current year, I see no *necessity* for that—unless, which I am far from thinking possible, Mr Lightfoot should press you for immediate payment. Several letters have passed between Mr Nicholson[5] and myself on the subject of reletting, but he is delicate and timid about undertaking the responsibility, and therefore as the best that can at present be done in my judgment, I shall today write to y[r] coz

---

[1] R. W.'s son.
[2] See previous letter.
[3] The Sockbridge estate. See also L. 972 below.
[4] John Studholme, land agent, of Finkle Street.
[5] See L. 972 below.

W^m begging him to go over from C.[1] and adv[ise] with Mr N.
and others as my representative on this business, so that with
your sanction, it may [   ]^2 effected, and everything else
be settled when you shall be at liberty [   ] in May.

If you can point out however the lands which you wish to be
sold and think it expedient to sell them *now*, and will give me
written authority to do so, they shall be *advertized* for immediate
Sale. Nevertheless I must repeat that I consider your presence
indispensible before a Sale can take place, and little less so, before
an advertisement is issued.

In the mean while I take it for granted that you will enter into
no arrangement or *personal obligation* without previously consulting the Trustees, whom your Father appointed. You must
reply to this without delay. No change in the state of your poor
Aunt has taken place since Dora wrote to you—and she herself is
much the same. A third Wm Wordsworth made his appearance
at the Rectory Workington on the 27th of Dec^r.[3]—We had
good tidings from Isabella herself this morning. Willy has not
been over this Christmas—if you come down perhaps he may
give you the meeting. We all join in love and good wishes, and I
remain d^r John always

Your affec Uncle
[*signed*] Wm Wordswhorth

967. W. W. to THOMAS NOON TALFOURD

MS. Dr. Douglas Horton. Hitherto unpublished.

[*In M. W.'s hand*]

Jan^{ry} 13th [1836]

. . . Honorable Member[4] of—I was going to say, a dishonored
House, I greet you well.

I remember Coleridge used to tell of one of his own puns,
that, when he was gravely asked by a sage citizen, who had a
smattering of natural philosophy, In what Stage of its processes

[1] Carlisle.
[2] *MS. torn.*
[3] See L. 957 above.
[4] Talfourd had been elected M.P. for Reading, his native town, the
previous year.

the blood acquired its sanguine color?—answered, In the *Redding Stage*, to be sure—*I* am sure that the Readingites will never have the blood to fly up into their faces, in blushes, for having elected you for their Representative.

To be serious, I should congratulate you heartily in having your talents, virtues and attainments thus publickly acknowledged did I not feel that as far as happiness is concerned a man is better any where than in the Hs of Commons.

As you so well know my opinions, which differ I believe in fundamentals from your own, I shall only say, respect them so far, as to think a little more about any course you might be inclined to take as a Member of the House, than you otherwise would have done, if you had not been aware that your notions of prudence and mine might be at variance.

Farewell—God prosper you!

[*signed*] Wm Wordsworth

Our united very kindest regards to Mrs Talfourd.

968. W. W. to CHARLES WORDSWORTH

MS. untraced.
Charles Wordsworth, Annals of My Early Life, p. 176.

Rydal Mount: Jan. 15, 1836.

My dear Charles,

Your marriage[1] was kindly announced to me by Chris, and I now write to congratulate you upon it, and to assure you how heartily we all wish for your happiness. I ought to have written sooner; but there is little courage in this house for writing to anyone: in fact, your aunt, Mrs W., is the only one of us who can write at all without inconvenience, and she is engaged from morning to night. It gives us all much pleasure to learn that your situation at Winchester[2] is so much to your mind, and I rejoice to find that you will have so much of the week at your disposal: *that* will leave you at liberty to add to your knowledge; for it must be a most melancholy thing for a young man to be

[1] Charles Wordsworth had married Charlotte Day (1817–39) in Norwich Cathedral on 29 Dec. 1835.

[2] He had been Second Master at Winchester since the previous summer (see L. 928 above).

perpetually going over the same ground with little or no means of advancing in any direction. This, most happily, will not be your case, and I doubt not you will profit by your privilege.

You are now with your bride, I understand, at Mrs Hoare's. Pray give my love, and that of this family to her, and our sincere and ardent wishes for every earthly comfort that may further, and not stand in the way of, her eternal happiness.

If I go to town in the spring, as not improbably I may, I shall certainly visit you at Winchester.

Your affectionate Uncle,
W. Wordsworth

969. W. W. and M. W. to ISABELLA FENWICK

Address: Miss Fenwick, Vicarage, Halse, near Milverton, Somerset. To be forwarded.
Stamp: Kendal Penny Post.
MS. WL.
LY ii. 774 (—).

Rydal Mount,
Jan^{ry} 18th, [1836]

My dear Miss Fenwick,

I am about to ask a favor of you, let me rather say another testimony of that friendship which Mrs W. and I value so highly. My eldest Son has just had a Son[1] born, his 2nd, the Boy is to bear my name. His Father, in consequence, looking beyond his Relations, is desirous of having a Sponsor among my Friends, and has just referred the matter to me. I have therefore turned my thoughts to you as in the first rank of those whom we love and esteem, and request you would do us the honor to undertake the office for the newborn. I am sorry that I cannot at present name the other Sponsors, but they will, I understand, be applied to upon the same principle.

Mr Henry Taylor probably told you that we had a glimpse of each other at Keswick[2]—We parted with some hope held out that he might call at Rydal on his return from Edin:—We were

[1] William Wordsworth, later Principal of Elphinstone College, Bombay.
[2] Henry Taylor had spent some days with Southey the previous October on the way to Edinburgh. See *Correspondence of Henry Taylor*, pp. 65–71.

much disappointed in not seeing him. Pray tell us how far you were satisfied with Mr Pickersgill's Portrait[1] of him.—

A friend of mine was lately visiting in the same house with the Duke of Wellington—he was in excellent health and high spirits, and is of opinion, *that we are looking up in the world.*—

I cannot guess how far the municipal elections will affect the future Parliamentary returns; not however I am sure to the degree that the Whig Radicals believe or pretend, nor on the other hand will they prove so insignificant as the Tories or Conservatives represent. It is affirmed that in those Corporations where the Whigs were before exclusively predominant, the elections of Councilmen etc are in favor of the Tories, and vice versa. If this is so, they are not so undeniable a proof as they would otherwise be, that the lower in the scale of society you go, the surer are you to find Radicals and revolutionists set upon the work of destruction without being capable of being turned aside by other considerations or passions.—

My poor Sister's health especially as affecting her mind is to us a constant source of anxiety, and my Daughter though much better is far from well.—We are going to Church, Mrs W. will add a few lines on our return. Farewell my dear Miss Fenwick, believe me with the highest esteem, most faithfully yours

Wm Wordsworth

[*M. W. writes*]

I cannot, my dear Friend, close my Husband's letter to you at this season of good wishes, without individually offering the very best my heart can conceive, in which I am affectionately joined by Dora.

It will be a great pleasure to us to hear from you and of you and trust you may be able to give a good report of your health. —Having mislaid your address; when I last wrote to you, I took the liberty to enclose to Mr Taylor—but, tho' I do not know where this may find you, I will direct to your own Home.

I wish I could have given a more favorable report of poor Mrs Southey[2]—but alas she still continues in the same melancholy state. Our friend, and his daughters bear up wonderfully, they are truly an example of Christian submission which is beautiful

---

[1] Untraced.
[2] Mrs. Southey had never fully recovered from her mental breakdown in Sept. 1834 (see pt. ii, L. 851).

to think upon. Mr W's eyes I am thankful to say, and I know you will be glad to hear, have been unusually well, thro' the winter thus far. Our melancholy household has been much cheered by the society, of the last 3 weeks, of our excellent F^d Mr Robinson—who you will recollect, as one of our visitors, when we had the great privilege of being of your household. He kindly came down purposely to see Mr W. and took lodgings in the village.—He joins our 1, oc dinner, and passes the rest of the day with us—accompanies Mr W. in his walks etc—a work of some charity. God bless you my d^r Friend

aff^ly yours
M Wordsworth

970. W. W. to ANNE HOOK

MS. untraced.
LY ii. 775.

Rydal Mount Jan. 21. [1836]

Dear Mrs Hook,

The Papers have just informed us of the loss which you have suffered in the decease of your Brother Sir Thomas.[1] Be assured we sincerely condole with you upon the melancholy event, for which Lady Farquhar[2] had prepared us; the case, we learned from her, admitting of no hope. Knowing the power of religious faith on your own mind and that of Georgina,[3] we do not presume to offer you any consolation, beyond that of the expression of our cordial sympathy, which perhaps will have still more value in your estimation as proceeding from friends afflicted as we are, and have been. May God support you through this and all your future trials.

With respect to our family I need not enter into particulars. In my poor Sister there is upon the whole no improvement and Dora's progress towards recovery under these sad circumstances cannot be expected to be other than subject to interruption. She was again bled last Saturday

---

[1] Sir Thomas Farquhar, 2nd Bart. (1775–1836), a banker and Treasurer of the Institute of British Architects, who had died on 12 Jan.

[2] Mrs. Hook's sister-in-law (not mother, as erroneously stated in pt. ii, L. 727), now married to Captain Thomas Hamilton. W. W. and H. C. R. had visited the Hamiltons at Elleray on 7 Jan. (see *HCR*, ii. 478).

[3] Mrs. Hook's daughter, Georgiana.

My daughter-in-law has got well through her confinement. Her new-born is a fine child, and is to bear my name.

I should not have adverted to public affairs but that I have just heard through a friend from one who is much among official persons in London, that if the King will consent, ministers will dissolve Parl^t before Easter; if not, they will resign;[1] after making allowance for loss in the Counties, they calculate upon an acquisition of 30 members upon the whole, which will enable them to keep their places. What a wretched condition is this country brought to!

The weather has with us been much less severe than you have had it in the South. Not a day has it prevented my taking my usual exercise.

We have staying with us a Mr Robinson, a friend whom we highly value who came down from London about a month ago. His society has helped us through the winter, by the interposition of many and chearful hours.

Believe me dear Mrs Hook with affectionate regards to Georgina in which we all unite   most faithfully yours

Wm Wordsworth

971. W. W. to SIR WILLIAM ROWAN HAMILTON

Address: Sir William Hamilton, Observatory, Dublin.
Postmark: 30 Jan. 1836.
MS. Cornell.
Hamilton. K (—). *LY ii. 776* (—).

[*In M. W.'s hand*]

Rydal Mount,
Jan^{ry} 26th [1836]

My dear Sir

You being a Father and a good Churchman, I have no Scruple in making the proposal I am about to do. You must know then, that my Son's new-born is to bear my name, and his Father being desirous that he should provide the Babe with Sponsors from among *my particular friends* you—as one whom I especially reckon upon as such, and furthermore as also bearing

---

[1] The Melbourne administration was going through a difficult period, but it survived until 1841.

the name of William—I hope will not object to stand in that interesting relation to my family. If I am not mistaken, it would give me great pleasure if you will write to my Son, who does not feel himself sufficiently acquainted, to have made this request himself, and propose doing him this honour. I know how much it would gratify both him and his wife. Should you have any conscientious or delicate Scruples upon this Subject, have no more hesitation in giving me a refusal than I have had in making the proposal.

I have no improved report to give you of the health of my poor Sister, nor does Dora make the progress towards recovery which we should look for did not the State of her Aunt cause so much anxiety to us all.

It will always my dear Sir be a great pleasure to us all to hear good tidings of you and yours—and with the united best wishes of this household, believe me ever to be very sincerely and faithfully

Yours
[signed] Wm Wordsworth

972. W. W. to JOHN LIGHTFOOT [1]

Address: Mr Lightfoot [*In M. W.'s hand*]
MS. Harvard University Library.
LY ii. 777.

Rydal Mount
Friday—29th Jan. 1836

Dear Sir,

It gives me pleasure to learn that you purpose to accompany John [2] to Penrith. Your advice and assistance cannot but be of great use to him—He tells me that you will undertake such processes as may be necessary for the recovery of arrears due from Jackson, [3] which as far as my Powers of acting Trustee extend, I authorize you to do.

I hope also you will advise with John and Mr Blamire [4] and

---

[1] The Keswick attorney who married R. W.'s widow.

[2]. R. W.'s son. He had now come of age, and the Sockbridge estate (see pt. ii, L. 648) was about to be sold. See also L. 981 below.

[3] Tenant of the farm at Tirril, on the road between Pooley Bridge and Penrith.

[4] Thomas Blamire, the Penrith solicitor.

Mr Nicholson,[1] as to the eligible distribution of the property in lots for sale. Lying scattered, as it does, much must depend, I should think, upon the judgement with which it is divided for sale into parcels.—

John is become of age this day; and I cannot conclude without expressing my trust that his affairs will be wound up in such a way as will prove satisfactory to himself and to all parties interested and concerned.

I remain dear Sir
sincerely yours
Wm Wordsworth

973. W. W. to EDWARD MOXON

Address: Edwd Moxon Esqre, Dover Street. [*In M. W.'s hand*]
MS. Henry E. Huntington Library.
K (—). *LY ii. 778.*

Jan^{ry} 30—[1836]

My dear Sir,

I am glad you like the verses;[2] I wrote them (how could it be otherwise?) with feeling for the subject. Do with them what you like as to the number of Copies you will strike off—I wish for 25—Only I submit that it would not be desirable they should get into the Athenaeum, or any other periodical, before they come out with the book.[3] I should not like it, nor would it be so respectful to dear Lamb's memory.

May I beg that you would send me down a Revise, through Mr Robinson who can promise me a Frank; should I think any alterations necessary I will return it immediately, if I do not, then take it for granted it is right, and the copies may be struck off.—

We feel ourselves greatly indebted to Mr Robinson, in giving us his Company at this time, and coming so far to see us.[4]

No material changes in our Invalids.

ever faithfully yours
Wm Wordsworth

[1] Unidentified: probably a local farmer.

[2] The poem to the memory of Charles Lamb. See L. 962 above.

[3] Talfourd's *Letters of Charles Lamb* (see L. 940 above). The verses were printed at the end of the second volume.

[4] This letter was probably taken to London by H. C. R., who left Rydal on 1 Feb.

974. W. W. to EDWARD MOXON

Address: Edward Moxon Esq, Dover St, London.
MS. Henry E. Huntington Library.
K. LY ii. 767.

Rydal Mount
Friday [? 5 Feb. 1836]

My dear Mr Moxon,

Thanks for the verses,[1] they will be quite correct when you have replaced the line

Otherwise wrought the will of the Most High:
Yet etc.[2]—

I do not forget your friendly invitation. Take care in respect to the Selections[3] that your liberality to me does not injure yourself. I think it probable that I shall be in Town in the Spring, and if it be after the earlier part of April, if you can make room for me for a little while I should be glad.—

I have never heard of Hartley's intention to write his Father's life, nor do I think it probable; but your message shall be conveyed to him. He is preparing for the Press another Vol. of Poems,[4] as I understand, and I shall recommend to him to publish with you if you will undertake the work.—

Since the above was written Mrs W. has seen H. C. He has no intention of writing his Father's life, but he has Poems and other works which he would be glad to publish with you.—

ever faithfully yours
W. W.

[1] The revise asked for in the previous letter.

[2] On second thoughts, W. W. put these lines back into the verses in memory of Charles Lamb. See next letter.

[3] The 2nd edn. of Hine's *Selections from the Poems of William Wordsworth*.

[4] This volume was not forthcoming, though Moxon replied to W. W. on 24 Feb.: 'I shall at any time be glad of either Prose or Verse from him, but if the latter I should not I fear be able to do more than print it at my own risk and divide the profits with him.' (*WL MSS.*)

975. W. W. to EDWARD MOXON

Address: Mr Moxon, Bookseller, Dover-street.
Postmark: 10 Feb. 1836. *Stamp*: Southampton [?Row].
MS. Henry E. Huntington Library.
K (—). *LY ii. 780.*

Monday 8th Feb^ry [1836]

My dear Sir,

I am quite ashamed of being so troublesome. Upon re-considering the Verses, I think the sense in one altered passage is not sufficiently clear if the line

'Otherwise wrought the Will of the most High',[1]

be omitted; therefore let it stand as before, and the line that follows thus—

Yet in all visitations, through all trials,
Still etc—

through instead of *and,* as I think it stood before.

Mr Pickersgill states and has found so many objections from the Engraver, that, being altogether indifferent on my *own account*, respecting the Engraving of the Portrait, I have abandoned the Project—

ever faithfully yours
[*not signed*]

I am glad you have seen Mr Robinson—he would tell you about us.—

[*Written at the side of the page*]

Dear Mr Moxon,

I am truly sorry to have caused you so much trouble about these unlucky verses, but all Poetry upon a domestic or personal subject especially if not helped by rhyme requires to be written with extreme care in all that concerns style, or it offends without the reader knowing why.—I have not yet seen H. Coleridge, he has been off on one of his drinking bouts.—

My dear Sir, Dont send more than 12 Copies of the Verses here, keep the rest for London distribution, and if not too late alter the line Aptly received etc. thus

Received, *there* may it stand, I trust, unblamed

---

[1] l. 100 of the verses to the memory of Charles Lamb. W. W. had thought of omitting the line (see previous letter), but he had second thoughts and it was added to the proof copy now in the *WL* and incorporated in the final text.

and print for 'Still were they faithful' 'Still they were faithful'.[1] You will notice the reason in the previous *inversion* of 'were they'.

W. W.

976. W. W. to C. W. JNR.

Address: The Revd C. Wordsworth etc. etc, Trin. Coll., Cambridge.
Stamp: Kendal Penny Post.
MS. Mr. William Wordsworth.
J. H. *Overton and Elizabeth Wordsworth, Christopher Wordsworth, Bishop of Lincoln, 1888, p. 78* (—).

Feb^{ry} 8th [1836] Rydal Mount.
My dear Chris,

Your letter of yesterday agreeably removed the uncertainty, I might say anxiety we have been in about your success.[2] For my own part, I was so much pleased with your spirit in standing forth as a Candidate, that, taking your youth into consideration, I should have felt almost sufficiently gratified by the attempt, even if you had not succeeded. Being quite certain that you are fitted for the office, and worthy of the honour conferred upon you, we heartily congratulate you, with best wishes for your health and happiness. W^m arrived here yesterday morning, and John left us on that morning for Keswick; I mean Sockbridge John; they both were highly pleased with the news of your success.—

We noticed in the Papers, some observations, not written in a friendly Spirit, upon the inexpedience and even injustice of selecting a public orator from Trinity; and other objections, of a worse character, founded upon your Relationship to the Master etc.—These latter, I hope would rather serve than prejudice you.—

We expect the Rector of Workington[3] tomorrow. His wife and children are well.—Sockbridge John is come down with a view to sell his Estate;[4] at least as much of it as shall be necessary to pay the heavy debt upon it.

[1] For these versions of ll. 47 and 102 see *PW* iv. 274–5, *app. crit.*
[2] C. W. jnr. had been elected Public Orator at Cambridge on 4 Feb. See also L. 981 below.
[3] i.e. John W.
[4] See L. 966 above and L. 981 below.

Your Father expressed a wish some time ago for Westmorland Freeholds for you all. Should you still have the same desire, an opportunity might now be had of procuring as much land as would make three Votes, and, I fear, at a very reasonable rate, as land now bears so low a price. If you have a wish to purchase, let me know and what sum you would go to for the purpose of having *3* Votes, or less, as you might wish. Even a *bidding* from any quarter might help John.

Of our Invalids I can say nothing very favorable. The State of your poor Aunt is such, and causes so much Distress to Dora, that *she* cannot I am sure recover; if she remains here. Nor am I sure that Dora can bear travelling — a few weeks ago she went out in our Carriage several times, and was much worse for the trial. — Your poor Aunt is in general bodily health much better — she is grown quite fat; but she cannot stand unsupported; and her mind, owing *we think* to some inflammatory action in the brain, is sadly weakened and disturbed.— We bear up under these trials as well as we can, of which after all the most painful part is the effect which her Aunt's illness produces upon the Niece. The poor Aunt is 64 years of age, but Dora is young enough to have looked forward to years of health and strength, which she will never attain unless it should please God that she should be enabled to quit her present abode, and exist in some quiet of mind, elsewhere. With best love to your Father and John I remain my dear Chris.

your affectionate Uncle
W. W.

You will have a Carlisle Paper with the advertisement of John's estates, sent you on Saturday. Mr. Robinson tells us that Mr Paynter,[1] a radical Friend of his, gave you a Vote not so much for your own merits, as in gratitude to your father, who protected him from insult at the time when he put the clerical M.A.[s] to the Bribery Oath; for this reason and also because you were 'a Poet's Nephew'. So that I have helped you a 'wee bit.'—

[*M. W. writes*]

Your uncle rec[d] a letter the other day from your friend

---

[1] Thomas Paynter (1794—1863), a barrister practising in Norfolk and Suffolk: Recorder of Falmouth, Helston and Penzance, 1838—41, and thereafter a police magistrate in London.

[? Handley]¹ who was pleased to see your name as a candidate for the P.O. He sent a *very* kind message, wishing you success— yʳ Uncle is Sponsor for his Son, together with the Q. Dowager of Bavaria² and others with names so long as that I cannot repeat them.—Your Aunt was much interested with and pleased with the success of yʳ Election.—When you write tell us what amount of filthy lucre is attached to your situation.

977. M. W. and W. W. to GEORGE HUTCHINSON and MARY HUTCHINSON

Address: Mr George Hutchinson, Sedberg, Kendal [*readdressed to*] Mrs Hutchinson, Brinsop Court, Hereford.
Stamp: Kendal Penny Post.
MS. WL. Hitherto unpublished.

[*c*. 9 Feb. 1836]

My dear George,

I take this long sheet, meaning to confine myself to the half of it, and you can write home upon the other.

With regard to the consideration which you, in so thoughtful and amiable a manner, set before us;³ there would have been less difficulty to giving our opinion, could we have been furnished with facts to rely upon, how far the situation offered to you is likely to lead to advancement, and indeed whether the Office is expected to be a *permanent* one, for if otherwise you might be turned adrift after a few years service. But I think your Father and Mother must have been satisfied as to this point, tho' her letter does not enter into this part of the subject. With her, I feel that I should have rather wished you to go to College, not because (as is her chief reason), 'I think you would there have less temptation to [fall]⁴ into snares and vices', but because I think your talents (could [they] command your will and attention to

---

¹ The reading is not very clear, but the reference is definitely to Edwin Hill Handley (see pt. ii, L. 569), as L. 1146 below makes plain.
² Widow of Maximilian I (1756—1825): formerly Princess Caroline Frederike of Baden. She died in 1841.
³ M. W.'s nephew George (see pt. ii, L. 769), at this time a pupil at Sedbergh, was hesitant about going on to Cambridge, and had written to the Wordsworths for advice on an alternative opening that had come up. See also *MW*, pp. 148—9.
⁴ *MS. torn.*

study) better fitted for that line of life, than for business,—for I trust your moral character and principles are such as to guard you against vice, which otherwise, may meet with temptation and encouragement as well at Coll: as elsewhere; and in some respects a youth is more protected from its influence in a public office, where full employment is the lot of every one rather than in Coll: where so much time is under your own control.

I have just read what I have said, and y^r Mother's letter and your own, to your Uncle, from whose mouth I now write.

'As you have now been in Sedberg several years with views, more or less fixed on the part of y^r friends, that you would be sent to Coll: in case you could command y^r attention to y^r studies, and proceed steadily and zealously in them, and you have been latterly aware of this; and do nevertheless at y^r age mistrust y^r ability to apply with pleasure and perseverance, I should be strongly inclined to recommend it to you to accept Mr Lewis'[1] kind offer, provided you were assured the Off: would continue, and that, if you behaved well you, in course of time, would be advanced: or if the off. were broked up you w^d after a certain years service in it, have claims to be transferred to some other. I take however this opportunity to press upon you, that either in this line of life, or in any other, you have no chance of ensuring success except by constraining every inclination that you might have that would interfere with your duty.'

I cannot dear George add any thing to the above farther than, that, whatever your decision may be, you shall have my fervent prayers it may lead to your temporal and eternal benefit—and may the Almighty direct you. With our united best love

Your Affec. Aunt M. W.

Do not forward this till Mr Wilkinson[2] gives you his opinion, on the Subject, and which you must transmit to y^r Father and Mother. Y^r Coz John is going to write to him.

My dear Mary

I shall write to you in a day or two by the parcel which now

---

[1] Probably Thomas Frankland Lewis (see pt. i, L. 46), landowner and neighbour of the Hutchinsons.

[2] Henry Wilkinson, headmaster of Sedbergh (see *MY* ii. 565). His opinion, quoted by George Hutchinson in his letter to his mother added at the bottom of the sheet, was that to succeed in the business referred to, George would need to be a barrister.

only waits for [?][1] letter to Eliz.[2] We rec[d] the Turkey etc etc all safe, and it has been thoroughly enjoyed by Willy, John's Brigham Curate, and Owen Ll.[3] The Rector himself did not arrive till after dinner, the day [it][4] was roasted, and as he does not eat meat at breakfast where it has appeared ever since (and has been cut [as] Willy says like a leg of veal) he has not been *hitherto* able to join in the praises of 'the first Turkey that ever appeared in West[d].'

They are both well and seem to accord in the opinion their father has given about dear Geo. I am very sorry to hear of MM's[5] illness. I trust however, she is better by this time—and that dear John's[6] eyes may not continue in the unpromising state your late reports have set before us. We feel very anxious about him, poor fellow! I think if Father does not accompany John back to Workington to be present at the Christening of his namesake, I shall venture to go for a few days. Mr Southey, Sir Wm Hamilton, the astronomical Proff. at Dublin, and our excellent friend Miss Fenwick are to be Sponsors. Willy refused to stand on the score, that he was so ill-godfathered himself, he would not be accessory to the like injury to his nephew. I cannot give you much of an improved account of our Invalids. I wrote to you by Mr Robinson when he left us last week. I hope you have received my letter by a frank from London.

With best love and good wishes, ever believe me my dear Sister

aff[ly] yours
M Wordsworth

We think it right to ask Mr W's[7] opinion regarding Geo's prospects at Coll, as he may have it in his power best to judge how far G's talents may be likely to fit him to make his fortune there. Before you come to a decision. It is only paying a proper respect to his Master.

[1] *Illegible word.*
[2] i.e. Elizabeth Hutchinson, M. W.'s niece.
[3] Owen Lloyd.
[4] *MS. torn.*
[5] Mary Monkhouse, daughter of the late Thomas Monkhouse (see pt. i, L. 50), now living at Brinsop.
[6] John Monkhouse of the Stow.
[7] Mr. Wilkinson's.

978. W. W. to JOSHUA WATSON

Address: Joshua Watson Esqre, 6 Park St, Westminster. [*In M. W.'s hand*]
Postmark: 12 Feb. 1836. *Stamp*: Chas St. West^r.
Endorsed: W Wordsworth Esq   9th Feb 1836 Cockermouth.
MS. WL.
LY ii. 781.

Rydal Mount
9th Feb^{ry} [18]36

Private

My dear Sir,

The Vicar of Brigham and Mr Hodgeson[1] his Curate are both now in my house; and the subject of a 2nd Church at Cockermouth[2] has of course been conversed upon in my presence.

The obstacles are as follows.

1st the character and dispositions of the Incumbent[3] of Cockermouth, who is indifferent or even averse to the Project:—which will prevent neighbouring Clergymen interfering for the purpose—

2nd a deadness in the body of the people which appears to be in no small degree consequent upon the character and disposition of their Clergyman.—The present Church is far from being filled; and therefore it is naturally enough said, 'that another is not wanted'.—

On the favourable side—

1st a strong sense in the minds of many persons, of the desireableness of the thing.—

---

[1] Probably the Revd. William Hodgson (1809−c. 1872), later perpetual curate of Brathay (1842−56).

[2] W. W. was now increasingly turning his attention to the problem of the provision of a second church in his native town of Cockermouth, which at this time formed part of Brigham parish. With the introduction of cotton and woollen mills and other manufactories, the population of the borough had almost doubled since the beginning of the century and now numbered about four and a half thousand; and the church of All Saints (1711), at the head of Kirkgate near the Castle, though enlarged in 1825, could only seat a fraction of this number. Dissent had flourished in the town since the Ejection of 1662: Quakers and Wesleyans were active, and there was vigorous opposition to the Established Church. As will become clear in later letters, W. W.'s efforts were finally unavailing: All Saints was completely rebuilt shortly after his death, in 1852, but Christ Church at the opposite end of the town was not added until 1865.   [3] For the Revd. Edward Fawcett, see L. 933 above.

2nd—an all but certainty that Lord Lonsdale would assist in it, as he has just offered to do in the case of Keswick, with which he is not by property connected; whereas he is Patron and Lay-impropriator of the parish of Brigham.—

3^d—Lord Egremont[1] has recently given [£]100 to Keswick, where he has *no* property, whereas as you know he is owner of Cockermouth Castle, and has a large estate immediately above the Town, and is furthermore known to be a munificent Person—

Now I take the liberty of asking two questions—1st I understand from Dr Wordsworth that 200 was lately offered to Kendal from a small surplus of the Church building society.[2]— Could any portion of that surplus not less than 200, be conditionally offered by the society as a nucleus for subscriptions to gather round.

2nd Does your experience enable you to suggest a plan by which the difficulty arising from the *covert* dispositions of the Incumbent could be got over; so that an attempt might be made?—

With regard to the former of these questions, I am aware that your Boards expect that the advance should be made, in the first instance, by the parishes themselves coming forward with a certain sum; but could not the general rule be dispensed with in a case like the present, particularly where you are so near the end of your fund?—

My Son having previously furnished you with the particulars of the case, I beg to refer you to his Letter, and have only [to][3] add that we should be much gratified if the scheme could be realized—

I remain my dear Sir
with the highest respect
faithfully yours
Wm Wordsworth

---

[1] For the 3rd Earl of Egremont, see pt. i, L. 124.

[2] The Church Building Society, with which Joshua Watson and C. W. were closely associated from its inception, was set up in 1817—18 alongside Lord Liverpool's Church Commission, to finance the provision of churches in the new centres of population.

[3] *Word dropped out.*

979. W. W. to SAMUEL ROGERS

Address: Sam¹ Rogers Esqre, St James's Place, London. [*In M. W.'s hand*]
Postmark: 18 Feb. 1836. *Stamp*: Kendal Penny Post.
MS. Sharpe Collection, University College, London.
Rogers. LY ii. 783.

Rydal Mount [*c*. 17 Feb., 1836]

Many and sincere thanks, my dear Friend, for your Grand
Present of Matthias's Gray,[1] which reached me a few days ago. I
have already skimmed the 2nd Vol. which was new to me; and I
hope for much pleasure and profit from the perusal of most of it,
at *leisure*. This last word, by the bye, reminds me of a reference I
found to Oldham, for the words—

I have not yet leisure to be good.[2]

You recollect that long ago I said to you I was sure the line
would be found somewhere, and if I am not mistaken you told
me, some time after, you had met with it in Owen Feltham's
prose.[3] Was this so?

I shall greatly value these two superb Volumes, and more for
your sake than for their own, and I hope that they of my family
into whose hands they may pass will also prize them as a
memorial of our Friendship.

I have not forgotten that I am in your debt for a Letter
received many months ago; and for which you would have
been thanked long since, if I could have added any thing
respecting myself or family which it would have gratified you
to learn. We struggle on, bearing up under our trials and
affictions as well as with God's help we can. My daughter is
some thing better, though not able to exert herself; but for my
poor Sister, though her bodily health is upon the whole better,
this blessing is more than counterbalanced by a disorder of the
mind, obviously proceeding from some inflammatory action
upon the brain. Mrs W. continues pretty well.—

---

[1] *The Works of Thomas Gray . . . To which are subjoined, extracts, philological,
poetical, critical, from the author's original manuscripts selected and arranged by T. J.
Mathias*, 2 vols., 1814. The editor was Thomas James Mathias (? 1754–1835),
satirist and Italian scholar. See *R. M. Cat.*, no. 546, which records the
autograph presentation, 'To William Wordsworth from Samuel Rogers—
January 27, 1836.'

[2] From John Oldham's *Satyr against Value*, stanza v. See also pt. i, L. 95.

[3] Owen Feltham (? 1602–68) published *Resolves, Divine, Morall, Political*,
c. 1620 (enlarged edn., 1628, etc.: 8th edn., 1661).

Last summer I saw a good deal of our excellent Friends both at Lowther and Whitehaven. Lady Frederick[1] was there, and you were often talked about. At Whitehaven I had frequent walks upon the cliffs, which were not unproductive of poetic *suggestions*, I do not presume to say inspirations.

Possibly, and even probably, I may visit London before the spring is over; if so, how happy shall I be to renew my conversations and walks with you. These are (truly may I say it) among the principal attractions London has for me. With kindest remembrances to yourself and Sister, in which my own poor dear Sister is still able to join with us all, I remain my dear Friend faithfully yours

W Wordsworth

Pray enclose this slip to Moxon.[2]

P.S. Be so good as to say to Moxon that I wish him to present you, as from me, a couple of copies of my verses upon Lamb, one for your Sister. I should have expressed this wish to himself upon the slip on the other side had there been room.

980. W. W. to JOSHUA WATSON

Address: Joshua Watson Esqre, 6 Park Street, Westminster. [*In M. W.'s hand*]
Endorsed: Wm Wordsworth Esq 19 Feb. 1836 Cockermouth Church.
MS. WL.
LY ii. 784.

Rydal Mount
Feb. 19th [1836]

Private

My dear Sir,

I was much gratified in learning from your Letter that you do not think Cockermouth is to be despaired of.[3]—Your proposal of naming the project to the Diocesan, is I think the best thing that can, at present, be done. It was upon the application of the Bp of Carlisle that Lord Egremont gave 100£ to Keswick, and when upon being applied to for the same place Lord Lonsdale offered to assist, it was with the Proviso that the Bp approved.—

---

[1] Lady Frederick Bentinck.

[2] The bottom of the sheet, containing the note to Moxon, has been removed.

[3] In the provision of a new church.

I am persuaded that if these two Noblemen were applied to through the Bp, they would both countenance and aid the Building of the Church, in a place where, to all but the indifferent or the prejudiced in religious concerns, it must appear to be so much needed. At present the main obstacle, is the slackness, and I fear aversion of the Incumbent;[1] but I feel confident that if these Noblemen would support the undertaking, we need not dread much from the covert indisposition of the Incumbent, which as things now are, would stand greatly in our way; though he would not openly oppose the attempt.

This is a matter of delicacy; and it is only to you that by Letter I would venture to speak as openly as I have done. If Lord Lonsdale had been in the North I would have seen him upon the subject, and treated this part of it with some thing of less reserve, than I feel necessary in communications by Letter.

A copy of your last has been forwarded to my Son, and no doubt he will have the papers filled up as desired, and sent.

There are in the manufacturing Districts many, many places far more destitute than Cockermouth; but surely for an encreasing population of nearly six thousand,[2] more than 100 free seats are required for the poor, and I question when the Sunday schools are supplied if there be that number in Cockermouth Church. But what makes the main difference between this place and the manufacturing towns and villages is, that there is ground for hope of success here notwithstanding the deadness of most of the Inhabitants; whereas in many parts of Lancashire and Yorkshire people spring up so fast, and float about so irregularly that the demand for religious instruction and consolation *cannot* be adequately supplied. Believe [me] my dear Sir

ever faithfully yours
W. Wordsworth

[1] Mr. Fawcett.

[2] Contemporary estimates put the figure rather lower, at about four and a half thousand. But W. W. is probably including the population of the outlying villages of Papcastle and Goat (see L. 1007 below).

981. M. W. to H. C. R.

Address: H. C. Robinson Esqre, 2 Plowden's Buildings, Temple.
Endorsed: 20 Feb: 1836, Mrs Wordsworth.
MS. Dr. Williams's Library.
K (—). Morley, i. 290.

Sat. Feb 20th [1836]

My dear Friend,

Thanks for your letter, which I assure you has been long looked for (not that we did not receive your short one on your arrival in Town)—and for its enclosures. But I wish you had told us something more of yourself—if you have got thro' your business, and whether your plan of travel is arranged[1]—or if you have determined upon your new Quarters? We feel as if we ought to know something more about you *Personally*. For ourselves we are going on just as you left us—I cannot report of the least change either for better or worse. We have had both our Sons over for a week or little more—which interrupted the sadness that followed upon our parting with you—*they* left us together last Tuesday, and had a stormy drive poor fellows! to Workington—their place was in part filled up by Sockbridge John next Coach-day, who is now with us—The sale[2] is advertized for the 9th of next Month.

We have now delightful weather—. W^m and I drove to Bowness on Thursday—to call upon the Pasleys,[3] who are come there to superintend the building of their house—thence round by Elleray where we found Mr Hamilton[4] quite recovered. Lady F.[5] and he enquired most particularly after you, as indeed do all our neighbours.

Your radical friends of Fox How were detained a few days by the illness of their Baby—but all was well again—and I have had a good report of their safe arrival at Rugby. Mrs A[6] speaks of a number of new Admissions, so that John Bull's[7] spite does not promise to injure the School.

---

[1] His proposed visit to Spain to see Barron Field.

[2] Of the Sockbridge estate, at the Crown Inn, Penrith. W. W. was now hoping to get back money which he had advanced to R. W. (see *HCR* ii. 486).

[3] For Sir Thomas and Lady Pasley, see pt. ii, L. 747.

[4] Capt. Thomas Hamilton.

[5] Lady Farquhar.

[6] Mrs. Arnold.

[7] Thomas Arnold's pamphlet on *The Principles of Church Reform*, 1833, and other writings which followed roused (as Morley notes) a storm of opposition

Your news of Mr Monkhouse[1] is very encouraging, having a while ago heard from his Sister, who was somewhat hopeless on the subject of his eyes. He will have left Town, or Wm would have requested you to order for *him* of Longman's (*at trade price*) a copy of Johnson's life which Mr M. wished to be sent to his lodgings, and for the Messenger to receive pay on delivery.

Dora with her tender love bids me tell you that your unlucky pocket Hk[f2] is safe in her hands, which she will take care of till she can restore it to you herself—She bids me add, that she has hitherto considered you a *true* friend, and ho[pes][3] you still are so—but if you are aw[are] of the flatteries which almost every other day her Father has poured in upon him you would be slow to encrease, *for our sakes*, the number. For he is really, she says, growing so vain *she* cannot keep him in any kind of order.

W. has just said to me that it is rather odd he should learn that the Church is strengthened *spiritually* by his humble exertions, at the moment when under many discouraging circumstances, he is doing his utmost for having an additional Church built in his Native Town of Cockermouth. He has nothing further to say than that the conduct of the Minister[s] and Radicals in the Carlo[w] affair[4] proves [? that] Hume[5] knew what he was about when he said that he would vote Black White and White Black, as suited his purpose.

God bless you my very d[r] F[d]
affly yours
M Wordsworth

in the Tory press which lasted at least four years. W. W. and H. C. R. had seen much of Dr. Arnold during his residence at Fox How over the Christmas holidays, and they had engaged in lively discussion on Church issues. 'Wordsworth did not hesitate to declare that he thought Dr. Arnold held opinions unbecoming a minister of the Establishment, yet he said this with the warmest love of him. And there was a like reciprocal attachment between the ladies.' (*HCR* ii. 476.)

[1] John Monkhouse of the Stow.　　　　　　　　[2] Handkerchief.
[3] *MS. torn.*
[4] O'Connell was accused of having corruptly sold a seat in Parliament after he recommended Alexander Raphael as one of the representatives for Co. Carlow in 1835, and Raphael was unseated on petition. O'Connell denied the charges, and was exonerated by a parliamentary committee which reported on 11 Mar. 1836.
[5] Joseph Hume, the radical politican (see pt. i, L. 27).

Do you know any thing of Mr Higgins[1]—Sec[r] of Nat His. at Guys Hospital? He has just sent us his little B[ook][2] upon 'the Earth'.

[*W. W. adds*]

Your Friend M[r] Painter[3] may be told that it is admitted by Johnians that the Nephew of the Poet and Son of the master was the better Man.[4] He may therefore be quite easy about his Vote.   W W

[*M. W. adds*]

Miss W. sends her love and bids me say that 'she has had many a *sad tug* since you went and that she has been very ill used, and has wanted you to protect her.'

982. W. W. to LINCOLN FAIRCHILD [5]

MS. Collections of the Poe Foundation, Virginia State Library.
LY ii. 785.

[*In M. W. 's hand*]

Rydal Mount Feb[ry] 23[d] [? 1836][6]

Sir,

Your letter with an enclosure from Mr Griscom[7] has been received. It will give me pleasure to pay to a Friend of that

---

[1] William Mullinger Higgins, physicist and geologist: author of *The Earth: its physical condition and most remarkable phenomena*, 1836.

[2] *MS. torn.*

[3] For Thomas Paynter, see L. 976 above.

[4] In the recent election for Public Orator at Cambridge, C. W. jnr. had been opposed by the Revd. John Frederick Isaacson (1801–86), Fellow of King's, but had won by nearly a hundred votes.

[5] An American traveller, but otherwise unidentified. No publication of his either in Britain or America can be traced.

[6] W. W. was at this time in process of changing his publisher from Longman to Moxon, as de Selincourt notes: hence the dating of this letter.

[7] John Griscom (1774–1852), Quaker educationalist, was Professor of Chemistry at Columbia College, 1813–20, instituted the Lancastrian system at the New York High School, 1825–31, and thereafter ran schools in Providence, R. I., and Burlington, N. J. He was the author of *A Year in Europe,* 2 vols., New York, 1823, in which he described his visit to W. W. in Apr. 1819.

gentleman such attention as my opportunities and engagements will allow.

At present I am not connected with any London Bookseller, and my acquaintance with that Body of Men is so confined, that not more than two of them are known to me even by sight, except those of the Firm of Messrs Longman, who were till lately my Publishers. I am sorry therefore that I cannot be of use to you in the way of introductions among them. Nor am I upon those terms of intimacy with any literary Men to allow me to take the liberty, at this distance, to introduce any one with whom I have not the honor to be personally acquainted.

Should you write to your friend Mr Griscom I will thank you to convey my respectful remembrances to him—I need scarcely add, that if you come into this Country in search of a Residence, I should be happy to give you all the assistance, as to that point, which I am able.

And am Sir your
obd^t S^t
[<i>signed</i>] Wm Wordsworth

983. W. W. to JOSHUA WATSON

Address: Joshua Watson Esqre, 6 Park Street, Westminster. [*In M.W.'s hand*]
Postmark: 8 Mar. 1836.
Endorsed: Wm Wordsworth Esq. 28 Feb. 1836.
MS. WL.
LY ii. 786.

Rydal Mount
28 Feb^{ry}—1836

My dear Sir,

I trouble you with this note on account of the Extract from an *intended* Tithe Commission Bill,[1] contained in a Letter of my Son Wm, which you will find on the other page. For myself I can give no opinion upon the matter, but if it have any promise about it, perhaps you would not object upon a fit occasion to

---

[1] In their previous administration the Whigs had proposed that tithes should be commuted for a rent-charge based on a septennial valuation made by special commissioners, but their Bill was rejected by the Lords. Lord John Russell was now introducing a new Bill on the same lines, which was to set up a board of tithe commissioners to settle disputed assessments.

mention it to the Archbishop. You know how anxious I am that my Son should obtain some office or situation in which his time might be turned to better account both for himself and for the publick than at present.—

I avail myself of this opportunity to condole with you on the death of the excellent B^p of Durham.[1] It is an event which every rational Friend of the Church must have long looked forward to, with mournful apprehensions. Then there are Salisbury, Ely, Peterborough all opening to receive any unworthy Person whom it may suit the purposes of unscrupulous men to appoint.[2] The Bp of Norwich[3] also cannot be expected to last long. Of Dr Hampden's opinions[4] I know no more than any one may have learned from the extracts from his Lectures in the newspapers—But surely it is astounding that he and others can remain in the Church at all. The notions of Dr H— (if correctly given in the Extracts) respecting Creeds declarations and articles appear to me irreconcilable with *any Church* however latitudinarian its character.—

I do not recollect whether I have written to you since Chris^t became public orator. As a personal question it seems every

---

[1] For William Van Mildert, the last Count Palatine of Durham, and founder of Durham University, see pt. i, L. 371.

[2] Thomas Burgess (1756—1837) was the present Bishop of Salisbury. He was succeeded by Edward Denison (1801—54). The Bishop of Ely was Bowyer Edward Sparke (1759—1836), who died this April and was succeeded by Joseph Allen (1770—1845), translated from Bristol. The see of Peterborough was occupied by Herbert Marsh (1757—1839), who was succeeded by George Davys (1780—1864), Dean of Chester. Lord Melbourne's ecclesiastical appointments were viewed with great suspicion by conservatives because he appeared to favour liberal churchmen who might be expected to support the Whig cause in the House of Lords.

[3] Henry Bathurst (see *MY* ii. 529) died in 1837 and was succeeded by Edward Stanley (1779—1849), father of Arthur Penrhyn Stanley.

[4] Renn Dickson Hampden (1793—1868), a liberal churchman and friend of Arnold and Whately at Oriel, was Bishop of Hereford from 1848 to 1868. In 1827 he published *An Essay on the Philosophical Evidence of Christianity*, and in 1833 his Bampton Lectures on *The Scholastic Philosophy, considered in its relation to Christian Theology*, which brought his orthodoxy into question. In 1834 he supported the admission of Dissenters to Oxford. His name came into prominence in 1836 when the Tractarians unsuccessfully tried to block his appointment to the Regius Professorship of Divinity on the nomination of Lord Melbourne, who refused to allow him to withdraw. In 1847 Lord John Russell raised another storm of protest by offering him the see of Hereford.

where admitted that he was the better man. His success gave us in this House much pleasure. With affectionate regards to Miss Watson, I remain dear Sir

most respectfully yours
Wm Wordsworth

[*In M. W. 's hand*]

Extract

'The only point remaining is the constitution of the B^d of Commiss^{rs}

'They are to be three, two appointed by the Secretary of State, one by the Archbp of Canterbury, and all removable only on the joint pleasure of the Secretary and Archbp: They are to be a body corporate, but to be appointed for 5 years only.

'They may appoint any number of *Assistant* Commiss^{rs} not exceeding *nine,* without the consent of the Treasury, and may delegate any of their powers to their Assistants, except the Acts required to be under their seal, such as confirming and authenticating agreements and awards.'

It is the *Assistant* Commiss^{rs} that my Son wished me to ask your opinion about—if the app^t could be held by any but a Barrister?

[*signed*] W. W.

984. W. W. to FRANCIS MEREWETHER

MS. Cornell. Hitherto unpublished.

Rydal Mount March 7th. [18]36

My dear Sir,

I wish I could have sent this Letter under Cover, as it will scarcely be worth Postage; but I cannot defer thanking you for the great pleasure which your excellent Sermon[1] gave me, and for which I beg you will accept my sincere thanks. It was well timed, and could not, I think, but do good.

Today I am going from home, and do not expect to be at Liberty to return for at least ten days. One of my objects is, to

---

[1] *Popery a new religion, compared with that of Christ and his apostles. A sermon preached in the Parish Church of Whitwick* . . . , Ashby de la Zouch, 1835 (3rd edn., 1836).

attend the Christening of my Grandchild[1] at Workington, who is to be called after me, and I hope will be taken to the font next Sunday. John was here not long ago and seemed to be a good deal dismayed at having ventured upon the sea of Authorship. The doctrines maintained in his sermon,[2] will be as I hope he is prepared to expect, obnoxious in certain quarters; but ours is at present truly a Church Militant, and it becomes every Soldier to be faithful to his duty and maintain his post.

Our Invalids are both better especially my sister, who has become quite improved, though still *enfeebled* in mind, and her bodily health is greatly improved. She is now making efforts to walk, though to her own great astonishment, as she feels so well, she can scarcely stand without some support. But if she goes on as she has done lately, she will soon be able to move about in her own room.

You will be pleased to hear that there are good dispositions among several of the leading gentry in our County and in Cumberland to support the establishment by enlarging and building Churches. A large new one is erecting, at Kendal,[3] one at Mil[n]thorp[e];[4] another within a mile or two of Ambleside.[5] My neighbour Lady Fleming has just subscribed £100 towards a new church at Keswick,[6] Lord Lonsdale will assist in the same work, and he has just given £100 towards enlarging the Church at Bootle[7] where a new Parsonage is also building; and I hope that both his Lordship and the Earl of Egremont will contribute to the erecting of a new Church in my native place, Cockermouth. It is a desperate stronghold of Radicalism; and the Inhabitants in general are little inclined to support the Undertaking; a proof how much, (circumstanced

[1] John W.'s second son, William.

[2] *Church Membership and Discipline should be better understood and more zealously maintained* . . . , Ashby de la Zouch, 1835.

[3] St. Thomas's, at the north end of Stricklandgate, in 'Commissioners' Gothic' by George Webster (1837).

[4] The church of St. Thomas, completed the same year in a similar style.

[5] Holy Trinity, Brathay, built by Giles Redmayne (see pt. ii, L. 758). Thomas Arnold preached there occasionally while in residence at Fox How.

[6] The new church of St. John the Evangelist, built at the expense of John Marshall and his family, was finally completed in 1838. See L. 933 above and Curry, ii. 453–4.

[7] Near Ravenglass, where Lord Lonsdale was the patron of the living. The ancient church was enlarged by the addition of north and south transepts in 1837.

as they are with only one Church for 6,000 Souls), they stand in need of it. We however hope to succeed in the end; the chief obstacle in our way, I regret to say, is the indifference or supineness of the Minister[1] himself of the present Church, which

[*cetera desunt*]

[*Fragment of postscript at side of letter in D.W's hand*] but was still poorly. Surely we shall be having direct news soon—but they are all so much and so exclusively involved in their own . . .

985. W. W. to LADY VANE[2]

Address: Lady Vane, Armathwaite, Cockermouth.
Stamp: Kendal Penny Post.
MS. Lord Inglewood. Hitherto unpublished.

Rydal Mount
16th March [? 1836]

Dear Lady Vane,

It was my intention to have left Workington yesterday for Armathwaite, but your Letter caused me to give up the pleasure of seeing you at present, notwithstanding your obliging Invitation that I would take Armathwaite in my way, and your offer of your Carriage etc.—A more advanced state of the season will be more favorable to the little excursions in your neighbourhood which Sir Francis proposed, but still I felt a little disappointed on the receipt of your's, and not a little sorry that Sir Francis should have to take so long a journey at this season, and upon an occasion any thing but pleasant. I wish heartily that he may arrive in time, and gain his point with his Brother.[3]

Yesterday I came through from Workington. On the outside of the Coach was a Mr Wright[4] who has resided some time at

---

[1] Mr. Fawcett.

[2] Diana (d. 1875), wife of Sir Francis Fletcher-Vane, 3rd Bart. (see L. 939 above), a fairly recent acquaintance of W. W.'s, who had called at Rydal Mount the previous December (*RMVB*). See also *MW*, p. 190.

[3] Frederick Henry Fletcher-Vane (1807–94), an army officer.

[4] Probably Charles Wright, who was employed as a guide at Keswick. See *RMVB* for Dec. 1837. The model of the Lake District was probably the one put on view in the Town Hall, Keswick, by Joseph Flintoff of Skiddaw Cottage, in the summer of 1839. (See *Cumberland Pacquet* for 11 and 25 June, 1839, and 28 July, 1840.)

Keswick. He has been some years employed in executing a model of the Lake District and other Parts of Cumberland and intended to call on Sir Francis that day; but on learning from me Sir F: was not at home he proceeded to Keswick. He seemed perfectly to understand his business and is taking wonderful pains ·about it.—

My Son begged your acceptance of those cards or Papers which you mentioned. He takes a lively interest in the success of your School.—

It was fortunate in one respect that I came home yesterday, as I found important Letters here requiring an immediate answer.

Believe [me] dear Lady Vane,
faithfully yours
Wm Wordsworth

986. W. W. and M. W. to H. C. R.

Address: H. C. Robinson Esqre, 2 Plowdens Buildings, Temple.
Endorsed: 16th March 1836, Wordsworth and Mrs Wordsworth.
MS. Dr. Williams's Library.
Morley, ii. 294.

March 16th I *think* [1836]
Thursday however.[1]

My dear Friend,

The oranges arrived safe and have proved most delicious to the Invalids of this House, to Miss Cookson,[2] and that poor young creature Miss Jackson[3] who we fear is dying of a consumption.

My Daughter guessed what your present would prove, which her Mother could not, nor could I when your Letter was forwarded to me. It has proved useful and also is ornamental, though Jane[4] thinks it much too good for the purpose. My best News is that our dear Sister is mightily improved in bodily health since your departure; her mind however is still feeble in all that relates to her illness, of which she has a strangely

---

[1] But Thursday was the 17th.
[2] Elizabeth Cookson.
[3] Daughter of Thomas Jackson of Waterhead (see pt. i, L. 63).
[4] Servant at Rydal Mount. The present was a coal scoop.

confused recollection. She now makes some little progress in walking though not without support.

We had no sale at Penrith for John's lands, there being no competition. He is endeavouring to. do better by private Contract—M[r] Lightfoot I do not much like, and he is of a bad stock,[1] but he *seems* well disposed.—in this matter.[2]

I am not sorry that you have given up the Spanish scheme.— Could I afford it I should take an Excursion upon the Continent in the summer, and should be heartily glad of your company. But my Stamp Off. income appears to be in such a rapid course of reduction,[3] that I shrink from avoidable expense. The Registration Bill, if carried, will take from me 70£ per Ann. Could you call at Moxons that he may talk with you about certain things I have mentioned to him relating to my Poems, in a Letter of this morning, to go by the same parcel as this.— He will furnish you with a copy of my Last Verses,[4] as an introduction from me[5] to S. Cookson[6] —

I wish your Friend Wood[7] could do something either for father or Son.—for poor Willy will be a Beggar.—He is now begging 10 per Ann: of me to enable him to go on. I must tell you that the Income of the Carlisle Sub Distribution is far short of what it appears to be on the Books; the Registrar exacting, under threats of applying to the Head Office in London for the Probate etc which he has occasionally done,[8] a large portion of the Poundage allowed.

As to the Irish Municipal Bill, [9] and the arguments in its

---

[1] His father Robert Lightfoot had been one of the witnesses to Raisley Calvert's will, but was distrusted by him (see *EY*, p. 133).

[2] These last three words added by M. W.

[3] H. C. R., who was called on to advise W. W. on his business affairs before he left Rydal, calculated W. W.'s income from the Stamp Office at about £450 per annum (*HCR* ii, 486).

[4] The verses on Charles Lamb.

[5] These two words added by M. W.

[6] Strickland Cookson.

[7] H. C. R. wrote in 1851: 'My Diary [for 1821] mentions "John Wood, a lively genteel young man!" Now he is a man of importance in the State, being the Chairman of the Board of Inland Revenue. He was previously the head of the Stamp Office and Chairman of Excise. In the latter capacity he lately effected great economic reforms.' (Sadler, ii. 220.)

[8] These five words added by M. W.

[9] For the proposed reform of the Irish corporations, see next letter.

support, what would you say to your shoes and mine being made off the same Last!—

farewell with love from all
affectionately yours
W Wordsworth

[*M. W. writes*]

My dear friend

I cannot put up this without expressing my own thanks for all your kindness—and as in duty bound more especially for your consideration of myself. William has been absent for 10 days— first at the intended sale—then at Workington to *assist* at the Christening of William the 3^d with whom and his Sister and Brother the old gentleman returned, as much delighted as any fond grandfather ever was since the world begun. I saw M^r and Mrs Harden[1] in their Carriage the other day who both asked particularly after you—M^{rs} H's feebleness of limb increases I am sorry to say—I assure you *all* your Acquaintance here retain a lively remembrance of you—and join in our wishes to see you among us again. I have no good account to send of Dora and she does not like my grumbling about her—So God bless you my dear friend

M. Wordsworth

We grieved to hear of poor Mary Lamb.

987. W. W. to JOSHUA WATSON

MS. WL.
LY ii. 789.

[*c.* 19 Mar. 1836]

My dear Sir

I am sorry that a wish to save postage caused so long a delay for my unlucky letter.—

The Papers relating to Cockermouth Church could not, as my Son and Mr Hodgeson his Curate thought, be filled up on account of the unwillingness of the Cockermouth Incumbent to stir in the business, without a request from the Bp. Accordingly

---

[1] The Hardens had now settled at Field Head, where H. C. R. had visited them during his recent stay at Rydal.

my Son wrote to his Lordship, stating particulars, and begging that he himself would write to Mr Fawcett. I left Workington last Tuesday, but the Bp's answer had not been received. I am not very sanguine, but still think the project ought not to be abandoned. Could we induce Mr Stanger[1] of Keswick to take it up and subscribe, as he was prepared to do at Keswick, there would be no difficulty, though the religious tenets of Mr Stanger are not what the judicious, I think, would approve. Lord Lonsdale has just given a 100 £ towards the enlargement of Bootle Church. That of Distington near Whitehaven wants it full as much and Maryport far more. The enclosed Paper gives an account of what is to be done at Keswick; with which Mr Stanger and his Party who were prepared with no less than 4000£, have nothing to do. And it is said he talks of building a third Church[2] at Keswick, where the *Gospel* may be preached. This would be a nuisance in so small [a] place. Mr Hodgson and Mr Hoskins[3] of the High near Bassenthwaite Lake have both a good deal of influence over Mr S— and may perhaps prevail upon him to favor Cockermouth.—

A thousand thanks for your kindness. I am *very* anxious on my Son's account, and not the less so, as my own Income from the Stamp off: has already been much reduced by various causes;[4] and if the Registrary is to be removed from Carlisle to London, as proposed in the new Bill, it will be reduced still further by 70£ per ann: This is rather hard after 23 years service, in which I have had from the first a Clerk, whose salary I cannot curtail, but would much rather encrease, so great are his deservings.—

The Chancellor of the Exchequer[5] is of my acquaintance, and I have reason to believe well-disposed to me, though not ignorant of my Politics. So no doubt is Lord Landsdown,[6] but as you will easily conceive it goes against the grain with me to ask any thing of these gentlemen that even looks like a government favor, I do so deeply deplore, and so strongly disapprove of their public conduct, especially in respect to the

[1] For James Stanger, the Evangelical churchman, see pt. i, L. 42.
[2] i.e. in addition to the church of St. John, then building.
[3] Thomas Alison Hoskins (b. 1800), educated at Rugby: High Sheriff of Cumberland, 1854.
[4] See previous letter.
[5] Thomas Spring Rice.
[6] Lord President of the Council under Melbourne. See L. 895 above.

Protestant Church in Ireland, and their municipal Bill for that wretched country.[1] As to the latter measure and the arguments by which it is supported what should we say of an order for two men's shoes being made off the same Last though their feet differed some inches in size! We have as yet little reason to applaud the new-casting of the Corporations for England;[2] but for Ireland and the Empire at large, the application of the same plan must in its tendency, be ruinous. But to return—I will consider seriously about writing to the Chancellor of the Ex: and Lord L: but I do not think I shall be able to prevail upon myself to take the step as I cannot ask any thing as a *favor*; if I thought they would admit that supposing my Son's qualifications sufficient for an office, I have a claim, from my writings and general character, in his behalf upon my Country, upon those terms but upon no other could I ask for an appointment. [As] to the good Archbishop I should feel no difficulty. It is time to bring this tedious Letter to a close. Believe me my dear Sir, under all circumstances,

most gratefully and respectfully yours
Wm Wordsworth.

Mr Moxon of Dover Street will send you three Copies of some printed, but not published Verses upon my deceased Friend Charles Lamb—one for Cambridge as soon as you may have an opportunity of giving it to the Doctor,[3] or either of [his] Sons, and one for Charles if they could convey it to him without expense—

My Sister is very much better in bodily health and so also in mind, though still feeble in certain points, from the effect of the late violent inflammatory actions upon the brain.—

Pray excuse this shabby paper which has been taken up inadvertently.—

---

[1] The Corporation Reform (Ireland) Bill was introduced in the Commons on 16 Feb. and was given a third reading on 28 Mar. But the Bill was altered in the Lords, and the Government refusing to accept the changes, it was dropped for the time being, and some reform was not finally achieved until 1840.

[2] See L. 913 above.

[3] i.e. C. W.

988. W. W. to EDWARD TWISTLETON [1]

Address: E. Twissleton Esq. [*delivered by hand?*]
Endorsed: March 20. 1836.
MS. Harvard University Library. Hitherto unpublished.

Rydal Mount
8—o clock
[20 Mar. 1836]

My dear Sir,
    The day being at present so promising if it should not change
for the worse allow me to propose our taking the walk this
afternoon which we were disappointed in yesterday. I shall not
stir from home till after three and so if you find it convenient to
call you will be sure of finding me.

truly yours
Wm Wordsworth

989. D. W., M. W., and W. W. to C. W. JNR.

MS. The late W. A. Wordsworth. Hitherto unpublished.

[*D. W. writes*]

[late Mar. 1836]

    My dear Nephew (formerly Christopher Wordsworth
Esquire of the University of Cambridge) now public Orator—
deputed to speak in the presence of Kings, Princes and
Bishops—I have to lay before you a case of distress. Your uncle,
the Poet of the Lakes, has been deputed by John Bolton Esqre of
Storrs Hall to lay the first stone of an Edifice to be erected at
Bowness—a Seminary for the youth of all generations to
come [2]—but alas! the poet is no Orator and he knows not what

---

[1] Edward Turner Boyd Twistleton (1809—74), friend of C. W. jnr. and
Charles Wordsworth: barrister and Fellow of Balliol College, Oxford,
1830—8. He served on many government commissions, and was chief poor-
law commissioner in Ireland, 1845—9. See also L. 1018 below.

[2] John Bolton had written to W. W., *c.* 20 Mar. (*WL MSS.*), to say that,
owing to illness, he would be unable to preside at the laying of the foundation
stone of the new school at Bowness on 13 Apr., and asking W. W. to take his
place. See L. 994 below. It is not clear how serious D. W.'s request to C. W.
jnr. in this letter was meant to be; but he replied on 2 Apr. (*British Library
MSS.*) that he was unable to help, as he was on the point of leaving Cambridge
to take up his new post of headmaster of Harrow (see L. 992 below).

to say on this important occasion. I therefore request *you* the first Orator of the Nation to make a speech for him which I will answer for it he will pronounce verbatim, his diffidence of his own powers being so overwhelming. I have got through a mighty struggle—and thank God am now as well as ever I was in my life except that I have not recovered the use of my legs. My Arms have been active enough as the torn caps of my nurses and the heavy blows I have given their heads and faces will testify. When are we to meet again at Rydal? I intend, God willing, to see you all at Cambridge in summer.

Ever your affec^{te} Aunt D. W.

[*M. W. writes*]

Your Aunt requires an immediate answer to her letter.

I hold the pen for your Uncle—who not being ready I will say a word for myself. When Charles was last here, your Aunt and he bargained for a copy of Sir W. Scott's 'Tales of a Grandfather', one series of which he had with him, and *left*—the other was to be *sent*, as I believe was agreed upon, to Brinsop, its destination (intended for a present to my niece your Aunt's God-daughter). Upon Elizabeth's enquiring after it when she was here last year, it struck me that I had observed some volumes of the said work when I was at Trinity Lodge, upon the little book case next [to] your Father's study door—in the Drawing room—and that the said volumes might be those in question. If I am not mistaken about such books being there, and without any other claimant, will you have the goodness to give them to Thos Hutchinson of St. John's for his Sister. Do you receive Richardson's Dictionary [1] regularly? We have got 15 numbers. I must not exhaust more of your Uncle's space. God bless you. M. Wordsworth.

[*W. W. writes*]

My dear Chris:

I wish I could leave you in the undisturbed possession of the pleasant feelings which the lively letter of your Aunt D. would naturally produce. She is indeed upon the whole in very much better bodily health than for a long time past—but she suffers not unfrequently a good deal of pain, but very much oftener

---

[1] *The New English Dictionary* was published in parts by Pickering from Jan. 1835 to Spring, 1837. The compiler was Charles Richardson (1775–1865).

what may be called uneasiness and discomfort. To this however we are reconciled, as her mind, tho' still very weak on some points, is far from being disturbed by fits of violence as it used to be. Pray keep your Aunt's letter, for if you had witnessed what we have done you would reckon it a great curiosity. Yet it would not have been sent at present if I had not had occasion to write to you upon a business of my own, in which, particularly if you are going to London this Easter Vacation, you might serve me.

Mr Longman writes to me that the Ex^n[1] is out of print (500 were published to be sold separately) and he proposes that as the Yarrow Re:[2] has been *stereotyped*, this should be done also with the Ex^n and the other 3 vols, of which not more than 180 are on hand. I have not replied to his letter, finding myself unable to determine from want of knowledge of particulars: because I am ignorant of the expence of stereotyping in the first instance, and of the rate at which any trifling alterations or corrections, for large ones are out of the question after that cost has been incurred, might be made. There is yet another objection. The proposed Ed: cannot be made uniform within and without, on account of there being so much less matter in the vol: Y. R. When it was proposed to me to stereotype this last, which *has* been done, I was led into a mistake, thinking the expressions were only laxly used, and that nothing more was meant by it than that the type should not be immediately broken up, but remain to supply the demand till after the 4 vols, were sold— when a new Ed. of the whole might be struck off. Under this mistaken impression, I did not give the subject half the consideration it was entitled to, and I am now hampered in the way I have told you, which becomes a serious matter—when the permanence of stereotype is to be decided upon. The Vol. of stereotyped Yarrow is of a type no larger than the last Ed: of the 4 vols. and extends to 324 pages besides 12 of Contents etc, so that thus far it would be uniform with the 4 vols. if reprinted as before—but then Yarrow contains only one sonnet on a page, and the other matter is somewhat in proportion, and this type is certainly smaller than I would have fixed upon, if I had previously had a thought of stereotyping the whole. If you have any temptation to run up to London during this Vacation, let

[1] *The Excursion.*
[2] *Yarrow Revisited.*

my embarrassment induce you to call at Longmans, and consult
with him as to what is best to be done. If it should be thought
justifiable to incur the stereotype expence for the whole, and
indeed whether so or not, I will forward a copy of the Ex^n to
you begging that you would be so kind as to look it carefully
over, both as to spelling and punctuation, and any improprieties
of style that would admit of being easily corrected—John
perhaps will also kindly help you in this labour—and then
forward it to Mr L. to be printed. As to my own feeling on the
subject in general I have only to add that, as the Yarrow has
already been stereotyped, and we are therefore, as has been
stated, in a difficulty out of which there appears to be no escape,
I am inclined to incur the expence of stereotyping the whole—if
it be judged prudent as it probably is or Messrs L. would not
have proposed it. The terms upon which I have published
hitherto are bearing 2 thirds of the profit. As Mr L. is silent on
the subject most likely he has no objection to the continuance of
those terms. But before I am bound in this permanent way, is it
not reasonable to ask what terms more advantageous could be
afforded me. On this point some other bookseller would of
course give a more disinterested opinion—Mr Moxon for
instance of Dover Street. I wrote to him on the subject some
little time ago,[1] but I fear my letter, which was sent thro' a
private hand, has not reached him. Much do I regret that we are
at such a distance from you and London, and that I have so many
reasons against my going from home of which a not inconsiderable one is expence. If the alteration in the Stamp duties be
carried into effect as proposed—my income will be so much
reduced that I must memorialize the Treasury who will I fear be
little inclined to attend either to me or any of my Brother-
Distributors on such an appeal. The transfer of the Registry
Office from Carlisle to London will alone take from me £70 a
year, and the reduction of the duties upon small conveyances
etc,—a regulation which I much approve—will, without
giving us an equivalent from increased duty upon large ones
(for these stamps are always got in London, unless you have
some interest to prevent it), probably lessen my income much
more. Then there are the Steam-boats which have put an end to
so many coaches—from which I, and in a still greater degree
William, were benefited.

---

[1] See L. 962 above.

I will conclude with the railways—but sufficient for the day is the evil thereof. The Treasury and the Whig head of the Board of Stamps,[1] tho' they know my politics well, are not personally ill-disposed to me, or I have reason to believe I should have been at present worse off than I am.

You have judged right about the Sockbridge freeholds. We could not sell anything in public, but 2 lots have since been very well disposed of, making together £140. The house has also been relet, but there is so much debt still upon the Estate, and John's mother, unfortunately married again, having so heavy a claim, the poor fellow is in sad spirits. I attended the sale[2] at Penrith, and did all I could to chear him.

I have lately seen a good deal of a schoolfellow of yours and a friend of Charles's—Mr Twisleton[3] who left the Assizes for the Lakes. He is very familiar with my Poems, and I hope has been benefited by them. He tempted me one evening in consequence of an observation which I had dropped upon Keble's style to illustrate my opinions upon poetic diction from his verses on baptism[4]—which Mr T. selected for the occasion, that piece being a favourite of his. I analysed it, and proved how vicious it was in diction—tho' the thoughts and feelings were quite suitable to the occasion. K. has been seduced into many faults by his immoderate admiration of the ancient Classics. A better service could scarcely be rendered to poetic literature than by shewing how far their style is entitled to studious imitation, and in what points owing to different laws of language and habits of thinking and feeling it cannot be copied without violation to nature and truth, and confusion and indistinctness in imagery.

Some verses of mine upon poor Charles Lamb may find their way to you—correct the line "He had a constant friend in Charity", and the following thus:

A Power that never ceased to abide in him
Charity mid a multitude etc.[5]

[1] For John Wood, see L. 986 above.
[2] On 9 Mar.
[3] See previous letter.
[4] From *The Christian Year*. The poem begins:

Where is it mothers learn their love?—
In every Church a fountain springs
O'er which the eternal Dove
Hovers on softest wings.

[5] See ll. 34—5.

"Tis well" read if you think it worth while, thus:

> 'Tis well, and tho' the record, in the strength
> And earnestness of feeling, overpassed
> Those narrow limits, and so missed its aim
> Yet will, I trust, upon the printed page
> Received, it there may keep a place unblamed. [1]

The verses were written in consequence of Miss L. expressing a wish for me to write her Brother's Epitaph. They will appear in Mr Talfourd's Memoirs prefixed to Lamb's Letters. Charles I understand from Mr T. is the candidate for Harrow. [2] He has our best wishes. Why has he not written to me since his marriage?

Your affectionate Uncle
W. W.

[*M. W. adds*]

Love from us all to your father and John, as well as yourself. God bless you. I cannot see to read over this crowded scrawl— so leave you to correct and make the best of it. Ever your affec. Aunt.

M. W.

990. W. W. to UNKNOWN CORRESPONDENT [3]

MS. Cornell. Hitherto unpublished.

[*c*. Apr. 1836]

My dear Sir,
    I hope you will not think that I am taking an unwarrantable liberty, when you hear what I have to say. You are a Cumbrian, have known the Bank of our beautiful Derwent from your Childhood, will you then assist in a project, which I have been the means of setting on foot for the benefit of one of the Towns upon the side of that stream, I mean Cockermouth. A new church is much wanted there, and efforts are making to that purpose. The inhabitants look towards me for help far beyond

---

[1] This was one of the alternative versions of ll. 47 ff. which was finally rejected. See *PW* iv. 274, *app. crit.*

[2] Charles Wordsworth, a Harrow man, had been mentioned as a possible successor to Kennedy, but he refused to enter the competition against his brother.   [3] Possibly Humphrey Senhouse of Netherhall.

what my little influence can do; yet I would do my utmost for I have the thing at heart, for reasons both general and particular. To you I need say no more; for I am sure you have a personal interest in the welfare of that neighbourhood: Some of your acquaintance who may have had pleasure from my Verses, may be inclined to repay their little debt of Gratitude by a kindness done to my birth place, and which had not a little to do with making me whatsoever of a Poet I may have grown up into. Contributions however small will be acceptable, the place being poor!

If you wish for particulars they are preparing and will be furnished. What at present seems most wanted is, a sum for authorizing an application to the building Societies.

most sincerely yours
W Wordsworth

991. W. W. to ELIZABETH PALMER PEABODY

Address: Miss Peabody, Boston, America. [*In Dora W.'s hand*]
Postmark: 30 May. *Stamp*: New York.
MS. Historical Society of Pennsylvania.
LY ii. 791.

Rydal Mount
7th April '36.

Dear Madam,

It is some time since I had the honour of receiving a Letter from you accompanying the Present of a Volume of your writing, The Records of a School.[1] For both these marks of your attention I beg to return you my sincere thanks, which ought to have been done sooner, and would have been so, but that I rarely write to any one. You may have perhaps heard that my eyes are subject to inflammations, which so curtail the little time I have for reading, that I have none almost for writing except what I am under the necessity of making. I cannot however omit thanking you both for the interesting Contents of your Volume, and for the account you are so obliging as to give me of the effects which some of my poems have produced upon the minds of young persons in your presence. Beyond

---

[1] See L. 937 above.

these acknowledgements I have nothing to add which would make my Letter more worthy of being wafted over the Atlantic, except the expression of my good wishes that your efforts for the benefit of the rising generation may be crowned with the success they so amply deserve.

Believe me to remain dear Madam with sincere admiration and respect

faithfully yours
Wm Wordsworth

P.S. Dr. Channing[1] lives, I believe, at Boston. Some time since I had a note from him announcing his intention of sending me, or his having sent me a Copy of a sermon of his recently published. If you be in communication with him will you be so kind as to express my thanks, adding that unfortunately I have not received his discourse.—

992. W. W. to JOSHUA WATSON

Address: Joshua Watson Esq^c, 6 Park St. [*In Dora W. 's hand*]
Endorsed: W. Wordsworth 10 Apl 1836 Cockerm° Ch.
MS. WL.
LY ii. 792.

Rydal Mount
10th April 1836

My dear Sir,

I enclose two Letters from Mr Wood[1] of Cockermouth. The 2nd is much more encouraging than the former had led me to expect.— I am particularly pleased with the subscription of the Indivi[d]ual of Papcastle,[2] as it was in no small degree with a

---

[1] For William Ellery Channing, see pt. i, L. 337. He had written again to W. W. on 19 Apr. 1835, paying tribute to Coleridge: 'Perhaps he has nowhere more enthusiastic friends and admirers than in this country, and among men of hostile sects. This is a proof that he is a teacher of universal truths. I hope he will find a biographer worthy of him, able to comprehend him, and just both to his excellences and *defects*. So much is known of him, that no record of him, but a faithful one, will obtain confidence. I am impatient to see his great philosophical work. His writings create a desire of something more from him to clear up what is obscure or carry out what is incomplete.' (*WL MSS.*)

[2] William Wood (see *MY* ii. 341), the attorney, now Law Agent to Lord Lonsdale.

[3] A village just outside Cockermouth on the north side of the Derwent, where the mills were situated.

view to the benefit of that place that I first pointed out Cocker-mouth as deserving your considering and that of the society.[1]—

I should be much obliged if you could furnish me with any Instructions towards answering the Queries in Mr Wood's first Letter, which I am almost ashamed to send you, it was so soiled in the pocket of a chaise-driver to whose care, for expeditions sake, it had been entrusted—

I shall be further obliged if you would circulate Mr Wood's Letter in any way which may seem likely to further the end we have in view. You will probably see the new Master of Harrow[2] very soon, pray shew it to him, or tell him of the Contents. I shall exert myself to the utmost among my Friends in all quarters.

Believe [me], my dear Sir
faithfully yours
Wm Wordsworth

[1] The Church Building Society.

[2] C. W. jnr. (see also L. 989 above), who left Cambridge to take up his new appointment on 18 Apr. In his letter to D. W. of 2 Apr. (*British Library MSS.*), he had set out at length his motives for resigning his Fellowship and his uncertainty of getting any preferment in the new situation created by the Ecclesiastical Commission. C. W. wrote on 17 Apr. that 'the superior temptations of Harrow in the way of emolument took him away', adding 'Chris's loss, you will easily believe, I shall feel very deeply . . . ', and the next day he wrote to Joshua Watson on the same theme: 'His public uses both to the College, and the University at large, were very great; and I do not know how they can be adequately supplied. Into this last office, the Public Oratorship, he would have thrown a grace and morale, which it has not been accustomed of late years to possess; which things alone, would have been of great value in these times more especially, when every thing is wanted to elevate the character of the Aristocracy, and to point out their importance to the public welfare.' (*WL MSS.*)

993. W. W. to WILLIAM WOOD[1]

Address: Wm Wood Esqre, Cockermouth.
MS. Harvard University Library.
LY ii. 793.

Rydal Mount
April 11th —36

Dear Sir,
  I am much obliged by your Letter reporting the proceedings of the Vestry-meeting for taking into consideration the desireableness of building a new Church or Chapel at Cockermouth. The Result of that meeting is exceedingly promising, and the mode of opening the business appears to me to have been very judicious. Till after next Wednesday I shall be a good deal engaged, but be assured that I will do all in my power to forward an affair, in which as you know I feel a strong interest, and that as speedily as possible.

I remain, dear Sir,
sincerely your obliged Serv^nt
Wm Wordsworth

994. W. W. and M. W. to SAMUEL and MARY STANIFORTH[2]

Address: S. Stanniforth Esqre, Liverpool.
MS. Mrs. Greenwood. Hitherto unpublished.

Rydal Mount
April 16th [1836]

My dear Sir
  Accept my sincere thanks for your obliging Letter received a few minutes since; and for all the particulars respecting Mr and Mrs Bolton and the family, we regret however that you did not mention Mrs Stanniforth. It gave me great pleasure to see your amiable son[3] at the meeting[4] who went through his part most

---

[1] See previous letter.

[2] Mrs. John Bolton's sister and brother-in-law (see pt. ii, L. 455).

[3] The Revd. Thomas Staniforth (1807–87), of Darnhall Hall, Yorks., and later (after Mrs. Bolton's death in 1848) of Storrs: rector of Bolton-by-Bolland, Yorks., 1831–59.

[4] On 13 Apr. W. W. had presided, in John Bolton's place, at the laying of

pleasingly. Knowing that Mr Graves[1] would write, I did not think it worth troubling Mr Bolton with a Letter, which would in many points have been only a repetition of what he would say. The stormy day was unlucky, but nevertheless the thing went off in a manner that gratified everyone, and not the less probably for their escape from the long speech I was disposed to inflict upon them; as you will have seen by the Wes. Gazette. It is correctly given except for one gross blunder—"the knowledge *within*" instead of, the knowledge *withers* and drops off. You would notice also in Mr Graves's beautiful Prayer *nature*, for *nurture*. As to the dinner I must say that it was excellent, and a meeting in which more kindly and sociable feeling prevailed could scarcely be seen. It was delightful to witness it, pray tell Mr and Mrs Bolton so *from me*. I know not how I should have got through the duty of chairman had I not been so admirably supported by the vice-president; and by Capt[n] Greaves,[2] who was the life of the company. To Sir Thomas Pasley also, I was much indebted.

You will excuse my saying more as I shall be occupied all day in writing Letters in aid of a Project I have been the means of setting on foot, the Erection of a new Church in my Native Town, Cockermouth, where one is much wanted. These are indeed, as you say, awful times; and the Church Establishment cannot stand unless exertions be made in every quarter where they are needed to support it.

Ever faithfully your obliged
W[m] Wordsworth

[*M. W. adds*]

My dear Mrs. Stanniforth, Mr W. has concluded his hurried letter in a characteristic manner and without adverting to your Husband's friendly enquiries after our Invalids. I have pleasure however in telling you, and dear Mrs B, that my sister is certainly better than she was last year—as we had proof

---

the foundation stone of the new school at Bowness, which Bolton was building entirely at his own expense. W.W.'s speech on the purpose and aims of education, a notable summary of the convictions of a lifetime, was published in the *Westmorland Gazette* for 16 Apr. and in *Mem.* ii. 195–204, and is reprinted with full discussion in *Prose Works*, iii. 291 ff.

[1] The Revd. R. P. Graves, curate of Windermere, who was in charge of the proceedings.

[2] Capt. Robert Greaves, of Ferney Green.

yesterday, upon her being taken into the garden; she was able to look about and enjoy all she saw—last summer she was unable to lift her head, the only time she was in the open air. Her memory too is come back to her—but her mind at times continues to be disturbed—her *bodily* health is good, and she is grown quite fat.—Dora too I am thankful to say is in many respects much better—tho' far from being well—but we encourage the hope that as the spring advances she may bear a little exercise in the open air, and that strength and health may be restored to her.—With affectionate regards to all my kind friends at Liverpool, and with best wishes that your sister may benefit by her visit to Leamington, and that we may see you all in comfortable health in the course of the summer at Storrs, believe me ever to be my dear Mrs Staniforth, your obliged

M. Wordsworth

995. W. W. to JAMES STANGER[1]

Address: James Stanger Esq[re], Lairthwaite, Keswick. [*In M. W.'s hand*]
MS. Cornell.
Mem. (—). K (—). LY ii. 788 (—).

Apr 16th [1836]

My Dear Sir,

Your obliging letter transmitted by Miss Southey, did not reach me, through an unusual neglect of the Carrier, till this morning—

The obstacle arising out of conflicting opinions in regard to the Patronage, one must be prepared for in every project of this kind. Mutual giving way is indispensable, and I hope it will not ultimately be wanting in this case.

The point *immediately* to be attended to is the raising a sufficient sum to ensure from the Church Building Society a portion of the surplus fund which they have at command, and which I know, on account of claims from many places, they are anxious to apply as speedily as possible. If time now be lost, that sum will be lost to Cockermouth.

In the question of the Patronage as between the people and the Bishop, I entirely concur with you in preferring the latter.

[1] The Keswick churchman and philanthropist. See L. 987 above.

Such is now the force of public opinion, that Bps are not likely to present upon merely selfish considerations, and if the judgment of one be not good, that of his Successor may make amends, and probably will. But elections of this sort, when vested in the people, have, as far as my experience goes, given rise to so many cabals and manœuvres, and caused such enmities and heart-burnings, that Christian charity has been driven out of sight by them. And how often and how soon have the successful party been seen to repent of their own choice!

The course of public affairs being what it is in respect to the Church, I cannot reconcile myself to delay from a hope of succeeding at another time.—If we can get a new church erected at Cockermouth, great will be the benefit, with the blessing of God, to that place; and our success cannot, I trust, but excite some neighbouring places to follow the example.

The little that I can do in my own Sphere shall be attempted immediately with especial view to ensure the coöperation of the societies. Happy should I be if you and other Gentlemen would immediately concur in this endeavour.

I remain my dear Sir,
with great respect sincerely yours
Wm Wordsworth

996. W. W. to THOMAS NOON TALFOURD

MS. WL.
LY ii. 793.

16th April [1836]

My dear Sir,

I wrote twice to Mr Moxon not long ago, through a sort of private channel and am not sure as I have not heard from him since that my last Letter has reached him. One of them contained corrections of the Verses upon Lamb, which I wished to be looked to when the Lines were printed in your Work.[1] They are as written down on the other leaf.[2]—

Have you any Friends, who out of joint attachment to the Church of England, to poetry, and to my attempts in that way, would assist in a Project of Building a Church, in my *native*

---

[1] *Letters of Charles Lamb.*
[2] The other leaf has been detached.

place Cockermouth. This Undertaking I was the means of originating, the good people who are any thing but rich depend upon my doing more towards it than my influence is equal to; but I will do my utmost having the thing much at heart. To you I need not say more.[1] No one needs to give his or her name (unless it be agreeable to do so), for publication of names of persons not locally connected might subject them to impertinent applications from other quarters.—

Messrs. Longman have proposed to me to stereotype my poems, and I think it will be done.

ever my dear Sir
affectionately yours
Wm Wordsworth

997. W. W. to H. C. R.

Address: H. C. Robinson Esq[re], Plowdens Build[ngs], Temple. [*In M. W.'s hand*]
Endorsed: April or May 1836, Wordsworth (Autograph).
MS. Dr. Williams's Library.
K (—). *Morley, i. 298.*

[mid-Apr. 1836][2]

My dear Friend

The Box has arrived a thousand thanks—but to whom was the packing entrusted, several of the Books, especially the new-bound Clarendon, have been a good deal disfigured for want of the precaution being taken of folding them up separately in paper, which ought *always* to be done. We fear you have robbed your own shelves—My little Library had long been disgraced by want of Gibbons decline a deficiency you have kindly supplied, and two Vols of my Clarendon had fallen into the Opium eaters hands—they were however I believe a present from him so I have not much reason to complain in this case. The Chiabrera[3] is a great acquisition—

---

[1] Talfourd replied on 27 Apr. (*WL MSS.*) that he was hoping to find subscribers, but 'Most of my friends who really love your writings are young men who have no money to spare, and the others do no associate your genius with the Church of England, being chiefly Dissenters from it.'

[2] This letter was received on 19 Apr. (*HCR* ii. 490): hence the dating.

[3] For Gabriello Chiabrera, see L. 940 above.

Have you Dissenter as you are, any Friends who would cooperate with a poor Poet, out of their love of his art and his attempts in it, and out of affection to the Church of England, in his endeavour to assist in building a new Church in his *native place* where it is much wanted.—Sums however small would be acceptable, and I the said Poet should be happy in being the medium of conveying them to the Committee, names mentioned or not—as agreeable—The people of C. are Poor, but we have some, and *even pretty good* hope of succeeding.—Pray do what you can for me, as they depend a good deal upon my exertions in their behalf.[1]

Dorina thanks you for the Rhine,[2] not inferior she thinks to the former Vol.

Tell Mr Courtenay to be so good as to look out for placing £2,500 for me which I shall have at command shortly.

ever faithfully yours.
[*unsigned*]

My arm aches with scrawling Letters this morning about my poor Church.

Our invalids pretty much as usual. My sister was out yesterday and wept abundantly at the sight of the Spring flowers.

[1] H. C. R.'s reaction was somewhat hostile: 'Your application to me to be a sort of *almoner* for your 'poor Church' troubles me—I see you take the matter to heart and I wish I could assist you—I cannot without exposing myself to something like ridicule or a serious charge of hypocrisy pretend to feel a personal interest in such a matter. And it so happens that in running over in my mind the names of those friends and acquaintances who are admirers, especial admirers of your writings I could not find above *three* who are attached to your Church—There are many whom I could ask to subscribe for a monument to you in any church, whom I could not ask to contribute to build a new church in the place of your birth.' (Morley, i. 299–300). Samuel Rogers's reply on 5 May (*WL MSS.*) to a similar application from W. W. was much more favourable: 'Though bred and born a heretick, my mother being a lineal descendant from a non-conformist whose life your Brother has circulated through the world, you may depend upon my doing my utmost for a church on such classick ground.'

[2] Possibly a sequel to Tombleson's *Views of the Rhine* (see pt. ii, L. 831); or another similar volume.

998. W. W. to EDWIN HILL HANDLEY [1]

Address: Edwin Hill Handley Esqre, Lower Wick, near Worcester. [*In M. W.'s Hand*]
Endorsed: 18 April 36, the poet Wm Wordsworth.
Stamp: Kendal Penny Post.
MS. Cornell.
Broughton, p. 73.

> Rydal Mount
> 18th April —36.

My dear Sir,

It is some time since I received a Letter from you, giving account how much you had been alarmed by the state of Mrs Handleys health after her confinement. As a letter in reply would have contained little more than expressions of sympathy and good wishes, for which I was sure you would give me credit I did not write; and I now address you upon something of a public occasion, and with less scruple because in your reply I shall have a report of Mrs H. yourself and my little Godson, how you all are—

Cockermouth is my native place. I have been the means of setting on foot a Project for building a new church there, where it is much wanted; and the Town, a poor one, depends more than, if they knew how little Influence I have they would be inclined to, on my endeavours to assist them.—To Cockermouth and its neighbouring scenes I owe much. They did not a little in making whatever of a Poet I may be. Now if, in the circle of your acquaintance you should know any persons, who, from united feelings of regard for the Church-establishment and gratitude to me for any pleasure my verses may have given them, would let me have a Contribution however small towards the good work, I should be well pleased and thankful—

You would rejoice in your Friend C's recent distinction and success. [2]

Believe [me] my dear Sir, with kind regards to Mrs H and a kiss to my Godchild,

> faithfully your's
> Wm Wordsworth

---

[1] See pt. ii, L. 569 and L. 976 above.
[2] C. W. jnr.'s appointment as headmaster of Harrow.

203

999. W. W. to THOMAS POOLE

Address: Thos. Poole Esqre, Nether Stowey, Somersetshire.
MS. untraced.
LY ii. 794.

Rydal Mount April 19th [1836]

My dear Mr Poole,

If I had been a money-maker instead of a verse-maker, though I often think of you as I trust you do of me, I should not have come a begging to you upon the occasion which has now tempted me, to take up the pen. I will be brief.

As far as concerns the Church of England, Cockermouth, my native place, is in a state of much spiritual destitution; nearly six thousand souls,[1] with only 300 sittings for the Poor, of which two thirds are taken-up by the children of two Sunday Schools. The place is poor, but increasing. I have been the means of setting on a foot the Project of erecting a new Church there; and the Inhabitants looked towards me for more, much more assistance than I can possibly afford them, through any influence which I possess. Nevertheless, I would gladly do my utmost, and therefore I have not scrupled to apply in many quarters, where I thought that I had friends, and even *Admirers* excuse the Word, who out of joint love for the Church and gratitude to me, for such pleasure as my verses might have given them, might be determined to give their beneficence a direction favorable to my wishes in this particular case.

Now, if there were any probability that any one of your wealthier acquaintances who had a trifle to spare would help me in this good work I should be truly thankful, having the thing much at heart. The time is not far distant, when unless great exertions are made, the same arguments of disproportion between church-men and non-church men which have been so ruinously applied to the Protestant Establishment in Ireland, will be brought to bear against the National Church of England. —Heaven forbid they should be successful. A 2nd Church is now building at Keswick,[2] one is just built at Kendal, another near Ambleside, and if we can succeed at Cockermouth, where there is a promising opening, we shall excite other Towns to follow our example.—I will leave the matter in your hands, knowing well how many claims so public spirited a man as yourself must

---

[1] See L. 980 above.

[2] See L. 984 above.

have upon both your time and your purse. A sum however small will be acceptable, name given or not, as agreeable.[1]

You were very kind in writing to me after your return to Somersetshire from the North. My family has been much afflicted since that time. We have lost dear Miss Hutchinson, my Wife's sister. At the time when she was taken from us, out of a family of eight, Servants included, four were confined to the Bed or the Sofa, and my poor Sister, one of them, expected to be called away every hour. She has survived almost miraculously, but she cannot walk, and scarcely can stand; my Daughter is a good deal better, but still a feeble Invalid. Mrs Southey's recovery is hopeless[2]—Southey and his Daughters bear up wonderfully. When are we likely to see you again among us? Your neighbourhood is very dear to me, the more so since poor Coleridge is gone.[3] If my daughter were strong enough to travel I certainly would visit you before the summer is flown. Farewell, Mrs Wordsworth, my Daughter and poor Sister unite in kindest remembrances. Ever yours,

W. Wordsworth

[1] In his reply of 13 Aug. (*WL MSS.*), Poole stated that he had approached his neighbour Sir Peregrine Acland, who had promised £20 for the new church. 'As for my *poor* self, I can only say . . . *I wish I were rich.* . . . However, as I have often had my Spirit carried out of the turmoil of the Hour by your "heavenly muse" —enjoying, apart, a better world—most ungrateful should I be, if I did not add my *mite* to promote any object you had at heart.' See also L. 1064 below.

[2] See Southey's letter to Joseph Cottle of 26 Feb. (Curry, ii. 441): '. . . her general state more resembles uneasy dreaming than any thing else.'

[3] In his reply Poole referred to the reminiscences of S. T. C. that were now appearing: 'Concerning all which has been done, and all which is doing by his *Friends* and *Friends to his Reputation*, I doubt not you know: but there is a party who from Vanity or still more worthless motives seem eager and proud to bring out all the little weaknesses existing among his extraordinary and admirable Faculties, which his too confiding Heart made manifest to them—as if a Man must be a Hero even to his valet de chambre!' The reference is probably to De Quincey's articles in *Tait's Magazine*, 1834–5 (see pt. ii, L. 844), and Thomas Allsop's more recent work (see above, L. 954).

1000. W. W. to JOHN GIBSON LOCKHART

Address: J. G. Lockhart, 24 Sussex Place, Regents Park. [*In Dora W.'s hand*]
MS. National Library of Scotland.
LY ii. 795.

> Rydal Mount
> April 27th—36.

My dear Sir,

Your Letter was duly received but I have hesitated about answering it on account of my intention to be in London in the course of a fortnight or so, when I could communicate in conversation all that I remember of your lamented Friend[1] at the period of our first acquaintance. In this I should be aided by a journal which my dear Sister kept of that interesting tour,[2] and which I would take with me. The notices there of Sir Walter are certainly not so copious as they would have been, had she anticipated what he was to become in the eyes of the world, but brief as they are they would, I am sure, interest you and Mrs Lockhart.

If anything should prevent my going to London, I will write again; I had totally forgotten that I wrote the Letter you allude to. His kindness to us claimed every sort of acknowledgment of looks, words, pen, and *actions* in grateful return, had they been in our power. Mrs W. my Sister and daughter, unite with me in cordial remembrances to yourself and Mrs Lockhart. Believe me, my dear Sir,

> faithfully yours,
> Wm Wordsworth

[1] Lockhart was now collecting materials for his *Memoirs of the Life of Sir Walter Scott, Bart.*, 7 vols., 1837–8.

[2] *Recollections of a Tour Made in Scotland* (1803). For their meetings with Scott see *DWJ* i. 387–406. The account in Lockhart's *Memoirs*, i. 403 ff. was drawn up after he met W. W. in London on 16 May and had heard the poet's recollections and extracts from D. W.'s journal.

1001. W. W. to H. C. R.

Address: H. C. Robinson Esqr, 2. Plowdens buildings, Temple. [*In Dora W.'s hand*]
Postmark: 2 May 1836. *Stamp*: Southampton Ct.
Endorsed: 27 April 1836. W: Wordsworth.
MS. Dr. Williams's Library.
K (—). *Morley, i. 301.*

Wednesday
27th April—[1836]

My dear Friend,

Offended! what could you be dreaming about![1]—I write now to tell you that I hope to be in London before three weeks are over at the latest; and yet circumstanced as we are all my hopes are but reflections from a troubling surface.

A thousand thanks for your Letter. My intention is to be on first going to town at my Friend Mr Watson's—6 Park street, for many reasons, and not the least that I shall then have an opportunity of meeting my Brother[2]—Pray thank Mr Courtenay for his Letter—all my money shall be at his disposal as soon as I can get it. He is one of the kindest of men, and has what neither you or I have, a genius for money-making.—

Could you contrive to let Longman know that I mean to be in town?—they must have been looking for a Letter from me; which they would have received three weeks ago, but that my man James forgot to post it; he has the worst recollection of any creature living.

If you see Landor, thank him for Pericles and Aspasia,[3] but

---

[1] See L. 997 above.

[2] W. W. would particularly want to discuss with C. W. the problem of the patronage of the proposed new church in Cockermouth, which he had already raised with James Stanger (see L. 995 above) and which C. W. had taken up in his letter of 23 Apr.: 'The matter of the Patronage is certainly a very important one. I am decidedly of the opinion that in all cases it ought to rest either in the Patron of the *Mother* Church (which, I suppose, in the instance of anything at Cockermouth would be Lord Lonsdale), or of the Incumbent of the entire parish (*your* Son John), or of the Bishop, if they please—but on no account, in any thing like popular election. To this last species, I have never given a sixpence, willingly and knowingly, and never will do so.' (*WL MSS.*) As will become clear from later letters, the Cockermouth scheme foundered because the question of the patronage could not be settled to the satisfaction of all parties, particularly the Evangelicals. See Ls. 1076, 1113, and 1116 below.

[3] Landor had now separated from his family and returned to England after an absence of more than twenty years. In Mar. 1836 he published *Pericles and*

207

tell him to leave the Church alone. He has lived too long in Italy to know how the Church of England is now working, and what it stands in need of.—

Our Invalids are much at one, my sister in rather a better way.

Pray remember me to Moxon and tell him that a Letter for him also was in the Cover which James forgot to post.—I shall see M— immediately upon my reaching Town, if I am able to go.

farewell
Most affectionately your
W.W.

[*Dora W. adds*]

This letter is all 'tell'—'tell'—'tell', but one important question is now to be asked? Will you embark with Father for any part of the Continent where travelling wont be more fatiguing than a man in his 67th year with 'all diseases that the spittals know' (in his fancy at least) ought to undertake—A thousand thanks from Dorina for y[r] beautiful gift[1] wh she thinks equals the 1st Vol in interest.

1002. W. W. to JOSHUA WATSON

Address: Joshua Watson Esq[e], 6 Part St. Westminster.
Postmark: 30 Apr. 1836.
Endorsed: W. Wordsworth Esq. 27 Apr. 1836 Visit etc.
MS. Mr. Jonathan Wordsworth.
Edward Churton, Memoir of Joshua Watson (—).

[*In Dora W.'s hand*]

Rydal Mount
April 27th 36

My dear Sir,

Remembering your kind invitation I venture to ask whether you could receive me at your house for a few days towards the close of the 2[d] week in May. I have had several invitations from other friends but prefer being with you at first should it suit

---

Aspasia, and the following month his *Letters of a Conservative*, in which he attacked the abuses of the Church Establishment. W. W. was to see a good deal of him in London the following month.

[1] See L. 997 above.

you—my intention was to have taken Cambridge in my way but a letter from the Master tells me that he will not be there. I ordered a West^d Gazette to be forwarded to you—in my address[1] therein contained the Printer has made several mistakes and one gross blunder 'the knowledge *within* drops off'—for *withers and* drops off—the conversations I have had with you on the subject of education tempted me to take the opportunity of making public some of my opinions on that subject w^h I am pleased to hear have met with good acceptance in this quarter, so much so that I have been requested to reprint the address, which I think of doing with a few corrections and additions.

With kindest regards from all here to yourself and Miss Watson

I remain my dear Sir
most faithfully yours
[*signed*] Wm Wordsworth

The forgotten Shawl-Plaid[2] shall be my Companion; and will prove useful if I take the outside: 'No—No'—say the Ladies here, 'it shall be packed up for fear you leave it behind also, and in a less romantic, not to say less honest, place.'—

1003. W. W. to JAMES SPEDDING[3]

MS. untraced.
T. J. Wise, Two Lake Poets. A Catalogue of Printed Books, Manuscripts, and Autograph Letters by W. W. and S. T. C., 1927, p. 28. LY ii. 796.

[Rydal Mount 28th April 1836]

. . . The Monody upon C. Lamb was given to my friend Serjeaunt Talfourd, Lamb's Ex^r, to be published with his Life,

---

[1] At the laying of the foundation stone of the new school at Bowness. See L. 994 above.

[2] Left behind when the Watsons visited Rydal Mount the previous summer.

[3] James Spedding (1808–81), third son of John Spedding of Mirehouse, intimate friend of Henry Taylor and Tennyson, and one of the original Cambridge 'Apostles', had first met W. W. in Dec. 1830 while he was an undergraduate at Trinity (see pt. ii, L. 582), along with J. W. Blakeley, Henry Alford and William Henry Brookfield. In 1835 he had been appointed to a temporary post at the Colonial Office, but he gave it up in 1841 in order to

Letters, etc. Moxon, with my permission, struck off a few copies for private circulation, one of which for yourself and another for Mr Taylor, if he wishes for it, it would give me great pleasure you should have.

1004. W. W. to EDWARD MOXON

Address: Edward Moxon Esqre, 44 Dover Street. [*In M. W.'s hand*]
MS. *Amherst College Library.*
LY ii. 797.

Rydal Mount 28th [April[1] 1836]
My dear Sir,
    The Bearer is Mr Spedding a particular friend of mine, and a man of first rate talents. (He is of the Colonial Off^e). Let him have two copies of my verses on Lamb, one for himself and one for Mr Taylor.[2]

devote the rest of his life to the study of Bacon, publishing the *Works*, 7 vols., 1857−9, and the *Letters and Life*, 7 vols., 1861−74. In 1847, when James Stephen retired from the Under-Secretaryship of the Colonies, Spedding was offered the post, but declined it; he also decline to succeed Charles Kingsley in the Chair of Modern History at Cambridge.

    [1] *Written* May: but the letter clearly belongs to April, before W. W. set out for London, and it was probably enclosed in the previous letter to James Spedding.
    [2] In a letter to I. F. of 24 May, Henry Taylor describes two parties he gave for W. W. on his arrival in London: 'I have given two breakfasts to Wordsworth, at one of which he was as brilliant as I have ever seen him, having the advantage of Charles Austin to elicit him. A more animated and vigorous conversation than they made of it between them I have never listened to. Edward Villiers, Spedding, Ferguson, and Carlyle were the others of the party, and made a good audience, but even Carlyle was little else than an auditor. The other breakfast was not so successful, for Charles Austin was not there, and no one else being bold enough to address themselves directly to Wordsworth across the table, I could not get the conversation generalised, and he gave himself to his neighbour. Moreover I committed the mistake of asking Rogers, which made two suns in one system . . . for Rogers's position does not admit of people treating him as a listener, and, as he cannot keep pace with Wordsworth, he must necessarily break a party into two conversations.' (*Correspondence of Henry Taylor*, p. 72.) Carlyle had already met W. W. the previous year at Henry Taylor's, but was not impressed with him: 'A genuine kind of man, but intrinsically and extrinsically a *small* one, let them sing or say what they will.' (James Anthony Froude, *Thomas Carlyle, A History of his Life in London, 1834−1881*, 2 vols., 1884, i. 31.)

I hope to be in Town in the course of three weeks at the latest. My first place of abode will be Park Street West[r], but I have not forgotten your most friendly invitation. I shall call on you the day after my arrival, wishing very much to talk with you about the intended stereotype of my Poems.

farewell
in great haste
affectionately yours
Wm Wordsworth

1005. W. W. to SIR GEORGE BEAUMONT

MS. Mr. W. Hugh Peal. Hitherto unpublished.

Rydal Mount
Ambleside
30 April [? 1836][1]

My dear Sir George,

On the 10th of May I mean to quit home for London, and should much like to take Coleorton in my way. I am called to Town by business, and one day for Liverpool, and one for Coleorton is all I can spare.—If you should not be likely to be at Coleorton on the 12th or 13th (and pray let me know) I should defer my visit till some more favorable opportunity.

Are Mr and Mrs Merewether likely to be found at home, at that time.

I hope that yourself and your little ones are well.—

Believe me my dear Sir George
faithfully yours
W[m] Wordsworth

[1] This letter seems most likely to belong to 1836. It was clearly written *after* the birth of Sir George's two children, and most probably after the death of Lady Beaumont, Dr. Howley's daughter, in 1834.

1006. W. W. to JOHN WORDSWORTH[1]

Address: John Wordsworth Esq, Keswick.
MS. WL.
LY ii. 798 (—).

[late Apr. 1836]

My dear John,

Business of different kinds makes it very advisable that I should go to London, before a fortnight is over.—Could not you contrive to despatch your business so that we might be Fellow travellers? I see Lectures are going to begin at King's Coll. At all events come over here, either at or before the end of the week; for I am anxious to bring our affairs to a settlement. Mr Courtenay is going soon on the Continent for 4 months, and he is my fac-totum in money matters, and I wish to have what is owing to your Aunt and me placed under his management, which has hitherto proved so advantageous.

We expect your cousin John in a day or two. Pray forward the enclosed to Mr Wood—

ever faithfully your affectionate Uncle
Wm Wordsworth

Invalids pretty much as usual.

Bring any papers with you which you think would be serviceable.

1007. W. W. to JOSHUA WATSON

Address: Joshua Watson Esq[re], 6 Park Street, Westminster, London.
Postmark: 7 May 1836. *Stamp*: Kendal Penny Post.
Endorsed: Wm Wordsworth Esq. 5 May 1836.
MS. WL.
LY ii. 797.

[*In M. W.'s hand*]

Rydal M[t]. May 5th [1836]

My dear Sir

My present intention is to profit by your hospitality on Tuesday night next, if I can find a place *in* or *out* of the Coach which quits Manchester at 5 oc in the morning and reaches London at 11 in the night—this will allow me to knock at your

---

[1] R. W.'s son, now a medical student in London.

door before twelve. I have therefore to beg you to be so good as to direct one of your Servants to sit up for me till that hour, as I have a particular objection to sleep at a London Coach Inn.

I much regret, along with you and Miss Watson, that neither my Wife, Daughter nor my poor Sister can accompany me— the Invalids not being in travelling condition, and Mrs W. of course unable to leave them. The Vicar of Brigham[1] is here at present, and will deliver a letter from me to Mr Wood tomorrow, in which I shall state your apprehensions,—and beg of him to forward under cover to you at the Society, every particular which may tend to enable us to get over that obstacle. This I know that Mr Fawcett the Minister of Cockermouth, admitted, that inclusive of the villages of Papcastle and the Goat, the population was now little less than 6000—and Mr Wood told my Son that there was a probability of a considerable increase in a short time. Land close to the Town which I myself sold as Exr: to my eldest Br. 20 years ago,[2] at less than a £100 an acre, has been resold—(a £1000 worth of it) at the rate of £1200 to build upon.

If I am disappointed of a place in *that* Coach at Manchester— you will see me I trust, in the course of the next day. But pray do not let either you or Miss W. derange any of your plans on my account, because, to use your own words, I shall regard your house as an Hotel till I have the pleasure of seeing the Host and Hostess.

You will be surprized when I tell you that the Chancellor of the Ex[r]:[3]—out of compliment to the Poet, and love of the Est[t]: has subscribed £10 to our embryo Church. 'What will they say of this at Cockermouth?'

With our united kindest regards from all here, I remain my d[r] Sir

very faithfully yours
[signed] Wm Wordsworth

[1] John W.
[2] See *MY* ii. 317.
[3] Thomas Spring Rice.

1008. W. W. to HIS FAMILY

MS. WL. Hitherto unpublished.

Wednesday Noon[1] [11 May 1836]

My dearest Friends,

Did not reach London till between one and two.—I hear my Brother's voice—he is come in, well. We were two hours later than our time, in consequence of a horse dropping down dead—and the tire of a wheel flying off, near Northampton. In other respects our journey was quite pleasant, except that being so late I was obliged to sleep at the coach Inn: breakfasted here. I will write again tomorrow if possible, I feel very well, only a little heated in the eyes—

I have had most anxiety about you all—Miss Watson is quite well—Mr W. has a cold—be particular about your health.

ever yours W. W.

1009. W. W. to HIS FAMILY

Address: Mrs Wordsworth, Rydal, Kendal [*readdressed to*] Rectory, Workington. [*readdressed to*] W. Wordsworth Esqre, Castle Street, Carlisle.[2]
Franked: London May fourteen 1836. Lonsdale.
Postmark: 14 May 1836. *Stamp*: Kendal Penny Post.
MS. WL. Hitherto unpublished.

Friday Morn [13 May 1836]

My dearest Friends,

Yesterday I called at Col: Off: saw Spedding, Taylor, and Mr Stephen.[3] Mr S— without my introducing the subject offered me 50£ for C.[4] Church; and kindly undertook upon my casual

---

[1] W. W. had now arrived at Joshua Watson's house in Park Street, Westminster, having travelled down in the company of his nephew 'Keswick John', whose affairs had now to be wound up on his coming of age. While in London, W. W. was also hoping to arrange terms for a new edition of his poems, and to bring to a successful conclusion the negotiations of the previous year to transfer his Distributorship to Willy W.

[2] M. W. sent this letter, with a covering note, to Isabella W., who in turn forwarded it to Willy W.

[3] James Stephen.

[4] Cockermouth.

allusion to the subject, to present to Mr S. Rice, [1] my Statement about the Stamp Off: so in the course of this day I should put it upon paper. He must be an excellent man, nothing could be so cordial and kind as his manner. H. Taylor is not satisfied with Moxon's dealing with him and is gone to Longmans, so I must treat even him as a Tradesman. Except my interviews at the Col: Off: yesterday, I did nothing being thrown out of my beat by Mrs Lawrence [2] who the day before earnestly begged me to call, leaving me the choice of Time till three. At two I called and she was not at home. She had offered to take me any way in her carriage, and I had thought of Chantreys: it was then too late in the day for the Archbishops and for Courtenay etc etc.—So I went to the Nat. Gallery, and dined here, having called both on Rogers and Lord Lowther—neither at home. The engagements of to day will not allow me to see Moxon, I dine at Lord Lonsdales, tomorrow go to Harrow, but it is of no use to tell you what I mean to do. Yesterday Quill: [3] called with note but I cant answer it, he not having given me his address. To day I shall see Landor and H. Robinson [4] who called yesterday. Mr Merewether breakfasts here this morning—Nothing yet has occurred to give me much pleasure except Mr Watson's interest in William and a hope from Mr Stephen's extreme kindness yesterday, that when I mention his case to him, I may interest him about the poor fellow. I have not yet seen Rogers who with his Sister called yesterday. I have called on him several times. I hope to add a few words before I close this Letter—

[unsigned]

[1] Thomas Spring Rice, the Chancellor of the Exchequer.

[2] Probably Mrs Rose Lawrence (see pt. ii, L. 685).

[3] E. Q. had now returned to London from Portugal.

[4] 'I had at breakfast Landor and Kenyon, and before twelve o'clock there came Wordsworth and his nephew and we had an agreeable chat till past two. Wordsworth and Landor agree on poetry better than on other matters, and where Wordsworth finds conformity in this he will be tolerant even of religious and political differences.' (*HCR* ii. 492.)

1010. W. W. to THOMAS NOON TALFOURD

Address: Mr Sergeant Talfourd. [*delivered by hand*]
MS. Cornell. Hitherto unpublished.

I am at 6 Park Street
Westminster
[*c.* 13 May 1836][1]

My dear Sir,

Many thanks for your very kind invitation, which I hope to profit by, before I quit London. I should have called upon you, but I have been run off my legs by business, since I arrived. I write at M[r] Moxons in the presence of Mr Rogers, at 11 at night, M[r] R. begs me to say that he shall be honored if you would breakfast with him the Sunday after next, Whitsunday. I shall have the pleasure of meeting you.[2] I am told you are so much engaged that it would be useless to call on you—is it so?

faithfully yours
W Wordsworth

[1] This letter was written shortly after 11 May, when W. W. arrived in London (see L. 1008 above), and rather more than a week before Whitsunday, which fell this year on 22 May.

[2] W. W. seems to have met Talfourd first at H. C. R.'s on the 16th, when, with Landor, they went to view the Elgin Marbles. W. W. and Landor dined with Talfourd on the 26th, before going on to the first performance of *Ion* at Covent Garden, with Macready in the title tole (*HCR* ii. 493−4); and at the supper-party which followed W. W. met Robert Browning (1812−89), who had published *Paracelsus* the previous year, Mary Russell Mitford (1787− 1855), Clarkson Stanfield, R. A. (1793− 1867), John Lucas (1807−74), who had just completed his portrait of Talfourd (see opposite p. 321), and many others, and renewed his acquaintance with Procter and Milman. (See A. G. L'Estrange, *The Life of Mary Russell Mitford*, 3 vols., 1870, iii. 44−5; *Macready's Reminiscences, and Selections from his Diaries and Letters*, ed. Sir Frederick Pollock, 2 vols., 1875, ii. 31−3.)

1011. W. W. to JOHN KENYON

MS. New York University Library. Hitherto unpublished.

Saturday morn: [14 May 1836][1]
6 Park Street
West.

My dear Mr Kenyon,
Without spectacles and with rather dim eyes I ran over your note at Lord Lonsdale's Door.[2] I gave a verbal message to your Servant, but to prevent mistakes I write to say that I shall be with you at 7 Thursday precisely. On Wednesday I dine with Courtenay. In my hurry for I was late, I overlooked the enclosed.

ever affectionately yours,
W. W.

1012. W. W. to JOHN WORDSWORTH[3]

Address: John Wordsworth Esq., 28 Great Ormond Street.
MS. WL.
LY ii. 800.

[mid–May 1836]

My dear John
I have unfortunately mislaid your letter, with Mrs Smith's[4] address, and know not where to call on her.
You will do right to call on Miss Rogers,[5] or upon any person at whose house you have been received.

---

[1] Dated by reference to *HCR* ii. 494, which records the dinner at Kenyon's on Thursday, 19 May. Landor and William Harness (see L. 1013 below) were also guests.

[2] Lord Lonsdale's town house was at 12 Charles Street, Berkeley Square.

[3] R. W.'s son.

[4] W. W.'s cousin, Mary Proctor Smith (see pt. ii, L. 455). She had visited Rydal Mount in June 1834 (*RMVB*).

[5] W. W. (possibly accompanied by his nephew) was at a party at Miss Rogers's on 16 May, where he met Milman and Sydney Smith (see *HCR* ii. 493). 'I never saw Wordsworth look so well, so *reverend*,' Sydney Smith recalled. 'And yet one fancies a poet should be always young.'

217

Mid— May 1836

I hope to call on you in a day or two.

Your affectionate Uncle
W. Wordsworth

I am sadly hurried.

1013. W. W. to WILLIAM HARNESS[1]

Address: Revd W. Harness, 19 Heathcote Street, Mecklenburg Sq.
Postmark: 16 May 1836.
MS. Cornell. Hitherto unpublished.

Park Street
11 Monday Morn. [16 May 1836]

My dear Sir,

How sorry I was to hear of your 2nd accident. As I shall have the pleasure of meeting you at Mr Kenyon's on Thursday, you will excuse the brevity of this note, which is merely to assure you that I am with great regard,

sincerely yours
W. Wordsworth

[1] The Revd. William Harness (1790— 1869), Byron's friend, and editor of Shakespeare (8 vols., 1825, etc.), Massinger (1830) and Ford (1831): incumbent of Regent Square Chapel, 1826—44, and perpetual curate of All Saints', Knightsbridge, from 1849. He had called on W. W. at Rydal the previous August (*R MVB*), with an introduction from Alexander Dyce, who emphasized that Harness was not 'one of those wandering bores who haunt your country during the fine weather' (*Dyce MSS., Victoria and Albert Museum*). W. W. dined with him on the 27th in the company of Mary Russell Mitford, Alexander Dyce, Henry Hope of Deepdene, Henry Chorley the musicologist, and others. (*Life of Mary Russell Mitford*, iii, 46.)

1014. W. W. to HIS FAMILY

Address: Mrs Wordsworth, Rydal, Kendal.
Franked: London May sixteen 1836. W. E. Gladstone. [1]
Postmark: 16 May 1836.
MS. WL. Hitherto unpublished.

[16 May 1836]

My dearest Friends,

I cannot get a pen to make a stroke. Two times tried to no account. Thanks for your joint letter. Best news I have is, that Mr Stephens [2] tells me Mr Spring Rice would not hurt a hair of my head. Tell this to J. C. [3] This morning I breakfasted with Mr Gladstone and saw H. Taylor and I have been putting the Stamp off. Statement in official form for S— Rice, who told Mr Stephen he should wish to see me. Yesterday breakfasted with H. C. R. met Landor who wrote the lines in D's album, [4] then

---

[1] William Ewart Gladstone (1809—98), the celebrated statesman, had visited Rydal Mount as a boy from the family home near Liverpool, where his father and W. W. had met at John Bolton's table; and subsequently Charles Wordsworth became his private tutor at Christ Church, 1830—1, and introduced him to W. W.'s poems. Gladstone was now M.P. for Newark and living in the Albany, and through his friendship with the circle of Henry Taylor and Spedding, he got to know W. W. well during this visit to London. They seem to have met on at least seven occasions, either at breakfast or dinner-parties. Gladstone introduced W. W. to Sir Francis Doyle (1810—88), later Professor of Poetry at Oxford, and Lord Mahon (see L. 1047 below), the historian, who had called at Rydal Mount in Sept. 1832 (*RMVB*); and W. W. renewed his acquaintance with Monckton Milnes, J. W. Blakesley, and Henry Hallam. Talfourd was their fellow guest on several occasions when the Copyright Question came up for discussion; and Gladstone also records W. W.'s thinking about the consequences of the Reform Bill, which 'had, as it were, brought out too prominently a particular muscle of the national frame: the strength of the towns; that the cure was to be found in a large further enfranchisement, I fancy, of the country chiefly; that you would thus extend the base of your pyramid and so give it strength . . . He thought the political franchise upon the whole a good to the mass—regard being had to the state of human nature; against me.' (See John Morley, *The Life of William Ewart Gladstone*, 3 vols., 1903, i. 135—7; *The Gladstone Diaries*, ed. M. D. R. Foot, vol. ii (1968), pp. 239—46.) Gladstone's final assessment of W. W., in a penetrating discussion of *Mem.*, appeared in *The Scottish Ecclesiastical Journal* for July, 1851.

[2] i.e. James Stephen.

[3] John Carter, W. W.'s clerk.

[4] See pt. ii, L. 705.

went to Rogers who took John[1] and me in his Carriage to his Sisters where we lunched, saw Eclipse, and went to Zoological Garden;[2] in the evening went to Sergeant Merewether's,[3] having first sat half an hour with Mrs Johnstone,[4] [who] sent you a message, dearest Mary. At the Sergeants, saw Mr and Mrs Merewether. On Sat: was at Harrow, Chris:[5] in high Spirits. Saw there the Hoares with whom Dr Wordsworth went back meaning to go on that day to Winchester. On Friday dined at Lord Lonsdales—met Rogers—was over done that day and slept ill . . .

[*cetera desunt*]

1015. W. W. to JANE MARSHALL

MS. Trinity College, Cambridge. Hitherto unpublished.

[20 May 1836]

Dear Mrs Marshall,

We of this family[6] dine today at Greenwich at six oclock; I much regret, therefore, that we must be gone before you call. In answer to Miss Marshall's[7] note, I have to thank her sincerely for her offer to take me to Harrow; but I *cannot* undo the engagement with my nephew any farther than to lengthen the morning to half past 4 or $\frac{1}{4}$ before five at the utmost, as he must be back to Harrow by eight. Mr Henry Coleridge is also to be here, and him I have not yet seen. I was not aware of the *length* of a London *morning* which I now find extends to $7\frac{1}{2}$ P.M.—

[1] R. W.'s son.

[2] In Regent's Park: laid out in 1827 by Decimus Burton, who added the Giraffe House this year.

[3] Henry Alworth Merewether (1780–1864), Francis Merewether's elder brother, was a Serjeant-at-law and Recorder of Reading. He was Town Clerk of London, 1842–59, and joint author of *The History of the Boroughs and Municipal Corporations of the United Kingdom*, 3 vols., 1835.

[4] Wife of the Revd. William Johnson (see pt. i, L. 1 and L. 872 above).

[5] i.e. C. W. jnr.

[6] i.e. Joshua Watson and his daughter.

[7] Mary Anne Marshall.

I am sorry for this awkward mistake, but hope that the postponed arrangement may not be wholly objectionable.

ever faithfully yours

Wm Wordsworth

[*In M. W.'s hand*]

A Birch of elegant and graceful form,
By Zephers loved and spared by every storm,
Lost, as it stood where Rotha murmurs by
Its health, its beauty; and I'll tell you why:
An active, staunch, scholastic Teacher came
To be its neighbour, one well known to fame.
The affrighted Tree, prophetic of a fate
At once both savage and indelicate
Sickened at Rugby's Lord, nor could abide
The thought of such disgrace, it droop'd and died.

[*W. W. adds*]

Another reading of the above important lines.[1]

1016. W. W. to HIS FAMILY

MS. WL. Hitherto unpublished.

[? 20 May 1836]

. . . Egremont,[2] and with that view I put into Lord Lonsdale's hand a Copy of Mr Woods Letter and of the Subscriptions.—I assure [you] I am busy from morning to night. Yesterday I talked over the new edition with Moxon at Mr Kenyons and I only wait for Rees[3] proposals to decide. My right eye continues a good deal distressed, the Sun is so glaring, and I fear I shall not be able to fill this sheet for want of time, as we dine at Dr Burneys[4] at Greenwich, Mr and Miss Watson also.—

---

[1] It is clear from L. 1073 below that this epigram on a birch tree in the grounds of Fox How was composed by the Revd. Charles Townsend (see next letter).

[2] The first part of this letter is missing. The reference appears to be to Lord Egremont, whose support was needed for the proposed new church in Cockermouth.

[3] Owen Rees (1770–1837), partner with Longman since 1794.

[4] The Revd. Charles Parr Burney, D. D. (b. 1786), ran a school in Greenwich, and was later Archdeacon of St. Albans and rector of Sible

Mr Gardner[1] called this morning—he gives an account which is hopeful of John—of whom I see a great deal. He will also supply me with a mild before dinner pill which he says will be beneficial as long as I can [?][2] and masticate. The Pills I had of Johnson[3] have done their duty abundantly. So I hope to go on well.

How I long to hear again how you are! pray send Mr Carr's account of Dora, and also John Carter's of the money arrangements, and also the earliest day when the Quarterly account can reach London for me to sign it. I am quite glad of the quiet evening before Mrs Marshall is to call here at 1/4 before six to settle about an engagement for to morrow, but I shall miss her: I see scores of people that are introduced to me but dont remember the names of one in ten. Crabbe[4] fell asleep last night at Kenyons table—he sate with his mouth open, as wide as the Lions when I have seen them roaring, but neither screamed nor snored. We[5] talk of a trip on the Continent together, but alas I feel the uncertainty of every thing. O that there was a railway to take me to Kendal or Lancaster or Preston, and then I should think of this scheme with pleasure, but to be so long absent from you all distresses me above measure.

Mr Townsend[6] says that Mrs Tillbrook[7] is well left. Till—had saved a good deal of money. Miss Watson has just come in, I placed the two medallions[8] before her, she scarcely recognized them. This moment Mr Wilkin has sent me half a dozen of his

Hedingham, Essex. He had called at Rydal Mount in the summer of 1832 (*RMVB*).

[1] John Gardner, to whom R. W.'s son John had been indentured.

[2] *MS. obscure.*

[3] Unidentified.

[4] The poet's son (see pt. ii, L. 810).

[5] i.e. W. W. and H. C. R.

[6] The Revd. Charles Townsend (1789—1870) a friend of J. C. Hare, H. J. Rose, Tillbrooke, and the Aylings, was curate of Preston with Hove, 1825—37, and thereafter rector of Kingston-by-the-Sea, Sussex. W. W. had corresponded with him over a number of years about his poems (*WL MSS.*), and he had recently succeeded in publishing *Winchester, and a few other compositions in prose and verse,* Winchester, (privately printed), 1835. See also L. 1073 below.

[7] See pt. ii, L. 639. Samuel Tillbrooke had died the previous year.

[8] Wyon's medallion portraits of W. W., and Southey, taken the previous summer (see L. 930 above), were to be exhibited at the Royal Academy. See also L. 1019 below.

Portraits.[1] Miss W. has kindly accepted one. She seemed pleased with the likeness—I must bid you good bye, ever and ever most affectionately your

W W.

Kindest remembrances to all the family.—

1017. W. W. to HIS FAMILY

MS. WL. Hitherto unpublished.

Sunday Morn: [? 22 May 1836]
Rogers's.

My Dearest Friends,

Here I have been breakfasting, the party—H. Taylor, Sergeant Talfourd, Mr Townsend,[2] Mr Empson[3]—I write by snatches. Yesterday I was with Mrs Marshall, her daughters, the Miss Rices,[4] Lord Northampton[5] etc at the Dulwich Gallery,[6] did not get home till after six, when I had a glimpse of Christopher[7] at dinner. Henry Coleridge was there and stayed the Evening—A note from Longman has vexed me; instead of sending the statement as he had promised; this note tells me that

[1] The lithograph of Wilkin's portrait of W. W. (see pt. ii, L. 639).

[2] The Revd. Charles Townsend.

[3] H. C. R.'s friend William Empson (1791–1852), Professor of 'general polity and the laws of England' at Haileybury from 1824, and a regular contributor to the *Edinburgh Review*, of which he became editor in 1847 on the death of Macvey Napier. He married Jeffrey's only daughter. W. W. had know him since at least 1832, when he called at Rydal Mount (*RMVB*).

[4] Thomas Spring Rice had three daughters: Mary (see pt. ii, L. 743); Catherine (1813–53), who married John Marshall's fourth son Henry Cowper Marshall (1808–84), of Derwent Island, in 1837; and Theodosia (1819–91), who married Sir Henry Taylor in 1839.

[5] Spencer Compton, 2nd Marquess of Northampton (1790–1851), of Castle Ashby, nr. Northampton, politician and patron of the arts: M.P. for Northampton, 1812–20; President of the Royal Society, 1838–49, and Trustee of the National Gallery and the British Museum. He called at Rydal Mount in the summer of 1838 (*RMVB*).

[6] The Dulwich College Art Gallery was built by Sir John Soane (1753–1837) between 1811 and 1814 to house the paintings inherited by Sir Francis Bourgeois from the art dealer Noel Desenfans, together with the collection of Edward Alleyn, founder of the College.

[7] C. W. jnr.

Mr Rees,[1] having gone out of Town for ten days, it cannot be sent, and begs that at the end of that time I would call. What are we now proceeding? I am very anxious to have the business settled. Chris: goes on the Continent but he cannot start till end of July.

Monday, 5 oclock afternoon—My dearest Sister a thousand thanks for your most welcome Letter received this morning. How sorry I am that [you] could not enjoy the eclipse;[2] but I hope you will soon be able to enjoy every thing. Thanks dearest Mary and Dora, for your Letters. How I long to be back again [with][3] you! This morning I breakfasted with Henry Taylor and from 12 to 5 made calls along with Mr Townsend, upon Mr Kenyon and Mr Darley,[4] and Mr Pickersgill, all of whom I found at home and upon John W. whom I did not. I have requested Pickersgill to get the Picture[5] framed, and then to send in his account. The blight I caught in my eye*lid* in coming from Mr Kenyons some nights past annoys me a good deal, and I am much heated by constantly moving about; after all the exertion of to day, I have to dine at Lord Lonsdales; and then we go to Mrs Marshall's concert. But what annoys me most of all is Longman's putting me off for ten or 11 days. Before the end of this week I hope to be at Mrs Marshall's. I have just received, tell John Carter, an Account of the Annuitants but I have not had time to look [it] over.—As soon as I have a morning to spare, I shall breakfast with Mr Courtenay, and then I hope to see my way on points of business. The life I am now leading must not last; tell me sincerely whether you think I ought to go abroad or not; I like the idea less and less every day, I so long to see you, and I feel so fevered.—This morning I have had a letter from Willy, how it came I know not. How thankful I was for your Letter of this morning. No body [can][6] ever grasp how anxious

[1] Owen Rees, Longman's partner (see previous letter).

[2] The eclipse of the sun on 15 May (see also L. 1014 above).

[3] *Word dropped out.*

[4] George Darley (1795–1846), poet, critic, and mathematician, whom W. W. had met in London in June 1828, just before his departure to the Continent with Coleridge (see C. Colleer Abbot, *Life and Letters of George Darley*, 1928, p. 73). Darley contributed to the *London Magazine* and *Athenaeum*, published tragedies *Thomas à Becket* (1840) and *Ethelstan* (1841), and edited Beaumont and Fletcher for Moxon in place of Southey.

[5] Pickersgill's portrait of W. W. 'in small' for Dora W., for which W. W. had sat the previous year (see L. 870 above).

[6] *Word dropped out.*

I felt about you all. Do write as often as you can. Yesterday was a bitter cold day.[1] I breakfasted with Rogers who had a Party—we walked in Kensington Gardens, called on Wilkins,[2] and Lord Holland.[3] I dined on cold meat at Rogers before his dinner; went to Church in Regent Street at 7, called on Mrs Johnson and sate with her till 9 when Mr Johnson came;[4] and reach[ed] Park street at ten.—If my business with Longman or Moxon were settled, I should go to rusticate quietly at Mrs Hoares.—I have just received 25£ from Mr Spedding, including Miss Fenwick's subscription, and 5 from himself but I find nobody like or in the smallest degree resembling Mr Stephen, who volunteered his 50.—Mr Kenyon will give John or me a few of his Books, viz, duplicates. My time is out, I must close with a thousand and ten thousand remembrances and love to you all, to you my dearest Sister, to you dearest Mary and to you dearest Dora. O when shall I hear that you are well; my stupid arm and hand aches and trembles—most faithfully yours. I keep up wonderfully; but every body being now in town, the work is ten times as hard, walking, talking, etc etc. as when, dearest Mary you and I were here last spring—Once for all remember me kindly to Mr Carter and to all the household.

W. W.

1018. W. W. to HIS FAMILY

MS. WL. Hitherto unpublished.

Wednesday morning. [25 May 1836]

My dearest Friends,

My last was sent off on Monday, I dined at Lord Lonsdale's that evening, he told me he was going down into Cumberland for a short time: If you enclosed to him I shall not get your Letter for some time. I have since heard from you again, enclosing Mr Carr's note, which I shall not deliver till I take up my quarters at Mr Henry Taylor's towards the end of this week.

[1] *Written* today.

[2] F. W. Wilkin, the artist (see previous letter).

[3] Chancellor of the Duchy of Lancaster in Melbourne's second administration, until his death in 1840.

[4] The Revd. William Johnson.

I hope the new carriage will suit Dora and that dearest sister may ride in it also.—Her letter must have been a great effort and I cannot say how thankful I was for it—the penmanship is not so good as that to Christopher[1] some time since, but I hope she will improve—she is not too old for it.—We have here a cold as bitter as Christmass, which prevents my right eyelid getting well. Yesterday after having squired Miss Watson through the exhibition, I went on to the Temple, called on Crabbe, Courtenay, Mr Twistleton,[2] Mr Graves,[3] and found no one at home; then went to Pater Noster row, to see what could be done, found Mr Orme,[4] whom I liked much better than Mr Rees, talked over the edition and he promised to send their proposals, which I anxiously expect. I then went to Charing Cross by appointment, with Mr Quillinan; when I had been there a quarter of an hour he appeared with Jemima, who was to proceed immediately with Mr Atherley,[5] per Coach to Brighton. Jemima is heavier faced and more dumpy than ever, but her father is told this will go off. When the coach left Charing Cross Q. and I walked in Hyde Park, and at last found a seat—tolerably sheltered where we sate down and talked about an hour and a half.[6] I then went to the Colonial off. saw Spedding, Taylor, and Mr Stephen who has again seen Mr Spring Rice who confidently assures him that I shall not be *hurt*. Perhaps you know that I dine with him on Sunday. This page I am writing at Mr Robinsons Chambers. I have just seen Mrs Smith[7] at her lodgings and find her northern journey put off to August.—And now about what you call my Continental trip. I find you dearest Mary under mistake as to the intended time; and for this and other reasons I feel strongly inclined to break from all my engagements here, in a week at the latest and run down to Rydal for three weeks; for I cannot bear the thought of

---

[1] i.e. L. 989 above.

[2] Edward Twistleton (see L. 988 above).

[3] The Revd. R. P. Graves was on a visit to London.

[4] Cosmo Orme (1780–1859), partner in Longman and Co., 1803–41.

[5] A friend of E.Q.'s, probably identical with the Mr. Atherley who stayed for a time at Rydal with his wife (see *SH*, p. 345), and was subsequently E.Q.'s neighbour in London.

[6] E.Q.'s MS. Diary for 24 May (*WL MSS.*) establishes the date of this meeting (which actually took place in St. James's Park), and consequently the date of this letter.

[7] Mrs. Proctor Smith, W.W.'s cousin.

being so long absent from you all as I shall be, if I remain here till the 5th of July and then start for the Continent. The objections to the scheme of going down and coming back are risk, expense, and fatigue; but I am tempted to brave these all, if you give me a word of encouragement, and pray write by return of Post, an unfranked letter and addressed to me at Mrs Marshalls, to tell me what you think, and encourage me, if you think it right, not else. If I do go abroad I should not like to have less than ten weeks. So that I feel decided altogether against going, if you don't approve of my coming down.

5 o clock Mr Watson's: on leaving Mr Robinson's I went to call on Strickland C——,[1] not at home, found Henry Coleridge— went with him to Montague's[2] room, he not at home, but found my old Friend Mr Dyce in his chambers, sate an hour with him, and H. C.[3] walked with me to Charing Cross. I went thence to the Colonial Off. for this Frank. Miss Fenwick, you will grieve to hear is far from well, threatened with something like dropsy of the Chest. I shall hear about her again from H. T.[4] On reaching home I found your Letter of Sunday, a thousand thanks for it and the favorable account of my dearest Sister. How comes it you did not mention Dora.—Mr Moxon expects to sell the 3000 in two years, but what if he should be disappointed—I am glad of having Mr Courtenay's Letter, and J. C.'s[5] notes—I shall put this [?][6] into Strickland Cookson's hands. Here I must make special appointment, I find he is so much from home. This very hour has come in one of the Mr Nicholsons who you recollect was at Rydal with his Sister.[7] He is most anxious to have Pickersgill's Portrait [?][8] and says that Cornaggie[9] the Printseller would he was sure, gladly undertake

---

[1] Strickland Cookson.

[2] Basil Montagu's.

[3] Henry Nelson Coleridge.

[4] Henry Taylor.

[5] John Carter's.

[6] *Blot on MS.*

[7] The *RMVB* records the visit of Mr. Nicholson of Rochester in 1830, and of Mr. G. Nicholson of Rochester and his two sisters in July 1833.

[8] *MS. illegible.* The reference is not to W. H. Watt's engraving of the portrait (see pt. ii, L. 717) for the forthcoming edition of W. W.'s poems, but to the full-length engraving commissioned shortly afterwards from R. C. Rolls (see L. 1048 below).

[9] Dominic Paul Colnaghi (1790–1879) had succeeded his father as head of the family firm in Pall Mall in 1833.

it. In consequence I shall call upon Cornaggie and see if the scheme be practical. I find many of my friends will be greatly disappointed if this opportunity be neglected, or rather refused.

Dearest Sister write to me again, a few lines, you Dora also— In consequence of loss of time by Nicholson's call, I must conclude. I am afraid there would be risk of delay if you should enclose your answer to Wm Marshall. And I forgot to ask Mr H. Taylor's, or Spedding's permission. Therefore I think the safest way would be to write without frank to me at Mr Marshall's Grosvenor Street. I will now tell you what you must on no account repeat, and what I am ashamed to mention as it proves what fits of absence I am subject to. At Lord Lonsdale's dinner the other evening what did I do—about 20 minutes before we went up to the Ladies, while I was sitting by my Lord Lonsdale, ten gentlemen or so being present, I found myself to my own great dismay with a decanter of cold water at my mouth, having drank out of it. How it happened I cannot possibly tell; guess how confounded I was, how many of the *Convives* saw me I know not.—I said nothing—took no notice and only took care to keep the Decanter so close to me afterwards that no one could have an opportunity to use it. In fact, being thirsty, I had totally forgotten myself, thinking only of the water. Nothing like this can happen to me again, nor shall I ever speak of it to any one, and I hope you will not, on any account. Lady Chantrey[1] said to me yesterday, every thing you say and do is talked about in London, you are so conspicuous a person. She little knows that this observation has lately brought up to my mind this abominable slip of recollection.—Here must just stop or I shall be too late for my Letter, Love to all

ever most affectionately yours
W W.

[1] Francis Chantrey had been knighted the previous year.

1019. W. W. to EDWARD WILLIAM WYON [1]

Address: E. W. Wyon Esq., 36 London Street, Fitzroy Squ[are].
Postmark: 27 May 1836. *Stamp*: Charing Cross.
MS. McGill University Library. Hitherto unpublished.

6 Park Street
West[r]
May 27th [1836]

Dear Sir,

I have to thank you for the present of the likenesses of Mr Southey and myself, from your hand. Since they have been in this House they have been seen by many Friends of Mr S. and also of my own, and by all have been approved as lively and striking resemblances.

I remain dear Sir
sincerely your obliged
W[m] Wordsworth

1020. W. W. to HIS FAMILY

MS. WL. Hitherto unpublished.

[*c.* 28 May 1836]

. . . in a proper train I trust for settlement.—but Mr Courtenay at least approves of the back business and thinks I shall make a good thing by coming to London. I *hope* so. All of the Stamp office forms I will if possible mail down [   ][2] I have another Frank for William's. Dear Willy—I could not meet his wish about [? instructions]. I have too a hundred little things to tell you.

The happiest day I have spent since I came to London was at Sergeant Talfourd's play and his supper.[3]

---

[1] See L. 1016 above.
[2] *Several illegible words.*
[3] For the first night of *Ion*, see L. 1010 above.

1021. W. W. to HIS FAMILY

MS. WL. Hitherto unpublished.

Sunday 3 oclock [? 29 May 1836]
Upper Grosvenor Street

My dearest Friends,

This morning I breakfasted with Dr H.[1] and at Mrs Hoare['s] saw also Mr Holland, a medical Man his Father. Dr Holland put into my hands Mr Carr's note, at the conclusion of which Mr C. states his anxiety that Dora should have change of air and scene, from which alone he expects benefit and adds (these are Mr Carr's words) that he looks forward with great dread to another winter spent at Rydal. Neither Dr H. nor his father could recommend medical [?][2] for improvement, except from change of scene. Dr H. said that the patient ought not to be deterred from making this trial by aggravations of pain at first, for he had known such pain often disappear (asked his father also) but he added that there could [be] no certainty that the *pain* would diminish after trial of motion persevered in, though the pain might have been at first disagreeable. Yet still he seemed of opinion and indeed decidedly so, that the trial ought to be made, indeed he recommended nothing but that, only he wished to hear the result of the [?][3]—And now my dearest Daughter, do let us try the effect of change of place. I shall be ready to quit this place on an instant and go with you any where. Don't mind expense; I have got *150* from Longman for the Yarrow[4] and hope for at least as much more for the Poems, so that we shall be quite rich.—Dr Holland was called out, and on the other side you see an opinion or two on some important points of his Father. Nephew John has just come in.

Monday morning. Have just breakfasted with Mr Gladstone and am going to Hampstead with Mrs Marshall. I have dined at Lord Lonsdale's—Lady Frederick[5] unwell. Last night I dined at Spring Rice's. Nothing said about Stamp Off: but I shall write to him before I leave Town. I have said that I read your Letter dearest Mary to Dr Holland, Mr Carr had noticed the faintings

---

[1] Dr., later Sir Henry, Holland (see pt. i, L. 42). His father Peter Holland, also a medical practitioner, came originally from Knutsford in Cheshire.

[2] *MS. obscure.*

[3] *MS. illegible.*

[4] The *Yarrow Revisited* volume.

[5] Lady Frederick Bentinck.

and shiverings; Dr H I think said they proceeded from Weakness. Moxon has sent me on new proposals which I have not had time to read, but Mr Graves calls it a *noble* offer.—

I write now from Mrs Marshalls, having just received your long and dear letters. Give a thousand loves to my dear Sister, and you dearest Dora get better and better, and bear with all my anxieties about you.—I cannot quit London, from business engagements before next Monday.

Dr Holland—

Saltwater hip-bath, dipping in three or 4 times, and not remain, friction afterwards with dry towels.—

Mr Holland's suggestions—(this bit was first written)

The pain appearing to be relieved by pressure Mr H. thinks it may be considered whether the application of a bandage of very thin flannel about a hand's breadth and cut from side edge to side edge to make it more [? close] might not be useful. Has a tepid salt bath ever been tried with a view to stimulating the system—

Mr Holland concurs with Dr Holland in opinion, that it is not improbable that perseverance in motion may (for this they have often known to be the case) gradually dimish the pain, which at present, and at first, it aggravates. And to the [?],[1] there would not appear to be grounds of objection, from the presence of inflammation in the parts which may be considered as proved from being relieved upon pressure.

1022. W. W. to WILLIAM STRICKLAND COOKSON

MS. Cornell. Hitherto unpublished.

Temple
Tuesday Morn. [31 May 1836]

My dear Sir,

Fearing I might not find you in your Chambers, I have enclosed a Letter from Mr Courtenay containing some pecuniary statements, with annotations of his made this morning. My object in calling was to ask the favor of your receiving for me in addition to what is or may become due upon the Guardian Shares the small sum which may become due or is due upon the Australian Agricultural Shares.—

---

[1] *MS. obscure.*

I have also taken the liberty of leaving with you a Copy of my late B^rs Will and other Papers—for the benefit of your advice, respecting such an Instrument as it would be proper to have drawn up, to release myself and my Brother from any claims which in future might rise out of our Executorship.—

I should be glad to see you, if I know at what time I should find you in Chambers.[1] Tomorrow I cannot however see you, as I am going to Harrow,[2] any other morning or afternoon of the week I should be at liberty.

Believe me my dear Sir
faithfully your obliged
Wm Wordsworth

1023. W. W. to HIS FAMILY

MS. WL. Hitherto unpublished.

Monday [late May 1836]

. . . have managed myself better since—but am not the Man I was a year ago. O that I could have better accounts from home—Have had Moxons proposals, dont much like them. Rees will meet me any day I appoint—but I want facts before I can determine, as to the new Edition.—This morning I should have called at the archbishops[3] but met Sir George B. in the Street, who told me there was a high life marriage in the palace. I should have gone to morrow to Lambeth, but am engaged to breakfast, and so for the next two or three days, most unluckily as I may find I have no chance of seeing the Archbishop after 12 and to him I want to mention W^m's Case. Mr Thornton[4] has just lost another daughter, married—She died in the last [? month]. I have not yet been at the Stamp off. nor seen Courtenay—I dine with him on Wednesday, but I shall not then be able to talk with him. What an execrable pen but no better to be had, no one in the House.

Monday, it is now a $\frac{1}{4}$ past three. I start for Lockharts, with D^r [?].[5] I am not to dine at Miss Rogers's. I wish the business of the

---

[1] W. W. met him that afternoon (see *HCR* ii. 495).
[2] For the installation of C. W. jnr. as headmaster.
[3] i.e. Lambeth Palace, residence of Dr. Howley.
[4] John Thornton of the Stamp Office (see pt. ii, L. 780).
[5] *Word dropped out.*

Poems were settled. The Stereotype Yarrow hangs like a millstone about my projects—it is so ugly a book. Moxon offers to print the whole in Six Vol. uniform with the Edit. of 1827, the Edit. to consist of three thousand, and to give two thirds of the profits, amounting to 771 to be paid in advance immediately after the publication of the 6th Vol; that is 771 for eighteen thousand volumes, miserable pay! The stereotype plates remaining mine or my heirs. I like not this at all.—

Thanks for the Extract from the W.[1] Papers. 600£ already subscribed, that is not an additional farthing, except what has come from my friends. This looks very bad indeed. I fear we shall not succeed, how is it possible unless somebody besides my self will come forward. I enclose Lord Lonsdale's note received yesterday, in answer to mine with the Church Book and Subscription. Lord Lonsdale has called on me this morning—unluckily I was out.—

Dearest Dora, I read your passage to Landor, about Lady Blessington[2] laughing heartily as he did—Keep Lord Lonsdale's offer quiet. I have written to Handley[3] the Enthusiast. What a miserable Letter is this, but bad pen, bad ink; and a bad arm, and a trembling hand, are all against me. People say I look well [? humoured]. A thousand blessings on you all! Dearest Mary, dearest Sister, dearest Dora—remembrances to all the Servants—I wish I had seen the Archbishop, that I might learn whether I have any thing to hope from that quarter for dearest William. Again adieu, I will write whenever I can.

Christ:[4] is to be paid by the Boarding members, a less agreeable arrangement. He is [?][5] dear fellow in happy Spirits. Most faithfully, most tenderly, and affectionately yours

W.W.

---

[1] Westmorland.

[2] Marguerite, Countess of Blessington (1789–1849), authoress and centre of a brilliant social circle, the friend of Byron, Count d'Orsay, and Landor. She wrote novels and edited the *Book of Beauty* from 1834 and *The Keepsake* from 1841. Dora W. had warned her father against visiting Landor at her house (see *HCR* ii. 509).

[3] Edwin Hill Handley (see L. 998 above).

[4] C. W. jnr.

[5] *MS. blotted.*

1024. W. W. to UNKNOWN CORRESPONDENT[1]

MS. Henry E. Huntington Library. Hitherto unpublished.

41 Upper Grosvenor Street
[? late May *or* early June 1836]

Dear Sirs,

A Letter addressed to me, and which came by the two-penny post on Friday last, has been mislaid without having been previously opened.

Was it from you? if so, be so good as tell me; if not, you need not give yourselves the trouble of answering this Letter, which I hope you will excuse.

Believe me dear Sirs
sincerely yours
W Wordsworth

1025. W. W. to JOHN WORDSWORTH[2]

Address: John Wordsworth Esq., 28 Great Ormond Street.
Postmark: 1 June 18[36].
MS. WL.
LY ii. 800.

Wednesday Morning [1 June 1836]
41 Upper Grosvenor Street

My dear John,

Could you get ¼ lb of Blue Pills and leave it at Mr Moxon's, directed for me. Mr Jackson[3] of Waterhead wants it for his Daughter.

Yesterday I left a note for you requesting you would go down with me on[? Sunday] by Steamboat to Woolwich to Mr Q.'s.[4]—

---

[1] Possibly Messrs. Longman and Co.

[2] R. W.'s son.

[3] See pt. i, L. 63.

[4] E. Q. was renting a cottage at Woolwich at this time. His MS. Diary (*WL MSS.*) records that W. W. dined at the cottage on Sunday, 5 June with his nephew, Moxon, and Frank Stone the artist, and returned to London the following day. Frank Stone, A.R.A. (1800–59), had executed portraits of E. Q.'s two daughters in 1833, and a copy of the one of Jemima (by Miss Withnall, one of the artistic ladies mentioned in pt. ii, L. 710) hung for

1 June 1836

Will you come also and breakfast here at half past nine that day, and then we can go down together.

ever your affectionate Uncle W. Wordsworth

1026. W. W. to DORA W.

Address: Mrs Wordsworth, Rydal, Ambleside.
Franked: London June three 1836. W. Marshall.
Postmark: 2 June 1836.
MS. WL. Hitherto unpublished.

Thursday June 2ᵈ [1836]
41 Upper Gros. Sᵗ.

Dearest Dora,

Miss Marshall holds my pen in consequence of one of my eyes being distressed but I hope it is nothing that will not go off with one day's care. You are being good in writing at such length about yourself. Your case is exceedingly perplexing such strong medical opinions even having been given in favour of your persevering in exercise, but on the other hand I cannot but feel that your own convictions are entitled to every possible consideration both on the part of your medical advisers and your friends. I should have grieved very much for the result of the first trial if it had not been clear from your own statement that you were too long out and attempted far too much. I hope you will proceed with more caution in future. Now as to an Airing in the boat, I cannot see the force of your opinion on giving it up. It seemed to me that a person of common sense who had never handled a pair of oars before might in calm weather row you as far as the Island at Rydal without your being sensible of the least jerk or disagreeable motion—What has he to do but slip the oars in gently, and draw them towards him as gently as possible—What I wish is that you should have the bracing effect of the air from the water, and under the shade of the Island if required. Surely some person man or woman might be found who could do this for gain. Remember what benefit old Mʳ Fleming[1] derived from the water. Yesterday I

---

many years in the sitting room at Rydal Mount. (See also *PW* iv. 120, 428.) W. W. had already met Stone during his previous visit to London in 1835. See also L. 1086 below.

[1] Probably James Fleming of Town End (see pt. ii, L. 507).

went to Harrow with Mr Lockhart and Mr Townsend, Cordelia Marshall and her brother Henry[1] and Mr Empson[2] was there also. I met Miss Hoare and Louisa Lloyd[3] and Sophy Pocock[4] there. We all enjoyed the day much. Were pleased with the delicacy of the Speeches, and the whole thing went off as well as possible. Christopher acquitted himself charmingly and seemed much pleased that I was there. We had a large party at home to dinner, Mr Marshall suffering under a cold. Sir W. and Lady Gomm[5] came in the evening. Lady Gomm looking as well as ever. They are going to Harrow. I have just had a letter from Miss Watson—her father is still very poorly and restricted from speaking. I have at last received Mr Longmans proposals and Mr Marshall is so kind as to. . . .[6]

1027. W. W. to MISS STANLEY[7]

Endorsed: Wordsworth June 2, 1836.
MS. Cornell. Hitherto unpublished.

41 Upper Grosvenor Street
[2 June 1836][8]

Dear Miss Stanley

Most fortunately I am disengaged on Thursday, and shall be happy to avail myself of the kind invitation of Sir John and Lady

[1] For Henry Cowper Marshall, see L. 1017 above.

[2] William Empson (see L. 1017 above).

[3] Probably C. W.'s niece Louisa, daughter of Charles and Sophia Llyod (see pt. ii, L. 562).

[4] Unidentified.

[5] See pt. ii, L. 816.

[6] W. W. apparently broke off so that William Marshall might frank the letter.

[7] Probably Maria (1798–1882), eldest daughter of Sir John Stanley, Bart., mentioned below.

[8] On 2 June W. W. accompanied John Kenyon, Miss Mitford, Elizabeth Barrett (1806–61), whom he had first met on 27 May at Kenyon's, Landor, and the Marshalls, on an expedition to the Duke of Devonshire's Palladian villa at Chiswick (see *Letters of Elizabeth Browning*, ed. Frederic G. Kenyon, 2 vols., 1897, i. 43, 47; *Elizabeth Barrett to Miss Mitford*, ed. Betty Miller, 1954, pp. ix–x).

Maria Stanley[1] to dine with them on that day.

believe me
dear Miss Stanley,
sincerely yours
Wm Wordsworth

1028. W. W. to BASIL MONTAGU

MS. Professor Mark Reed. Hitherto unpublished.

41 Upper Grosvenor Street
Friday 2.[2]
[? 3 June 1836]

My dear Montagu,
    Accept my thanks for your very kind note. I came to Town on several matters of business which have occupied my time along with other engagements in a most perplexing way.
    Do not trouble yourself to call here, as I am scarcely ever at home, my kind friends allowing me to make their house an Hotel for my convenience. I shall make every endeavor to see you before I quit Town, or start for The Continent Which I have some intention of doing.
    We have been sadly afflicted at Rydal since I last saw you.

ever faithfully yours
Wm Wordsworth

[1] Sir John Thomas Stanley, 7th Bart. (1766–1850), later 1st Baron Stanley of Alderley, and his wife Maria (1771–1863), daughter of John, 1st Earl of Sheffield. Their nephew Arthur Penrhyn Stanley (1815–81), the future Dean of Westminster, now an undergraduate at Balliol College, Oxford, was already known to the Wordsworths, having visited Rydal Mount with Dr. Arnold in Aug. 1833. (See R. E. Prothero and G. G. Bradley, *Life and Correspondence of Arthur Penrhyn Stanley, D. D.*, 2 vols., 1893, i. 100–1; and *RMVB*.) The Stanleys were connected by marriage with the Hares, and it was probably through Julius Hare that W. W. came to know them.

[2] i.e. 2 p.m.

1029. W. W. to MARY WATSON

Address: Miss Watson, 6 Park Street, Westminster.
Postmark: 3 June 1836.
MS. New York University Library. Hitherto unpublished.

Friday Morn. [3 June 1836]

My dear Miss Watson,

I write this not without hope of getting down to Park Street in the course of the morning, but I am too well aware that I may be prevented. How it would have rejoiced me to hear a still more favorable account of your dear Father's convalescence. Be assured I left your hospitable roof with sadness not seeing [you][1] on account of your illness, your Father being so poorly also—

Christopher did his part to admiration at Harrow,[2] and everybody seemed pleased with him. The party that partook of the Collation under his roof was large, and were doubtless particularly gratified.

Dr Holland[3] could not say much to cheer me; he had nothing to advise but fresh air, as much exercise as could be borne, and change of place as soon as it could be effected.

Pray thank my kind correspondent for his compliance with my request in writing so punctually.

Hoping soon to see you I remain
my dear Miss Watson
with earnest good wishes
faithfully yours
Wm Wordsworth

1030. W. W. to HIS FAMILY

MS. WL. Hitherto unpublished.

Mr Marshall's 6 oclock [early June 1836]

My dearest Friends,

I sent off a sad scrawl to you this morning and now sit down to write a few words before I go to dress.—Mr Marshall tells me Mr Spring Rice assured him that none of the meditated changes could injure us Distributers (this can't be correct) and some

---

[1] *Word dropped out.*
[2] See L. 1026 above.
[3] See L. 1021 above.

would serve us, for they were going to reduce the Discount allowed at the Head Office, so as to take away the temptation to get the larger stamps in London. For my own part tell Mr Carter I see no way of preventing the Rydal off: being injured, but raising my poundage; and this I shall not scruple to press on the said S. R.—

Here follows Moxon's 2nd proposal received this morning—

Mr M. to print stereotype and pay all the expenses of an Edition of 3000 copies of Mr W.'s P. works in 6 vols similar to the Edit. in 5 vol 1827.

Mr M. for the same to give Mr W. 1000 £ the whole to be paid in cash immediately after the Publication of the 6th vol: (this I shall stipulate to be in 6 months).

Mr M. to give Mr W. for every future edit. of 1000 Copies 400, to be paid in Cash within 6 months of the day of publication.

The Copyright and stereotype plates to be Mr Words-worth's—

So you see dearest Friends there is nothing like standing up for one's self, and one's own legitimate interest.

I have not yet seen Longmans again though this was the day they appointed for me at Pater Noster Row—

I shall perhaps call upon them tomorrow, as I mean to breakfast with Mr Courtenay.—

I have seen this afternoon Mrs and Miss Hoare and [? Louisa][1] Lloyd at Hampstead, but could not call at the Coleridges[2] to my great regret, Mrs Marshall returning another way.

If I could have a decided account of Dora's being better, and recovering the flesh I am sure she has lost, and being able to bear motion, I could give up the hope of seeing you again before I start for the Continent. Dearest Mary I will attend to your Commission from Mr Jackson,[3] but I fear I shall not be able to do so to morrow. I have just been[4] calling on Col[l] and Mrs Howard,[5] both suffering from the Influenza—the Col. I did not see. They go out of Town to morrow for health's sake, as I did not see the Col[l] I did not mention the C:[6] Church.—They are

---

[1] *MS. obscure.* But see L. 1026 above.

[2] Sara and Henry Nelson Coleridge, now living on Downshire Hill, Hampstead.

[3] Thomas Jackson of Waterhead. See L. 1025 above.

[4] *Written* being.

[5] Of Levens (see pt. i, Ls. 203 and 303).   [6] Cockermouth.

going down to West^nd early.—Tuesday Morn. Mr Courtenay
has breakfasted here, and all my business with Mr Courtenay is
settled—he recommends our not meddling with the money due
from John's Estate till we return from the Continent. At
present, owing to the rash of speculation, in railways etc etc—
things are so unsettled that he does not like to recommend any
particular investment, and means to leave a large sum of his own
to wait his return. You were so against my coming down to
West^nd that I gave up the thought for the present at least,
trusting that my last respecting dear Dora will produce its effect.
Miss Fenwick is not in so alarming a state as was thought. D^r
Ferguson[1] has received a statement of the case, he had been in
Town, and concludes from what we saw[2]

farewell—

1031. W. W. to HIS FAMILY

MS. WL. Hitherto unpublished.

Sat: 4th [June 1836] ½ past 12.

My dearest Friends,
    I have been breakfasting with Mr Carey[3] at the British
Museum, and here I am at Moxons, waiting for him with a view
to enter upon and conclude with him a Bargain for my new
edition. His proposals being decidedly more advantageous than
Longmans:—Yesterday I dined at home, and went in the
evening with the Miss Marshalls to a party at Lady [   ] well's;[4]
the last evening party I shall go [to] for I cannot bear the lights.

---

[1] Dr. Robert Ferguson (1799—1865), Sir Walter Scott's physician and a
writer for the *Quarterly*, became Professor of Obstetrics at King's College,
London, in 1831. In 1840 he was appointed gynaecologist to the Queen, and
attended at the birth of all her children. W. W. was consulting him about
Dora W.'s health.

[2] W. W. was apparently interrupted and left his last sentence unfinished.

[3] Henry Francis Cary (1772—1844), the translator of Dante's *Divine
Comedy* (1805—14), had been Assistant Keeper of Printed Books at the British
Museum since 1826. W. W. had first met him at Rogers's in 1823 (see pt. i,
L. 97), when Cary had been much struck with his 'frankness and fervour' (see
R. W. King, *The Translator of Dante, The Life, Work and Friendships of Henry
Francis Cary*, 1925, pp. 157—8); and W. W. had subsequently dined with him
before setting out for the Continent in June 1828 (see *Lamb*, iii. 167).

[4] *MS. torn.*

At dinner I can protect [them ver]y well with my shade, but only then, and my eyes are weak to day from having been a great deal distressed last night. Mrs Marshall did not dine with us, she was unwell in a cold which had taken away her voice, and Mr Marshall and Cordelia dined out. I think I told you that M. offers me £1000 for the right of publish[ing] an Edition of 3000 the stereotype plates to be mine—I shall hereafter send you his papers and Longman's Statements that the profits of my last edition have been 687—received or to be received at midsummer, which will be about 370 for this year in addition to the Yarrow,[1] 350 after deducting for lost [?],[2] so that the whole Sum will scarcely be less than 500£ which may be reckoned as a sort of Godsend.

If I go abroad I should wish to start as soon as I have signed the Quarterly account,[3] if I do not I shall certainly be at home about the middle or at latest later end of July. I am sad at the thought of leaving England without seeing you, all and each of you; and most anxious for another Letter, which I hope may come to day. What a joy would it be dearest Mary and Dora if you could come so that we might pass quietly a few days together at Hampstead; Joanna[4] being with dear Sister[5] till Mary could return. This would rejoice me above measure but I fear it is too good a thing for this world. O that there were a railway from Kendal.—I write on and Moxon does not make his appearance—What answer can you suppose I shall give to the enclosed stray or love note? Can it think you? be a Hoax? The Ladies appear to be my chief admirers, and whatever the creatures may think of me I appear in the absence and default of others perhaps to be grown into popularity.—I called yesterday at Mr Watsons,[6] did not see him—He is no better. Walked with Whewell, Blakesley[7] and Julius Hare.—Pray send me for Miss Courtenay's Album the 2nd Stanza of my little Poem to the Moon[8] (I recollect the rest of the Poem before The Moon. . . .

[*cetera desunt*]

[1] The *Yarrow Revisited* volume.
[2] *MS. obscure.*   [3] For the Stamp Office.
[4] Joanna Hutchinson was on a visit to Brinsop from the Isle of Man (see *MW*, p. 153).
[5] i.e. D. W.   [6] Joshua Watson's.
[7] J. W. Blakesley, the Cambridge 'Apostle' and Classical scholar (see pt. ii, L. 706).
[8] It is not entirely clear which poem W. W. is referring to here

1032. W. W. to MESSRS. LONGMAN AND CO.[1]

MS. WL. Hitherto unpublished.

41 Upper Grosvenor St.
June 6, 1836—

Dear Sirs,

Your statement and proposal were duly received.—After giving them the most careful consideration, and comparing your terms with those offered by Mr Moxon, I am of opinion that his are more advantageous to me, and therefore I purpose to accept them. Let it be understood that this preference does not imply on my part any sense of your offer not being creditable to yourselves, it being obvious that it may not suit a house with a long established and widely extended business like your's to make engagements such as may be convenient and beneficial to a publisher differently circumstanced.

Mr Moxon will wait upon you with a view to the settlement of the affair in a manner which, I trust, will be satisfactory to all parties.

I remain, Dear Sirs,
Yours truly
W. Wordsworth

1033. W. W. to HIS FAMILY

MS. WL. Hitherto unpublished.

Monday evening ½ before 7
[6 June 1836][2]

My dearest Friends,

I have a minute to spare before Rogers calls to take me to dine with his Sister. A thousand thanks dearest Dora for your minute account—it proves to demonstration that you are not yet fit for carriage motion—I will shew it, however, to Dr Holland. Your

---

[1] Longmans, who had recently sent detailed estimates for a new edition of W. W.'s poems in seven, six or five volumes (*WL MSS.*), replied to this letter at once on 7 June, dismayed that W. W. should treat these estimates as definite proposals. But W. W. stuck to his determination to transfer the proposed new edition to Moxon. The text here is W. W.'s copy of the letter actually sent.

[2] Dated by reference to E. Q.'s account of W. W.'s visit to Woolwich in his MS. Diary (see L. 1025 above).

6 June 1836

dear Mother's account of Mary H.[1] grieves me much, poor thing I hope they are alarmed more than is needful. I will see Mrs and Miss Hoare, by all means. I like dear Dora very much your notion of going to the sea side; but if you could cross the sands it would be far better, as the Grange[2] is I fear a close relaxing place with little of sea air; but I hope all will be done for the best; and do for heaven's sake let care be taken not to exasperate the spine. Neither your mother nor you say a word about your appetite. You said tooth-ache took your flesh away—is it coming back now that tooth ache is gone—

I will now tell you of my proceedings, yesterday, I went down with John[3] and Moxon to Woolwich when we found Quillinan waiting, and we proceeded to Nightingale Vale, no 6—it is I assume a sylvan situation—a very small cottage, but neatly furnished. Poor Rotha is plainer I think than ever, the spreading age she has reached, but the lengthier one she I fear will never attain—and yet why despair? She *seems* dearest Mary much shorter than when you and I saw her last spring, but it can only be *seems* shorter, which effect is produced by her encreased width. She speaks as low, and appears as shy as ever. About one yesterday, the day raw cold and somewhat rainy, we set off and walked among the woody dingles, and upon the upper grounds which command a view of the River, on our return [at] half past 4, found Mr Stone[4] waiting for us. They three[5] left us at eight for the Coach. I slept there, was up at 6 this morning, and at 7 set off with Rotha for a walk of an hour. I told her about Rydal and her Rydal Friends. This morning at 9 her Father and I walked down to the River side, he crossed for Essex whither he was going to vote for an election of a County member.[6] I

[1] Mary Hutchinson, M. W.'s niece, whose health was declining.

[2] i.e. Grange-over-Sands, a tiny watering-place before the arrival of the railway.

[3] R. W.'s son.

[4] Frank Stone the artist.

[5] Presumably W. W.'s nephew John, and the other dinner guests at E. Q.'s cottage, Stone and Moxon.

[6] The South Essex election opened at Chelmsford on 7 June and closed two days later. George Palmer (1772–1853), an East Indian merchant and bulwark of the National Lifeboat Institution, was elected against Mr. Champion Branfill by a large majority, and served until 1847. (See *The Times* for 10 June 1836.) E. Q.'s connection with Essex is not entirely clear, but he must have possessed property there to qualify for the vote.

returned by Steam—did business at two offices in the City, one for the Australian and the other for our Guardian shares, took a seat on a omnibus and discovered when I reached [?][1] Hill that I had left my umbrella somewhere, went back to the nearest off., found it not, but to my great joy at the farther one. I say great joy for, dearest Mary, I have lost 2 of my silk handkerchiefs. I hear Rogers' knock.

Tuesday morning

Upon looking this morning at the returned paper I find that Mr W. S. Cookson's name is there instead of Mr Courtenay's. Pray look at my directions and tell me by whose fault; another paper will have to be sent, yours writing Mr Courtenay's name instead of Mr S. Cookson's: Thomas Philip Courtenay Esq[re] 23 Montagu Street, Russel Sq.

I have got a very bad head-ache to day, partly from exhaustion of yesterday, in talking etc, and partly I think from drinking some bad ale at Miss Rogers instead of wine. In future, I shall confine myself to one glass of sherry, unless when I can also get a little porter, without which I can rest well, keep my body open, and I find at fashionable Houses Porter is not be be had. Now judge of my loss; this morning breakfasted with me here the Revd Mr Judkin[2] who swears he gave me another picture, Mr Collins,[3] and Capt[n] Washington,[4] Bella Askew's Husband. I suffered myself foolishly to be involved with this latter Gentleman in an altercation and dispute about Pagan mythology, astronomy, etc, which exhausted me much, and to get rid of the subject I read them all passages of the Excursion relating to that subject which exhausted me still more. Then came two French Gentlemen of my acquaintance who wanted my opinion on French affairs, and this knocked [me] up altogether. Since I came in, I have been writing Letters to Mr Courtenay on business and Mr Strickland Cookson. I am to dine with Mr Gladstone so that I scarcely know I shall get through the day. I long for quiet, when I may prepare at least

---

[1] MS. *illegible*.

[2] See pt. ii, L. 678.

[3] Probably William Collins, the artist (see *MY* ii. 490).

[4] Captain, later Rear-Admiral, John Washington (1800–63), hydrographer: Secretary of the Royal Geographical Society, 1836–41. In 1833 he had married Eleanora, younger daughter of W. W.'s distant relative the Revd. Henry Askew (see pt. ii, L. 463).

three vols of my poems for a new edition before I go abroad, which if done at all will be as soon as possible before I have agreed to the Quarterly account.—Pray ask Mr Carter how we are to provide for the two payments. 13 July 250. D° October, for the latter something may be had I should suppose from John's property and in a few days I shall learn whether I have any thing to receive through Mr Courtenay. My teeth if I get them will cost £50. Then there is Pickersgill's portrait[1] to be paid for, and my continental journey—The sum from Longman in [?][2] of Yarrow will be 450—

I now lay aside my pen, the clock having just struck. God bless you. How is dearest Sister, better[3] I hope. Mr Moxon will be glad to publish her journal, which shall be done next Spring,[4] and with the money we all take a tour together.

farewell   W. W.

1034. W. W. to DERWENT COLERIDGE

MS. Cornell. Hitherto unpublished.

Wednesday afternoon [early June 1836]
41 Upper Grosvenor
Street.

My dear Derwent,

I should be most glad to see you, and Mr Marshall with whom I am staying begs me to ask if you can breakfast with us on Friday next at half past nine.

Ever faithfully
yours
Wm Wordsworth

[1] See L. 1017 above.

[2] *MS. obscure.*

[3] better *written twice.*

[4] In 1822 W. W. had enlisted Rogers's help in finding a publisher for D. W.'s *Recollections of a Tour Made in Scotland* (1803), but the scheme had fallen through (see pt. i, Ls. 76 and 88); and the new proposal from Moxon also came to nothing.

Address: Mrs Wordsworth, Kendal, Ambleside.
Franked: London June ten 1836. W. E. Gladstone.
Postmark: 10 June 1836.
MS. WL. Hitherto unpublished.

[10 June 1836]

. . . I will send you down Longmans accounts that you may see if they are correct—

I am afraid I shall not have time to look after odd vols. of Registers or novels.

Moxon wanted to purchase a Copy of the Edition of 27 for our one—he was asked 4.10 for it bound in calf.—A Bookseller told Mr Harness[1] that scarcely a Day passed in which he did not sell a Copy since the price was lowered in the last Edition—My Poems are making their way in France[2] and the whole have

---

[1] William Harness (see L. 1013 above).

[2] For Hippolyte de la Morvonnais and his translations from W. W., see L. 1107 below. A number of other translations and notices appeared in French reviews in the eighteen-twenties and thirties, but W. W.'s aims and methods were often misunderstood, and no complete translation of all his poems into French is recorded during his lifetime. His principal followers in France were Philarète Chasles (1798—1873), who visited the Lakes in 1818 (see his *Mémoires*, 2 vols., Paris, 1876, ii. 69—78; and E. M. Phillips, *Philarète Chasles, Critique et Historien de la Littérature Anglaise*, Paris, 1933); Amédée Pichot (1795—1877), whose *Voyage Historique et Littéraire en Angleterre et en Ecosse*, 3 vols., Paris, 1825, and *The Living Poets of England*. 2 vols., Paris, 1827, mark a significant stage in the appreciation of the Lake Poets in France (see L. A. Bisson, *Amédée Pichot, A Romantic Prometheus*, 1943); and Sainte-Beuve (1804—69), whose poetry shows a distinct influence of W. W., following his visit to England in 1828. But there is no evidence that W. W. had any personal acquaintance with any major French critic before June 1843, when Pichot came to Rydal Mount *(R MVB)*. See Maxwell Austin Smith, *L'Influence Des Lakistes sur les Romantiques Français*, Paris, 1920; Eric Partridge, *The French Romantics' Knowledge of English Literature (1820—1848)*, Paris, 1924; and Kathleen Jones, *La Revue Britannique, Son Histoire et Son Action Littéraire (1825—1840)*, Paris, 1939. In a letter to Dora W. on 27 May 1835 *(WL MSS.)*, E. Q. had drawn attention to an article by Xavier Marmier, a member of Sainte-Beuve's circle, in the *Revue de Paris* on 29 Mar. 1835, which mentioned W. W. in the course of a discussion of 'Poètes de Province'. Marmier had written: 'Il y a même, il faut en convenir, tel genre de poésie qui ne peut guère être bien senti que loin de la rumeur des grandes villes, au milieu du silence et

been[1] translated into French Prose, so that I hope Moxon wont lose by his liberal terms—My admirers are greatly increased among the female sex.

I am still in doubt about my teeth.

I was 2 hours with John yesterday. Mr Watson is very poorly and not allowed by his Physicians to speak. So that I cannot answer Willy's queries. This is very unlucky. I shall call again at Lambeth with a hope of seeing the Archbishop. Love to dearest Sister whom I have not mentioned but let her not suppose that I am not now and perpetually thinking of her.—And you dearest Mary I have not named you, nor Kate Southey. When Dora goes to the sea side, you must go down with her to see that she does not tire herself in the journey, and you dearest Dora must submit to your dear Mother's suggestions, requests, and wishes, and entreaties. God bless you all. Love to dear Kate S.—I meet her Uncle Dr S.[2] at Lord Beresford's[3] on Wednesday. I hear nothing of the other [?].[4] Poor dear Mary Hutchinson.[5] How sorry am I for them all.

[unsigned]

des riantes images de la campagne. Nous croyons, par exemple, que Burns n'eût pas fait dans le tourbillon d'Edimbourg les ravissantes élégies qu'il a faites dans sa ferme. Nous croyons que les poètes de Westmoreland, et en particulier Wordsworth, eussent mis moins de fraîcheur, moins de simplicité, et de grâce naïve dans leurs chants, si, au lieu de s'inspirer au bord de leurs beaux lacs, ils étaient allés chercher l'inspiration dans un *rout* de la cité.'

[1] been *written twice.*
[2] See pt. ii, L. 522.
[3] William Carr Beresford, Viscount Beresford (d. 1854), a distinguished army commander in the Peninsular War. His brother, Admiral Sir John Beresford, Bart. (1766—1844), successively M.P. for Coleraine (1812—23), Berwick (1823), Northallerton (1832), and Chatham (1835), was also known to W. W. (see *RMVB* for Sept. 1834).
[4] *MS. obscure.*
[5] M. W.'s niece, now seriously ill.

1036. W. W. to HIS FAMILY

Address: Mrs Wordsworth, Rydal.
MS. WL. Hitherto unpublished.

8 oclock Monday morn.
[13 June 1836]

My dearest Friends,

I breakfast with Rogers at eight, and he Hallam[1] and I are going to Windsor. —Miss Marshall will write you a few lines. I enclose a draft, which I spoke of sometime since—the money is made up, tell J. Carter, of what I brought for us here, of Longman's draft for the Yarrow,[2] and Mr Spedding's money for the Church.[3]—Strickland Cookson is sure he never received the power of Att^y[4] but dearest Mary no bad use can be made of it. I shall apply to Talfourd, and Henry Taylor, but I fear they will not be able to give an extract of it.—I was at the Horticultural Show on Friday a bitter cold day, and I caught some cold; but it is going off. This day week I go to Moxon's, and then shall shut myself up to prepare the new Edition. Quill^n will be there also.—Yesterday we heard Mr Benson[5] preach at the Temple Church, he read the communion service most impressively. I could not distinctly hear his sermon.—The Church is a most beautiful one. The weather is still very cold here. How I long to hear about you all: dearest Sister and Dora, how I long to hear that you are better. I hope in the course of this week to get through business with Mr Addison and to settle with Mr Courtenay, whom I am surprized I have not heard of, since I returned the MS. signed Papers. I hope I shall find a Letter from you to morrow—farewell—dearest Friends—

W. W.

[1] Henry Hallam the historian.
[2] The *Yarrow Revisited* volume.
[3] The proposed new church at Cockermouth.
[4] Attorney.
[5] The Revd. Christopher Benson (1788—1868), son of a Cockermouth solicitor: educated at Eton and Trinity College, Cambridge, Master of the Temple, 1826—45, and Canon of Worcester from 1825. A noted Evangelical preacher and opponent of the Tractarians.

1037. W. W. to HIS FAMILY

MS. WL. Hitherto unpublished.

Tuesday morning 9 oclock [14 June 1836]
Mr Horace Twiss's.[1]

My dearest Friends,

I am come here to Breakfast: Last night dearest Mary returning from Windsor, I received your anxiously-expected Letter, which pleased me with the prospect of Dora having the benefit of change of scene.—How I wished you could have added that she was in the way of recovering flesh instead of losing it. God grant I may [have][2] such news, before I quit England if that is to be.—Last night I found also Mr Graves's parcel, if possible I will call upon his Mother[3] to day; but I have been sadly tired of late, partly in consequence of some cold caught in my face and limbs at that weary flower-show, whither I went to gratify the Miss Marshalls. Tell dearest Sister, that we went all through Windsor Castle, with the exception of the Library and St Georges Chapel.[4] It is very greatly altered since the Renewal,[5] scarcely to be recognized, the Round Tower by being raised and I think spoiled, but the whole greatly improved and the appearance of the Courts from the living Rooms is most magnificent. Upon the whole the day was agreeably spent except for fatigue, went down to Eton, and saw Edward Coleridge[6] and his wife both looking marvellously well and prospering abundantly; went also under the guidance of the provost[7] through the Lodge. I forgot to mention that we passed

---

[1] Horace Twiss (1787–1849), lawyer, politician and wit, at this time M.P. for Bridport: author of *The Public and Private Life of Lord Chancellor Eldon*, 3 vols., 1844. He had called on W. W. in Aug. 1834 (*RMVB*).

[2] *Word dropped out.*

[3] She was Helena, eldest daughter of the Revd. Charles Perceval, rector of Bruhenny, Co. Cork, and widow of John Crosbie Graves (1776–1835) of the Irish bar, chief police magistrate of Dublin.   [4] *Written* castle.

[5] Sir Jeffry Wyatville had transformed the external appearance of Windsor Castle in the later 1820s, remodelling the royal apartments and raising the Round Tower by some 30 feet. D. W. would recall the older building which she had known as a much younger woman when she stayed in the Cloisters with her uncle Canon William Cookson in 1792 (see *EY*, pp. 81 ff.), and again with W. W. in 1802, just before his wedding.

[6] S. T. C.'s nephew, see pt. i, L. 126.

[7] Dr. Joseph Goodall (1760–1840), headmaster of Eton, 1801–9, and thereafter Provost.

the Queen and some ladies in the long Corridor; I rather think they had heard of us and came out on purpose. From Windsor we went to Mr Jesse's,[1] Hampton Court, a beautiful ride along the Thames. He lives in a wren's nest of [a] cottage, small as the smallest Lodging house in Ambleside, beautifully situated with a Grand Park behind and a beautiful village green in front. Mrs Fraser[2] was there, I liked her much—I think she has sound sense. Her little Boy is a fine child, but when I kissed him he made an ugly face, a trick, his mother said, taught him by his Grandfather who spoils him a little. Mrs Jess is a fine looking woman for her years. Hallam tells me that he has made upwards of 700£ by his books since he told me himself that he is going to publish another. This one will pay for the enlargement of his House which he is going to undertake. Mrs Fraser expressed much interest in you dearest Dora, she talks of going to the North in August. Judge how my time is spent when I tell you that at 8 this Monday I received a Card with the name of Mr Conolly[3] upon it. He was waiting below, he had heard of my being in Town from the newspapers and called thus early to pay his respects. He took a high tone of admiration. He is an American, a converted Catholic, having been a protestant minister in America. His wife and family are at Rome, where he *himself* lives a good deal with Lord Shrewsbury.[4] He returns to Rome in September.

---

[1] Edward Jesse the naturalist (see pt. ii, L. 748), author of *Gleanings in Natural History* (1832−5), and deputy surveyor of royal parks and palaces.

[2] W. W. is apparently confusing names. He seems to be referring to Jesse's daughter, Mrs. Matilda Charlotte Houstoun, the novelist, whose late husband had visited W. W. when an undergraduate at Cambridge. In her memoirs she describes producing her infant son for the poet's inspection during his visit to Windsor, and gives a somewhat unflattering picture of W. W.'s unprepossessing demeanour: 'I could . . . have well nigh wept over his big nose and general coarseness of appearance.' (*A Woman's Memoirs of Well-known Men*, 2 vols., 1883, i. 112 ff.)

[3] Pierce Connelly, an episcopal clergyman, was received with his wife into the Roman Catholic Church in 1835, and ten years later he entered the priesthood. His wife Cornelia (1809−79) entered a convent and became foundress of the Society of the Holy Child Jesus in Derby. He subsequently renounced the Catholic faith, and became rector of the American episcopal church in Florence. Their son was Pierce Francis Connelly, the sculptor.

[4] John Talbot, 16th Earl of Shrewsbury and Waterford (1791−1852), of Alton Towers, Premier Earl of England and a leader of the Roman Catholic laity, who devoted his enormous wealth to the Catholic cause. See Denis Gwynn, *Lord Shrewbury, Pugin and the Catholic Revival*, 1946.

Having to be here at 9 I walked him down with me to the end of the street. — I am sorry you were disappointed in not having a Letter from me when you expected it but I assure you I have written as much and as often as the state of my eyes and engagements will allow. I have no pleasure equal or comparable in the slightest degree to writing to you.—When I get to Moxons I will make up a parcel to send you, though I fear it will contain little that will much interest you.—My engagements are as follows: today, dine at Home, evening a Levée. Tomorrow breakfast with Lord Northampton,[1] dine at home. Thursday dine with Mr Courtenay; friday with Lord Liverpool,[2] Saturday Sir Robert Inglis. Mr Twiss is coming and I must conclude—

W. W.

1038. W. W. to JOHN WORDSWORTH[3]

MS. WL.
LY ii. 799.

[? 15 June 1836]

My dear John,

I leave Mr Marshall's Monday next for Mr Moxon's.

I am now going to call at Gray's Inn with a chance of finding Mr Addison[4] at home. If I do not I shall leave a note for him, begging an account of your affairs as far as he had to do with them.

You have not written me your wish about the army,[5] and the particulars; for as I told you I cannot bear them in mind.

The accounts from Rydal are much as usual.

Your affectionate Uncle
W. Wordsworth

I breakfast at home tomorrow, if it should suit you to call.

---

[1] See L. 1017 above.
[2] For the 3rd Earl of Liverpool, see pt. i, L. 76 and pt. ii, L. 592.
[3] R. W.'s son.
[4] Richard Addison, partner of the late R. W. and one of his executors.
[5] John Wordsworth wished to enter the Army Medical Service.

1039. W. W. to JOHN WORDSWORTH

Address: John Wordsworth Esq., 28 Great Ormond St.
MS. WL.
LY ii. 799.

Lincoln's Inn.
Wednesday afternoon [15 June 1836].

My dear John,

Pray breakfast with me at Mr S. Cookson's, 45 Torrington Square at 9 on Saturday next, and bring with you any statements of accounts you have relative to your father's affairs. I have been at Mr Addison's and seen him.—

If you can't come be so good as let me know.

Ever yours
W. W.

1040. W. W. to JOHN DAVY[1]

Address: Dr Davy, Fort Pitt, Chatham.
Franked: London June sixteen 1836 W. Marshall.
Postmark: 16 June 1836.
Endorsed: Mr Wordsworth.
MS. Lilly Library, Indiana University.
LY iii. 1378.

41 Upper Grosvenor Street.
Thursday, June 16th [1836]

My dear Sir,

A few days ago I availed myself of your permission to forward to you the account of the injurious effects of carriage motion on my poor Daughter and other particulars of her case. And now I cannot forbear sending you a Transcript of a Letter just received from her.—She says, 'Tell Dr Davy that the acid has been applied to my side but I don't think it does any permanent good. While it acts, it certainly removes the aching in the side, but I think it only sends it to the back (under the shoulder) and when I lay it aside the aching comes back again as fresh as ever. I have been better since the bleeding, and my appetite is much improved.'

---

[1] For Dr. John Davy, see L. 921 above.

The necessity for having recourse to bleeding, as stated in her former letter, was brought on by persisting in carriage-motion.

Believe me my dear Sir
gratefully
Your much obliged
Wm Wordsworth

On Monday I go to Mr Moxon's, Dover Street.

A thousand thanks for your most kind and considerate Letter, received since the above was written—it will be forwarded by this day's post to Rydal.—I shall go to the Continent and as far as Rome if possible, if I do not receive unfavourable accounts from home.

As your Letter slightly alludes to shampooing, I have enclosed a slip of a Letter written some little time ago, in consequence of an account I had sent her in a Letter from a female Friend of successful treatment in that way, by a Miss Walker who lives at Barton[1] in Westmorland.

I cannot conclude without adding that it would give me sincere pleasure to profit by your most friendly invitation, at any time, and I much regret my inability. Do not trouble yourself to return this slip of paper.

1041. W. W. to HIS FAMILY

MS. WL. Hitherto unpublished.

[*c.* 17 June 1836]

My dearest Friends,

My heart fails—I am so sad in a morning when I wake and think that more than 4 months will elapse before I see you again, if I go to Italy and after an absence of I believe 7 weeks. I cannot bear to think of it having reached the age that we all have except you dearest Dora—I should have thought nothing of it 20 years ago—but now I sicken at the scheme as I draw near to the appointed time. Do let me put it off, and try the events of another year, that may [have][2] produced favorable changes among us; if not it will be no disappointment to me.

---

[1] A small village between Sockbridge and the head of Ullswater.

[2] *Word dropped out*

I think I will return with Mr Graves, and do not scold me if I should. To say the truth in another point also—I have been much exhausted by these long London tete a tetes with people, foreigners among others, who wish to hear me talk and never are at rest. I shall see Mr Quillinan in an hour's time. I dine at Lord Lonsdale's. I had a call this morning from Sir Robert Inglis.

ever affectionately
most affectionately yours—
[*unsigned*]

I have been again to the Dentist, and with Constable[1] the Painter. God bless you again and again. Mr Graves is very well.

1042. W. W. to HORACE TWISS[2]

Address: Horace Twiss Esq. [*? delivered by hand*]
MS. Swarthmore College Library. Hitherto unpublished.

[*c.* 18 June 1836]

My dear Sir,
Upon carefully reviewing all that passed between us, and consulting with a judicious Friend who knows me well, my situation in life etc—I feel obliged to give up the pleasing hopes your conversation raised, and have returned the paper unsigned, without even consulting Mr Courtenay.

The same considerations had they presented themselves to my mind with equal force, would also have prevented me from hazarding the other adventure small as it is. But to that I consider myself bound unless with entire convenience to yourself you could release me from it—which I should prefer, but solely on the condition already mentioned—

believe me my dear Sir, ever faithfully
Your obliged
W Wordsworth

If I had not been engaged to breakfast for several successive mornings I should have preferred the medium of conversation to this Note—
41 Upper Grosvenor Street is my address till Monday next, then Mr Moxon's Dover Street—

---

¹ See L. 1048 below.

² See L. 1037 above.

1043. W. W. to THOMAS NOON TALFOURD

Address: Mr Sergeant Talfourd, Russell Square.
Postmark: (1) 21 June 1836 (2) 22 June 1836.
MS. Bookfellow Foundation Collection, Knox College. Hitherto unpublished.

Tuesday afternoon [21 June 1836]

My dear Sir,

Your Letter, for which pray accept my thanks, has summoned me to a further consideration of the subject, and the result is that I think it better I should not go.[1]—I will tell you why when I have the pleasure of seeing you, which I trust will be on Saturday afternoon at the latest.[2]

ever faithfully yours
Wm Wordsworth

1044. W. W. to WILLIAM BLACKWOOD[3]

Address: W. Blackwood, Esq.
Endorsed: W. Wordsworth. June 22.
MS. National Library of Scotland. Hitherto unpublished.

London
44 Dover Street
June 22nd. [1836]

My dear Sir,

I take the Liberty of enclosing for your perusal a Tale, by a female friend of mine, with which I have been much pleased.

It is the work of Mrs Bedingfield,[4] formerly Bryant, who has

---

[1] The reference seems to be to W. W.'s postponement of his plan to visit the Continent until the following year.

[2] W. W. went to stay with Talfourd on the 25th. There, on the 27th, he saw Harrison Ainsworth (1805–82), author of *Rookwood*, etc., and John Forster, the *Examiner* critic (see pt. ii, L. 659). Lamb had given Ainsworth an introduction to W. W. as early as 1823 (see *Lamb* ii. 412), and they may well have met before this. The novelist visited W. W. in 1843 (*RMVB*).

[3] In writing to the firm W. W. seems to have been unaware—or to have forgotten—that William Blackwood had died in Sept. 1834, and had been succeeded by his sons Alexander and Robert.

[4] Mrs. Mary Bedingfield, authoress of *Longhollow*, 1829, and other tales. In Sept. 1836 *Blackwood's Magazine* carried a story called 'Poor Will Newbery!' which is attributed to Mrs. Bedingfield in the Contributors List (*National Library of Scotland MSS*.) See also L. 1072 below.

published several things, in prose and verse, which have not obtained the notice they merited.—She is desirous (from the state of her circumstances with reference to her children by her former marriage) to turn her literary talents to some pecuniary account; and wishing to befriend her, I have sent you the enclosed, being myself persuaded that it has great merit, and hoping that you will be of the same opinion. Should that fortunately prove so, will you have the goodness to write to the Lady (Mrs Bedingfield Stow Market) and let her know what you could give her for this specimen of her talents or for any other tales that might suit you.

If the MS now sent should not prove likely to answer your purpose, pray be so kind as carefully to preserve it, till you may have an opportunity of having it safely conveyed to Rydal Mount, or till you may receive directions from the authoress herself how she wishes to have it disposed of.

I remain dear Sir
faithfully your obliged
Wm Wordsworth

1045. W. W. to HIS FAMILY

MS. WL. Hitherto unpublished.

4 oclock Dover Street
[*c.* 23 June 1836]

My dear Friends,

I attempted to write at the Dentist's as you will see by the cover. From his House or rather from Holborn I took an omnibus and made three or 4 farewell calls, Lord Lonsdales included, at Houses where I had dined. On arriving here I was delighted by the sight of your Letter, which had been forwarded by the two penny, and now sit down merely to thank you all, sister above all, for her Note; and dearest Dora I hope you are decidedly better though you do not say so, yet I cannot but infer it—

I have not yet seen Mr Robinson or heard of him;[1] but I am resolved to return to Rydal, and I hope to set off on Tuesday week at the latest. My reasons are my faint-heartedness and

---

[1] H. C. R. had been away in Bury St. Edmunds since the middle of the month. He returned to London on the 25th.

those I have already given. As to my health I cannot expect to be strong in my muscles while I live in this place, with these profuse night meals. My right arm is certainly no worse but better, and the fingers much less numb, and also the back of the hand, but my left without being positively numb, has sensations more easily produced in it by awkward positions than formerly, sensations such as one feels when one says ones arm or leg is asleep, but this is in so very small degree that I never should have noticed it, but for the state the other arm was thrown into long ago, and for a general loss of muscular strength about the wrists and in the fingers of both arms, when I exert them in packing etc—so that I really wish to be quit—the more so, on account of slight pains and uneasinesses in the crown of my head, when I have much exerted myself in walking. But dont say any thing of these matters even to Mr Carr, as to consulting anyone, that can be of no use. I must avoid heating or stimulating things and labours. You may remember I have often said that salt and seasoned meals during my whole life have caused perspiration to start from the crown of my head, and this is so now in a much greater degree with a slight pricking pain; which first I felt in Church at Rydal. But far far too much of this you shall hear no more of it I hope—I shall write again on Monday—How I long to see you. To day I met at Sir Robert's[1] Lord Sandon,[2] Sir Stratford Canning[3] etc. Copy right was talked over; I shall be the means of bringing about a favorable change in the law in that particular, I have no doubt. O for a sight of you dear James[4]—and the trees of Rydal. Adieu adieu, again adieu. My dearest Sister and others and thanks for your Letter; Keep a glass of Mary Fisher's Elder wine for me. God bless you.

W W.

[1] Sir Robert Inglis's.

[2] Dudley Ryder, later 2nd Earl of Harrowby (1798—1882), M.P. for Tiverton (1819—31), and for Liverpool (1831—47); member of the Ecclesiastical Commission, Secretary of the India Board (1850—1), Chancellor of the Duchy of Lancaster under Palmerston and then Lord Privy Seal (1855—7).

[3] Sir Stratford Canning, 1st Viscount Stratford de Redcliffe (1786—1880), doyen of nineteenth-century diplomats, had been British ambassador at Constantinople and negotiated the settlement of Greek affairs with France and Russia (1828) after the battle of Navarino. Thereafter he entered Parliament as M.P. for Old Sarum (1828), Stockbridge (1830), and King's Lynn (1835—41), returning to Constantinople in 1842, where he conducted the negotiations with Russia which ultimately terminated in the Crimean war.

[4] James Dixon, gardener and handyman at Rydal Mount.

1046. W. W. to H. C. R.

Address: H. Crabb Robinson Esq., Bury St. Edmunds, [*readdressed to*] 2
    Plowden Buildings, Temple, London.
Franked: London June twenty four 1836 W.E. Gladstone.
Postmark: 27 June 1836. *Stamp*: Bury St. Edmunds.
Endorsed: 24th June 1836, Wordsworth Autograph.
MS. Dr Williams's Library.
K(—). Morley, i. 304.

44 Dover Street
[24 June 1836]

Tomorrow at Sergeant Talfourd's for a couple of days

My dear Friend

I have been expecting to hear from you or rather to see you
every day; And now feel not a little ashamed to tell you by
Letter what I wished to say *viva voce*, that after having been 2
months without seeing the faces of those at home who are so
dear to me, I have not courage to prepare for our continental
journey. To add 4 months, probably, of absence to the two
already elapsed I do not feel equal to—Pray come up and set me
at ease upon the point of my feeling as if I were using you ill, in
declining to go abroad at present. I shall say no more at present.

ever affectionately
Yours
W Wordsworth

P.S. My London life has much exhausted me, notwithstanding my abstinence. The accounts from home are rather better.

1047. W. W. to HIS FAMILY

MS. WL. Hitherto unpublished.
Friday [24 June 1836]
44 Dover [St]

My dearest Friends,

Having breakfasted at Rogers's I had an opportunity of
procuring this frank of Mr Gladstone who was there.—I also
wrote a short note to Mr Robinson, to let him know that I really
had not courage to go abroad at present; and begging he would

come up to Town that I might give him my reasons and set myself right in his opinion.—I have been calling this morning on Mr and M[rs] Lester[1] and Lord Mahon,[2] and in half [an] hour Rogers will be here and we [are going][3] to an Exhibition or two. By imprudently sitting yesterday while I was at the Dentists, opposite to an open window, I have caught a disagreeable sneezing cold which affects my eyes a great deal, and my throat somewhat.—I do not mean to tire myself any more, and hope to recover some of my lost strength.—Mr Quill: and Rotha are still here and his Brother is in the House also having just arrived from Oporto.—I have given up all notions of returning by Hull, it would take 4 or 5 days, I shall return as I came, but in the inside instead of the out.—I shall write again to morrow in all probability, as I can easily procure a frank and Sunday is not a post day. I am rather vexed about this cold as the running of the eyes weakens them, when they were improving much; it was the cold east winds and the light which hurt them.—

I have seen Mr Trench[4] author of that vol. of excellent poems, and Mr Strong the Sonnetteer,[5] Mr Sharp's and Miss

[1] W. W. is probably referring to Henry Thomas Lister (1800–42), one of Henry Taylor's circle, author of *Granby* (1826) and other popular novels, and Registrar General of England and Wales from 1836. His wife Maria (d. 1865), daughter of the Hon. George Villiers, youngest son of the 1st Earl of Clarendon, wrote *Lives of the Friends and Contemporaries of Lord Chancellor Clarendon*, 3 vols., 1852, and other works. They had both visited the poet in 1831 (*RMVB*).

[2] Philip Henry Stanhope, Lord Mahon, later 5th Earl Stanhope (1805–75), of Chevening, nr. Sevenoaks, Kent: M.P. for Wootton Bassett, 1830–2, and for Hertford, 1835-52; Under-Secretary for Foreign Affairs in Peel's first administration, and later Secretary to the Board of Control; a prime mover in the foundation of the National Portrait Gallery (1856) and the Historical Manuscripts Commission (1869); author of a *History of the War of Succession in Spain, 1702–1714*, 1832, *The History of England from the Peace of Utrecht to the Peace of Versailles, 1713–1783*, 7 vols., 1836–53, *The Life of the Right Hon. William Pitt*, 4 vols., 1861–2, and numerous other historical works and essays. He had already established himself as one of the leaders of the movement for Copyright reform, and this may have prompted his visit to W. W. as early as Sept. 1832 (*RMVB*). See also L. 1236 below. His wife, Emily (d. 1873), whom he married in 1834, was daughter of General Sir Edward Kerrison, Bart.

[3] *Hole in MS.*   [4] R. C. Trench (see L. 949 above).

[5] Charles Edward Strong (b. 1815), Fellow of Wadham College, Oxford, published translations of Italian sonnets (1827) and his own *Sonnets* (1835).

Kinnaird's Torquay friend. He told Mr Moxon, who invited him to breakfast that he would have given 50 pounds for the pleasure. So my dearest Sister, you see that your old Brother is still in request. I had an odd adventure the other night between nine and ten when Mr Moxon and I went to hear Lord Melbourne's trial;[1] I will tell you it when I get to Rydal. Dearest Dora get well, and we will go to Italy together at . . .

[*cetera desunt*]

1048. W. W. to HIS FAMILY

MS. WL. Hitherto unpublished.

Saturday 2 o clock [25 June 1836][2]

My dear Friends,

I am writing in Mr Marshall's room, John[3] opposite me, copying a form of letter kindly sent me by Mr Courtenay to be addressed to Messrs Bell[4] requesting an account of the Government Annuities, what sums have been received upon them and to whom and where paid. This morning I met John at Breakfast at Strickland Cooksons, that he might receive instructions from him, John has got a paper, which he will take down in July, and proceed to settle his affairs.—On my return here, I found your Letters. Glad I am of such favorable accounts; but dearest Dora we cannot go bleeding for ever; I am now as much afraid of carriage exercise for you as before. I wish and pray from the bottom of my heart that you may not be so much hurt by your intended journey to the sea-side as to require bleeding again. Let

[1] The action brought by the Hon. George Norton (1801–75), a commissioner in bankruptcy, against Lord Melbourne, the Prime Minister, for having had 'criminal conversation' with the plaintiff's wife, Mrs. Caroline Norton (1805–77), the well-known poetess, society beauty and wit. The trial opened in the Court of Common Pleas on 22 June, Sir William Follett (see L. 1049 below) appearing for the plaintiff, and Talfourd for the defence, and Melbourne was acquitted. The evidence adduced was so weak that it was thought at the time that the trial was deliberately engineered to discredit the Prime Minister and the Whig government. See David Cecil, *Lord M.*, 1954, pp. 154–65.

[2] This letter was written from John Marshall's house, where W. W. called on his way to spend the weekend at Talfourd's.

[3] R. W. 's son.

[4] The stockbrokers.

every possible precaution be used. A few mornings ago I called on Mrs Graves, she not there, but almost the first word Miss Graves [1] spoke, when she had enquired after you was a dagger to me. She said her Brother told her that bleeding in spinal cases was quite exploded; it had harmed the patient so much, and it does seem reasonable to bear in mind that ease must not be procured by bleeding and merely to be thrown away, long exertion, there again, cannot be accused of this fault. But take more and more care, if it were not that I thought it *right* that I should go abroad, as a thing which if [not done] [2] will never be done, I should most certainly go down to Westmorland—to be with you by the Sea side following W[m] Crackanthorp's [3] example, who will leave London the moment he hears that his Sister is strong enough to be moved. I saw him yester-evening at Mr Hallams.—Be not alarmed about my speculating turn. I have resolved not to venture the £100, nor even a sixpence, in the way I talked upon the suggestion of Horace Twiss, [4] and I have no money to provide except for my teeth, beyond what Mr Carter knows and a trifle for John's pressing expenses.

Now dearest D— for your questions. Capt[n] Elliot [5] is of R. N. and a brother of Mr Elliot formerly of the Colonial Off. whom you dearest Mary will remember we often saw at Miss Fenwick's with his Wife a Daughter of Mr Perry [6] formerly Editor and proprietor of the Morning Chronicle. Mr Taylor [7] was directed to have the tea sent, by a conveyance which Mr Marshall always employs, Pickfords most likely, he is not in the House or I would ask. I shall also ask Henry Taylor. — I have

---

[1] Clara (d. 1871), R. P. Graves's sister. In 1843 she married Leopold von Ranke, the historian, who visited W. W. in October of that year (*RMVB*).

[2] *Words dropped out.*

[3] Of Newbiggin Hall, W. W.'s cousin. His sister was Miss Sara Crackanthorpe, also of Newbiggin.

[4] See L. 1037 above.

[5] Captain, later Admiral, Sir Charles Elliot (1801—75), afterwards (1841) a controversial Minister Plenipotentiary in China, was brother of Frederick Elliot, Henry Taylor's colleague at the Colonial Office, who was now serving as Secretary to Lord Gosford's Commission of Inquiry into Canadian affairs. See *Autobiography of Henry Taylor*, i. 164 ff.

[6] James Perry (1756-1821) edited the *Morning Chronicle*, the leading Whig paper, to which Lamb, Coleridge, and Hazlitt contributed, from 1789.

[7] Apparently an associate of Twining, the tea merchant.

seen Mr Westall[1] twice—told him you owed him £10—but I
had not wherewith to pay him. He was quite easy about that;
and begged, dearest Mary, you would ask T. Troughton[2] to
send him his account, and what No. of Engravings he had on
hand. Have seen Boxall[3] twice, at his own house, but only for a
few moments, shall see him again in the course of next week. Mr
Harness[4] walks well, and was improving daily after his 2nd
accident, I have seen him several times, he contrived to use a
stick.—Alas! I have not yet seen Mr Aders,[5] shall, when Mr
Robinson returns from Bury where he has been upwards of a
fortnight. Have not seen Derwent's wife[6]—they did not come
on account of the Baby's illness, who I learn from the News
papers is since dead. Pick's Picture[7] is to be twice engraved, first
the head and upper part as vignette for the new Edition, and the
whole length for sale. About Chris's marriage intentions[8] I
know nothing—nor am I likely to see Charles and his Bride, or
to have time to see Dr Watson.[9] The Master of Trinity passed
through London on Tuesday, but I had no notice of his
intention and of course saw him not as he did not call. It is Chris:
who means to travel during his Holidays. You may depend
upon having his Book.[10] Constable's India paper Proof prints,[11] a

[1] William Westall the artist (see pt. ii. L. 636).
[2] Thomas Troughton, the Ambleside bookseller.
[3] William Boxall, the portrait painter (see pt. ii. L. 603).
[4] William Harness.
[5] Charles Aders, H. C. R. 's friend (see pt. i, L. 342).
[6] Derwent Coleridge's wife, Mary, had just lost her second child Emily.
[7] Pickersgill's protrait of W. W. For the vignette engraving by W. H.
Watt, see pt. ii, L. 717 and L. 1078 below. The full-length engraving by R. C.
Rolls was eventually published in *The Modern Poets and Artists of Great Britain*,
ed S. C. Hall, 1838.
[8] C. W. jnr. did not marry until well over two years later. See L. 1284
below.
[9] Joshua Watson's elder brother, the Revd. John James Watson, D.D.
(1768—1839), rector of Hackney (1799) and of Digswell, Herts, (1811),
Archdeacon of St. Alban's (1816), and Prebendary of St. Paul's (1825).
[10] *Athens and Attica: Journal of a residence there,* 1836.
[11] W. W.'s friendship with John Constable (1776—1837) the landscape
painter, dates from 1806, when Constable was staying with John Harden of
Brathay, and painted portraits of Charles and Sophia Lloyd. They subsequently met at Sir George Beaumont's , probably in the spring of 1807 (see
HCR i. 312), and again in May 1812; and possibly as a result of a further
meeting in the spring of 1835, Constable contributed a poem in praise of

handsome Present, will go down with the Marshalls. I thought
Cordelia would like to see them at leisure perhaps, copy some of
them or parts of them. I will see Mr Twining,[1] I hope the tea
will soon reach you. Mr Quillinan and Brother will both be at
Mr Moxon's today, I go there on Monday.[2] I had no business
with Mr Addison but to request a statement of John's accounts,
Receipts and payments, as far as he had himself been concerned
with them. Copley Fielding[3] has just this moment sent back the
album, with a very nice drawing in it. He said it would have
been much better but that [the] Paper was too soft. Love to Kate
S.[4]—sorry I cant see her sweet face at Rydal. I promise you, my
legs shall never save my purse[5]—but I am a little sorry that Mr
Robinson is so fond of diligences for economy and gossip's sake.
I have told him I never will travel in one or in the night through
a beautiful country; this I have expressly stipulated for.—And
now my dearest Sister, let me thank you for your delightfully

W. W.'s patriotism, dated 28 June 1835, to Dora W.'s Autograph Album
(*WL MSS.*). In 1836, when Constable's *Cenotaph* was sent to the Academy, he
inserted in the Catalogue one of W. W.'s Coleorton inscriptions (see *PW* iv.
196). For a full discussion of their early relationship, see *John Constable's
Correspondence*, Vol. v, ed. R. B. Beckett, Suffolk Records Society, 1967,
pp. 73—8. Constable had now written on 15 June (*WL MSS.*), asking W. W.
to accept 'my Little Work—(on the Chiar oscuro) . . . the subjects of which
are for the most part in the neighbourhood of Dedham—in Essex—one of the
Early and favorite haunts of our valued friend the late Sʳ George
Beaumont . . . I feel that I am endebted to him for what I am as an artist—and
it was from his hands that I first saw a volume of your poems—how then can I
ever be sufficiently gratefull . . . ' He acknowledged with pride that W. W.
had attended one of his recent lectures at the Royal Institution, and expressed
the hope that he would see him again at the last lecture, on the following day.
Constable's *English Landscape* was published in five volumes of four prints
each, consisting of mezzotints by David Lucas (1802—81), between 1830 and
1832. W. W. later recalled with gratitude the artist's gift in a letter to
Constable's daughters, 6 June 1844 (in next volume). See also L. 1052 below.

[1] Richard Twining, the tea merchant.

[2] E. Q.'s brother arrived from Portugal on Friday, 24 June (see previous
letter), the day before this letter was written. W. W. left John Marshall's on the
20th, stayed at Moxon's till the 25th, and thereafter spent the weekend at
Talfourd's, before returning to Moxon's the following Monday.

[3] Anthony Copley Fielding (1787—1855), President of the Water-Colour
Society, was contributing to Dora W.'s Album.

[4] Kate Southey.

[5] A reference to the proposed Continental tour with H. C. R.

penned Letter; how shall I rejoice were you well enough to go to Rome with me, but I go now least[1] I should soon be as disabled as you are. This London life wears me out—these long tete a tetes with strangers, and late dinners and in the morning hours would soon make an end of me. My right hand is almost as numb as Mrs Hardens,[2] and my left little better, and with night I perspire as much as you will remember I did in that close room at Calais.[3] I have thrown off my breast plate, my [?][4] Belt, and my Leather-waistcoat. Apropo of dress, I ordered a plaid jacket and waistcoat, and by a stupid error of Mr Courtenays eldest son I have got two, costing together above sixpound— the poor Taylor was so dismayed when I told him I had only ordered one that in pity to him I took the other. And now my dearest dearest Sister Goodbye—how pleased I am to hear you are so much out. Yesterday I called at Lambeth, did not see the Archbp[5] but left a message with Mrs H. commending W^m to her, and speaking warmly of his anxiety to prepare himself for any duty to which through his Grace's goodness, he might be called. This is all I could do, but probably I shall write to the Arch^b before I leave England. Mr Watson[6] I saw yesterday, he is better but prohibited from talking. I found Cambridge John[7] had been there—he is at Hampstead—he has not called here. My heart is aching sadly but I go on, depend upon it my dearest wife that I will not forget our Son, I will do all that is possible for him. Yesterday I dined at Lord Liverpools—a most splendid and beautifully situated house;[8] saw Lady Catharine[9] and her unmarried Sister,[10] both enquired dearest Dora particularly of you. The Botched Ivy Cot.[11] is just what I expected. The answer

[1] lest *written* least.

[2] Mrs. Harden of Field Head was in declining health (see L. 1056 below).

[3] W. W. is apparently recalling the Continental tour of 1820 (see *MY* ii. 623 and *DWJ* ii. 11 ff.).

[4] *MS. obscure.*

[5] Dr. Howley.

[6] Joshua Watson.

[7] C. W.'s son.

[8] The reference seems to be to Lord Liverpool's town residence, Fife House in Whitehall Yard. His country seat was Coombe House, Kingston.

[9] Lady Catharine Cope Jenkinson (b. 1811), Lord Liverpool's eldest daughter, Lady of the Bedchamber to the Duchess of Kent, married in 1837 Col. Francis Vernon Harcourt, son of the Archbishop of York.

[10] Lady Louisa Cope Jenkinson (b. 1814).

[11] In 1835 the Ivy Cottage, Rydal, had been rented by William Ball (1801−78), a Quaker from Tottenham, and a connection of the Frys, who had

to my letter to the Bells,[1] and Mr Courtenay's statement by which it will be followed, will shew what funds we have at command—demands for travel will be upwards of £100, teeth 50, so that the Yarrow[2] will be swallowed up by these personal expenses. There remains I hope about 300 due from Longmans for the Poems. . . .

[*cetera desunt*]

1049. W. W. to HIS FAMILY

Address: Mʳˢ Wordsworth, Rydal Kendal.
Franked: London June Twenty-seven 1836 T. N. Talfourd.
Postmark: 27 June 1836.
MS. WL. Hitherto unpublished.

Moxons Monday afternoon
[27 June 1836]

My dearest Friends,

A Frank being so easily procured, I write again though with little or nothing to say.—Mr Courtenay has sent me in his statement, which I shall either forward in a day or two or bring with me.—By this account, as far as appears, the only very promising part of the concern at present, is the Government annuities. Of these Mr C. says, 'I reckon that investment in these has produced you a profit of £500 beyond 5 per cent in your Capital embarked, reckoning what you have received and the balance of what remains. And to shew you that I am sincere in this Estimate, I am willing to give you £500 for your bargain, after allowing you five per cent on your money, on what you have paid and received. I offer you this, also, in case you wish to realize profits etc.' To morrow I shall breakfast with Mr Courtenay, and talk these matters over; but for this intention, I would forward to Mr Carter his statement today.— Enough of money. This morning I breakfasted with Mr Spring

---

been in practice as a solicitor in Bristol for some years; and he and his wife struck up a friendship with the Wordsworths (see *RMVB* for 1835). Soon afterwards, Ball purchased the property, enlarging it to the residence which survives today, and renaming it Glen Rothay; and there W. W. met many of his Quaker friends. Ball published nine volumes of poetry, including *Nugae Sacrae*, (anon.), 1825. See *Annual Monitor*, 1879, pp. 8–54.

[1] i.e. to Bell Bros., the stockbrokers.
[2] i.e. the payment for the *Yarrow Revisited* volume.

Rice, and talked the matter of Copy right over with him. He seems determined to take or have it taken up with spirit, so that I have no doubt it (the term) will be greatly extended. Do consider that The Excursion has only 6 years to run if I should die. I am happy in having been the means of putting the measure of justice in train.—Yesterday Sir Wm Follett[1] dined with us. On account of his health he does not go out to dinner, but he made an exception and came to gratify me, and as he said for the pleasure of making my acquaintance.—Since I wrote the above that was written at Moxon's I have been 2 hours engaged with him in arranging and distributing the Poems for the intended Edition in six volumes, Excursion included. I feel rather fatigued, the cold I so foolishly caught in sitting at the Dentist's before an open window in a blowing wind, and after a long walk became weaker in my eyes and relaxed my body very much.

The Poems will stand thus as to pages

1st vol	384	5th vol:	428
2	382	Excursion	422.
3	368		
4	421		

Mr Robinson with his usual goodness (though disappointed) chearfully lets me off; and in consequence, God willing, I shall be at home on Thursday Evening, meaning at present to go to St Albans on Tuesday afternoon, sleep there and proceed to Manchester on Wednesday, Mr Graves I hope will accompany me and not impossibly Mr Quillinan, whom I have seen to day. Could not James come to meet me at Kendal on Thursday with the Carriage. It would save expense. I am sure I am quite right in returning. Mr Robinson thinks so, and especially on account of settling with John,[2] and making out the accounts previous to his signing a Release. This now strikes me of more importance on account of the difficulty of getting correct Statements of the money that has been paid and received by Mr Addison and Mr Hutton.[3] Mr Hutton especially has been very forgetful. Miss

---

[1] Sir William Webb Follett (1798−1845), one of the greatest advocates of the century: M. P. for Exeter (1835−45), Counsel to the University of Cambridge (1836), Solicitor General in Peel's first and second administrations (1834−5, 1841−4), and Attorney General (1845).

[2] R. W.'s son.

[3] The late R. W.'s executors (see *EY*, p. 645; *MY* ii. 328).

Fenwick is no longer an Invalid. Tomorrow at 12 I conclude with the Dentist and I mean to dine at Hampstead. I have just received the Enclosed from Dʳ Davy. What a good creature and a thoughtful one he is. It is an answer to the slip of your Letter which I enclose also.—How sorry I am that I shall not see Cambridge John¹ at Hampstead, he is gone (I told you) to Winchester. Dearest Sister, I shall give all your loves to Sara Coleridge and I hope to see Christopher,² and Mrs Gee³ etc. farewell again farewell.

I hope my arms will strengthen and my legs too when I get to the [?]⁴ of Rydal.

1050. W. W. to ALEXANDER DYCE

MS. Victoria and Albert Museum. Hitherto unpublished.

[? late June 1836]

My dear Mr Dyce,

I regret that I cannot have the pleasure of breakfasting with you being engaged for the whole of the week; and I shall probably be out of Town the week after.

If you could contrive to be at home on Tuesday next—¼ after two, I should have an opportunity of calling upon you; but pray don't give yourself the trouble of answering this note.

Ever my dear Mr Dyce,

faithfully yours
Wᵐ Wordsworth

1051. W. W. to HIS FAMILY

MS. WL. Hitherto unpublished.

[28 June 1836]

My dearest Friends, here I am at the Dentist's, meaning to go hence into the City after he has done with me. John here also. To day I leave Mr Talfourd's and go to Hampstead, to remain I

---

¹ C. W.'s son.
² C. W. jnr.
³ Of Hendon (see pt. i, L. 327).
⁴ *MS. blotted.*

hope no longer than Friday.—I have been breakfasting with Mr Courtenay who repeats his offer of 500, and to pay 5 per cent for the money vested in the annuities.—I am to advise this day with my Brother in the City, whether I should do well to accept this offer. Mr Courtenay says that I have been luckier thus far than I have a right to expect—If I can see Strickland Cookson, I should be glad of his advice. I write not merely that you may see my handwriting for I have nothing to say, but to acknowledge the receipt of your most welcome Letters this morning, and to beg that you would continue to write through Sergeant Talfourd, as late as by Saturdays post but no later, because I think of sleeping at St Albans on Tuesday night.

Since breakfast I have called on Mr Justice Coleridge,[1] his family are coming down to the Lakes, there also I saw Mrs Patteson,[2] having intended to call upon her.—What a happy thing would it be if dearest Dora could get well enough to start in the autumn. We might both go with Miss Fenwick, travelling leisurely, and for the benefit of us all. She says she could not have you dearest Mary, but surely Joanna would come to you, and she might be at ease on that point.—John thanks Dora for her Letter, and sends love to you all, and wishes he had been going down with me but cannot until the end of July.—Dearest Sister I will think of your dresses. I did not take Mr Partridge's[3] watch myself, but it went through one of Mr Marshall's Servants, you had therefore better send the address.

ever affectionately yours,   W. W.

Love to all yourselves and to all the Servants.

My cold is a good deal better, but my arms do not strengthen, and I perspire terribly in the night, and I shall do, till I get to Rydal.—

---

[1] After a sound, if not brilliant, career at the Bar, Sir John Taylor Coleridge (see *MY* ii. 235) had been appointed a Justice of the King's Bench in 1835. For his visit to Fox How, see L. 1073 below.

[2] Sister of Sir John Taylor Coleridge and Henry Nelson Coleridge (see pt. ii, L. 564).

[3] Mr. Partridge of Ambleside.

1052. W. W. to HIS FAMILY

MS. WL. Hitherto unpublished.

Wednesday noon [? 29 June 1836]
44 Dover street—

My dearest Friends,

I am now writing at Moxon's with John[1] beside me,
preparing some comments upon Mr Addison's Bill of Monies
received and applied.—Yesterday I had a pretty hard day,
concluding with dinner at Mr Moxon's with Quillinan and
Brother, and an evening Party at Sir Wm Gomm's, in discharge
of the last of my engagements except one to Breakfast on
Saturday pressed upon me so by Sir Robert Inglis that I could
not refuse. On that evening I mean to sleep at Sergeant
Talfourds and on Monday or Tuesday propose going to
Hampstead for a few days; then I shall return hither; and now
for the point of points—

When I consider how long I have been from home already,
and that if I go abroad probably 4 months will be added to that
time my heart sickens at the thought, and I cannot muster
courage for the undertaking, at our time of life—

2^ndly every body tells me that it is scarcely safe to descend into
Italy, unless one keeps entirely in the north, until October.

3—If I start now three months there must be employed in
Germany, which is more than twice the time I wish to give to
it.—

What I propose then is, to return to Rydal in about a
fortnight for at least 2 months and then start for Italy, or give up
the thing for another year, which may produce formidable
changes, or changes so unfavourable as to make me cease to
want to go—

4 In fact I am heartsick and homesick, and have been a good
deal exhausted by the life I have here—which I feel chiefly
though this you need not mention to any one, in my arms, that
are strangely languid, with a sort of numbness in my fingers,
much less than I care to have in the right hand after the scalding,
but still a weakness in both arms and hands, which makes me
afraid at present of the hard service I might be tempted to put
myself upon: There is probably something of fancy in this
feeling and I hope it may go off at least in part when I shall be

1 R.. W.'s son.

269

more quiet, and less fevered, for every night I break out in to violent perspirations, and yesterday I had a severe head ache with throbbing in the arteries of the temples, and shooting pains.[1] I look well enough, Mr Liddel,[2] Dora, told me I looked ten years younger than when he saw me at Abbotsford. But still I do feel a difference, such as you will find described in the beginning of Sir Humphrey Davy's complaint—[3]

I have proposed to Mr Quillinan to go down with me; in which case I should stop a day or two with Dr Davy at Chatham and proceed by Steam to Hull, whence there is a railway to Selby,[4] and a conveyance to Leeds etc.

What has tired me most in London is tête a tête with strangers and the late dinners.—I have the satisfaction however of having done my duty. All I regret is that I did not refuse many invitations which I accepted. Were I ever to come to London again, I should boldly say at once that I was engaged, whenever I thought proper, whether I was or not.—I am quite well to day, except that I don't feel quite as strong as I ought to be especially as I said before in my arms.—My head-ache is gone, and my eyes are good.

The Marshalls are gone to day. They will stop a few days at Leeds, and then go to Halsteads. Pray write to them there, tell them how you are, and thank them all for their goodness to me. They will visit you soon. They have Constable's prints[5] with them and one or two things more.—

Mrs Partridge's watch was sent to the watchmaker, but I have not his address or Mr Graves would bring it down. Let me know the watchmaker's address—James[6] could call for it—

Among the duties of yesterday I called at Mr Twinings—told him about the tea-present, at which he laughed heartily. The tea was sent by Pickfords Boats, at least that was the direction given

---

[1] It is evident from earlier letters that W. W. feared that these were preliminary symptoms of a stroke.

[2] Henry Thomas Liddell (see L. 875 above), whom W. W. had met during his visit to Sir Walter Scott in 1831.

[3] In the last years of his life Sir Humphry Davy suffered increasingly from muscular paralysis, following a stroke at the close of 1826. See J. A. Paris, *Life of Sir Humphry Davy* . . . , 2 vols., 1831, ii. 300 ff.

[4] W. W. is mistaken. The Hull and Selby railway was not opened until 1840.

[5] See L. 1048 above.

[6] Handyman at Rydal Mount.

to Mr Taylor,[1] who no doubt would act upon it; but I shall
ascertain the truth. I forward[ed] part of Dora's Letter to D[r]
Davy yesterday—it seemed. . . .

[cetera desunt]

1053. W. W. to M. W.

Address: Mrs Wordsworth, Rydal Mount, Kendal.
Franked: London July One, 1836. E. Strutt.[2]
MS. WL. Hitherto unpublished.

[Hampstead]
Thursday morning [30 June 1836]

My dearest Mary,

Your letter of Monday has just reached me. I rejoice that
Dora is in *your* opinion 'now really improving'—and grieve
much that my Letters have made you unhappy. All I have to say
is that as you put it, upon a point of domestic duty, I will lay
bare all my symptoms whether real or imaginary to D[r] Holland,
if possible on Saturday, but I fear Mr Moxon may have engaged
some persons to meet me at Breakfast, there on Sunday.—I
cannot put off my journey home; for I am quite tired of this
mode of life and worn out with it. It is easy for you to say go and
spend a quiet day here or there, it is not in my power to spend a
quiet day any where. People put so many questions to me, and
think it so necessary to endeavour to put me upon something,
and to talk to me. You quite forget too my situation and my
disposition when you talk to me of quiet and preservation from
exhaustion. Should I go to D[r] Davy's he would invite his friends
to meet me and so on.

On Tuesday there was a party here to dine, Mr
Cunningham,[3] vicar of Harrow, and Henry Coleridge of the

---

[1] Twining's associate (see L. 1048 above).

[2] Edward Strutt, 1st Baron Belper (1801−80), a 'philosophical radical' and
friend of Bentham, the Mills and Macaulay: M.P. for Derby (1830−47),
Arundel (1851−2), and Nottingham (1852−6), chief commissioner for
railways (1846−8), and Chancellor of the Duchy of Lancaster under Lord
Aberdeen (1852−4). See also pt. ii, L. 602.

[3] The Revd. John William Cunningham (1780−1861), curate to John
Venn at Clapham, 1805−11, and thereafter vicar of Harrow: a noted
Evangelical, and editor of the *Christian Observer*, 1850−8.

271

number, Gurney[1] and another of the Hoares, Mrs Joanne
Baillie[2] etc etc. Mrs Henry Coleridge and Mrs C.[3] came in the
evening—Sara neither looking well nor strong. Yesterday I
called on them and should have called also on Miss Trevennan,[4]
but she was gone to London. I dined at Mr Longmans, a party of
20, with numbers in the evening.—This morning I go to
Hendon, and at one must be back at Henry Coleridges where I
am to meet at Luncheon Miss Trevennan, Derwent and his
Bride etc. Chris:[5] dines here at 3 and I expect Mr Crabb
Robinson and Sockbridge John, and John Wordsworth[6] from
Winchester. To morrow I shall return to Moxons, and on
Tuesday, God willing, shall sleep at St Albans in my way home,
meaning to be with you, notwithstanding all you have said to
the contrary, on Thursday evening. Every Body is pleased with
my teeth, and so am I except for one cause; owing I imagine to
the 2 teeth left in on the left side, the springs on that side cause an
irritation in that cheek, or blister, which prevents my wearing them, as I could otherwise do without the slightest
inconvenience, though of course I cannot masticate with them
yet, but very slowly. I hope the Dentist will be able to obviate
this inconvenience of the blister, or little lumps which they
cause in the left cheek; for there is nothing of it in the other. The
teeth look perfectly natural. My profuse night-sweats continue,
and will do so I am sure till I get to Rydal, unless I have the
resolution to abstain from drinking (water I mean) in consequence of these late dinners that make me so thirsty, though I
never take more than a couple of glasses of wine and a half at the
utmost, and eat the plainest things at table. As to my hands and
arms of which I have said so much I can only say that the right
arm, which you know was injured last summer is upon the
whole very much better, but I shall have in it and indeed in the
other also in some degree a sense of muscular weakness about

[1] John Gurney Hoare (1810−75), younger son of Samuel Hoare III
(1783−1847), had become head of the family bank on the death of his elder
brother, Samuel Hoare IV (1807−33). He had visited W.W. in 1830
(*RMVB*).
[2] Joanna Baillie, who published three volumes of *Dramas* this year, was
permanently resident in Hampstead.
[3] i.e. S. T. C.'s widow.
[4] Emily Trevenen (see pt. ii, L. 463).
[5] C. W. jnr.
[6] C. W.'s son.

the wrist, and also in the injured arm about the little finger specially, and sometimes on the back of the hand, a faint numbness something like, when a leg or arm has been in the state of being asleep, from a constrained position. Now I will tell you frankly and honestly, these sensations are not worth speaking of, nor would ever have been mentioned by me, if one had not heard so much of them or similar ones as precursors of paralytic affections. At this moment I am quite well, except merely that having written this long letter, and another to Mr Courtenay my right wrist, and fingers attract a little attention, but I am ashamed to advert to it, it is so very trifling.—

I shall consult Dr Holland to gratify you, and as far as my judgement is concerned, further regulation of my diet.[1] If he (Dr Holland) thought I could do without wine, I should much prefer that plan. But Basil Montagu by hard work and low living, as Procter[2] told me, brought himself into great pains, his body breaking out into Boils etc etc. I shall pay Jannetta[3] her 2—10.—If my Dentist can prevent the mischief in my Cheek, I am sure you will greatly approve of what has been done.—I could not have gone abroad in any Comfort of mind. I had quite miscalculated what would be my feelings towards home when July came. Had we been 40 years of age instead of nearly 70 I could have done it—at present it is quite out of the question, and in prolong[ing] my stay from home any where else would not answer for the reasons I have given. Therefore do not [? constrain] me my dearest friends. I am the best judge of my own heart! And to dearest Sister, I am glad of the proposed [?][4] into her room. My right arm is now free from sensation and the other attracts no attention. farewell.

Thursday evening

My dearest Friends,

Chris. has been dining here and Mr Robinson also who will take this to London to have it franked and sent for tomorrow's post. Mr Moxon has also been here and he and Mr R. will go with me to Hallams on tuesday afternoon, as will Mr Graves, Mr G. to proceed with me to Kendal.

On Saturday morning I shall see Dr Holland—I have lunched today with Miss Trevennon where I saw Mrs Derwent Coleridge

---

[1] W. W. has apparently lost the thread of his sentence here.
[2] Bryan Waller Procter, 'Barry Cornwall'.
[3] Mrs. Gee's daughter.   [4] *MS. illegible.*

and her Son. She is a very nice and I think sensible woman and their boy a very fine fellow. Sarah C. was looking much better. I did not find any body at home at Hendon but Miss [   ][1] a Niece of the Lockyers with whom I left 2 – 10 for Janetta. Chris. I think will come and see us—Cambridge John expected any minute, but I must close.

Farewell also to friends. How sad I am at the thought of having distrusted you. Derwent came this morning for the sake of company merely. Mrs Hoare rode with me to Hendon and I had to talk against [the] wheels the whole way to H. Then I had to talk at Miss Trevennans nearly three hours, then half an hours tete a tete with Derwent and ever since with Chris: or Mr Robinson so that my very head aches and [?][2] with it.

Mrs and Miss Hoare send best love—are both quite well. I shall not have [? a chance] of seeing Mrs Gillman. My cold is going off—I shall know on Saturday whether Mr Quillinan can come down. I will bring down your [?][3] dearest Mary.

1054. W. W. to JOHN EDWARDS[4]

MS. Mr. R. E. Whitaker. Hitherto unpublished.

Hampstead Heath.
Friday [1 July 1836]

My dear Mr Edwards,

It is some time since your very friendly letter and elegant verses (elegant and vigorous) upon the Eclipse were forwarded to me. I thank you sincerely for both, and write to say that I purpose to pass through Derby next Wednesday in or on the Telegraph Manchester Coach (Telegraph I think is its name)—I mean the Coach that goes from the Bull and Mouth through to Manchester in one day. You will be able to learn at Derby at which hour it reaches that place and I hope it may be convenient to let me have the opportunity of shaking you by the hand as we pass through.

Believe me my dear Sir,
with faithful regard
sincerely yours
Wm Wordsworth

---

[1] *Hole in MS.* [2] *MS. faded.*
[3] *Illegible word.* [4] See *MY* i. 470; ii. 562.

1055. W. W. to HENRY WILLIAM PICKERSGILL

MS. Cornell. Hitherto unpublished.

44 Dover Street
1ᵗ July 1836

My dear Sir,

My departure draws nigh, not for the continent but for home, as I find I have not courage to face another long absence without seeing my family. Next Tuesday noon I leave London for St Albans, to be there taken up by the Manchester Coach the day after. I write this partly to bid you farewell, and partly to say how happy I should be could you make me the Conveyer of your charming Picture¹—if finished to your mind, as I am sure so beautiful a performance if it accompanied me could not fail to add to the pleasures of my day of welcome. Should not the alteration be completed to your satisfaction the Picture might afterwards be sent to Mr Moxons, and My Nephew would gladly charge himself with it on his journey to the North, a month hence.

Let me add, if you [are]² tempted to revisit the Lakes it would give me great Pleasure to shew you the Beauties of Rydal Mount.

Believe me my dear Sir
with much respect
Your obliged
Wᵐ Wordsworth

1056. M. W. to H. C. R.

Address: H. C. Robinson Esqʳᵉ, Plowdens Buildᵍˢ, Temple, London.
Postmark: 6 July 1836. *Stamp*: Kendal Penny Post.
Endorsed: 4 July 1836, Mʳˢ Wordsworth.
MS. Dr. Williams's Library.
K (—). *Morley, i. 305.*

July 4ᵗʰ [1836]

Thank you heartily my dear Friend for your addition to W's letter, which affords us an opportunity of bidding you good bye

---

¹ The copy of his portrait of W. W. which Pickersgill had made for Dora W.

² *Word dropped out*

before your departure; and of telling you how much we feel your good-tempered bearing towards your vacillating *fellow-traveller that was to have been.* God bless you! I trust you will have an agreeable journeying meanwhile—and if after all, you are *together* to prosecute your visit to Rome, may you meet him in a mood of better promise to be a desireable Companion, than if you were to start now when he either is, or thinks himself exhausted by the business and bustle of London.

I do not wait for W's arrival at home before I despatch this farewell note—lest it should miss you altogether, (and for the same reason I do not spare you postage) and I also wish to remove the idea, which report, you say, has suggested—'that we have not informed W^m of all—'. We hope that he will not find his sister worse, than when he parted from her—and she has continued during his absence quite as well—and indeed in some respects she is better, even than when you saw her. Her bodily health continues good: tho' sad indeed is the feeling that now abides with us, and how removed the hope we had encouraged of her mind strengthening as a consequence of her being able to get out and be amused in the fresh air—She has now her drives—and daily exercise in a Merlins chair, in the Garden— and for a time enjoys it—and she is very happy—but no permanent change follows. She is, as you know at times, and for a *short space* her own acute self, retains the power over her fine judgment and discrimination—then, and at once, relapses into child-like feebleness—and gives vent to some discomfort by merry sallies or with the impatience of a *petted child* contrives one *want* after another, as if merely to provoke contradiction. But she *has no delusions*, and we can only consider her state poor thing, as that of premature Dotage.—We do not at all like the notion that you say has gone abroad of our having prepared disappointment for poor W. by holding back any additional cause for anxiety—we have too much *self-love* to have allowed him, and indeed *encouraged* his going abroad if any unfavorable change had taken place—so if any of our friends, who are kind enough to be interested about us, are anxious, you can assure them that their friend is not returning to a more unhappy home than he left.

As for our younger Invalid—I have more confident hope that she is getting well—than I have hitherto encouraged—and we are looking forward to a decided improvement if, by God's blessing, we can but see her accomplish, without injury, a short and *easy* journey (by means of a boat down Windermere, and driving along Sands) towards the Sea Coast—this we mean to attempt before the end of the month and I know my dear friend we shall have your good wishes to attend her.

Miss W. and She, join me in affectionate love to you—and we hope you will come to us at Xtmas, if the Italian trip does not interfere, and tell us all your German Adventures. Miss Cookson, who is with us for a few days, begs likewise her kindest regards—You will be sorry to hear that poor M[rs] Harden is declining very fast—the paralysis is making rapid progress *internally* and decided dropsy having commenced, her death I apprehend is daily expected. Her cheerful resignation, I am told, is *beautiful*. Her Son Allan and his Wife[1] are at Field Head—and John,[2] who is established, with great prospect of success in his profession, at Liverpool pays his Mother frequent visits—Sisters, and Cousins innumerable have been leave-taking—and in the middle of excitement which to most Persons would have been distressing in like circumstances—M[rs] H. h[as][3] been able to support her spirits in a thankful state of calmness that has astonished all her friends. We see very little of our Elleray friends—The Harrisons[4] are all at Allonby—as are Miss Luff and Owen Lloyd—Willy too has joined their Party, for a few days from Carlisle as he tells me in a note this morning. M[r] Carr[5] often enquires after you—You will be glad to hear that his Wife's health is improved—this I fear, from the nature of her complaint, is but a temporary amendment—but they are cheered for the present.

Should you have any communication with the Clarksons before your departure pray say all that is affec from us—and to poor Miss Lamb.

Ever my dr Sir faithfully your obliged

M. Wordsworth.

---

[1] Mrs. Harden's eldest son Allan, and his wife Mary, lived in Edinburgh.

[2] John William Harden, Mrs. Harden's third son.

[3] *MS. torn.*

[4] The Benson Harrisons.

[5] Thomas Carr had impressed H. C. R. when he had called on him in Ambleside the previous January: 'a retired surgeon, a superior man . . . a man of thought and reading. Somewhat deaf and afflicted with a painful malady, he soon became an object of pity . . .' (*HCR* ii. 482.)

1057. W. W. to EDWARD QUILLINAN

Endorsed: From Mr Wordsworth 5th July 1836. Recd 9th—E. Q.
MS. Harvard University Library.
LY ii. 801.

Tuesday Noon [5 July 1836]

My dear Mr Quillinan

I am ashamed of myself, in having forgotten a commission of my Friend and Neighbour the Revd Robert Graves of Bowness. He has two Sisters,[1] *young* Ladies, who want to go to Bowness, but are unable to accompany him at present, and are anxious for the benefit of an Escort within the next fortnight or three weeks; in other words as soon as convenient to you after a week is over.[2] I am able to say that they are young Ladies who will give you little trouble, and Mr Graves would meet them at Kendal. I may add that you would find them very interesting Companions, and it would give me great pleasure to know that this request is one which you are able to comply with. If so, or rather in any case, be so kind as to let their Mother Mrs Graves know. Her address is 28/B/Devonshire Street, Portland Place, Corner of High Street.

ever faithfully yours
Wm Wordsworth

1058. W. W. to LADY THEODOSIA SPRING RICE[3]

MS. untraced.
LY ii. 801.

44 Dover Street
5th July 36

Dear Lady Theodosia

I cannot promise myself the pleasure of being one of your Party on Thursday Evening, as by that time I hope to be at Rydal Mount. I leave London this afternoon at three o'clock,

---

[1] Clara (see L. 1048 above), and Caroline (1819–55).

[2] According to his MS. Diaries (*WL MSS.*), E. Q. left Woolwich on 15 July and after a visit to Brighton, set out for Rydal on the 30th accompanied by the two Miss Graves, travelling by steamer to Hull and Selby and thence by railway to Leeds and coach to Rydal.

[3] Thomas Spring Rice's first wife (d. 1839), 2nd daughter of Edmund, 1st Earl of Limerick.

for St Albans. I need not repeat how happy I should be to see
you and the young Ladies[1] at my beautiful place of Abode.

With kindest regards to all around you, I have the honor to be

dear Lady Theodosia
faithfully yours
Wm Wordsworth

1059. W. W. to EDWARD MOXON

MS. Henry E. Huntington Library. Hitherto unpublished.

[Rydal Mount]
[*c.* 9 July 1836]

My dear Mr Moxon,

Got here on Thursday after noon, after a pleasant journey.
Excuse extreme haste. Kindest remembrances to Mrs Moxon
and your Sister and a Kiss to Emma.—

All at home pretty well.

affectionately yours
W. W.

1060. W. W. to H. C. R.

*Endorsed: 11*th *July 1836, Wordsworth (Journey).*
MS. Dr. Williams's Library.
K. Morley, i. 308.

July 11th [1836]

My dear Friend

I congratulate you on the decision in your favor, and meet
your proposal with very strong inclination, and even all but a
promise and a positive engagement, which after what has
passed, I could not enter into, nor do you wish that I should.[2]

In one point, however, I must deal frankly with you, I feel
that I am far from being as strong in body as you; and I must
have some more distinct notion than I can form at present, of the
fatigue which I am to encounter. To spare bodily exhaustion I

---

[1] For Mary, Theodosia, and Catherine Spring Rice, see L. 1017 above.
Their subsequent visit to Rydal Mount later this month is recorded in *R MVB*.

[2] W. W. was now thinking of postponing the proposed tour of the
Continent until the autumn; but it was eventually arranged for the following
spring. See also H. C. R.'s reply to this letter (Morley, i. 310).

am prepared to incur more expense than would perhaps suit your plans. I told you that I dreaded long lumberings in foreign diligences, and could not by night bring myself to having any thing to do with them. What do you say to our looking out for a Companion, so that we might proceed at less expense when the hiring of a carriage was required; there would I think also be other advantages in a third Person if well chosen.

To this scheme however there appears to be one almost insurmountable objection—it would *bind* me to go if possible.—Boxall[1] the Painter described Rome to me as an execrable climate from the middle of November till towards the end of January. He said he went in November from Florence to Rome, through dismal cold and rain, and a more uncomfortable Residence than he found there for the next two months, is not to be imagined—it threw him into an illness, which left him before he had been a week in Naples, after two months weary residence in Rome.—Rome is said to be delightful in October, but we could not get there in time for that month, if we could, we might proceed to Naples and come back to Rome at a proper season. But all this your experience will be able to throw light upon.—It seems to me that the best plan would be to reverse our former scheme and go strait through France down the Soane, and the Rhine, and by the Cornice Road, and return by Venice and the Tyrol, etc, as we should have no time to explore that region so late in the year. But there is time to digest all this. We are glad you are going into Wales,[2] but you should begin with the Wye—Chepstow, Tintern Abbey; Monmouth, Goodrich Castle, Ross, etc. At Brinsop Court within six miles of Hereford live Mr and Mrs Hutchinson, and Mr Monkhouse is not far from them. He lives

---

[1] W. W. had met William Boxall again at a party at Moxon's on 3 July (*HCR* ii. 497), just before he left London. E. Q., John Kenyon, and Abraham Hayward the jurist (see pt. ii, Ls. 761, 800) were also there, and J. M. Lappenberg (1794–1865), the German historian, who subsequently visited Rydal Mount (*R MVB*). Lappenberg had met W. W. in Edinburgh in 1814, and subsequently in London, and he wrote to the poet on 30 May 1832 (*WL MSS.*) to introduce his brother-in-law Dr. G. Baur, the Biblical scholar (*R MVB*), to outline his plans for a history of Britain, and to acknowledge his debt to W. W. 'Allow me once more to repeat to you, that your poems have ever since been to me an inexhaustible spring of life, vigour and delight.'

[2] H. C. R. left on a tour of Wales with his friends the Masqueriers on 19 July.

upon the Wye, at *The Stow*. They would all be delighted to see you. You might from there go up the Wye, by Hay and Builth, Rhaiodwor Gawy,[1] and so to the Devils Bridge and onward through North wales, from Bangor you might make an excursion to Conway for the Castle's sake, and so up the Conway to Llanrwstr, and by Capel-Kerig back to Bangor, whence you might take the Steamer to Liverpool, and from Liverpool there is a Steamer to Ulverstone, from which if convenient see Furness Abbey, and come to us by Windermere, up which Lake there is at present a Boat in connection with the Liverpool Steamer to Ulverstone. After a few days' stay with us, all being well and promising, I should be delighted to return with you to London, and strait for the Continent, this leading Proviso always bearing in mind, that I must not weaken my old frame by fatigue that can be spared.

I have done well to return home; My Conscience as well as my yearnings of heart urged me to it. Indeed it would have been quite unjust both to myself and you, if I started without first coming hither; I find our Invalids as well as I had reason to expect.— I have no more to say, but I hope this pleasant scheme may be realized. God bless you, love from all.

Affectionately yours
W. W.

We had a most pleasant journey hence. I was delighted with St Albans and its neighbourhood.—

1061. W. W. to EDWARD MOXON

MS. Carl H. Pforzheimer Library. Hitherto unpublished.

[late July *or* early Aug. 1836]

My dear Mr Moxon,

To save the Post my last through Mr Stephens[2] was sent off in so great a hurry as not to leave time to my Daughter to thank you for your Present. Never was a gift more happily chosen; she is delighted with the Book, so is her dear Mother, and so would my poor Sister have been, had it pleased God to leave her in full possession of her powers of mind. Pray be so kind as to forward

---

[1] i. e. Rhayader, or in Welsh Rhaiadr Gwy.
[2] James Stephen, of the Colonial Office.

the corrections on the other leaf to Mr Evans. [1] And let us know
his address, as it might save trouble and time perhaps if we were
to enclose the sheets, under cover to him, sometimes, without
their passing through your hands, though I shall like you to see
them all before struck off.

affectionately yours
W Wordsworth

I shall now proceed to correct the Excursion and the Poems
regularly, [2] and hope that the work will advance at a good pace,
as it is not impossible that I may go abroad in the Autumn.

We have sent a small Parcel, to your care, for my nephew
John Wordsworth. It contains a Watch, be so good as to take
charge of it till he calls for it.

1062. W. W. to ROBERT SOUTHEY

Address: R. Southey Esq. [*delivered by hand*]
MS. Cornell. Hitherto unpublished.

[Aug. 1836]

My dear Southey,
    The Bearer of this note is meaning to call upon you. I offered
to give him an Introduction, thinking it might be more

---

[1] Of Messrs. Bradbury and Evans, who were to print the new edition of the
Poetical Works which Moxon now had in hand.

[2] The task of revising the poems was well under way by early August, after
E. Q. 's arrival at Rydal Mount, and his MS. Diaries (*WL MSS.*) for 3 Aug.
onwards record a good deal of 'tinkering' (the word was W. W.'s) with the
poems, in particular with *The Female Vagrant* and *Alice Fell* ('restored at my
request') on the 4th and the 5th. 'Descriptive Sketches.—Mr W today, and
subsequently has given these *Alpine Sketches* a careful revision and correction,
and has, I think, very greatly improved them, as this juvenile production was
as full of corrupt diction as of vigorous poetry. Mrs. W. says full of "swagger
and flourish".' W. W. was still 'tinkering' with *Alice Fell* (in proof) and with
An Evening Walk on 1 Sept., and on the 3rd E. Q. records some alterations to
The Idiot Boy, 'one of Wordsworth's early poems, one of those that has been
most ridiculed . . . but full of nature and tenderness. There are delicate and
subtle touches in it that are admirable. Here and there I would quarrel with an
expression . . . but the whole is so good and complete, that it would be rash
perhaps to suggest troublesome objections. Mr W. says he never wrote
anything more currently than this poem, nor when he was in a happier and
more poetical state of feeling.'

agreeable to him to present himself in that way. He is Mr James Alexander Stewart Mackenzie[1] Member for Ross and Cromartie, a Reformer. He married the widow of Sir Samuel Hood, who has succeeded to her Father's Estates the late Earl of Seaforth. Mr M. has been residing some time in Ambleside, along with his Son.[2] He is intimate with Mr. Rickman,[3] Rogers, and several of our common Friends. You will find him a very intelligent person. We have conversed upon the subject of literary Copy right, and he is well disposed to exert himself for procuring an Extension of the term.—

We shall be sorry, truly sorry, to part with Bertha.

Most affectionately yours,
W. W.

1063. W. W. to H. C. R.

Address: H. C. Robinson Esqre.
Endorsed: Augt or Septr 1936, Mrs Wordsworth and W abo^t the journey.
MS. Dr. Williams's Library.
K (—). *Morley, i. 313.*

[*In M. W.'s hand*]

[16 Aug. 1836]

My dear Friend

I have been very uneasy for some time in not knowing how to communicate with you, and principally from a fear that you may be relying too confidently upon our journey being begun

---

[1] The Right Hon. James Alexander Stewart (1784–1843), nephew of the 7th Earl of Galloway, had married in 1817 Mary (1783–1862), widow of Sir Samuel Hood, 1st Bart. (d. 1814), eldest daughter and co-heir of Francis Mackenzie, Lord Seaforth (1754–1815), and had assumed the surname of Stewart-Mackenzie. He was Governor of Ceylon, Lord High Commissioner of the Ionian Islands, and had been M.P. for Ross and Cromarty since 1831. The *RMVB* records his visit to W. W., and fixes the date of this letter.

[2] Keith William Stewart-Mackenzie (1818–81), of Seaforth.

[3] John Rickman, the statistician (see also *MY* ii. 561), a clerk in the House of Commons since 1814, had accompanied Henry Taylor and Southey to Holland in 1826 (see pt. i, L. 176), and had planned to write jointly with Southey a sequel to the *Colloquies*, which however was never published. His house in London was a favourite port of call for the Southey family. See Orlo Williams, *Lamb's Friend the Census-Taker. The Life and Letters of John Rickman*, 1912.

by the middle of next month. Do not think me liable to be turned by every piece of information from every quarter, but I cannot refrain from mentioning what has had a good deal of influence upon my own mind, the decided opinion of Dr Arnold that all that I could wish to see in Italy might be seen in three months—and that from the middle of March till the middle of June would be the best season. Lady Davy[1] who was here the other day, and who has been much in Italy, is also of the same opinion: a few days ago I saw a letter from Boulougne, dated 26th last month: in which the writer said that her[2] Banker in Florence, whom she had seen that day, told her that he did not know how he should get back to the City on account of the Cholera, which tho' not actually in Florence, was in Milan Genoa and several other cities, including Rome. Now, tho' you might not dread the Cholera quite so much as I should do, I am sure you would have an equal fear of Quarantine not merely on account of loss of time—but the wretched manner in which People are huddled together in the places where they are stopped. Thus much for generals, for personals I will mention two or three reasons which make me desirous of deferring the [3] commencement of our journey till the middle of Febry sh^d it suit you. First, my nephew's affairs are not yet settled, 2dly I have a wish to superintend the printing of the Stereotype Ed: of my Poems, which I can get thro' before the end of the year, as two presses are proposed to be set to work 3dly my Son John will have 3 months nearly at his disposal, and is anxious to accompany us, if possible. Lastly, I have a hope that my daughter will improve in health before that time: her back is already much better and her side also—but I am not easy about her—she is so exceeding thin, and has a cough on a slight occasion. My poor Sister is much as she was when you were here. I have only to add that it would rejoice us all if you would spend your Christmas here, and we would start together in the middle of February—

Dr Arnold went off yesterday[4] with a detachment of 10—by the Lake Tourist—meaning to take the Steamer for Dublin at

---

[1] Lady Davy (1780—1855), Sir Humphry's widow, formerly Mrs. Apreece: a friend of Mrs. Fletcher and Sydney Smith.

[2] *Written* his.

[3] *Written* twice.

[4] His departure on 15 Aug. is recorded in E. Q.'s MS. Diary: hence the dating of this letter.

Whitehaven—Young Bunsen[1] was of the Party—The cross of Prussian and English, with Italian air to boot, has not produced beauty in this instance, but he is said to be amiable and promising. farewell—Mr Quillinan is here, and sends kind regards. Mrs W. my sister, and Dora their love.

Believe ever your faithful friend[2]

Wm Wordsworth

What more changeful than the sea?
Yet over his great tides
Fidelity presides.

The quotation is by Dora, from the description of herself in the Triad; but here applied to the old gentleman, her Father, and his travelling inclinations.

1064. W. W. to THOMAS POOLE

Address: Thos. Poole Esqre, R. King's Esqre, Redcliff Parade, Bristol.
MS. untraced.
LY ii. 802.

Rydal Mount
Aug. 20th 1836

My dear Friend

Your Letter[3] gave me great pleasure. I was fully assured that you would do your best to promote the good object I have in

---

[1] Henry George Bunsen (1818–85) matriculated at Oriel College, Oxford, later this year, and was vicar of Lilleshall, Shropshire, 1847–69, and a Prebendary of Lichfield. He was the eldest son of Baron Christian von Bunsen (1791–1860), also known as the 'Chevalier Bunsen', German diplomat and liberal theologian: Niebuhr's successor as Minister at the Prussian legation in Rome (1823–39), and Prussian ambassador in London (1841–54), where he was regarded as the outstanding representative of European Protestantism in England, and pioneered the scheme for a joint Lutheran and Anglican Bishopric in Jerusalem. Bunsen was a great admirer of the Church of England, and a close confidant of Arnold, Hare, and the broad-church party. In 1817 he had married an English lady, Frances (1791–1876), daughter of Benjamin Waddington, of Llanover, Monmouth. C. W. jnr. had met Bunsen's family in Rome in 1833, and W. W. met him there in 1837. See Frances Baroness Bunsen, *A Memoir of Baron Bunsen*, 2 vols., 1868.

[2] These five words and the signature in W. W.'s hand.

[3] See L. 999 above. W. W.'s reply here is his last recorded letter to Poole, who died suddenly the following year, on 8 Sept. 1837.

view, and therefore relied upon hearing from you in due course of Time. Thanks for your exertions; and for your contribution. By this day's post I shall write to Sir P. Ackland[1] as you suggest. His liberal contribution was grateful to me, both upon public and personal considerations.—As to the draft, I am sorry to be obliged to request you would keep it as well as your own contribution till the Project takes a more substantial Shape. My own little influence has not been exerted in vain, but a great disappointment has occurred in a high quarter. The Earl of Egremont is Lord of the Castle of Cockermouth and has a large property in the neighbourhood. Knowing his munificence I had over confidently relied upon his support. He thought it better, in which view he is quite mistaken, to enlarge the old Church and encrease the Endowment. But even to this I fear he is not likely to contribute; as he has just made an offer of two thousand pounds to the Inhabitants, to be disposed of for the benefit of the place in any way which they may approve. Preferring temporal things to spiritual they have chosen to have a new Market place with Buildings etc. This was wanted, and therefore one cannot complain. The other and still higher want will and must be supplied in course of time. I shall shortly go over to Cockermouth and learn the state of things upon the spot. In the meanwhile let me beg of you either to take charge of Sir Peregrin's subscription till you hear further from me, or if you prefer it return the draft to him, taking for granted it may be called for if the project be not dropped.

You express yourself as becomes an old and most valued Friend upon the affliction of my family. Of dear Miss Hutchinson I shall say no more than that her memory is consecrated in our hearts. My poor Sister cannot stand unsupported, and she suffers daily in body, but we trust by no means to the degree that a Stranger might suppose. If her *mind* had not been impaired by the disease its pressure would have been very much lighter upon the body. And this thought, Melancholy as it is, affords us some consolation.—My Daughter is certainly better as far as concerns pain: but the inflammation in the spine returns with carriage motion so therefore she cannot benefit by change of air; so that her strength comes back slowly

---

[1] Poole's friend and neighbour Sir Peregrine Acland, 2nd Bart. (b. 1789), of Fairfield, nr. Bridgewater: 'a mild and very obliging man', according to Southey who visited him in November.

if at all. Had she been able to travel the hope I had encouraged of seeing you and Stowey and Alfoxden would certainly have been fulfilled. As it is, we must submit to God's will.—My Wife and your old Friend my dear Sister, unite with me in the kindest remembrances, as does my daughter also.—With what you say upon our dear departed Friend Coleridge I entirely concur.

Ever faithfully yours
W. Wordsworth

Dora would be hurt to see a letter from her Father to you, in which her name was omitted among those of the Family who bear a delightful recollection of your friendly, tho' short visit at Rydal Mount[1]—Most respectfully d[r] Friend

Yours W. Wordsworth

1065. W. W. to JOSHUA WATSON

Address: J. Watson Esq[re], 6 Park St, Westminster. [*In M. W.'s hand*]
Endorsed: W Wordsworth Esq 22 Aug 1836 Cockerm° Chapel.
MS. WL.
LY ii. 803.

Rydal Mount
August 22 [1836]

My dear Sir,
 I have just received the enclosed from Mr Stanger; my answer, which I hope you will approve, was that I could not concur in his proposal.[2]
 I should be glad if Mr S—'s Letter should suggest any observations to you, to have the benefit of them.

Ever faithfully yours
Wm Wordsworth

[1] In 1826 (see pt. i, L. 259).
[2] James Stanger already seemed hesitant, if not uncooperative, about the proposed new church at Cockermouth, as Lord Lonsdale noted in his letter to W. W. of 24 Aug.: 'If Lord E[gremont] is to be prevail'd on to give Money for the Building a Church, it will require more address than Mr Stanger is possess'd of to win him over—I don't take Mr S. to be one of the veni, vidi, vici Gentlemen.' (*WL MSS.*)

1066. W. W. to ROBERT SOUTHEY

MS. Cornell. Hitherto unpublished.

[3 Sept. 1836]

My dear Southey,

The Bearer of this Letter is M[r] Henry Robinson,[1] (my Cousin), solicitor for Admiral Tatham, in the great Will cause[2] now pending, and he wishes to consult you, or rather have your opinion upon an important point in the case.

Ever affectionately yours
W. W.

[1] See pt. ii, L. 434. Henry Robinson's visit to W. W. is recorded in E. Q.'s MS. Diary for 3 Sept.: hence the dating of this letter. He returned on the 5th to make final arrangements for W. W.'s appearance at the Lancaster assizes. See next letter.

[2] The cause of Wright versus Tatham was one of the most celebrated and prolonged cases in 19th-century legal history. John Marsden (1758–1826), of Hornby Castle, Lancs., had bequeathed his estates to his steward Wright; but the will was disputed by the heir-at-law Admiral Sandford Tatham (d. 1840), on the ground that Marsden was of unsound mind and incapable of making a testamentary disposition of his property. The case turned on a number of letters supposed to have been written by Marsden, which, it was argued, proved (or disproved) his competence to make a valid will. The penultimate trial came on at Lancaster in Aug. 1834, and a verdict was given in favour of Wright; but two years later there was a new trial, before Lord Justice Coleridge (see L. 1073 below), and W. W., Southey, Lingard the historian (who lived at Hornby), and Robert Shelton Mackenzie (see L. 1110 below) were summoned as expert witnesses. 'The point at issue', as Southey explained on 10 Sept. to Henry Taylor, 'was, whether certain letters produced in the testator's handwriting could all be composed by the same person, or whether they did not imply such a difference of intellect, and contain such different peculiarities of spelling and style, as to be proofs of a long-laid scheme for defrauding the heir-at-law.' W. W. drew up a careful classification of the letters (now in the *WL MSS.*), and decided that they must have been composed by different persons, some educated, some illiterate, while another person copied them out fairly for the post. His conclusion, Shelton Mackenzie recalled, was 'thought piled on thought, clear investigation, careful analysis, and accumulative reasoning.' W. W. was called to the witness box on 7 Sept., but it was decided that his evidence was inadmissible. A verdict was however eventually given for Tatham. (See Southey, vi. 298–300; Martin Haile and Edwin Bonney, *Life and Letters of John Lingard, 1771–1851*, [1911], p. 254; Lord Hanworth, *Lord Chief Baron Pollock, A Memoir*, 1929, pp. 119–39.)

1067. W. W. to SIR BENJAMIN COLLINS BRODIE[1]

MS. Mr W. Hugh Peal. Hitherto unpublished.

Rydal Mount
[6 Sept. 1836]

Mr. Wordsworth begs to present his Compliments to Sir Benjamin Brodie, with sincere thanks for his obliging note. Most unfortunately for Mr Wordsworth he is obliged to go from home this day upon important business;[2] but as he passes through Ambleside about a quarter before 3, he will do himself the honor of calling upon Sir Benjamin. Fearing however that he may not be so fortunate as to see Sir Benjamin, he begs leave earnestly to request that Sir Benjamin, and Lady Brodie, would call at Rydal Mount either this afternoon, or any hour that may suit them tomorrow. Mrs Wordsworth will be at home, and happy to receive them. Mr W. will certainly return to Rydal on Thursday, at the latest; and it is not impossible that he may be able to reach home tomorrow night.

Thanks for Dr Holland's Letter.

---

[1] The physician (see L. 875 above). His visit with his family is recorded in *RMVB*. According to E. Q.'s MS. Diary, they returned to tea at Rydal Mount on the 8th, after W. W.'s return home. In a later letter of 5 Nov., Brodie looked back with pleasure on his ramble with W. W.: 'One advantage of my visit to the Lake country is that it has enabled me to understand better those Lyrical Ballads which I learned to admire when I was yet a boy, and to which I have continued faithful, in however much I may have been altered otherwise by thirty years of active engagements in the unpoetical world.' (*WL MSS.*)

[2] The Great Will Cause at Lancaster. See previous letter and next letter.

1068. M. W. to SIR WILLIAM ROWAN HAMILTON

Address: Sir Wm Hamilton, Observatory.
Postmark: 13 Sept. 1836.
MS. University Library, Davis, California. Hitherto unpublished.

Rydal Mount
Sepr 7th, 1836

My dear Sir,

Dora being about to write, to congratulate her friend[1] in Phoenix Park on the birth of her Daughter, affords me an opportunity to thank you for your communication from Bristol—which I doubt not, Mr W. would have done himself, but he is absent—*for a day or two*[2]—not gone to Rome—*that* project being deferred till the middle of Feb^ry, when God willing, he still thinks of starting—if all goes on well at home. You will be glad to hear that both Miss W. and Dora are better than when you last heard from Rydal, and we both look forward with hope to the latter being eventually well, but her complaint is a tedious one, and we must hope *with patience.*

We are always happy to hear of the well-doing of you and yours, especially delighted to find that your Sister Eliza is going on prosperously and that She is reaping the reward of her enthusiasm. We hear of her, and of her kind remembrance to us, occasionally, thro' the Graves whose society we consider an acquisition to our neighborhood. When you write to your Sister pray make our affectionate remembrances to her, with a thousand good wishes, and hopes that we may meet again.

I shall probably be the bearer of your note to my daughter-in-law, whom I intend to visit, at their new Parsonage of Brigham next week, and be *first* introduced to your Godsosn, of whose

---

[1] Maria Drummond.

[2] At the Lancaster assizes. See L. 1066 above. According to E. Q.'s MS. Diary, he left Rydal with W. W. and Southey on the afternoon of the 6th, and that evening they conferred with Admiral Tatham's lawyers at Lancaster. 'Mr W was examined as to his opinion of the letters passed off as Tatham's, and he pointed out the discrepancies of style and expression as well as spelling which convinced him that they could not be the product of the same mind. Mr Southey said nothing but in brief and emphatic assent to Mr W's opinion which was stated lucidly and strongly much to the satisfaction of the counsel and Dr. Lingard.' E. Q. gives a long account of W. W.'s examination in the witness box on the 7th. (*WL MSS.*)

pleasant looks and sweet disposition I have heard much. I shall have great pleasure in uniting his Godfather's blessing with that of the Grandmother.

With the united regards of this family to yourself and Lady H.

believe me, dear Sir W^m
to be very sincerely yours
M. Wordsworth

1069. W. W. to UNKNOWN CORRESPONDENT

MS. untraced.
LY iii. 1379.

Rydal Mount, Kendal, Sepr 10th [1836]

Dear Sir

In remembrance of a few days pleasant intercourse with Members of your family some years ago, at the Lakes, I venture to address you on a Matter in which I think you possibly have the power to be useful to me, as I feel assured you will have the *inclination* provided my request does not interfere with your own views or convenience.

One of my two Sons,[1] encouraged by his friends at Birmingham[2] has offered himself as a Candidate for the Secretaryship to the Birmingham and Derby Railway—and knowing your influence in the latter Place to be of the first importance, it has struck me that by timely application for your interest, you might be inclined to put it forth for the benefit of my Son. If I am mistaken in this conjecture, or if my wish interferes with your engagements, I can only hope that you will excuse the liberty I have taken, and with kind remembrance to your family, in which Mrs W. begs leave to join

believe me to be faithfully
Your's Wm Wordsworth

[1] i.e. W. W. jnr.
[2] The Lloyd connections.

MS. untraced.
Transactions of the Wordsworth Society, no. 6, p. 113. K. LY ii. 812.

[*In M. W.'s hand*]

[*c.* 24 Sept. 1836]

My dear Mr Kenyon,

I won't waste time in thanks, having told you heretofore thro' Mr Moxon how much I was obliged by your letter.

You ask how the Muses came to say, 'weep in the public roads *alone*.'[1] Did you ever attend an execution? Funerals, alas! we have all attended, and most of us must have seen then weeping in the public roads on one or both of these occasions.

I was a witness to a sight of this kind the other day in the Streets of Kendal, where male mourners were following a Body to the grave in tears. But for my own part, notwithstanding what has here been said in verse, I never in my whole life saw a man weep *alone* in the roads; but a friend of mine *did* see this poor man weeping *alone*, with the Lamb, the last of his flock, in his arms. I hope you are satisfied, and willing that the verse should stand as I have written it.

Dear Mrs Kenyon was right as to the *bare*—the contradiction is in the *words* only—bare, as not being covered with smoke or vapour;—clothed, as being attired in the beams of the morning. Tell me if you approve of the following alteration, which is the best I can do for the amendment of the fault.

> The city now doth on her forehead wear
> The glorious crown of morning; silent, bare,
> Ships, towers, etc.[2]

It was in the English tongue[3]—you say 'is not this, in an English poem, superfluous?' Surely here is an oversight on your part; whether the poem were in English, or French, or Greek is a matter wholly indifferent as to the expression I have used. She came from afar. The Emigrant Mother came from France, as is

---

[1] See *The Last of the Flock* (*PW* ii. 43), l. 4. John Kenyon had written on 22 Aug., suggesting a number of corrections to W. W.'s poems: 'I am going to take a liberty with you or your verses—The latter I have loved for more than thirty years thro evil report and good report—and therefore they are bound to consider that I now speak about them in the Spirit of Love.' (*WL MSS.*)

[2] See *PW* iii. 38. The alteration was fortunately not adopted.

[3] *Her Eyes are Wild* (*PW* ii. 107), l. 10.

told in that other Poem, but I do not think it necessary to say, in this latter case, that her griefs found utterance in French—only that I have put them into verse. But in the instance to which you object it was expedient to specify, that—though she came from far, English was her native tongue—which shows her either to be of these Islands, or a North American. On the latter supposition, while the distance removes her from us, the fact of her speaking our language brings us at once into close sympathy with her.

As to the *Old forest of civility*,[1] you are, I fear, right; I say *fear*, because I may have much trouble in correcting the passage. I had no particular allusion in my mind; the line before spoke of the *citadels of truth*, and the Forest was intended, in like manner, as a metaphor to express those usages and habits of civilization, which from their antiquity may be compared to a forest whose origin is unknown.

I *do* rejoice at my change of plan: two or three days ago I heard at Lowther[2] that Lady Westmorland[3] had just been stopped at Pavia, on her way to Rome, in consequence of the Cholera. I have had a great deal of dry and wearisome labour, of which I do not repent, however, in preparing my Poems for the new Edition, especially those which were among my first attempts.

I hear from many quarters of the impression which my writings are making, both at home and abroad, and to an old man it would be discreditable not to be gratified with such intelligence; because it is not the language of praise for pleasure bestowed, but of gratitude for moral and intellectual improvement received. Do not suppose, however, that I am not prepared for the language of censure and discouragement from many quarters. I hear of that also occasionally, and should be sorry were it otherwise; for I should then be sure that the igneus vigor and cælestis origo did not belong to me, but that I was of

---

[1] *Thanksgiving Ode* (*PW* iii. 155), ll. 108–9. In the new edition the 'old forest' was altered to the 'fair gardens'. In his letter Kenyon had objected that 'the two words 'forest' and 'civility'—both in derivation and in their actual usage—contradict each other.'

[2] This was most likely his visit with Mr. Justice Coleridge (see L. 1073 below) on 21–2 Sept., as recorded in *Mem.* ii. 303. Hence the dating of this letter.

[3] The 10th Earl's second wife, Jane (d. 1857), of Apthorp, Northants., Lady Lonsdale's sister-in-law.

the world, worldly, and of the earth, earthy—but too much of this. I trust that, if I am to go to the Continent, I shall see you in passing thro' London.

My Church[1] is, after all, likely to be built and endowed, notwithstanding you, one of the most valued of my friends, will not assist me. But I know that half a finger's breadth, if it be near enough to the eye, will blind. Mrs Wordsworth says O the impudent man! To-morrow we are to have a Chapel[2] consecrated within less than 3 miles of this place; there is no situation out of the Alps, nor among them, more beautiful than that where the building is placed. Mrs Wordsworth and I walked thither this afternoon. You know the River Brathay—the Chapel stands upon a rocky knoll above it, and commands a view of the stream to Langdale Pikes, which this afternoon were white with snow, as was also nearly half the mountainside below them. The meadows were as green as the after-grass could make them, and the woods in the full foliage of many-coloured Autumn. I wish you had been with us, and I am sure you would have subscribed for a peal of bells, that their harmony might be wafted up and down the river. How glad we were that we were not dissenters—likewise that we were true Conservatives.

We are something better at home—at least we hope so. Why did you not mention your Brother—we are always glad to hear of him.

Affectionately yours,
[*signed*] Wm Wordsworth

[1] At Cockermouth, which W. W. had visited on 18 Sept. to confer with William Wood, while staying for a few days with John W. at Brigham.
[2] Holy Trinity, Brathay (see pt. ii, L. 758).

1071. W. W. to JOSHUA WATSON

Address: Joshua Watson Esqre, 6 Park Street, Westminster.
Endorsed: Wm Wordsworth 26 Sept 1836 Cockerm° Ch.
MS. WL.
LY ii. 804.

[*In M. W.'s hand*]

Rydal Mount Sepr 26th —36

My dear Sir

In regard to Cockermouth Church my prospects brighten. But first let me tell you that in passing thro that Town the other day, I had a meeting with 4 Gentlemen who had taken an interest in the Subject: one, the Mr Wilson[1] who had proposed to subscribe a £100—but I am sorry to say with the exception of Mr Wood, who is Lord Lonsdale's Law Agent, I found them all most unfavourably disposed to the old mode of Patronage, and strongly tinctured with what you will allow me to call Saintship and Simeonism.[2] But to come to the point. I am sure it will not have escaped your memory, that you said to me 'Get the Church endowed by — — and we will build it'. Now I am prepared to say that a friend of mine, in every respect unobjectionable as a Patron will endow the Church if we will engage to build it. I told the Person, whose name in the present stage of the business I am not at liberty to mention, that less than £150 p^r ann—proceeding from the endowment, and the letting of the Pews *in the Gallery*, the amount of which was an uncertainty would not suffice: he agreed with me in this, so that I have no doubt that he will act liberally. I told him that the Body of the Church, as the New Ch:[3] at Workington, must be free sittings.

Now my dear Sir, can the Church be built by us, if the Radicals and Ultras of C— refuse their aid, which I fear many of them may? If it can it will be a great and good work, and all will be well. It would have grieved you to hear the account of the emptiness of the old Church, as I had it, and it was painful also to hear the present Incumbent[4] spoken of in respect to his Ministry as I did.

---

[1] Probably John Wilson, a cotton and linen manufacturer.

[2] See L. 1076 below.

[3] St. John's, built by Thomas Hardwick in 1823; an unusually substantial building for a Commissioners' Church.   [4] Mr Fawcett

295

In a few days I shall have an interview with Mr [St]anger, but I do not expect that we can come to any terms. Pray let me have an answer at your earliest convenience that I may know whether the hope you held out can be fulfilled, in order that I may communicate with the Individual who is so well disposed towards the Place.

With our united affectionate remembrances to yourself and Miss Watson; I remain my d^r Sir

faithfully yours
[signed] Wm Wordsworth

Our Invalids are better—

1072. W. W. to WILLIAM BLACKWOOD [1]

Address: W. Blackwood Esqre, Edinburgh.
MS. Cornell. Hitherto unpublished.

[*In M. W.'s hand*]

Rydal Mount
Sep^{tr} 27th (1836) [2]

My dear Sir,

Your last Parcel, thro' Mr Hamilton containing a No of your Magazine and £8 for Mrs Bedingfield was duly received, and has already been placed by a friend of mine in the hands of Mr Moxon of Dover St—Mrs B. having been advised by me that the Mag. with the enclosure is there waiting her order. I have to thank you for your attention to my request on Mrs Bedingfield's behalf—and also for a Copy of Miss Bowles' Poems [3]—and for your kindness in sending me your Magazine. Miss Bowles' volume has been read with great pleasure in this house; and as far as I can judge is likely to do her much credit.

Perhaps you may have heard that Mr Moxon is printing a new Edition of my Poems in six volumes, to be published monthly—he hopes that the first will be out on the 1st of

---

[1] But see L. 1044 above.
[2] Year added in another hand.
[3] Caroline Bowles (1786–1854), who was to become Southey's second wife, had contributed to *Blackwood's* and the Annuals, and published *Chapters on Churchyards*, 1829, and *Tales of the Factories*, 1833. *The Birthday; a poem, in three parts: to which are added occasional verses*, appeared in 1836 (*R. M. Cat.*, no. 526).

November. He has dealt with me on such liberal terms, that I should be sorry if the Publication does not answer. Since Mr Hamilton's removal to Elleray we see very little of him or Lady Farquhar, to our great regret.

As I hope to procure a frank for this letter it may be a few days after its date. Pray remember this family to Professor Wilson. I cannot conclude without saying, that your hope that I continue to derive pleasure from your Magazine is well founded.

Believe me dear Sir to be
Sincerely yours
[*signed*] Wm Wordsworth

1073. M. W. to H. C. R.

Endorsed: 28 Septr 1836, Mrs Wordsworth Epigram.
MS. Dr. Williams's Library.
Morley, i. 317.

[28 Sept. 1836]

My dear Friend

Your long and very interesting Letter was most welcome this morn^g. yet when I came to its end, a blank was left upon my mind no mention being made of any intention of your coming to us before your departure on y^r tour—which is a point that Dora and I insist upon—in vain did my eye go before me as I read, but not an allusion to your Christmas visit. In all other respects your letter was most satisfactory. Here we are *in the Hall* up to the ears in a muddle of counting lines to fill the *2nd vol* [1]—a body of finished sheets from the first, having arrived along with your letter—and their appearance after many changes gives great satisfaction to the Poet and his Clerk—His *Journeyman* in the Person of Mr Quillinan [2] having left us last week, to my

---

[1] The revision of the poems had been under way since the beginning of August (see L. 1061 above).

[2] E. Q. entered some record of W. W.'s conversation at this period in his MS. Diaries (*WL MSS.*), e.g. under 2 Sept.: 'Mr. W. said tonight that there was no immortality in laughter in reference to the effect produced on mankind by authors.—That there was not a jest nor a stroke of humour from beginning to end in the sacred writings.—That Aristophanes and the other Greek and Roman writers of comedy were not really popular, and that even Shakespeare's comedies did not *lay hold of us.*—That Don Quixote was admirable, but rather melancholy than laughter-moving.—That the most pathetic of all passages were to be found in the Scriptures and in the Greek

great regret, for he supplied my place, which he filled most admirably, and has quite thrown me into the shade. However the Poet is obliged to be thankful for his old helpmate and a busy house we have—working steadily till dinner time—and in a *disorderly* manner the rest of the day: tho' he finds time to walk with Mr Justice Coleridge, [1] who with his family are residing in Fox-how.—By the bye, do you remember a dying birch tree upon the good Doctor's ground, I must give you an Epigram that was brought in after a walk, by Mr Townsend [2] (I know not that he is of your acquaintance—he was till of late Curate of Preston nr Brighton—and has published a small volume entitled 'Winchester and other pieces') a friend of our's who visited us in the way you did, for a short time, but instead of lodging at Agnes's [3] he was in Mr Fleming's (our Clergyman's) late lodgings—but to the Epigram.

A melancholy Fact.

A Birch of elegant and graceful Form,
Loved by the Zephyrs, spared by every storm
Lost (tho' refreshing Rotha murmured by),
Its health, its beauty—and I'll tell you why.
   An active, staunch, scholastic Teacher came
To be its neighbour, one well *known* to fame.
The Tree thro' fear of being put, by fate,
To use both savage and indelicate,
Sickened at Rugby's Lord, nor could abide
The thought of such disgrace, it drooped and died

30th August 1836

Tragedians, and in Shakespeare.—He thought the French writers of light dramas the most effective and laughter-moving—but no wit, founded on manners or fashions, could endure, however good.'

[1] After presiding at the Lancaster assizes earlier in the month, Sir John Taylor Coleridge was now spending six weeks holiday with his family at Fox How, which had been lent him by the Arnolds. He contributed a long reminiscence of the Wordsworths during this period to *Mem.* (ii. 300–15).

[2] The Revd. Charles Townsend (see L. 1016 above) was spending the summer at Fieldfoot, Loughrigg. He was, according to E. Q.'s MS. Diary, 'ruddy, square, and strong, and a famous walker, cricket and tennis player. He is gentle in manner, rather elaborate and drawling in his enunciation, and has considerable pretensions to talk in literature and art.'

[3] Presumably Mrs. Atkins, with whom H. C. R. had lodged at Rydal.

Now for *your private* amusement I have only transcribed this—being not quite sure that our friend Mrs A. to whom I sent it, liked the joke. The *ghost* or corpse of the birch is now laid low, and it was only from a mistake that it had been left by the family, to have been the occasion of exciting the poetical railing of our agreeable Visitor.

We heard of you with great pleasure as having been at Brinsop, but regretted you could not go to the Stow—I hear Mr Monkhouse is again in London. Thanks for your brief detail of your Welsh travels—I think William agrees with all you say about your intended tour, only *you misunderstand* that he is *limited* to 3 months however all the work, which you *foolishly* recommend to be left midway and 'to be considered as a delightful occupation' to return to finish, will be completed before you set out—else your *journeyings* will not always be the most laborious part of your travels. The juvenile pieces have caused great labor; but, as we proceed, we hope to go on with less difficulty—and that the Poet may leave home with a perfect holiday before him—and, but, I dare not say so—return to *the Recluse*;—and let me charge you, not to encourage the Muse to *vagrant* subjects—but gently recur, upon such indications should they arise, to Rogers' hint that 'jingling *rhyme* does not become a certain age.' entre nous—

John has the strongest wish to go with you—but this must depend upon his being able to have his Parish served during his absence—They have got into his new Vicarage where Father and Mother visited them last week for 3 days—to our great satisfaction—the healthiness of the situation has given fresh looks to the whole household—and the prospects from their windows are most beautiful.

Willy is at present a Candidate for the Secretaryship to a Railway[1]—alas for the *Poets* Son! he is supported by his Uncle D^r W's connections the Lloyds—but being late in the field his expectation of success is not very sanguine.

Now for our Invalids—our dear Sister is very well and generally very happy—but her Mind does not strengthen—tho her memory is now good, that is *partially*—And it is most strange, as you will think, when I tell you that sometimes she amuses herself by pouring out verses—as by inspiration—in a moment and seemingly without thought she will write down

---

[1] See L. 1069 above.

(and in as good a hand as ever she wrote) 6 or 8 very respectable lines—generally addressed to her attendants,—the subjects are not very elevated. She reads the Newspapers, but an old one—read a doz times—pleases equally with a new one. Dora is certainly better—And

[*cetera desunt*]

1074. W. W. to EDWARD MOXON

Address: [Edward Mox]on Esqre, [44 Dov]er Street[1] [*In M. W.'s hand*]
Stamp: Strand.
MS. Henry E. Huntington Library. Hitherto unpublished.

Tuesday—[Sept. 1836]

Dear Mr Moxon,

I liked the appearance of the sheet sent me much. But pray let me have more as speedily as may be, for I am not without hopes of going abroad before the Autumn is past.

Pray ask your Brother if any parcel was sent to you from Rydal, some months ago, to be forwarded to Mr or Mrs Bedingfield Stowe Market.

ever faithfully yours
W W.

[*M. W. adds*]

Mrs W. will thank Mr M. to send the enclosed note to the twopenny post.

---

[1] *Half of sheet missing.*

1075. W. W. to SIR JOHN TAYLOR COLERIDGE

Address: Mr Justice Coleridge. [*delivered by hand*]
MS. British Library. Hitherto unpublished.

[late Sept. *or* early Oct. 1836]

Ambleside Kendal by the Glasgow mail—It goes I believe from the Swan with two necks.[1] I have a call to make in Ambleside after dinner, but will be at Fox how immediately after that to walk with you.

W. W.

1076. W. W. to JOSHUA WATSON

Endorsed: Wm Wordsworth Esq Oct. 5. 1836 Cockermᵒ Ch.
MS. WL.
LY ii. 805 (—).

[*In M. W.'s hand*]

Rydal Mount Octᵇʳ 5ᵗʰ [1836]

My dear Sir

Your letter has rather discouraged my hope of succeeding in the way I mentioned to you, so that I was glad to avail myself of an opportunity for a second interview, which I had with Mr Stanger yesterday. The result is, that if my Friend who offered to endow the Church provided it could be built, does not disapprove, or feel hurt, I am disposed to co-operate with Mr Stanger, if sanctioned in such a measure by your judgment. As I found that so large a sum, as will appear by the enclosed was likely to be at Mr S—'s disposal I thought it expedient that I should give way to him, and the more so, because I am persuaded, that in so doing those Inhabitants of Cockermouth who have shewed the most favorable dispositions, would be best pleased; I wish I were at liberty to treat this part of the subject more openly.

Finding that I could not induce Mr S. to join in my plan beyond a small contribution towards erecting the Church, and

---

[1] Presumably travelling instructions for J. T. Coleridge, or for someone who was visiting him at Fox How. The Swan with Two Necks was the mail coach terminus in Warrington.

301

feeling very loth to let so large a sum as he offers be lost towards the Place, I proposed—first stipulating for time to consult my friends—to aid him to the utmost with such subscriptions as I could raise—but upon these conditions. 1st that the Trustees of Mr Simeon[1] should have nothing to do with the concern, and 2d^{ly} that in preference to Elective trustees of any kind, the Patronage sh^d be lodged in one Individual and that I had no objection to that Individual being himself on account of the large sum he was prepared to advance. He replied, that tho' very unwilling to undertake the responsibility of Presenting, yet rather than lose my cooperation he would do so—consenting further, for, for this I stipulated, that in case of his death the Patronage as far as was in his power, should be preserved in one hand. He then said, if he survived his Brother, it should pass to him—or otherwise, he should leave it to some one who, to the best of his judgment—would act towards the trust conscientiously.

Now my dear Sir, I am well aware that this plan cannot be carried into effect without the sacrifice of the first presentation at least—being under the *influence* not to say dictation, of the Simeonites. But is not this better much, than that the Church should not be built at all, where it is so deplorably needed? Will you then assist cordially in this project? And give me the benefit of your directions how to proceed?

I remain dear Sir
faithfully y^{rs}
[*signed*] Wm Wordsworth

N.B. I ought to say that Mr S. is a Conservative in politics—so there is no fear of a Radical being appointed.

Mr. Stanger thinks, that with his own Contribution, and those which the Residents in, and near Cockermouth have

---

[1] Charles Simeon (1759–1836), the acknowledged leader of Evangelical churchmen, and from 1783 vicar of Holy Trinity, Cambridge, was one of the founders of the Church Missionary Society (1797), and a prominent supporter of the British and Foreign Bible Society. He founded a body of Trustees for acquiring Church patronage and administering it according to his own views. Whereas Stanger was an Evangelical and sympathetic to Simeon's principles, W. W. was profoundly distrustful of Evangelical methods and the 'instant' conversions that went with them. C. W. was actively engaged in discussing the Cockermouth plan with Joshua Watson at this time, and wrote to him on 11 Oct. about 'the uncatholic spirit' of the Simeon Trustees (*WL MSS.*).

proposed to advance, he may have £4000 or £4500 at command.

Mr Stanger himself believes that the Parties, who would make up this sum, also prefer, that the Patronage should be vested in the Trustees appointed by Mr Simeon; but in order to secure the cooperation of those who take an interest in the proposed new Church, but entertain decided objections to this Scheme of patronage, he would not object to having the Patronage vested in himself, as probably the principal Contributor.

N.B. The above is copied from a paper in Mr Stanger's hand— but it be added, that Mr S. admitted that he was not sure of quite so large a sum as £4500, unless the Election were in Trustees. From what Mr W.[1] saw of certain persons in Cockermouth lately, he thinks they are not disposed much to the Patronage being in *Mr Simeon's* Trustees, only in Trustees rather than being in the hands of one Individual.

1077. W. W. to SIR JOHN TAYLOR COLERIDGE

Address: Mr Justice Coleridge, Fox How. [*delivered by hand*]
MS. British Library. *Hitherto unpublished.*

Friday Morn.
[7 Oct. 1836][2]

My dear Sir,
    I am engaged to go to Bowness to day. If you are at liberty (though I am loth to propose any thing that should take you from the company of Lady Coleridge)[3] I suggest that we might go together in my Vehicle. My scheme is, that we should alight at Low wood and go up to Troutbeck on foot, and be taken up by the Carriage five miles further on the road to Bowness; and from Bowness should return by Elleray, Mr Hamilton's. My business at Bowness is to advise with Sir Thomas Pasley[4] about

---

[1] Mr. William Wood.

[2] Dated by reference to *Mem*. ii. 308, which records the expedition proposed by W. W. in this letter.

[3] Mary (1788–1874), daughter of Dr. Gilbert Buchanan, rector of Woodmansterne, Surrey, whom J. T. Coleridge had married in 1818. She was, by all accounts, something of a valetudinarian.

[4] See pt. ii, L. 747, and L. 981 above.

the grounds of his new House. But this would not be lost time to you, as the views are fine from the place.

W. W.

I propose to set off about 11 or a little later should it suit you better.

1078. W. W. to EDWARD MOXON

Address: Edward Moxon Esqre, 44 Dover S^t. [*In Dora W.'s hand*]
MS. Harvard University Library.
LY ii. 806.

[*In M. W.'s hand*]

Octr 10th [1836]

My dear Sir

The Box has just arrived, and I have only time to thank you cordially and say a very few words.

The Print as far as we can judge seems excellently engraved[1]—but for my own part I cannot but think, (wishing it may be liked by others) that in following the plan of giving the head and part of the Person, independent of the reclining attitude, an air of feebleness is spread thro' the whole; which is the more felt from a fault in the original Picture, of a weakness of expression about the upper lip.

I shall write to Mr Judkin[2] as soon as I can command a moment's time—but I have been sadly hampered by some corrections of minor import which have taken up my time in a way which I cannot excuse myself for. I am at this moment far from well in consequence.

You say you have sent the *remainder* of the Sheets—but are you aware that what you before sent only commence at the 145th Page—so that you must kindly forward those which precede in order to hunt out errors—Mrs W. says why did Mr Moxon tear the heads from the worthies whose Autographs are sent me for a sample?

[1] The engraving of Pickersgill's portrait by W. H. Watt (see also L. 1048 above), intended as the frontispiece of the new edition. E. Q. shared W. W.'s misgivings about the print: 'It wants the vigorous character of the poet's countenance', he complained in a letter to M. W. on 29 Oct. (*WL MSS.*).

[2] The Revd. T. J. Judkin, who had offered to illustrate the new edition (see L. 1080 below).

Messrs Masterman's Bank is the one in connection with Wakefields, of Kendal and who will receive on my account with that Bank, what you have to transmit to me.

Ever dear Sir, with our united best regard to you and yours,

[*signed*] Wm Wordsworth

We will be much obliged by y^r having a doz. more prints struck off for us.

1079. W. W. to JOSHUA WATSON

Endorsed: Wm Wordsworth Esq 17 Oct. 1836. Cockerm° Ch.
MS. WL.
LY ii. 807.

[*In M. W.'s hand*]

Rydal Mt Octr 17th [1836]

My dear Friend

I will plague you no further, than merely to ask you, If I can get a Church at Cockermouth endowed—and by my own efforts raise perhaps £6 or 700 towards its erection—can you aid me from the Societies etc—to complete the Building?— When I have an answer to this, I must either determine to give up the scheme altogether to Mr S—,[1] who is prepared to build in union with the People of C— who generally entertain his views, or, *we* must proceed independent of him; in which case he will apply his money to the building a Chapel, having as he told me, another neighbouring Place in view. So that you see the £3 or 4000, which he has at command, *is* to go forth to propagate Simeonism, and in a worse shape than I had brought him to consent to. Therefore, you will perceive, that there was policy in my attempt to draw him from investing Patronage in the Trustees of Mr S.[2]

It grieves me to ask for an early reply knowing how valuable your time is, but I am anxious to give my final answer to Mr S.[3]

ever faithfully
your obliged
[*signed*] Wm Wordsworth

[1] Mr. Stanger.   [2] Mr. Simeon.   [3] Mr. Stanger.

Pray be so good as to tell how your health is, and Miss Watson's.—This is sent through the twopenny post—to save time.—

1080. W. W. to THOMAS JAMES JUDKIN[1]

Address: Mr Geo T. J. Judkin, 6 Holly Terrace, Highgate Hill.
MS. Yale University Library.
T. J. Wise, Two Lake Poets. A Catalogue . . ., 1927 (—). *LY ii. 809* (—).

[*In M. W.'s hand*]

Rydal Mount Oct[r] 20th [1836]

My dear Sir,

Your Picture was very welcome, I think it decidedly improved by the suggestions you were kind enough to work upon, and by the additional figure. The whole has an air of animated seclusion which is very agreeable to the feeling, while the Picture is in my judgement exceedingly well painted. It continues to give encreasing pleasure to us all, as we become better and better acquainted with [it],[2] and we hope that at some time or other we may have the pleasure or shewing you, how well it looks, and in what good company it hangs. Its immediate neighbour is a Picture by my late valued friend Sir Geo Beaumont—*The White Doe*.[3]

I am truly sensible to your kind offer to assist in illustrating my Poems, I regret that this was not thought of when we met in Town, and something might have been contrived for our mutual satisfaction—It is now too late for the present Edition, but I shall nourish the hope that at some future time our labours may be united in a manner so agreeable to my feelings.

I ought not to omit mentioning that your print of the Crucifixion has been *more* than admired—it has been deeply *felt* in this house: and by Strangers—competent Judges.—I still intend being in London about the middle of February—or rather the end of that month—but as my plan is merely to pass thro', I shall hardly be able to avail myself of your kind invitation, tho' I hope we shall effect a meeting.

I have desired Mr Moxon to send you my volumes as they come out, in the first, if you think it worth while to compare the Pieces entitled Evening Walk, Descriptive Sketches, and the

---

[1] See L. 1078 above.   [2] *Word dropped out.*   [3] See *MY* i. 196, 392.

Waggoner[1] with the preceding Ed: you will find I have made
very considerable alterations, which I trust will be found to be
improvements—at all events they ought to be so, for they cost
me much labour.

Believe me to be my d^r Sir
very sincerely yours
[*signed*] Wm Wordsworth

1081. W. W. to EDWARD MOXON

Address: Edward Moxon Esqre, 44 Dover Street.
MS. Henry E. Huntington Library.
LY ii. 808.

[*In M. W.'s hand*]

Octr 20th [1836]

My dear Sir,

I have looked over the 1st Vol, and with the exception of the
one erratum in the table of Contents—and one Stanz: in which
there are two gross errors, which by the bye arose out of a
correction without a revise, I have no blunders to lay to the
charge of the Printers—though there is one serious one for
which I am myself accountable. I have enclosed by this Post a list
of Errata and emendations for Mr Evans.[2]

The book I think executed in a way which will do the Printers
and yourself credit—As to the Portrait I am still of opinion, in
which others concur, that the attitude has an air of decrepitude
in consequence of the whole Person not being given—it appears
to me to be beautifully engraved; and pray tell the Artist[3] with
my compliments that I think so.

I have heard such strong opinions given respecting the
disadvantages the Ed: will labour under in not having one
illustration at least for each Vol. that I regret much for your sake
that an arrangement was not made between us, with a proper
sacrifice on my part, to include this. It is now I fear too late. I

---

[1] For the recent revision of *The Waggoner*, see Sir John Coleridge's diary
quoted in *Mem.* ii. 310.

[2] The printer.

[3] W. H. Watt, the engraver.

hope however that the apprehensions which have led me to speak in this way may prove groundless.

I wish Copies to be sent in my name *before* publication, as the vols come out to,

Mr Stephen, Colonial Office
Sir Ben: Brodie Bar^t, or rather to Lady B.
Mr Quillinan
Mr Judkin and to my nephew J. W.[1] who will call for it, likewise to Sir Charles Bell,[2] Edinburgh and to Mr Montgomery,[3] Sheffield.

We hope Mrs Moxon and your Baby are well—and dear Miss Lamb, to whom always remember us with love. Thanks for the journals you have sent us.

Before you pay any money for me into the Bank, let me beg you to make out my account which has been of long standing, and settle it.

With our united regards to you and yours, I remain sincerely yours

[*signed*] Wm Wordsworth

1082. W. W. to JAMES STEPHEN

Address: James Stephen Esqre.
MS. Harvard University Library.
K (—). *LY ii. 810.*

Rydal Mount
October 24th 36.

My dear Sir

I am sorry for the Printers carelessness by which you were left in doubt as to the destination of the Pacquet. I reckon it one of the happinesses of my life to have had few secrets either of my own or of others to take care of—and should such another instance of neglect occur, you need not scruple to be as bold as you have been.

And now let me thank you gravely and cordially for the service you have done me in press-reading the proofs of this

---

[1] i.e. 'Keswick John'.
[2] The neurologist. See L. 1084 below.
[3] James Montgomery (see pt. i, L. 125).

Publication. We have already got through 2 Volumes and part
of a third. I have directed Mr Moxon to send them to you in
succession, as they come out. I am sorry to say that the first
Volume has several Mistakes, for which I am answerable
mainly, having trusted to the Printer, in several cases where
alterations were made in the proofs, without having a revise sent
down. The Excursion (the last of the six volumes) is one of those
already printed, and will be sent shortly for your kind
acceptance; in this I hope few errors will be found, but I have not
seen it yet.

May I beg that some one about you would take the trouble of
correcting in your Copy the Errata with a Pen, at least the most
important of them.

Repeating my thanks for this kind service, I remain

> My dear Sir
> faithfully
> Your much obliged
> Wm Wordsworth

1083. W. W. to SIR BENJAMIN COLLINS BRODIE[1]

MS. untraced.
Bookseller's Catalogue.

> Rydal Mount
> [? Nov. 1836]

. . . looking at her[2] case under the two aspects of dim-
inution of pain and increase of strength, she is without doubt
considerably improved . . .

As your Son[3] is a lover of Poetry, he might be interested in
comparing in some points, this first vol. with the corresponding
ones[4] in former Editions. Some of the Pieces, the Juveneal ones

[1] See Ls. 875 and 1067 above.
[2] i.e. Dora W.'s.
[3] Sir Benjamin Collins Brodie, 2nd Bart., F.R.S. (1817–80), Professor of
Chemistry at Oxford from 1865, was about to enter Balliol College as an
undergraduate.
[4] W. W. had asked Moxon to send Brodie the volumes of the new edition
as they appeared.

in particular, have undergone a good deal of correction. . .

[My sister] talks of the pleasure she had in seeing you, tho' for so short a time—she remains much in the same state, certainly not worse. . .

1084. W. W. to SIR CHARLES BELL[1]

MS. Hunter Baillie Collection, Royal College of Surgeons of England. Hitherto unpublished.

[Nov. 1836]

Dear Sir Charles,

I have long been anxious to write to you, but put it off in the hope of giving greater value to my letter by being enabled to communicate decisive accounts of the improved health of the Invalid whom you kindly came so far to visit. This you will be glad to hear I can now do, my Daughter is certainly very much better since she had the benefit of your advice. She is now enabled to ride on horseback every 2^d or 3^d day, a couple of miles, and she walks in the garden on the intermediate days—remaining in the open air from half an hour to an hour at a time: but this is always attended by some fatigue and at *first* the exercise was followed by pains in the head and sleepless nights.

Among the unpleasant symptoms still left—are the pains in the side, about the shoulder and down the arm; and the palpitation of the heart, the latter a good deal diminished—the former not so much. I observe also a short tickling cough which seems to depend upon damp weather—and has its seat in the throat: also I think myself that it is apt to come on after exercise or excitement. Her appetite is so much improved that it may now be said to be good, and in consequence she gathered flesh, as Mr Carr thought, too fast, as her strength and power of exertion, rather diminished than increased—accordingly he thought it expedient that she should take less nourishing food. On the whole I trust however she is doing very well.

[1] Sir Charles Bell (1774–1842), the neurologist, published *The Nervous System of the Human Body* in 1830; his Bridgewater Treatise on *The Hand, its Mechanism and Vital Endowments as evincing Design* in 1833; and in 1836 he joined with Brougham in annotating Paley's *Natural Theology*. He taught at the Middlesex Hospital and for a short time at the new London University, and in 1836 was appointed Professor of Surgery at Edinburgh. He had come to Rydal the previous August to see Dora W. (*RMVB*).

I need scarcely add that if anything may strike you, upon this statement, by which she could benefit—it would be gratefully received.

It gives me great pleasure to add that not long after you had seen my daughter, we had the gratification of a visit from Sir Ben: Brodie[1] at Rydal, who kindly listened to a statement of her case. And as far as I could collect, his opinion coincided with your own. We cannot be sufficiently thankful, that as the Invalid could not travel, she had in this way the friendly advice of two gentlemen so eminent in the Profession. Indeed we have every reason to be grateful for the services of Members of your Profession—Dr Holland, tho' he never saw her, having taken great pains in considering her case—and Dr Davy having done the same, last year,[2] with the advantage of personal interviews.

Mr Fleming,[3] whom you will recollect having seen at Ambleside, called here yesterday. On telling him I was about to write to you, he was much pleased to have an opportunity of thanking you for the great benefit he had derived from your advice—he said you saw into his case at once and had, to use his own expression, set him upon his legs again. He certainly looks infinitely better and is much stronger, both for exercise and the duties of his profession.

I have directed my Publisher to send you a Copy of my Poems, (now coming out monthly) as they appear. Some thing in them perhaps may interest you in your leisure moments—at all events Lady Bell will not I trust find it difficult to spare time to look into them. I hope you find your pursuits at Edinburgh as agreeable as you anticipated; and that the loss of London society, where you will be much missed, is made up to you. With many thanks, in which Mrs W. and my Daughter cordially join, I remain, dear Sir Charles, very faithfully

Your much obliged
Wm Wordsworth

I ought to have mentioned that my daughter's sight is not strengthened—rather, she seems to herself to be more dim—and short-sighted—but probably this may not be so—in fact she may be more conscious of the weakness, as she stirs more about and the eyes are called more into action.

[1] See L. 1067 above.
[2] See L. 921 above.
[3] The Revd. Fletcher Fleming, incumbent of Rydal

1085. M. W. to H. C. R.

Endorsed: 1 Novr 1836, Mrs Wordsworth.
MS. Dr. Williams's Library.
K (—). Morley, i. 322.

Rydal Mount Novr 1st [18]36

My dear Friend

Thanks for your letter, which we had long been wishing for, and tho' it does not convey the desired information—we must not grumble; but I must tell you, that, we Females were not so disinterested as to beg for your company this time, merely for the sake of *the Poet*—but for *our own* gratification. *He* will have his full share of your cheering Society when you run off together—and we poor things! would fain have had our part: however selfish schemes ought not to prosper and we must reconcile ourselves to our disappointment as well as we can; Nevertheless we shall owe that *Italian Man* a grudge, if he really be the main bar to our seeing you—two days *in* Italy would bring back the language to you better than all your plodding at it, in Plowden's Buildings.—

I do beg your pardon for not having adverted to all the interesting communication your former letter conveyed to us—but you ought to have borne in mind that the few lines I wrote almost at the moment it was received, was not intended as a reply to *that* letter which was to William—but because I could not help expressing our general pleasure in having heard from you, and having the opportunity to enclose a scrap in a cover, which I was in the act of aiding my husband to despatch—and the little time I then had to give to you was *won* from his pauses. Let me now tell you once for all, that it always delights us to follow you on your excursions—and that your visit to Bristol[1] was peculiarly interesting. Dora and I were *with you* in Cottle's Sanctum, where some 7 or 8 years ago[2] we too, were favored

---

[1] On 29 Aug., on his way home from Wales, H. C. R. had called on Joseph Cottle, who was preparing to publish his controversial *Early Recollections; Chiefly Relating to the Late Samuel Taylor Coleridge*, 2 vols., 1837, which naturally gave the Wordsworths some cause for concern. In his last letter but one, on 12 Sept., H. C. R. had given W. W. a long account of his visit to Cottle, who was familiarly known as 'the regicide' in the Wordsworth circle on account of his tragedy *Alfred*. See Morley, i. 315–16, and *HCR* ii. 500–3. H. C. R. regarded the book as 'a poor thing' when it appeared (see *HCR* ii. 534).   [2] In 1828 (see pt. i, L. 347).

with a sight of the Portraits[1]—to the best of *my* recollection we were most pleased with that of Southey—in wh^{ch} we saw, or fancied we saw, the spirit of the embrio Poet—Dora said that of her Father's reminded her of her Brother John. With regard to the benevolent Regicide's intended Book—I need only say that he *has* behaved disingenuously—If Southey saw all the M.S. he could not and does not, approve[2]—the story is too long, and too intricate for me to enter upon—William (who was shewn letters by Judge Coleridge which prove that Cottle was resolved to publish the objectionable matter, before he received *that* letter of Mr Gillman's, which he afterwards asserted had determined him *to* publish) will tell you all about it. Southey will see Cottle soon, who has commenced making a Progress[3] with his Son, and will skim the South and West of England, to introduce Cuthbert to his old friends, and the interesting haunts of his youth; calculating upon an absence from Keswick of at least 3 months, before they part at Tarring—the Vicarage of his son-in-law—where, probably he may be introduced to, and give a blessing to his second Grandchild—as Edith is expecting her confinement before that time.

I hope your expectations of receiving Lamb's letters from Bristol are fulfilled—I had much rather they were really in Talfourd's hands, than left to the mercy of C. With you I do not regret the publication of our dear friend's *Remains* (to use the fashionable designation)—Dora, who is rumaging her

---

[1] In 1798 Cottle had commissioned William Shuter's portrait of W. W. (now at Cornell); and in 1796−8 the drawings by Robert Hancock (1730−1817) of S. T. C., Southey, W. W., and Lamb, which were engraved as illustrations to Cottle's *Early Recollections*, and which eventually found their way to the National Portrait Gallery after his death. See Blanchard, *Portraits of Wordsworth*, pp. 41−3, 140−2. 'As to your own picture, 'H. C. R. wrote on 12 Sept., 'you have taken abundant care to let the world know that you did not marry Mrs W: for her beauty. Now this picture will justify the inference that she too had a higher motive for her acceptance of you.'

[2] Cottle had sent his MS. to Southey in the spring of this year in an attempt to placate the Coleridge family who wanted the book suppressed; but he failed to satisfy their objections, and in June James Gillman threatened to take Cottle to court. Later, when it became clear that Cottle was going ahead with publication, J. T. Coleridge sought Southey's help in persuading Cottle to omit certain objectionable passages referring to S. T. C.'s use of opium and a gift of £300 from De Quincey. See Curry, ii. 444 ff.

[3] See Southey, vi. 306−26, and Warter, iv. 472−95. Southey also visited Thomas Poole at Nether Stowey.

portfolio, has just given me a copy of one of his invaluable letters—which I will enclose, thinking it not an improper one to publish—as expressing a right feeling in his own delightful language and playful manner. I trust this, and all the letters we have sent may be preserved and restored to us. We have rec[d], but I have scarcely looked into, Coleridge's 'Literary Remains'.[1]

The Tragedy[2] is in existence—but say nothing about it, lest its destruction should follow.

Mrs Hemans's letters etc.[3] we consider as a very flimsy Publication—and not at all likely to support the opinion of those who have extolled her genius—I must not say it disappoints me—from my personal knowledge, it is exactly what I should have expected—But we have strong evidence that her mind was steadied, and she became much more interesting, after she went to Dublin,—that is, she discarded what to us seemed to be a lightness and affectation of manner. The Mr Graves, who saw much of her in Dublin, to the last— quite reverence her.—and you know they are sensible Persons not likely to be carried away by what is superficial. Poor woman! she was sorely tried—and a beautiful trait in her character was, that she never uttered a complaint of her Husband.[4]

[1] Henry Nelson Coleridge had just brought out the first volume. 'It is quite provoking', H. C. R. had written to M. W. on 27 Oct., 'to see an attempt made to exhibit one of the profoundest thinkers and most splendid talkers of his age, as vulgarly orthodox.' (Morley, i. 320)

[2] *The Borderers*, published 1842. 'Among the letters destined to appear', H. C. R. had written on 12 Sept., 'is one in which Coleridge extols your *tragedy*—he says It makes him feel *less* than he ever did—That there are weak points in Shakespear and Schiller but none in this etc etc—Your own silence about this tragedy (for I never heard you allude to it,) assures me that your own opinion is different—Still I hope it is not destroyed—It ought to be preserved at all events as a curiosity—There have been instances in which works rejected by their author have been published in an Appendix—And were this play ever to appear as the *dramatic experiment* of a great philosophic and lyric poet, in a way that shewed the author's own consciousness that tho' poetic it was not dramatic, it could not lessen him in the opinion of the few.' For S. T. C.'s letter to Cottle in praise of *The Borderers*, see Griggs, i. 325.

[3] Henry F. Chorley, *Memorials of Mrs Hemans*, 2 vols., 1836.

[4] Captain Alfred Hemans, who had served at Corunna and in the Walcheren expedition. The couple had lived apart for seventeen years.

Your Epig^m i.e. C's[1] we knew—yet it was new to poor Miss W's mind as many *gone-by* things are—and it made her laugh heartily—You ask if W.ever wrote an Epigram—I believe he once did, and if I am not mistaken I will send it in my next—I shall not have time or opportunity perhaps at present.

He and his Son W. are journeying to day from Brigham—where they met on Saturday—The father from Whitehaven, last Tuesday he accompanied Lady F. Bentinck thither to pay his respects to the Lowther family, as being more convenient to him (in this season of business) than if he had gone to Lowther, where a longer visit would have been looked for. The proofs have been forwarded during his weeks absence, and no time has been lost. He gets on with his work very well—The Juvenile Pieces [2] cost him much labor—but *then* he had a useful Assistant in Mr Quillinan; and his presence here was a Godsend to me.

We had not heard of the Aders' misfortunes—for which we are very sorry—heartily do I wish that Wm could think himself justified in giving aid to Mrs A's praiseworthy undertaking[3]—it will be a privilege to be housed under such superintendence, and there seems little doubt but that her undertaking will answer—he has not, of course, yet heard of the scheme, or the cause of it—Willy's project[4] failed—and he is still upon the look out—His two journeys to Birmingham, tho' success on that occasion did not follow, were not I trust thrown away altogether—for he seems to have made many friends, and recommended himself by his activity—and desire for suitable employment.

I am glad you see John [5] sometimes—He has been fortunate in the Sale of his Lands. You are very kind in continuing to be interested in the settlement with the Trustees—he now has all things in his possession to enable Mr Cookson to give the Trustees a *release* (or whatever you call it) and if you could, when you meet with the Parties, suggest or enquire if this is

[1] S. T. C.'s epigram *Extempore on a steamboat*, quoted by H. C. R. in his letter of 27 Oct. (Morley, i. 321.)

[2] Principally *An Evening Walk* and *Descriptive Sketches* (See L. 1080 above): after 1836 the group was renamed *Poems written in Youth*.

[3] Aders had gone bankrupt and his wife proposed starting a boarding house in Brussels, for which enterprise she needed from £600 to £700 capital. (Morley's note.)

[4] To be appointed Secretary to the Birmingham and Derby Railway.

[5] 'Keswick John'.

done, with a view to remind that it ought to be—it would be satisfactory to have all settled before W. leaves England.

And here I am on the last page without having spoken of our Invalids—which used to be my all-involving subject—you will suppose from this that they are going on well—and so it is, comparatively. Miss W. to us seems quite delightful—tho' my sister Joanna, who joined us only last week [1]—is greatly shocked at the change that has taken place in her—and almost wonders to hear us congratulate ourselves. Yet our cause for thankfulness *is* great. [2] Dora's health too, is *slowly* improving—if, as I would fain hope, a fearful oppression or catching of the breath, and a pain in the side, is only indicatory of *weakness*—for her looks are greatly improved—and she has, to a considerable degree, resumed her domestic activities—and she goes into the open air, for about an hour every day—sometimes upon the Poney— hitherto, not without this exercise being followed with considerable fatigue—but when she first began to go out, fatigue was not the only consequence—it brought on pain in the head and feverish sleeplessness. This having passed off, she is encouraged to persevere—and we hope she may gain strength. Do not allude to this detail, when you write—which, pray do not delay to do at your leisure—I must have tired you out—yet I shall probably prose a little longer to you to morrow—after the two Williams' return—meanwhile I will spare you.

ever faithfully your obliged and affectionate
M. W.

W. is come home, but too late for me to say more than that he

---

[1] From Brinsop.

[2] M. W. had given an account of D. W.'s health in a letter to Mrs. Coleridge on 11 Oct. (*Harvard University Library MSS.*): ' . . . Her intellect was never brighter than *at times* it now is—She amuses herself with composing verses, which she can do without apparent thought or effort, and she *writes* them with a rapidity that would astonish you, and in a far better and straighter hand than she used to do—her performances are far from contemptible, indeed there is often much beauty in what she thus throws off— generally the subject is called forth by a present occurrence and addressed to some of her attendants or visitors. She is interested about all her friends, and does not confine all her thoughts and feelings, as she used to do, to herself, which is a great improvement . . . She is herself happy—and is most entertaining company, on an evening when, perhaps for an hour together, we can keep her interested in our sitting-room, tho' she is always glad to get back to her own . . . '

is well—his eyes have not suffered from his drive, thro' the cold misty air.

To[1] shew you that *we* can write an Epigram—we do *not say a good one.*

On an Event in Col: Evans's[2] redoubted performances in Spain

> The Ball whizzed by,—it grazed his ear,
> And whispered as it flew,
> I only touch—not take—don't fear
> For both, my honest Buccaneer!
> Are to the Pillory due.

The Producer thinks it not amiss as being murmured between sleep and awake over the fire while thinking of you last night!

1086. W. W. to EDWARD MOXON

Address: Edward Moxon Esqre, 44 Dover Street.
MS. Henry E. Huntington Library.
K (—). *LY ii. 810.*

[*In M. W.'s hand*]

[? early Nov. 1836]

My dear Sir,

I was looking somewhat anxiously for your letter which I rec^d this morning. I entirely concur with you in all you say; and if you can get the 3000 disposed of in a reasonable time, we

---

[1] This p.s. has become detached from the letter to which it belongs, but it is probably part of this letter (or possibly of L. 1094 below).

[2] George de Lacy Evans (1787–1870) fought under Wellington in Spain and at Waterloo (where he had two horses killed under him), and later commanded a division in the Crimea. He came forward as radical M.P. for Rye in 1830; and in 1833 he was elected M.P. for Westminster, defeating John Cam Hobhouse, and holding the seat until 1841, and again 1846–65. In 1835 he took command of the British levy raised for the service of the Queen Regent Christina of Spain against Don Carlos. He was defeated at Fuenterrabia in July 1836 and at Hernani in Mar. 1837, but retook them both in May 1837, before the legion, its term of service expired, returned home. Evans was awarded the K.C.B. for his services. See also L. 1219 below.

can try our fortune with illustrations. Both Mr Stone[1] and Mr Judkin have [?][2] drawings gratis—an artist whom I met with the other day promised to send me a finished drawing from a sketch which he had made of the Valley in which I have placed the Solitary and which would be an appropriate ornament for the Excursion. I have no doubt but that I could procure drawings from various artists, so that the expense would be confined to engraving and striking off—Many years ago I mentioned to Messrs Longman a Scheme of printing in one volume, for the purpose you advert to, but they thought it would leave so little profit to me, that it would be ineligible. I did not press the matter upon them, tho' I was unconvinced.

We have not yet seen the Excursion, but when it reaches us—which it may do along with the other Volumes, 12 copies, (and the sooner the better) it shall be carefully looked over—and the errata made out.

I am convinced that if any alterations be made in the proofs, which one is tempted often to make, it is impossible to have a book correctly printed without a Revise. There are now and then blunders, in rhyme and metre which are inconceiveable sense—some of which however, are not always to be ascribed to the Printers, but arise from neglect on our part (when a change has been made) to erase the old text.

Let the copy of the Excursion, which you send down to have the errata made out, be bound up in cloth before it comes, and pray send also a print to bind up with the sheets of the first Volume, which was sent for the same purpose.

I am contented that my small account should remain unsettled as you wish, rather than disturb the generous arrangement you have made—and I sincerely wish that the bargain may be as advantageous to you as it is to myself, compared to any of my previous ones; and independent of this consideration, it is a great pleasure to be thus connected with you. With best regards to Mrs M. in which Mrs W. and my Daughter join, believe me   sincerely yours
[*signed*] Wm Wordsworth

[1] Frank Stone, the *genre* painter (see L. 1025 above), had offered illustrations for the new edition free of cost; and as E. Q. explained to M. W. in his letter of 29 Oct. (*WL MSS.*), 'though he is not a Turner he flatters himself he would not disgrace Mr W.'

[2] *Illegible word.* K reads 'offered' which gives the right sense (see L. 1080 above), but that is definitely not what is written.

1087. W. W. to HENRY TAYLOR

MS. Bodleian Library.
LY ii. 814 (—).

[*In M. W.'s hand*]

Rydal Nov[r] 4th [1836]

My dear Mr Taylor

I have been moving about, or your letter would have been earlier noticed. The enclosed which I hope it will be convenient to you to get franked if you do not happen to learn that Sir G. Beaumont is at Lambeth Palace, is upon the subject. For your sake and other friends I wish Sir G. B. would entrust the Bust to Chauntry[1]—and in some degree I wish it for my own—since I have seen the print designed for the new Ed: of my Poems: It is well engraved but partly owing to a fault about the upper lip, and still more to its having preserved the inclination of the body (natural in a recumbent attitude) without an arm to explain it or account for it, the whole has an air of feebleness and decrepitude which I hope is not yet authorized by the subject. It was an unfortunate suggestion from Mr Rogers that the portrait should be given in this half sort of way.

I am glad that you are about to see Misss Fenwick again in London, and rejoice in that re-establishment of her health which allows her to quit her country home. She will be glad that we think Dora a good deal better. She moves about pretty freely in the house, and walks out, or rides a little almost every day. My poor Sister is no worse. I have thought a hundred times of writing to Miss Fenwick—but it seemed I had so much to say, that it ended in a feeling that I could say nothing.

Ever faithfully yours
[*signed*] W[m] Wordsworth

Sir George Beaumont's address if he is not at Lambeth is Coleorton Hall Ashby de la Zouch

The pleasure of being with Miss Fenwick and you during my short stay in London will be one of my great inducements to

---

[1] For an engraving to be made. The bust of W. W. which was executed by Chantrey in 1820 for the late Sir George Beaumont, was widely considered to be the most impressive likeness of the poet. It was finally engraved by William Finden, to take the place of the Pickersgill portrait in the *Poems* of 1845. See also pt. ii, L. 500.

leave home. My intention is to set out from Rydal towards the end of Feb^ry. W. W.

1088. W. W. to ISAAC GREEN[1]

Address: Revd I. Green, Sedbergh.
Stamp: Kendal Penny Post.
MS. Cornell. Hitherto unpublished.

[*In M. W.'s hand*]

Rydal Mount
Novr 5th [1836]

Dear Sir,

Having been from home I am sorry not to have been able to reply earlier to your letter. It will give me pleasure to mention the intended rebuilding of Howgill Church to Dr Wordsworth—tho' I cannot press the matter upon his attention as freely as I might otherwise have done if I had not lately been applying to him upon the subject of building a New Church at Cockermouth, our native Place: where an additional one is much wanted. To this he has subscribed £50 and I am doing my utmost among my friends to procure aid in the same good Work. After all, as your application to him is, I suppose, as the Head of the College, I do not see how my intervention could under any circumstances be of much use. I will however with pleasure do as you desire—and will also put the circulars you have sent me, in the way of such Persons of my Acquaintance, as may seem most likely to take the subject under consideration. But for the reason mentioned above, I have not much hope of success.

It was very gratifying to me to see your own generous Subscription—it ought to encourage others in the neighbourhood, and I hope will do so.

The very pleasing Drawing you have sent, I infer, is from the pencil of Mrs Green—with her permission, to whom we beg our kind regards, we should wish to retain it.

---

[1] Brother of the late Daniel Green, curate of Langdale. See pt. i, Ls. 108 and 365.

THOMAS NOON TALFOURD, M.P.
from the portrait by John Lucas, 1836

I remain dear Sir, with a strong desire you may succeed in your pious undertaking,

Sincerely yours,
[*signed*] Wm Wordsworth

1089. W. W. to THOMAS NOON TALFOURD

Address: Mr Sergeant Talfourd M.P., Russell Square, London.
Postmark: 18 Nov. 1836. *Stamp*: Kendal.
MS. Harvard University Library. Hitherto unpublished.

[*In M. W.'s hand*]

Rydal Novr 16th [1836]

My dear Friend,

It would have given me great pleasure to have signed the paper you have sent me, but for two reasons, which will appear to you I think sufficient. First, I cannot speak of my own knowledge to the very important fact of English books being garbled by American Publishers at all, much less for any sordid purpose. The only two books printed in America which I have had an opportunity of looking into—are Tacitus' Works in Latin,[1] and my own Poems in 4 Vols[2]—given me by an American Friend—which are certainly not altered in the least from the original text. Therefore I feel it would be wrong in me, upon hear-say evidence merely (tho', of course not doubting the fact) to join in so grave a censure of American Publishers.

Secondly, I submit whether it would be politic to condemn those Publishers in such strong language; if the Agent for the American Publishers who communicated with Mr Moxon last Summer be trust-worthy, they as well as the American Authors are anxious to have English-Copyright established in America, and have for this purpose drawn up a petition, either jointly or

---

[1] Probably the New York edition (1825) of the *Histories, Germania* and *Agricola*.

[2] The Boston edition of 1824 (*R.M.Cat.*, no. 692). The printers reproduced Longman's edition of 1820, including 'whatever is peculiar in Orthography, Punctuation, and the Use of Capital Letters'. See *Cornell Wordsworth Collection*, no. 74. The first complete American edition in one volume appeared in 1836.

severally, which is to be introduced by Mr Clay[1] to Congress, next Session.

Now if this be so, I must repeat my doubt whether it be politic to put forth, from English Authors in a body, such an accusation, so strongly expressed, as it might irritate the American Publishers, and in consequence their tempers might stand in the way of their interest.

Sometime ago I wrote rather a long letter to Sir R. Inglis[2] upon Copy-right—tho' being then, and still continuing to be, unpossessed of accurate historical knowledge of the Subject. I am not aware that there was any thing important to you in that letter, but still I should like you to see it; and if you know Sir R. I. it might not perhaps be disagreeable to you to express to him my wish.

If I were Master of the facts historically, and had access to the arguments which have been used on both sides, when the question has been brought before the courts of law, or Parliament, I would readily give my best judgment to the consideration of the whole case. As it is, I feel incompetent to treat it in a manner to be of use to you.

Am I mistaken in supposing that I mentioned to you the name of Mr Stewart Mackenzie,[3] as a Member of Parliament who would support the side of justice in this matter?

Looking at it practically it is a mere question of degree—the Statute by assigning a term,[4] has relinquished the abstract ground of denying Copyright in the productions of Mind altogether: and by the same restriction, it has refused to admit the doctrine of independent perpetuity of Copyright in literature. So that we have, in the existing law, or any law upon the subject, a compromise between two principles. The practical question then is, does the existing law allow a *sufficient*

[1] Henry Clay (1777–1852), Congressman and Senator, Secretary of State under John Quincy Adams, 1824–8, made a report to Congress in 1837 in favour of an international copyright law, and pressed the claims of British authors in the Senate against the vested interests of American publishers. For the Petition to Congress by English authors, see L. 1189 below.

[2] This letter has not survived: it must have been an important early statement of W. W.'s position, perhaps arising out of his discussions in London the previous summer (see L. 1049 above).

[3] See L. 1062 above.

[4] The Act of 1814 limited an author's copyright to a term of 28 years from the date of publication, or for the remainder of his life, if he outlived that term.

recompence—to which, along with every thinking and un-prejudiced Man, I should say no—without going further than my own case I feel the grievous injustice of the law as it now exists—but with this point you are fully acquainted. Neverthe-less I would not appear as a Petitioner, but in the last extremity.

I am sorry that I have not time to add more. Believe me, with kindest regards to Mrs T. in which Mrs W. and my Daughter joins

Ever faithfully Yours

[*signed*] Wm Wordsworth

At your leisure will you be so good as direct, and forward the enclosed.

1090. W. W. to C. W.

Address: The Rev Dr Wordsworth, Trinity College, Cambridge.
Franked: London November nineteen 1836 T. N. Talfourd.
Postmark: 19 Nov. 1836.
MS. WL.
LY ii. 815.

Novr 16, [1836][1]

My dear Brother,

My Friend Lady Frederic Bentinck, when I saw her lately, mentioned an engraved Portrait, in the possession of Mr Roper, who inherited through Lady Sunderlin, Mr Malone's pro-perty.[2] Mr R— is desirous to have some explanation of this portrait, and I observed to Lord L—[3] that from your minute acquaintance with those times, I thought it not unlikely that you would be able to throw some light upon it. If you can do so, I shall be glad to hear from you upon the subject at your perfect leisure, but that I fear never comes,—at all events at your convenience.

[1] Year added by C. W.

[2] Many of the engraved portraits belonging to Edmond Malone (see *EY*, p. 499) passed on his death to the Revd. Thomas Rooper (1782–1865) of Brighton, a relative of Malone's sister-in-law Lady Sunderlin (d. 1831). In his reply of 28 Nov. (*WL MSS.*), C. W. conjectured that the portrait in question belonged as frontispiece to Richard Carpenter's *Astrology proved harmless, useful, pious,* 1657, a sermon on Genesis 1. 14, dedicated to Elias Ashmole.

[3] Presumably Lord Lonsdale—but the MS. reading is unclear.

I have just received a Letter from Mr John Ellis,[1] upon the subject of his political projects in connection with the Borough of Cambridge, and requesting my interest in his behalf, upon the ground of our coincident opinions. I wrote to him in answer, that having received some time since a circular Letter from the Board of Stamps forbidding the Distributors to interfere in Elections, upon pain of their severest displeasure, and informing us that certain functionaries had been superseded on account of interference, I must decline meddling and could only wish him well which I heartily did.

Now as Mr Ellis has his fortune to make in the world, I have to beg that, as he tells me he has called upon you, you would not be a jot the less guarded with him on account of any knowledge which you may suppose I have had of him. He came down into this country with Henry Curwen on a visit to the Island, he then called upon me; he also called upon me in London, and I dined at his House; he has been a week in my Son John's house at Brigham, and passed an evening in mine, a few weeks ago. Upon all these occasions he invariably maintained conservative opinions, and at his own house in particular in opposition to some of his Guests who held the contrary. But my knowledge of him extends no further; he is of a gentleman's family of the West, his Brother an Ultra Radical and Candidate, as he told me in his Letter, for one of the divisions of Cornwall. Mr Ellis is of gentlemanly manners as you would see, and I believe ready and ingenious both with tongue and pen.—

You would hear of Wm's disappointment,[2] nothing could be more kind than Mr Frank Lloyd[3] and all his connections were to Wm and I am not sorry that he made the attempt, though it was of course attended with expense—He made two journeys to Birm^g.

[1] Probably John Ellis (b. 1812), a Cornishman, who was later M.P. for Newry, 1837–41. W. W. consulted him in 1838 about the Copyright Bill. No one of this name stood for Cambridge Borough in the election of 1837, Thomas Spring Rice and Professor George Pryme (1781–1868) being returned again.

[2] He was a candidate for the post of Secretary to the Birmingham and Derby Railway.

[3] Francis Lloyd (1803–75), partner in Taylors and Lloyds Bank in Birmingham, 1828–39. On he death in 1828 of Charles Lloyd, snr. (see pt. i, L. 152), the succession in the Birmingham Bank passed through his younger son James (1776–1853), to James's three sons, James, Thomas and Francis. See R. S. Sayers, *Lloyds Bank in the History of English Banking*, 1957, p. 27.

I am sadly hampered about Cockermouth Church. Lord Lonsdale is in the best disposition, and would write to Lord Egremont, but I cannot go forward, Mr Fawcett, the Minister of Cockermouth, having declined as Mr Wood informed me, to make the official Returns, indispensible for Mr Watson, before he can give an assurance of what may be expected from the Societies. How would you advise me to proceed, in order to procure these returns. The Bp of Chester[1] wrote sometime since to the Secretary and he to Mr F, but the returns have not been made.

Unless something considerable can be had from the Societies, I am afraid the thing will fall into the hands of Mr Stanger and the Simeonites and my Friends and I will be obliged to withdraw altogether except for my own Individual trifling sub[2]—which I must give to Mr Stanger he having promised me a small contribution if he were to have no further interest in the Concern.

Love to all. Dora is better though still suffering much from her side—Sister no worse—

ever most affectionately yours

Wm Wordsworth

[*M. W. adds*]

We want to hear of our Nephews'—as well as of your own health.

---

[1] John Bird Sumner (see pt. ii, Ls. 426 and 455). The diocese of Chester included Cumberland south of the Derwent until 1856.

[2] £30, according to the List of Subscribers (*WL MSS.*).

1091. W. W. to JAMES MONTGOMERY

Address: James Montgomery Esq., The Mount, Sheffield.
MS. untraced.
Holland and Everett, Memoirs of James Montgomery, v. 202. K (—). *LY*
ii. 818 (—).

[Rydal Mount]
[30 Nov. 1836]

My dear Friend,

Through the kindness of Mr Younge[1] your volumes, and the little book belonging to my daughter,[2] which you have been so good as to enrich with a most valuable contribution,[3] were received yesterday at Rydal Mount. For these tokens of your regard, and for the accompanying letter, accept our joint thanks. I can assure you with truth that from the time I first read your *Wanderer of Switzerland*, with the little pieces annexed, I have felt a lively interest in your destiny as a poet; and though much out of the way of new books, I have become acquainted with your works, and with increasing pleasure, as they successively appeared. It might be presumptuous in me were I to attempt to define what I hope belongs to us in common; but I cannot deny myself the satisfaction of expressing a firm belief that neither morality nor religion can have suffered from our writings; and with respect to *yours*, I know that both have been greatly benefited by them. Without convictions of this kind all the rest must in the latter days of an author's life appear to him worse than vanity. My publisher has been directed to forward to you (I suppose it will be done through Messrs Longmans) the first volume of my new edition, and the others as they successively appear. As the book could not be conveniently sent to you through my hands, I have ventured to write a few lines upon a slip of paper to be attached to it,[4] which I trust will give

[1] Probably Montgomery's friend William Younge of Endcliffe, Sheffield.

[2] Dora W.'s Autograph Album.

[3] The lines to W. W., quoted in *Memoirs of James Montgomery*, v. 201–2. In his accompanying letter of 15 Nov. Montgomery wrote: 'May you long live to enjoy the felicity of having won an honest fame, as one of the benefactors of your contemporaries . . . ' (*WL MSS.*)

[4] 'In admiration of genius, and as a grateful token of profound respect for the pure and sacred uses to which that genius has been devoted, these volumes are offered to James Montgomery by his sincere friend, William Wordsworth. Rydal Mount, Nov. 30, 1836.' (K's note.)

you a pleasure akin to what I received from the lines written by your own hand on the fly-leaf of your first volume. With earnest wishes that time may deal gently with you as life declines, and that hopes may brighten and faith grow firmer as you draw nearer the end of your earthly course, I remain, my dear sir,

Faithfully yours,
W. Wordsworth

Pray excuse my employment of an amanuensis; my eyes require that help which Mrs Wordsworth is ever ready to give.

1092. W. W. to JOSHUA WATSON

Address: Joshua Watson Esqre
Endorsed: W. Wordsworth Esq rec^d 4 Decr 1836. Cockerm^o Ch.
MS. WL.
LY ii. 819.

[*In M. W.'s hand*]

Dec. 4 [1836]

My dear Friend

I have had a great deal of mortification about Cockermouth Ch: When I passed thro' the place some little time ago, I learned from Mr Wood that Mr Fawcett had declined to send the official returns, as requested by the Bp thro' his Secretary—I was so much hurt at this, that I did not like to trust myself with a conversation with Mr F.—nor did chuse to take upon myself to write to the Bp: I simply applied to Mr Stanger, with a request that if he were personally acquainted with Mr F. and had no objection to speak to him upon the subject—that he would try to induce him to make the returns. You may think this was injudicious—but indirectly I had heard from Mr Stanger and having occasion to write to him—I thought it might be as well to use that mode of coming at our object. I have however heard no more of him.

I also mentioned the subject, being unwilling so often to trouble you, to Dr Wordsworth, and he tells me that I must apply to you. I hope that in so doing I do not press too much upon your health, which was in so delicate a state, when I last had the pleasure of being with you.

I am happy to say that Lord Lonsdale is in the best possible disposition for having the thing done, and for keeping it out of the hands of the Party.[1]

I think it may not be superfluous to send you the accompanying papers rec^d from Mr Wood.

Hoping that yourself and Miss Watson bear this unfavourable season without injury to your health. My Sister remains in her usual uncomfortable state—but you will both be glad to hear that my daughter is gradually improving—Mrs W. and myself well and we all unite in affectionate regards

ever faithfully yours
[*signed*] Wm Wordsworth

1093. W. W. to HENRY TAYLOR

MS. Bodleian Library.
LY ii. 820.

[*In M. W.'s hand*]

Rydal Mount Decr 19th [1836]

My dear Sir,

I have received your interesting communication,[2] and cannot apply to the Marshalls as you suggest—because I have, more

---

[1] The Simeonites.

[2] On 12 Dec. Henry Taylor had sent to W. W. 'an account of a poetical vagabond for whom Mr Gladstone and I are raising a subscription to send him to College', and asking him to put the case before the Marshalls (*WL MSS.*). A penniless youth of 19, Henry Thompson, son of the tax surveyor at Oakham, had stopped Gladstone on Constitution Hill the previous year, and asked for money wherewith to publish his poems. Both Gladstone and Taylor thought well of his verse, but felt that he would be better served by giving him the chance of some further education. Gladstone found him a temporary post as usher at a school near Liverpool, and with Taylor raised money to send him to Magdalen Hall, Oxford, Gladstone undertaking to be responsible for any deficiency in the sum subscribed. Thompson graduated in 1840, but thereafter nothing more is known of him. In a further letter of 4 Jan. 1837, Henry Taylor declined to accept any contribution from W. W., 'for to receive contributions from any but very affluent people on this account w^d be a departure from the principle by which I determined to be governed in this matter.' (*WL MSS.*)

than once, heard Mr Marshall express his disapprobation of attempts to raise people from their station in this way. The whole family are, according to their own views, charitable and generous—and even munificent. But Mr Marshall, as I know, having once contributed to like patronage, discontinued his Subscription, from a belief that he was not acting judiciously, tho' the young man fully justified the expectations of those who took him up from a very low condition.

Mr Bolton, my neighbour, is one of the most generous of men—but as he is upwards of 80 years of age and his powers of duly considering any point that may be laid before him somewhat impaired, I feel some little reluctance in applying to him as I have hitherto done, on the subject of Cockermouth Church, never having mentioned it to him. But fortunately I know he has a very high opinion of Mr Gladstone, which will encourage me to send the Papers to him, as I shall do by this day's post. Had your letter reached me a few days ago while I was visiting at Lowther, Levens and elsewhere in this neighbourhood, I might have done something by conversation, which I do not like to introduce by letter.

There is a class, I hope I do not deceive myself in thinking I am worthy of being reckoned one of them, whose outgoings in this line fully keep pace with their incomings, be they what they may; and on this account I must confine myself to so small an *anonymous* contribution as £3—fearing that if my name were attached [it] might prevent others out of delicacy from giving as much as they would else have done.

The particulars of this case upon the whole, seem promising—but weak eyes and ill health are spoken of—and Mr G. and you must be aware, that one of the evils to be apprehended in projects of this sort, is that the Student may destroy his health by over-application from an anxious desire to prove himself worthy of what has been done for him. One sees the result in far less urgent cases. Travellers sent out at the expence of Societies, or of Governments, perish in far greater numbers than those whose expences are met by their own means. From my connection with the University I have seen a good deal of these experiments, but tho' several to my knowledge have failed, the balance has been upon the whole decidedly in favor of such as have come under my notice.

The Cholera frightens me, but say to Miss Fenwick, with our joint love (and thanks from Mrs W. for her last kind letter) that under any circumstances I trust I shall see her, either in London or at her own home, in the course of the Spring. Dora thank God! is so much better that she talks confidently of being able to go to Leamington in Feb^ry—and after conducting her thither, if I do not go to Italy, I am under engagement to pay a few visits in Warwickshire and Leicestershire and shall extend my journey either to London or Somersetshire as may best suit Miss F.'s arrangements—Should I find her in Town, would it be possible to tempt her back with me into the North?—but this is Castle-building!

Farewell—remember me kindly to Spedding[1] and Mr Gladstone and other friends and believe me faithfully y^rs

[*signed*] Wm Wordsworth

I have heard nothing more of the Bust.[2] Chauntry would be your best Informant. I have no doubt Sir G. Beaumont would apply to him, as stated in his letters, which I forwarded to you. I regret much that Miss F. is not quite pleased with your Portrait. The expression she complains of was certainly there when I saw it—

1094. M. W. to H. C. R.

Endorsed: 19 Decr 1836, Mrs Wordsworth.
MS. Dr. Williams's Library.
K (—). *Morley, i. 334.*

Rydal Mount
Decr 19—[1836]

My dear Friend

Last evening when we were all sitting drowsily over the fire, I sagely observed—'I think Mr R. has *cut us*' to which Dora replied 'Will the sun cut us?'—truly, however *he* has nearly done so of late—but indeed if you will not come to see us, you ought now and then to send us one of your nice close written letters to pore over, to break the chain of those everlasting Proofs that Mr Evans sends us day after day to blind our eyes with—I seldom open one of his covers without expecting to find a Sibylline from you within.

---

[1] James Spedding.
[2] See L. 1087 above.

—I know not where you are or if you are to be found, so this in case it should reach you is but to remind you that we are alive—and not only so, but that we feel Dora is improving more rapidly than heretofore—our poor Sister is in her usual way. And *my* sister Joanna, who is with us, is not very flourishing—W^m and myself quite well.—Tell us what you think about the *Italian* Cholera.

Ever faithfully yours, with our united love
M. Wordsworth

D^r and Mrs A.[1] are expected next Sat: with 3 of their young ones—a detachment of 6 with Nurses, Governess etc—arrived a fortnight ago.—

By the bye did you receive a nice letter of poor C. Lambs—which I found, and enclosed to you some time since?

1095. D. W. and M. W. to JANE MARSHALL

Address: Mrs Marshall, Heddingley, near Leeds.
Stamp: Kendal Penny Post.
Endorsed: Mrs Wordsworth and Dorothy 1835? John's death.
WL. WL.
LY ii. 822.

[*D. W. writes*]

Christmas Eve [1836]

My dear good Friend,

My heart is too full for many words. May God comfort you under your heavy loss! and he *will* comfort you—all things here below will speak to you of your dear Son's[2] goodness. I have had a tremendous struggle. This morning, I trust, has brought the last of it.

A thousand thanks for your kind presents. The Turkey will be our Xmas day dinner—but I cannot tell all over—thank you for all, and may God bless you and all yours.

Dorothy Wordsworth

[1] Arnold.
[2] Her second son, John Marshall, jnr., had died on 31 Oct.

331

Christmas Eve 1836

How my heart yet beats at the sound of Christmas Day—
[*M. W. writes*]

Your precious letter addressed to Dorothy—was felt by us all—and to myself so touchingly, as a Mother, that it would be unjust to you and to my own feelings to dwell upon the several situations you placed before me, at the close of a letter—but thoughts were raised, that, if it please God we should meet, will revive in my mind; as does the animated countenance of your now blessed Son, when I think of *your own* as first presented to me—at the door of my Brother's farm-house in Yorkshire when you called to inquire for your beloved friend.[1] The change that took place, when I told you 'she was gone' will never be forgotten—the look is always like a visitation that I can call up.

Your letter dear friend with its enclosures I took to Dorothy—she gave me *her* portion, to take care of, till she considered what to do with it—The other £5 you have so kindly entrusted to me, is most acceptable, and has anticipated a petition I meant to make to you for a little assistance to a poor family whose worthy head is now in the aşylum at Lancaster—his wife and 5 children living in our village, meanwhile, have 4 shillings a week allowed by the Parish, and she makes a couple of shillings more by going out to wash—but the children are young—and this, without aid, is a poor pittance. She is however well taken care of, but as the family are not within the pale of the Rydal Hall charity, I thought I might be authorized to ask for your help—which you have supplied me with *unasked*—and so liberally as will be felt beyond this individual family. God bless you for it, and for all your kindness.

I take a greater liberty with you than common by forwarding *such* an untidy and I fear *illegible* letter, and must pray your forgiveness—writing with a Poet beside me ought not to be an excuse—tho'—as at this moment, he takes the pen, bad as it is, literally out of my hand. This reminds me of what *you* say of his *alterations*, or corrections. I must say that he never makes one that he does not *seem* to convince my understanding and judgment—but like you, not always my *feelings*—however we must give him credit for being right—and *we* can always cherish where we like, what we have loved and cling to—and hope that

---

[1] In Sept. 1802: see *EY* p. 377.

332

those to whom the Poems are new, may find a higher—I am sure not a *deeper*, pleasure from them than we have done.

Best love to Mr M. and every one from all. I feel deeply for dear Dora[1] and her household—of Ellen[2] we have not heard any late news—hope for good. Of the afflicted ones at Scarboro'—we shall be glad to hear when they are returned home. Alas! my first introduction will be to the widow—not to the happy wife of your beloved son!

Most aff^{ly} yours

M. Wordsworth

Does not this little uncouth letter remind you of one of D.'s youthful epistles? I mean in appearance.

1096. W. W. to HENRY TAYLOR

Address: H. Taylor Esqre, Colonial off.
MS. Bodleian Library.
LY ii. 822.

[*In M. W.'s hand*]

[late Dec. 1836]

My dear Sir,

I enclose the reply which I have rec^d from Sir G. Beaumont upon the application for the Bust.[3] I am afraid it will not be practicable upon the plan proposed—but I hope Sir F. Chantrey will be able to remove Sir George's apprehensions of injury to the Bust.

We have not heard from Keswick for a week—before that time our accounts of poor Mrs Southey were not more unfavorable than when her Husband was at home.[4]

We shall be glad to hear good tidings of dear Miss Fenwick, who we surmise is in London by this time—and that you are

---

[1] i.e. Mrs. Jane Dorothea Temple, Mrs. Marshall's fourth daughter. Capt. and Mrs. Temple had called at Rydal Mount in 1832 (*R MV B*). They lived in Hampshire.

[2] The invalid daughter.

[3] See Ls. 1087 and 1093 above.

[4] Southey was now away on his tour of the West Country. See L. 1085 above.

enjoying the Society of each other. With love to her from Mrs W. etc, very sincerely but in haste, yours

[*signed*] W Wordsworth

1097. W. W. to UNKNOWN CORRESPONDENT

MS. Toronto Public Library. Hitherto unpublished.

Rydal Mount
Decr 29—1836

Dear Sir,

I was not acquainted with the passage of Ausonius[1] to which you allude, nor with any part of his writings at the time nearly 50 years since when I composed the lines which you quote—I perfectly remember the very moment when the Poem in which they occur fell from my lips, I do not say my pen for I had none with me. The passage in Ausonius does not put the case so strongly as mine, as the mere word gaudere is not perhaps much more than a strong expression for 'thrive'—

The interest you take in this little matter is gratifying to me as a proof of sympathy between us, and emboldens me to subscribe myself

sincerely
your much obliged
Wm Wordsworth

1098. W. W. to HENRY TAYLOR

Address: H. Taylor Esqre, Colonial Office.
MS. Bodleian Library.
LY ii. 824.

[*In M. W.'s hand*]

Rydal mount Decr. 31st [1836]

My dear Mr Taylor,

My application to Mr Bolton in behalf of our young Poet[2] has I am sorry to say proved unsuccessful. Mr B.'s answer being

---

[1] Apparently an alleged echo from Ausonius's poem on the Moselle in W. W.'s *Descriptive Sketches*. But the exact passage cannot be identified.

[2] Henry Thompson. See L. 1093 above.

that owing to the innumerable distressed Persons with whom he is in various ways connected—and to other calls for his money, he cannot feel himself justified in making advances for a Stranger. Knowing how munificent and charitable he was, I ventured to ask him, but only on account of the respect which I knew he entertained for Mr Gladstone. Circumstanced as I am amongst my other neighbours I have no hope of being useful on this occasion, which I assure you I regret much. Be so good as to advance the £3 for me which shall be repaid, either thro Moxon, or when we next meet.[1]

I hope that Miss Fenwick and you stand the severities of the Season—with every good wish in the old-fashioned way to you both—in which my Wife and Daughter unite,

I remain, d[r] Mr Taylor, faithfully yours

[*signed*] W[m] Wordsworth

Would it not be well that I should return the Papers, to be used in some other quarter?

I hope you have good news of Mr and Mrs Taylor[2]—Pray remember us respectfully to them.

1099. W. W. to JOSHUA WATSON

Endorsed: W Wordsworth Esq 31 Dec. 1836.
MS. WL.
LY ii. 825.

[*In M. W.'s hand*]

Rydal Mount Dec[r] 31st, 1836

My dear Sir

Many thanks for your letter and for the kind interest and all the trouble you have taken and are prepared to take about Cockermouth Church.

Your communications have furnished me with an occasion to address Lord Lonsdale again on the subject, and as soon as I have his answer I shall know how to proceed—and then I shall write to you—meanwhile accept my best thanks.

---

[1] Taylor in fact declined the offer.
[2] Henry Taylor's father and stepmother.

It delights us, to learn that your valuable health is amended, and as you do not mention Miss Watson, we trust she is well.

We have had a long letter from Chris: to-day with the comfortable news that the Master of Trinity is particularly well—and that Charles takes kindly to his Profession—finding the labour easier and the pleasure more, than at first. My daughter I am thankful to say is much better—my poor Sister struggling on as before—but without loss of strength. Perhaps you heard of the pains my Son Wm took about a situation at Birmingham—they proved unsuccessful, further than that I believe he recommended himself in his Canvass—to many Persons—some of whom possibly may hereafter befriend him. You will be glad to hear that neither he nor I suffered by the great failure of the Forster's Bank[1] at Carlisle—we had however a narrow escape.

The Ed: of my Poems now going thro' the Press, I hear is selling very well.

With our united kindest remembrances, and every good wish of the Season, which you feelingly call holy and happy, to you and Miss W. I remain my dear Sir your faithful and affectionate friend,

[*signed*] Wm Wordsworth

1100. W. W. to EDWARD MOXON

MS. Henry E. Huntington Library.
K (—). LY ii. 826.

[*In M. W.'s hand*]

[late Dec. 1836]

Dear Mr Moxon,

Thanks for your letter. Notwithstanding my double responsibility at Carlisle (for my Son is my Subdistributor there) we have not suffered from the failures,[2] tho' we had a narrow escape: and I assure you the state of the commercial world does not leave me free from anxiety—both with respect to my

---

[1] The firm of Thomas Foster and Co., Castle Street, founded *c.* 1750, stopped payments on 18 Nov., after a number of local businesses went bankrupt, and financial dealings in Carlisle remained unstable until the following spring.

[2] The failure of Foster's Bank. See previous letter.

Office, and some other concerns. I hope you will be able to take care of yourself, for I apprehend the storm is coming.

Your account of the sale of the book[1] is as favourable as I ventured to expect: being myself quite at ease in regard to the reception which writings, that have cost me so much labour, will in the end meet with, I can truly say that I have not the least anxiety concerning the fate of this Edition, further than that *you* may speedily be repaid what you have generously advanced to me. The labour I have bestowed in correcting the style of these poems now revised for the last time according to my best judgment no one can ever thank me for, as no one can estimate it. The annoyance of this sort of work is, that progress bears no proportion to pains, and that hours of labour are often entirely thrown away—ending in the passage being left, as I found it.

I hope that Mr Evans will comply with my request, to send clean sheets *as they are struck off*—along with the succeeding proofs—and if it were possible to do this so that an opportunity may be given to us to return readings perfectly correct before the stereotype plates are taken—At all events, if the plan be adopted the errata may be sent *in time*—and perfectly correct.

You will remember I mentioned to you, by note, that I had been applied to by the Editor or Publisher of the Ch of Eng. Mag:[2] for permission to introduce the Ecclesiastical Sonnets into his Publication. In my hasty reply to this Gentleman I neglected to notice his obliging offer to send me his Mag: an omission for which I am sorry. Will you if you pass that way be kind enough to mention this, and add that I should be glad to receive it from him.

With our united regards to Mrs Moxon and your Sister, and with best wishes to yourself believe me to remain dear Mr M. sincerely yours

[*signed*] W Wordsworth

The Pub^r of the Ch of E. Mag: has an Agent (a bookseller) at Kendal by name Dawson, thro' him Mr Troughton of Ambleside receives copies, and the one intended for me might be sent thro' Mr D. in Mr Troughton's parcel.

The parcel containing the 2 Vols prepared for me may be sent to Messrs Whitaker, Ave Maria Lane—to be enclosed in Mr Troughton's parcel—to Ambleside.

[1] The *Yarrow Revisited* volume.
[2] A new periodical started this year, which ran until 1875.

1101. W. W. to EDWARD MOXON

MS. Henry E. Huntington Library. Hitherto unpublished.

[*In M. W.'s hand*]

[late 1836 *or* early 1837]

My dear Sir

I am very sorry any delay should have occurred by the missing of the Sheets which has prevented the Errata being sent—having at length rec[d] them, it shall be prepared as soon as possible, and I shall be glad now to have the proofs sent as speedily as possible.

In future, instead of making payments into Masterman's Bank, I will thank. you to pay the money to my professional friend W. Strickland Cookson, 6 Lincolns Inn—whom I have requested to receive the same for my use. Mrs Wordsworth will be obliged to you to procure from Longmans, (if he still has possession of the work) 2 Copies of the 2[d] Ed. of Yarrow revisited, and send with the 12 Copies of the 2[d] vol of the new Ed:—probably we may shortly meet with an opportunity of having the parcel called for.

With best regards
very sincerely y[rs]
W Wordsworth[1]

1102. W. W. to JOSHUA WATSON

Address: Joshua Watson Esq[re], 6 Park St., Westminster.
Endorsed: W[m] Wordsworth Esq Jan[y] 1837.
MS. WL.
LY. ii. 778.

[*In M. W.'s hand*]

[8 Jan. 1837]

Extract of a Letter from the Earl of Lonsdale

'On this subject (Cockermouth Ch:) I know not what to add to what I have already said upon it—I am ready to provide an Endowment to the amount of one Hundred and Fifty Pounds

---

[1] Not signed by W. W.

per ann: and I presume, as in all such cases the Clergyman
derives some Benefit from Pews'

My dear Sir,

The above noble offer I have this morning received from
Lord Lonsdale,[1] with authority to mention his name, so with
what may be fairly expected from the Pews in addition, the
Minister, as times go, would have a respectable Endowment. By
tomorrow's post I shall write to Mr Wood—and if necessary
will go over to Cockermouth. Could Lord Egremont be
prevailed upon to contribute somewhat generously towards the
Building, the way would be pretty smooth before us; tho' I am
certain that the most zealous part of the People of C. are not
favorable to the Patronage being vested in our Friend,[2] not
from personal objections to his L^dsp, but preferring popular, or
other Patronage, and therefore I do not expect any considerable
Contributions from the Place—and for my own ability to raise
money among my Friends etc, I fear must not be rated at more
than 7 or 8 hundred pounds, but I cannot say, till it is fairly
tried—as it *now shall* be—it is proper for me to *restate* this,
because in a former letter from you, I observed you had misread
or I had miswritten, the amount—as you understood me to
have said 17 or 18 hundred—which must be very *very* far
beyond what I can raise.

In answer to your question of 'how we are to proceed as to
the return made by Mr F.'[3] I should say, that such are his
dispositions as to allow no hope of more favorable returns being
extorted from him, either thro the Bp: or otherwise. But if Mr
F's return could be by you laid before the Board, with liberty on
your part to accompany it with such information as has been
given by Mr Wood—and the rules of the Boards would permit
them to act upon such colateral[4] representation, then I think it

---

[1] Lord Lonsdale's letter (*WL MSS.*) is dated 5 Jan. 1837, which helps to
establish the date of this letter. De Selincourt incorrectly placed it in Jan. 1836,
in spite of the endorsement.

[2] i.e. Lord Lonsdale.

[3] Mr Fawcett, curate of Cockermouth. Lord Lonsdale had written of him,
'If Mr Fawcett was expected to answer all the Questions contain'd in the Form
of Enquiry issued by the Church Building Commissioners He has contented
himself with furnishing very scanty Information on the Subject—No doubt
he is adverse to the Erection of a new Church, His own being very badly
attended.'

[4] *Written* colatteral

would be best, to proceed in this manner. It is of great importance that we should know as soon as possible what extent of aid we may look for from the Societies—the fact respecting the Endowment being settled.

As to the Vicar of B—,[1] he is so circumstanced in respect to Cockermouth, and has so much to do among the Dissenters in his own district—and thro' the whole Parish, in which they swarm—that he cannot afford to place himself in hostility with his B[r] Minister at Cockermouth, as would be the case, if he should take the part you allude to in this business—Furthermore, *his* active interference would place me in an invidious situation among the Inhabitants.

I shall trouble you again when I have communicated with Mr Wood meanwhile, believe [me] ever my dear Sir faithfully and very aff[ly] yours

[*signed*] Wm Wordsworth

Our kindest remembrances to Miss W.

1103. W. W. to C. W. JNR.

Address: The Rev[d] Chris: Wordsworth, Trinity Lodge, Cambridge.
Stamp: Kendal Penny Post.
Endorsed: Cockermouth Church etc.
MS. *British Library.*
Mem. (—). *Grosart* (—). K (—). LY ii. 780 (—).

Rydal Mount Jan[ry] 9th [1837]
(I hold the pen for your Uncle. M. W.)

My dear Nephew,

It was very kind of you to write us so long and so pleasant a letter—but lest you should take too much credit to yourself, let me tell you, that the evening before yours reached us, Dora had destroyed the last we had had from you. She had been in the habit of keeping your letters, each, till another made its appearance; but finding that you had been silent for a year! she burnt as I have told you the last token of your regard of this kind with a spice of indignation. You have however made amends, and we are all in good humour with you. Scarcely so with

[1] The vicar of Brigham, John W.

Charles who, we cannot help thinking, might have given us a couple of lines by the young Arnolds,[1] to let us see that he was aware that he had Relatives of the name of Wordsworth, living at a place called Rydal Mount.

In the first place, we rejoice to hear that your Father is so well. Next, that Charles likes his situation; as we hope you do yours, since you say nothing to the contrary. As the feet of young and old in this house are somewhat tender, I am glad of your improved gravel walks[2]—and I assure you should be most happy to tread them again, especially if your Cousin[3] was with me. This subject puts me in mind of a little fact, which it may be worth while to make known among your Invalid friends— Dora, you will be pleased to hear, is now able to walk two hours or more at a time—a power which she owes entirely to the situation, and *form* (if I may call it) of one of our Terraces. It is airy, and about 70 paces in length, level at each end, with a gentle inclination—a curve—in the middle. She has positively assured me, she is less tired by walking 2 hours upon this terrace than a quarter of an hour on any other walk we have, all of which are equally smooth on the surface—one being of turf. Let me tell you here that I like your book upon Athens and Attica[4] *very much.* Has it been noticed in any of the Reviews? Thank your Father for *his* valuable gift[5]—I wish I had been younger for the benefit I might have derived from it. We have read the preface and looked over other parts, and it will be in our house, as I trust it will in a thousand others, a standard book. John who spent 3 days with us last week, (having walked from Brigham), took his Copy home—with which he was most gratified—and as he knew we were going to write immediately to Cambridge, he expressed a hope that his Uncle would accept his best thanks, thro' our letter. They have been settled in their new Vicarage 6 months. I expect that Isabella caught a severe cold lately, by going to see her Mother—the health of the whole family has been much improved since their removal to Brigham. The

[1] Matthew and Thomas, spending the year at Winchester.
[2] At Harrow.
[3] 'Keswick John', who had accompanied W. W. on many of his visits in London the previous spring.   [4] See L. 1048 above.
[5] C. W. jnr.'s letter to W. W. of 27 Dec. 1836 (*British Library MSS.*) was accompanied by two sets of C. W.'s *Christian Institutes*, one for W. W. and one for John W. The work was published in 4 vols. early in 1837, the Preface being dated 13 Dec. 1836

House as you know, tho' exposed, is charmingly situated—commanding beautiful views up and down the river, with Cockermouth Castle in the middle distance, and Skiddaw in the back ground, from one of them. H.Curwen is gone into the Rectory-house at W.[1] and is at present serving as assistant-Curate to John—and will himself be inducted to the Living shortly. We are almost as anxious about your brother John succeeding to the Professorship,[2] as you can be. We look, but in vain, for his appointment in every Newspaper that comes into our hands—being quite of your opinion, that Person and Thing would suit each other exactly.

Now let me tell you, but more for your Father's ear than yours'—that in a letter which I received from Lord Lonsdale yesterday, he generously proposes to endow a New Church at Cockermouth with £150 per ann.[3] From a conversation with him in the Autumn I expected he would do as much—tho' he did not then permit me, as he has done now, to mention it publicly. Your Father knows what impediment lies in our way—but if this offer should encourage the Societies to help us liberally and Lord Egremont could be prevailed upon to give his aid to the project, I trust we shall then be able to keep it out of the hands of a certain Party[4]—who, if we renounce, will certainly take it. I must frankly tell you however, that I do not look for much pecuniary assistance on the Spot—the Patronage being, where of course it ought to be, with the Endower—to whom they have no *personal* objection, but it is a very Radical Place—and the religious part of the community are strongly inclined to the Saints—and no wonder—the present Minister being so inefficient. It will now be my duty to exert myself to the utmost, and if you—or any one of our friends would lend me a hand in aid of the good work, I should be thankful. Miss Hoare readily opened her purse strings for us![5]

[1] Workington, where John W. had held the living until Henry Curwen was ready to accept it.
[2] It was incorrectly rumoured that James Scholefield (1789–1853), Professor of Greek at Cambridge, was about to resign, and C. W. jnr.'s brother John had the support of three out of the seven electors as his successor. As C. W. jnr. remarked in his letter, 'John and the Greek Professorship were made for one another.' But Scholefield retained the Chair until 1853.
[3] See previous letter.
[4] The Simeonites.
[5] Miss Hoare had promised £10.

9 January 1837

We wish your letter had mentioned the Hoares—as it is some time since we have heard from them. Nor has Owen[1] heard, who by the bye, is far from well, and causes us all, much anxiety. John and he skated together upon the Lake, and Owen was pleased to see him; but he is in very low spirits. We try to persuade him to take Pupils—but he shrinks from it, as a task to which he is unequal—tho' we are sure he was never as well, as when so employed. He has not unfrequently preached lately at Ambleside, and with great effect— especially 2 or 3 Sermons upon the vice of drunkenness—which he was solicited to publish, for distribution in the neighbourhood—but he declined, I rather think on account of his dejection.

We have had little snow here, at the utmost not more than 4 inches deep—and the Coach between Kendal and Whitehaven has never been delayed for an hour—neither had we a single bough torn off—during your late whirlwind. But the summer was very wet with the exception of eleven days, which were beautiful—and during the whole of the Autumn, the Country had much more than its usual allowance of rain, which you will know is enough. You must not suppose however that it rains here the *whole year round*, for the Month of May and the former part of June were almost without a shower.

The best news about ourselves is Dora's health being much improved. She takes a great deal of pains to be well, and strictly follows Sir B. Brodie's advice—but the pain in the side and about the heart is not removed—and the least possible addition to the small portion of animal food she takes, or a sip almost of wine puts the heart wrong immediately. We still hope that in a few weeks she may [be able][2] to accompany me Southward.

I cannot speak for much change for the better in your poor dear Aunt. Her bodily uneasinesses would seem to us distressingly great, were we not sure that they appear more deplorable on account of the weakening of her mind than they really are— tho' no doubt this very weakness, as it disqualifies her from keeping them down, aggravates them. She has however cheerful and happy intervals, and is always pleased to receive notice from her absent friends.

I think of the Portrait[3] just as you do, and could explain were

[1] Owen Lloyd.

[2] *MS. damaged.*

[3] C. W. jnr. shared W. W.'s dislike of the engraving of Pickersgill's portrait, which served as the frontispiece of the new edition of the *Poetical*

it worth while, how it has got that air of decrepitude, and the maudlin expression about the upper lip. If we live to see another Ed: an engraving from Chantry's Bust shall replace it. I have sometimes been working unmercifully hard, giving my last corrections to the Poems, and do not regret the labour—because I *know* them to be much improved. I would not however advise any one who is anxious about the finish of his style to run a monthly race with the press, volume by volume—as I have been doing, and after all, as there has not been time to receive revises—the edi[tion] for a stereotype, will be far short of what I could wish. The 4th Vol will close with the Ecc.Son:[1] which I have now reached, and shall have little trouble with them: and by the middle of next month my work will be done. Give my cordial congratulations to Mr Rose[2] and with our united love to all, including *particularly* my Niece[3] whom we have not had the pleasure of seeing—I remain my dear Chris:

Your affec Uncle,
[*signed*] Wm Wordsworth

[*M. W. writes*]

My d^r C.

The Longmans not having sent in their last year's bill or any report of the 'Yarrow Revisited'—I am still unable to account to you for the expenditure of the £20 you entrusted me with. I hope you have rec^d the Richardson's di[ctionar]y very regularly—*we* have reached [?][4]   M. W.

We think you ought to pay us a visit during your Vacation—your B^r Schoolmaster Dr Arnold finds it easy to run down with his wife and children and a host of nurses etc., *twice* a year—and it is not to say how much they enjoy the country, at all seasons!

Works. 'I wish it had been the *Bust*, instead of a bad engraving of the *picture*,' he wrote.

[1] *Ecclesiastical Sonnets.*

[2] H. J. Rose had recently been appointed Principal of King's College, London, in succession to Dr. William Otter. But his health broke down soon afterwards, and he died at Florence in Dec. 1838.

[3] Charles Wordsworth's wife, Charlotte.

[4] *Seal.* For Richardson's Dictionary, see L. 989 above.

1104. W. W. to UNKNOWN CORRESPONDENT

MS. Cornell. Hitherto unpublished.

[*In M. W.'s hand*]

Rydal Mount
Jan^{ry} 10th 1837

Sir,

Incessant engagements have prevented me from giving your letter an immediate reply.

Be assured that I am sensible of the honour done me by the Society,[1] whose Organ you are, in the resolution which they have passed for electing me a Member of it: and let me thank you for the flattering terms in which you have conveyed to me that intelligence.

The expressions 'honorary and *corresponding*' are, I take for granted, ordinarily used upon these occasions—otherwise it would be right for me to say, that I could not accept the honor, if it involved me in any engagement to communicate with the Society, by letter. I am too far advanced in life to be at liberty to add to my literary occupations, as the Society are probably aware.

With best wishes for the Success of the Institution, and not without regret it is not in my power to contribute my Mite to the Contributions by which I doubt not the Liverpool literary, scientific and commercial Institution will be distinguished,

I have the honor to be
Sir, faithfully yours'
[*signed*] Wm Wordsworth

---

[1] The Royal Institution, in Colquitt Street, Liverpool, founded 1814.

1105. W. W. to EDWARD MOXON

MS. Henry E. Huntington Library.
LY ii. 827.

[*In M. W.'s hand*]

Rydal Mount
Jan^{ry} 14th [1837]

My dear Sir,

If you can procure for me a Copy of Dr Wordsworth's late Publication entitled 'Christian Institutes'[1] and at Rivingtons at the Trade Price, I will thank you to procure it for a friend of mine.—It may be forwarded as I before directed—packages for me to be sent thro' the Kendal Monthly Parcel from Whitakers for Mr Troughton, Ambleside.—But it seems that there is some delay by this channel for we have not *yet* received the 2^d Vol: of the new Edition. Pray mention what Rivington charges the Copy of Christian Institutes.

They are getting rapidly thro' the 4th Vol—but Mr Evans has not attended to my wish, by forwarding clean sheets as quickly after they are struck off as convenient—that I might collect the errata in time to make the stereotype plates as correct as we can. Let us have a line to say how you, Mrs M. and the Little ones stand this severe season—and with our united kind regards believe me sincerely yours

W. Wordsworth[2]

1106. W. W. to JOSHUA WATSON

Endorsed: W. Wordsworth 14 Jan 1837.
MS. WL.
LY ii. 828.

[*In M. W.'s hand*]

Rydal Mount Jan^{ry} 14th [1837]

My dear Friend

I enclose you a letter which I have received from Mr Stanger[3] to which I shall reply by this day's post, and tell him of Lord

---

[1] See L. 1003 above.

[2] Not signed by W. W.

[3] James Stanger had written from Cheapside on 10 Jan. (*WL MSS.*) that Mr. Fawcett, the incumbent of Cockermouth, had promised to see Mr Wood

Lonsdale's offer, and which, if I have any thing to do with the business, decides where the Patronage must rest. If, dear Sir, you have no objection to meet Mr S., and think there is the least probability of any good being done by your taking this trouble, a note from you, to the address he gives, would be answered I doubt not, by a call from him at any time you might propose, within the next 10 days.

I have not heard from Mr Wood since I sent him your dispatches.

With our united kindest regards to Miss W. believe me faithfully and aff ly yours

[signed] Wm Wordsworth

1107. W. W. to SAMUEL CARTER HALL

Address: S. C. Hall Esqre, Elm Grove, Kensington Gravel Pits.
Postmark: 16 Jan. 1837. *Stamp*: Fleet St W.C.
MS. Harvard University Library.
LY ii. 828.

[*In M. W.'s hand*]

Rydal Mount
Jan^{ry} 15th 1837

My dear Sir

Accept my thanks for your elegant present of the two volumes of the Book of Gems,[1] which I received two days ago, and also for the very friendly letter that accompanied them. You speak feelingly of the pleasure which you and Mrs Hall had in seeing me some years ago[2]—be assured that it was reciprocal, and nothing but overwhelming engagements, more than at my

and to fill up the official returns for the parish in order to ascertain if the Church Building Societies would grant any assistance towards building the new church; and Stanger himself was willing to meet Joshua Watson to discuss further what might be done. But W. W. was already doubtful whether the requisite information could be got out of Fawcett (see L. 1102 above), and Lord Lonsdale's unequivocal offer of an endowment had raised anew the vexed question of the patronage.

[1] *The Book of Gems: the poets and artists of Great Britain*, 3 vols., 1836–8.
[2] In the spring of 1831.

years I ought to have exposed myself to, could have prevented me seeking you out when I was in Town last Spring.

Being much engaged in a monthly race with the Press—in which a new Edition of my Poems has involved me, I have not had time for more than a glance at your part of the Volumes—but I must say how much I was pleased with your notice of our Westmorland Poet, Langhorne—The Critique is very judicious, both as to his merits and his faults—I do not wonder that you are struck with his Poem of the Country Justice—You praise it, and with discrimination—but you might have said still more in its favour; as far as I know, it is the first Poem, unless perhaps Shenstone's Schoolmistress be excepted, that fairly brought the Muse into the Company of common life, to which it comes nearer than Goldsmith, and upon which it looks with a tender and enlightened humanity—and with a charitable, (and being so) philosophical and poetical construction that is too rarely found in the works of Crabbe. It is not without many faults in style from which Crabbe's more austere judgment preserved him—but these are to me trifles in a work so original and touching.

You ask me to furnish you with a few notices of my life—an application to the same effect was lately made to me by a french Gentleman[1] who had been engaged upon what he calls a 'long labor upon my works'—a translation I believe of many parts of them, accompanied with a commentary. My answer was, that my course of life had been altogether private, and that nothing could be more bare of entertainment or interest than a biographical notice of me must prove, if true. I referred him to Gagliani's Ed:[2] which, as to the date and place of my birth, and the places of my Education is correct—the date of my publications is easily procured—and beyond these I really see nothing that the world has to do with, in my life which has been so retired and uniform. Since the beginning of the year 1800 I have had a home either at my present residence or within two

---

[1] Probably Hippolyte de la Morvonnais, the Breton poet, who was preparing a study of Wordsworth in 1834. The work was never published in full, but parts (including translations of several of the *Lyrical Ballads*) found their way into *La Revue Européenne* for July and Sept. 1835. He published further translations in the St. Malo newspaper *La Vigie de l'ouest* during 1839. See E. Fleury, *Hyppolyte de la Morvonnais*, Paris, 1911, pp. 180–2, 224–9, 262.

[2] Galignani's edition of 1828 contained a brief Memoir of W. W.

miles of it—tho', as appears from my writings, I have made excursions both on the Continent and on our own Island—and also that I have sometimes sojourned in Leicestershire.

With my cordial regards to Mrs Hall and every good wish to both of you whom I have often thought of with sincere esteem believe me to be truly yours

[*signed*] Wm Wordsworth.

1108. W. W. to FREDERICK EVANS[1]

MS. Wellesley College Library. Hitherto unpublished.

[*In M. W's hand*]

[early 1837]

for Mr Evans

Sir,

Finding that the 2ᵈ vol is considerably short of matter, I have sent another Poem[2] which can be spared from the 5ᵗʰ vol. I wish it to come in before the Devotional Incitements and in printing it I am anxious that it may be so arranged, as for the conclusion of the 4ᵗʰ Stanza to appear upon the same page with the line immediately preceeding, and with which it is connected by the rhymes.

W W.[3]

---

[1] Printer of the new edition of the *Poetical Works*. This letter is tipped into the third volume of the Wellesley College copy of the edition of 1832, opposite p. 242.

[2] W. W. was now moving the *Vernal Ode* from *Poems of Sentiment and Reflection* to *Poems of the Imagination*.

[3] Not signed by W. W.

1109. W. W. to FREDERICK EVANS[1]

Address: Mr Moxon, 44 Dover St.
MS. Wellesley College Library. Hitherto unpublished.

[early 1837]

Mr Evans,
Dear Sir,
    Be so good as to alter two passages in the 2nd Book of the
Excursion as below

W W.

On page 67 read thus

> Will last for ever. Oft on my way have I
> Stood still, though but a casual Passenger,
> So much etc[2]

and page 77 read thus

> Beside a fire whose genial warmth seemed met
> By a faint shining from the heart, a gleam
> Of comfort spread over his pallid face.[3]

1110. W. W. to ROBERT SHELTON MACKENZIE[4]

Address: R. Skelton Mackenzie Esqre, Liverpool,—Journal Office.
Stamp: Kendal Penny Post.
MS. Cornell.
K (—). *LY ii. 830* (—).

[*In M. W.'s hand*]

Rydal Mount, Kendal
Jan^{ry} 24th 1837

Dear Sir,
    I ought to have replied to your very obliging letter
immediately, but I have had many engagements pressing upon

---

[1] Tipped into the fourth volume of the Wellesley College copy of the
Poetical Works of 1832, opposite p. 76.

[2] *Excursion*, ii. 553—5.

[3] *Ibid.*, 884—6.

[4] Robert Shelton Mackenzie (1809—80), author and journalist: in 1833
editor of the *Liverpool Journal*, and from 1834 to 1851 correspondent of the

me, and have therefore trusted to your kindness for excusing a little delay. The particulars you told to Mr Southey and myself about American periodical Literature amused and interested us much; and the Newspaper you have sent with your communication forcibly illustrates what you stated at Lancaster. Allow me to say that I was much pleased with your frankness in making a public declaration of the mistakes you had been led into concerning Mr Southey's character, and without giving ourselves credit for deserving all the agreeable things you say of us, I will venture to affirm, the tenor of the whole article[1] is entitled to much praise for its candour, openness, and spirit—and the ease with which, as a literary composition, it is written.

The Sonnets are elegant and harmonious, and much too good to be confined to the columns of a transatlantic Newspaper.

Let me thank you kindly for your offer to send me the American Publications. There is a direct communication from Liverpool—by Coach daily—and every other day one passes thro Rydal—therefore if your Parcel leaves Liverpool by a Tuesday's or Thursday's Coach, and is directed, to be forwarded, by the 'Lake Tourist'—it will reach me the following morning.—

If there be in America such a demand for English Literature as your information respecting the recent Edition of my Poems[2] implies, is it not reasonable—that English Authors should have some compensation in the way of Copyright in that Country? particularly as American Authors have that privilege in England—surely the advantage ought to be reciprocal.

In a day or two the printing of the last Vol: of the Ed: of my Poems now going thro' the Press will be commenced—when it is completed I should like to beg your acceptance of a Copy, if

New York Evening Star. He settled permanently in America in 1852. His principal works were a novel Titian, 3 vols., 1843; an edition of Maginn's Miscellaneous Works, 5 vols., 1855—7; an edition of Noctes Ambrosianae, 5 vols., 1866; and biographies of Dickens (1870) and Scott (1871). He had met W. W. and Southey the previous September during the trial of the great Will Cause (see L. 1066 above).

[1] An article in a New York paper, probably the Evening Star. Shelton Mackenzie mentioned it in his reply of 10 Feb. (WL MSS.), in which he defended his own change of political views.

[2] Either Yarrow Revisited, and Other Poems, 2nd edition, Boston, 1836, or the Poetical Works, in one volume, New Haven, 1836. See Cornell Wordsworth Collection, nos. 98 and 99.

you will let me know how I must desire my Publisher to address it to you.

I remain dear Sir,
sincerely your obliged S^t.
[*signed*] W. Wordsworth

P.S. I laughed heartily at the blunders of the American Press—particularly at Purgatory for Paraguay—this is the more droll when one remembers the Poem of Mr S. against which such an outcry was raised—his Vision of Judgment.

1111. W. W. to EDWARD MOXON

Address: Edward Moxon Esqre, 44 Dover Street.
MS. Henry E. Huntington Library.
K (—). *LY ii. 830* (—).

[*In M. W.'s hand*]

Rydal Mount Jan^{ry} 28th [1837]

My dear Mr Moxon,

I have rec^d your letter this morning along with 2 Proofs bringing the 4th vol to page 336. These two, with *one* on Monday, are all I have had this week—Something less than 2 sheets more will, I expect, conclude this volume. I regret that the Memoir[1] (making part of the notes to this volume) as it has been very much read, was not printed in larger type, the same as the Essay on Epitaphs, at the close of the Excursion. But Mr Evans is in no fault, as I forgot to give directions to that effect. The Printer has already been furnished with nearly two thirds of the Copy for the 5th volume, so that he can have no excuse, if he be not punctual.

I will tell you at once about the new pieces which this Ed: will contain; they are inaccurately stated in the 1st Vol:. One of the Political Sonnets is now *first printed* viz 'What if our numbers barely could defy.'[2] In the Miscellaneous Sonnets is the one you have noticed, and in Eccl: Sonnets is one upon the Norman Conquest, beginning 'Coldly we spake the Saxons over-

---

[1] The *Memoir of the Rev. Robert Walker* (*PW*. iii. 510–22), an extended note to *The River Duddon* sonnets.
[2] *PW*. iii. 120.

powered'.[1] In the same volume is a short Poem beginning 'O life without the chequered scene'[2] of which the second Stanza is new, the first being taken from one in the same class, so that together they make an add[l] piece. A new Stanza, or rather additions to the amount of a new Stanza in the 3 Cottage Girls.[3] In the 5th volume, I have added from my Mss 2 Poems to the class of the Evening Voluntaries,[4] one 72 lines the other 50 odd, and also a Poem upon a drawing of the Bird of Paradise,[5] and an additional Epitaph from Chiabrera,[6] which with the Lines to the memory of dear Charles Lamb,[7] and those upon the death of Hogg[8] make a considerable increase of new matter in this last volume—But after all, the value of this Ed. in the eyes of the judicious, as hereafter will be universally admitted, lies in the pains which has been taken in the revisal of so many of the old Poems, to the re-modelling, and often re-writing whole Paragraphs, which you know have cost me great labour and I do not repent of it. In the Poems lately written I have had comparatively little trouble.

We are sorry to hear that you have been plagued with the Influenza in your house—thus far we have escaped it, for which we are thankful. My Sister is rather better than worse, and I rejoice to say that my Daughter's health is greatly improved. (Cannot you tell us something about Miss Lamb, we are always anxious to hear of her). We talk confidently of moving southward, if all be well, in the course of the latter half of next month.

God bless you and yours and believe me faithfully and aff[tly]

your Friend
[*signed*] W[m] Wordsworth

[*W. W. writes*]
How is dear Mr Rogers?, and his Sister?

[*M. W. writes*]
I hope the Books have been regularly sent to the Printers and especially to Mr Stephen[9] to whom we have given so much

---

[1] *PW*. iii. 357.   [2] *After-Thought* (*PW*. iii. 174).   [3] *PW*. iii. 186.
[4] The two poems *To the Moon* (*PW*. iv. 14, 16).
[5] *PW*. ii. 320. This poem was published in the new edition of the *Poetical Works* (v. 139), and not in 1842, as de Selincourt states.
[6] *PW*. iv. 249 ff.   [7] *PW*. iv. 272.   [8] *PW*. iv. 276.
[9] James Stephen (See L. 1082 above).

trouble. Our parcel with the 2ᵈ vols have not reached us. The little parcel directed to my daughter recᵈ through Mr Stephen to-day was intended to be sent by your next parcel—we did not mean to trouble Mr S. to frank it.

Many thanks for your kindness in procuring for me the new Books at Trade price. The proofs concluding the 4 vol: have reached us *this* morning and will be returned by this night's Post. Jan 29ᵗʰ.

1112. W. W. to H. C. R.

Endorsed: Jan 1837. Wordsworth Intended journey.
MS. Dr. Williams's Library.
K (—). *Morley, i. 334.*

[*In M. W.'s hand*]

Rydal Mount Janʳʸ 28ᵗʰ [1837]

My dear Friend

We are a letter in your debt—and that letter spoke of discomforts to which your Brother had been exposed, and of a severe domestic distress[1]—It seldom happens that friends can do more upon such occasions than express assurances of sympathy, which we have all sincerely felt with you upon this. Moxon tells us you have returned to town—and we trust you have left your family more reconciled to their heavy loss, than you ventured to hope—the blessings of Christianity are in nothing more deeply felt than in its power to dispose the mind to resignation under the pressure of like afflictions. And not only to do this, but to turn them into sources of something more than cheerfulness—as being more exalted than mere cheerfulness can be—Today we have heard of the disease of a most amiable young Person about 20 years of age—in whom we were much interested—She is the 6th Child that her Parents have lost within the last 2 years—most of them (within a very few years) of the same age. Both from letters and conversation I have learnt and I have also seen, that the Parents have been supported under these afflictions in a manner which you would have delighted to witness.

---

[1] The death of his brother's grandchild (Morley's note).

Dr Arnold and his family are here and have been enjoying themselves much.—the D^r takes very long walks, and I sometimes fear Mrs A. is tempted to do more in this way than she ought. The Winter has been with us, I should say, an agreeable one—on account of its great variety—Frost—snow—rain, bright and gleamy sunshine, such as we have had to-day—the mountains being most beautiful—and we have had many such days; and the winter upon the whole has been far from severe. We have had primroses in blow thro' the whole of it.

In two or three days I hope the printing of my last Volume will be begun, the whole of the Verses are corrected for the Press—But I must have another *tug* at the Postscript on the Poor Laws,[1] and other things, in which I wish you were here to help—Mary wishes it still more—

What do you think of an edition of 20,000 of my Poems being struck off at Boston[2]—as I have been told on good authority—An Author in the English language is becoming a great Power for good or evil—if he writes with spirit.

Now for our travels—I trust I shall be ready to start from home by the end of the 3d week in Feb^{ry} I shall land Dora at Leamington, where I must be obliged to stay at least two days —then direct for town—I hope this will suit you, but pray write immediately and let me know what way we had best take, I suppose it will be of course to enter Italy by the Cornice road. How can we most agreeably and best get thither, I must repeat that I am not equal to lumbering night and day, in a french diligence—else we might go that way to Chalon sur Soane and so float down that river and the Rhone [? at][3] Avignon—but in this I submit entirely to your experience. Here let me say, that I have lately rec^d a most friendly letter from Barron[4] Field,

---

[1] The *Postscript, 1835.*

[2] See L. 1110 above.

[3] *Written* a.

[4] *Written* Baron Field. He had written from Gibraltar on 17 Dec., expressing his pleasure with the *Yarrow Revisited* volume. 'Your genius only mellows with your age. Not the smallest spark of decay is visible yet. Oh! continue the "Recluse". I wish I was Moxon. I would make you such an offer for it as would ruin me to enrich my children. . . . I really think from what Murray said to me, two or three years ago, he would give you £1000 for the rest of the "Recluse".' And he singled out *On The Power of Sound* for special praise. 'Even in versification, how deeply you have studied the sound as well as the sense of poetry, will one day be acknowledged.' (*WL MSS.*)

355

inviting us to the South of Spain, but this is out of the question at this time of the year—For never will I trust myself in the Atlantic in a steam boat between the Autumnal and Vernal equinox. Nor would you I think, if you had read a most interesting letter which we had lately from Mr Quillinan[1]— giving an account, poor fellow, of his wretched situation with his daughter and 40 Passengers, who were on the brink of destruction off Cape Finnesterre—and in much danger for 5 days—all owing to the rascallity of the owners and agents of the Steam Vessel—sending her out again at that season—a week after her return from Madeira and Gibraltar, when, as the head Engineer told Mr Q. after their disaster, she stood in need of at least repairs which would have taken 3 weeks. I wish you could see Mr Q's detail, for it is very touching and beautifully written.

It is late, and I must conclude—pray let us hear[2] from you—I have been 7 hours walking this day—A blank post day *to* London giving me a holiday. Do not imagine from this bravado as it may seem, that I am too youthful to be your Companion— Alas! I feel how far, how very far I am below you in muscular strength—but let me be thankful for what is left—farewell! with love from all—Dora is much better in health—and my poor Sister no worse, but rather more comfortable.

Ever most faithfully yours
Wm Wordsworth

[1] E. Q. had returned to Portugal the previous November. On 14 Nov. he sent Dora W. a brief account from Lisbon of his near-escape from death: 'I will only now tell you that on Thursday night in a furious gale of wind we were drifting fast on a lee shore, off Cape Finisterre, near the rocks of which we were so near that they were now and then discerned in a flash of lightning. Otherwise the night was as dark as it was wild; and when I add that we were crippled, both engines being damaged and useless, you may imagine our situation; having nothing to trust to but the two or three scanty sales of the steamboat which appeared quite incapable of urging the bulk of a steamer away from the shore . . .' And on the 25th he followed this up with a dramatic and moving account of the mounting crisis after they had put to sea with crippled engines. 'I had made up my mind that it was better that Jemima and I should stay without the possibility of being separated, in the cabin, and so have it over the sooner, as the vessel would fill from below.' (*WL MSS.*)

[2] *Written here.*

1113. W. W. to LORD LONSDALE

MS. WL.[1]
LY ii. 833.

Rydal Mount Feb[ry] 1st 1837

My Lord

It is mortifying to me after having given your Lordship so much trouble upon the matter of the intended Church at Cockermouth, to be obliged to send you the enclosed. Mr Stanger's letter[2] and the ext[t] from Mr Watson's would have been forwarded earlier, but I thought it better to wait for Mr Wood's reply[3] to mine, written immediately after your Lordship empowered me to make known, where I thought it would be serviceable, your very munificent offer. Mr Wood's letter came this m[g] and notwithstanding the encouraging expectations of support from the Societies held out by Mr Watson probably you will be of opinion, when you have read Mr Wood's letter, that the project must be suspended or given up as far as yourself and your friends are concerned: for my own part, *my* present feeling is, that unless you differ from me, we should leave the people of Cockermouth to take their own course; and this opinion I entertain, not so much in consequence of what Mr Wood says of the withdrawal of such and such subscriptions from Persons on the spot—as from what he says of the decided hostility of the people, and their present temper upon Church matters.[4]

---

[1] A draft of the letter sent, probably the copy sent with the next letter to Joshua Watson.

[2] James Stanger had written on 23 Jan. to say that he, and most of the other subscribers in Cockermouth, would withdraw their offers of support if the patronage of the new church were to be vested in Lord Lonsdale; and in protesting his desire to see the church in Cockermouth divested of all appearance of party, he suggested as an alternative that it should be vested in the Bishop instead. (*WL MSS.*)

[3] William Wood wrote W. W. a long letter on 31 Jan. about the hostility of the Cockermouth radicals to the Established Church: '. . . it is with deep regret that I am obliged to confess that I see no prospect of getting through with our intentions, for want of the cordial support of the higher and middle classes of the inhabitants. . . .We must let the popular clamor for church Reform subside before we can hope to get on with vigour and unanimity.' (*WL MSS.*)

[4] Lord Lonsdale replied on 6 Feb.: 'As Matters stand at present I am of opinion that all farther Discussion respecting the New Church at Cocker=

I expect Mr Stanger to call in a day or two, when I shall strongly express my regret that your Lordship's proposal has been so unwort[hily] received; and shall state that I await your final answer and also the opinion of Mr Watson, before I can give my own, but if he presses for my *present* opinion I shall say that neither my feelings nor my judgment will allow me to apply to my friends in any quarter;—on the contrary, I shall return what sums I have rec^d upon personal application, and what has been offered me by Strangers—and shall take no active part in what his Party may be disposed to do: but that if they build and endow, and the patronage be lodged in the *Bishop of the Diocese* (tho' not holding a favorable opinion of such Bps as we are likely to have in future) I would give my own mite, so convinced am I of the spiritual destitution of the place.

I cannot conclude, my Lord, without expressing what a pleasing and deep sense I have both from general and personal considerations, of

[*cetera desunt*]

1114. W. W. to JOSHUA WATSON

Endorsed: Wm Wordsworth Esq. 1 Feb. 1837.
MS. WL.
LY ii. 832.

[*In M. W.'s hand*]

Rydal Mt Feb 1st [1837]

My dear Sir

I thank you cordially for your last letter—I have not seen Mr Stanger yet but enclose an extract of a letter[1] from him— also one from a letter from Mr Wood received this morning— for which I have been waiting, and also a rough draft of my own letter addressed to Lord Lonsdale this morning, which will put you in possession of my present notions.

mouth be suspended as the Steps already taken appear so distasteful to those who appear'd to be most anxious for its Establishment, [but] are now most opposed to it.' He stated that he had in any case been in favour of transferring the patronage to the Bishop. (*WL MSS.*)

[1] See previous letter.

I must however repeat to yourself directly, that it is the *hostility* of the people of C and their perverse notions of Church matters and not the withdrawal of the subscriptions which would deter me if Ld L. continued to support us—from proceeding in the matter, encouraged as I am by y^r last letter respecting what might be looked for from the Societies.

I hope you and Miss W. keep clear of the Influenza, as I am thankful to say we have hitherto done. Pray let me hear from you at your convenience.

With affec regards from all, ever faithfully yours

[*signed*] Wm Wordsworth

1115. W. W. to H. C. R.

Address: H. C. Robinson Esqre, 2 Plowdens Buildings, Temple.
Endorsed: 11th Feb: 1837, Mrs Wordsworth and W. W.
MS. Dr. Williams's Library.
K (—). Morley, i. 337.

[*The first part in M. W.'s hand*]

Rydal Mount
11th Feby 1837.

My dear Friend

Thanks for your letter, the reasonableness of w^h throughout, I acknowledge—My present wish is, if you approve to go from Brighton by Steam to Dieppe, to Rouen and Paris: this shortens the land journey much—then to Challons and down the Soane and Rhone and by all means by the Cornice road forwards into Italy—

I like your account of your friend, and shall be glad that he or any other eligible person sh^d accompany us—there are many reasons why three persons are preferable to two, though of course there are objections. My son has spent too much money about his new house to be able to go along with us.

Now my dear Friend, consult with Mr Moxon, how my last vol: can be pushed thro' the press as fast as possible—all the copy is in the hands of the printer, except the postscript,[1] which I

---

[1] The *Postscript, 1835*. In his letter of 3 Feb., H. C. R. had suggested the omission of this item from the new edition, and its separate publication as a

could leave to be done by Mrs W. and my Clerk—There is nothing (except some fear of the Influenza seizing us on the road) save the printing of this work to prevent our setting off for Leamington in a very few days

Most faithfully
Yours
Wm Wordsworth

All going on as usual at Home. Dora's health improving.

1116. W. W. to JOSHUA WATSON

Address: Joshua Watson Esqre, 6 Park Street, Westminster.
Postmark: 14 Feb. 1837. *Stamp*: Kendal Penny Post.
Endorsed: Wm Wordsworth 14 Feb. 1837 Cockermouth Ch.
MS. WL.
LY ii. 834.

[*In M. W.'s hand*]

[14 Feb. 1837]

My dear Sir

I enclose a Copy of Lord L's letter just received—Your own, for which I feel *very greatly* obliged to you, has come by the same post—

Lord L's letter is so express upon the point of the business being suspended, that I must have submit[t]ed to his judgment even if it had not been in concurrence with my own. Nevertheless I cannot but regret that his Lordship did not before mention to me his disinterested dispositions[1]—as you will find

pamphlet; and he went on to look forward to a collected edition of W. W.'s prose works. 'Hereafter perhaps the lovers of your poetry may be desirous to have your collected prose writings—your Convention of Cintra—your Letter on Burns, your poor law investigation and those other unacknowledged brochures which I have heard imputed to you—The *Guide* notwithstanding its humble title is much more congenial with your poems than any of these controversial writings. The *Epitaphs* you have very properly included—' (Morley, i. 337.)

[1] i.e. his expressed wish that the patronage of the new church at Cockermouth should be vested not in himself, but in the Bishop. He had written to W. W. on 12 Feb. reiterating his view that the matter was best left to lie for the present: 'The objection to leaving the appointment of the Minister

them expressed in his letter. To day I shall write to $L^d L$. to let him know that I shall not proceed with the affair—but hope however that he will permit me to make known in certain quarters the manner in which he intended in all probability to have acted.

I am indeed much mortified—My Neighbours Lady Fleming and Mr Bolton have both promised subscriptions—and Mr Benson Harrison of Ambleside had increased his sub^n to £50—so that I had every prospect of effecting a good deal, thro' my own applications—and with your inestimable assistance the thing might have been done notwithstanding the withdrawal of the Cockermouth subscriptions. But neither on acc^t of my respect for $L^d L$, yourself, and the societies, which are so much indebted to your labours, nor above all, of my veneration and love for the genuine Ch: of England, can I attempt to force upon the Inh^{ts} of C.[1] a Church of which the present generation at least, appears so unworthy.

Mr Stanger being disappointed in not finding his own Carriage at Ambleside, proceeded to Keswick by the Coach—so that I have not seen him—and must write to him to-day.

I hope to have a peep at you in passing thro' London—before three weeks are over. I should have thrown myself upon your hospitality, but not having seen my good Friend Miss Fenwick when in town last Spring—I have been many months pre-engaged to sleep under her roof. My intention is to accompany Dora to Leamington—and if all goes well with her, she will probably proceed to Hampstead in April or May—when I trust she may renew her acquaintance with yourself and Miss Watson—to whom and to you we all beg our united affectionate remembrances. My Sister is no worse, and we have all thus far kept clear of Influenza—except my Son Wm who is

with me will have its Influence with many—but it must exhibit a stronger Hostility to the Church Establishment than some of them may wish to have Credit for, if they reject the Nomination of the Bishop. . . . I believe I said to you before that it is the usual Course in these Cases that the Patronage follow'd the appointment—but I think under the Circumstances it will be better with the Bishop. I speak generally as to *the* Bishop, as it may happen, that there might not be at this time much Difference in the Choice of a Minister between the present Diocesan and Mr Stanger.' (*WL MSS.*) Dr. Sumner, the Bishop of Chester, was widely suspected of Evangelical leanings.

[1] Inhabitants of Cockermouth.

now with us pining for a sphere of action more suitable to his age, than his scanty employment at Carlisle

Ever most faithfully
Your obliged friend
[*signed*] Wm Wordsworth

1117. W. W. to H. C. R.

Address: H. C. Robinson Esqre, 2 Plowdens Build^gs, Temple.
Postmark: 18 Feb. *Stamp*: Kendal Penny Post.
Endorsed: Feb: 1837, Wordsworth Autograph.
MS. Dr. Williams's Library.
Morley, i. 338.

[*c.* 17 Feb. 1837]

My dear Friend,

The Epidemic has seized Dora, and she has been 4 days confined to her bed, and is very weak. I write this from fears that our setting off may be retarded by it. Mrs Wordsworth and I are yet untouched by the disease; but two of our servants have had it, one of whom is still in bed. My Sister keeps clear and is as well as usual. I will let you know in[1] this same channel how we go on. Mrs Wordsworth['s] Brother Mr Thomas Hutchinson (of Brinsop) has just had a fearful accident.[2] His Horse fell with him; and the spinal marrow has been much injured in consequence, so that the use of his limbs was taken away. We *hope* he is doing as well as can be expected after so dreadful a shock.

Ever faithfully yours
Wm Wordsworth

Perhaps you have not been told that Dora is intended to be her Father's fellow traveller as far as Leamington.[3]

---

[1] through *written in above.*
[2] See *MW*, pp. 154–5.
[3] Where Mrs. Hook was living.

1118. W. W. to FRANCIS FOLJAMBE COURTENAY[1]

MS. Mr. Arthur Houghton, Jnr. Hitherto unpublished.

[Following signed copy of 'She dwelt among the untrodden ways', as in P. W. ii. 30]

Rydal Mount
20th Feb^{ry} 1837

My dear Sir,
   I send you in my usual hand neither worse nor better the two transcripts you desired. I hope to see your father shortly, but when exactly I know not, as my Daughter whom I was to have attended as far as Leamington is laid up with influenza . . .

[cetera desunt]

1119. W. W. to H. C. R.

Address: H. C. Robinson Esqre, 2 Plowdens Buildings, Temple, London. *[In M. W.'s hand]*
Stamp: Kendal Penny Post.
Endorsed: 20 Feb: 1837, Wordsworth Enquiries abo^t Cholera.
MS. Dr. Williams's Library.
Morley, i. 339.

Tuesday 20th [Feb. 1837]

My dear Friend,
   I write to you *principally* to entreat that you would endeavour to *ascertain* as speedily as you can, by application to the Representatives of the Italian Courts, or by Traveller, or through any persons who are in correspondence with Italy, what degree of impediment, we are likely to meet with, from quarantine, sanitary or political, on entering Italy or travelling there—This, I feel indispensible for pacifying dear M^{rs} W^s mind, who has had such unfavorable accounts upon this subject, one yesterday, very strongly expressed from Lady Frederick

---

[1] b. 1818, third son of Philip Courtenay, W. W.'s financial adviser: admitted to Jesus College, Cambridge, and the Inner Temple, 1834; transferred to Trinity, 1836.

Bentinck who has much communication with Foreigners. Poor dear Mary, is full of fears, and in dejected spirits on account of the sad intelligence from her Brothers House at Brinsop. His daughter[1] appears to be in a hopeless state of sickness, and Mary is anxious to go thither to assist her Sister-in-law, in nursing the Invalids. But this cannot be done at present, on account of Dora's being reduced by the Influenza. If Dora recovers her strength, so that it may be deemed reasonable for her to move, Mother and Daughter *will move* as soon as possible, and I shall accompany them if your answer be favorable so that M^{rs} W^s mind shall be tranquillized, I mean to accompany them as far as Manchester, and give up going to Leamington. In that case I should be in Town two or three days earlier. If Dora should not be well enough to start, it will then be for me to consider, whether I should not start this day week which, I for myself, am quite prepared to do.

This, I fear, will be found to be a confused letter. The sum is, Learn about the cholera, and write *immediately* and if your answer be favorable I shall probably be in Town in ten days at the latest.

ever affectionately yours
Wm Wordsworth

Tuesday.

I think I told you before that poor Mr Hutchinson of Brinsop had lost the use both of his legs and arms, by injury to the spinal cord, from his horse falling with him—so that you may judge of the distress of that House, the daughter dying, and the father in that state—!

---

[1] Thomas Hutchinson's second daughter Mary, who died of consumption later this year.

Address: R. Shelton Mackenzie Esqre, Liverpool. [*In M. W.'s hand*]
Stamp: Kendal Penny Post.
MS. Historical Society of Pennsylvania.
LY ii. 835 (—).

Feb^{ry} 23^d [1837]

My dear Sir

Your newspaper and obliging Letter were duly received and would have been earlier acknowledged, but for reasons which I am sure you will deem sufficient, viz incessant occupation preparatory to my leaving home for some time, hurry in carrying through the Press the Edition of my Poems of which the last Volume is now done, and finally the influenza which, thought it has not yet touched me, has sadly disabled most of my family—

Your verses[1] written under such affecting circumstances do great honour both to your heart and head, especially the former copy, which is indeed very touching. I thank you for sending them to me.—The American Editor has misled you in respect to the Elegiac poem of mine which you have republished.[2] It is not a new thing, but has been several times reprinted among my collected works, and you will find it in the 4th Volume of the one now in course of publication, which shall be forwarded to you according to the received address as soon as I reach London, which I hope will be in ten days time at the latest.[3]

Many thanks for your interesting information about american piracies. At Keswick the other day I saw at Mr Southey's the newspaper you mentioned in your Letter as containing the whole of the Souvenir.[4] It is a curiosity. If I can contrive to see

---

[1] In his letter of 10 Feb. (*WL MSS.*), Mackenzie had enclosed a poem on the recent death of his daughter.

[2] The reference is apparently to the *Elegiac Stanzas* on F. W. Goddard (*PW* iii. 193), reprinted by Mackenzie in the *Liverpool Mail* from the *New York Mirror.*

[3] 'I find Mrs W has already given directions that the volumes shall be sent to your address.' (Added in M. W.'s hand.)

[4] Actually *Friendship's Offering* for 1837, which was reprinted in the *Philadelphia News* on 26 Nov. 1836. In his letter Mackenzie had mentioned that American authors had already petitioned Congress on the Copyright

the Chancellor of the Exchequer for a few minutes at this busy time, I will mention the particular to him. I think I told you before, that he is interested in the general subject of international law upon this question. Connected with copyright is a point, to me of much more importance, viz the lengthening the term. When I was in Town last spring I took much pain in drawing the attention of leading Members of the House of Commons of all parties, to this portion of the question. Sergeant Talfourd means to make a motion upon the subject, which I hope will be entertained by the House as it ought to be. I am not without hope of proceeding this Spring to the Continent, and soon after I reach London, but as this is very uncertain, I don't like to talk about it, because these things get into the Newspapers. Believe me dear Sir, with much respect

sincerely yours
Wm Wordsworth

[*In Dora W.'s hand*]

The Newspaper containing your first copy of verses was laid aside with the intention of having the lines transcribed into a book; unfortunately it has been torn up (I have this moment discovered) by one of the servants, and that part of it wh. contains your verses—To the line

'Wilt thou not hover round that home of wh. thou art the light' is preserved. Might I trouble you to have transcribed for us the remaining portion, it can be enclosed in the parcel along with the books—this accident has annoyed us much.

question: ' . . . I shall keep the ball up in the Liverpool Mail. I may claim the credit of being the first person, 4 years since, to state to American authors (thro the medium of their own periodicals) the Evil of the wholesale pirating system—as regarded *their* interests.'

1121. DORA W. to H. C. R.

Address: H. C. Robinson Esqre, Plowdens Buildings, Temple.
Postmark: 1 Mar. 1837. *Stamp*: Fetter Lane.
Endorsed: 27th Feb. 1837. Wordsworth (Autograph).
MS. Dr. Williams's Library.
Morley, i. 342.

Monday Febry 27th. [1837]

My dear Mr Robinson,

Father desires me to thank you for your very satisfactory letter received this morning and to say that he hopes to be in town this day fortnight[1] (Monday 6 March) and will be ready to start for Italy as soon as he has paid his visit to Miss Fenwick— He accompanies my Mother and me to Leamington and will give a day to Dr Arnold.—We have had a very good account of my Uncle Hutchinson who is going on as well as possible but alas for his poor Daughter she cannot long be among us—My Mother proceeds to Brinsop from Leamington without halting at all—

Did you receive a note from Father, enclosing a letter for Miss Hutchinson,[2] enclosing a copy of a letter from Mr Quillinan? if you have not would you beg Mr Moxon to make enquiries for it from his printers Bradbury and Evans to whose care your letter was sent—it left Rydal last Saturday fortnight—

With kindest love and best wishes from all

Very affect^ly yours
Dora Wordsworth

Aunty is very nicely I have had a slight return of the Influenza w^h prevents our starting this week as was our intention; we have fixed next Tuesday for our departure

[*W. W. writes*]

I am quite satisfied with your account,[3] and M^rs W seems to be so too. I cannot say how much I was grieved at what you say about your health. I hope the journey will do us both good.

ever affectionately yours
W. W.

---

[1] But there was a change of plan. See next letter.
[2] Joanna Hutchinson.
[3] H. C. R.'s letter of 24 Feb. (Morley, i. 340) had given a reassuring account of the progress of the cholera in Italy.

1122. W. W. to H. C. R.

Address: H. C. Robinson Esqre, Plowden's Buildings, Temple.[*In Dora W.'s hand*]
Postmark: 6 Mar. 1837. *Stamp*: Fleet St W.C.
Endorsed: March 1837. (Wordsworth) before the journey.
MS. Dr. Williams's Library.
K (—). *Morley, i. 343.*

Rydal Mount
Thursday March 2^d [1837]

My dear Friend

We have just receieved your 2nd Letter. All had been previously settled for our departure, though Dora is still troubled with cold and susceptibilities of taking cold—reliques of the influenza. This is Thursday and on Monday morning we mean to quit Rydal, hoping to reach Manchester that night, Birmingham on Tuesday night Whence Mrs W will hasten to her Brother's, and we two be I hope at Rugby, early on Wednesday. On Friday I shall proceed to London, and after a few days, very few, given to friendship under the Roof of Miss Fenwick, and to calling on other Friends, and to business passports etc., I shall be eager to depart: in order to have the benefit of the spring of Italy, and its beauty as early as possible. I say this being well aware that you will readily meet my wishes.—Mrs W— confides in our united prudence, and for myself I have not a jot more fear of apprehension than I should have, of being carried off at home, by influenza, apoplexy, palsy, or any other of Death's ministers.—

Two or three days ago died my good old Friend Mr Bolton; [1] my friend and neighbour Mr North [2] was in extreme danger for several days with influenza, and this morning has died of the same complaint, my excellent neighbour and friend Mrs Freeman, [3] who only a week ago or less last Friday talked with Mrs W— and me with all the animation of a person of 20, being quite well.—

I long to see you that we may plan our journey and be off with as little delay as possible. We have now here the most

[1] John Bolton of Storrs.

[2] Ford North of Ambleside, who occupied Rydal Mount before the Wordsworths.

[3] Mrs. Lydia Freeman of Clappersgate, whom H. C. R. had met in Jan. 1836: 'a fine old woman of eighty-three . . . a pleasure to see such a person' (*HCR* ii. 480).

beautiful weather, celandines and daisies smiling upon the sun, in abundance. I trust that the Stamp office will have no objection to rather a prolonged stay on my part; I cannot banish the hope of having a peep at Sicily[1] if you approve, and the Steam boat to Palermo shall be found doing its duty.—

I still incline to going by Dieppe to Rouen and so on to Paris. The only part of the journey which is to me uninviting is the space between Paris and Chalons sur Soane. Nismes we will see if you approve—farewell.

Most affectionately yours
[*unsigned*]

Monday

P.S. Our intended departure has been hastened a day since Dora wrote. Mrs Hooke cannot receive us, so that she will go to Dr Arnolds[2] first, which allows me to be in Town three days earlier, than her Letter would lead you to expect. There was a mistake in her Letter, she wrote, as she afterwards remembered, Monday 6th instead of Monday 13th. Unless some thing happens which I can't foresee, I shall be at Miss Fenwicks on the evening of the tenth, and happy to see you there on the eleventh. No. 1 Portugal street South Audley street is her residence.

No 1. Portugal S[t 3]

1123. W. W. to M. W.

Address: Mrs Wordsworth, M[r] Hutchinson's, Brinsop Court, Hereford.
MS. WL. Hitherto unpublished.

Monday morning [13 Mar. 1837]

My dearest Mary,

I am afraid of a sad blunder, which will have caused[4] a Letter intended for you, and despatched on Saturday, to go to Rydal, and in this fear I will repeat part of its contents as briefly as possible—

---

[1] Cf. *Prelude* (1805), x. 1007 ff.:

> Child of the mountains, among Shepherds rear'd,
> Even from my earliest school-day time, I lov'd
> to dream of Sicily . . . (*Prel.*, p. 424.)

[2] At Rugby.
[3] Added by Dora W.   [4] *Written* called.

Mrs Arnold will have told you about Dora. She has been faring wonderfully. I left Rugby Friday morning, got to Town before six—Saturday saw Mr Robinson, Strickland Cookson and others. National provincial[1] doing well, have not yet seen Mr Courtenay, will try to do so to day.—I hope we shall get off on Saturday—for Boulogne but will write again.—I have received your Letter and am anxious for one sent to Dora. To morrow Mr Rogers will take me to Hampstead. I am now writing in Sir Robert Inglis's off: near Westminster Bridge, having been to call at the Archbishops after breakfasting at Mr Watsons and parting with my Brother who is gone to Cambridge. Did not find the Archbishop at home; sate some time with Mrs Howley. Francis Beaumount,[2] Sir George's Brother just dead very suddenly. Miss Howley[3] to be married in a few days. Met Mr Hugh Rose[4] in the Strand, looking very ill. Yesterday settled with Mr Robinson and others all the particulars of our journey. Mr Moxon goes with us to Paris. Shall be able to write to you without expense of Postage. Miss Fenwick is in weak health. I dine out no where; saw the Marshalls all well on Saturday, Wm starting for the north. Shall call on Dr Holland and Brodie. I saw John Wordsworth[5] yesterday.

I must now conclude. Love and best wishes to all

Your affectionate Husband
W Wordsworth

Yesterday I called on Miss Rogers and the Lockharts, Mrs Lockhart dangerously ill.[6]

[1] i.e. W. W.'s National Provincial shares.
[2] William Francis Beaumont (1803–37), of Buckland Court, Surrey, had died on 10 Mar.
[3] Anne, Dr. Howley's second daughter, married William Kingsmill (d. 1865), of Sydmonton Court, Newbury, on 16 Mar. 1837.
[4] Hugh James Rose. See also L. 1103 above.
[5] R. W.'s son.
[6] Mrs. Lockhart's illness at the beginning of March had interrupted work on the *Life of Scott*. She died on 17 May.

1124. W. W. to DORA W.

Address: Miss Wordsworth, Revd Dr Arnolds, Rugby.
MS. WL. Hitherto unpublished.

Monday between one and two
[13 Mar. 1837]

My dearest Dora,

I am now writing in Sir Robert Inglis's off: vile pen, and worse ink. Arrived safe in Portugal street, Miss Fenwick poorly. Saturday given to business, saw Mr Robinson, Strickland Cookson, etc etc, but have not yet see[n] Mr Courtenay. Yesterday settle with Mr Robinson every thing about journey, hope to get off on Saturday. I have seen Mr Moxon twice, says nearly 2000 of the Edition are disposed of. Called at the Printers, a short time there as busy as man will be—Saw Dr Wordsworth three times at Mr Watsons, he is just gone to Cambridge. I have been calling at the Archbishops, did not see him but saw Mrs Howley, Francis Beaumont, Sir G.['s] Brother just dead suddenly—poor Tom Clarkson[1] killed by a fall from his Gig. To morrow Rogers takes me to Hampstead, and on Saturday I hope we shall be able to start, but this I see I have said before. I have called at the Stamp off. [   ][2] there, passports will be prepared tomorrow—Yesterday called at Miss Rogers and Mr Lockharts—Mrs Lockhart dangerously ill. Mr Hugh Rose I met in the street, looking very [ill].[3] Shall call on Sir Benjamin Brodie, Dr Holland, and Judge Coleridge.[4]

I hope dearest Dora your health improves. As I shall be able to write to you free of postage, you and your Mother will hear from us at least once a week. Kindly accept this Scrawl for I must off. Best remembrances to D^r and Mrs Arnold, and all—

ever affectionatly your father
W Wordsworth

---

[1] C. C.'s son (see pt. i, L. 4), at this time one of the Thames police magistrates. See also L. 1134 below.

[2] *MS. illegible.*

[3] *Word dropped out.*

[4] Sir John Taylor Coleridge.

1125. W. W. to DORA W.

MS. WL. Hitherto unpublished.

[*c.* 15 Mar. 1837]

private

My dearest Dora,

Dear good Miss Fenwick wishes to invest four hundred pounds to accumulate till the age of 15 or so for the benefit of the education of her Godson[1] at the University or in such way as may suit his father's circumstances and the boy's Talents; and if he should die be sure as to go to like purpose for the benefit of one of his Brothers.——

She wished first that this money should be transferred to John's name, to this I objected on account of his circumstances as a poor Clergyman and other wise, also, I thought he would be more likely to [be][2] watchful over his expectations, and also to exert himself, if kept ignorant of this resource.

I objected on accounts which I named to Miss Fenwick. She then suggested that the money should be transferred to your name, this I thought far the best plan, and trust that you will have no objection—and I now write solely to ask your permission for that being done and in the hope of your approving of my not having it lodged wherever it may be lodged, in John's name, and also that you would think it much better neither he nor Isabella should know any thing about this resource.

Pray write by return of Post under cover to Mr Stephen and Mr Taylor; and be particularly particular about your health. I have seen the Hoares at Hampstead, the Coleridges etc etc, all well. We shall not depart till Sunday morning at the earliest when we shall take the Steamboat at The Tower, for Calais. We have got our Passports. I have seen Sockbridge John here— Love to all the Arnolds great and small—

[*unsigned*]

---

[1] John W.'s son William. See also L. 1130 below.
[2] *Word dropped out.*

1126. W. W. to D. W.

MS. WL.
LY ii. 836.

Friday afternoon [17 Mar. 1837]

My dear and very dear Sister,

Here I am waiting on the Dentist and have snatched a moment to tell you, that I am worn out with hurry.—You will be surprized but I hope not grieved to hear that I am starting for a trip upon the Continent with Mr Robinson. Our passports are procured, our carriage bought and we shall embark at the Tower Stairs on Sunday morning for Calais. How I wish you could have gone with us; but I shall think of you every where, and often shall we talk of you. I have seen the Marshalls, who made a thousand enquiries after you,—Mrs and Sara Coleridge who did the same. It is a week today since I arrived here and I long to be gone for I am fairly worn off my feet with flying from one part of the town to the other, and so many things to do. We shall write from abroad at length, and I hope you will be amused. Tell dear Joanna[1] that I have just got her letter to Mary giving an account of her proceedings—

I should have written to you before, but I had not a moment's time when I forwarded Mary's and Dora's Letter, which told you about every thing.

Farewell my dearest Sister and farewell my dear Joanna, and kindest remembrances to all the household James, Anne, Jane and Dorothy;[2] and mind that you all take care of yourselves and of each other.

Your most affectionate Brother
W. Wordsworth

[1] Joanna Hutchinson, who was looking after D. W. while M. W. was away at Brinsop.

[2] i.e. James Dixon, the gardener, and the three housemaids. An additional maid had been taken on some time before this to look after D. W.

1127. W. W. to ROBERT SOUTHEY

Address: Robert Southey Esq., Keswick.
MS. Pierpont Morgan Library.
K. LY ii. 837.

No 1. Portugal Street
Saturday Morning
[18 Mar. 1837]

My dear Southey,

To-morrow morning Mr Robinson and I depart by the Steamboat for Calais. I cannot leave England without saying farewell to you, and the expression of good wishes and prayers for yourself, your dear daughters, their afflicted mother, your Son, and all your family.

I have just been a week under the roof of our excellent friend,[1] and enjoying the company of Henry Taylor.

I will now transcribe a few words from a Letter of Mr Quillinan addressed to Dora, upon which for Landor's sake I shall make no comment.—I received the Letter this morning, and never heard a word on the subject the passage treats of.

Extract—

What has Mr Wordsworth done to that Welsh Furioso, Wal Landor the Savage, to excite his madness to such ludicrous malignity and grandiloquent vituperation.[2] Madmen are some-

---

[1] I. F.

[2] At the close of 1836 Landor had published *A Satire on Satirists, and admonition to detractors* (*Works*, ed. Welby and Wheeler, xvi. 217 ff.), in which he launched an unexpected attack on W. W. for denying all merit to his contemporaries, Southey included, and for depreciating Talfourd's *Ion*, the first performance of which W. W. had witnessed in Landor's company (see L. 1010 above).

> Amid the mighty storm that swell's around,
> Wordsworth was calm, and bravely stood his ground.
> No more on daisies and on pilewort fed,
> By weary Duddon's ever tumbled bed,
> The Grasmere cuckoo leaves those sylvan scenes,
> And, percht on shovel hats and dandy deans,
> and prickt with spicy cheer, at Philpot's nod,
> Devoutly fathers Slaughter upon God. (ll. 234–41)

Landor also accused W. W. of plagiarizing his lines about the sea-shell (*Excursion*, iv. 1132–47) from *Gebir*, i. 170–7. When he read the poem the previous

374

times very subtle in malice. What of his trying to blow up a flame of discord between your Father and Mr Southey! as if two such long-tried friends could quarrel at this time of day about the opinion that one or the other might or might not entertain as to the value of the other's poetry. Byron or Landor might give up an old Friend for such a cause, but Southey is too right minded to believe that W ever seriously disparaged his talents, or to be very irate if he really had had the bad taste to do so. I am sorry for Mr S., for Landor is also a very old and prized friend of his. It is remarkable with respect to L. himself, that he is the man of all the literary men of the day, Southey perhaps excepted (he forgets Coleridge or speaks perhaps only of the living) to whose ability and classical attainments I have most frequently heard your father bear testimony, and that in the most decided manner.

His wrath at Mr Wordsworth for having plagiarized his lines about the shell is capital fun.

Thus far Mr Q., and not a word of all this did I ever see or hear of before. Farewell again, and again.

[*unsigned*]

1128. W. W. to LORD LONSDALE

MS. Lonsdale MSS. Hitherto unpublished.

Portugal Street
London
Sunday [19] March [1837]

Dear Lord Lonsdale,

Meaning to take the Steamboat to-morrow for Calais, I cannot leave England without a parting expression of good wishes for yourself, Lady Lonsdale, Lady Frederick, Miss Thompson and all my dear and valued friends of your family, who may be at Cottesmore.

December, H. C. R. had remonstrated with Landor (see Morley, I 326—33) about the injustice of the attack and its all-too-obvious affinities with Byron's satire; and along with W. W.'s other friends he tried to keep the poet in ignorance of Landor's strictures. But now for the first time W. W. had heard of them from E. Q. in Portugal. But to judge from H. C. R.'s account of his state of mind (*HCR* ii. 516), W. W. does not seem seriously to have been put out by them, though his relations with Landor were permanently affected.

I had seen Lady Anne,[1] and also Lord Lowther and Sir John Beckett, all looking well, and this morning I mean to call in Bruton Street.[2]

I reached London a week ago, but have been far too busy among my friends, and with my little concerns, to have had time to look at the papers, so that I know little about what is going on.

I conducted my Daughter to Rugby, and on Monday she goes to Leamington. She bore her journey wonderfully; so that we all hope her health will be restored.

I hope to be back in England in six months at the latest. My Companion is a retired Barrister, Mr Robinson, with whom I have travelled before.

And now, my Lord, let me express my deep sense of all your kindness to me and my family, of which I trust none of them will ever prove unworthy, and believe me faithfully

Your obliged
Wm Wordsworth

Mrs Wordsworth is now in Herefordshire, in attendance upon her Brother and his family, who are suffering from sickness, as I mentioned to Lady Frederick. My Sister is left under the care of a Sister of Mrs W.

1129. W. W. to WILLIAM STRICKLAND COOKSON

Address: W. Strickland Cookson Esq, Clayton & Cookson, Lincolns Inn.
Postmark: 20 Mar. 183[?7].
Stamp: S. Audley S^t.
MS. Cornell. Hitherto unpublished.

[19 Mar. 1837]

My dear Sir,

Will you be so kind as to answer this demand, just received. Does it not look like an unpromising business.

---

[1] For Lady Ann, Lord Lonsdale's third daughter, and her husband Sir John Beckett, the banker, see *MY* ii. 515.
[2] The residence of Col. H. C. Lowther.

As soon as the Master of Harrow's[1] consent is procured Miss F. will appoint a meeting

Faithfully yours
W Wordsworth

1130. W. W. to C. W. JNR.

Address: The Revd Christopher Wordsworth, Harrow.
Postmark: 29 Mar. 1837.
MS. British Library. Hitherto unpublished .

Paris Thursday Evening
March 23rd [1837]

My dear Chris,

Here we arrived a little after six yesterday afternoon, having left London, by steam-boat, on Sunday Morning. We were detained till between one and two on Monday at Calais, and obliged to stop at Samers, about six in the afternoon, it blew and *snew* so hard. Next morning the ground was white with *deepish* snow so that we got on slowly, through severe cold; but here we are, and I have been rambling about Paris the whole of the day, in a common Frock-coat, while 3 fourths of the persons one meets are wrapped from the heels to the upper lip in blue cloaks.

But now for business. I have a favour to ask of you which I trust it will give you pleasure to grant. You must know, but this is a secret and you must keep it, that my excellent and amiable Friend Miss Fenwick, who was kind enough to stand Godmother, for John's second son, named Wm Wordsworth, is desirous of placing £500 to accumulate for the purpose of his future education. She wished me to be a Trustee, but I declined on account of my advanced age. I have therefore to beg what would much gratify her, that you would act in my place. Three trustees are desirable and your Colleagues will be your Cousin Dora, and Mr Strickland Cookson, a Solicitor of Lincoln's Inn, who is a most excellent man, and a tried Friend. He will manage the business part, and it will be for you and Dora, to determine hereafter how the money can be best applied to answer Miss Fenwick's benevolent purposes. If this Child should die, it is Miss Fenwick's wish that the money with the accumulation

---

[1] C. W. jnr. The reference is to the trust fund set up by Miss Fenwick on behalf of her godson, which is described in the next letter.

377

upon [it]¹ should go to complete the education, of any other of John's Children, according to your judgement and Dora's.

Now as Miss Fenwick is anxious that this trust deed should be executed as soon as possible, I do request my dear Nephew that you would consent to act, and signify without delay your consent to Mr Cookson. His address is W. S. Cookson Esquire, Clayton and Cookson, Lincoln's Inn.

I should have written to you before I left London, but I knew you were moving about, and I was not made acquainted with Miss Fenwick's intentions till a couple of days or so before our departure.

The money will be placed in the funds, there to accumulate and to be applied as above stated. It was much more agreeable to Miss Fenwick that John should not know any thing of this; and for other reasons I think it best.

On Saturday or Monday, we depart for Lyons. We bought a carriage in London, and it promises well.

Farewell my dear Nephew, and remember me to all enquiring Friends, I need not say to your Father and Others. This is taken by Mr Moxon who came with us thus far, *and it will pass through Mr Joshua Watson's hands to whom I have written.*²

most affectionately Yours
W Wordsworth

1131. W. W. to ISABELLA FENWICK

MS. WL.
LY ii. 838.

Paris friday 24ᵗʰ March [1837]

My dear Miss Fenwick

To spare your eyes to save time I shall write journal-wise.— Arrived at Calais between nine and ten, after a passage sufficiently trying for those who are subject to sea-sickness. Poor Mr Moxon suffered greatly, I not at all; for I went to bed at 3— o'clock, and as advised by Mr Rogers closed my eyes. The next morning snow and chill blasts; detained at [? Parcs] by the

---

¹ *Word dropped out.*
² The words in italics have been erased by W. W.

Customs house, pass-ports, etc till half-past one. Snow fell so heavily that we could not get further than Samer and saw little of the country. Tuesday; snow heavy on the ground which obliged us to take, in one place, an additional Horse. The day and road improved, and we passed frequently through a pleasing Country of hill and vale; Montreuil strikingly placed upon a moderate eminence, Abbeville with its Cathedral still more agreeably in a Valley. But all this every body knows. The landscapes though often agreeable to look upon are almost every where disfigured more or less by long lines of threadpaper trees placed so near each other that they cannot but spindle as they do: multitudes of *lopped* trees, in lines by the way side, and the *pollards* where ever seen *all* so close together as to have no tops worth looking at. The peasantry appeared every where taller and stouter than those of England are in a great number of Counties; say Cambridgeshire, Herefordshire all Wales and many other parts. At the close of the long war they had become a dwindled race, the Conscription having swept away the flower of the Youth. They seem now greatly improved in strength and stature. Slept at Grandevilliers. Wednesday; severe frost, not a sign of Spring upon the trees; nevertheless small birds chirping among the bushes here and there, and one lark heard warbling aloft and soaring, as if he wished to get out of the frosty region through which we were travelling. We were much struck with the appearance of Beauvais and went into the Cathedral, many persons at Mass,[1] 10 women for one man, but men of all ages, and a few, a very few, boys.—The day was bright, and by walking up the hills often we contrived to keep ourselves warm, and were much pleased. Went into the Cathedral of St Denis, which has been undergoing extensive repairs. I am no critic in Architecture of any age or Country but I was much gratified with what I saw there. In a recess in one of the side aisles, some priests were engaged in some sort of service, one boy chanting, but none of the people present. Candles were arranged thus[2] and one might almost have thought that they were objects of worship; and a book, a large one was turned to and fro incessantly with the stand upon which it was placed, all this is no doubt well understood by Roman Catholics, but to an ignorant spectator, it has an air of mummery, form without spirit.—Walked on before the Carriage and almost reached

[1] It was the Wednesday of Holy Week.
[2] W. W. adds a drawing.

Paris before it overtook me. The variety of Voitures on the road, their shapes, and the pompous names of some of the public vehicles amused me much, while the rays of the setting sun made the clouds of dust glitter around those that took either side of the pavement. The pace of some was furious. I observed several horses slip on the pavement and then rear, but neither driver nor passengers seemed to care a jot about the matter.—I have nothing to say about Inns etc which would be useful to you, only don't embark at the Tower stairs in a *low-priced steamboat*. We had no choice, being so anxious to get on; but 5 shillings is a price so low as to tempt many persons of coarse habits and mean condition. You or any other Lady would have been annoyed, though a great part of our fellow voyagers were very respectable.—We paid 3£ for the freight of the Carriage.[1] It seems likely to answer our purpose well.—Observe also not to bring with you any clothes which have the appearance of being *new*. The man who rummaged my portmanteau, observed a plaid jacket, he turned it over to another, a tall person who would have been handsome if he had not taken so much snuff; *he* turned it over to a third, named the Inspector, who decided that I must pay ten francs for the entry of this precious piece of raiment into the Kingdom of France. I was *horrified*! assured the Inspector in the best French I could command, that the habit was made 10 months ago, and that I had worn it several times for half a day or so. 'Monsieur votre parole est *infiniment respectable* cependant l'habit est neuf', and he pointed to the collar in proof that he had a right to contradict me, though as politely as possible. Take care therefore that you dont get into the same sort of scrape, and have your veracity put to the same sort of test. The best way perhaps is to write one's name, if it be possible, on some part of the garment. I got off however without paying the fine.—What shall I say of Paris? Many splendid edifices and some fine streets have been added since I first saw it at the close of the year —91.[2] But I have had

[1] They had bought a carriage for the tour in London for £70.

[2] W. W. had spent a few days in Paris, 30 Nov.– 5 Dec., at the close of 1791, before going on to Orléans. The task of opening up and remodelling the ancient city had been begun soon afterwards by Napoleon, and several new avenues (including the Rue de Rivoli) were planned on church lands confiscated during the Revolution. These public works were continued under the Restoration. Among the new buildings only recently completed were the Arc de Triomphe and the church of the Madeleine.

little feeling to spare for novelties, my heart and mind having been awakened everywhere to sad and strange recollections of what was then passing and of subsequent events, which have either occurred in this vast City, or which have flowed from it as their source. Sat. morning—Yesterday, Friday, spent 7 hours nearly in rambling on foot up and down. The frost severe, the poor Swans in the basins of water in the Thuilleries gardens, hiding their bills and as much of their necks as they could among the pure white feathers of their wings: one pair were standing upon the ice, another couched upon the wooden platform in front of their little huts or kennels—The lions of the fountains spouted out vigourously their glittering waters, in striking contrast with their long beards of icicles.—Went to the Louvre. The old Pictures removed to make room for the annual exhibition of French art. We were sorry for this, as the new things gave us but little pleasure, though not uninteresting as shewing the present state of French art, which really does not seem to have much to boast of. The most impressive picture we noticed, has for its subject Lord Strafford kneeling down on his way to his place of execution to receive the benediction of Archbp Laud.[1] This is said to be purchased by the Duke of Sutherland;[2] he has done well—for the artist deserves encouragement. Here we met Lord Lyndhurst.[3] Mr Robinson reintroduced me. I had once been two or three days with him at Lowther; but he seemed neither to remember my name nor person, making a cold formal bow, as to a perfect Stranger. Is it that when raised in the world we have eyes and minds only for those above us? or that his Lordship did not catch my name, and had forgot my person? We then went to the Luxemburg, a number of French artists copying there pictures which had

[1] A painting by Delaroche, 'very well conceived', according to H. C. R.'s MS. Travel Diary for 1837, 'but Laud is a caricature, his hands stretched out of the prison over the victim. Neither seeing the other is a happy thought . . .' (*Dr. Williams's Library MSS.*). Paul Delaroche (1797–1856), the historical painter, completed 'The Earl of Strafford on his Way to Execution' in 1835. For Haydon's opinion of it, see his *Dairy* (ed. Pope), iv. 446.

[2] George Granville Leveson-Gower, 2nd Duke of Sutherland (1786–1861).

[3] Lord Lyndhurst had retired from the Lord Chancellorship with the fall of Peel in 1835, but he held the office again in Peel's second administration from 1841. W. W. had met him as Attorney General in Aug. 1826 (see pt. i, L. 246).

better be buried. Here remembrances pressed upon me, some tragical, and some my dear Mary and dear Sister (for this letter is intended also for you) of very different character. Do you recollect how pleased we were,[1] in the gardens of this palace, to see the Boys rolling and sporting and hiding themselves among the heaps of withered Leaves, as they do with us among haycocks? From the Luxemburg we went through a part of Paris that is very interesting to me, the fauxbourg, S[t] Germains to the Elysian fields. In the fauxbourg observed two splendid new Houses rising up among the forlorn Hotels of the extinct nobility. We were told these belonged to rich individuals. One would have thought these parvenus might have pleased themselves by purchasing some of the old Hotels of the nobility. But there are qualities enough in human nature to account for the preference of new to old independent of modern comforts.—Went on to the Longs champs to see the parade of equipages in which the French indulge themselves there on Good Friday. There were a few splendid ones—one of them with four horses belonging to the Duke of Orleans. We were told he was in the Carriage, and if there fearless, I hope, of assassins. What pleased me most was to see the number of shabby vehicles, hackney coaches, cabriolets etc, several of them crowded with children who seemed to enjoy themselves in spite of the severe cold. The triumphal arch which terminates the alley of the Longs champs is a grand structure, worthy of being the entrance of this city or rather of announcing your approach to it. But why does not modern art dress her France and her victories with their wrongs? Dined at a Restaurateur's after a walk of six hours without resting, and should have spent the Evening in writing Letters but I was afraid of hurting my eyes.—2 o'clock Saturday—Have been calling with Mr Robinson upon a friend of his.[2] He will be of great use in furnishing us with the signatures of all the Ambassadors for our pass-ports. This gentleman is high in the foreign office. He resides in rather a fashionable street and after mounting 92 steps we came into what proved a suite of commodious apartments elegantly furnished. He is a great collector and fashioner of illustrations for scarce and beautiful books, goes to the expense of eight

[1] During their visit to Paris in Oct. 1820. See *MY* ii. 641–7; *DWJ* ii. 330.
[2] An official named Feuillet. 'I read to him some of W.'s poems', H. C. R. noted, 'but he has no sense of their peculiar charm.'

pounds sometimes in binding a single V. He showed us Rogers's Italy embellished with 100 additional engravings; is illustrating my Poems, and has sent some of the Volumes (the present Edition) already to the Binder; one would be anxious to see what sort of embellishments he rakes together. Rogers's Italy is a much easier affair. But far more than with all his books was I pleased with his two Children, one a little fairy of a girl with dark hair curling about her temple and forehead, and the other a fine Boy of about twelve years. Allow me to say also, dear Mary, that the mother of these children had as sweet a countenance as one could wish to look upon, with features as handsome as any woman of sense need desire. Her Husband was a handsome man about forty years of age, and spoke of French Literature and particularly of Molière, La Fontaine, and Bossuet with much animation. More of this when I see you all. Now dont you think, this is a pleasing specimen of French life; humility and elegant luxury happily combined—humility in living 92 steps above the street door, and elegance in these pursuits of taste, which no one, I think, would be cynic enough severely to condemn. From this gentleman's house Mr Moxon and I went to Montmartre, for the sake of viewing the city. There was the gigantic triumphal arch far to the right, the columns of the beautiful church of the Madeleine below us, the dome of the Invalides, the house of one of the assemblies formerly the Hotel de Bourbon, the column in the place Vendôme with Napoleon in his bronze greatcoat and cocked hat on the top of it, and we saw nearly one half of the vast City in clear prospect; bridges river and all, the other half glimmered through smoke much thinner and lighter of course than ours, with a kind of ghostly indistinctness. We descended from the windmill, on which we stood, and looked back; there was the miller looking out of a square open window with his brown face, and cap as white as snow, not apparently at us, but upon the City, with the nonchalance of the Philosopher in Lucretius, who from the eminence of his wisdom regards the world and all its wanderers as something far beneath his anxieties.—Met soon afterwards, among the quiet Houses upon Montmartre, a Man and Woman decently dressed followed by a little rabble of 40 or 50 boys and girls between five and 6 years of age, all singing or making strange cries. Behind the pair of adults came a female with an infant in her arms; they had been baptizing it at a neighbouring church; and the small children were begging, or giving thanks for, small pieces of money liberally scattered among them; soon after passed a sweet little girl tripping down the Hill and singing to herself. I wished to know whether a Hymn or a chanson, but she was afraid of being asked, and stepped aside into a door. Entered an omnibus which was empty, and filled gradually: women of rather the upper class came in smirking, but a peasant girl sat down by my side with her embrowned face, and stiff and fixed features, as if they were not free to smile, at least in the dignified company of an Omnibus.—

I have written till my fingers are frozen, so good bye and God bless you all; if we can get our passports we shall set off tomorrow for Fontainebleau. I forgot to say that an Englishman, a foreman of Gagliani,[1] only confesses to the printing of 3,000 copies of my Poems, a very different story from what I had heard. These Printers however are destroying each other's trade by underselling, and Gagliani would be glad, he says, to have copyright extended to Foreigners.—Farewell once more.—Yours W. Wordsworth.

Dear Miss Fenwick, remember me most kindly to Mr Taylor, and beg him to forward this scrawl to Mrs Wordsworth. She will send it to Dora; pray supply all words that are missing, and turn what I have endeavoured to write into sense if you can. If you are so kind as to favor me with a Letter, address à Rome, poste restante—dearest Mary do you the same. I have written by Mr Moxon to the Master of Harrow.—I have attempted to read over this whole writing by candlelight, but in vain, so turn into sense if you can and think it worth while. God bless you, my dear Friends.

Postscript. I am ashamed of this scrawl, Dear Miss F.—send it to Mrs W. as soon as you are stopped by the vile penmanship.

[1] Galignani.

1132. W. W. to D. W.

Address: Miss Wordsworth, Rydal, Kendal.
Franked: London March twenty nine 1837 G. Grey.[1]
Postmark: 29 Mar. 1837.
MS. WL.
LY ii. 844.

Saturday Paris 25th March [1837]

My dearest Sister,

It is now near twelve at night and my eyes are worn out. I have only to say I have written at length to Miss Fenwick, to be forwarded to Mary and then to you, or perhaps first to Dora as nearest. We set off tomorrow for Fontainbleau on our way to Italy; how I wish your strength had been equal to the journey. I have seen the Baudouins[2] all well, a thousand kind inquiries after you. We reached Paris on Wednesday evening, and I have rambled about every where. God bless you and dear Joanna and kind remembrances to all the servants. And pray tell Mr Carter that I shall be greatly obliged to him, if he will correct the misprints of the Stereotype of the Yarrow and send the corrections up to Mr Moxon, who is desirous to strike off from the Stereotype thus corrected a new edition with the additional Poems of the last, for the purpose of accommodating the purchasers of the Edition of 1832.

farewell again farewell my dear Friends.

[*unsigned*]

---

[1] Sir George Grey (1799–1882), M.P. for Devonport (1832), Under-Secretary for the Colonies under Thomas Spring Rice (1834), Judge Advocate General (1839–41), and Home Secretary under Lord John Russell from 1846, a post he held for nearly twenty years. He franked this letter in London, Moxon having brought it over from Paris.

[2] According to H. C. R.'s MS. Travel Diary (*Dr. Williams's Library MSS.*), W. W. saw the Baudouins on 22 and 23 Mar., and again on the 26th.

1133. W. W. to DORA W.

Address: Miss Wordsworth, Mrs Hooks', Leamington.
Franked: London March twenty nine 1837 G. Grey.[1]
Postmark: 29 Mar. 1837.
MS. Cornell. Hitherto unpublished.

Paris
Saturday
twelve o'clock
at night
[25 Mar. 1837]

My dearest Dora,

You must have thought we were lost: I write now merely to tell you, we start tomorrow for Fontainebleau on our way to Lyons, and that I have written at great length what you will receive from your Mother, through Mr Stephen. We got here on Wednesday; and I have never rested since. To morrow in the Carriage we shall be quiet; as we mean to leave this place about 12 or one oclock.—I hope you take care of your health; I am well. Much love to Mrs and Miss Hook, and God Almighty bless you and grant us all a happy meeting. Mr Moxon came with us to Paris and will be the Bearer of this and all our other Letters. farewell again and again farewell.—

Your most affectionate Father
W Wordsworth

Pray beg of Mrs Hook to thank her son for the invaluable book[2] he sent me.—

---

[1] See previous letter.

[2] W. F. Hook, *Five sermons preached before the University of Oxford*, 1837 (see *R. M. Cat.*, no. 254). Dr. Hook (see pt. ii, L. 726) had dined at Rydal Mount the previous August, according to E. Q.'s MS. Diary. (*WL MSS.*)

1134. W. W. to CATHERINE CLARKSON

MS. untraced.
LY ii. 845.

Paris, Easter Sunday [26 Mar. 1837][1]

My dear Mrs Clarkson

I could not bring my mind to break in upon your grief after the sudden loss of your Son;[2] nor can I now quit Paris where Mr Robinson and I crossed last Wednesday, without a word of sincere and affectionate condolence, which in deep sympathy I offer to yourself and your afflicted Husband. The sad tidings were told me by our common friend Mr Robinson at his chambers. May almighty God support you and your husband through this and all trials that await the remnant of your days; and may he give his blessing to the widow now bereft of her support, and to their poor child!

Mr Moxon who has kindly accompanied us thus far, will be the bearer of this to London. We are going, God willing, as far as Naples. Farewell my dear friend,

Yours most faithfully
Wm Wordsworth

1135. W. W. to HIS FAMILY

Address: Mrs Wordsworth, Brinsop Court, near Hereford, Angleterre.
Postmark: (1) 8 April 1837 (2) 14 Apr. 1837. *Stamp*: Toulon-sur-Mer.
MS. WL.[3]
K (—). LY ii. 845 (—).

Toulon 8th April [1837]

My dearest Friends,

I will ask a few questions first. How are you dearest Mary in health—How is the pain in your chest and from the dropsical

---

[1] According to de Selincourt, who saw the MS., this letter was postmarked 28 Mar. But it was probably posted in London on the 29th by Moxon along with the two previous letters.

[2] Thomas Clarkson, jnr. had died on 9 Mar. after a carriage accident (see also L. 1124 above): he left a son Thomas (1831–72).

[3] Enclosed with this letter is one from H. C. R. to M. W., describing their itinerary.

swellings, and Dora! How is every one at Rydal Mount, you my dearest Sister, and Joanna and Isabella and all friends at Brinsop, and the servants, all friends, Mrs Luff Mr Carr Mr Carter etc and Mary in particular. Tell me about these things whatever you write. And write again à la Poste Restante à Rome. I should have written particulars at Lyons but for a horrid cold in my head and nose and eyes which I caught on crossing the mountain Tarare 3000 feet high between the country of the Loire and the Rhone. This cold quite blinded me with streaming eyes, and took away the strength of which I was so proud. I am now recovering, but I have not yet learned the art of managing myself as to eating and drink. The diet varies so much and the strength of the wine differs so much in different places, that I have suffered from headach; my wish would be to confine myself to milk with coffee or chocolate but milk I find binds the body; but no more of this, if anything serious happens to the health of either of my eyes I shall [? starve]. Upon the whole in despite of the coldness of the season such as has not been known for a century, we have had a great deal of enjoyment; but the annoyance has been great also. I will just mention what pleased me most. The day at Vaucluse,[1] where I was enchanted with the power and beauty of the stream, and the wildness and grandeur of the rocks, and several minor beauties which Mr R. has not noticed, and which I should have particularised but for this blinding cold. I was much pleased with Nismes, with Marseilles, but most of all with the drive between Marseilles and Toulon, which is singularly romantic and varied. From a height above Toulon, as we approached, we had a noble view of the purple waters of the Mediterranean, purple no doubt from the state of the atmosphere; for at Marseilles, where we first saw it, the colour was not different from the sea of our own Island. At Nismes the evening was calm, the atmosphere unusually clear, and the air warm, not from its own temperature, but from the effect of the sun. I there first observed the stars, as appearing brighter and at a greater variety of depths, i.e. advancing one before the other more than

[1] 'Wordsworth was strongly excited, predetermined to find the charm of interest, and he did. There is no verdure, but perhaps on looking more closely Petrarch may not have praised his retreat either for shady groves or meadows—and the stream of the Sorgues is eminently beautiful.' (*HCR* ii. 517).

they do with us.—I could mention a hundred little things that
have interested me, and all of which would have been recorded,
but for the bitter cold in my fingers, and streaming eyes.—One
of the few promises of summer which we have had is the peach-
blossom abundantly scattered over some parts of the country,
and very beautiful, especially when neighboured by the cypress,
a tree that is plentiful in this part of the south of France. We
cannot thus far have been said to be unlucky except in being
obliged to *post* from Lyons to Avignon instead of floating down
the Rhone which would have been delightfully done except for
the bad weather on one day and at less expense a good deal
whereas it took better than two days. Our Carriage has stood
the journey capitally; —Mr Courtenay gave us a calculation of
expenses thus, 180 days at 1 pound 1. £200; living expenses
(they don't amount to so much as we find); carriage duty etc
35—2500 miles travelling at 1 shilling per mile 125, but we shall
probably have to go much farther, perhaps 700 miles; extras 10
shillings per day 90 pounds, for unforeseen contingencies 50
pounds, in all 500—but for the one great mistake as to distance,
and barring serious accident to the carriage, or illness, this
calculating would somewhat exceed the requisite Sum.

We have escaped the Gripe by which 6000 people in
Marseilles alone have suffered, of the cholera we hear nothing. It
is rather fortunate that yesterday my 67th birthday was
decidedly the most impressive and agreeable since we left Paris
though no part of it equal to the two hours at Vaucluse and one
hour of Nismes. Vaucluse was to me worth 50 perusals.

[   ] to be able to say that I have learned the art of
managing myself as to diet [   ][1]

[*unsigned*]

1136. W. W. to D. W.

MS. WL.
K (—). LY ii. 847.

April 10th [1837]

My dearest Sister,
I sit down to write to you at the City of Nice where we
arrived two hours ago. You know that the place is celebrated for

---

[1] *MS. illegible.*

the softness and purity of its air but thus far we have rather seemed to be flying from the spring than approaching it. Yesterday we came from a place called Luc to Cannes. It snowed, it hailed, it rained, it blew, and lucky it is for you, notwithstanding the beauty of the country, that you were not with us. For in our half-open Carriage you would have perished with cold; our fingers were frozen so as to be almost useless. We passed by Frejus founded by Julius Caesar, and much enlarged by Augustus. It stands near the Mediterranean and abounds with Ruins and fragments of Roman antiquities; in particular, the remains of an amphitheatre and an Aqueduct. The road from Frejus towards Cannes is of an Alpine or rather Appennine character, mountainous and richly wooded with pines, which though none of them very large trees refreshed our sight much by a vast expanse of verdure (for the green was light-coloured), after being detained so long among the arid and bare hills and mountains which appeared to be almost everywhere spread over the south of France at least as far as we have seen it. The first fine spreading and climbing wood we saw was on the road between Marseilles and Toulon. It was of pines. I will not fatigue you with descriptions of scenery and Towns which would give you no distinct impressions, but will simply say that from Avignon by Nismes, Aix, Toulon, Marseilles etc to this place the face of the Country has much surpassed my expectations. The olive groves, when they first made their appearance, looked no better than pollard willows of bushy size; but they are now become trees, oftener a good deal larger than our largest hollies, though I have seen none so large as our best birch-trees. But they suffice to give a sylvan character to the whole Country, which was long wanting. Orange-trees also now occur frequently, in plots; and on entering this Town we first saw them with the fruit on, which on account of the severity of the winter is not good this year, being very sour. You can buy 12 in the street for three half-pence. At Cannes we saw the villa which, with a taste sufficiently odd, the owner of Brougham Hall is building there.[1] Beautiful and splendid as the situation is, I should much prefer Brougham hall, with its

---

[1] Brougham's career in public life had virtually ended in 1834, when he ceased to be Lord Chancellor. Early in 1835 he bought land at Cannes on which to build a villa.

Lowther woods and two flowing streams,[1] clear and never dry. Imagine to yourself a deeply indented bay like that;[2] on the right hand lofty mountains, and on the left hand, the ground sinking down into a low point of land, so as almost to meet an island upon which stands a fortress, famous as being the place where the Man of the *Masque de fer*[3] was confined. Such is the general description of the bay of Cannes. The Town lies behind the projection, under which I have placed a cross; that projection is of rock, and adorned with the ruins of a castle, with a church still in use, and also with some decayed buildings of a religious kind. Lord B.'s villa stands upon olive and orange groves that slope down to the Mediterranean, distant about a quarter of a mile or less, a narrow beach of yellow and smooth sand being interposed. Broken ground runs behind the house, scattered over with olive and other fruit-trees, also some pines; but the frost had sadly nipped the oranges, and their leaves were scattered pretty thick under the trees. If the dry channels of the ravines worn by the occasional floods were constantly filled with pure foaming water, and the rocks were of less crumbling material—they are a sort of sandstone—this situation would be enviable, and yet still it would want our oaks and birches, etc., as it does actually want the chestnut and walnut trees that adorn, as you know well, many parts of the north of Italy and Switzerland. Do not think I say too much of Cannes when I tell you that beyond the left or eastern horn of this bay, and near the Road leading to Antibes, which, as the Map will shew, is the next town on the road leading from Cannes to Nice, Bonaparte disembarked from the island of Elba. The Postilion pointed out the spot. Antibes is the frontier town of France; like all the Towns of which I have lately spoken except Aix, beautifully situated, Mountains in the distance, and the blue waters of the Mediterranean in front, and on one side. I am now writing on the 11th after a pleasant [walk][4] yesterday evening and another this morning before breakfast in the environs of Nice. My dear

---

[1] Brougham Hall stands near the confluence of the Eamont and Lowther rivers. [2] W. W. adds a drawing.

[3] Usually identified as Count Ercolo Antonio Mattioli (1640–1703), Senator of Mantua, and private agent of the Duke Ferdinand Charles, who was imprisoned for twenty-four years, first at Pignerol and finally in the Bastille, for deceiving Louis XIV in a secret treaty for the purchase of the fortress of Casale, the key of Italy.

[4] *Word dropped out.*

10 April 1837

Sister and all my dear Friends how I wish you could see it, it is so charming a neighbourhood. The Town like all these Towns almost stands in a deep bay and near the centre, where a river (large at some times if one may judge of its power from the width of its channel now almost dry) flows into the sea. As in the bay of Cannes there is a rocky projection such as I have marked crowned with forts etc that hides the Town of Nice from the harbour. The Town is richly decorated with Malls or public walks and built, in all that the stranger passing through it without stopping, is likely to see, in a stately not to say splendid style; but there are in it many streets and some half a mile in length almost that are not more than 4 yards wide. These are shady and cool; filled with the noise of artisans and the bustle of shops. This morning after having had my eyes dazzled with the sunshine and the glare of white streets and houses I was much refreshed by walking nearly half an hour in their long and cool vistas, for so I will call them. I said I would not tire you with descriptions and yet you have had nothing else. Tomorrow we shall take the road to Genoa, whence I hope to despatch this Letter, so I will say no more than that I am getting rid of the ugly cold in my head and also of something worse, a lameness in my right hip, as I once feared, dearest Mary, something like your sciatica; for I could not stoop or lean forward without sharp pain. It was brought on by sitting so many days in a *constrained* position in the carriage to make room for a Nightbag and a Carpet-bag, which I ought to have placed under my knees, where now I have put them, and find them to be no annoyance. The pain was brought on in this way and then it [?][1] till it became much worse by rash and hasty climbing among steep and slippery rocks for the sake of commanding points of view: this injury however is almost entirely passed away, so also I hope is one that Mr R. caught somewhat in the same way—a violent sprain in the ancle by slipping on a steep rocky descent—his ancle swelled instantly to the size of a hen's egg, but the sprain is doing well so no more of mishaps or infirmities. So farewell, all dear friends, till we have been a day or two at Genoa.—

God bless you all! It is now two o'clock at noon, my eyes as this Letter shews are much recovered from the effects of the cold in my head; but be you all assured, that in such a month as this,

[1] MS. *illegible.*

392

this cannot but be one of the most unhealthy spots in Europe, exclusive of those where malaria prevails. It is so hot and so cold, just as you happen to be in the sunshine or shade. Again Farewell.—

[*unsigned*]

1137. W. W. to D. W., M. W., and DORA W.

Address: Mrs Wordsworth, Mr Hutchinson's, Brinsop Court, near Hereford, Inghilterra.
Postmark: 13 May 1837. *Stamp*: London.
MS. WL.
K (—). *LY ii. 851.*

Rome Saturday 27th or 28^{th1} April [1837]

My dearest Sister, I begin with you because I wrote to you two sides and a half of close-penned lines from Nice on the 10th of this month, meaning to finish when I had been a day or two at Genoa; but I was prevented by a hundred causes. On Thursday afternoon we arrived at Rome, a Letter posted at Toulon will have told you of my proceedings to that place. The other, which I shall not send gave particulars of our journey to Nice Alps and over part of them to Genoa, so on to Massa then to Lucca and Pisa and by Volterra and Siena to Rome; where I confidently expected at least one Letter but found none. Today is a post day and if I do not hear from Mary I shall be certain there has been some mistake and I shall pass the next month nearly without the hope of tidings from any of you. From Paris I sent by Mr Moxon a double Letter to Miss Fenwick to be forwarded through Mr Stephen to Mary and then to Dora and you; where and how Mary and Dora are I cannot guess. Unluckily I said to Mary that, as Mr Stephen had requested, her Letter might be forwarded to him to save the English postage, whereas if this had not been [?]² and she had paid the postage to Rome, which must be done, surely I should have heard of you. Now I know not where to address this for a speedy answer, pray dearest Mary write the moment you receive this addressing to

---

¹ Saturday was the 29th.
² *MS. obscure.*

Rome. Hoping the best of you all here let me say that we have both been quite well since I threw off my cold; only as I fully expected my bowels, owing to mistiming, to heat of travelling, over-exertion sometimes or a want of choice in diet, have been rather too torpid but without the slightest inconvenience, only one does not like this to continue, and now that we shall be comparatively at rest for a fortnight or three weeks things will I trust be soon as I could wish.

We are most agreeably lodged in the Piazza d'Espagna, and while we stay here shall live at little expense, nothing at all indeed compared with that of travelling. I have been delighted with a hundred things since we left Toulon but I should be lost if I went into details. Mr Robinson does not return from the office so I have given up all hope of hearing from you. This is a most grievous disappointment, and I fear will sadly interfere with my enjoyment but I must bear it as well as I can. Dearest Dora where and how are you—I know nothing and tomorrow it will be six weeks since we left London. Of all things that I have seen at Rome the inside of St Peter's has most moved me. I have not yet been in the Vatican and have thus far contented myself with rambling under Mr R.'s guidance through the streets of Rome looking at few interiors except the four principal Churches, St Peter's of course being one of them. On Monday we shall go to the Vatican, and there examine the principal pictures, then make little excursions in the neighbourhood to Tivoli, Frascati, Albano, in short to see whatever is thought most worth seeing, and in the 4th week from this time at the latest we shall proceed either to Naples or turn our faces northward to Florence. I speak thus doubtfully because five or six cases of Cholera having appeared lately at Naples the Papal Government which is unusually strict has revived the Quarantine so that though people are free to go from Rome to Naples, they are not free to return. Nevertheless Mr Collins[1] the Painter and his family are going there on Monday having time at their command and no fear of the disease; neither have we but depend upon it if the quarantine be not taken off or mitigated, we shall, though to my infinite regret, give up Naples, and do as I have said. How much do I wish that you were all healthy strong and at liberty to pass the ensuing months with us here; nothing can exceed the

---

[1] For William Collins, R. A., see *MY* ii. 490—1. He spent two years in Italy at this time.

interest of Rome but though I have seen the Coliseum the Pantheon and all the other boasted things nothing has in the least approached the impressions I received from the inside of St Peter's.—Mr Francis Hare[1] has just called. We have seen Mr and Mrs Ticknor[2] and Sismondi[3] the Historian, his Wife and her two Sisters old acquaintances of mine, and dearest Sister one of them of yours when we were at Coat-How house, Mr John Wedgwood's near Bristol. They were rejoiced to see me. Miss Mackenzie[4] whose sister the Mr Mackenzie who was at Ambleside last summer married and took her name, has been very kind to us. She is an old Friend of Mr Robinson and is a great admirer of dear Chris.[5] But I will not trouble you about Persons, and were I to begin with things there would be no end. Notwithstanding a season of unprecedented severity, so severe that not a green leaf is to be seen scarcely or the promise of one, on any deciduous tree till we came near Rome, I have been enchanted with the beauty of the scenery in innumerable places,

[1] Francis Hare (1786–1842), elder brother of Augustus and Julius Hare and a close friend of Landor, lived in Italy. According to H. C. R.'s MS. Travel Diary (*Dr. Williams's Library*) it was on 11 May at Hare's table that W. W. saw Baron Bunsen (see L. 1063 above), whom he had already met on other occasions during this visit to Rome, and also Nicholas Wiseman (1802–65), the future Cardinal, at this time rector of the English College.

[2] George Ticknor, Professor of Spanish at Harvard and one of W. W.'s earliest American visitors (see *MY* ii. 504), had visited Rydal Mount with his wife on 1–3 Sept. 1835 (see L. 920a above). Thereafter they had travelled extensively on the Continent, arriving in Rome early in 1837; and it was here, on 27 Apr., at Miss Mackenzie's, that they renewed their acquaintance with W. W. They met again at Como, Venice, and Munich. See *Life, Letters, and Journals of George Ticknor*, i. 432–4; ii. 85–6, 97–9.

[3] Jean Charles Léonard Simonde de Sismondi (1773–1842), the Swiss historian, whose *Histoire des Républiques italiennes du moyen âge* was published in Paris in 16 vols., 1809–18 (English version, 1832). In 1819 he had married Jessie, daughter of John Bartlett Allen of Criselly, Pembroke, and sister-in-law of Sir James Mackintosh. Her sister Louisa had married John Wedgwood (see *EY*, p. 199), who was now a banker in London; and another sister, Elizabeth, married his younger brother Josiah (see *EY*, p. 213), who was M.P. for Stoke-on-Trent, 1832–5.

[4] Frances Mackenzie (d. 1840), younger daughter of Francis Mackenzie, Lord Seaforth: 'a woman of taste and sense, and the friend of artists,' according to H. C. R., who had met her in Rome in 1830. Her elder sister Mary married James Alexander Stewart (see L. 1062 above).

[5] C. W. jnr. had met her in Rome in 1833.

though almost in full as many there is a deplorable want of beauty in the surface, where the forms are fine. Speaking of the Apennines in contradistinction to the maritime Alps, for one scarcely can say where one begins and the other ends, I should say that, as far as I have seen, they are both in beauty and grandeur immeasurably inferior, often lumpish in their forms, and oftener still harsh, arid, and ugly on their surface; besides these mountains have an ill habit of sending down torrents so rapidly that the rivers are perpetually changing their beds; and in consequence the vallies, which ought to be green and fertile, are overspread with sand and gravel. But why find fault when much that I have seen is so enchanting. We had scarcely been two hours in Rome when we walked up to the Pincian hill, near our hotel; the sun was just set, but the western sky glowed most beautiful. A great part of the City of modern Rome lay below us, and St Peter's rose on the opposite side; and for dear Sir George Beaumont's sake I will mention that at no great distance from the dome of the church on the line of the glowing horizon was seen one of those broad-topped pines,[1] looking like a little cloud in the sky, with a slender stalk to connect it with its native earth. I mention this because a friend of Mr Robinson's whom we had just accidentally met told us that this very tree which I admired so much had been paid for by our dear Friend, that it might stand as long as Nature would allow. Mr Robinson not yet returned so no letters!—God grant that you may all be well. I do not send love and remembrances having so little space but give them to all friends or relatives at Brinsop, at London, at Rydal, at Keswick, at Ambleside, at Brigham and do not forget Dear Wm at Carlisle nor Miss Fenwick wherever she may be, nor the Arnolds; but what does all this avail? Give me credit for thinking and feeling as I ought being so far from you all. Dearest Joanna how are you? and my dearest Sister I trust you do not stick so close to your fire; and Dora are you improving and Mary are you strengthening and how are the Invalids of Brinsop? The other side of the sheet shall be left for Mr R.[2] It is

---

[1] See *The Pine of Monte Mario at Rome* (*PW* iii. 212, 493—4). The friend of H. C. R.'s, whom W. W. goes on to mention, was the sculptor William Theed, the younger (1804—91). He was a pupil of the doyen of Roman neo-Classical sculptors, Bertil Thorwaldsen (1768—1844), whom H. C. R. (and probably W. W.) visited at his studio on 17 May (Sadler, iii. 123).

[2] H. C. R. added a note to D. W., describing their journey: 'I have been gratified by finding that your brother has not postponed his journey too

now three o'clock and I am going to Dinner. We walked from 8 till eleven and I shall walk from half-past four to half-past seven. I feel quite strong except that sometimes I have an aching between the shoulders at the back of the neck such dearest Mary as I have heard you complain of. My eyes for them are wonderfully well as this letter written at a sitting will shew, and written after an hour's reading. Write instantly paying postage to Rome and not troubling yourself dearest Mary to send through Mr Stephen. God bless you all ever your affectionate Husband Brother and Father

[*unsigned*]

1138. W. W. to M. W. and DORA W.

Address: Miss Wordsworth, John Marshall Esq, Upper Grosvenor St, London, Inghilterra.
Postmark: 20 May 1837. *Stamp*: London.
MS. WL.
K (—). *LY ii. 854* (—).

[6 May 1837]
—This will be in London in eleven days.—
Saturday

My dearest Mary,

Yesterday put an end to my anxieties and depression of mind by bringing me your most welcome Letter of the 17th April with a postscript from Dora of the 19th. Mr Stephen had kindly sent it to the English ambassador which perhaps occasioned delay of a day or two but I believe I had been unreasonable in calculating so confidently upon an answer to my Toulon letter upon my arrival at Rome. I have therefore to beg your pardon for writing in such bad spirits as I did. Dearest Dora your mother speaks of a letter from yourself to me but I have not received it. How glad I was to have so good an account of your health, and most thankful to Drs Holland and Brodie and to all your kind friends for their goodness to you. I rejoice that you are in Town, thank Mrs Harrison[1] in my name with my best

long—he is not insensible to the beauties that have met us on every side—especially he seems to have been impressed by St. Peter's.'

[1] Probably Mrs. Benson Harrison.

love and give the same to one and all of the family with whom you are. I cannot feel sufficiently grateful to God for the good account of you all except your poor dear Cousin[1] at Brinsop, for whom there appears to be no hope. Of Sister and Joanna also the accounts are good to my heart's delight.—Your Letter took off such a weight from me as I cannot describe, for I feared I should have no news till your answer came to mine from Rome, which would have had to follow us to Florence, for there is not the least chance of our being able to include Naples in our tour, on account of the Quarantine. In the course of next week we shall go to Tivoli etc etc and 3 or 4 days after our return will suffice for Rome. You will naturally wish for details, but what can I select out of such a wilderness of sights antient and modern, though I have not seen a 100th part of the indoor attractions, not yet even the Vatican, to which we go on Monday under the guidance of Mr Gibson[2] the Sculptor. Several times however I have been at St Peter's, have heard Mass before the Pope in the Sistine Chapel, and after that seen him pronounce the benediction upon the people from a balcony in front of St Peter's and seen his Holiness scatter bits of paper from aloft upon the multitude, indulgences I suppose. Of the outside of Rome, and the ruins and the modern town, antient walls etc I have seen a great [? deal] both on foot, and in a carriage, for which latter accommodation we are indebted to the kindness of Miss Mackenzie[3] an old Friend of Mr R. and Sister-in-law to the Mr Mackenzie who with his son was at Rydal last summer. She is an amiable person and nothing can exceed her attentions. Mr Collier[4] also, an acquaintance of Lord Lowther, has accompanied me on two excursions in the neighbourhood, one to the Monte Mario which commands the most magnificent view of modern Rome the Tiber and the surrounding country. Upon this elevation I stood under the pine redeemed by Sir G. Beaumont, of which I spoke in my former Letter. I touched the bark of the magnificent tree and could almost have kissed it out of love for his memory. One of the most aggreeable excursions

[1] Mary Hutchinson, who was dying.

[2] John Gibson, R. A. (1790–1866), neo-Classical sculptor: protégé of Sir George Beaumont and pupil of Canova at Rome, where he had lived since 1817. See Sadler, iii. 120–1. H. C. R. and W. W. first met him on 2 May.

[3] See previous letter.

[4] The name occurs several times in H. C. R.'s *MS. Travel Diary*, but no further information about him or Mrs. Collier is forthcoming.

we have made was with Miss Mackenzie and Mr Collier to the Tomb of Cecilia Metella and the other antiquities in its neighbourhood. This was on the first of May. The air was clear and bright, and the distant hills were beautifully clothed in air and the meadows sparkling with rich wild flowers. In our ramble after alighting from the carriage we came to the spot which bears the name of the fountain of Egeria; but this is all a fiction, nevertheless the grotto and its trickling water and pendent ivy and vivid moss, have enough of Poetry and painting about them to make the spot very interesting independent of all adjuncts whether of fact or fiction. Dearest Dora say to the Miss Marshalls that I hope they will one day see most of what I have seen, particularly the Cornice Road and Rome and its neighbourhood; as to yourself, notwithstanding your own and your Doctor's good report I fear you will never feel strong enough to adventure so far. I do not think dearest Dora that you could stand it, and after all it is very trying at this season of the year, and through all the summer and in winter the weather appears to be often very rainy and what may be called bad. This morning we have been with Mr Severn[1] the Painter a friend of Keats the Poet. He has excellent health in Rome summer and winter; but his House stands clear of Malaria and how does he live in Summer? Why he is out in the open air at five in the morning with his Wife and children when she is well enough, returns at 7, paints all day and does not stir out again till an hour or so after sunset. But this sort of life you see ill suits anyone but a person with occupations like his. Upon the whole the weather since we came, or rather the state of the atmosphere, has not except upon the first evening of our arrival been favorable to landscape beauty. We have several times been out as early as six in the morning, but then the sun has too much power for beauty, and the evenings have all, since that one, been without fine nights. Of Villas and their gardens I have seen I can scarce tell you how many, some from the views they command of the city, old and new, very impressive. But of churches and

---

[1] Joseph Severn (1793–1879), the artist, whom W. W. had met many years before in London at Haydon's house at the close of 1817, when Keats and Leigh Hunt were also present. (See William Sharp, *Life and Letters of Joseph Severn*, 1892, p. 33.) Severn had accompanied Keats on his last journey to Italy, and thereafter had settled in Rome, where H. C. R. had seen him in 1830. W. W. and H. C. R. met him first on 29 Apr. On 12 May he escorted W. W. round the Vatican Galleries. See also *HCR* ii. 520.

pictures and statues in them I am fairly tired—in fact I am too
old in head, limbs and eyesight for such hard work, such toiling
and such straining and so many disappointments either in
finding the most celebrated picture covered up with curtains, a
service going on so that one cannot ask to have a sight, or the
church closed when one arrives at the door. All this will
however be forgotten long before I get back to dear England
and nothing but the pleasure, I hope, survive. The only very
celebrated object which has fairly disappointed me on account
of my ignorance I suppose is the Pantheon. But after all it is not
particular objects with the exception perhaps of the inside of St
Peter's that make the glory of this City; but it is the boun[d]less
variety of combinations of old and new caught in ever varying
connection with the surrounding country, when you look
down from some one or other of the seven hills, or from
neighbouring eminences not included in the famous seven.
Tomorrow we are going into the Campagna to see a sheep-
shearing upon the farm of a wealthy Peasant who lives in that
sad and *solemn district*, as I believe it is around his abode, which
lies about four miles along the Appian Way. And there this
hospitable Man dwells among his herds and flocks with a vast
household, like one of the Patriarchs of old.—

I write with watering eyes; caused I think by the glare of the
sun, but some tell me it is a slight touch of influenza. I wish it
may and then it will go off. The influenza has been travelling
with me or rather I with it since I left Rydal. I found it in
London in Paris every where in the south of France and even
greatly prevalent in Rome though abating. I should not have
mentioned my eyes, but to account for this penmanship even
more wretched than usual—nor should I have written today but
to beg you to direct to Florence, 'poste restante', and remove
your regret at my not having heard from you before. Your
Letter, Dearest Dora may be forwarded instantly through Mr
Stephen to the Minister at Florence, so I should suppose, but that
you can ascertain through Mr Taylor or himself and if there be
any doubt of the elegibility of that mode of conveyance,
notwithstanding the postage, pray write instantly by post, à la
Poste Restante or as you may learn to do best, for I believe in
some parts of the continent the post off: will not charge itself
with Letters so directed. This however is not the case at Rome.
If you can send through the Minister so much the better, pray
write instantly without waiting for Mother's reply to this and

even if you cannot send through her write by the Post. Say if the Master of Harrow undertook the off:[1] and tell me all the news you can of our Friends. I fear the legacy story is too good to be true. We live for nothing almost here, but travelling Post is for one cause or another more expensive than we were led to expect. Here comes Mr Robinson to whom I resign the Pen.[2]

With love and blessings to all. W. W.

1139. W.W. to HIS FAMILY

Address: Miss Wordsworth, J. Marshall's Esq., Upper Grosvenor St, London, Inghilterra.
Postmark: 3 June 1837. *Stamp*: (1) Albano (2) London.
MS. WL.
K (—). *LY ii. 858* (—).

Albano—Friday May 19th [1837]

My dearest Friends,

It is just three weeks and two days since we reached Rome, and on Tuesday next we shall leave it to take the road for Florence. Since my last I have worked hard to see the most remarkable things in Rome and its immediate neighbour-hood—Churches, Palaces, Villas, Ruins, Eminences—not Cardinals, though I have seen numbers of these, but command-ing points of view, and all these with very great pleasure, and only one drawback—the never-wanting proof that I am rather too old for such *excessive* exertions, and that my bodily strength is diminished within the latter part of these labours. But my health thank God continues very good, so I have every reason to be thankful. We have passed a day at Tivoli with much enjoyment, and another at the Shepherd's hut in the Campagna. On Wednesday we came to this place, went the same evening to see the neighbouring Lake of Albano, and yesterday made a Tour round its sister lake or rather Volcanic pool of Nemi. The day was charming for our purpose, though every body here cries out against the weather as worse than ever was known, for 200 years, at this season. That excellent Creature Miss Macken-zie brought us hither in her Carriage, and we are lodged in the

---

[1] The trusteeship mentioned in L. 1130 above.
[2] H. C. R. added a few lines.

same Hotel. Our intention is to return to Rome on Sunday, and as I have said leave it on Tuesday morning. Today we shall ascend Monte Cavo if the weather which is but lowering will permit, and on our journey back to Rome we mean to visit Frascati, Grotto Ferrata[1] etc.—I would gladly single out from what we have seen something the description of which might interest you, but I seem to have little talent for dealing with objects so new to me and with impressions in every respect so different from what others receive. Of adventures we have had none; of persons we have seen not many, and these chiefly English Artists who by the by seem to live at Rome on very good terms with each other. One of them Mr Severn, the Friend of Keats the Poet, has taken my portrait,[2] which I mean to present to Isabella. I fear you will not, nor will she, be satisfied with it, it is thought however to be a pretty good likeness as to features, only following the fact, he has made me look at least 4 years older than I did when I walked 7 hours in Paris without resting and yet without fatigue. Mr Severn this Monday had one of his children christened[3] in one of the villas near Rome, Miss Mackenzie was Godmother, I attended and after dinner an Italian Gentleman, who had sung several charming airs, Roman, Neapolitan, Milanese and Venetian, recited a Poem which he had composed in Italian to my honor—I shall bring a copy of it to England. At Miss Mackenzie's where most of our evenings have been past, I saw a young Italian Lady, who was so struck with my resemblance to her deceased Father that, as she told Miss Mackenzie afterwards, she had been unable to suppress her feelings and had retired and burst into tears.—

We are told that the cholera if existing at all at Naples need not be regarded; but the quarantine we both dislike so much that we keep, as I have said, to our resolution, and to tell you the truth I am not sorry to be so near the time of turning my face

[1] i.e. Grottaferrata, on the lower slopes of the Alban Hills. The Basilian abbey, a centre of Greek learning in Italy, was noted for its Byzantine frescoes and mosaics.

[2] This portrait of W. W., seated and holding an umbrella, arrived in Grasmere in August, and received fairly favourable comment from the family (see *MW*, p.177). It was duly given to Isabella W. and passed from her to her son William, but it subsequently disappeared (see Blanchard, *Portraits of Wordsworth*, p. 163).

[3] According to Sheila Smith, *Against Oblivion*, 1943, p. 159, W. W. stood as godfather to the child.

homewards; for the Tour of Italy is too much to be taken in less than 8 months unless a person be young and very strong. The country is inexhaustible for those who are well read in antient story and classical Poetry, and its natural beauty tempts you to exertion in every direction. Of the character of the people I can scarcely speak but by hearsay; for one's own transient observations often only serve to mislead one, at least it very often happens so—for instance, yesterday, in passing through the romantic little Town of Nemi, that crests with its picturesque towers and roofs a steep and lofty [? hill] on the shores of the lake of Nemi, I was grieved to see not less than 20 stout men lounging together in a small square about two o'clock. What a sad state thought I must these people be in, either without work of if they have it, too idle to turn to it. In the evening I learned from an intelligent Italian Physician who called on Miss M. that from about the middle of May to the middle of July the peasants of these little Towns and Villages rise at one or two o'clock in the morning, sometimes at midnight, and work in their vineyards till 8, and pass the middle of the day in chatting together or amusing themselves at some game or other. They go to work so early because when the Sun becomes powerful as the morning advances young shoots and buds of the vine would be injured by rubbing their clothes against them or touching them I suppose in any way. The spot from which I write is surrounded with romantic beauty and every part of it renowned in history or fable. The lake of Nemi is the celebrated Speculum Dianae, and that of Albano is still more famous as you may read in Livy the Historian. The window of the room from which I am writing has a fine view of the Mediterranean in front. The house was formerly a palace of the King of Spain, in the court below is a fountain, water spouting from the mouths of two lions into the same basin. Thence descends a flight of steps 80 in number, into a large Italian garden; below that the ground falls in a slope thickly set with olives vines and fruit trees, then comes a plain or what looks like one with plots of green corn, that look like rich meadows, spreading and winding far and wide, then succeeds a dusky marsh, and lastly the Mediterranean Sea. All this is part of the antient Latium the supposed kingdom of Æneas which he wrested, along with the fair Lavinia, from Turnus. On the right, a little below the Hotel, is a stately grove of Ilex belonging to the Palace or Villa Doria. This neighbourhood did till lately abound in magnificent trees

403

oaks and elms and others; some of these survive but a Laurel, about a mile hence, [?] be felled, to meet the gaming propensities of a Duchess, I believe the wife of their [?].[1] I must now think of concluding. At Florence no doubt I shall have a letter; *immediately* on receiving this do you dearest Dora, if in London, write to me at Milan by Post; and you dearest Mary write within a week after you receive this to me at Venice (poste restante both places). I shall write again as soon as I get your expected letter at Florence. Dearest Sister and Joanna I hope you are going on well, this letter is for you if you can read it. Give my love to everyone, I name no one for I have no room; but I think of you all a thousand times a day and often wish I were back again at dear Rydal.—From Milan we shall go to Como and, for the sake of old times, take the steamboat up to the head of the Lake, returning by it the same day. But farewell and God bless you all; when you write to Miss Fenwick say with my love that sometimes I am tempted to wish I had put off my journey to winter quietly with her at home. But this seems ungrateful, as I have had so much pleasure.

Wherever you may be remember me affectionately to the Marshalls one and all.—

My eyes are again in their best way.

Pray tell me above all about your health all of you.

[unsigned]

1140. W. W. to DORA W.

Address: Miss Wordsworth, Mrs Gee, Hendon.
Postmark: 12 June 1837. *Stamp*: Charles Sᵗ Westʳ.
MS. WL.
LY ii. 861.

Wednesday 30th May[2] [1837] Florence

'Vallombrosa I longed in thy shadiest wood
To linger reclined on the moss-covered floor!'[3]

This longing was fulfilled yesterday. We left Rome Tuesday

---

[1] *MS. illegible.*   [2] Wednesday was the 31st.

[3] The opening lines of *Stanzas, Composed in the Simplon Pass* from *Memorials of a Tour on the Continent, 1820* (*PW* iii. 189). W. W. imagines himself following in the footsteps of Milton, who is reputed to have stayed at

last, as my letter from Albano posted there on the Saturday before said we should do, and after three diversions to each of the three great Tuscan Sanctuaries as they are called, viz Laverna, Camaldoli, and Vallombrosa we reached Florence at six yesterday evening having given a week to the journey. This is the 30th of May and this morning I have been at the post-off: where to my infinite mortification I find no Letter from anyone. I then went to the English Minister but was told that I could not see his secretary till half-past 12. Thither I shall go again, but with the faintest or rather no hope as my direction to you was that Letters forwarded through Mr Stephen should be 'poste restante'. Ten weeks have I been from England (we left London on the 19th March) and only have received one Letter. You cannot conceive how this disturbs my mind and darkens my spirits; and not the less so because I believe it to be in a great degree my own fault. On leaving England I ought to have said, write me every 12 days so and so, in succession, naming the places, according to my best conjecture as to where we should reach, and how long we should remain in them. Well let me hope the best, and keep my thoughts as quiet as I can. Here we shall stay six days, we thought ten, but visits to the three monasteries were included in that calculation and these we have already taken in our way. Now to resume from the point of my Albano Letter. We were there 4 days but during two the weather was so bad that we could do nothing, and accordingly left Frascati and Tusculum etc unseen. We however saw the best things, namely, went to the top of Monte Cavo, the antient Mons Albanus, and thoroughly explored the immediate neighbourhood of the two lakes Albano and Nemi. The journey from Rome hither has been a succession of delights. The Country beautiful and the weather favorable. Of the things which charmed me most I will mention Nervi, the fall of Terni, much the most impressive waterfall I ever saw, Spoleto and its neighbourhood, Perugia, the drive up the Arno to Beviena on our way to the Convent of Laverna, and along the banks of the same river towards Camaldoli, Laverna itself, Camaldoli and Vallombrosa, all of which retreats are deserving of their high reputation, and lastly Florence itself, the external appearance of which has been praised as much as it deserves. I should like to

the monastery in Vallombrosa in 1638 (see William Riley Parker, *Milton, A Biography*, 2 vols., Oxford, 1968, ii 825)

enter into the details of many of these things but it would be endless and I reserve particulars till my return; only I will tell you that I spare no pains, for example, yesterday I was on *Horseback* at five in the morning! to go to Vallombrosa, with a man on foot as my Guide. Mr R. judiciously declined going as he had visited the place at leisure six years ago. The distance from my starting place Ponte Sieve [1] is nine miles, 4 or more of steep ascent up a lofty mountain. As we ascended I looked back on the long winding vale of Arno, in several reaches of which the river and its banks were hidden by the vapours that had risen from it, and we proceeded first through vine and olive yards then through groves of oak and chestnut up and down for several miles. My Guide unfortunately was fond of short cuts, and took one of these against my wish, and pursued the path contrary to my advice, till it was lost in the thick wood and wholly ceased. Here I was obliged to dismount and we foundered about for a considerable time, at last by aid of a man who was attending one of the Charcoal pits, we regained the road; and after three hours of pretty hard labour for man and horse reached the Convent; where I was conducted by a Monk about the Church and the library, and shown a specimen of the chambers of the Monks and everything deemed interesting in the Convent. I was then furnished with a guide, and explored for two hours the holy places in the surrounding woods. Vallombrosa is somewhat improperly named, for in fact it is no valley at all, the place where the Convent stands, but rather what we should call a cove, or small level place on the side of a steep and lofty mountain, by the side of a torrent not very large which immediately behind the convent throws itself down a precipitous rock; and hurries on down what we should call a Ghyll into a deep yet rapidly declining mountain valley richly clothed in chestnut woods. Immediately surrounding the convent pine trees grow in abundance, with a few beeches and chestnuts, but right above these pine trees grow woods of beech and spread along a region in which snow is lying. It is remarkable that both at Camaldoli and Laverna also beech trees grow upon the loftiest ground, as if they were hardier than pine trees, which does not seem to be the case among the Alps. About half past three I returned to Ponte Sieve having had a good dinner at the Convent where I left according to custom a small

---

[1] Pontassieve.

sum for the *poor*. The hot weather has at last set in; and the deciduous trees are looking green but not the oaks in the lofty situations where we have been nor the chestnuts in the loftiest. In ascending to Laverna, among the sternest solitudes of the Appennines I first heard the cuckoo; Mr R. had heard it the day before. Then also I saw primroses and daisies blooming side by side, and the same at Camaldoli, in which spot primroses will be found I should suppose a week hence. One of the great pleasures of our tour has been that passing through so many elevations of Country we have had the spring renewed upon us repeatedly. The white thorn and the broom have greeted us in full blow over and over again during the last eight weeks. And now I must quit my pen to go again to the English Minister—oh that I may have a Letter. This morning I read Talfourd's admirable speech upon copyright[1] in which he makes honorable mention of me. Adieu my dearest Friends!—

[1] Talfourd had introduced his Copyright Bill in a major speech in the House of Commons on 18 May. Its main provision was to increase the duration of copyright to sixty years following an author's death. His speech had included an eloquent tribute to W. W.: 'Let us suppose an author, of true original genius, disgusted with the inane phraseology which had usurped the place of poetry, and devoting himself from youth to its service; disdaining the gauds which attract the careless . . . not seeking to triumph in the tempest of the passions, but in the serenity which lies above them—whose works shall be scoffed at—whose name made a by-word—and yet, who shall persevere in his high and holy course, gradually impressing thoughtful minds with the sense of truth made visible in the severest forms of beauty, until he shall create the taste by which he shall be appreciated—influence one after another, the master spirits of his age—be felt pervading every part of the national literature, softening, raising and enriching it; and when at last he shall find his confidence in his own aspirations justified, and the name which once was the scorn admitted to be the glory of his age—he shall look forward to the close of his earthly career, as the event that shall consecrate his fame and deprive his children of the opening harvest he is beginning to reap. . . . This is no imaginary case—I refer to one who . . . has opened a vein of the deepest sentiment and thought, before unknown—who has supplied the noblest antidote to the freezing effects of the scientific spirit of the age—who, while he has detected that poetry which is the essence of the greatest things, has cast a glory around the lowliest conditions of humanity, and traced out the subtle links by which they are connected with the highest—of one whose name will now find an echo, not only in the heart of the secluded student, but in that of the busiest of those who are fevered by political controversy—of William Wordsworth.' The Bill proceeded to a second reading, but lapsed with the dissolution of Parliament following the death of William IV.

1 o'clock—I am just returned from the Minister Mr Abercrombie[1] to whom I sent in a slip of paper with these words 'Mr Wordsworth will be greatly obliged to Mr Abercrombie if he will let him know whether any letters for Mr W. have lately arrived under cover to Mr Abercrombie'. The answer by an Italian servant was none—and now I must go by appointment to feast upon one of the Galleries with what appetite I may—I have only to add, that spite of all my gratifications I shall be heartily glad to be in England as speedily as I can, having seen what is proper to see—Venice will be the last spot in Italy, thank God, where we shall be detained. I never was good at sightseeing, yet it must be done. Dearest Sister how I wish I knew how you are and you Dora are you improving and you Mary and how is Joanna and the fireside of Brinsop and how are John and Isabella and their little ones and Wm?—I have brought away from Rome a small portrait[2] of myself for Isabella.

Thursday morning June 1st—I have been again at the post-off: but no Letter and I am quite at a loss how to direct this; whether to you dearest Dora at Mr Marshall's to all of whom present my love, or to your mother at Brinsop. If you be, Dora, with Mrs Hoare give my love to her and Miss Hoare and to the Master of Harrow of whom I often hear. For example yesterday Mr Ingram[3] you may tell him inquired very cordially after him. Everybody seems glad of the fine weather as they call it and so it is but I have been better pleased with the unseasonable cold and wet, on account of my eyes which till yesterday have been for some time in their very best way. But yesterday dazzling sun and two unlucky hours of lamp and candle light at Mr Hare's, who is on his way to Munich, have put one of them into an irritated state. The health of both of us is good. Much as I am pleased with this place, for I have had a walk this morning as I had one of two hours on the banks of the Arno yester evening, I long to be on the move to bring me nearer to you all. Let your

[1] Raph Abercromby (1803–68), later 2nd Baron Dunfermline: British Minister at Florence, 1835–8.

[2] Severn's portrait (see previous letter).

[3] 'An old Roman acquaintance' of H. C. R.'s: 'an old Whig', who had engaged in controversy with Henry Phillpotts, Bishop of Exeter (see pt. ii, L. 722), when the latter was rector of Stainton-le-Street, Durham, about the grounds on which the Church of England had separated from the Church of Rome.

next be written instantly to Venice poste restante, paying what is required and ten days after at the latest write to me again directing to Salzburg, Germany; if this Letter should be long in reaching any of you still write to Venice, for both there and at Milan directions will be left at the post-off: for forwarding the Letter. As we shall remain here 5 or 6 days I shall hope to hear from you—then please tell her on Tuesday next at the latest a day will take us hence to Bologna then we go by Modina, Reggio, Piacenza, Pavia, Milan where a day by steam up the Lake, Lecco, Bergamo, then we shall see the lakes of Isea, and Garda, Brescia, Verona, Padua, Venice where we mean to stop a week or so then for Trieste, Innsbruck, Salzburg, the Austrian lakes near it, then Munich, and so to Heidelberg and London. How I long to hear from you—farewell one and all, dearest Mary I hope you have taken every possible care of your health and that you Dora are going on well and Sister and Joanna but all this I said before. Mr Robinson sends his love, again and again farewell.

[*unsigned*]

1141. W. W. to DORA W.

Address: Miss Wordsworth, Hendon. [*readdressed to*] Marshall's Esqᶜ M. P., Upper Grosvenor Street.
Postmark: (1) 19 June 1837 (2) 20 June 1837.
Stamp: Charles Sᵗ Westʳ.
MS. WL.
LY ii. 865 (—).

Sunday 4ᵗʰ June [1837] Florence

A thousand thanks dearest Dora for your most welcome [letter], which I received two or three hours ago. My anxiety to hear from England had depressed my spirits so that I scarcely enjoyed any thing; and now your long Letter has made me quite easy and comfortable. I delight to hear that you are gaining strength, and that Mother has got back to Rydal, where she found Sister and Joanna so well. Poor dear Mary H.[1] though you do not say so, is I conclude no more. God bless her innocent

---

[1] Mary Hutchinson had died on 27 Apr. (see *MW*, p. 156).

spirit—I loved her much. Mother's health you do not mention but I hope she strengthened—I shall be grateful to hear that she had taken the Baths at Leamington; my anxious thoughts about her symptoms have haunted me sadly since I left home. And now dearest Dora let me talk about meeting and the thought I have that we may return together to Rydal. Your visit to [? Taring],[1] and afterwards to the Coleridges,[2] will detain you till we shall be so far on our way home that I trust it will suit you to wait for me; and I often think with delight of our visiting Lord Bacon's tomb[3] at St Albans together on our way home; we taking our places by the Manchester Telegraph and being taken up at St Albans at 7 next morning as Mr Graves and I were when dear Mr Rogers was so kind as to accompany me so far on the way. I wrote on my arrival at this place last Wednesday—but was quite uncertain how to direct—I think in my eagerness to hear from you I did wrong to beg of you in my letter from Albano to write to Milan—There will I fear not be time but your letter will follow us to Venice where labour and pleasure, which have both been great (the labour for me, though nothing for my companion whose strength is wonderful). Since my last on Wednesday or Thursday I have been incessantly employed in visiting Churches, Galleries and spots in the neighbourhood that command views of Val d'Arno and the city which I find to be a most charming place, and one that for a residence is preferable to one [?   ][4] so, unless one's purse were so full as to make money no object. Everything here is within comparatively easy reach, Libraries, Galleries and the country. Yesterday I walked to a point called Bello Sguardo, as the name implies it commands a splendid prospect. Our Companion was a Gentleman Mr Spence[5] who has married a lady of Florence and he took a villa upon this point. It is roomy and elegant quite private, with a garden coachhouse etc and he pays only 12 pounds a year for it, using it only in the summer months. I ought to add that he has it at this price ready furnished, though he says

[1] MS. *obscure.*
[2] i.e. Sara and Henry Nelson Coleridge in Hampstead.
[3] In St. Michael's Church.
[4] MS. *faded.*
[5] William Spence, F. R. S. (1783–1860), entomologist and economist, whom H. C. R. had got to know in Rome in 1830 (see Sadler, ii. 486): author of *Britain Independent of Commerce*, 1807, and (with William Kirby) of *An Introduction to Entomology* (see pt. i, L. 288).

not very well. His fuel during the whole winter cost him 50 shillings, so that with 300 a year a Man at Florence might live quite in style! and with 800 like a prince. The evening before we were at a hill on the opposite side of the vale—Fiesole mentioned in the first book of the Paradise Lost, and this evening though I have been out 4 or 5 hours I shall go to the Cascina, the public evening walk and drive of the Inhabitants; where I suppose I shall be in the midst of a few acquaintance I have either met or made at Florence. Yesterday at Mr Hare's I met Lady Susan Percy,[1] her brother Charles, both Coleorton acquaintance, and two days before Lord Charles Hervey[2] whom I had known in London. He is an intimate Friend of the Master of Harrow. By the by I have not yet learned whether dear Miss Fenwick's [*erasure in MS.*] Do not fail dearest Mary to write to her and give her my love, saying how often I wished that we had been together at Rome. Of this be assured that I never shall go from home for any time again, without a female companion. My evenings would have been very dull at Rome, if it had not been for dear Miss Mackenzie, to whom I became quite affectionately attached as I believe she did to me. You know I cannot read by candle-light, so that without her house to go to I must have gone to bed every night at nine.—

Monday morn. So I did last night and have got up before five this morning to finish my Letter. I was much grieved dearest Dora to hear so unpromising an account of your Uncle Thomas's future recovery[3] and poor Mrs Lockhart![4] I had read her death in the Newspaper for which I had been in part prepared, as Dr Ferguson[5] her physician told me in London that her constitution which had always been a bad one was dreadfully impaired. Her poor Father would have deplored her

---

[1] Lady Susannah Percy (d. 1847), younger sister of George, 2nd Earl of Beverley and 5th Duke of Northumberland, and of Dr. Hugh Percy, the Bishop of Carlisle. Lord Charles Percy (1794–1870) was their youngest brother.

[2] Lord Charles Hervey (1814–80), fifth son of the 1st Marquess of Bristol (see pt. ii, L. 696): a friend of C. W. jnr.'s at Trinity, 1833–6, and rector of Chesterford, Essex, from 1839.

[3] Thomas Hutchinson had been crippled after a riding accident (see L. 1117 above).

[4] For Mrs. Lockhart's fatal illness, see L. 1123 above. She was Sir Walter Scott's eldest daughter, and had married J. G. Lockhart in 1820.

[5] For Dr. Ferguson, see L. 1030 above.

loss bitterly. I have spent my time very pleasantly at Florence; it is so much less fatiguing a place than Rome; but even here one has to *waste* a great deal of labour in sight-seeing on account of Churches and Galleries being closed when you expect them to be open. Yesterday I had no less than three pretty long walks which turned to no account—the places being shut up, though I was under the guidance of an Italian who lives in Florence.[1] In the afternoon we had an awful thunderstorm and heavy rain; it cleared up and I went to the Public Drive where I saw most of the fashionables of Florence; more than one half of them I thought English. The ride is under trees and the ground is very damp. This place I am told is very injurious to health and often avoided by the Florentines, at times when the English crowd thither to the great benefit of the purses of their physicians. Florence you know lies low in a valley which widens a good deal below the City, but the bases of the hill immediately opposite are not more than a mile and a half apart. This makes the air sometimes intensely hot, and no doubt it must often be very cold on account of sweeping winds. Everybody complains of a great change in climate in Italy within the late few years. Mrs Landor,[2] who was visited yesterday at Fiesole by Mr Robinson and called in her carriage to give us an airing or rather as it proved a damping in the Cascina says they have had eight months winter here, a strong expression but really though we have had very hot *hours* to encounter while we have been in Italy, some parts of the day, particularly the evenings, have been so chill that a fire (by the way the Italians are quite afraid of fires) would have been almost always agreeable. I do not suppose I shall have time to fill the remainder of the sheet, as I have to go to the great Gallery for the last time and to several other places, and shall have much to do in preparation for our departure before five tomorrow morning, as we mean to go through to Bologna in one day—a long journey.

[1] Enrico Mayer, who had taken W. W. and H. C. R. to the Santa Croce on 1 June, 'a church of great interest, from the noble characters whose monuments adorn it—Galileo, Dante, Michael Angelo, etc.' (Sadler, iii. 127–8). W. W. was to meet Mayer again in 1839. See L. 1331 below.

[2] H. C. R. had offered to call on Mrs. Landor in the hope of healing the breach between her and her husband. 'Mrs Landor is certainly a very weak woman, but I think respectable in her conduct. My suspicions on this head are removed, and I have no doubt her provocations have been very great indeed.' (*HCR* ii. 523.)

4 June 1837

I am not surprized at the effect of Sergeant Talfourd's speech [1] which I had read at length in the Times. It is judiciously and eloquently done, and I trust it will produce its effect, and that you all, my dear Children, may derive some little benefit from the measure it will lead to, after I am gone. The notice the Sergeant kindly took of me may excite some envy and spite, but upon the whole it will tend to swell the stream of my reputation and so widen the circulation of my works; for the good of readers I hope and also for Mr Moxon's sake, for I shall be delighted when he gets his money back. Do not my dearest Dora be hurt at your Uncle's [2] coldness—I called him the bad Brother, he gave me so little of his time, not more I think than twenty minutes at the very utmost when I saw him in town. It is their way, and we must make allowance, taking people as they are. My dearest Mary how I long for a line from you, and a few words from my poor Sister, how is she about her fire and does she complain of her 'struggles' as formerly? Pray remember me to everyone in our household in particular and to the neighbours, to Mr Carr, the Dowlings, Mr Robinson, [3] Mrs Robinson, Mrs Luff, the Cooksons one and all, in short say I forget nobody. Travelling would agree well with me if I had not quite so much to do at the places I come to and could keep free of constipation of the bowels which is impossible without using more medicine than I like. This is owing to change in diet and being mistimed as to meals. Now at Florence I am beginning to do well as I was at Rome when I came away, but tomorrow's long journey, and the irregularities, unavoidable ones, before us will mistime me again. My eyes keep marvellously well which is a great blessing, owing I believe in no small degree to the *faintly* blue spectacles I brought with me. These take away entirely the glow of the sun and I trust that with them on I shall be able to face it when it grows still more powerful. Blue spectacles or green, but nothing like so good as these, they are far too blue, are used by thousands in these places. For myself I have been most lucky in the forethought with which I have provided and clothed myself. Tell Mr Carter my long blue coat the same as his has been of inestimable use to me; I am now writing in it, I have worn it much and shall do in the carriage, it

---

[1] See previous letter.

[2] The reference is probably to M. W.'s brother, George Hutchinson.

[3] Capt. Charles Robinson of Ambleside.

413

has served me over and over again as an additional blanket, and when I suspected damp sheets I slept upon it. The shoes which Sprott made me proved most excellent. I have worn them constantly, the soles keep out cold, for the floors indoors are often very cold and in the Churches in particular; it keeps out also the heat of the pavement in the streets which is often burning, and of course the damp. I got also in London an excellent pair of black wire spectacles which will guard my eyes from dust in the carriage, so that I hope to return in tolerable plight. Mr Robinson is naturally not so anxious to be at home as I am; who trust now that in the first week of September we shall be in England; except in Venice I think we shall not be detained more than two or three days anywhere, and this only at the Austrian or Bavarian Lakes near Salzburg and at Munich. To this last place write to me as soon as you receive this. I have already directed you I think to write to Salzburg; if not address me there instead of Munich. I would gladly beg for an answer to this at Venice but it would be imprudent, as I trust we shall have left that place before one could reach me, so write rather to Munich that I may not be disappointed. And now my dearest friends I must conclude with a God bless you all from the bottom of my heart. Love to John and Isabella and their little ones and to dear William and to London John[1] of whose prize I was glad to hear. Give my love to Edith and her Husband [2] and to all the Southeys and to the Coleridges, but there is no end to this. I shall write again from Venice certainly and if I find a letter at Milan perhaps from that place. Mr Robinson sends his love as usual—I have not time to read over this so make it out as well as you can. Again farewell W. W.

I am quite undecided whether to address this, Mary, to you or to Dora. Were I sure it would find her at Hendon it should be there.

The kindest regards to all at Hendon.

Pray Dora see if something cannot be done in London to stop the decay of your tooth by filling it.—

Tell W^m that I shall see today one of the Tobins[3] who is here copying pictures at the Gallery. He means to be a painter—

[1] R. W.'s son.
[2] Dora W. was going to visit the Warters at their Sussex rectory.
[3] Unidentified.

1142. W. W. to JAMES STEPHEN

Address: James Stephen Esq etc etc etc, Colonial Off., London.
MS. Cornell.
LY ii. 870 (—).

Florence, June 5th —37.

My dear Sir,

I had the pleasure of receiving by the ordinary Post yesterday, a letter of the 24th Ult: which was most welcome. I feel somewhat fatigued by great, over great exertions in sight-seeing but am quite well in health, as is my Fellow traveller. We both promise ourselves great pleasure in telling you some thing of our adventures in Autumn. I trust we shall reach London by the beginning of Sept^{br}. To-morrow morning we start for Bologna. I have been much gratified by our six days stay in Florence.

With kind regards to Messrs Taylor and Spedding, I remain my dear Sir

Ever faithfully your
much obliged
Wm Wordsworth

[*H. C. R. adds*]

Allow me to add my hope that I shall find you in Autumn perfectly well and not indisposed to hear some account of our agreeable adventures.

H. C. R.

1143. W. W. to DORA W. and M. W.

Address: Mrs Wordsworth, Rydal Mount, Kendal, Inghilterra. Single Sheet.
Postmark: 3 July 1837. *Stamp*: (1) Venice (2) London.
MS. WL.
LY ii. 870 (—).

Padua June 21st Wednesday [1837]

My dearest Dora,

I begin with you to thank you for your Milan Letter which I had the happiness of receiving the day we left that place. My last was from Florence. It has taken us 16 days to reach this place; our journey having lain through Bologna where we slept two nights, Reggio, Modena, Piacenza, Parma, Milan, Bergamo, Brescia, Verona and Vicenza which we left this morning. The mere posting might have been performed in a very few days but out of the 4 when we slept at Milan we gave one to Como, and one to the celebrated Carthusian Monastery called the Certosa near Pavia, two days we gave to the lake of Iseo and three to that of Garda: fortunate diversion for otherwise the long journey first to Parma from Bologna along the dead flat plain of Lombardy coasting the Appennines and from Milan along the same sort of country precisely coasting the Alps, would notwithstanding the attractions of the several towns, have proved at this season very tedious. But helped out by our incursions into the Alps among those magnificent lakes the whole thing has answered very well. Tomorrow will take us to Venice with the wonders of which City I shall consider our Italian tour as concluding. Then we shall set our faces fairly towards England; not to arrive there as soon as I could wish, for some sacrifices must be made for my fellow-traveller who has done so much to meet my wishes. But my dearest Friends you see that his situation and mine are in important respects very different. He has no home to turn to and I am anxious to be again at mine. He feels that we have incurred a good deal of expense and therefore when at a pleasant place is more disposed to linger longer than I have any inclination to do, so that to my great regret he talks of giving a fortnight to the Austrian and Bavarian lakes in the neighbourhood of Salzburg: this my dear Dora will tend to prevent my reaching London in what I feel to be what you call *decent* time. Yet still we will return together; whether by Brinsop or no must depend upon our convenience. After so long a ramble, I should certainly have put off that visit till another year, had it not been for Uncle Thomas's illness— this weighs much with me and I will strain a point to see them at Brinsop along with you if we are both tolerably well. But I assure you as the trembling of my hand shews this hot weather is playing the deuce with my nerves. My wrists are deplorably unstrung and my muscular strength much diminished. We have had no spring properly speaking, about three weeks since the Summer burst out at once into a profuse heat, and ever since we have been perspiring and drinking cold water from morning to night. Commend me to an English climate in preference a thousand times to what I have known of an Italian one. What I have seen both of Nature and Art in Italy have delighted me much, but I am convinced that none but young people, and strong ones too, should attempt to explore Italy with less than twelve months time at their command, and abundance of money also to spare them bodily fatigue whenever money can do it. We have been generous to ourselves in this way, but not as far as moving about goes (especially in Towns) to the extent of what would have been for me expedient; for as I said before nothing is so exhausting as seeing sights in hot weather in large towns. My dearest Mary and Sister, no words can describe my delight in seeing the first objects in Milan which I recollected we had seen together[1]—though there were several things visited by us in company that I was obliged to leave unseen, in particular the Ambrosian Library and Leonardo da Vinci's Last Supper,[2] but I went to the Brera and to the Cathedral several times, not omitting to mount among the Statues as high as the circle of metallic stars; higher I did not venture, my head was too giddy and my dearest Mary I wanted the support which your firmness gave me when we ascended together. At three o'clock in the morning we took the diligence for [? Cernobbio][3] got there by eight embarked on the steamboat and I went to the head of the Lake; Mr R. stopped to visit a friend at Menaggio where you recollect he and dear Mr Monkhouse[4] passed such a terrible night among thousands of fleas. It would be idle to attempt to express my feelings upon that expedition, whether I thought of my walk with dear Jones,[5] or of our enjoyment at so much later a period of life upon the same ground. Though Mr and Mrs Ticknor and their son and daughter went in the same boat as far as Bellaggio, for we fell in with them at Como, I kept much to myself, and very often could I, for my heart's relief, have burst into tears. I wish Dora that you had been with me, that I might have pointed out to you all the spots that your Mother your Aunt and I had been delighted with. This would make the happiest day of all my tour. In passing Cadenabbia things came upon me as fresh as if they had happened the day before, and delighted I was to find how little the forms and colours [of] objects had faded from my memory. At six we were again in the Diligence an omnibus chokefull and everybody gasping with

---

[1] During the Continental tour of 1820. See *DWJ* ii. 233 ff.
[2] See *PW* iii. 183.
[3] *MS. unclear.*
[4] M. W.'s cousin, Thomas Monkhouse, who was one of the party.
[5] i.e. the 'pedestrian tour' with Robert Jones in 1790.

heat. Between eleven and twelve we got back to Milan. The lakes of Iseo and Garda were well worth the time we bestowed upon them; at the head of the latter we stopped a whole day, of which I employed 8 hours in rambling among the Alpine heights. The scenery is magnificent and I was well repaid for my labour. When we meet I will tell you some of my little adventures, and endeavour to describe what we saw and did there as well as at Iseo—At Venice we shall see the Ticknors again and though I expect much pleasure there, and shall I trust carry away much that will remain in my memory for future delight, I frankly tell you, that my gladdest moment, after receiving your Letter if it bring no bad news, will be the one when I am in motion again for Dear England. I could tell you a hundred things of what I have seen, if I had space or were fonder of writing, or could write legibly, but I feel disposed to give utterance rather of thanks to God in which I am sure you will join who has enabled us to make so long and in some respects hazardous a journey without one ill accident or moment's illness to either of us; except if it deserves to be named the cold I caught in France. We have both escaped the influenza and all attacks of fever which, I assure you, is not a little to be dreaded from sudden checks of perspiration and other causes incident to this climate so different from our own. Yesterday we had a vitious horse put into the carriage, who backed dangerously at the first bridge we came to on leaving the post Town. I insisted upon another being brought, and not without difficulty prevailed. Such a horse in many places where we have been might have caused our destruction. When I think of Thomas's[1] sad situation I am deeply thankful that all has gone well with us. Dearest Dora be assured that I will curtail our stay among the Austrian lakes as much as I can, with due regard to Mr Robinson's wishes, in order that I may reach London in as good time as possible. At Munich we shall be detained at least 4 days, and at least two at Heidelberg but not half a day anywhere else. If anyone would take a fancy to our carriage when I shall consider our *touring* is fairly over, we should most gladly sell it; and make our way direct by steam to Rotterdam and London. That would spare both time and fatigue but it is not likely because we cannot sell it without being repaid the deposit of duty we were obliged to make at Calais, so to that place I suppose we shall be

---

[1] Thomas Hutchinson.

compelled to go! I leave the rest of the space to say a word from Venice to acknowledge I hope the receipt of your letter.

Venice Friday 23 We reached this place yester evening after stopping 5 hours in the heat of the day at Mestre. We are well lodged where John W.[1] recommended us to go. We are close by the place of St Mark, a splendid spot! What I have seen of Venice has fully equalled my expectations. No letter from you; yet surely I directed you to address me hither. I must bear my disappointment as well as I can. Dearest Dora, I am truly sorry for your tooth-ache, and Mary tell me about you all and dearest Sister how is she. Love to you all and kindest regards to the servants one and all and to Mr Carter and to all friends. The day you receive this dearest Mary write to me directly to Munich. How I long to be through all the sights of this place. The weather is insufferably hot; every now and then as I am writing such a cramp comes into my right hand, the hand with the little lump in the palm, that I am obliged to lay down my pen. Dora I am sorry about the leaves. I ought to have had a little Box for that purpose as the leaves and the flowers I plucked in different places have all crumbled away. Give my love to Edith and her husband, to the Watsons if you be with them and to all friends. We left Mr Augustus Hare[2] seriously ill at Florence. I find a letter in the post-off: today from Mrs Hare telling me he is a good deal recovered. I think him however a man old for his years—Dearest Mary and Sister, Venice in situation very much resembles Amsterdam as Lombardy does Holland in general very much, but the architecture of Venice is wonderfully more splendid than Amsterdam. It is quite unique, inferior only to Rome and scarcely that. Again and again farewell. If I have no letter at Venice I shall scarcely write again till we get to Salzburg.

W. W.

I have not yet been told whether Christopher accepted the trusteeships.[3] Love to Miss Fenwick—

We have spent 100 pound a piece, the prices of the Carriage not included. This is very fair.

I do not regret our not going to Naples as it would have been too much for our time—

---

[1] C. W.'s son, John.
[2] A slip for Francis Hare. Augustus had died in 1834.
[3] See L. 1130 above.

1144. M. W. to EDWARD MOXON

MS. Mitchell Library, Sydney. Hitherto unpublished.

Rydal Mount
June 21st [1837]

My dear Sir,

This morning's post brought me the letter[1] upon which I write—and not feeling comfortable that Mrs Hazlitt[2] should remain under the notion that Mr Wordsworth had neglected all respect towards his dear and lamented Friend's[3] memory, it has struck me, that the best mode of answering her letter, in the absence of my husband, is, to request you will send her a Copy (if you possess one) of the lines to our friend's memory which you printed—pamphlet-wise.[4] And further, that you will *give Mrs H's letter to Mr W. on his return*—for I dare say, *were it in his power*, knowing that the wish remains with Miss Lamb that the blank space on her Brother's Tombstone should be filled by him, he would do his best to gratify her feelings; but probably the space is intended to remain, till the Pair are reunited.

Our dear friend, since her Brother's death, having shrunk from the proposal to see us, when I was in Town—(and probably the like was the reason why Mr W. and she have not met since that time)—I do not seem to be at liberty to write to her—much as it would gratify me to communicate with one so tenderly beloved by this Family—but, never being sure what state of health she may be in, and fearful of calling out mournful or old associations that might be too much for her—I dare not avail myself of the address to herself, that Mrs H. has furnished me with. Nor perhaps would it be proper to mention Mrs H.'s interference on this subject. *You* will judge of this—and may I beg, that if you send the lines to Mrs H. that you will acquaint her, with my respects, of Mr W^s absence. And whenever you find dear Miss Lamb able to speak of friends that have been silent since her sad bereavement, fail not to give our tenderest love to her.

I continue to have good tidings regarding the health and well-doing of our Travellers. I think we shall see them sooner

[1] A letter addressed to W. W. at Rydal Mount, franked M. J. O'Connell [M.P. for Co. Kerry], London, June eighteen, 1837.

[2] Widow of John Hazlitt (1767–1837), the miniature painter, elder brother of the essayist.

[3] Charles Lamb.

[4] See L. 962 above.

420

than at one time I looked for. My next letter to them (but they have been unlucky in not receiving letters) will be directed to Heidelburg.

May I ask how the Ed: goes off? I see Mr Talfourd's *Lamb*[1] is published—what a masterly Speech he made on Copy-right—we may all feel grateful to him. Dear Sir, I hate to trouble you, but it would be very *convenient* to me to see your account against us—for I cannot *settle* with friends (whom you kindly allowed us to oblige—and who are importunate to pay their debts) for want of knowing certain charges—as for instance Richardson's Dic:ʳʸ Mr Wˢ Poems etc—

I hope Mrs Moxon and the Children, as well as yourself, are well—and with best regards to one and all, believe me dear Sir to be very sincerely yours

M. Wordsworth

P. S.   Could I have commanded a frank I would have written to Mrs Hazlitt—pray tell her so, if you communicate with her. If from any cause, *you* decline doing so, acquaint me, as I should not wish to be so uncivil as not to notice her kindly-meant letter.

1145. W. W. to HIS FAMILY

Address: Mrs Wordswoth, Rydal Mount, near Kendal, England.
Postmark: 13 July 1837. *Stamp*: (1) Salzburg (2) London.
MS. WL.
K (—). LY ii. 874 (—).

[Salzburg]
[5 July 1837]

My dearest Friends,

Here we are at Salzburg having arrived this morning, and found, dearest Dora, your welcome letter. But I must go back; and speak about your letters. Mary, yours reached me at Venice, the day after I had written; one from Dora as I must have told you most fortunately the day I left Milan, so that in all I have received four; and shall confidently expect another when we reach Munich, where we shall not be for some little time, for Mr R. much to my regret talks of taking not less than a

---

[1] *The Letters of Charles Lamb.*

fortnight among what are called the Austrian Lakes not far from
this place. I hope he will change his mind, as he has made so
many sacrifices for me, I must make some for him. How
thankful I am dear Dora that you are relieved from your
suffering. Most earnestly do I pray that this may be the last of the
kind you will have to suffer. Thank you again and again for
your entertaining letter; and you dear Mary for yours, which
brightened my stay at Venice. Our abode of six days would
have been most delightful, but for two unlucky circumstances,
the extreme heat of the weather and the smallness and aspect of
my bedroom which during four nights (the two last I was able
to procure a better) made me very uncomfortable indeed,
endeavouring to sleep while I was actually in an oven. Our
journey of six days or seven (Mr Robinson is out and he keeps
the dates) from Venice through an Alpine country to this place
has been charming; the weather though very hot sometimes for
a few hours in the day mightily improved and my *perspirations*
at an end. But I expect to have enough of them, when we get
again into the plain country. But for your letters, I have received
five, one from Mary at Rome date Brinsop April 17th one from
Dora, Florence, another Milan, one from Mary, Venice, and
lastly this of to day Salzburg. I began and wrote half of a letter at
Venice but I thought it better not to finish it, and as it is now out
of date I shall not send it. My health has been good, but certainly
my Frame is weakened by the journey as I feel in many ways, as
for instance the bodily exertion of rummaging in my trunk for
something I wanted since I began this Letter, has brought a kind
of cramp of pain to my stomach such as I have often felt upon
like occasions but never used to have. This stomach weakness
may be in part accounted for by the quantity of liquid which
from extreme thirst I have been tempted to take, and it has been
increased I will confess by the less excusable fault, the labour I
have lately undergone in correcting a little Poem[1] of 76 lines

---

[1] W. W. and H. C. R. had visited Assisi on 25 May (see Sadler, iii. 125),
and Laverna three days later (see L. 1140 above). The first draft of *The Cuckoo
at Laverna* (*PW*. iii. 218) was begun on 30 June (see *HCR* ii. 528), and later
expanded into a poem of 112 lines by the addition of the passage about
St. Francis (ll. 49—73). See L. 1261 below. 'It was at Laverna', H. C. R. later
recalled, 'that he led me to expect that he had found a subject on which he
would write; and that was the love which birds bore to St. Francis. He
repeated to me a short time afterwards a few lines, which I do not recollect
among those he has written on St. Francis in this poem. On the journey, one

which I was tempted to write. This work disturbed or rather broke my rest for two or three nights when I might have had the benefit of the cool air of the Alpine country with sound sleep to recruit me. As these verses have cost me in this way more than they ought to have done I shall be much mortified if you do not like them and think them pretty good. I promise you solemnly that I shall attempt nothing of the kind again during this journey. The mistiming of meals, which is often unavoidable, and employment that would rob me of rest in the night are too much. As to over-hurrying, or rather mine, you are a good deal mistaken on this point. Six days apiece were quite enough for both Florence and Venice unless one had meant to make a study of the works of art there; so was the time we gave to all the other Italian cities unless we had had the same object. And as to posting, that, as our journey from Venice will shew, we have taken at leisure. Indeed I never wish to do otherwise except when the face of the Country is wholly uninteresting. I could write to you Volumes in the way of letters were I [to][1] touch upon all that I have seen felt and thought.

I have, however, to regret that this journey was not made some years ago,—to regret it, I mean, as a Poet; for though we have had a great disappointment in not seeing Naples, etc., and more of the country among the Apennines not far from Rome, Horace's country for instance, and Cicero's Tusculum, my mind has been enriched by innumerable images, which I could have turned to account in verse, and vivified by feelings which earlier in my life would have answered noble purposes, in a way they now are little likely to do. But I do not repine; on the contrary, I am very happy, wishing only to see all your dear faces again, and to make amends for my frequent bad behaviour to you all. Absence in a foreign country, and at a great distance, is a condition, for many minds, at least for mine, often pregnant with remorse. Dearest Mary, when I have felt how harshly I often demeaned myself to you, my inestimable fellow-labourer, while correcting the last Edition of my poems, I often pray to God that He would grant us both life, that I may make some amends to you for that, and all my unworthiness. But you know

night only I heard him in bed composing verses, and on the following day I offered to be his amanuensis; but I was not patient enough, I fear, and he did not employ me a second time.' (*Mem.* ii. 330.)

[1] *Word dropped out.*

into what an irritable state this timed and overstrained labour often put my nerves. My impatience was ungovernable as I thought *then*, but I now feel that it ought to have been governed. You have forgiven me I know, as you did then, and perhaps that somehow troubles me the more. I say nothing of this to you, dear Dora, though you also have had some reason to complain.—But too much of this—I hope I shall be able to write the rest of this sheet more legibly as I have just been watering the ink which had got unmanageably thick as these few great blots shew. How sorry, dear Dora, I am for poor Mr Hallam;[1] he had just been touring in the beautiful country where now we are before he lost his son so suddenly. Beautiful indeed this Country is; in a picturesque and even poetic point of view more interesting than most of what we have seen. It is something between the finest part of Alpine Switzerland and the finest parts of Great Britain; I mean in North Wales, Scotland, and our own region. In many particulars it excels Italy, I mean of course what I have seen of it; and also, greatly indeed, the south of France. The mountains are finely formed, and the Vales not choked up, nor the hillsides disfigured by the sort of cultivation which the sunshine of Italy puts thereupon— vines, olives, citrons, lemons and all kinds of fruit-trees. Yesterday we passed through a country of mountain, meadow, lawn, and the richest wood spread about with all the magnificence of an everlasting Park, such a character as we often find in England, but these things here are on so vast a scale compared with our landscapes. But I must not run on in this strain, but leave the rest of this sheet as you would wish Mary to Mr Robinson.[2] How glad was I to have your account of my beloved Sister; oh my dear Sister do try to renew your love of

[1] Henry Hallam's son Arthur had died at Vienna on 15 Sept. 1833 (see pt. ii, L. 784).

[2] H. C. R. adds a note at the foot of the letter: 'The only German inconvenience my friend suffers from is the necessity of choosing between a scanty coverlid that leaves his extremities both length and breadth bare or a suffocating feather bed that requires kneading and modelling to fit the body and keep on. He however, tho' perhaps he wont confess it, I believe really feels better than he did in Italy—for how else did it happen that the *fit* did not come on till he was got among the Alps and was homeward bound. A certain degree of repose of mind must have been the cause tho' you know it is not the effect of the exercise of verse making. You are to have the product from Munich, and will be well pleased with it I promise you . . .'

Nature. How I wish I had you here for a few minutes, notwithstanding your love of your own Chair and your fire! Write to me at Heidelberg and that may be your last letter. Dora you shall hear of the time when I hope to be in town, as soon as I can come at all near a determination. You have never told me anything about the last Edition, how it has sold, how it is liked, and what John Carter thought of the printing of the latter part. But farewell and God bless you all and love to all the family every where and to all friends again farewell—I shall certainly write from Munich; and perhaps begin my Letter before.—

W. W.

1146. W. W. to M. W.

Address: Mrs Wordsworth, Rydal Mount, Kendal, Angleterre. Single Sheet.
Postmark: (1) 17 July 1837 (2) 24 July 1837. *Stamp*: Munchen.
MS. WL.
K (—). *LY* ii. 878 (—).

Munich Monday July 17th [1837]

My dearest Mary,

Twelve or thirteen days ago I wrote to you from Salzburg acknowledging the receipt of your most welcome letter. This morning we came hither, and I had the pleasure of finding another from you. I grieve much to learn that Dora's jaws still torment her. Poor Creature what is to become of her? How happy am I on the other hand to learn that you are so well, and my dear Sister is better. Thank her affectionately for the few words she wrote me. Since my last we have had a delightful ramble amongst the Austrian lakes which we have seen completely as we should have done also those of the valley but that the weather broke 4 days ago, and cut short our expedition though we did see three of these latter. At present I consider our *Tour* finished; and all my thoughts are fixed upon home, where I am most impatient to be; and conscientiously so, for I have hurried over nothing, notwithstanding your frequent hints to the contrary; which have rather hurt me, particularly as there are (as must be the case with all companions in travel) so many things in habit and inclination in which Mr R. and I differ. Upon these I shall not dwell at present, as the only one I care

425

about is this; he has no home to go to but chambers, and wishes to stay abroad, at least to linger abroad, which I, having the blessing of a home, do not. Again, he takes delight in loitering about towns, gossiping, and attending reading-rooms, and going to coffee-houses; and at *table d'hôtes*, etc., gabbling German, or any other tongue, all which places and practices are my abomination. In the evenings I cannot read, as the candlelight hurts my eyes, and I have therefore no resource but to go to bed, while I should like exceedingly, when upon our travels, if it were agreeable to him to rise early; but though he will do this, he dislikes it much, so that I don't press it. He sleeps so much at odd times in the day that he does not like going to bed till midnight; and in this, and a hundred other things, our tastes and habits are quite at variance; though nobody can be more obliging in giving up his own; but you must be aware it is very unpleasant in me to require this. In fact, I have very strong reasons for wishing this tour, which I have found so beneficial to my mind, at an end for the sake of my body; for certainly either the diet or some other cause has very much shaken my nerves as this trembling of my hand writing, and the frequent cramps I have had in my hand since I began this page, sufficiently shew. My bowels have latterly been in better order and I have no pain anywhere, but my head is often cloudy and my nerves as I have said are much deranged. I sometimes think that the coffee and beer I take, for I have nearly left off wine, are too much for my nerves. If I dared do so I would leave off beer and wine altogether and coffee also, but milk I know is binding. Excuse all this; not a word of which would have been said had not both you and Dora blamed me so much for hurrying. In fact I have not hurried, but been very patient, considering the tiresome way in which when in towns I have been obliged to spend so many hours. If the state of my nerves and stomach would allow me to write verse I should never want employment, or if my muscular powers were as great as they have been so that I could walk all day long it would be the same, but that time is passed away, and I want the sight of your faces and the sound of your voices, when I can do neither the one nor the other, nor read to beguile the time. Therefore find no more fault, I undertook this journey as a *duty*, I have gone through with it as such, and except that as far as concerns my health having had a most unsuitable companion in Mr Robinson I have in consequence made many sacrifices of which he was not aware, I have kept duty constantly in my eyes, and have greatly enriched my mind; and I hope when I get home that I shall find my health not at all worse. So let us all be glad that I have made this upon the whole so delightful journey. I shall have a thousand things to tell you; and if I had ten years before me of such strength as I have had, you would see my future verses animated in a way that would please you all. Now for other and more agreeable things; but I find my handwriting shockingly unsteady.—Yet how can I say agreeable for to tell you the truth I fear that public affairs will now take a wretched course and that the young Queen[1] under unwise guidance will abandon herself to the foolish and selfish Whigs. The elections about to be will I fear run much against the conservatives, indeed on these points all my thoughts are gloomy—so no more about them—

How long Mr Robinson will be loitering here I know not. The exterior of the place has for me no interest; but I believe it contains a large collection of works of Art some of which must no doubt be interesting, and tomorrow I shall begin with them—and I hope on the fourth day at the latest, I wish the third, we shall start for Heidelberg where we shall stay I suppose two days at least—All the rest will be straightforward travelling, so that I hope by the end of the third week from this time we shall be in London or perhaps a few days later. I wrote thus far before dinner at 2. From 3 to 5 I tired myself in walking about the place under the guidance of a friend[2] of Mr Robinson, I have since been in my room alone. It is now $\frac{1}{4}$ past 7 and before 9 I shall be in bed, for sheer want of something to do, unless I tire myself with composition[3] which I am resolved not to meddle

[1] Queen Victoria (b. 1819) had acceded to the throne on the death of William IV on 20 June, and a General Election followed in which the Tories gained 37 seats, but the Whigs still retained office with a majority of 38. Lord Melbourne undertook the delicate task of guide and mentor to the young queen, much to the discomfiture of the Tories.

[2] Clemens Brentano (1778–1842), the German Romantic poet: 'He rattled about religion in a way that could but half amuse and half disgust W.', H. C .R. recorded in his MS. Travel Diary, 'for B. is a strange mixture of drollery and assumed earnestness in religious matters that amounts to fanaticism.' (*Dr. Williams's Library MSS.*)

[3] W. W. was evidently thinking of expanding the first draft of *The Cuckoo at Laverna* (see previous letter), and had been seeking further information about St. Francis. On 17 July, according to his MS. Travel Diary, H. C. R. introduced W. W. to Johann Joseph von Görres (1776–1848), Professor of

with. I wish I could single out any part of our tour to give an account of, but we have no adventures, and since we left Venice, have had nothing to see but the fine country we have passed through and the employments of the people and their appearance. Yesterday was Sunday, we passed the greatest part of the day near one of the Bavarian lakes where the Queen Dowager my Co-Sponsor[1] has a palace. The scenery compared with most we have seen since we entered the Alps is of a mild character more like our own but very agreeable. The People were all assembled in the little town for Church and I was much amused with their appearance. The women are the most gigantic race I ever saw and they wear a dress which makes them appear very high-shouldered and short-necked (like our Barlow jug[2]). The men are a fine race, most of them wear bonnets shaped exactly like, and in height the same, as those of our old puritans. Some had a feather, like Hofer's,[3] stuck on one side sometimes with a flower but most only a flower in this hat or bonnet, and the flower never in front but almost always directly behind, which has a singular appearance. They pride themselves much upon the quality and workmanship of their stockings; one man's were so elabourately figured that I could not but ask him the price, he told me as much as 7 or 8 shillings, rather six or seven, I expressed my wonder, and he told me he had had those stockings and regularly worn them, I suppose on Sundays and feast days, for twenty years. I employed myself for more than 3 hours in walking about this beautiful valley, and conversing as well as I could with its interesting Inhabitants who have however one great fault, they are extremely fond of beer and drink immense quantities. But if we were to judge from the size and neatness and apparent comfort of their habitations, which however are built almost entirely of wood, from their dress, and

History at Munich since 1827, and author of *Die Christliche Mystik* (1836–42); and some days later they were reading Görres's pamphlet on St. Francis the troubadour. 'It has a few passages only about St. Francis's power over animals which Wordsworth may make use of.' (*Dr Williams's Library MSS.*) For another possible influence on the poem, see Alan G. Hill, 'Wordsworth and the Two Faces of Machiavelli', *RES* xxxi (1980), 285–304.

[1] As godparent to Edwin Hill Handley's child. See L. 976 above.

[2] Apparently a type of Staffordshire pottery.

[3] Andrew Hofer, the Austrian hero, who led the Tyrolese against the French in 1796, and again in 1809 when the French were in alliance with the Bavarians. He was captured and executed in 1810. See *PW* iii. 129 for W. W.'s tribute to him.

the fertility and beauty of their country they are in an enviable condition.

I shall not send off this Letter till we have left or are on the point of leaving this place. At Heidelberg I shall inquire after Willy's lodgings, but this will be my last letter as I shall be in London I trust within not much more than a week of the time of your receiving this. Write to me by all means at Mr Moxon's through Mr Stephen. How I long to see you dearest Mary and all of you again. As to going to Bath or Brinsop I will do whatever is thought best; I feel that dear Thomas and Mary have strong claims upon me, and if both Dora and I are [we]ll, I hope I shall have courage to go and see them; b [ut I][1] do long to [be at] rest under our own roof! The verses may wait till I send them from London. Mr R. has had today a letter from a Money-friend in London who has a great deal to do with our joint-stock bank. He says many unpleasant things have come out respecting concerns of this kind; but none at all affecting the character of ours; so that if it continues to stand the test of examination and it is under excellent management I doubt not it will not only survive the storm but thrive upon the ruin of others. As you do not mention James I hope his health is restored; pray remember me most kindly to all the servants; Mr Carter also and to all friends. You little know how I love you all.

A man must travel alone, I mean without one of his family, to feel what his family is to him! How often have I wished for James to assist me about the carriage, greasing the wheels, etc a most tedious employment, fastening the baggage, etc., for nothing can exceed the stupidity of these foreigners. Tell him how I wish I had been rich enough to bring him along with me! But I must leave a scrap of paper for another day.—I have no cramp in my fingers since I began to write this afternoon and my hand is steadier, though the writing is execrable. God bless you all.

Thursday morning 20th. It is fixed that we leave this place tomorrow noon. I think we should be four or five days getting to Heidelberg as the German postilions are so slow, and we shall stop at least half a day at Stuttgart at Ulm and Augsburg. So as you know the distance from Heidelberg to Calais you will be able to calculate within 2 or 3 days the time of our arrival in London. I am quite tired of this place, the weather has been very

[1] *MS. damaged.*

bad, and after the galleries close which is at 12 o'clock and one, I have nothing to do, and as I cannot speak German my time moves very heavily. The Ticknors are here and I have passed a couple of hours every evening with them. God bless you again.

Mr Robinson would have written on this sheet but unluckily I have left no room for him. He is quite well and strong, and does much better than I do in places like this, where there is no natural beauty and nothing interesting in the architecture,[1] the town being new.

[*unsigned*]

1147. W. W. to EDWARD MOXON

Address: Mr Edward Moxon, Bookseller, Dover Street.
Postmark: 4 Aug. 1837.
MS. Henry E. Huntington Library.
LY ii. 882.

Brussels 2nd August [1837]

My dear Mr Moxon,

Here we are after a most pleasant Tour, in good health and spirits. I write now to tell you that I hope to be in London, on Monday evening next, and I shall make my way directly to your hospitable door.—

Pray inquire after my Daughter at Mr Henry Coleridge's, or if it suits to write to Hampstead Heath, at Mrs Hoare's, at one or other house you will be sure to hear of her, and let her know my intention.

Remember me most kindly to Mrs Moxon and your Sister and Brother; and believe me faithfully and affectionately yours

Wm Wordsworth

---

[1] But in the remaining days of their visit, they saw something of the church revival in Munich, and on 20 July visited the Ludwigskirche where they met Peter von Cornelius (1783–1867) at work on his fresco of the Last Judgement, surrounded by his pupils. See Sadler, iii. 137.

1148. W. W. to DORA W.

Address: Miss Wordsworth, Mrs Hoare's, Hampstead Heath. An answer required.
MS. WL.
LY ii. 883.

Tuesday 8th [Aug. 1837] Dover Street—44

My dearest Dora,

Here I am; arrived at the Custom house yesterday at half-past 2, and got to this House between 7 and 8 where I found Mr Moxon and one of his Sisters. He had kindly come up from Ramsgate to welcome me. Why did not you mention your mouth, about which I am so anxious, in your kind note. Here I found also a short Letter from your Mother.—As I have much to do, I shall not stir out till after three today; if Mrs Hoare to whom and Miss Hoare give my kind love, could come with you, or send you over in her carriage that I might have a few minutes talk with you, I should be greatly obliged. At all events let me have an answer by the Bearer.

Ever your affectionate Father
W. W.

1149. W. W. to HIS FAMILY

MS. WL.
LY ii. 883.

Wednesday morning [9 Aug. 1837]

My dearest Friends,

On Monday at half-past 2 reached the Custom house—was detained several hours till our baggage could be examined and did not reach Mr Moxon's till near eight. Kind creature he had come up from Broadstairs, where his wife sister and children are for sea-air, on purpose to meet me. I received, dear Mary, your 2nd Letter at Munich—the one for Heidelberg did not reach that place till we had left it though 26 days had passed between my Salzburg Letter and the day we left Heidelberg—it followed me however to Brussels where I got it after much trouble, particulars of which I defer till we meet. Mr Moxon was so kind as to send his Boy over to Hampstead yesterday morning, and the consequence was Mrs Hoare brought Dora over to see me. I did not myself think her improved in looks, but that might be owing to the flurry of seeing me. I questioned her pointedly as could be about her health, and she answered frankly 'I certainly am better, except for my face I have little pain, and my appetite is good, but I do not gather strength as I expected. In short I can do little, that is a little exertion is too much for me.' But Mr Rogers is so kind as to take me over today to Hampstead where I shall see her again and I will write to you either tomorrow or next day. Her respect for Mr Carr's opinion, as being best acquainted with her constitution, has I think quite reconciled her to pass this winter in the South, which I rejoice in. Our plan is, as probably she has told you I am obliged to write this before I have seen her letter, is to go together to Chatham in the earlier part of next week; I will try also to manage for her going to Broadstairs for a week's sea-air and bathing, and I will remain with her there. The Rogers have a spare bed in their lodgings and I can easily get one in the place; we will then go to Brinsop together, if all goes on well, so that alas, alas! our meeting and the sight of my dear Sister and all Rydal friends must be deferred for some time. Thanks for your Letter which I found here—The memorandum will be attended to. I rejoice to hear that you are all well and that my dear Sister can walk by aid of a stick; we shall do great things together when we meet again.—

From Munich we came through Augsburg, Ulm, Stuttgart to Heidelberg, where we slept three nights, and I went everywhere especially to the places where we had been together; the weather very fine. From Heidelberg through Mannheim Worms Mainz Coblenz Cologne etc to Brussels, from Brussels to Antwerp by railway, and returned to Brussels the same day—this was to me a delightful day of recollections of you and Dora,[1] from Brussels through Tournay and Lille to Cassel a charming place and St Omer with which I was much pleased, to Calais where we arrived about two in the afternoon and embarked about two in the morning; for the first three hours, the sea being rough, I was tremendously sick, and feel the inconvenience in my throat to this hour.—Dear Miss Fenwick is in town, she arrived yesterday. I called at her Lodgings, and saw

---

[1] i.e. the recollections of D. W. and M. W. of the tour of 1820, and those of Dora W. of the tour of 1828.

her looking well for a few minutes. Today I shall see her again before I go to Hampstead. I also called on Mr and Mrs Johnson [1] yesterday. Rogers called on me here, and I dined with him, [2] but only stopped an hour and a half, having passed almost the whole day within always waiting for Dora and with her all the evening. I have sixty pounds left of the 200 I took with me, there is also the Carriage that cost us 70 pounds, but by that I fear we shall lose greatly, it is now at the Coach Makers. Pray give my affectionate regards to Mrs Bolton, [3] I mean to write to her as soon as I can find a moment's leisure.

What a sad thing this Workington affair [4] is; but tell dear Isabella with my best love that I trust in God's goodness and that it will ultimately tend to the good of the whole, and every branch of the family. Congratulate John and Isabella also on the birth of their Son, [5] with a thousand good wishes that he may prove a blessing to his Parents; say also all that is kind to Mr and Mrs Curwen from me. I would write to them, but they can easily understand how overwhelmed I must be with answering Letters that have accumulated for me here. I am glad to hear that James is recovered and hope that Anne Jane and Dorothy [6] are all well. Tell Lady Farquahar I had the pleasure of meeting her sister Lady Cumming [7] and Amelia with another sister and I believe a third but I am not sure; she was of the family at Louvain on their way to Baden-Baden. They were well.

[unsigned]

[1] The Revd. William and Mrs. Johnson.

[2] W. W. and Thomas Moore dined with Rogers on the 8th, and again on the 10th when they were joined by Henry Taylor and Edwin Landseer the artist (see L. 1338 below). See *Memoirs, Journal, and Correspondence of Thomas Moore*, vii. 197–8.

[3] W. W. had apparently just received a legacy from the late John Bolton's estate (see *MW*, p. 163).

[4] The flooding of the Curwen mines. See L. 1157 below, and *MW*, pp. 169, 177–8. Tunnelling had proceeded too near the sea bed and three mines had been engulfed. 25 men and two boys were drowned, and hundreds were thrown out of work.

[5] Their third son John (1837–1927). See *MW*, p. 158.

[6] Maids at Rydal Mount.

[7] H. C. R.'s MS. Travel Diary records the meeting with Lady and the Miss Cummings at Louvain on 2 Aug. They were apparently the wife and daughters of General Sir Henry Cumming (1772–1856), a distinguished commander in the Peninsula, who was a neighbour of the Marshalls in Upper Grosvenor Street.

Address: Mrs Wordsworth, Rydal, Kendal.
Franked: London August ten 1837 Jas Stephen.
Postmark: 10 Aug. 1837.
MS. WL.
LY ii. 885.

[10 Aug. 1837]

My dearest Friends,

I was obliged to send off yesterday a scrawl unfinished. I went with Mr and Miss Rogers to Hampstead—they to Miss Baileys[1] I remained at Mrs Hoare's from half past two till six when they took me up, and Mr R. brought me to Miss Fenwick's 19 Lower Grosvenor Street where I remained till ten. Dora is in excellent spirits and I cannot but think a good deal improved in health. Everybody seems delighted with her. I have looked over her letters and find she has mentioned my toe. I must therefore add that in the great toe of my right foot I have had a slight aggravation of a redness and heat that I have had a little of for some years—I trust it will not prove anything but it attracted my attention in rather a disagreeable way which it never did before. I think this was owing in great measure to fatigue and heat and to broken sleep caused partly by the Poem[2] I now send you getting into my thoughts in the night-time. But far too much of this I hope insignificant affair.—This morning I am going to the Colonial Off:, Stamp Off:, Strickland Cookson, the Dentist, I have lost my last tooth but one, and Courtenay's if possible, so that I shall have enough to do. It is now eleven o'clock. Rogers, Moore, and Kenyon have been breakfasting here.—I enclose a note from Mrs Hook whom I have not yet seen. I shall be obliged to conclude this letter as the last probably without a signature. Have you packed up my Mr Moxon's two additional volumes of Cowper[3] which have been waiting for some time, to be called for by someone as you told him they would be; what is to be done with them. How to proceed about pupils for John,[4] I know not, but I will do my best.—Mrs Howley begged me when I was last in Town to let

---

[1] Joanna Baillie.

[2] *The Cuckoo at Laverna.*

[3] Southey's *Works of William Cowper, with a Life of the Author.*

[4] John W. was now in financial difficulty, following the losses that had struck his wife's family, and was seeking ways of supplementing his income.

her know of my return and she would come up to Town to
fetch [me][1] to visit them.[2] I fear I shall not have time to do this, I
long so to be at home. But something might come of such a
visit. Pray write by return of post if you can to this place.

I have this moment read your last letter to Dora to which I
find nothing to answer—I am delighted you have got Henry[3]
with you and [? charmed] that you like him so much. Love to all
friends whom I have not time to mention, W. W.

Tell me whether you get into the Poem at once, and how you
like it.—

1151. W. W. and H. C. R. to FRANCES MACKENZIE

Address: Alla nobile Donna La Signora Mackenzie, (Inglese), Alla Cava della
Signora Camporesa, Via Gregoriana, Roma.
Postmark: 30 Nov. 1837. *Stamp*: (1) Temple (2) Calais (3) Roma.
MS. Cornell. Hitherto unpublished.

11th August [1837]
Mr Robinson's Chambers, London.

Dear Miss Mackenzie,

I promised myself, before we left Rome, the pleasure of
writing to you from Munich. We remained there four days but
it rained all the while and in consequence I found the place so
dull that I could not bring myself to approach you in such a state
of spirits—you to whom I had been indebted for so many
delightful hours, of which be assured I shall ever retain a grateful
remembrance. You will naturally be desirous of knowing
something of our Movements after we left Rome. The road to
Florence with the diversion to the three Sanctuaries,[4] I found
most interesting. At Florence we remained six days, saw every
thing with much pleasure; thence to Bologna and Parma, to
Milan where we slept four nights, saw the Lake of Como, went
by Bergamo etc., saw the Lakes Iseo and di Garda, with both of
which we were much pleased, Verona, Vicenza and Padua, and
remained six days at Venice. There also I was delighted; from
Venice we went to Salzburg by what is called the new German

---

1 *Word dropped out.*
2 At Addington Palace.
3 The eldest grandson.
4 Laverna, Camaldoli, and Vallombrosa.

[?]¹, spent days among the Austrian Lakes with very much pleasure, and proceeded by the Bavarian Lakes to Munich; but we were unable to make as complete a Tour of these on Account of bad weather which drove us into Munich. From this place we went by Augsburg and Ulm to Heidelberg, where we slept three nights, thence down the Rhine to Cologne, and so on to Brussels, saw Antwerp and landed at the Custom house on Monday 7th of August after a most agreeable tour, without sickness, accident, or any unpleasant delay. And now let me go back again to indulge in grateful recollections, my dear Miss Mackenzie, of your kindness, of which I think over and over again, and of which I am tempted to speak oftener than perhaps you would like, but not oftener than they who love me are pleased to hear. It is not my object in sitting down to write you an entertaining Letter, I am too much hurried to endeavour any thing of the kind, besides, I should be quite at a loss what portion of so interesting a tour to select. I cannot conclude, without urging upon you to bear in mind the hope which [you]¹ so kindly held out to me that Mrs W. and I might have the pleasure of having you for our guest, at Rydal Mount; and requesting you to be so good as to repeat the assurance, if you can; and to let me know where and how you have passed the summer.

Believe me, dear Miss Mackenzie, with a thousand good wishes

faithfully and gratefully yours

Wᵐ Wordsworth

The Poems² will be sent along with a Copy for Mr Severn to whom and his Lady I wish to be kindly remembered, through Mr Westmacott³ as Mr S. desired.

[*H. C. R. writes*]

2, Plowdens Building, Temple. 17 Novʳ 1837

My dear Madam,

You will not suspect the *poet* of ingratitude or inattention, whatever you might have done as to his companion. The letter

¹ *Word dropped out.*

² Presumably the new edition of the *Poetical Works.*

³ The reference is probably to the sculptor Richard Westmacott, R. A., the younger (1799–1872), who had studied in Rome, 1820–6, rather than to his father, Sir Richard Westmacott, R. A. (1775–1856), the pupil of Canova.

on the other side, coming from such a man, you will place among your literary *pretiosa*—I rejoice at having been the medium of so much enjoyment to both of you. You certainly were Wordsworth's good Angel at Rome. But for you his evenings would have been sad and even his days imperfectly enjoyed. I will *not* say that I feel grateful to you for your great attention to him tho' I am for those conferred on me, because I know that they had their own reward and that you received as much as you gave. But I do rejoice exceedingly that you saw so much of each other and have left such mutual recollections and feelings, as will prevent your ever forgetting or being indifferent to each other. I do hope that before many years elapse you will visit him and as you must pass thro' London, I trust you will find me out. For the present there is no likelyhood of my leaving chambers. And I trust you will allow me to inform you from time to time of whatever change of residence may take place. You will bear this in mind, Should you ever be in London and not know precisely where I am, that you can obtain information at the *Athenian Club Waterloo Place*.

I must explain the delay in sending this letter which has at last lain longer than I intended by me. I should have sent it long ago, but for the knowledge that the Cholera being at Rome would prevent your return till the memory of it almost was gone. I have enquired of your few acquaintance Eastlake [1] and Uwins [2] but they could not tell me of your actual return. However now, you must be returned, if ever you do return.

We reached England so much earlier than I intended that I wished to make a sort of supplementary journey and I accompanied Mr Wordsworth into Herefordshire. But the weather did not allow of a tour on the Wye, our project. I have since been travelling in the North West of England and in three days saw more rich Verdure and beautiful trees than on our long five months tour.

You have from the poet himself a short Itinerary. I have little to add. The spots he deeply enjoyed were the three Sanctuaries.

---

[1] Sir Charles Eastlake (1793–1865), historical and landscape painter, had lived in Rome from 1816 to 1830. He became Keeper of the National Gallery in 1843, and President of the Royal Academy in 1850.

[2] Thomas Uwins, R. A. (1782–1857), a successful water-colourist, painted in Italy, 1824–31, and returned to England to establish a new reputation as a painter of Italian scenes in oils. He succeeded Eastlake as Keeper of the National Gallery in 1847.

He began one poem on hearing the *Cuckoo at L'Averna* which I trust he will finish. I fear we are not entitled to expect much beyond—'I have', he said, 'a fund of thoughts and suggestions, if I had but youth and health to work them up'—You know how painfully he writes. But then when produced how glorious, how perfect the works are!

You must have observed how intensely as well as how delicately and discriminatingly W. enjoys the beauties of nature. He cares rather less than I wish for works of antiquity—he has a fine sense for the charms of colour, but is less susceptible to beauty of form either in Sculpture or Architecture. I overheard him exclaim with rapture at the sight of two children playing by the Amphitheatre at Nismes 'Oh that I could steal those children and carry them off to Rydal Mount!' And on top of the Colosseum he was admiring the rich verdure beyond as much as the sublime edifice below. He ought to have visited Italy many years before—Most likely I should, he said, but for the Edinburgh Reviewers. He sent a message to this effect to Jeffery. I have no space for news. The queen is very popular and not liked the worse because it is known that she is a bit of a hoyden. She received the Bishops with great dignity, but when she had quitted them was seen thro' a glass door to run off with a skip like a school girl. And she said lately to a new Maid of honour—'I do think it good fun to play Queen'. This is just as it should be and justifies our hoping that the high spirited girl of eighteen will turn out the prudent Woman of thirty. What more could she be? Until she is a wise matron, she can not be a fit Queen. And now let me also express my gratitude to you for all favours begging for a continuation of them in the shape of an early letter—

Your obliged friend   H. C. Robinson

Among the agreeable incidents of the journey were the frequent Meetings with the Ticknors whom we fell in with at *Como, Bergamo, Venice* and *Munich.* I meant to add to the Monasteries as the spots W. rejoiced in—Lovere and Riva at the head of the lakes of *Iseo* and La Garda. Also many places in the Salzkammergut of Austria. Due remembrances to the Hares— the Bunsens if at Rome. Report says they have left [? Kesher][1]. Will you forgive my deforming the poet's letter by these unworthy accompanyments? I have not yet heard from

---

[1] *MS. obscure.*

W. S. L.[1] I tried to do good at Florence and made his daughter[2] write to him. But I fear nothing can be done—he is an impracticable man with all his genius.

If *Schmidt*[3] the painter and his brother in law *Spence* and his beautiful wife should be in Rome this Winter my kind remembrances—

1152. W. W. to HIS FAMILY

MS. WL.
LY ii. 886.

Monday morning Mrs Hoare's, Hampstead
[14 Aug. 1837]

My dear friends,

I have been very busy since my last; but I have mislaid your paper of Memorandums which I hope however is at Moxon's, so that I cannot at present say what I have left undone. On Saturday I walked hither, calling by the way upon Miss Fenwick, Mr Spring Rice, I saw the ladies but not him, he was at Downing Street, Mrs Hook and Miss Rogers.— Yesterday evening I was at Sir Benjamin Brodie's[4] and he has kindly allowed me to take Dora to him which cannot be before Friday next, on which day or Saturday I hope we shall go to Chatham when also she will see Dr Davy, so that she will have the best medical [advice]. I mentioned incidentally our poor Brother Thomas's case; his answer was very encouraging, he says he has lately had two cases under his care of two gentlemen who by accidents had lost the use of arms and legs; they are both recovering the use of them, though of course slowly, one of them is 70 years of age. He does not rely upon medicine, he says Time and care must do the work, the patient using as much exercise as he can bear. I said Thomas had been at Bath, he did not think much good likely to come of that; but that whatever

---

[1] Walter Savage Landor (see also L. 1141 above), who settled in Bath towards the end of this year.

[2] Julia, now aged sixteen, had formed an attachment for her cousin Edward Wilson Landor. See *HCR* ii. 523–4.

[3] An artist whom H. C. R. had known in Rome in 1830. He had married an Italian lady, sister of the wife of William Spence (see L. 1141 above).

[4] He lived on Hampstead Heath.

strength[ens] the general health, such as good air exercise and cheerful spirits and a tranquil [?][1]; to these the sufferer must chiefly look for restoration, and he did not seem to doubt that in time it would come. I have seen much more of Dora; she certainly is not strong, I observe from time to time she puts her hand to her side as formerly, and shrinks a little in her posture. But then surely she must be upon the whole much better. Yester morning she was at Church which I think however a little too much for her, and thence she and I drove in a car to Hendon, of course she was a little tired on our return and lay down on the sofa, but I trust she will do well. She seems reconciled to staying for the winter in the south as we all desire it so much. Miss Fenwick means to pass the winter somewhere on the southern coast, and will be most happy to have Dora with her as long as she can, and will bring her down into Westmorland, in spring or early in the summer. Is not that a nice plan; dear good Creature Miss Fenwick is! She comes this morning to fetch me and she will talk over the matter with Dora, and I dine with her today to meet Mr Stephen and Mr Taylor. Tomorrow I breakfast with Miss Rogers to meet the American Minister[2] and his lady. I have seen Courtenay twice, and shall see him again. He has just received rather more than 200, due on the annuities, with which he will purchase India Bonds as a present investment adding them to the

[*cetera desunt*]

1153. W. W. to M. W.

MS. WL.
LY ii. 888 (—).

August 15th Tuesday [1837]

My dearest Mary,

Your pacquet reached me yesterday. The frank I was to have sent off on Monday, proved of a wrong date; and most unfortunately a pretty long letter I had written for you must

[1] *Word dropped out.*

[2] Andrew Stevenson (1784–1857), Congressman, Speaker of the House of Representatives (1827–34), and Minister to the Court of St. James (1836–41).

have been left at Hampstead yesterday, now I have inflammation in my right eye and cannot write at length. I know not
what to say to Wm's proposal, but that he must examine
carefully before he mixes with anything of the kind.[1] I had from
Mr Courtenay papers of the annuities, a dark and unpromising
account. We erred in not accepting his proposal which would
have put 500 into our pockets. I have such a hot skin and such
feverish nights, that I am anxious to be gone from London.
Yesterday I dined at Miss Fenwick's, dinner not till eight as
Mr Stephen could not come before, remained till 12, I have not
been up so late for 5 months and consequently a disturbed night
and the inflammation in my eye—on Friday Dora will see Sir
Benjamin Brodie with me and on Saturday I hope we shall be at
Chatham. Sir B. says he has lately had two patients like Brother
Thomas[2] both recovering though slowly. Time, exercise,
cheerful spirits, and hope must do the work, and not medicine.
[?   ][3] I can write no more on account of the anger in
my eye. Love to dearest Sister, farewell my dearest Mary I wish
I were quietly at Rydal.

W. W.

On opening Dora's Letter I find this, my own to you
enclosed.

1154. W. W. to DORA W.

Address: Miss Wordsworth, Mrs Hoare's, Hampstead Heath.
Postmark: 15 Aug. 1837. *Stamp*: Piccadilly.
MS. WL.
LY ii. 888.

[15 Aug. 1837]

My dear Dora,
    These came yesterday. How unlucky I am, the Letter I wrote
to your mother under a wrong frank must have been left at
Hampstead where you made the objection to its being crump-
led up. I do not find it in my pocket-book neither can I find any

---

[1] W. W. jnr. apparently had some scheme for seeking employment in a
Brewery Company (see *MW*, p. 171).

[2] Thomas Hutchinson.

[3] *MS. illegible.*

where a letter for the Isle of Man, from your Mother, which I was to have got franked. I must also have left at Hampstead a pair of mottled half-stockings. I have got an inflammation in my right eye in consequence of a dinner deferred at Miss Fenwick's last night till 8 and not coming away till 12. I am anxious to be out of London and to be living somewhere in quiet—I feel I am living too fast—I had a very feverish and hot skin last night. God bless you—you will be expected at Mrs Hook's on Thursday. I found Sara Coleridge looking very ill—God bless you my dearest Dora, kindest remembrances to all.

W. W.

P.S. Upon opening your Letter to Mother, I find my own enclosed

pray be so good as to look for my stockings

1155. W. W. to JOSEPH COTTLE

Address: Joseph Cottle Esq^e, Bedminster, n^r Bristol. [*In Dora W.'s hand*]
Postmark: (1) 20 Aug. 1837 (2) 21 Aug. 1837. *Stamp*: Chatham.
MS. Cornell. Hitherto unpublished.

London August
19th 37

My dear Sir, or rather
My dear and good old Friend,
    Upon returning from the Continent where I have been travelling for more than four months past I find your Letter[1]

---

[1] Cottle had written on 29 Apr., enclosing his *Early Recollections; Chiefly Relating to the Late Samuel Taylor Coleridge*. 'In a work of this nature, I could not well help introducing your name, occasionally, but it has ever been with respect, and such as I hope will merit your cordial approbation. Had I possessed the privilege of living in your vicinity, you might, in a personal conference, have favoured me with some useful suggestions, both as to additions and omissions. It may not still be wholly unavailing to receive from you any remarks which might be suggested to your mind, in the perusal. . . . May I be permitted to ask, also, whether you think I have been too full of my disclosures respecting our friend Coleridge?' (*Bristol University Library MSS.*) See George Lamoine, 'Letters from Joseph Cottle to William Wordsworth: 1828–1850', *Ariel*, iii (Apr. 1972), 84–102.

with Many others waiting for me in London. Be assured that I set a due value upon the expressions of affectionate remembrance with which it abounds, and that I often think with the most lively interest of the happy days I formerly spent in your company and at [?][1] and in the neighbourhood of Bristol. The volume which was the occasion of your Letter I have not yet seen, nor shall I be able to have seen for several weeks, as I shall be unavoidably detained in the south of England, and by a journey which I have to make into Herefordshire to see my Brother in Law Mr Hutchinson, who has had the Misfortune to lose the use of his limbs from a violent concussion of the spinal chord occasioned by his horse falling with him.

Since the decease of our great Friend S. T. Coleridge Many things have been written and published about him, with few of which I am at all acquainted. It may be a weakness on my part, but I will say to you frankly, that so much sadness weighs upon my mind, when I think of those whom we have lost and are losing, that I cannot bear that the Public should be made Confidants of several friendships and affections almost as soon as one or both of the partners are laid in their graves. My judgement upon your book or any other upon the life of Coleridge, would therefore be of little value; and it would be painful to myself to give a better.[2] It would give me great pleasure to see you again, but that is not likely. My poor Sister, of whom you kindly inquire is much of a wreck both in mind and body, but not so as to be insensible of or indifferent to your remembrance of her.

Mrs W. is pretty well, so is my daughter.

Believe me my dear Sir
very faithfully your obliged Friend
Wm Wordsworth

[1] *Word missing.*
[2] Seven lines are obliterated at this point, not apparently by W. W.

1156. W. W. to HENRY REED[1]

Address: To Henry Reed Esqre, Philadelphia.
Endorsed: Rec^d Oct. 21.
MS. Berg Collection typescript, New York Public Library.
Mem. (—). *K* (—). *Wordsworth and Reed, p. 4* (—).

London, August 19, 1837.

My dear Sir,

Upon returning from a tour of several months upon the Continent I find two letters from you awaiting my arrival, along with the edition of my poems you have done me the honour of editing. To begin with the former Letter April 25, 1836.[2] It gives me concern that you should have thought it necessary not to apologize for that you have not done, but to

---

[1] Henry Hope Reed (1808–54) of Philadelphia, a grandson of General Reed, Washington's secretary, practised law for a time and taught moral philosophy, but ultimately became Professor of Rhetoric and English Literature in the University of Pennsylvania (1834), a Chair he occupied with great distinction until his premature death in the shipwreck of the *Arctic* on his way home from a visit to Europe. In 1837 he produced the first American edition of W. W.'s *Complete Poetical Works*. Broughton gives a full list of his numerous other publications (*Wordsworth and Reed*, p. xiv). He married Elizabeth White Bronson, a granddaughter of William White, the first Anglican Bishop of Pennsylvania.

[2] Reed had addressed a long letter to W. W., assuring him of 'the strong *personal* attachment of at least one of his American admirers'. 'This letter is not written with the vain purpose of communicating opinion or of paying compliments. The time has gone by when Mr Wordsworth might have set some value on an individual's judgment—when he might have been gratified at learning that he had won his way into some hearts. . . . Nor is this letter with the least presumptuous thought of taxing you with correspondence. It *is* written only as an expression of *feeling*. . . . You would be the last to check the flow of gratefulness, which so naturally gushes to light from the secret channels of the heart. . . . I know your own sense of thankfulness to the Poets for "the nobler loves and nobler cares" that are given by them . . . My single-hearted wish is to express to you, in this form of confidential intercourse, the same sentiment of gratitude. It cannot for a moment be confounded with flattery: no one can, I trust, question the sincerity of what is written under such circumstances—so privately—so free from ulterior motive. I am seeking for the pure pleasure of doing so, to tell you of my sense of obligation: The salutary warnings from your pages have, I persuade myself, not been addressed in vain: communing with you there, I have felt my nature elevated—I have learned to look with a better spirit on all around me.' (*Wordsworth and Reed*, pp. 1–3.)

444

PROFESSOR HENRY REED

from a portrait attributed to Thomas Sully, *c.* 1838

explain at length why you addressed me in the language of affectionate regard.—It must surely be gratifying to one whose aim as an author has been to reach the hearts of his fellow-creatures of all ranks and in all stations to find that he has succeeded in any quarter, and still more must he be grateful to learn that he has pleased in a distant country men of simple habits and cultivated taste, who are at the same time widely acquainted with literature. Your second letter,[1] accompanying the edition of the poems, I have read, but unluckily, have not before me. It was lent to Sergeant Talfourd on account of the passage in it that alludes to the possible and desirable establishment of English Copyright in America.

I shall now hasten to notice the Edition which you have superintended of the poems. This I can do with much pleasure, as the Book which has been shewn to several persons of taste, Mr Rogers in particular, is allowed to be far the handsomest specimen of print in double Column which they have seen. Allow me to thank you for the pains you have bestowed upon the work. Do not apprehend that any difference in our several arrangements of the poems can be of much importance; you appear to understand me far too well for that to be possible. I have only to regret, in respect to this Volume, that it should have been published before my last Edition in the correction of which I took great pains as my last labour in that way, and which moreover contains several additional pieces. It may be allowed me also to express a hope that such a law will be passed ere long by the American legislature as will place English Authors in general upon a better footing in America than at present they have obtained, and that the protection of Copyright between the two countries will be reciprocal.

The vast circulation of English works in America offers a temptation for hasty and incorrect printing; and that same vast circulation would, without adding to the price of each copy of an English Work in a degree that could be grudged or thought injurious by any purchaser, allow an American remuneration which might add considerably to the comforts of English Authors who may be in narrow circumstances, yet who at the same time may have written solely from honorable motives.— Besides, justice is the foundation on which both law and practice ought to rest.

[1] This letter is lost.

Having many letters to write on returning to England after so long an absence I regret that I must be so brief upon the present occasion. I cannot conclude, however, without assuring you, that the acknowledgements which I receive from the vast continent of America are among the most grateful that reach me.[1] What a vast field is there open to the English Mind, acting through our noble language! Let us hope that our Authors of true Genius will not be unconscious of that thought or inattentive to the duty which it imposes upon them of doing their utmost to instruct, to purify and to elevate their readers. That such may be my own endeavour through the short time I shall have to remain in this world, is a prayer in which I am sure you and your life's partner will join me.

Believe me gratefully
Your much obliged friend
Wm Wordsworth

1157. W. W. to M. W. and D. W.

Address: Mrs Wordsworth, Rydal, Kendal.
Franked: London August twenty five 1837 Jas Stephen.
Postmark: 25 Aug. 1837.
MS. WL.
LY ii. 889 (—).

Broadstairs, Wednesday 23 August [1837]

My dearest Friends
I arrived here this morning. But I will take things in order. On Thursday last I dined with Mrs Hook in Regents Park,

---

[1] 'It is the happiness of even married life that has been heightened by the spirit of your Poetry,' Reed had written. 'Could your fancy have transported you across the Atlantic, how completely domesticated would you have found yourself in our tranquil study! How often has its fireside been gladdened by you! Some of our happiest hours—the duties of the day fulfilled—have been spent over your pages;—again and again are they read to my *one* listener—the best kind of audience in the world. When after some lapse of time we have recurred to our cherished volume, we have felt that you were aiding us in "binding our days together by natural piety". . . . What is more, in your example I have discovered the best elements of a true and rational patriotism, and guided most safely by the light of your feeling, I have a deeper love for my own country.'

whither Dora had come in the afternoon. On that night as on the night before I slept at the Roger's,[1] where on Friday morning Dora joined me in a Fly and we went to Sir Benjamin B's. What passed between them I do not exactly know, but on joining them he told me that nothing serious ailed her and that she only wanted strength. He approved of her remaining the winter in the South, which he said it would be well to try. From Sir B.'s we went back to Rogers, and then in a Coach to London Bridge wharf, where after waiting half an hour we embarked for Gravesend. We had a pleasant passage, a fine breeze, which she much enjoyed. At Gravesend we got into an Omnibus and reached Chatham Docks, just as they were at dinner, between five and six. She bore the fatigue of the day very well, but next day she was very *yawnative*, and more exhausted than I was prepared for. Mrs Smith[2] took us in a carriage to call on the Nicholsons[3] and upon Mrs Fletcher at whose house we met Dr and Mrs Davie[4] and their children. Miss Fletcher[5] quite well and strong. On Sunday morning Dora did not go to Church, but the Nicholsons after offered to lend their carriage to take us to the Cathedral, Mrs Smith, she and I went. On Saturday I called on Colonel Pasley[6] who has been ill, but is getting better,

---

[1] W. W. had dined at Rogers's on Wednesday the 16th with H. C. R., Courtenay, and Empson. Later on, Moxon and Talfourd joined them. 'Talfourd was a great acquisition. His vivacity and good humour are quite inspiring.' At breakfast the following morning H. C. R. and Empson came again, and W. W. spoke about his poetry. 'He repeated emphatically what he had said before to me, that he did not expect or desire from posterity any other fame than that which would be given him for the way in which his poems exhibit man in his essentially human character and relations—as child, parent, husband, the qualities which are common to all men as opposed to those which distinguish one man from another.' (*HCR* ii 535.)

[2] W. W.'s cousin Mrs. Proctor Smith, resident at Chatham.

[3] Of Rochester (see L. 1018 above).

[4] Dr. John Davy (see L. 921 above) was now stationed at Chatham, and W. W. had visited him and his family at Darland on 19 Aug. For some account of the impressions he gave them of his recent Italian tour, see *Autobiography of Mrs. Fletcher*, pp. 227–8. 'He spoke with most interest of the ruin at Nismes, and said he saw nothing in Italy equal to the combined effect of the situation and edifice of the Pont du Gard at Nismes. Of the maritime Alps route also, and of the Mediterranean generally, he spoke with much delight.'

[5] Mary Fletcher (1802–80), who married Sir John Richardson (1787–1865), the Arctic explorer, as his third wife in 1847.

[6] Col. Charles William Pasley (see pt. ii, L. 396).

in an inflammation of the trachea. On Monday Dora remained at home. I called on Dr Davey and he took me to Cobham House, 4 miles from Rochester, a seat of Lord Darnley's.[1] On that day (viz. Monday) Dr D and Mrs Fletcher and Miss dined at Mrs Smith's; and Tuesday noon I left Mrs Smith's with a hope of getting on to Canterbury in time to be brought hither by Mr and Miss Rogers, but the 2 first Coaches were full, so I arrived too late, and was obliged to sleep at Canterbury which with the expense of travelling from Canterbury cost me 12 shillings, but I missed their company also. Dora thought it better on every account she should remain at Chatham, in which she was quite right as the journey hither would have fatigued her much; besides her stay at Chatham would otherwise have been too short. Having now seen a good deal of her, I can say, that I am rather disappointed as to the state of her strength; in other respects not so.—Therefore my dearest Friends let us live in hope that she will be restored in time. At Chatham she received your 2nd Letter; your first with Isabella's enclosed I found here and shall forward to her through Mr Stephen. I cannot say anything fixed yet about our movements; but I shall not stay here more than a week. Rogers and his Sister are both here; Moxon and I dine there today. If possible I will go for two nights to the Archbishop's[2] and then for Herefordshire. Dora wrote to Charles Wordsworth to receive her for a night or two, and Mr Smith will convey her up to Town. Tell Mr Carter I will call at Bell's.[9] As to her Chair for Thomas,[3] I talked to Dr Davey about it, but he seemed to be without distinct ideas on the subject, and thought nothing so likely to answer as a Sedan Chair; so that until I shall have seen Thomas I fear I can do nothing in the matter. I have not been able to make out much of Isabella's Letter, so that I know not if it may require any comments from my pen. I hope John, our John, will be very careful what he says, or writes, of the Curwen affairs—his words misled me a good deal about the supposed amount of the loss. This must be a very meagre Letter. I think I told you if I had had the prospect of Dora's being at the seaside with Miss Fenwick or any other friend I should never have thought of coming here, but gone straight into Herefordshire, but having

[1] John Bligh, 6th Earl of Darnley (1827–96).
[2] At Addington Palace.
[3] W. W.'s stockbrokers.
[4] i.e. for the crippled Thomas Hutchinson.

entangled myself in engagements with Mr Rogers and Mr Moxon I could not break through.—Your account of little Henry[1] delights me much. I hope you will be allowed to keep him till my return, pray do. I was up this morning at four, and had a dull ride hither. Yesterday I went in to Canterbury Cathedral and if it had been only 2 miles instead of 4 to Lee Priory I should have walked thither. Dora was much mortified when she learned I had directed my Letters through Mr Stephen to be forwarded hither, and I am myself sorry that I did so. This is Wednesday, by next Wednesday or Thursday at the latest I hope to be in London. So that a Letter in answer to this may be directed to Mr Moxon's. I had a violent [? Lax][2] for 2 days in London but it is gone off and I am well except the heat in the toe and something of numbness in my hands which I think is always worst after drinking a little, however little, more than usual. I feel strongly persuaded that I should do best to leave off fermented liquors altogether. How I long dearest Mary to see you again and you my dearest Sister, and all of you. Farewell W. W.

Thursday. My dearest M. I could not send this letter off yesterday as I intended. I am afraid you will be impatient for news. I am sorry to learn from the enclosed which I took the liberty of opening that Dora says her heart beats more lately. She never mentioned this to me, and I do not like to teaze her with questions about her health. Neither do you mention your own health, pray do, how is your chest? This must say I have contrived to read Isabella's Letter[3] which does her great credit.

Ever yours—

P.S. Thursday the numbness in hands is better today—

[1] Their grandson.
[2] *MS. obscure.*
[3] Presumably about her family's financial losses and the suffering of the people of Workington, following the mining disaster.

1158. W. W. to DORA W.

Address: Miss Wordsworth, W. Smith Esq, Chatham Docks, Chatham.
Franked: London August twenty five 1837 Jas Stephen.
Postmark: 25 Aug. 1837.
MS. WL.
LY ii. 891.

Broadstairs Thursday morning
[24 Aug. 1837]

My dearest Dora

Mr and Miss Rogers were gone when I reached Canterbury, it was not till near six; so I had to sleep there which with expenses of coaches before I got here cost me 12 shillings. I was called at 4 in the morning, hired a fly at Ramsgate, reached this door between 7 and 8. I wished much to write to you yesterday as I did to Mother, but I was engaged in various ways till it was too late: I found much difficulty in reading the enclosed Letter as I fear you will also. Yesterday was shocking bad weather, today is bright and pleasant, which I am especially glad of for your sakes, as you will I trust enjoy your trip to Sheerness. This is a very pleasant, though not a particularly amusing place; but the drives are agreeable; yesterday I went with Rogers to Margate, and to Kingsgate but it rained so we could not get out of the Carriage. We shall go again. Next Wednesday, I trust, I shall be in London. Probably today I shall write to Mrs Howley, and if convenient I will go for two days to visit them, perhaps it would be as well you should stay at Chatham till my return, but all this may be fixed in time. The air is very bracing here today, and I think would agree well with Miss Fenwick and yourself. But Ramsgate may be as good and is no doubt much more amusing on account of the size of the harbour, the fine quays or piers, and the multitude of vessels.—I am quite sorry this Letter was not sent off yesterday but really my dear Child it was no fault of mine. Love to Mr and Mrs Smith and your Cousin Mary[1] and kind remembrances to Mr [?][2]

affectionately
W. W.

---

[1] Mary Smith (b. 1818), who lated lived at Rydal.
[2] *MS. obscure*. Perhaps Mr. Nicholson of Rochester.

1159. W. W. to M. W.

Address: Mrs Wordsworth, Rydal, Kendal.
MS. WL.
LY ii. 892.

Broadstairs Monday Augst 28 [1837]

My dearest Mary,

I have heard from Mrs Howley. The Moxons dont leave this place till Friday; I had meant to go on Wednesday, but they have prevailed on me to stay to go along with them. On Saturday I shall go to the Arch B^{p's} and return with him to Town on Tuesday morning, and on the Saturday following at the latest I trust that dear Dora and I will have reached Brinsop.—I have not heard of her since I came here but I shall write to her today with an account of my movements. Her intention was to go to Charles Wordsworth's if they could receive her. She cannot go to Mr Moxon's on account of the house being newly painted, nor shall I.—In the Letter I mean to write to Dora today I shall beg of her to let me know by post where she goes. She will of course remain at Chatham till I quit this place.

Lord Holland has begged through Mr Rogers that I would give them one day which perhaps I may do, but this will depend entirely upon Dora's convenience. I wish she could have been with me here, for this is a very pleasant place with delightful air at this season of the year, though it must be very cold in winter, as indeed it is now, being full as nipping an air as in October with us.—But Dora would have enjoyed it, and both Mr and Miss Rogers have their carriages here, so that she could have had an airing every day along the high grounds. We have been three times at Margate, and once at Ramsgate, and probably may go as far as Dover. I should have written more at length but my right eye is rather inflamed having been struck by the coldness yesterday in Mr R's carriage, and I was so imprudent as to read a good deal after dinner, when I felt it affected. Love to dearest Sister, ever most affectionately yours

W. W.

1160. W. W. to DORA W.

Address: Miss Wordsworth, W. Smith's Esq., Chatham Docks, Chatham.
Stamp: Ramsgate Penny Post.
MS. WL.
LY ii. 893 (—).

No. 5 Prospect Place, Broadstairs
Monday noon, 28ᵗʰ. [Aug. 1837]

My dearest Dora,

The Moxons leave this place Friday next, and have prevailed upon me to put off my departure, which I intended for Wednesday at the latest, to go along with them, by steam, embarking at Margate by ten on that morning.

On that day I hope to call at Bell's on account of the annuities, and on Saturday having heard from Mrs Howley, I shall go to Lambeth, probably to return with the Archbᵖ who comes every Tuesday to Lambeth; if not with him, at all events I shall return on that day at the latest.—Pray write to me by Post and tell me where you will be in London. The best place for us both would have been Mr Moxon's, but you must not be trusted there on account of the newly painted House. I mean to sleep on Friday at Mr Rogers, and the same on Tuesday when I return from Addington Park. Lord and Lady Holland have warmly requested me through Mr Rogers to give them one day; but in this I should be entirely guided, my dear Child, by your convenience; being determined, if it suit you, to be at Hereford on Friday night, at all events on Saturday at the very latest.

I have again mislaid the paper of Mother's commissions, if you have it not; but I do not recollect anything in it which we could effect, except to apply to Macrone, the Publisher, for Sir E. Brydges Edit: of Milton,[1] which Mr Moxon has undertaken to do.

You would have enjoyed yourself here much, we have a comfortable Lodging with plenty of room for you, and both Mr and Miss Rogers have their carriages here, with their horses, so that you might have had an airing every day. This is a quiet pleasant place with agreeable drives; we have been thrice at Margate, and once at Ramsgate. I hope you saw from Chatham Docks the glorious sunset we had on Saturday evening.

---

[1] See L. 888 above.

We shall embark on Friday at Margate for London at ten in the morning, but probably you will not be inclined to leave Chatham till my return from Addington Park, otherwise I might have had the pleasure of seeing you on Friday, which would be much to me, for I find it is a little mortifying to be so near you, and not be with you, especially when we shall have to part so soon and for so long a time.—

Write to me by all means here if you can so as that Letter may be here by Thursday morning, on Friday it would be too late, as the Letters are not delivered till nine, when we may be at Margate—if you have not fixed anything pray write to me at Dover Street as soon as you have, but at all events let me hear from you as soon as you can. Love to all kind friends about you, your affectionate father.

W. W.

I wrote through Mr Stephen enclosing Mother's letter to you.

I have caught a little irritation in my right eye, from the sharp air while riding with open windows—

1161. W. W. to RICHARD HOWITT [1]

MS. untraced. [2]
Carl R. Woodring, 'Peter Bell and "The Pious": A New Letter', Philological Quarterly, xxx (Oct. 1951), 430–4.

Rydal Mount, Aug. [? Sept.] 30, 1837

Dear Sir,

I have to thank you for your proof-sheet and letter received this morning. The stanzas in 'Peter Bell' [3] had been objected to as irreverent and they were omitted accordingly, as stated to your

---

[1] For Richard Howitt, see pt. ii, L. 608.

[2] The MS. was mislaid by the owner, Miss Maisie Howitt, shortly after she had published this letter in the daily *Argus* of Melbourne, Australia, for 4 Mar. 1933, and consequently her dating to August, which was accepted by Woodring, cannot be checked. But W. W. did not return to Rydal Mount until the end of September, and the letter was most likely written at that time.

[3] See pt. i, L. 366. William and Mary Howitt had stayed with the Wordsworths in July 1836 (*R MVB*), while W. W. was revising his poems for the new edition, and they had probably discussed this stanza (see *Mary Howitt*,

brother and sister, not with the approbation of my own judgement, but in deference solely to that of another. You can easily understand how unwilling I should be to shock any pious person with unjustifiable approximation of sacred topics to profane, but I cannot think it wrong to restore the passage since you, who have manifestly entered into the spirit of the poem, regret its omission, and, if I recollect right, your brother and sister did also. I have been very much pleased with your verses, [1] and think my own honoured by being interwoven in a poem on such a subject, treated with such depth of feeling. I recollect with pleasure the brief interview I had with you at Nottingham. Accept my kind remembrances and don't omit to mention to your brothers and sisters that our obligations to them are a source of great pleasure to my wife, my daughter, and myself.

Believe me, dear sir, faithfully yours,
Wm Wordsworth

An inflammation in my eyes has obliged me to employ an amanuensis.

1162. M. W. to H. C. R.

Address: H. C. Robinson Esqre, 2 Plowdens Build^gs, Temple.
Endorsed: August 1837 M^rs. Wordsworth
MS. Dr Williams's Library.
Morley, i. 346.

[late Aug. 1837][2]

My dear Friend
   The pleasure of expecting the enclosed will find *you all* assembled in your *dusty rooms* induces me to forward a few lines, for the sake of that pleasure, under cover to you. At the same time I am afforded an opportunity to thank you for all your

An Autobiography, 1889, i. 254). Shelley had used it to open *Peter Bell the Third* in 1819.
   [1] Probably (as Woodring notes) *A Sabbath Pilgrimage*, in Richard Howitt's *The Gipsy King, and Other Poems*, 1840, p. 99. A sonnet, *On Visiting Rydal Mount*, appears in the same volume, p. 87.
   [2] But probably written on 2 Sept., as the somewhat confused postscript might suggest.

delightful scraps—and to say how glad I am that you are yet to be the Poets fellow-traveller[1] a fair proof to me that your long ramble has not sickened you of each others society.[2] Besides Dora in this case will have an opportunity to ascertain how far my opinion of your qualifications as a travelling companion is correct. I hope before you part you will settle about your Xtmas visit to the *home staying* at Rydal

ever faithfully and aff^{ly} yours

M. Wordworth.

I send this by Mondays post—Tuesday's would possibly have done to meet my object—but it might not have reached Plowdens Build^g this the 2^d before this Thursdays breakfast Party broke up

1163. D. W. to HANNAH HOARE

Address: To Mrs Hoare, Hampstead Heath, near London.
MS. WL.
LY ii. 898.

[Sept. 1837]

My dear Friend

I know not when I last wrote to you—and now I have a hard task to write at all among the many thoughts which press upon me—I have had a long long struggle; but through God's mercy here I sit on my chair—with a clear head—and a thankful heart. I will give you some of the many verses which have slipped from me I know not how—since I cannot now so well express my thoughts and feelings to you.

To my kind Friend and medical Attendant T. Carr composed a year ago—or more.

Five years of sickness and of pain
This weary frame has travelled o'er
But God is good—and once again
I rest upon a tranquil shore.

---

[1] To Brinsop.

[2] Relations between W. W. and H. C. R. had been somewhat strained on several occasions in the course of their Continental tour. On their return, H. C. R. was relieved to discover that W. W. had not apparently disclosed this. See *HCR* ii. 533–5.

I rest in quietness of mind,
Oh! may I thank my God
With heart that never shall forget
The perilous path I've trod!

They tell me of one fearful night
When thou, my faithful Friend,
Didst part from me in holy trust
That soon my earthly cares must end.

On that night Mr Carr left me because he could do no more
for me, and my poor Brother went to lie down on his bed
thinking he could not bear to see me die.

I hope I may recover the use of my legs, though at present I
cannot walk without props to bear my whole weight.

It grieves me that poor Dora is not likely to come home this
autumn or winter. God grant my dear Brother may soon arrive
in safety! Pray give my best Love to Miss Hoare. I venture to
hope that I may see you both again—

God bless you—
ever your affect^e

D. Wordsworth

When you see Charles or any of my nephews give my kindest
love to them.
Monday—the day of Month I know not.
Do you ever see Sir Benjamin Brodie? If you do tell him I often
and often think of him—and pray give him my kindest regards.

1164. W. W. to MARY HUTCHINSON

Address: Mrs Hutchinson, Brinsop Court, Hereford.
Franked: Croydon Sept four 1837 W. Cantuar.
Postmark: 4 Sept. 1837.
MS. WL. Hitherto unpublished.

Saturday Septr 2nd [1837]

My dear Mary or Mrs Hutchinson,
whichever you like best,
We have fixed our departure for Friday next, by the Mazeppa
for Hereford. As the journey will be a long one pray be so good
as to secure us three bed rooms at Hereford on that night, three I
say, for Mr Robinson is with us, *he* wishes to sleep at the best Inn

where the newspapers are kept.—[We] wish for nothing more than neat beds in quiet rooms. On Saturday morning, if convenient you will be so kind as to send for us,—and let the Servant bring word whether Mr Monkhouse will be at home, and can receive Mr Robinson, who in that case will go on to the Stowe, to visit him for 2 or 3 days.—

We have made and will make enquiries about a carriage[1] but, I fear, there is little chance of success; besides, I am somewhat afraid of the responsibility, not having notions sufficiently distinct of what would best answer the purpose. As I write in a great hurry, having a world of matters to do this morning before I start for Addington Park, where I am going to remain till Tuesday on a visit to the Archbishop of Canterbury. Best love to Thomas, yourself, and all yours.

most affectionately   W Wordsworth

[Dora W. writes to Ebba Hutchinson]

Dear Ebba I have written to Mrs Gee about M. M.[2] and will bring her reply. Mr Robinson will see about the Italian books— he will *not* go to Brinsop except for a call so don't dream of preparing aught for him. Mr R., Father and I have a scheme of which you are to be one if you will and can of going to Tintern and—but more of this when we meet. God bless you Darling— not time for another [?][3]

Dora Wordsworth

[1] For Thomas Hutchinson. See L. 1157 above.
[2] Mary Monkhouse, daughter of the late Thomas Monkhouse, now aged 16. She was perhaps going to Mrs. Gee's school at Hendon.
[3] *Word dropped out.*

1165. W. W. to CHARLES ROBERT LESLIE[1]

Address: C. R. Leslie Esq., Pineapple Place, Edgware Road.
Postmark: 4 Sept. 1837. *Stamp*: Piccadilly.
MS. Cornell. Hitherto unpublished.

44 Dover street
2nd Sept^{br} —37

Dear Sir,
    I am gratified to hear of the intention to pay a tribute of respect to so admirable an Artist as Mr Constable in the way you mention; and it will give me pleasure to have my name down as a subscriber, for one guinea, which may be had from Mr Moxon 44 Dover street whenever called for—

I remain with much respect
sincerely yours
Wm Wordsworth

1166. W. W. to M. W. and D. W.

MS. WL.
LY ii. 895 (—).

Dover Street 2nd Sep^{br} [1837]

My dearest Friends,
    The Enclosed Paper is for Mr Carter's custody. I called yesterday at Mr Bell's and expect to receive today his account of the monies paid to Mr Courtenay which I will either send or bring.—
    Dont send the portrait[2] to Isabella till I come. I will get it framed if she thinks it worth it, which I fear she will not, nor you either. The little drawing of Dora is charming, very like her; you would prize it highly.—Dont let any volumes of the Poems which you will find in the box be sold separate.—They sell very slowly at present, indeed no books at all sell. Today we shall see about the remaining Volumes of Sir Egerton's

---

[1] For C. R. Leslie, see pt. i, L. 139. He had just set on foot a subscription to purchase Constable's *The Cornfield* for the National Gallery, in memory of the artist who had died on 1 Apr.
[2] For Joseph Severn's portrait of W. W., see L. 1139 above.

Milton—at 4 I leave this place for the Archbishop's, he sends a servant and a carriage for me, and shall remain till Tuesday, and on Friday we shall start for Hereford.

On Thursday I had a delightful excursion with Mr Rogers to Dover; the place is mightily improved as to new buildings since we were there, and I think it would suit admirably Miss Fenwick and Dora.—

As Mr Rogers will not be in London to go with me to Holland House, I shall content myself with breakfasting there, on Wednesday, and that day I shall dine with Dora at Henry Coleridge's, and we both sleep that night and the next at Mr Rogers', and depart thence on Friday morning.—So you are now aware of our movements.—As I find that Dora and I are writing the same things I shall give over, with my best love to Sister and a kiss to Henry.[1] How I long to see you all—most tenderly and affectionately yours

W. W.

I think Dora is stronger.
Mr Robinson is not so much pleased with Dora's Portrait as I am though he allows it to be a likeness.[2]

1167. W. W. to SIR GEORGE BEAUMONT

MS. Cornell. Hitherto unpublished.

Addington Park
Sept^b 3^d 37

My dear Sir George,

Allow me to thank you for your kind Letter, and to express my regret that I am unable to take Coleorton in my way to the North. I am obliged to cross the Country to the neighbourhood of Hereford, in order to visit a Brother of Mrs Wordsworth, who, by a dreadful accident, has lost the use of his limbs. Whenever I may be called to London again, depend upon it, I shall see you at Coleorton, should you happen to be there. I have

---

[1] Their grandson.
[2] H. C. R. added a note, giving his opinion of the portrait (which has not been identified). The whole letter is written on the back of a letter from John Wood Warter to Dora W.

not yet seen little Constance, [1] but I learn that she is quite well, so are the Archbishop and his Lady, and both looking well. Pray mention my name to my little Godson [2] whom I long to see, and believe me, my dear Sir George

faithfully your obliged
Wm Wordsworth

1168. W. W. to H. C. R.

Address: H. C. Robinson Esqre, Temple.
Endorsed: Sept. 1837. Wordsworth. Autograph.
MS. Dr. Williams's Library.
Morley, i. 347.

44 Dover street
Tuesday afternoon [5 Sept. 1837]

My dear Friend,

It was inconsiderate in me, on my Daughter's account, to engage to breakfast with you on Thursday.—I knew it would fatigue her much, and it is necessary for her to start as fresh as possible on her long journey.—M^r M— and I have therefore undertaken to set Mr Cookson free from his engagement to you, and on that condition he has promised to breakfast here on Thursday at nine, Mr Moxon not doubting that you will readily do the same. M— and I called at your chambers this morning, after having been with M^r C, but you were not at home—

farewell, faithfully yours
W Wordsworth

---

[1] Sir George's only daughter, now staying with Dr. and Mrs. Howley, her grandparents.

[2] Sir George's younger son William.

1169. W. W. to THOMAS POWELL[1]

Endorsed: Sep: 7th Gave to Wordsworth Coleridge's Greek Testament.
MS. Doheny Memorial Library, St. John's Seminary, Camarillo, California. Hitherto unpublished.

7 Sept[r] [1837]
Dover Street

My dear Sir,

Tomorrow morning I depart, but I must snatch a moment to express my regret that your engagements did not allow you to breakfast with us this morning; and above all to thank you for the very valuable testimoney of your kindness, which I found on my return from the Country.

The book will be placed among my choicest treasures of that kind, and after my day will I trust pass into the hands of my elder Son, who is a Clergyman, and will know how to use and prize it.

With kind regards to Mrs Powell, and to your Brother, believe [me]

my dear Sir
in great haste
most sincerely your
much obliged
W[m] Wordsworth

[1] Thomas Powell (1809–87), dramatist and miscellaneous writer in prose and verse, was employed by the City merchant Thomas Chapman in the eighteen-thirties, and used his contacts to ingratiate himself with leading writers of the day. In 1838–9 he projected *The Poems of Geoffrey Chaucer Modernized* (published 1841) to which W. W., R. H. Horne, Leigh Hunt, Elizabeth Barrett, and others contributed. In 1842 he published two verse plays, *The Count de Foix* and *The Wife's Revenge*, the latter dedicated to Talfourd, and the following year a third, *The Blind Wife*, dedicated to Robert Browning. In 1844 he collaborated with R. H. Horne in *A New Spirit of the Age*. Powell had met W. W. by 1836, when he asked permission to dedicate his anonymous volume *Attempts at Verse* (1837) to him, and on receiving a favourable reply, Powell wrote W. W. a rhapsodic letter on 10 Oct., recalling the effect that his poetry had had on him: 'A strong delight came over me—a sunbeam seemed to stir the inmost depths of my Soul' (*WL MSS.*). Thereafter he cultivated W. W. assiduously, sending him books and presents of cheese, until his criminal activities became known, and he was forced to flee to America where he passed the rest of his days.

1170. W. W. to ISABELLA FENWICK

MS. Cornell. Hitherto unpublished.

[*In Dora W.'s hand*]

Brinsop Court
n^r Hereford
Sepr 13th 18[3]7¹—

. . . and will be most happy to join you when or wheresoever it may be convenient to you to receive her² after that time— Pray remember us both kindly to Mr Taylor and

believe me my dear Miss Fenwick
with Dora's love   Your faithful and affe^{te} Friend
[*signed*] Wm Wordsworth

1171. W. W. to EDWARD MOXON

Address: Edward Moxon Esq^e, 44 Dover S^t, Piccadilly.
Postmark: (1) 15 Sept. 1837 (2) 16 Sept.
MS. Henry E. Huntington Library.
LY ii. 895.

[*In Dora W.'s hand*]

Brinsop Court
n^r Hereford.
Sep^t. 13th [1837]

Dear Mr Moxon,

We had a beautiful day and reached Hereford in good time, Dora not being very much fatigued—The weather is at present so broken that we are unable to fix a day for setting off on our excursion for Tintern. Mr R.³ is with Mr Monkhouse, 14 miles from this place up the Wye, but he will dine here to-day—he enjoyed himself as usual. I have contrived to get an inflammation in one of my eyelids in w^h the eye of course participates but I sh^d be ashamed of being dejected by such, I hope, passing

---

¹ *Written 1827.*
² Dora W., who was to stay with I. F. for the winter.
³ H. C. R.

privation when I see Mʳ Monkhouse on the verge of blindness as cheerful as the brightest day of Spring, he is indeed a noble example for every afflicted person—

I find that I have brought away only one Vol: of Cowper[1] which is more than enough, for neither are wanted here—Dora will therefore bring back with her to London this one and you will be so kind as to take the other out of my portmanteau.

I have nothing more to add than kind wishes in which Dora joins and a hope that you all continue well

Ever faithfully yours
[*signed*] Wm Wordsworth

I shall remain at this place till about Tuesday 26ᵗʰ when I start for the north and on Thursday Evᵍ hope to be at home.

1172. W. W. to EDWARD QUILLINAN

Address: Edward Quillinan Esqʳᵉ, Post Office, Falmouth.
Postmark: 21 Sept. 1837.
Endorsed: 1837 Brinsop Mʳ Wordsworth Septʳ 20. Dora and Ebba—Recᵈ at Falmouth Sunday Octbʳ 8ᵗʰ Ansᵈ same day to Rydal Mount.
MS. WL.
Mem. (—). *Grosart* (—). *K* (—). *LY ii. 896.*

[*In Dora W.'s hand*]

Brinsop Court, Wednesday Sept. 20ᵗʰ [1837]

My dear Mr Quillinan,
(I hold the pen for Father)
We are heartily glad to learn from your letter just received that in all probability by this time you must have left the unhappy country in wʰ you have been so long residing. I should not have been sorry if you had entered a little more into Peninsular politics, for what is going on there is shocking to humanity, and one would be glad to see anything like an opening for the termination of these unnatural troubles—the

---

[1] Southey's new edition.

position of the Miguelites[1] relatively to the confliction of so-
called liberal parties is just what I apprehended and expressed
very lately to Mr Robinson, who would not hear of it; very
inconsiderately, I think, setting down that body as all but
extinguished. He came down with us to Hereford with a view
to a short tour on the banks of the Wye w[h] has been prevented
by an unexpected attack of my old complaint of inflammation
in the eye; and in consequence of this Dora will accompany me
home with a promise on her part of returning to London before
the month of Oct[br] is out. Our places are taken in to-morrow's
coach for Liverpool, so that since we must be disappointed at
not seeing you and Jemima here, we trust that you will come to
Rydal from Leeds. This very day Dora had read to me your
Poem[2] again; it convinces me along with your other writings
that it is in your power to attain a permanent place among the
poets of England, your thoughts, feelings, knowledge, and
judgement in style, and skill in metre entitle you to it; if you
have not yet succeeded in gaining it the cause appears to me
mainly to lie in the subjects w[h] you have chosen. It is worthy of
note how much of Gray's popularity is owing to the happiness
with which his subject is selected in three pieces—his Hymn to
Adversity, his ode on the distant prospect of Eton College, and
his Elegy. I ought however in justice to add that one cause of
your failure appears to have been thinking too humbly of
yourself, so that you have not reckoned it worth while to look
sufficiently round you for the best subjects or to employ as
much time in reflecting, condensing bringing out and placing
your thoughts and feelings in the best point of view, as is
necessary. I will conclude this matter of poetry, my part of the
letter,[3] with requesting that as an act of friendship at your

[1] See pt. ii, L. 781. In Sept. 1836 the liberals or Septembrists had seized
power and exiled their opponents, the supporters of the late King Pedro's
charter for parliamentary government within the control of the monarchy.

[2] Unidentified.

[3] W. W.'s letter was followed by notes from Dora W. to E. Q. and
Elizabeth Hutchinson to Jemima Q. E. Q.'s last two letters to Dora W. from
Oporto (*WL MSS.*), which W. W. had not seen, suggest how far their
relationship had deepened since his escape from shipwreck. In the first, on 7
Mar., he hinted that Dora W. should bring young Mary Hutchinson out to
convalesce in Portugal: 'But I am too unfortunate a man for any event so
auspicious ever to cheer me in this world—you do not know what yearnings
of the heart you have awakened in me by your remarks about Willy and his

convenience you would take the trouble, a considerable one I own, of comparing the corrections in my last edition with the text in the preceding one. You know my principles of style better I think than any one else, and I should be glad to learn if anything strikes you as being altered for the worse. You will find the principal changes in The White Doe, in w^h I had too little of the benefit of your help and judgement: there are several also in the sonnets both miscellaneous and political—in the other poems they are nothing like so numerous, but here also I should be glad if you w^d take the like trouble. Jemima, I am sure, will be pleased to assist you in the comparison by reading new or old as you may think fit. With love to her I remain my dear Mr Quillinan, faithfully yours,

[signed] Wm Wordsworth

1173. W. W. to LORD LONSDALE

Address: The Earl of Lonsdale, Lowther, Penrith.
Stamp: Kendal Penny Post.
MS. Lonsdale MSS.
Mem. (—). *K* (—). *LY ii. 899* (—).

[*In M. W.'s hand*]

Rydal Mount
Sept. 27th [1837]

My dear Lord Lonsdale,

An attack of my old enemy, Inflammation in one of my eyes, makes it necessary for me to employ Mrs Wordsworth's pen to

love; how differently might many of my past years have gone by, if I had been wiser in money-guarding, and wiser in woman's heart. But pshaw! such regrets must sound ridiculous to you from a man of 45.' And then more fretfully, on 11 Apr., in answer to a letter from Dora W. rejecting any possibility of marrying him: 'So you are not only *not* coming, but you *would* not if you could! . . . Then you add that I shall like you better for such a resolution: now there you are mistaken: I *could* not have liked you better than I did, but I do like you a little less for this confession of yours.—Never mind, I shall be hard enough in time (it is high time I should petrify) . . . It is best that you should be there, and I should be here; it is best that you should be a Nun at large and your own Lady Abbess; and it is best that I a widower of 45, not inexperienced in troubles, should at last look out for a rich widow or a maiden heiress . . . "It is best as it is"—God bless you for that and everything, I shall be a philosopher in time.' See L. 1189 below.

enquire after your Lordship, Lady Lonsdale, and all my friends who may be at Lowther; and to express my regret in not being able to pay my respects to you in Person, as I had hoped to do. After having had excellent health during my long ramble, it is unfortunate that I should thus be disabled at the conclusion; the mischief came to me in Herefordshire, whither I had gone on my way home, to see my Brother-in-Law, who by his horse falling with him some time ago, was left without the use of his limbs.

My son William, from a modesty that is natural to him, was doubtful about accepting *singly* an invitation in which you had done him the honor of joining him with Lord Gifford,[1] but as a similar compliment had been paid him once or twice before, he relied upon a favorable interpretation of the motive which has induced him to present himself at Lowther.[2]

I was lately a few days with Mr Rogers at Broad-stairs, and also with the Archbishop of Canterbury at Addington Park— they were both well. I was happy to see the Archbishop much stronger than his slender and almost feeble appearance would lead one to expect. We walked up and down in the Park, for 3 hours one day and nearly 4 the next, without his seeming to be the least fatigued. I mention this as we must all feel the value of his life in this state of public affairs.

The Cholera prevented us getting as far as Naples, which was the only disappointment we met with; as a Man of Letters I have to regret that this most interesting tour was not made by me earlier in Life, as I might have turned the notices it has supplied me with, to more account than I now expect to do.

With respectful remembrances to Lady Lonsdale and to your Lordship, in which Mrs W. unites, I remain my dear Lord, faithfully

Your much obliged St

[*signed*] Wm Wordsworth

Our staunch Conservative friend Mr Partridge[3] called on me

[1] Robert Francis, 2nd Baron Gifford (1817–72), son of the Lord Chief Justice (see pt. i, L. 16).

[2] Lord Lonsdale replied on 27 Sept., congratulating W. W. on his safe return home, and adding, 'We have great pleasure in seeing your Son William, whose amiable Manners cannot fail to recommend Him to any Society into which he may happen to be introduced.' (*WL MSS.*)

[3] Robert Partridge, the Lowther supporter from Ambleside.

this morning, he made some enquiries about my late tour; and in answer to them, I having occasion to mention *Genoa*, Mr P. with more spirit than is now usual in his conversation, said, 'Aye, that's the velvet Country—it's somewhere up in the Mediterranean'—You know, perhaps, that Mr P. was for a long time a Haberdasher in Tavistock St.

May I request your Lordship to direct and forward the enclosed at your perfect convenience.

1174. DORA W. to MARY GASKELL[1]

Address: Mrs Gaskell, Thornes House, Wakefield [*readdressed to*] Harden Grange, Bingley.
Postmark: 3 Oct. 1837.   *Stamp*: Penrith.
MS. St. John's College, Cambridge. Hitherto unpublished.

Octr 3^d 1837.

My dear Madam,

I fear you must have thought me strangely negligent—but your kind note was only received by us two days ago, having followed us from place to place and at last overtaking us in our own home among the mountains whither we had been driven earlier than was intended by a return of my Father's old enemy—a severe attack of inflammation in the eye. Had not other causes made it impossible for us to have profitted by your most hospitable invitation this must have put an end to any hope of the kind—a melancholy end—and yet it has been the source of no small pleasure to me for I was to have been left behind in Herefordshire; but thanks to the eye, that furnished me with an excuse for coming home as my Father's escort. You will, I feel

---

[1] A new acquaintance of the Wordsworths. She was Mary (d. 1845), eldest daughter of Dr. Brandeth of Liverpool, and in 1807 had married Benjamin Gaskell (1781–1855) of Thornes Hall, nr. Wakefield, M.P. for Maldon, 1812–26. She was, according to Dibdin, 'an intellectual Circe, and can charm a Whig into a Tory'. (See T. F. Dibdin, *A Bibliographical, Antiquarian and Picturesque Tour in the Northern Counties of England and in Scotland*, 3 vols., (privately printed), 1838, i. 154–5.) In 1840 she was instrumental in obtaining for W. W. the Wordsworth family aumbry from the Beaumont family. See pt. ii, Ls. 648 and 672, and Ls. 1364, 1410, and 1415 (in next volume). De Selincourt confused Mary Gaskell with her more famous namesake, Elizabeth Gaskell, the novelist.

sure, be happy to hear that the attack is subsiding and we trust without even a temporary loss of sight tho' there is the same sort of formidable speck upon the eye which caused blindness three years ago. It is a little hard upon him, is it not? after so long an absence to come home to be shut up in a dark room this lovely weather when the country is in its greatest beauty; and yet we are but too thankful he is at home and that his eyes served him during his long and interesting wanderings from which he returned in perfect health and strength—and without having been detained for a single moment by sickness or any accident however trifling. He unites with me in Comp^{ts} to you and best thanks for your wish to see him at Thornes House, and with my Mother, bids me add that should you or any of your family be in this neighbourhood he trusts you and they will give him the pleasure of making your acquaintance and thanking you *viva voce* for your kindness.

Believe me to remain dear Madam
Very faithfully yours
Dora Wordsworth

1175. W. W. to C. W. JNR.

MS. British Library. Hitherto unpublished.

[*In M. W.'s hand*]

Rydal Mount Oct 5th [1837]

My dear Nephew,

I hope you will not take it ill, if I reply to your letter received by Dora this morning. *We* were driven from Brinsop by an inflammation in one of my eyes, for which the way was certainly prepared by reading in the coach that took us thither, your Father's pamphlet upon the Church Commission.[1] I was

---

[1] *The Ecclesiastical Commission and the Universities; a Letter to a Friend*, 1837, a defence of the traditional role of the Universities as power-houses of theological learning, and of the patronage system, whereby Professors and Heads of Houses (like C. W. himself at Buxted) were able to combine their University positions with parochial responsiblity, to the mutual benefit of each. C. W. characterized the changes proposed by the Commission as 'a mere concern of dry arithmetical and financial computation'.

anxious to put myself under Mr Carr's care and Dora could not bear to let me come home in that helpless state by myself, and to say the truth it was a great consolation to me to know that she would have this opportunity of seeing her Mother and Aunt before her winter campaign in the South—whither she will return under the escort of Mr Henry Cookson,[1] about the 18th inst. Her destination is London (probably Mr Johnsons[2] 107 Regent Street) for two or three days and then Dover till Christmas, when she goes to Mrs Gee's—then to Hampstead. Your 3 Cousins (the 2 Johns) and William have been assembled under this roof to meet us, on our return. *Sockbridge*[3] took leave yesterday for London—Brigham John is naturally anxious for Pupils—how otherwise is he to maintain a wife and 4 children, whose living is not more than £180 a year. Pray bear him in mind, and do what you can for him. There are two reasons why, *at first,* he would prefer Boys under 15 years of age—not having been accustomed to tuition he would like a little experience before he undertook those whose education was further advanced—and Isabella would rather have to do with *boys* than Young Men, provided the remuneration were sufficient to make it a substantial object. He has only accommodation for two, therefore the terms must not be low—but on this point he would like to submit to your experience, and that of his other friends in the South. I need scarcely say that the house is charmingly situated on the banks of the Derwent—and the communication by Railway and steam boat from the South is very expeditious—as you travel from Birmingham to White-haven in 15 hours. A seam of Coal that promises well has been discovered at Workington, in an abandoned pit—but your Aunt and I are both of opinion, such is the pecuniary situation of Mr Curwen thro' embarrasments *inherited* from his Father, and *others taken* upon himself; and such his own deplorable unfitness for all business, and so disposed to expence are the Young Men of his family—that there is no hope of Isabella ever receiving out of savings from an entailed Estate, what her Father intended for her;—in short I do not see what prospect there is of any thing coming to her. So that it behoves John as he has got himself into

---

[1] Henry Cookson was now a Fellow of Peterhouse and proceeding to Holy Orders.

[2] The Revd. William Johnson.

[3] R. W.'s son.

this situation to make up his mind to support his family in future by his own exertions. His amiable wife is disposed to accommodate herself to their changed circumstances most pleasingly —their eldest Son has been under this roof for several weeks— a fine manly Boy of 3 years as ever was seen—and we shall feel a great loss of his sweet company, when he leaves us, as he must do—together with his father and Uncle—next week, to make way for poor Mr and Mrs Merewether who purpose setting out from Coleorton on the 9th to visit us, as well as John and Isabella at Brigham.

You need not have been so timid about the Chapel of Harrow School,[1] as I can sympathize thoroughly in your anxious wish to have the thing done. My objections are strong, but I think they ought not to be insurmountable—to my name appearing among the list of Subscribers upon the terms you propose. Money as you rightly conjecture, I have none; more than I can spare being destined for Cockermouth Church if that is to go forward: and I own I rather shrink from the disingenuousness of seeming to give money, above all for a religious purpose, when I actually do not. This objection I could not get over were it not that I feel convinced, if I had the sum to command—other claims considered, it would go with my whole heart to your purpose. Another reason is, that it seems to imply, on my part, too high an estimation of my own name, and importance in Society—but my near Connection with you, (and our bearing the same name must make it generally known), seems to justify me in waiving this objection. So that if you continue in the same mind, after what I have said, you may put down my name for a not unbecoming sum.

Your subject of my poetical predecessors and their travels in Italy, is too comprehensive for a Sonnet—the case of Milton hurrying out of Italy, and giving up Greece, in his youth—to mix with the troubles of his own Country—and my coming back in age to a land so disturbed by conflicted parties as this is— might be presented in a few lines that would not be without

[1] Pupils at Harrow had hitherto attended the Parish Church, where special galleries had been provided for their accommodation; but now C. W. jnr. was about to launch an appeal for a school chapel. The foundation stone was laid by Lord Aberdeen on 4 July, 1838, and the building was completed the following year to the designs of C. R. Cockerell, and consecrated by the Archbishop of Canterbury. This chapel was later replaced by the present building, designed by Gilbert Scott in 1854—7.

interest. At Valambrosa I was pleased to find, that they have attached the name and memory of Milton to a dependency of the Convent—a small house situated upon a rock a little above the main building—but no doubt you have been there. I delivered your book to Mrs Bunson[1] a day or two after our arrival at Rome—he himself was very ill in the Influenza, which stuck to him the greatest part of the time I was there so that I saw but little of him.

My opinion of Ireland—people and face of the Country, is just what you express—the County of Kerry with its mountains and boldly indented shores is not inferior to any part of these Islands, and the coast of Antrim is truly grand—but the rest of the Island is much inferior to the fine things in Wales, Cumberland, Westmorland and Scotland. The Lakes made by the outspreading of the Shannon are particularly so; and gave to my eye the disagreeable appearance, for the most part, of a flooded Country.

I now come to the most important part of your letter, which is the state of your dear Father's health. I had previously been anxious about it. In his answer to a letter from your Cousin John—he made use of strong expressions upon this subject—saying that he was growing very old, and that his digestion was weak and sadly deranged—and that he had too much work before him. Can nothing be done to divert his mind from these voluntary labors, at least? His pamphlet takes the right view of the case, only he has left untouched—and how could he touch it? the great abuse of Church Patronage in this department—for which, human nature being what it is, there appears to be no remedy. As I find dictating rather a worrying thing to my eye, I must abruptly conclude with saying that I found your Aunts much as I left them, only your Aunt D. had acquired the ability of balancing herself for a few steps without support—Love to John and Ch:[2] and his Wife when you see or write to them—and with affec love from all ever most faithfully yours

[*signed*]   Wm Wordsworth

[1] i.e. Baroness Bunsen (see L. 1063 above).
[2] Charles Wordsworth.

1176. D. W. to EDWARD FERGUSON [1]

MS. Cornell.
K (—). *LY ii. 900* (—).

Sunday—Rydal Mount
[8 Oct. 1837]

My dear Cousin Edward,

A Madman might as well attempt to relate the history of his doings and those of his fellows in confinement as I to tell you one hundredth part of what I have felt, suffered and done.

Through God's Mercy I am now calm and easy, and I trust my dear Brother's eyes are in a fair way of perfect recovery. They all feared he would lose his sight; but now he is very much better.

Your last letter has interested me exceedingly—Our poor good old Aunt [2] and her patient nurse, how I feel for them! but God is Merciful.

I am glad to hear of Eliz[th] Ferguson's [3] happy prospects. Pray with my love to her tell her that I wish her and her Husband all the happiness this world can give. I do not mean the *wealth* of the wealthy; for that can do little for us.

My B[r] C[r] is, as you say, but in delicate health. His Sons are quite well—one at Winchester—another at Harrow, and the third (but oldest and therefore ought to have been *first* mentioned) a Lecturer at Cambridge.

My Niece looks charmingly, and is now I trust quite well. My Nephew John is here with his eldest Son, a charming little Boy, whose prattle amuses me (old Aunty, as he calls me) very much. My dear Sister is well. Happily for all the house her health has been, on the whole, very good.

I have not seen dear Charles Lamb's Book. [4] His Sister still survives—a solitary twig, patiently enduring the storm of life. In losing her Brother she lost her all—all but the remembrance of him—which cheers her the day through.

---

[1] Mrs. Rawson's nephew (see *EY*, p. 42). This letter is written by D. W. in a clear vigorous hand without a blot. It came as an agreeable surprise to the Wordsworth household, as M. W. explained in her covering note of 9 Nov. (*MW*, p. 193).

[2] Mrs. Rawson, who died on 23 Dec.

[3] Edward Ferguson's niece (see pt. ii, L. 463).

[4] Talfourd's *Letters of Charles Lamb.*

Give my best Love to your Sister, and Aunt if she can understand it—

May god bless you.

Yours ever truly
Dorothy Wordsworth.

I *must* send you some of My Many Verses.—Observe the Lines were composed a year ago.

To Thomas Carr, My Medical Attendant.

Five years of sickness and of pain
This weary frame has travell'ed o'er
But God is good—and once again
I rest upon a tranquil shore.

I rest in quietness of mind.
Oh! may I thank my God
With heart that never shall forget
The perilous path I've trod!

They tell me of one fearful night
When thou, my faithful Friend,
Didst part from me in holy trust
That soon my earthly cares must end.

True it is, and I doubt not M[r] Carr was *surprized* the next morning to hear that I was alive.

1177. W. W. to THOMAS SPRING RICE

MS. Cornell.
Broughton, p. 74.

[*In M. W.'s hand*]

Rydal Mount
Oct. 17th [1837]

My dear Sir

I have deferred replying to your obliging letter, from the hope of being able to do it with my own pen—which an inflammation in one of my eyes has prevented for several weeks, and tho' I am much better, it is still hazardous for me to write—

so that you must excuse both the delay, and my now employing an Amanuensis.

I am pleased that you thought so highly of the American printing of my Poems,[1] the book may be sent to Mr Moxon, Bookseller 44 Dover St, where, in compliance with his wish, it will remain till I send for it—meanwhile he will shew it as a specimen.

As among my young Female friends there are few that rival your daughter Mary in my sincere regards, I felt a strong desire to gratify her by throwing off some lines on the interesting subject you propose and *did* make an attempt, but wholly without success. The tune is so deservedly popular that words for other music would not be received by the Nation, and *Victoria* is not only an unenglish word, but, in that metre, almost unmanageable; and it clashes most provokingly with Victorious; but I entirely agree with you that it is highly desireable to have something dignified and appropriate, sub-stituted for some of the vulgar trash of the old verses. Possibly a happy moment may come—when I may be more fortunate—tho' I do not think it likely. Besides there is the Laureate, on whose province I should seem to be trespassing—at present however *his* thought must be occupied by domestic affliction—his poor wife, who has been labouring long with mental derangement, is sinking fast under her malady.

Pray ask Mary (I use her name by her desire without prefix) whether she has ever heard of a little prodigy of a Poetess, by name Emilie Fisher,[2]—she is the daughter of a Prebendary of Salisbury of that name, and her mother is my first cousin. The Queen has heard of her, and been much pleased, I am told, with some of her productions—one in particular, of which her Majesty was the subject. This child now[3] about 11 years of age appears to be really an inspired Creature—having composed at the early age of eight very touching verses, which would do no discredit to the first writer of the age. I have mentioned this not without some faint hope, that her sensibility to music, for which she is almost as remarkable, as for her feeling of Poetry, may put her at *some time* upon doing what you suggested to me.[4] I shall

---

[1] The Philadelphia edition, edited by Henry Reed (see L. 1156 above).
[2] For Emmeline Fisher and her poems, see Ls. 1185 and 1188 below.
[3] now *written twice*.
[4] That W. W. should compose some new words for the national anthem.

myself, tho' I have not had the happiness ever to have seen her, name the subject to her.

Our Country is at present in most exquisite beauty; this morning the splendid foliage, the green lawns, and the broken rocks, with the gleaming waters of two lakes, as seen from different terraces in my little pleasure-ground, perfectly enchanted me. Excuse this long letter, which will I feel encroach too much upon your time.

And believe me, with respectful remembrances to Lady Theodosia, and love to my young friends of your family, to be, my dear Sir,

faithfully y^r obliged
[*signed*] Wm Wordsworth

Mrs. W. takes the liberty to enclose a letter to be directed and forwarded at Mr S. Rice's convenience

1178. W. W. to LADY FREDERICK BENTINCK

MS. WL transcript. Hitherto unpublished.

[late Oct. *or* early Nov. 1837]

. . . Sergeant Talfourd means to resume the Question of the Copy-right Bill[1] as soon as possible after the opening of the Session. If you should be in the way of any member who is in favour of this most just measure which is also so desirable for raising the character of our Country's literature, pray press their attendance, especially upon the 2nd reading. What the Serg^t fears is, that the dull-headed and cold-hearted economists will endeavour to have the Bill referred to a Committee and also defeat his purpose altogether. Mr Holmes[2] I understand during last Session was active with his usual zeal in support of the Bill. I hope he will not slacken when it comes on again. If you should meet pray present him my sincere and cordial thanks. It has been thought advisable (and so much was said on the other side for the petitions from Booksellers and against the Bill, while

---

[1] See L. 1140 above. The new session of Parliament opened on 15 Nov., and Talfourd was given leave to introduce a new Bill on 14 Dec.

[2] William Holmes (see pt. i, L. 240).

authors were silent) that *individual* petitions should now proceed
from them. I have accordingly drawn up a petition[1] in my own
name with a view to have it presented, should the plan be acted
upon. But this is all between ourselves, as the thing if done at all,
will be in a quiet way.

[*cetera desunt*]

1179. M. W. to ROBERT PERCEVAL GRAVES

Address: Revd Robt Graves, Bowness.
Stamp: Kendal Penny Post.
MS. Cornell. Hitherto unpublished.

Friday Morn^g [3 Nov. 1837]

My dear Sir,

Altho' Mr W'^s eyes, I am happy to say, are considerably
amended—he regrets that he dare not venture to expose them,
by going to Bowness to call upon Mrs Hughes and her
nephew;[2] he is therefore much obliged by your endeavour to
arrange for his having the pleasure of seeing her at Rydal,
together with Charles. He begs me to say, that he is under
engagement to go to Lowther, if possible, on Monday—so
that I can only propose for your friends coming to Rydal
tomorrow—and at as early an hour as their convenience and the
weather may suit. Our dinner hour—is (for the accomodation
of our Guests, who, when the weather will permit are exploring
the neighbourhood), now 3 oC—too late for us to expect your
Party to join us, but if you will partake of Lunchen with us at
1 oC—this hour, or as much before as you like, will be quite
convenient to Mr Wordsworth.

Mr Merewether[3] thanks you for your kind wish that he
should revisit Bowness—but the bad weather had been such a
hindrance to their seeing what they wish—and as they leave us
on Tuesday—he does not think it will be in his power to avail

---

[1] See L. 1231 below.

[2] Mrs. Hemans's son Charles and her sister (see *MW*, p. 192).

[3] Mr. and Mrs. Merewether, together with their son and daughter, were
on a visit to Rydal Mount and Brigham Rectory.

3 November 1837

himself of your kindness. He with the rest of our Party beg their compt⁵. Pray give my regards to Mrs Graves and yʳ Sister and believe me dʳ Sir

Yours sincerely
M. Wordsworth

1180. W. W. to DORA W.¹

Address: Miss Wordsworth, 3 Clarence Place, Dover.
Franked: Penrith November twelve 1837 Lonsdale.
Postmark: 12 Nov. 1837. *Stamp*: Penrith.
MS. WL. Hitherto unpublished.

[Lowther]
[12 Nov. 1837]

My dearest child,

I have opened this merely to say that my eyes, though weak, are not, I think, worse. I am yet uncertain whether I shall go tomorrow, and meet your Mother at Keswick with a view of proceeding to Brigham or wait here till Wednesday for the same purpose. The family are all well and go either on Tuesday or Wednesday.

Kindest love to dear Miss Fenwick

affectionately yours
W. W.

Is your appetite come back?—

¹ Dora W. had now joined I. F. at Dover. W. W. added this note to a longer letter from M. W. to Dora W. (see *MW*, p. 191), after he had arrived at Lowther Castle.

Address: Mrs Howley.
Endorsed: Ans^d—Decr 6—1837.
MS. Lilly Library, Indiana University.
Russell Noyes, 'Wordsworth and Sir George Beaumont's Family', TLS, 10 Aug.
1962.

[In M. W.'s hand]

[20 Nov. 1837]

Dear Mrs. Howley,

I left Addington Park with an intention of writing to you soon after, upon a melancholy subject which pressed much upon my mind, but I was prevented by an inflammation in my eyes—nor am I yet able to use my own pen without injury—I therefore employ Mrs. W. as my am[an]uensis. When I wrote to you from Broadstairs I was ignorant of the domestic affliction, with which, not long before, you and the Archbishop had been visited—and when on returning to London the event came to my knowledge, I was much hurt at the thought of being liable to a charge of want of feeling in not having condoled with you upon that sad event, in my letter. During my stay at Addington Park I hoped in vain for an opportunity of adverting to the subject without indelicacy; and I came away resolving to discharge that duty, for such I felt it to be, by letter. Let me now then, late as it is, assure you that we do truly sympathize with you in your severe trials, and sincerely pray to God to support you under them.

Mr. and Mrs. Merewether have been visiting us, with some benefit I trust to the health and spirits of both—their daughter came with them, and for part of the time their eldest joined them. With Mrs. M. I had much conversation concerning Coleorton; She is, I think, a Person of sound judgment, and well-regulated mind. It would give me pleasure at some future time, to talk with you upon the particulars of our conversation; I will content myself at present by saying, how much I was delighted with the report she gave, of the characters of your two Grandsons. [2]—You know how deeply I am interested in all that concerns that Place and Family.

---

[1] Mary Frances Howley (1783—1860), wife of the Archbishop of Canterbury, was the eldest daughter of John Belli of Southampton. This letter is dated from a later endorsement.

[2] Sir George Beaumont's two sons.

You may perhaps have forgotten, that I reported rather a slighting expression which Mrs. W. has used in a letter respecting Mr. Augustus Hare's Sermons;[1] she is desirous of recalling it since she has seen more of the volumes of which we both think highly—tho' she retains the opinion, in which I concur, that there is an over-familiarity in some of the metaphors and illustrations, used by the Preacher, in order to bring down his language to the comprehension of the most illiterate. This practice may perhaps be beneficial in districts where numbers cannot read, but in our neighbourhood, it would be felt by the Peasantry to be below the dignity of the Pulpit and they would even take it rather as an insult, to their capacities.

You know how much I was pleased with the improvements at Addington Park, I therefore do not scruple to mention, that there is one feature in your beautiful Lodge, which I could not bring myself to be pleased with; it is the Armorial Bearings over the entrance. Decorations of his kind do not seem to me to suit a rustic Fabric, and especially one built principally of wood—and therefore of perishable materials. Let me recur also to the favourite old English flower the holly-hock; I told you how much I missed it in the grounds. The other day I saw at Lord Lonsdale's in front of his stately Mansion several very lofty ones—not less than 12 or 13 feet high—almost in full flower at this late season,—and in my own Garden on this 20th of November there are several that are still ornamental. It is scarcely to be borne that the Dhalia, and other foreigners recently introduced,[2] should have done so much to drive this imperial flower out of notice.

Pray excuse this long letter, and believe me, with kind remembrances in which Mrs. W. joins, my dear Madam, sincerely yours.

[signed] Wm Wordsworth

I hope Constance is well.[3]

[1] The posthumous *Sermons to a Country Congregation*, 2 vols., 1836 (5th edn., 1841).

[2] Lady Holland (see L. 1160 above) is credited with the reintroduction of the dahlia into England.

[3] Sir George Beaumont's daughter.

1182. M. W. and W. W. to DORA W.[1]

Address: Miss Wordsworth, 3 Clarence Lawn, Dover.
Franked: London November twenty five P. Courtenay.[2]
Postmark: 25 Nov. 1837.
MS. WL. Hitherto unpublished.

[*c.* 23 Nov. 1837]

. . . are come down in to the back room, and James's bed head put against the Stamp-press, so that if there *was* any force in your fears (which they all laugh at) of his suffering from the warmth of Miss W''s fire, you may be at ease in that score—I like to tell you all our movements to have you at home as much as we can, and that you may correct our mistakes when we make them. Mr Carter is very dutiful in his enquiries after you, and they all send love and all good wishes. We have got excellent Potatoes and apples from Mr Pearson—I am reminded of this, by fancying I hear his Carts, which he said he would send with straw this week. Sir P. Malcolm[3] said he never eat such good Potatoes. I do not know the price for the measures differ—but as [? Cath:][4] said Keswick ones would be 5/— a bushel without carriage. We seem to make out that we get *2 bushels and a ½* for 10/—. I will now be done as I am descending too far into domestics—and will only beg you to spare your eyes, and with tenderest love and good wishes to dear Miss F— Here Father calls upon me to write "Dearest child, a thousand thanks *from me* for your delightful letter. I walked thro' a fierce storm yesterday to A.[5] with the vain hope of such a reward as we have received today. We have here water and wind without ceasing, but nothing that deserves the name of cold—here and there is a hollyhock in the garden with a few flowers remaining as fresh as in early autumn. I walk without injury at least 3 hours a day. What arrangement is to be made for your returning to dear Miss F? Old engagements must not be broken, no old friends

---

[1] Written on a letter from Thomas Powell (see L. 1169 above) to W. W.

[2] Philip Courtenay, W. W.'s man of business, was now M.P. for Bridgewater.

[3] Admiral Sir Pulteney Malcolm (1768–1838), brother of Sir John Malcolm (see *MY* ii. 110, 216), had been Commander-in-Chief of the Cape Station (1816–17) at the time of Napoleon's banishment to St. Helena.

[4] *MS. obscure.* The 'Catherine' apparently referred to is unidentified.

[5] Ambleside.

sacrificed to one however dear, unfortunately of but recent date.
Still I cannot help grudging such time as may materially break
in upon your engagement with her—tell her so with my love.
And that I should indeed be grateful to the powers of air if they
would waft me and your Mother to Dover and back again at
our wish. I rejoice that you have stood on Shakespeare's cliff—I
did so a few weeks back. Blessed be his name. I wish a thousand
places in England were called after him.

At Canterbury is a very agreeable public walk called the
Dungeon,[1] I fear you did not see it. It commands a striking view
of the Cathedral.—Poor Southey was able to give me three
hours of conversation with entire command of himself.[2]

Your affectionate Father
W. Wordsworth

1183. W. W. to UNKNOWN CORRESPONDENT

MS. Henry E. Huntington Library. Hitherto unpublished.

Rydal Mount
24th Nov^b —37.

Sir,

You wish for my handwriting, you should have had a sample
of it long ago, but an inflammation in my eyes prevented my
complying with your request.

I remain
sincerely yours
Wm Wordsworth

[*Two separate signatures in W. W.'s hand are added at bottom of
letter*]

---

[1] i.e. the Dane John, an ancient fortification near the city walls.
[2] Mrs. Southey had died on 16 Nov. See Southey, vi. 347—8.

1184. W. W. to ROBERT SHELTON MACKENZIE

Address: R. S. Mackenzie Esqre, Liverpool.
Stamp: Kendal Penny Post.
MS. Historical Society of Pennsylvania.
LY ii. 901.

[*In M. W.'s hand*]

Rydal Mount Novr 25th [1837]

My dear Sir

Your parcel reached us on the 19th. The state of my eyes obliges me to employ Mrs W's pen to thank you for it, and for the enclosed letter. As it is not prudent for me to write with my own hand, I cannot of course have yet become acquainted with much of the contents of the books and papers which you have so kindly sent—The Herbarium is a truly valuable one and will be much prized by my daughter who is fond of such collections—meanwhile, her Mother begs you to accept their joint thanks for it, and the Forget-me-not,[1] you so kindly have presented to them. We have turned to the Poems in the Annual you have directed us to, they are remarkable both for tenderness and poetical spirit; the one upon your departed Child, is not unworthy of ranking with the Mother's lays of Miss Browne[2] which we have read, and been much pleased with; as also, the animated piece in which the course of a river is traced from its fountain to the sea: this was not less interesting to me on account of its reminding me, of Mr. Coleridge's *intention* of writing a poem to be called 'the Brook'[3] and of my own Duddon. These two pieces are all that we have yet found time to read of Miss B's little book—for in truth, we have had three other volumes sent us (within the last 10 days) to look over—besides arrears of other accumulations. If I could with prudence put my eyes to this work, it would not require a 4th part of the time occupied by things being read aloud. And now, not to speak of other

---

[1] The Annual. Mackenzie had written briefly on 17 Nov. (*WL MSS.*), enclosing this volume and a collection of American flowers.

[2] Phoebe Hinsdale Brown (1783–1861), American hymn writer. She contributed to *Spiritual Songs*, 1831, and *The Mother's Hymn Book*, 1834, and published didactic works in prose, *The Tree and its Fruits* and *The Village School*, both in 1836.

[3] See *Biographia Literaria*, Ch. x, and the I. F. note to *The River Duddon* (*PW* iii. 503–4).

demands, and parliament being sitting, the Newspapers cannot be neglected. I therefore need give no further explanation of my inability to report impressions—or give opinions with respect to the American publications—as soon as I am able, I shall glance my eye over them. In the mean while let me repeat my thanks for the copious specimens you have sent me, and in particular for Mrs. Sigourney's[1] volume—which, judging from the 'Mother's Sacrifice', and 'the American Indians', especially the former, I cannot but expect much pleasure from. I see there is a prose tale of yours—but you will not be hurt when I frankly say, I have not read it—for it is not once in a hundred times, that for many years past, I have been able to find time for reading prose fictions in periodicals—and too seldom indeed for the most celebrated novels.

What a pity a Man so wealthy did not provide in his will for the poor orphan Mourner—the story, as you have given it, is truly affecting; and the Sonnet gives the essence of the incident in a manner that does you much credit, and it is much to be regretted that you have not more time to give to the Muses, whom you serve so willingly and well. Are you aware that Cowper has been beforehand with you in the Ice-palace?[2]

Bryant's[3] poems we have not yet looked into, but if you are

[1] Lydia Huntley Sigourney (1791—1865), of Hartford, Conn., a prolific American magazine writer in prose and verse, known as the 'American Hemans'. She came to Europe in 1840, visiting W. W. and Southey (see L. 1452 in next volume): the following year she published *Pocahontas, and Other Poems*, and *Poems, Religious and Elegiac*. As de Selincourt notes, she was especially famous for her obituary poems which, it was said, added a new terror to death. She edited the *Lady's Book*, which is probably the volume referred to here. She had written to W. W. on 14 Nov. 1836 (*WL MSS.*), asking for a contribution to the *Religious Souvenir*, an annual which she was editing at that time. See also Gordon S. Haight, *Mrs. Sigourney, The Sweet Singer of Hartford*, New Haven, 1930.

[2] See *The Task*, v. 127—76.

[3] William Cullen Bryant (1794—1878), friend of Channing, Allston, etc., and editor of the New York *Evening Post* from 1829, had published a small collection of his verse (including *Thanatopsis*) in 1821, and a much larger volume, *Poems*, 1832, which was published in England with a dedication to Samuel Rogers, and won praise from Professor Wilson in *Blackwood's* for its 'Wordsworthian' qualities. Bryant had been an early admirer of the *Lyrical Ballads*. 'He said that upon opening the book, a thousand springs seemed to gush up at once in his heart, and the face of Nature, of a sudden, to change into a strange freshness and life ' (Park Godwin, *A Biography of William Cullen*

in communication with the Gentleman who sent the vol: to me, pray be so good as to thank him in my name—several of Mr. B's pieces have fallen in my way from time to time, some of which had merit of a very superior kind.

I must not conclude witho[ut] thanking you for your Portrait, it is a spirited and a very good likeness.

Excuse my writing so briefly in answer to your interesting communications—yet I feel I needed not to have made this apology, after what has been said above—and believe me to remain

faithfully, your much obliged

[*signed*] Wm Wordsworth

Our little County has just been disgraced by a horrible Murder[1] to which cupidity appears to have been the sole motive—thus placing us if possible below the most savage Irish.

Bryant, 2 vols., New York, 1883, i. 104.) See also letter of 14 July 1845 (in next volume).

[1] The local papers reported the perpetration of 'a most foul and horrible murder' at Langdale, near Orton, on the night of 18 Nov. One Thomas Hunter, a carrier, had been waylaid and shot, and his pocket book and the bag in which he carried his silver taken. (See *Westmorland Gazette* for 25 Nov.) On 17 Feb. 1838, the trial opened at Appleby before Mr. Justice Coleridge of a notorious poacher named Wills, who was suspected of the crime, but he was eventually discharged from lack of sufficient evidence.

1185. W. W. to ELIZABETH FISHER[1]

Address: Mrs Wm Fisher, Poulshot Rectory, Devizes.
Stamp: Kendal.
MS. Cornell.
Rosalie Masson, 'An "inspired little creature" and the Poet Wordsworth',
    Fortnightly Review, xciv (Nov. 1910), 874—89 (—).

[*In M. W.'s hand*]

[Nov. 1837]

My dear Cousin,

I have long been in your debt—probably dear Sarah Crackanthorpe[2] has told you what privations an inflammation in my eye has caused me: this has passed away, but has left a weakness which still makes reading and writing injurious to me, so that I scarcely venture upon either the one or the other. The thanks for your letter, and the Poems it accompanied, which I had hoped to give from my own pen, I am obliged to express from Mrs Wordsworth's which necessity has on the present occasion an advantage in it, as she has not been less pleased with our little Cousin's (her's, independent of me) astonishing productions.[3] It is impossible to foretell what may come in future time out of these promises but I have met in the language of no age or country, with things so extraordinary from so young a Person. I am afraid of writing this—lest it, or something like it, should come to her ears; and I cannot conceal

---

[1] W. W.'s cousin. His uncle, Canon William Cookson, had two surviving daughters, who married sons of John Fisher (1748—1825), Canon of Windsor and Bishop of Salisbury. The elder daughter, Mary, married Archdeacon John Fisher (1788—1832), Canon of Salisbury, vicar of Osmington and of Gillingham, in Dorset, and friend of the artist John Constable. It was the younger daughter Elizabeth (to whom this letter is addressed) and not Mary, as erroneously stated by de Selincourt and in pt. i, L. 8, who married Canon William Fisher.

[2] W. W.'s cousin (b. 1794), visiting from Newbiggin early in November (see *MW*, p. 194): younger sister of William Crackanthorpe.

[3] The poems of Emmeline Fisher (1825—64), Mrs. Fisher's daughter, had been submitted to W. W. for his opinion. In 1850 she married the Revd. Charles Hinxman, rector of Dunmore, Stirlingshire, and Barford St. Martin, Wilts. (1860—86), and eventually published a volume of *Poems* in 1856 (2nd edn., 1857), but she hardly lived up to her early promise. Many of her MSS., including the verses referred to in this letter, are preserved among the *WL MSS*. See also Ls. 1177 above and 1188 below.

from you that I look with a thousand apprehensions upon what may be the fate of one, in whom such powers are so early displayed. It would avail little to enter into particulars, for throughout the Poems, are scattered indications of all that can be desired—an observant eye, feeling, thought, fancy, and above all imagination, as evidenced especially in the Poem of Secrecy, and even still more in the Verses on the strange noise heard in a serene sky—in part of these last there is the very spirit of Milton himself. But pray keep this in your own heart—or mention it only to your husband. Of the not unfrequent, and inevitable faults in language I forbear to speak—and wish others to do the same—let her yield to the impulse of her feelings unembarrassed about minutiae of style, or even correctness or incorrectness in the use of words. At her age this could not but be injurious, both for her mind and body also. For to produce accuracy, does, in the most expert, often prove a teasing employment.

The Verses, upon the Queen, especially in the translation from the Star to the living Person, are exquisite, and tempt me to ask, tho' not without hesitation, that as Emmie has, I am told, such a fine feeling for Music, that she would make an attempt to fit the noble music of 'God save the King' with better and more appropriate words, than those that are ordinarily joined with it. A request to this effect was made to myself, from a person high in Office[1]—I tried, but could not succeed. Your inspired little Creature may be more happy in her effort—and so I told my Correspondent.

My dear Cousin, it is rather a sad thing to me, that neither yourself nor your Sister, nor indeed any of your Brothers[2] have ever set foot on the soil of Westmorland or Cumberland. I would have given not a trifle if you and little Emmie[3] could together, have seen the sun-rise from my door this morning— the glowing sky above the Mountain top—the miles of silver

[1] Thomas Spring Rice, the Chancellor of the Exchequer. See L. 1177 above.

[2] Mrs. Fisher had two surviving brothers, William (now vicar of Broad Hinton, Wilts.), and George (now rector of Writhlington, Somerset, and vicar of Powerstock, Dorset); and one sister, Mary, now a widow (see L. 1323 below). Her eldest brother Christopher, an officer in the Indian Army, had died in 1834.

[3] Emmie visited Rydal Mount in 1841 and 1845.

lake in the distance,—the green quiet valley between, and the mists curling on the hill-sides that enclose it!

I must not end this letter without a word about that poor Sufferer, my dear Sister. She is not wholly without enjoyment, as probably Sarah C. would tell you—but the many un-comfortable hours she has to go thro', often make our hearts ache. Dora is now at Dover—she goes to Cambridge about the 19 of next Month, upon the invitation of her Uncle, there she will meet her Cousins—among whom I include Charles's Wife, whom she has not seen—but my paper fails me and I can only add our united love to yourself and all your family, and believe me your affec Cousin, and sincere friend,

[*signed*] Wm Wordsworth

1186. W. W. to ROBERT SHELTON MACKENZIE

Address: R. Shelton Mackenzie Esqre, Liverpool.
Endorsed: Decr. 1837.
Stamp: Kendal Penny Post.
MS. Dr. Douglas Horton. Hitherto unpublished.

[*In M. W.'s hand*]

Rydal Mount Decr 8th [1837]

My dear Sir,

Your kind and obliging letter of the 1st ins^t would have rec^d an immediate answer, but being unwilling that you should be charged with a 2^d postage, I thought it best to await the probable arrival of the American books which you hoped to forward in a few days. As the parcel has not reached me, I do not like to seem any longer inattentive to your letter, or to delay my thanks for the newspaper which preceded it.

Mr Southey cannot fail I think to be pleased, as I was, with your volunteered defence of his character[1] in a point where it has been often, so stupidly and maliciously attacked: what should we say of a Poet who wrote no better at the age of 40 than at 20, or under? And what a blockhead must a man be deemed, who, in questions of polity, ecclesiastical or civil,

---

[1] Shelton Mackenzie had reviewed the new edition of Southey's poems (10 vols., 1837—8) in the Liverpool newspaper which he conducted.

became no wiser in mature life than he had been in his nonage? Yet it is made a matter of reproach to Mr S. that he had not retained thro' life, the crude notions of his boyhood—almost. You, with a manly indignation have repelled this charge, and in emphatic language, that does you honour.

Mrs W. and myself, who have had like losses of our own, were much moved by your elegiac verses,[1] which are worthy to take their place with the preceding ones, which the same mournful subject has called for.

It will give my Wife and Daughter great pleasure to receive the little book of facsimilies, which you propose to prepare for them, as a token of your regard, and for its own sake.

My late tour on the Continent proved every thing that I could wish; except that the Cholera and the Quarantine deterred our getting further than Rome, and it was impossible to give up Naples and its neighbourhood without some painful regret. My health during the whole time was excellent, tho' the fatigue of sight-seeing was sometimes too much for me. Since my return however to England I have had an attack of my old complaint, inflammation in my eyes, which, tho' I am now recovering from it, has caused many letters still to remain unanswered, and compels me now, in writing to you to employ Mrs Wordsworth's pen.

Believe me my dear Sir, to be with sincere regard,

faithfully your obliged
[*signed*] Wm Wordsworth

1187. M. W. and W. W. to DORA W.[2]

Address: Miss Wordsworth, Clarence Place, Dover.
MS. WL.
MW, p. 200.

[11 Dec. 1837]

Father says 'thank her for the paper of acc^{ts} and tell her that my eyes are very much better'—(but look at them at this

---

[1] *The Departed*, elegiac verses on his daughter, dated Liverpool, 1 Aug. 1837, and printed in the *Dublin University Magazine*.
[2] Part of a much longer letter of M. W.'s.

moment) 'no bloodshot—but that I cannot read without watering, etc.'—When I read about the winds of Dover—he said that will never do for my eyes,—but he bids me now say to Miss F. 'Be assured that it would give me infinite pleasure to be with you at D. and not a little to be your escort to Paris, but as to Dover not only the winds, but the saline air, the white cliffs and dazzling waters are all enemies that I am afraid of. I am not sure but my late attack was prepared by my ' residence at [? Broadstairs] for it was there I felt the first approaches of injury, and really at present I dare not commit myself to any engagement, lest this infirmity should make me a burthen instead of a chearful and useful companion to those whom I love. But things may change in the next 4 months.'

I did not mean dear D. you should have troubled yourself about a gown for me—but many thanks—did you not receive this notice from me? We have got no box from Moxon yet—

Again from Father—'reading the n.papers aloud is a slow process and they have taken up far too much of our valuable evenings—but the subjects they turn upon have, since the meeting of P^{t1} been so important that I can not be easy without *having* the papers read to me. You know how deeply I am interested in the education, above all the religious education of the People, and what a scheme is that of the poor lost creature, Ld Brougham[2] who professing to be afraid of the Gov^t having the management of it, is for setting up a London Board of Comm^{rs} with whom and under whom, are to act those precious bodies the Municipalities, and where they are not, the members of Mechanic Institutes, etc, etc, to determine where and how Schools are to be erected, and the people taught—The Clergy not being alluded to in his pranks.—In short there is no end to his absurdities. Then there is the ballot, the extention of Suffrage etc, which schemes if they go forward, and particularly the latter, it will be impossible to avoid a Revolution—Enough'.

---

[1] Parliament.

[2] In 1835 Brougham had moved that Parliament should vote grants for the extension of national education, and that a board of commissioners should be appointed to supervise the allocation of the money granted. On 1 Dec. 1837 he had reintroduced these proposals embodied in two new Bills for developing a national educational system.

1188. W. W. to ELIZABETH FISHER

Address: Mrs Fisher, Poulshot Rectory, Devizes.
Stamp: Kendal Penny Post.
MS. Cornell.
Rosalie Masson, 'An "*inspired little creature*" *and the Poet Wordsworth*',
    Fortnightly Review, xciv (*Nov. 1910*), *874*—89 (—).

[*In M. W.'s hand*]

Rydal Mount Dec[r]. 15th
[1837]

My dear Cousin,

It would have been inconvenient to me to reply earlier to your two last kind letters. As I was sure you would give me credit for being duly Sensible of your attention, I have felt no uneasiness on this account. I now thank you sincerely for both the letters and the Poems;[1] and especially for the Anthem, undertaken upon my suggestion. When I made the vain attempt myself, my wish was to steal into the subject, by using as much of the first Stanza of the old Song, as possible—but I found the name Victoria as a substitute for Great George utterly unmanageable. And this discouraged me so, that tho' I did compose 2 Stanzas, in place of the vulgar stuff about 'knavish tricks, etc.,' I did not think it worth while to *write* them, and they are now forgotten. My young Cousin, for I love to call her so, found, I suppose, the same difficulty insurmountable; and has given an entirely new thing, with which we are not a little pleased; and perhaps I may forward it, with your permission, to my friend Mary Spring Rice—(who as you know is one of her Majesty's Maids of honor) whose Father suggested to me to do, as a most agreeable thing to his daughter, what I in vain attempted.

The reason why I have used the word 'perhaps' is solely because that copies of Emmie's verses, *in my opinion*, ought not to be widely spread; her mind ought to grow up quietly and silently; and her extraordinary powers should be left to develope themselves *naturally*, with as little observation as possible. You have probably as strong reasons, as a Mother can have, for supposing that notice and admiration do in no degree stain, disturb, or alter the current of her thoughts and feelings—

---

[1] More of Emmie Fisher's poems. See L. 1185 above.

but you cannot be *sure* of that: she herself may receive from such quarters injury of which she is not at all aware, and even if she should be so, her efforts to prevent it in future might be unsuccessful, the human heart being so subtile in deceiving itself.

But it is time I should say a word or two upon the poems last sent. The corrections for the Anthem are decided improvements, and prove that her judgement keeps pace with her other faculties. Of her other Poems, the least remarkable is that to her Cousin. The most is the dialogue between the Earth and the Wind. I should have thought this, had it been produced some thirty years ago, a piece entitled to great praise as *coming from any one*—but Verse has been so much written, and read within that period, and so many things produced in the same strain, that these verses, which would otherwise have been *truly astonishing* in a Child, tho' still having claim for very high admiration, are not so much proofs of *originality* of mind, as of sensibility and aptitude for sympathy with beauty and grandeur as she must have found them in part expressed elsewhere. These observations lead me to speak with regret that Mrs Hemans's Poems have been put in her way at so early an age; towards the close of my 6th Vol: will be found a poem occasioned by the death of the Ettrick Shepherd, [1] which shews that I think highly of that Lady's genius—but her friends, and I had the honor of being one of them—must acknowledge with regret, that her circumstances, tho' honorably to herself, put her upon writing too often and too much—she is consequently diffuse; and felt herself under the necessity of *expanding* the thoughts of others, and hovering over their feelings, which has prevented her own genius doing justice to itself, and diminished the value of her productions accordingly. This is not said with a view to the withdrawing M^{rs} H's works, but with a hope that it may be a caution for you to place those of the elder Writers in your daughter's way, in preference to modern ones, however great their merits. And in this implied recommendation, I do not speak without allusion to my own. Wherever I have written better than others, as far as style is concerned, it has been mainly owing to my early familiarity with the Works of the truly great Authors of past times—and where I have the least pleased

---

[1] The *Extempore Effusion* was placed in the 6th volume of the new edition of the *Poetical Works*.

myself in style or versification I can trace it up to early communication with inferior writers. One of my Schoolmasters,[1] whom I most respected and loved, was, unfortunately, for me, a passionate admirer of Dr Johnson's prose; and having not been much exercised in prose myself, I have not till this day got over the ill effects of that injudicious [   ]^2 upon my own way of expressing myself. Both the 'Stricken Village' and the 'Frozen Army' are additional evidences of this young Creature's unrivalled powers.

Your wish to see my daughter shall be communicated to her—but she is so deep in engagements for the prescribed time of her absence from home, [as] will scarcely allow her to profit by it. Next week she meets her Cousin Charles in London, to accompany him and his wife to Cambridge, to pass about a fortnight with her Uncle. As to myself, I could have answered confidently that I would have made a point of seeing you and yours, had I been some years younger—but on the 7th of April I shall enter my 69th year, and cannot of course encourage hopes, which are so likely to be disappointed.

My Wife and Sister join me in [   ]^2 believe me

faithfully your affec Cousin,
[*signed*] Wm Wordsworth

I much regret that we have not at this moment the convenience of a frank—and am unwilling to detain my letter.

---

[1] For a list of the masters at Hawkshead Grammar School when W. W. was a pupil there, see T. W. Thompson, *Wordsworth's Hawkshead*, ed. Robert Woof, 1970, pp. 342–3.

[2] *MS. torn.*

1189. W. W. to H. C. R.

Address: H. C. Robinson Esqre, Atheneum.
Endorsed: Decr 37. Wordsworth. Family matters, Hutchinsons and business.
MS. Dr. Williams's Library.
K (—). Morley, i. 349.

[*In M. W.'s hand*]

Decr 15 [1837]

My dear Friend

We were glad to see your handwriting again, having often regretted your long silence. To take the points of your letter in order. Sergeant T.[1] did forward to me a petition[2]—and I objected to sign it, not because I was misinformed, but because allegations were made in it, of the truth of which, I knew nothing of my own knowledge; and because I thought it impolitic to speak of the American Publishers who had done what there was no law to prevent them doing, in such harsh and injurious terms. This I thought would exasperate them, and put some of them upon opposing a measure, who might otherwise have felt no objection to it. Soon after this I had the pleasure of seeing a very intelligent American Gentleman at Rydal—whom you perhaps have seen—Mr Duar[3]—to whom I told my reasons for not signing the Petition—he approved of them, and said that the proper way of proceeding, would have been to lay the case before our foreign Secretary, whose duty it would be to open a communication with the Aⁿ[4] foreign Sec^{ry} and thro' that channel, the correspondence would regularly proceed to Congress. I am however glad to hear that the Petition was rec^d as you report.—When I was last in London—I breakfasted at Miss Rogers' with the Aⁿ Minister, Mr Stephenson,[5] who

---

[1] Talfourd.

[2] See H. C. R.'s letter to W. W. of 11 Dec. (Morley, i. 348). Harriet Martineau (see next letter) had organized during the previous year a Petition from English writers to the American Congress on the subject of Copyright, which had been taken up by William Cullen Bryant (see L. 1184 above) in the pages of the New York *Evening Post*. A Bill was brought forward in Congress and passed unanimously, but like Talfourd's measure in the House of Commons, it lapsed at the end of the session.

[3] See *R M V B*, Nov. 1836. The reference is to William Alexander Duer (1780–1858), jurist and educationalist: President of Columbia College, New York, 1829–42.

[4] American.

[5] For Andrew Stevenson, see L. 1152 above.

reprobated, in the strongest terms of indignation, the injustice of the present system. Both these Gentlemen spoke also of its impolicy, in respect to America, as it prevented Publishers, thro' fear of immediate underselling, from reprinting valuable English Works. You may be sure that a reciprocity in this case is by me much desired—tho' far less on my own acc^t, for I cannot encourage a hope that my family will be much benefited by it, than for a love of justice, and the pleasure it would give me to know that the families of successful Men of letters, might take such station as proprietors which they who are amused or benefitted by their writings in both Continents seem ready to allow them. I hope you will use your influence among y^r Parl^{ry} friends to procure support for the Sergeant's motion.[1] I ought to have added that Spring Rice was so obliging as to write to me upon the subject of the American Copyright which letter I answered at some length—and if I am not mistaken that correspondence was forwarded by me to Serjeant Talfourd.

Either of the plans of travel for next Summer that have been presented to you, would [I][2] think answer for your amusement. Both I believe are somewhat fatiguing; but if you avoid, which you must do, overstraining yourself by walking—above all up hill, I have no fears for you on that account. Mr Quillinan's Father who was a very strong Man, did on one occasion over-exert himself, lost his life by putting-off wearing a truss till it was too late, and last week a worthy man of Ambleside died also, as Mr Carr told me, from not submitting to an operation which became necessary, from the same cause. Therefore let me earnestly beg that you never would travel in foreign Countries unprepared with one of these accommodations in case you should stand *in the least need* of it.

I am uneasy in being so long in Barron Field's debt, he having favored me with another letter of criticism[3] upon my last Ed: Some of the remarks will be useful but in others I differ from him *toto caelo*—for example he proposes to read, for

'His eye thro' the lost look of dotage is cunning and shy'[4]
His eye thro' the *last* look and—

---

[1] i.e. the new Bill he had introduced the previous day.

[2] *MS. torn.*

[3] In his letter of 15 Sept., Barron Field wrote, 'You have . . . done me the honour to adopt some of the few suggestions I made to you in my letter of December last',—and he added some more. (*WL MSS.*)

[4] See *The Two Thieves or, The Last stage of Avarice* (*PW* iv. 245), l. 22.

As probably you will have to write to him again, pray thank him for his kindness, and say that it is only the state of my eyes that prevents me from writing to him myself. In fact I am not yet able to pen more than a few lines at a time without injury, and to you I will mention what has *not* been said to anyone else that Mrs W. who is my only Secretary suffers so much from a pain in her wrist from an old sprain and Rheumatism that every line which she writes gives me some uneasiness. (*He* compells me to say this M W) So that you see we are in no great plight for keeping up correspondence—even with our dearest friends—Then there are those abominable Albums and Autographs, with which I am cruelly pestered. Now *mind* that this does not prevent *your* writing to us. Only do not take it ill if you are not answered so much at length as we could wish—the inconvenience Mrs W. feels in writing, is only *temporary*.

Poor dear Kenyon![1] but I had foretold in my own thoughts and said also to Mrs W. that I feared it would not be long before he would have some dangerous seizure—I apprehended something of an apoplectic kind, for he is of far too full a habit— and so I rather think I told him. He is a generous and noble Creature, and one for whom I have the highest respect—Pray when you see him, tell him we were much troubled to hear of his indisposition.

Dora will pass thro' London from Dover on the 18th and will be with Mrs Hoare at Hampstead till the 21st when she intends, God willing, to proceed with her Cousins to spend some little time with her Uncle at Cambridge—She has been much benefitted by her residence I hope at Dover—but from presuming too far upon her returning strength—she has walked too much and in some degree her uncomfortable feelings at her chest have come back upon her.

Of the Southeys we hear nothing but well, except that M[r] S. does not sleep as well as could be wished—and his daughters say that at times he looks thin and worn.

I have become indisposed rather to publish my Sister's Scotch Tour at present.[2] I have no good reason for thinking that the

---

[1] In his letter H. C. R. had given an account of Kenyon's severe illness.

[2] In 1836 Moxon had prepared detailed estimates for printing the *Recollections of a Tour Made in Scotland, 1803* (*WL MSS.*), but nothing came of them, and the work was not published until 1874. See also L. 1195 below. Talfourd had written on 22 Nov. (*Cornell MSS.*) 'I am sure your admirers— now happily embracing all who love English poetry for its own sake—will see

taking it thro' the Press would be a *profitable* stirring of her mind, at all, and the hope of this result was my only inducement to undertake the experiment. Besides, we both feel there would be some indelicacy in drawing public attention to her in her present melancholy state. Before I was forced to take this view of the case it had given me much pleasure, and I had corrected and enlarged two little Poems upon the subject of Burns[1] which would have seen the light for the first time in this Publication.—

And now for a more important subject of private business. Mr Hutchinson of Brinsop made his will, leaving all his property to his Wife, for her time, to be distributed equally among his 4 children after her death. I pointed out to him the probable great injustice of this, after he had been at the expense of giving a University education to his two Sons; and furthermore showed him, that if any of his Children should get into difficulties—it would be much better to interpose a more dispassionate judgment, than a Mother's can be supposed to be for regulating the mode and degree of relief which it might be proper to afford them. I therefore, with the entire approbation of Mrs H. and her most ready concurrence, proposed that the Property should be placed in the hands of Trustees—in the manner in which my own is. Mr Monkhouse and my Son W^m are, much to the satisfaction of the Parties, ready to undertake this office—and presuming upon your never-wanting kindness I have ventured to say, that you would assist them in drawing out a form for the accomplishment of this good purpose—And I now beg that for the sake of this excellent family you would do this—putting yourself into communication by letter with Mr M.—who is aware of what I meant to propose to you, as soon as you can find it convenient.

Cannot you, either during the winter, or the Spring run down and give us a month of your company—which we so much value. It took Dora only 12 hours to go from Kendal to Birmingham—the journey from Warrington by Railway and from Kendal to Warrington by Mail—we can meet you at K. so that you need not stop there—so that from B. to us would take no more than 14 or 15 hours time.

with unmingled pleasure the republication of your poems in the setting of Miss Wordsworth's work . . . '

[1] See *PW* iii. 65, 67, and L. 954 above.

We have had Mr Quillinan with us for the last fortnight—[1] who having business at Leeds kindly came on—he leaves us on Saturday—meaning to take up his Daughter at Brinsop.

Glad to hear that Miss Lamb is well—our kind love to her— We have been looking for some time for a package, which Dora announced to us was to be sent from Mr Moxon—Say to him, if you please, that if he could get from M'Crone Sir Egertons Milton, [2] which he recollects I was promised—to enclose in the parcel. M. I understand has been something disappointed in the sale of the Ed: I fear he is a little too. sanguine—because he told me he expected a greater sale of Lambs works—A friend of mine, tells me that he heard from Mr Marshall (Marshal and Simkin[3] Paternoster Row) that the demand for my 6 vols was steadily encreasing. Kind remembrances to all who enquire after us, and with affectionate remembrances from us all to yourself, believe me ever faithfully

Your's [*signed*] Wm Wordsworth

---

[1] E. Q. had returned to England in October, and reached Brinsop after W. W. and Dora W. had left. He thereafter proceeded to Leeds, where on 24 Nov. he received a letter from Dora W. in which she tried to clarify her feelings for him. 'My love for you is a spiritual Platonism such as man might feel for man or woman for woman . . . I wish for your own sake you were fairly married to some one else.' To this E. Q. replied from Rydal Mount on 8 Dec., calling her advice heartless: 'I am not spiritualised enough for you— you—frigid disagreeable thing! . . . it is a woodpecker's tap on a hollow tree in my ears: it is a squirt of lemon-juice in my eyes, and it is gall and wormwood on my tongue.' It was while writing this letter, as E. Q.confessed much later (in his letter of 17 Apr. 1839), that M. W. entered the room and seeing Dora W.'s letter on the table asked to see it. According to his own account of the incident, he was 'evasive and ingenuous', and offered to read her part of the letter, on which M. W., seeing his embarrassment, remarked that if she could only hear a part, she would rather not hear any of it. (*WL MSS.*) See also L. 1225 below.

[2] See L. 1160 above.

[3] The London publishing house.

1190. W. W. to THOMAS NOON TALFOURD

MS. Harvard University Library. Hitherto unpublished.

[*In M. W.'s hand*]

Rydal Mount Dec 15th [1837]

My dear Sir,

I am glad that you found my notices not without value—I hope to see Mr Southey and will give him your opinion; but our Parliamentary friends are for the most part, persons who will support the bill[1] without application from us, or they are the same individuals. We shall not forget to remind them when the day for the 2^d reading approaches.

Mr Robinson, you will probably have heard has lately seen Miss Martineau,[2] who assures him there can be little doubt that Copyright will be secured ere long in America for English Authors. Should this be effected, it will prepare the way for the same measure taking effect on the Continent, in which case successful English Authors may look forward to more than competence, arising not from bounty in any quarter, but from justice—which is a great pleasure, that so distinguished a friend of my own as yourself, should be the principle Instrument in bringing about so much good.

My eyes are much better—but still I am obliged to abstain from exercising them, by reading or writing. My Spirits have, of course suffered a good deal from privation, but as to nothing, thank God, to complain of.

Very affly, yours, with best regards from Mrs W. to yourself and Mrs Talfourd.

[*signed*] Wm Wordsworth

---

[1] The new Copyright Bill. Talfourd had written on 22 Nov., thanking W. W. for his 'notices', 'which will be of great use to me in the event of a serious opposition to my Bill.'(*Cornell MSS.*)

[2] Harriet Martineau (1802—76) a Unitarian and an advanced liberal in politics, had travelled in America, 1834—6, and published *Society in America* in 1837, a novel *Deerbrook* (1839), *Letters on Mesmerism* (1845), and numerous other works. In 1845 she came to live at the Lakes in a house she built for herself, The Knoll, Ambleside, and came to know the Wordsworth circle well. Her *Autobiography* appeared in 3 vols., 1877. See also previous letter.

498

1191. W. W. to THOMAS SPRING RICE

Endorsed: W. Wordsworth. American Copyrights.
MS. National Library of Ireland. Hitherto unpublished.

[Dec. 1837]

Private.

My dear Mr Spring Rice,

Be so good as to cast your eye over the enclosed advertisement, cut out of a New York Paper which has reached me this morning. I am induced to send it on account of your late obliging communication respecting American Copy-rights.

If Lady Theodosia and my young Friends of your family be with you pray present to them my very kind regards.

And believe me faithfully yours
Wm Wordsworth

1192. W. W. to SIR WILLIAM ROWAN HAMILTON

Address: Sir Wm Hamilton, Observatory, Dublin.
Postmark: (1) 21 Dec. 1837 (2) 23 Dec. 1837.
Stamp: (1) Kendal (2) Dublin Penny Post.
MS. Cornell.
Grosart. Hamilton(—). *K*(—). *LY ii. 903.*

[*In M. W.'s hand*]

Rydal Mount Decr 21st [1837]

My dear Sir W^m,

The Papers had informed me of the honor[1] lately conferred upon you, and I was intending to congratulate you on the occasion, when your letter arrived. The Electors have done great credit to themselves by appointing you, and not a little by rejecting the Ultra-liberal Archbishop,[2] and that by so decided a majority. We are much pleased that your Sister, who we conclude is well, has sent her Poems to press,[3] and wish they may obtain the attention we are sure they will merit. Your own

---

[1] Hamilton had just been elected President of the Royal Irish Academy.

[2] For Richard Whately, Archbishop of Dublin, see pt. ii, L. 833.

[3] Eliza Hamilton's *Poems* were published in Dublin in 1838.

two sonnets, for which I thank you, we read, that is Mrs W. and myself (Dora is in the South), with interest—But to the main purport of your letter. You pay me an undeserved compliment in requesting my opinion, how you could best promote some of the benefits which the Society, at whose head you are placed, aims at; as to patronage, you are right in supposing that I hold it in little esteem for helping genius forward in the fine arts, especially those whose medium is words. Sculpture and painting *may* be helped by it; but even in these departments there is much to be dreaded. The french have established an Academy at Rome upon an extensive scale, and so far from doing good, I was told by every one that it had done much harm. The Plan is this: they select the most distinguished Students from the School or academy at Paris and send them to Rome, with handsome stipends, by which they are tempted into idleness and of course into vice: so that it looks like a contrivance for preventing the french nation, and the world at large, profitting by the genius which nature may have bestowed, and which left to itself would in some cases, perhaps, have prospered. The principal, I was indeed told the *only*, condition imposed upon these Students is, that each of them send annually some work of his hands to Paris. When at Rome I saw a good deal of English artists. They seemed to be living happily and doing well—tho' as you are aware, the public patronage any of them receive is trifling.

Genius in Poetry, or any department of what is called the Belles Letters, is much more likely to be cramped than fostered by public Support; better wait to reward those who have done their work, tho' even here national rewards are not necessary, unless the Labourers be, if not in poverty, at least in narrow circumstances. Let the laws be but just to them, and they will be sure of attaining a competence, if they have not misjudged their own talents, or misapplied them. The cases of Chatterton, Burns and others, might, it should seem, be urged against the conclusion that help beforehand is not required—but I do think that in the temperament of the two I have mentioned there was something which however favourable had been their circumstances, however much they had been encouraged and supported, would have brought on their ruin. As to what Patronage can do in Science, discoveries in Physics, mechanic arts, etc. you know far better than I can pretend to do.

As to 'better canons of criticism, and general improvement of

Scholars', I really, speaking without affectation, am so little of a Critic or Scholar that it would be presumptuous in me to write upon the Subject to you. If we were together , and you should honor me by asking my opinion upon particular points, that would be a very different thing, and I might have something to say, not wholly without value. But where could I begin with so comprehensive an argument, and how could I put into the compass of a letter my thoughts, such as they may be, with any thing like order. It is somewhat mortifying to me to disappoint you—You must upon reflection I trust perceive, that in attempting to comply with your wish I should only lose myself in a wilderness. I have been applied to to give lectures upon Poetry in a public Institution in London, but I was conscious that I was neither competent to the Office, nor the public prepared to receive what I should have felt it my duty to say, however in [adequately]. [1]

I have [had] a very pleasant and not profitless tour on the Continent, tho' with one great drawback, the being obliged on account of the cholera to return without seeing Naples and its neighbourhood. Had it not been for the State of my eyes which became inflamed after I got back to England, I should have been able to take Liverpool in my way home, at the time you were there. The attack continued for a long time, and has left a weakness in the organ, which does not yet allow me either to read or write; but with care I hope to come about.

My Sister continues in the same enfeebled State of mind and body. Mrs W. is well—but your Godson we hear is suffering from derangement of the Stomach, so that at present he is not a thriving child, but his elder brother is now remarkably so, and he about the same age was subject to the same trials. We trust that your little family are all flourishing, and with our united affectionate regards believe me, faithfully

Dear Sir W. yours
[*signed*] Wm Wordsworth

I am sorry that I cannot send this thro' Lord Northampton, [2] because he tells me he is coming northward.

---

[1] *MS. torn.*

[2] See L. 1017 above. In 1837, with the help of Richard Monckton Milnes, Lord Northampton edited a volume of miscellaneous poems by various authors under the title of *The Tribute* (*R. M. Cat.*, no. 600).

1193. W. W. to ALEXANDER DYCE

Address: The Revd Alex^r Dyce, 9 Gray's Inn.
Postmark: 25 Dec. 1837. *Stamp*: High Holborn.
MS. Victoria and Albert Museum.
Mem. (—). *Grosart* (—). *K* (—). *LY ii. 906.*

[In M. W.'s hand]

Dec. 23, 1837

My dear Sir,

I have just rec^d your valuable Present of Bentley's Works[1]—
for which accept my cordial thanks, as also for the elegant little
Vol: dedicated by you to the Author, and for the leaf to be
added to Akenside[2]—the one to Mr Southey shall be delivered
to him, with your best respects, as you desire.

Is it recorded in your Memoir of A,—for I have not leisure
nor eyesight at present to look,—that he was fond of sitting in St
James's Park with his eyes upon Westminster Abbey? this, I am
sure, I have either read or *heard* of him; and I imagine that it was
from Mr Rogers. I am not unfrequently a visitor on Hampstead
Heath, and seldom pass by the entrance of Mr Dyson's[3] villa on
Goulder's Hill, close by, without thinking of the pleasure which
Akenside often had there.

I cannot call to mind a reason why you should not think some
passages in 'The Power of Sound' equal to anything I have
produced;[4] when first printed in 'Yarrow Revisited', I placed it
at the end of the Volume, and in the last edition of my poems, at
the close of the Poems of Imagination, indicating thereby my
own opinion of it.

---

[1] *The Works of Richard Bentley*, edited with notes by Alexander Dyce, 3
vols., 1836 and 1838. Richard Bentley (1662—1742), was a predecessor of
C. W.'s as Master of Trinity (1700—42).

[2] For Dyce's edition, see L. 870 above. The leaf added to Akenside
contained the saying of Henderson the actor, that 'Akenside, when he walked
in the streets, walked for all the world like one of his own Alexandrines, set
upright.' This story, as de Selincourt notes, had been reported to Dyce by
W. W. on the authority of Rogers.

[3] Jeremiah Dyson, Akenside's patron and friend. See L. 879 above.

[4] In his letter of 7 Dec., Dyce had written of his enjoyment of W. W.'s later
poetry: 'I have now *got up* all your later poems, and often repeat parts of them
to myself with great delight. Perhaps I am wrong in thinking that the *Ode on
the Power of Sound* contains some passages as magnificent as any you have ever
written.' (*Dyce MSS., Victoria and Albert Museum.*)

How much do I regret that I have neither learning nor eyesight thoroughly to enjoy Bentley's masterly *Dissertation on the Epistles of Phalaris*;[1] many years ago I read the work with infinite pleasure. As far as I know, or rather am able to judge, it is without a rival in that department of literature; a work of which the English nation may be proud as long as acute intellect, and vigorous powers, and profound scholarship shall be esteemed in the world.

Let me again repeat my regret that in passing to and from Scotland you have never found it convenient to visit this part of the Country. I would be delighted to see you, and I am sure Mr Southey would be the same: in his house you would find an inexhaustible collection of books, many of them curious no doubt; but his classical Library is much the least valuable part of it. The death of his excellent Wife was a deliverance for herself and the whole family—so great had been her sufferings of mind and body.

You don't say a word about Skelton, and I regret much your disappointment in respect to Middleton.[2]

I remain, my dear Sir,
faithfully, your much obliged
[*signed*] Wm Wordsworth

[1] Bentley's *Dissertation on the Epistles of Phalaris . . . and the Fables of Aesop* was published in 1697.

[2] Dyce's edition of Skelton appeared in 1843; his edition of Thomas Middleton in 1840. In his letter to W. W. he stated that two volumes of the latter had already been printed, but were held back by the publisher who was 'frightened at the state of the trade'.

1194. W. W. to SAMUEL CARTER HALL

Address: S. C. Hall Esqre, care of Messrs. Whittaker and Co., Ave Maria Lane.
Postmark: 25 Dec. 1837.
MS. Historical Society of Pennsylvania.
LY ii. 907.

[*In M. W.'s hand*]

Decr 23rd [1837]

My dear Sir

I have been anxious for the arrival of your volume,[1] both on its own account, and that I might be at liberty to answer your last obliging note. The Book only reached me yesterday, it having been delayed at Mr Moxon's until he could send it in the same parcel with the new Ed: of Disraeli's 'Curiosities of Literature'.[2]

Absurdly unreasonable would it be in me, if I were not satisfied with your notice of my writings and character—All I can say further is that I have *wished* both to be what you indulgently affirm they are. In the few facts of your Memoir, there is only one mistake or rather ina[c]curacy. You say he was educated *with* his almost [equally][3] distinguished Brother—My B^r D^r W— he it is true was brought up at the same school—but being upwards of 4 years younger than myself—we could scarcely be said to be educated together—and I had left College before he came there. In Mr Chorley's[4] account of me in his 'living Authors' just published, there are several gross errors— among others he says my appointment as Distributor of stamps took place no less than 11 years after the date he assigns it.[5]

You will be sorry that the Copy of the Gem sent to me is imperfect—the pages from 128 to 137 being wanting—I shall

---

[1] The third volume of *The Book of Gems* (see L. 1107 above), which opens with a Memoir of W. W. and a number of his poems.

[2] *Curiosities of Literature* by Isaac D'Israeli (1766–1848) appeared anon., 1791: 9th edn. revised, 6 vols., Edward Moxon, 1834.

[3] *Word dropped out*: equally *supplied from Book of Gems.*

[4] Henry F. Chorley, *The Authors of England, a Series of Medallion Portraits of Modern Literary Characters Engraved by Achille Collas, with Illustrative Notices,* 1838. The Preface is dated Oct. 1837. See also L. 1200 below.

[5] W. W. means that his appointment took place eleven years after the date to which Chorley assigned it, which was c. 1803. The error was uncorrected in the second edition, 1861.

therefore take the liberty of sending it back, thro' my Kendal Bookseller to Whittaker and Co, to be exchanged.

Not long after my arrival here I had the pleasure of seeing your B[r] who came, as he may have told you, with Mrs Curwen, my daughter-in-law's Mother. We talked a good deal ab[t] you and Mrs Hall, and I was much gratified with his intelligent conversation. I have not been able to do more than look into the Gem—my eyes being to[o] weak—tho' much amended. Pray accept my best wishes for Mrs Hall and yourself, and believe m[e] dear Sir to be faithfully y[r] obliged

[*signed*] Wm Wordsworth

1195. W. W. to EDWARD MOXON

Address: Edward Moxon Esq[re], 44 Dover Street.
Postmark: 25 Dec. 1837.
MS. Henry E. Huntington Library.
LY ii. 908.

[*In M. W.'s hand*]

[23 Dec. 1837]

My dear Mr Moxon,

The parcel arrived safely yesterday and I thank you, both on my own part and that of my Son's for the handsome vol:[1] from you, which it contains. I forwarded Mr Southey's, as well as my Son's, by yesterday's Coach. Thank you also for your note, if Mr Quillinan had not told me that the Edition was reduced to 700 Copies I should have been pleased to hear from yourself (as he said he had done, some little time ago) that 900 only were on hand—as it was I was a little disappointed—more for your sake than my own. I will inform my daughter of Mrs Moxon's and your kind invitation to Dover Street, but I believe her engagements will not admit of her availing herself of your friendly proposal—She is now I trust at Cambridge and must return to Dover as soon as she has paid a long-promised, and often-interrupted visit, at Hampstead.

I *had* hoped that my carrying my Sister's journal[2] thro' the

---

[1] *The Book of Gems.* See previous letter.
[2] See L. 1189 above.

press might prove a salutary interest to her—but as I no longer can cherish that hope, I must defer the publication—we find that the work perhaps would not interest her at all, or if it did, like every thing that excites her, it would do her harm.

Mr Hall's Gem being imperfect, wanting no less than 9 pages, we shall be obliged to return it to be exchanged for a perfect Copy, and will take that opportunity of *safely* sending the Autographs for the two Copies of my Poems. My F^d Mr Powell tells me that Mr Marshall (of the firm of Simkin and Marshall) had mentioned to him that the Sale of my 6 vols was steadily encreasing, and that he was persuaded an edition in one vol would sell. It w^d be still for us to consider, however, and for me especially on acc^t of the stereotype, wh[ether][1] such an Ed: might not put a stop to the Sale in 6 vols: and therefore be unadvisable if the 900 now on hand were reduced even to 200 (tho' you recollect we talked of entering upon such an Ed: when it should be reduced to 500)—Is the Coloquies on Religion[2] sent from you or [the] Author? If from you accept my thanks—if from [him] pray present my acknow[ledgements.]

My eyes are nearly well, but do not allow me to read much. Kindest love to Miss Lamb. We rejoice to hear she is so well.

faithfully y^rs
[*signed*] W W.

[1] From this point on, the side of the MS. is worn away.

[2] F. W. Faber, *Colloquies on Religion and Religious Education*, 1837 (*R. M. Cat.*, no. 229). Frederick William Faber (1814–63), poet, Tractarian, and Oratorian priest, had become an enthusiastic disciple of W. W. while still a schoolboy at Harrow, and had called at Rydal Mount in 1831 (*RMVB*). The following year he went up to Balliol College, Oxford, transferring to University College as a Scholar two years later; and in 1836 he won the Newdigate Prize with a poem *The Knights of St. John*. In the summer of 1837, following his election to a Fellowship at University College, Faber took a reading-party to Ambleside, assisting the local clergyman and winning fame as a preacher and as 'a perfect *model* of what a deacon of our church ought to be' (see *MW*, pp. 176, 187–8); and he returned the following summer (*RMVB*), thereby cementing his friendship with the Wordsworth circle. See F. A. Faber, *A Brief Sketch of the Early Life of the late F. W. Faber, D.D.*, 1869, pp. 13 ff.; and John Edward Bowden, *The Life and Letters of Frederick William Faber, D.D.*, 1869, pp. 70 ff.

1196. W. W. to EDWARD FERGUSON

Postmark: 1837.
MS. Mrs. Finch. Hitherto unpublished.

Rydal Mount
Dec 30th [1837]

My dear Sir,

Sincerely do we thank you for your kind Letter, communicating the tidings of the Decease of our excellent Relative, Mrs Wm Rawson.[1] This event which, if it had happened some time ago, would have caused us all, particularly my dear Sister, much sorrow and regret, is now only to be regarded as a merciful release. To every one of her kindred and friends looking back upon the course of her long life, as at this time they will be naturally summoned to do, it will appear that there is abundant cause of congratulation, nor can they doubt that as a good Christian she is gone to her reward.

We lament to hear that your liberty of moving is restrained by infirmities, and cordially wish and pray, that your own course and that of those you best love, may be, through God's mercy, much smoother to that rest which cannot be far from any of your contemporaries.

My poor sister continues much the same in bodily health, but from weakness of frame affecting the strength of her mind, she is unable to keep her attention sustained upon things that formerly used to interest her. She talks much however, of her Aunt, as you know she was used to call her Departed Relation[2] and friend, and indeed of Halifax and all her early connections there; nothing indeed seems to employ her thoughts so much.

Mrs Wordsworth is well, so am I. Our Daughter is now at Cambridge with her Uncle and Cousins; her health is much improved, but she has suffered lately from being tempted to exert herself too much.

With affectionate remembrances to your self and sister, in which Mrs W. and our dear Invalid unite,

believe me to be your much obliged
Cousin
Wm Wordsworth

Sarah Crackanthorpe[3] has been written to.

---

[1] Mrs. Elizabeth Rawson had finally died on 23 Dec.
[2] She was strictly speaking a cousin of D. W.   [3] See L. 1185 above.

1197. W. W. to SIR WILLIAM ROWAN HAMILTON

Address: Sir Wm Hamilton, Observatory, Dublin.
Postmark: (1) 4 Jan. 1838 (2) 6 Jan. 1838. *Stamp*: (1) Kendal (2) Dublin Penny
Post.
MS. Cornell.
Grosart. Hamilton (—). K (—). LY ii. 910.

[*In M. W.'s hand*]

Rydal Mount Jan^{ry} 4th [1838]
My dear Sir W^m,

From a hope of something starting up in my mind which might prevent my letter from being an utter disappointment I have not answered yours as I wished to do, by return of post. But I am really still as much at a loss how to make my letter worth reading as if I had replied immediately. Allow me however to thank you for your last, which has completely done away with the vagueness of the former. I now distinctly understand you, and as to one of your leading points, viz, availing myself of publication through your Society,[1] I may say that, if there had been among my papers any thing of the kind you wish for, I should have gladly forwarded it to you. But it is not so, nor dare I undertake to promise anything of the kind for the future. Though prevailed upon by Mr Coleridge to write

---

[1] In his letter of 30 Dec., Hamilton had spoken about the role of the Royal Irish Academy in the encouragement of science and literature: 'What I look to . . . is the drawing forth of *critical essays*, more philosophical and elaborate than would suit the taste of the mere ordinary reading public, by inviting and encouraging the presentation of such essays to its *Transactions*. May I dare to illustrate my meaning by applying it to your own case? Suppose that *you* could be induced to favour us with any critical reflections . . . embodying or sketching out any views of yours respecting the spirit and philosophy of criticism, or the nature and essential laws of poetry, or the objects and prospects of literature, . . . suppose this done with so little adaptation to prevailing popular tastes, that in whatever manner the work might be published it must be as bread cast upon the waters, to be found only after many days; yet not, like poetry, appealing to the universal *heart* of man, but rather to the calm deliberate *judgment* of the thoughtful student or philosopher: I think that no more appropriate mode of publishing such a composition could easily be devised, than by presenting it to a literary society like ours, whose published *Transactions* have among learned men an increasing circulation, at home and abroad . . .' (*Hamilton*, ii. 230.)

the first Preface to my Poems—which tempted, or rather forced, me to add a Supplement to it—and induced by my friendship for him to write the Essay upon Epitaphs, now appended to The Excursion, but first composed for The Friend, I have never felt inclined to write criticism, tho' I have *talked*, and am daily talking, a great deal. If I were several years younger I would, out of friendship to you mainly, sit down to the task of giving a body to my notions upon the essentials of Poetry, a subject which could not be properly treated without adverting to the other branches of fine Art; but at present, with so much before me that I could wish to do in verse, and the melancholy fact brought daily more and more home to my conviction that intellectual labour, by its action on the brain and nervous system, is injurious to the bodily powers, and especially to my eye-sight, I should only be deceiving myself and misleading you, were I to encourage a hope, that much as I could wish to be your fellow-labourer, however humbly, I shall ever become one.

Having disposed of this rather painful part of the Subject of your letter, let me say—that though it is principally matters of science in which publication through your Society would be serviceable, and indeed in that department eminently so, I concur with you in thinking that the same vehicle would be useful, for bringing under the notice of the thinking part of the community critical essays of too abstract a character to be fit for popularity. There are obviously, even in criticism, two ways of affecting the minds of men: the one by treating the matter so as to carry it immediately to the Sympathies of the many, and the other by aiming at a few select and superior minds, that might each become a centre for illustrating it in a popular way. Mr Coleridge, whom you allude to[1] acted upon the world to a great extent thro the latter of these processes; and there cannot be a doubt that your Society might serve the cause of just thinking, and pure taste, should you, as President of it, hold up to view the desirableness of first conveying to a few, thro' that channel, reflections upon Literature and Art which, if well meditated would be sure of winning their way directly, or in their indirect results, to a gradually widening circle.

---

[1] Hamilton had reminded W. W. that Coleridge's essay *On the Prometheus of Aeschylus* was published in the *Transactions of the Royal Society of Literature*, after being delivered as a lecture on 18 May, 1825. See Griggs, v. 143; vi. 712.

May I not encourage a hope that during the ensuing Summer, or at the worst at no distant period, you and I might meet, when a few hours' conversation would effect more than could come out of a dozen letters dictated and *hastily*, as I am obliged to dictate this, because of an unexpected interruption when Mrs W. and I were sitting down, with the pen in her hand.

You are right in your recollection that I named to you the Subject of foreign Piracy as injurious to English Authors, and I may add now that if it could be put a stop to, I believe that it would rarely happen that successful writers in works of imagination and feeling at least, would stand in need of pensions from Gov^t, or would feel themselves justified in accepting them. Upon this Subject I have spoken a great deal to M.P.s of all Parties, and with several distinguished Americans. I have also been in correspondence with the present Chancellor of the Exchequer[1] upon it, and dwelt upon the same topic in a letter which I had occasion to write to Sir R^t Peel. Mr Litten Bulwer,[2] as perhaps you know, drew the attention of Parl^t to it during the last Session. Ld Palmerston[3] said in answer to him, that the attention of Gov^t had already been directed to the measure, and that it would not be lost sight of, or something to that purpose. I may claim some credit for my exertions in this business, and full as much, or more, for the pains which I have taken for many years, to interest men in the H of C. in the extension of the term of copy-right,—a measure which I trust is about to be brought to a successful close by the exertions of my admirable friend Sergeant Talfourd. To him I have written upon the argument more than once. When this is effected I trust the other part of the Subject will be taken up with spirit; and if the foreign Sec^{ry}, in whose department the matter lies, should be remiss, I trust he will be stimulated thro' Parl^t, to which desirable end the Services of distinguished Societies like yours, and the notice of the question by men of letters, in reviews or otherwise, would greatly contribute. Good Authors, if justice were done to them

[1] Thomas Spring Rice had spoken in support of Talfourd's first Bill the previous summer.

[2] Edward Lytton Bulwer, 1st Baron Lytton (1803–73), dandy, politician, and novelist: as M.P. for Lincoln, 1832–41, a reformer and supporter of copyright: author of *Falkland* (1827), *Pelham* (1828), *The Last Days of Pompeii* (1834), *The Last of the Barons* (1843), etc. He had met C. W. jnr. in Rome in 1833. Along with Peel and Benjamin Disraeli he spoke in support of Talfourd's new Bill on 14 Dec. 1837.   [3] The Foreign Secretary.

by their own and foreign countries, now that reading is spread and is spreading so widely, would very few of them be in need, except thro' their own fault.

When I was in Town last Aug: the American minister Mr Stephenson spoke to me with much indignation of the law and practice by which copy-right was secured in England for American authors, while there was no reciprocity for english writers in America.

But I must conclude, or I shall miss the post. The Father of your Godson[1] is here, and begs to be remembered to you. Did I ever mention to you that owing [to] the sea having swallowed up his Father-in-Law's coal pits, his income is much reduced, and he therefore feels it necessary to endeavour to procure a couple of Pupils who could afford to pay rather handsomely for the advantages they would have under his roof. By this time he would have succeeded, but Parents in the South have an unaccountable objection to sending their Sons so far north. As the same might not be felt in Ireland, I take the liberty of mentioning his wish to you, being persuaded that if you can you will assist him in his views. If y[r] address to y[r] Society should be published, could you send it me, and acquaint me with what you have done.

Aff[ly] yours
[*signed*] W[m] Wordsworth

1198. W. W. to THOMAS NOON TALFOURD

Address: Mr Sergeant Talfourd M.P., Russell Square, London.
Postmark: (1) 8 Jan. 1838 (2) 10 Jan. 1838.
Stamp: Kendal Penny Post.
MS. Broadley Collection, Archives Department of the Westminster Public Libraries. Hitherto unpublished.

[*In M. W.'s hand*]

Rydal Mt
Jan 8th [1838]

My Dear Sir,

As the time draws near when your bill[2] is to be brought in to Par[t] would you be so kind as to name the day, for the 2[d]

[1] John W.

[2] The new Copyright Bill. For the vicissitudes this measure suffered until it was finally passed in 1842, see Moorman, ii. 550–5.

reading—that I may apprize the few personal friends whom I may have in the house—and urge them to attend. Mr Southey tells me that he knows not one to whom he could apply beyond those whom he is sure will attend without such application. We are reading the 6th Vol. of Lockhart's life of Scott—what a deplorable picture of distress and humiliation all to be traced up to one mis[take]¹—an undervaluing of the dignity and importance of literature in comparison with what is called *rising in the world*, and those indulgences, and that sort of distinction which the acquiring money with rapidity, and spending it with profusion, afford.²

Wishing you and yours a happy new year in which Mrs W cordially joins with a request that you will send the enclosed to the twopenny post, I remain

dear Sir, ever faithfully yours

[*signed*] Wm Wordsworth

¹ *Seal.*

² See Mrs. John Davy's MS. Journal of 1837 (*WL MSS.*), which records some of W. W.'s conversation during his visit to the Davys at Chatham (see L. 1157 above): '. . . Something which was said concerning Lockhart's Life of Scott, by my mother, brought him forth in great vigour, and we all agreed we had never heard him discourse more like the "fervent Angel". He was afflicted at the view opened by Lockhart of Scott's occupation of mind in money concerns and love [? of] haggling—and pained to think that the person he had walked with over field and fell, and thought a "light airy creature" devoted to nature's enjoyments, should have had, as he now discovered another mind, and separate train of thought and anxiety, which as he truly said, ought to have poisoned all. . . . We all agreed that Wordsworth was . . . true to his character as a poet, in his lamentation that Scott should so have under valued his high destiny as a man of genius, and so have over valued possessions in house and land—as to become a trader and speculator with tradesmen. . . . Nothing but hearing his living utterance can never convey to you the impression made by his grand simple earnestness of manner—with his racy yet elaborate English diction, his words waiting on him like servants on a Master, whom they love to be used by, or more like still perhaps to spirits called up by a magician . . . '

MS. *Doheny Memorial Library, St. John's Seminary, Camarillo, California.* Hitherto unpublished.

[*In M. W.'s hand*]

Rydal Mount Jan^{ry} 9th [1838]

My dear Mr Powell

I have deferred replying to your last very kind letters enclosed within the parcel which I duly received free of charge—until Mrs W. had procured information to enable her to answer your question relative to the little Boy about whom I ventured to trouble you.

Pray present my thanks to Dr Smith[1] for his attention in transmitting me, thro' your hands, his valuable work on 'the Philosophy of health'; which, advanced in life as I am, I am not without hope of profitting by. I am pleased to see large extracts from the book in the Penny Magazine, and wish it all the circulation and success which, as far as I am enabled to judge, it abundantly deserves.

Your notice of Mr Chapman[2] a pious and conscientious Minister interested me much, and Mrs W. and I thank you for those effusions of his devout Spirit which you presented to us. Our sympathy with religious feelings is not limited to the members of our own church, attached as we are to its faith and Ordinances, and like yourself preferring them to any other; and strenuous, according to our narrow influence, in upholding them. Pray thank most cordially Mr. An: Chapman[3] for the readiness with which he has promised to meet my wishes in the question of Copy-right. It is well to be prepared to frustrate opposition, tho' it is to be hoped no party will disgrace itself by

[1] Thomas Southwood Smith (1788–1861), sanitary reformer, author of *Illustrations of the Divine Government*, Glasgow, 1816, and *The Philosophy of Health*, 2 vols., 1835–7: became a Unitarian minister at Edinburgh and at the same time studied medicine: helped to found the *Westminster Review* (1824), the Society for the Diffusion of Useful Knowledge, and similar organizations; served on several committees of enquiry on factory children and the poor, and wrote many valuable reports on the control of epidemics and sanitary improvement. See also L. 1260 below.

[2] Perhaps the Revd. Edwin Chapman, a minister at Deptford, who edited the *Unitarian Magazine and Chronicle*, 1834–5.

[3] Aaron Chapman, M.P. for Whitby, a partner in the firm of John Chapman and Co., for which Powell worked.

standing in the way of a measure of justice—so obvious to the disinterested.

I now turn to a Subject which I cannot begin upon without first making my sincere acknowledgments for the manner in which you have rec[d] our request. In addition to what was said before, I must state more distinctly that we wanted our nephew[1] to be educated with as little expence, as to food, clothing, and tuition as might be consistent with his well-doing. We are ignorant however what foundations are open to one so circumstanced. As to the Blue Coat School, or Christ Hospital as it is called, could he be admitted there that would be all we would desire—but we apprehend that for this purpose one of two conditions is indispensable viz that he should either be the Son of a Clergyman or of a Freeman of the City, and he is neither the one nor the other. Several of my friends, and some among the most distinguished, Coleridge and Lamb, were brought up at this school; and at a time when in some respects, especially as to diet, it was nothing like so well managed as it has been since. If however any course should be open for introducing the Boy there, which perhaps your friendly enquiries might ascertain, we will endeavour to avail ourselves of it in his behalf. For assuredly, as we said in our last, the case for the reasons there given, is urgent. The particulars concerning the Boy I will transcribe from the letter received this morning:

'John Hutchinson was 8 years old last Christmas Eve, and for his age writes a good hand, reads well (for a Country Lad) and can cast up a short question in Addition—he is a fine healthy looking Boy, very good tempered and obedient, and shews much application'. To this Mrs W. may add, that having seen her nephew she certainly thinks him a fine promising Child— and she will ever consider herself most grateful to you, should you be able to put her in the way of training him to be a good and useful man.

Since you mentioned the desirableness of printing my poems in a single volume, it has been suggested to me, and not for the first time, that many would be gratified by having all the Sonnets, which amount to upwards of 400, published in a single and separate volume. What do you think of this? I have requested my daughter, who is at Hampstead at present for a

---

[1] John Hutchinson (1829–1916), eldest child of George Hutchinson, M. W.'s brother. See also *MW*, p. 217.

few days to call upon Mr Moxon and mention the subject.

Believe me to be ever faithfully your obliged
[*signed*] Wm Wordsworth

I believe I hailed you and yours upon the New Year in my last—if not, pray except[1] for yourself and all belonging to you our joint best wishes.

1200. W. W. to ROBERT SHELTON MACKENZIE

Address: R. Shelton MacKenzie Esqre, Liverpool.
Postmark: 26 Jan. 1838. *Stamp*: (1) Kendal (2) Liverpool.
MS. Berg Collection, New York Public Library.
Hitherto unpublished.

[*In M. W.'s hand*]

Rydal Mount Jan^{ry} 26 [1838]
My dear Sir,

Assure yourself that I could only take as a compliment what upon the suggestion of Mrs M. you thought required an apology. The expression of your regret that particular accounts had not been given of the circumstances under which the Poems[2] were written was obviously a proof of the interest you took in them, and therefore, could not reasonably give offence, tho' the delicacy of Mrs M'^s mind made her fear it. Such notes were not given for several reasons, the practice has to me an air of attaching more importance to miscellaneous productions than to many they may appear to possess; in some cases also the prose might take from the natural independent poetical effect, and I have observed, with regret, that if poetry and prose present themselves to the eye upon the same page, a large majority of readers will take to the prose in preference, which is rather humiliating and mortifying to a pains-taking Poet! Besides I was unwilling to swell the book,—6 volumes cannot be sold at too great a price, for thousands whom I would wish to have as Readers, and I am confident that the Authors of the present day must, with very few exceptions, put themselves into

---

[1] i.e. accept.

[2] Some poems of W. W.'s, which Mackenzie had mentioned in a previous letter.

less room if they would have their works go down to Posterity in a body.

You enquire if Mr Chorley's biography of me[1] be correct. It is not in several instances: viz. page 89 'The same enthusiasm made him partaker of certain fierce Poems of the hour, long since forgotten, or disavowed'—The nonsense that follows in the same sentence is below comment—but what the *fierce Poems* were, I am utterly at a loss to conjecture; all that I know is, that when I was a very young Man the present Archdeacon Wrangham and I amused ourselves in imitating jointly Juvenile's Satire upon Nobility—or rather parts of it.[2] How far the choice of a Subject might be influenced by the run at that time against Aristocracy, I am unable to say, and am inclined to think that if the 3ᵈ and 10ᵗʰ Satire had not been so well imitated by Dʳ Johnson, we might as easily have chosen one of them to amuse ourselves or try our skill upon. Not a word of this essay was ever, to my knowledge, printed, and fierce poems upon political subjects from *my* pen, could never have been suppressed or forgotten for they were never written. (Again, on the same page). In 1803 he married etc etc etc and about the same time his being nominated to the office of the Distributor of Stamps.' Here are two errors. My marriage took place in 1802 and I did not enter upon the office till May 1813—eleven years after.

As your purpose to write about my poems induced you to make the request I have thus far answered, I will add for your information, that till the age of 17 years and a half I lived among the mountains or near the lakes and rivers of Cumbᵈ and Lancashire, from that time till my 30ᵗʰ year, almost entirely in Cambridge, in London, in France or Germany, travelling or resident in many districts of England and Wales. Since the year 1800, I have had a home where I now reside, or within 2 miles, —but as my Poems shew, my excursions both at home and abroad have been frequent, as of course have been my visits to London.

I gladly avail myself of the present occasion to thank you for the Copies of the Liverpool Mail, which from time to time you have been so kind as to send me and also for the no: of the Glasgow Constitutional.[3] The panegyrical notice of me is

---

[1] In *The Authors of England*. See L. 1194 above.

[2] In 1797: see *EY*, pp. 172–7.

[3] A twice weekly paper, which ran from 1836 to 1855.

obviously the work of a *young* man, and in a few years, if he
remembers it, he will think the Style too florid, and his praise, I
fear, too high-flown—but extremes of this kind are not I think
unpromising in a youth, on the contrary if I may judge by what
I remember of my friends, and myself—Mr Coleridge in
particular—they are of good omen. The admiring *Orator* must
have my poems at his finger ends, for I took the trouble to
number the quotations from [me]¹ in that short speech and
found them not less than 13! Poets and Artists are thought to be,
I know not whether justly or not, fonder of praise than other
men, but for my own part I can sincerely affirm, that I set
infinitely less store by it than for those involuntary effusions of
love and affection and gratitude which have reached me either
directly or indirectly from many Strangers to my Person. Mr
Blackwood sends me his Mag: but to save the expense of
carriage only once a quarter, so that I may not have a sight of the
Poem you mention for some little time.

If you are in communication with Miss Edgeworth pray
thank her for her message, and say that I think with lively
interest of my visit to Edgeworth-town some years ago,² and
wᵈ be much pleased could I cherish the hope of repeating it, but
I have reached that age when one feels habitually, sit modus
lapso maris et viarum.

Pray keep your eye upon the 2ᵈ reading of Sergeant
Talfourd's motion upon copy-right, and as far as it may suit yʳ
convenience, beg of yʳ friends in Parlᵗ to support with their
votes a measure so just.

Heartily do I wish that you were at liberty to follow yʳ
inclinat[ion] to devote more of your time to an art, in which I
am strongly persuaded you are fitted to excel.

I remain, with kind regards to yourself and family, in which
Mrs W. concurs, sincerely

your obliged
[*signed*] Wᵐ Wordsworth

My eyes are better
W W.

---

¹ *MS. torn.*
² In 1829.

Address: Edward Moxon Esqre, 44 Dover Street.
Postmark: 5 Feb. 1838. *Stamp*: Cornhill.
MS. Henry E. Huntington Library.
K (—). LY ii. 914.

[*In M. W.'s hand*]   [*c.* 3 Feb. 1838][1]

My dear Mr Moxon

About a Month ago having occasion to forward (thro' Hudson and Nicholson Kendal) an imperfect Copy of the Gem[2] (which was sent me by Mr Hall) to be corrected at Whitaker's, I enclosed the fly leaves which were intended for Mrs M.'s and Emma's copies of my Poems—not having had any report of the arrival of this book in Ave Maria Lane, and as your letter does not notice your having rec^d the said leaves, I think it proper to apprize you thereof, that you may enquire after them—they were simply returned in the stiff paper in which I received them, and directed to you.

I am rather pleased that you approve of the Sonnets in a separate volume, not that I care much about it myself, except for the money that it would bring (and that mainly on account of an unfavourable change in the circumstances of my Son) but because requests that I would print such a volume have reached me from many quarters. Mr Powell tells me that one of the City Publishers (Smith Elder and Co[3]) to whom he had mentioned the subject said he was sure such a Publication would sell. You somewhat surprize me in purposing to print *one* Son:[4] on a page, the whole number being I believe 415. Your plan and consequent price would make it a book of luxury, and tho' I have no objection to that, yet still my wish is, to be read as widely as is consistent with reasonable pecuniary return. A day or two ago Dr Arnold shewed me a letter from a Clergyman, an

---

¹ Written at the beginning of February, and taken by a visitor down to London for posting.

² *The Book of Gems.* See L. 1194 above.

³ The firm founded in 1819 by George Smith (1789–1846), who migrated from Elgin to London and worked for a time with Rivington and John Murray, before launching out on his own in partnership with Alexander Elder. The younger George Smith (1824–1901) was founder and proprietor of the *Dictionary of National Biography*, the *Cornhill Magazine* and the *Pall Mall Gazette*.   ⁴ Sonnet.

accomplished Scholar besides, entreating of me to publish my works in 'brown' paper, that was the word, meaning I suppose the cheapest form, for the benefit of readers in the humblest condition of life—being convinced from his own experience, that my works were fitted to touch their hearts, and purify and exalt their minds. These were not his words exactly, but they were to this effect. Miss Martineau I am told has said that my poems are in the hearts of the American People.[1] That is the place I would fain occupy among the People of these Islands. And I am not at all sure that the abstract character of no small portion of my own poetry will at all stand in the way of that result. Though it would not in *itself* recommend them to the mass of the people.

These observations are merely thrown out as springing up naturally on this occasion. I leave the mode of publication entirely to your superior judgement being persuaded that whatever there may be, in these or my other works, fitted for general sympathy, *that* will find its way as education spreads to the spirits of many. I ought to add as a personal motive for preferring a vol: printed as you recommend that it will gratify my daughter, whom I am always happy and proud to please— and before you decide, as to type and shape of page, would you take the trouble to communicate with her, and send a specimen to No. 3 Clarence Lawn, Dover.

I will write to you in reply to your query about the arrangement in a day or two—

Mrs W. joins me in thanks to you and Mrs M. for your kind invitation which we will remember should we leave home— but I do not at present feel inclined to encounter the excitement of a Spring in London. With our joint affec regards believe me sincerely my d[r] M.

Yours
[signed] W[m] Wordsworth

P.S. I see an advertisement of a pamphlet[2] written against the extension of Copy-right, but have met with no notice of it,

---

[1] See *Society in America*, 3 vols., 1837, iii. 219.

[2] Probably *Observations on the Law of Copyright, in reference to the Bill of Mr. Sergeant Talfourd, in which it is attempted to be proved that the Provisions of the Bill are opposed to the Principle of English Law; that Authors require no additional Protection; and that such a Bill would inflict a heavy blow on Literature, and prove a great Discouragement to its Diffusion in this Country*, 1838. The author was

either in Newspaper or review. Have you any reason for believing that Sergeant Talfourd's motion will meet with any opposition in the house—at all formidable? After all, about the Sonnets, may not there be some risk—*this* I should not like to encounter, much less should I chuse to throw it upon you. What say you of this important point which unaccountably I had overlooked?—

1202. W. W. to EDWARD FERGUSON

Address: Edward Fergusen Esqʳᵉ, near Halifax. *Double paid*. [*In M. W.'s hand*]
Postmark: 7 Feb. 1838. *Stamp*: Kendal Penny Post.
MS. Cornell. Hitherto unpublished.

Rydal Mount
7ᵗʰ Febʳʸ [18]38

My dear Mʳ Ferguson,
    I enclose my Sister's Receipt for the Legacy left her, by her Aunt,[1] as she used to call her. You will see by the Handwriting that afflicted as she is both in mind and body, her nerves are as steady as ever. Though we have the company of our younger Son from Carlisle, ours is but a dull house. Our Daughter is at Dover, and we have good accounts of her health; but John has had a severe cold with so much fever (the typhus raging in the neighbourhood) as caused his poor Wife great alarm.
    Pray remember us most kindly to your Sister,[2] and, believe me

dear Mʳ Ferguson
faithfully yours
Wᵐ Wordsworth

probably Thomas Wakley (1795–1862), the medical reformer, a vociferous opponent of the Bill. He was founder of *The Lancet* (1823), M.P. for Finsbury (1835–52), and Coroner for West Middlesex from 1839.
    [1] Mrs. Rawson.
    [2] Anne Ferguson.

1203. W. W. to H. C. R.

Address: H. C. Robinson Esqre, 3 Plowdens Build^gs, Temple.
Stamp: Fenchurch St.
Endorsed: Feb 1838 Wordsworth on public affairs.
MS. Dr. Williams's Library.
Morley, i. 353.

[In M. W.'s hand]

[Feb. 1838]

My dear Friend

Thanks for your two letters. As we are now so far advanced towards Spring, when Carriages must be more in request, I quite agree with you, and my Son W^m is of the same opinion, that we have a right to look for £35 clear of the expense of removing the Carriage,[1] *at the lowest*—that sum would be just ½ of what it cost us in London, and you know there were other considerable expences in fitting it out at Paris. You cannot however come to any resolution respecting it, with which I shall quarrel. We have written this morn^g to Brinsop, reporting the substance of your letter—M^r H's feeble state, tho' his health has been improving, must be taken as an excuse for their dilitoriness—*We* have not heard from them lately.

The weather has not been anything like so severe with us as in the South, and not an inmate in this house has suffered in the least from cold our situation is so warm, and sheltered.

Before you go to Norway don't fail to read Samuel Laing Esqre[2] Journal of a residence in Norway *1836* published by Longman—for a book professing to be written in English, it is in style the worst I ever read; and the Author in some important points, is an ill reasoning and an inconsistent theorist. But his book contains a good deal of valuable information, respecting a Country little visited, and where there have existed for many many Centuries Institutions, and a state of Society worthy of being considered, by a more comprehensive mind than this Traveller's.

Mr Moxon has consented to publish the Sonnets in a separate vol: and seems pleased with the project—but he proposes to print them only one in a page—which will make a Vol of not

---

[1] The carriage which had been used for the Continental tour the previous summer. The Hutchinsons seem to have been interested in acquiring it.

[2] Samuel Laing (1780–1868), traveller and author, also published *A Tour in Sweden*, 1838. He was very critical of Swedish domination of Norway.

less [than]¹ 420 pages the price to be 9/ at least—of course it will then be a book of luxury—which may be better tolerated in this class of composition than others, as the structure of the Sonnet is so artificial. But what do you say to his plan? you have a special right to be the [first] consulted, having been the first to suggest to me such a publication and [having] been one of his best Patrons. Pray confer with him about it. By the next post, I hope to send off a list of corrections, chiefly errors of the press, and amended punctuation. There will be one add¹ Son:² which I composed yesterday for a conclusion to the class of our Continental Tour in —20—and I think of writing another by way of finale for the whole Volume.

Thanks for your notices of public affairs, I am glad of what you say of Fonblanc,³ nothing upon that subject from him has fallen in my way; but I have lately seen in an extract, from him that he is as bigotted about the ballot as ever. I learn from a pretty good quarter that the Tories are building high hopes upon the humiliation of the present Ministry. I wish I could share them, but I see no prospect of forming a Govᵗ at present in which any one Party in the State, can take the lead without compromises, and inconsistencies which are likely to make common honesty a thing no longer to be looked for, in public men. The Canadian Rebellion⁴ could have never broken out but from the weakness of our Govᵗ at home; upon this, the Agitators upon both sides of the Water built; and it⁵ is this which has called out the insolence the American Govᵗ is now manifesting—the root of the whole, being the distracted state of public opinion among ourselves.

¹ *Word dropped out.*
² *At Dover* (*PW* iii. 198), incorrectly dated by de Selincourt to 1837. The volume finally contained twelve new sonnets.
³ Albany Fonblanque (1793–1872), radical reformer and journalist, noted for his humour and sarcasm: associate of Bentham, the Mills, and Grote, and a leading contributor to the *Westminster Review*: John Forster's predecessor as editor of *The Examiner*, 1830–47. In 1837 he published *England under Seven Administrations*. H. C. R. saw much of him at the Athenaeum.
⁴ The Canadian Rebellion of 1838 was caused by the disputes between French and British settlers in Lower Canada, and the struggles for representative government, led by William Lyon Mackenzie, in Upper Canada. It was easily subdued, but led ultimately to the triumph of the Earl of Durham's colonial policy which resulted in the unification of Canada into a self-governing dominion. The Canada Government Bill was passed in July 1840. See also L. 1281 below.   ⁵ it *written twice.*

Dr Arnold was truly sorry to leave Fox How sooner than he needed to have done—to attend to what he deemed his duty in the thing called University Col.[1] (I believe) do not the words of the Charter say that the object of the Institution is to provide a regular and liberal course of education? How is this to be done, if Christianity as promulgated in the Greek Testament, is as a matter of fact to be excluded? Plague upon such liberality, and shame upon a Ministry who could consent that under this mask of old names and honors, such a system should be smuggled into a Country, with whose laws and institutions Christianity is so intimately blended, as with ours. Is it possible that a Body of Teachers, of whose very existence such jealous precautions are deemed an indispensible condition can long work together for a good purpose.

Do you mean to embark for Norway from London—the communication from Stockton upon Tees is frequent and direct. Stockton is about 70 miles from us, and by antedating your departure from town a fortnight or so we might have the pleasure of seeing you here before your departure. Mrs W. has a Cousin at Stockton—who trades with Norway and the Baltic.—And from him she could learn particulars that might serve yr convenience previous to embarkation, and no doubt could give you useful introductions. If you could come round this way, I think I might engage to go with you to Stockton by the rail-way from Carlisle to Newcastle[2]—now one of the most splendid Towns I am told in England.[3] Probably you might embark from that Place.

With our united love your
affectionate Friend
Wm Wordsworth.

[1] Thomas Arnold had accepted nomination to the Senate of the newly-founded London University in 1835, in order to try to preserve its Christian, but non-sectarian, character, against pressure from unbelievers on the one side and high churchmen on the other. On 2 Dec. 1837 he contrived, against mounting opposition, to carry a resolution that all graduates should have passed an examination in Scripture; but on the following 7 Feb. this was overruled, and the proposed test was made voluntary. Arnold remained a member of Senate for a few months longer in the hope of making the examination a success, but finally withdrew in Nov. 1838. See Stanley's *Life of Arnold*, Ch. viii.

[2] The Newcastle and Carlisle Railway was opened in 1835–6.

[3] In the eighteen-twenties and thirties Richard Grainger, a successful local builder and speculator, had enlisted the services of John Dobson (1787–1865)

February 1838

Willy will be obliged to you if you will get the enclosed forwarded for him at your *perfect convenience.*

1204. W. W. to DORA W.

MS. British Library.
Some Unpublished Letters of William Wordsworth, Cornhill Magazine,
xx (1893), 257—76. K. LY ii. 916.

[Feb.—Mar. 1838]

My dear Dora,

Read the following remodeling of the Sonnet I addressed to S;[1] the personalities are omitted, a few lines only retained:

> Oh, what a wreck! How changed in mien and speech!
> Yet, though dread Powers that work in mystery, spin
> Entanglings for her brain; though shadows stretch
> O'er the chilled heart—reflect! far, far within
> Hers is a holy Being, freed from sin:
> She is not what she seems, a forlorn wretch;
> But delegated Spirits comfort fetch
> To her from heights that Reason may not win.
>
> .   .   .   .   .   .
>
> Inly illumined by Heaven's pitying love,
> Love pitying innocence, not long to last,
> In them, in Her, our sins and sorrows past.

The sonnet, as first sent to you and S., may be kept, if thought worthy, as a private record. The meaning in the passage you object to is certainly not happily brought out; if you think it better thus, alter it:

> Over the sacred heart compassion's twin,
> The heart that once could feel for every wretch.

The thought in the sonnet as it now stands has ever been a consolation to me, almost as far back as I can remember, and

and other local architects in laying out a classical city centre, including the celebrated Grey Street, with the monument to Earl Grey (1838) as its focal point.

[1] Southey. See *PW* iii. 56, and *app. crit.*, for the earlier version written soon after Mrs. Southey's death on 16 Nov. 1837 and making explicit reference to D. W.

hope that, thus expressed, it may prove so to others makes one wish to print it; but your mother seems to think it would be applied at once to your dear Aunt. I own I do not see the force of this objection; but if you and Miss Fenwick and others should be of the same mind, it shall be suppressed. It is already sent to the Press,[1] but not as it now stands; if you think it may be printed without impropriety, pray be so good as to superintend the Revise which I shall order the printer to send you: this would save time, for I could not entrust the revise to the Printer only.

The following is sent for your amusement; it will go by Mr Fleming to Cambridge for your cousin John, to be printed without my name, if he thinks it worth while, in the —[2].

[*Here follows Sonnet 'Said Secrecy to Cowardice', as in PW iv. 129, but in l. 14 read 'Grote'[3] for* —]

[*unsigned*]

1205. W. W. to SIR JOHN TAYLOR COLERIDGE

Address: The Honble. Mr Justice Coleridge, Carlisle or elsewhere on the Circuit.
Postmark: 21 Feb. 1838. *Stamp:* Kendal Penny Post.
Endorsed: 1838 Feb^ry 21st W. Wordsworth Rydal Mt.
MS. British Library. Hitherto unpublished.

Rydal Mount
Feb^ry 21 —38.

My dear Mr Justice Coleridge,

Your Letter, just received, was most welcome, only less so than the sight of yourself would have been. It would indeed have been a high treat could you have found time to give us a couple of Days. We will hope to be more fortunate on some future occasion. Your good news of Lady Coleridge gave

---

[1] For the forthcoming volume of *Sonnets*.

[2] It is clear from L. 1209 below that W. W. meant to write the *Cambridge Chronicle*.

[3] George Grote (1794—1871), the historian of Greece, and one of the 'philosophical radicals', was M.P. for the City of London, 1832—41. His name was particularly associated with the principle of voting by ballot, on which he wrote a pamphlet in 1821, and which he advocated in the House in four motions (1833, 1835, 1836, 1839), and two Bills (1836 and 1837). His cause was only gained shortly before his death.

Mrs W. and myself, very great pleasure, and we trust that by perseverance in the rules laid down, she will escape the recurrence of any serious attack: You will be glad to learn that Hartley[1] has for many months been very regular, not having slept more than twice out of his lodgings. We see him from time to time. He is very instructive,—and agreeable also, but for a habit of contradiction, and a fondness for Hartley paradoxes.

I am not aware whether you saw Dr Arnold lately in Town. The *principle* has been sacrificed, and I hope it will not be long before he leaves University College (is that its name?) altogether.[2]

I rejoice to hear that your eyes serve you so well. I was rather in fear about them, having suffered so much and been so long disabled in that way. I have had an attack of long duration since my return from the Continent. I am now, thank God, much better.

My Daughter is now at Dover and we have much pleasure in thinking that she will soon be under your Brother Henry's[3] roof, for some little time, if convenient to them.—I am glad you think the Tatham cause[4] is likely to come to an end, both on account of the Parties concerned, and still more for the credit of the Law.

Your report of the unsatisfactory conduct of our Justices in the Westmorland Murder[5] does not surprize me. It is the worst case, and *almost* the only one, as far as I know, that has occurred, in the County, for above half a century. The Prisoner has long borne a bad character, and nobody seems to doubt that he committed the crime; but it is a thousand times better he should not have been tried, than that he should have come off after trial for want of evidence. We had some years back a horrible Murder and robbery committed at Hawkshead upon a poor

---

[1] After spending the earlier part of 1837 teaching at Sedbergh in place of his friend the Revd. Isaac Green, who had been ill, Hartley Coleridge was now back in Grasmere; and Mrs. Fleming having died, he was now lodging with the Richardsons, who occupied her house. He returned to the school a year later, in the spring of 1838, as acting headmaster, on the sudden death of Mr. Wilkinson. See *Poems of Hartley Coleridge, with a Memoir of his Life by his Brother*, 2 vols., 1851, i. cxiv ff.

[2] See L. 1203 above.

[3] Henry Nelson Coleridge.

[4] For the cause of Wright versus Tatham, see L. 1066 above.

[5] See L. 1184 above.

Woman of unsound mind, which as she had no Relatives was scarcely inquired into at all, and the Perpetrator, though the strongest suspicions fell upon a person in the neighbourhood remains unpunished to this day. Happily enough in some respects for them, people in this neighbourhood don't know how to go about the detection of such Offenders, and I have always thought that a police officer from London or Liverpool should immediately be sent for after such crim[es.]

Pray present my respects to Mr Justice Patteson,[1] and kindest remembrances to Lady Coleridge in which Mrs W. unites and believe me to be, faithfully

Your obliged Friend
Wm Wordsworth

Why did you give yourself so much trouble about the Derbyshire Guide? It has not yet found its way hither, but surely will.

1206. W. W. to MRS. J. M. MULEEN

Address: Mrs J. M. Müleen, 21 Heriot Row, Edinburgh. [*In M. W.'s hand*]
Postmark: (1) 28 Mar. 1838 (2) Mar. 1838. *Stamp*: Kendal.
MS. *Pierpont Morgan Library*.
LY ii. 921.

Rydal Mount
28th Feb^{ry2} —38

—'I cannot doubt that they whom you deplore
Are glorified; or, if they sleep, shall wake
From sleep, and dwell with God in endless love.'[3]

Wm Wordsworth

You tell me that my writings have been your comfort and solace in sickness and affliction; it was kind in you to do so; for I meet with no reward comparable to such assurances.

[*signature cut away*]

[1] Sir John Taylor Coleridge's brother-in-law.
[2] Perhaps, as de Selincourt suggests, miswritten for 28 Mar. in view of the postmark. W. W.'s correspondent is untraced.
[3] *Excursion*, iv. 188–90.

1207. D. W. to DORA W.

MS. WL.
LY ii. 930.

[c. Mar. 1838][1]

My dearest Dora

They say I must write a letter—and what shall it be? News—news I must seek for news. My own thoughts are a wilderness—'not pierceable by power of any star'[2]—News then is my resting-place—news! news!

Poor Peggy Benson lies in Grasmere Church-yard beside her once beautiful Mother. Fanny Haigh is gone to a better world. My Friend Mrs Rawson has ended her ninety and two years pilgrimage—and *I* have fought and fretted and striven—and am here beside the fire. The Doves behind me at the small window—the laburnum with its naked seed-pods shivers before my window and the pine-trees rock from their base.—More I cannot write so farewell! and may God bless you and your kind good Friend Miss Fenwick to whom I send love and all the best of wishes.—Yours ever more

Dorothy Wordsworth

[*M. W. adds*]

The Doves have lived by day in Aunt's room ever since we went to Brigham when no fire was in the sitting-rooms—at night they are in the office and James likes their company.—Miss Belle is a wretched object to all but Anne.

---

[1] This letter may be dated, as de Selincourt notes, by the fact that Mrs. Rawson died in Dec. 1837, and Peggy Benson in Feb. 1838, and that Dora W. was staying with I. F. in the early months of 1838.

[2] Spenser, *Fairie Queen*, i. i. 7 (misquoted).

1208. W. W. to JAMES STEPHEN

Address: J. Stephen Esqre. [*In M. W.'s hand*]
MS. Cornell. Hitherto unpublished.

Rydal Mount
Ambleside
March 5th 1838

My dear Sir,

Several of my friends being desirous of having all my Sonnets under their eye at once, I have yielded to their request, and am about to print them in one Volume. It will contribute to making this a correct Book, if you will permit me as heretofore, for which I shall be greatly obliged, to let the sheets pass through your hands.[1]

Let me avail myself of this opportunity to thank you for the service you have rendered Mrs Wordsworth, my Daughter and myself thro the medium of Mr Taylor by forwarding Letters between us during our long separation, which will not terminate till towards the beginning of June.

The severe winter has been a very healthy one in this neighbourhood, not a tithe, as our medical Attendant has told me, not a twentieth part of the sickness of last year. He does not recollect so healthy a season since he began practise here, many years ago. I hope neither you nor yours have had cause to complain. We of this Household have been quite well.

Believe me my dear Sir

faithfully your
much obliged
Wm Wordsworth

---

[1] Stephen replied from Downing Street on 7 Mar.: 'There must be some things which even you cannot imagine. One of them is the strangeness of the contrast which the mention of your Sonnets, in a note from yourself, produces to the ordinary tenor of my pursuits in this office. Need I say that I shall be happy, or rather honoured, in being the channel of communication between you and your printer? It is something to be a minister, however humble, in the communications which God has instructed you to make to the busy, care worn, generation among which my life is passing.' (*WL MSS.*)

1209. W. W. to JOHN WORDSWORTH[1]

MS. untraced.
K (—). LY ii. 917.

Saturday, Mar. 10th, [1838]

My dear John,

. . . In compliance with your wish, and that of other friends, I am carrying through the press an edition of *all* my sonnets in a separate volume. . . . I was myself for making the edition not expensive by publishing two sonnets on a page; but Dora disliked this, and Mr Moxon thought that we should have a better prospect of selling seven hundred and fifty at nine shillings than fifteen hundred at a considerably lower price, two sonnets on a page. . . . Four new sonnets will be added, which I have composed since the resolution of printing them in this shape was taken. The whole number will scarcely be less than four hundred and twenty.

. . . People compliment me upon my looks, but I feel myself a good deal older within the last two years. I think my Continental exertions, and perhaps the heat of the climate, were something too much for me; but what agrees with me worst of all is residence in London, late hours of dining, and talking from morning to night.

This morning brought me a letter from Lady Frederick Bentinck, containing the sad news of the death of my excellent friend, Lady Lonsdale.[2] She was in her seventy-seventh year, but when I saw her last November she had little or no appearance of infirmity. I loved her with sincere affection. . . . She has been as kind to me as an elder sister. . . .

I have sent you a sonnet[3] which I shall not print in my collection, because my poems are wholly as I wish them to continue, without *personalities* of a vituperative character. If you think it worth being printed, pray have it copied and sent to the *Cantabridge Chronicle*, without a name. . . .

And now farewell.

Your affectionate uncle,
Wm Wordsworth

---

[1] Son of C. W.

[2] Augusta, Lady Lonsdale had died on 6 Mar.

[3] *Said Secrecy to Cowardice and Fraud.* See L. 1204 above. The sonnet was in fact included in the forthcoming volume of *Sonnets*, but in a note appended to *Protest Against the Ballot* (*PW* iii. 411). See *PW* iv. 431.

1210. W. W. to EDWARD MOXON

Address: Edward Moxon Esqre, 44 Dover Street.
MS. Henry E. Huntington Library.
LY ii. 918.

[*In M. W.'s hand*]

13th March [1838]

Dear Mr Moxon,

When I see Mr Southey's Madoc[1] containing 478 pages including titles, dedication prefaces with embellishments I shrink at the idea of one volume being charged according to your calculation 9/- as it cannot amount with notes and five new Sonnets and a short preface, to more than 440 pages at the utmost—but of course I submit to your superior knowledge and experience if you continue in the same mind.

May I trouble you to settle the enclosed bill for me at Longmans—Have you rec^d the fly leaves yet? I found on enquiry of my bookseller on receiving your letter, that the parcel which contained them, was still lying at Kendal, he not having had an opportunity of sending it to Whitaker—as he receives parcels weekly from that house, we foolishly overlooked that he did not also send thither frequently, or we might have found other means of conveyance ere this.

I have had this morning rather a melancholy note from dear Southey who has just lost his Brother the Capt.[2]—who died on his voyage from Demerara, and I grieve to say speaks of himself as being in depressed spirits and deranged health. Pray tell Mr Robinson when you see him that we had been looking for a letter from him for some time—My son John recovers very slowly from the Typhus fever—he is strong, but has scarcely slept at all for several weeks—it is seven since he was first seized.—My daughter is now at No 10 Chester Place Regents Park at Mr H. N. Coleridge's, where I am sure she would be glad to see you—as they do not keep a carriage it will not be in

---

[1] The fifth volume of the new edition of *The Poetical Works of Robert Southey*.

[2] Capt. Thomas Southey (1777–1838), Southey's younger brother, had seen distinguished service during the Napoleonic period, but had fallen on hard times since, and at one point contemplated emigrating to Canada. He published a *Chronological History of the West Indies*, 3 vols., 1827. See Curry, ii. 504.

531

her power to make many calls during her short stay in Town—
With kind regards to Mrs M and y^r Sister in which Mrs W. joins

believe me ever y^{rs}
[*signed*] W. Wordsworth

1211. W. W. to ROBERT SOUTHEY

Address: Robt Southey, Esqre. [*In M. W.'s hand*]
MS. *St. John's College, Cambridge. Hitherto Unpublished.*

Friday morning
[? 16 Mar. 1838]

My dear Southey,

We condole with you sincerely upon the death of your Brother.[1] His loss must be most severely felt by his Widow and family; and we much fear that a still heavier pressure, in consequence of this Event, may come upon your self and your Brother Dr Southey. My own Brother has been very much indisposed for several months, but we have learned today that he is somewhat better; his illness was the consequence of great fatigue, caused by the necessity, in addition to his other labours, of examining all the deeds, Statutes, and other writings, concerning his College, previous to the intended proceedings of the Commission of enquiry.[2]

By the decease of Lady Lonsdale, I have lost one of my most valued Friends. I feel it sharply. A more humbleminded Person could not exist; she was affectionate, courteous, kind or charitable to everyone according to the relations in which they stood towards [her].[3] Poor Lord Lonsdale! It must be a sad blow to him; they had been married 57 years.

---

[1] Thomas. See previous letter.

[2] In Apr. 1837, the Earl of Radnor had moved the second reading of a Bill for the appointment of a Commission of Enquiry into the working of the statutes and the application of the revenues of the Halls and Colleges of Oxford and Cambridge; and to avoid having reform thrust upon them, the Colleges had reluctantly set about putting their houses in order. The Master and Seniors of Trinity had agreed to revise the College statutes, but little progress was made while C. W. was Master. Later on, by 1844, some limited reforms were made under Whewell.

[3] *Word dropped out.*

Your account of your State of health and spirits grieves me much. But as to the hernia, it being inguinal and not femoral, there is no danger in it if a good truss be *constantly* used; this I know, not from [my] own experience, but from that of several Friends. Mr Crabbe Robinson has had this infirmity, but the swelling disappeared by the use of the truss; so did it with my Sister. But a Person who has once been affected in this way, though all outward signs may have disappeared, should never go from home without that support at hand. Mr Robinson alarmed me a good deal in Italy by not having taken this precaution. He had overstrained himself in two days' long walking up the Appennines, and the threatening pain returned; but afterwards he became more moderate in his exercise and no further mischief ensued. It is absolutely necessary for ease and comfort that the pad of the truss should not be too large. The best, Mr Carr says, is Salmon and Oddys opposite-sided truss.— But in London you can suit yourself, only for heaven's sake provide the best you can immediately. Mr Quillinan's father lost his life because he would not submit to the inconvenience of putting up with a Portuguese one till a better could be had from London.

I forward a letter and shall also send a Pamphlet[1] from Mr Merewether as in duty bound: but I shall tell him that it is quite out of your power, for sundry weighty reasons, to pay the least attention to the subject at present, if ever; so don't trouble yourself even to think about it for a month.

Thanks for Madoc, he is an old and highly valued Friend. But what a cheap Book![2] Mrs W. has been reading the Poem and is charmed with it. What is to come of you and me as Poets in future times, it would be presumptuous to aim at determining, but surely we shall have a better chance of being remembered than some others who have figured in our day.

How sorry I am that your engagements don't allow you to come over with Bertha. I do not like the thought of your long absence, and still less if you are to go without my seeing you.[3]

---

[1] Francis Merewether does not appear to have published a new pamphlet recently. The reference is probably to a later edition of his *Popery a new religion, Compared with that of Christ and his apostles. A Sermon* . . . , 1835, which had reached a 3rd edn. by 1836.

[2] i.e. compared with Moxon's estimates for the forthcoming volume of *Sonnets*.

[3] Southey was about to go up to town to consult Sir Benjamin Brodie.

Would it inconvenience you if I should come over for a night. God bless you.

Most affectionately yours
Wm Wordsworth

1212. M. W. to H. C. R.

Address: Henry Crabbe Robinson, 2 Plowdens Buildings, Temple.
Endorsed: 18 Mar 1838, Mrs Wordsworth.
MS. Dr. Williams's Library.
Morley, i. 358.

18th Mar. [1838]

My dear Friend

I have but a moment to thank you[1] in our joint name for your kind letter—and to tell you that the little parcel which accompanies this—is some certain Popish charm which has followed W^m from his Holiness from Rome and which you are to seize some favorable occasion to forward to his friends[2] in Paris—You know their address and by doing this service you will add to the number of the innumerable kind things you have done for us.

Southey who will be in Town only for a couple of days is the Bearer of this.

Ever faithfully
Y^{rs}
M Wordsworth

W. says, 'as they meant to change their residence you had best direct to Mon. Boudouin Mont de Pietè'
'The Thing'[3] is not arrived—He will be a very welcome Guest when he does appear——

---

[1] *Written* your.
[2] The Baudouins.
[3] Probably the bust mentioned in L. 1219 below.

1213. W. W. to [?] FRANCIS AGLIONBY[1]

Endorsed: Letter from Wordsworth the Poet. Answered forthwith.
MS. *St. John's College, Cambridge. Hitherto unpublished.*

Rydal Mount
Kendal
23^d March 1838

Dear Sir,

It may perhaps have passed from your recollection that many years ago we met under the roof of the Earl of Lonsdale; without looking therefore for a formal introduction, upon that ground, and as a Member of Parliament for one of the Divisions of my native County, I take the liberty of addressing you upon a subject in which as a Man of Letters I am not a little interested.

The second reading of Sergeant Talfourd's Copyright Bill stands for Wednesday April 11th. If you approve of the motion, which can not be rejected without great hardship and injustice to every Author who would wish to produce works of permanent value, I venture to request that you would take the trouble of supporting the Sergeant in his laudable endeavour by your vote and interest among your Parliamentary Friends.

I have the honor to be
sincerely yours
Wm Wordsworth

---

[1] Major Francis Aglionby (see pt. i, L. 3) was one of the Members for Cumberland, and the most likely recipient of this letter. He replied on 26 Mar. that he was very flattered by W. W.'s 'remembrance' of him, but regretted that he would be unable to attend on the second reading of the Bill, as he had to be present at the Sessions in Cockermouth on that day: 'I send you a Print of the Bill which I have perused and am favourable to the principle, and I shall feel much obliged by your making any marginal Observations which may occur to you and forward the Bill to me at Nunnery in the Month of April, and I will pay every attention to your Suggestions.' (*Cornell MSS.*)

1214. W. W. to WILLIAM EWART GLADSTONE

MS. British Library.
K. LY ii. 919.

Rydal, Kendal, March 23ᵈ, 38.

My dear Mr Gladstone,

Most probably I am putting you to unnecessary trouble by this Letter, which is written solely to remind you that the 2nd Reading of Serjeant Talfourd's Bill stands for Wednesday, April 11ᵗʰ. In a Letter received this morning Serjeant Talfourd[1] tells me that the Booksellers[2] (rapacious Creatures as they are) are getting up a very strong opposition to his motion, and will be supported by the Doctrinaires (who are they? Warburton[3] and Grote,[4] and id genus omne, I suppose). Upon the general merits of this question it would be presumptuous in me to enter in a Letter to you. But as to my own interest in it, it may not be superfluous to say that within the last three years or so my poetical writings have produced for me nearly 1,500 pounds, and that much the greatest part of them either would be public property to-morrow, if I should die, or would become so in a very few years. Is this just, or can a state of law which allows the possibility of such injustice be favorable to the production of solid literature, in any department of what is usually called Belles-Letters?[5]

ever faithfully yours,
Wm Wordsworth

I need not say how much I would rejoice to see you at Rydal Mount.

---

[1] In his letter of 21 Mar. (*Cornell MSS.*) Talfourd wrote: 'I trust this will reach you in time to enable you to exert any influence you can command to secure attendance and support.' He stressed the need for Members to attend, not only in case there was a division, but also in order to secure a quorum of the House, 11 Apr. being the day before the Easter Recess.

[2] Principally Thomas Tegg (see L. 1235 below), but also more recently firms like W. and R. Chambers of Edinburgh, who had moved into the popular market. On 26 and 27 Mar. the London booksellers and publishers organised a petition against the Bill.

[3] For Henry Warburton see pt. ii, L. 681.

[4] George Grote (see L. 1204 above).

[5] Gladstone replied on 26 Mar.: 'I am firm and staunch in support of Talfourd's bill, and I confidently hope we shall be able to carry him through. It may not be able to save our literature permanently but its tendency is that way,

1215. W. W. to PHILIP HENRY HOWARD[1]

Endorsed: 1838. Mr Wordsworth the Poet to P. H. Howard Esq MP.
MS. Johns Hopkins University Library. Hitherto unpublished.

Rydal Mount
Kendal—March 23^d —38

Dear Sir,

Though I have not the honor of more than a slight personal acquaintance with you, I venture to address you as representing the chief place of my native County upon a question in which as a Man of Letters I am much interested. I am further induced to take this step, by bearing in mind that the illustrious name of Howard stands high in the literature of our common Country, and especially so in the department of its Poetry.[2]

The second reading of Sergeant Talfourd's Bill for the extension of Copy-right stands for Wednesday, the 11th of April: If you are favorable to the Measure, allow me to entreat that you attend the House on that day in support of a Motion which cannot be rejected without severe injustice to Authors, who look beyond the making of immediate impression by their works, and would wish to leave behind them permanent Memorials of their endeavours to benefit their Country and Mankind.[3]

I have the honor to be
faithfully and respectfully
yours
Wm Wordsworth

and this should be enough. A ground not less strong I certainly recognise in the anomaly now existing and the extreme disadvantage at which literary property stands as compared with other and meaner kinds.' (*British Library MSS.*) See also Russell Noyes, 'Wordsworth and the Copyright Act of 1842: *Addendum*', *PMLA* lxxvi (1961), 380–3.

[1] M.P. for Carlisle (see pt. ii, L. 610).

[2] W.W. is thinking particularly of Henry Howard, Earl of Surrey (1517–47), soldier and poet, executed by Henry VIII, and remembered for his sonnets and blank-verse translation of parts of the *Aeneid*.

[3] Howard replied on 11 Apr. (*Cornell MSS.*) that the opposition to Talfourd's proposals was so strong that he was in favour of a Select Committee being set up to consider the whole problem further. See also L. 1229 below.

1216. W. W. to SIR WILLIAM MAYNARD GOMM[1]

Address: Col: Sir William Gomm, 6 Upper Grosvenor St. [*In M. W.'s hand*]
Postmark: 27 Mar. 1838. *Stamp*: Store St.
Endorsed: Mr Wordsworth 24th March /38. On the Bill of Copy right. Ans^d—
MS. *Cornell*.[2]
LY ii. 920.

Rydal Kendal
24th March 38.

My dear Sir William,
   Knowing your attachment to literature, I venture to solicit
your support by application to your parliamentary Friends in
favor of Sergeant Talfourd's Copyright Bill; the second reading
of which, stands for the 11th of april, *Wednesday*. The success of
this measure is to me as a Man of letters not a little interesting
though far less so than to many of my Contemporaries. I have
however exerted myself for many years past to have it brought
before the House, and am now taking much trouble to promote
its success by application to my friends, among whom I could
not but enumerate yourself. Of the Justice of the proposed law, I
need not speak to one so enlightened as you are, nor need I insist
upon its tendency to promote sound literature, without
cheapning in the least degree its circulation, for the vast encrease
of Readers will make it the interest of authors to publish in a
cheap form.[3]
   With respectful Compl^s to Lady Gomm

I remain
dear Sir William
faithfully yours
Wm Wordsworth

---

[1] For Sir William Gomm, see pt. ii, L. 816.
[2] Photostat: original untraced.
[3] Gomm replied on 30 Mar.: 'Would that my influence were a thousand
times more extensive and commanding than I feel it to be! . . . I have nothing
more at heart than the advancement of sound Literature, and the prosperity of
those to whom we owe its development . . .' (*Cornell MSS.*)

1217. W. W. to HORACE TWISS[1]

MS. Cornell.
Paul M. Zall, 'Wordsworth and the Copyright Act of 1842', PMLA lxx (1955), 132–44 (—).

[c. 24 Mar. 1838]

My dear Mr Twiss,

Allow me to remind you that Sergeant Talfourd's Bill for the Extension of Copy right will be read the 2nd time, if possible, on the 11th of April, Wednesday. Unfortunately, and to my great regret, you are not in Parliament, but you have much influence, and pray do your best to induce your friends to attend on that day in support of a measure, which cannot be rejected without the utmost injustice.

Ever faithfully yours
W Wordsworth

I hope Mrs Twiss and your family are well and pray present to her my regards.

1218. W. W. to RICHARD MONCKTON MILNES[2]

Address: B. M. Milnes Esqre MP, London. [In M. W.'s hand]
Postmark: (1) 26 Mar. 1838 (2) 28 Mar. 1838. Stamp: Kendal Penny Post.
Endorsed: Be so kind as send the enclosed to the 2d Post Off.
MS. Trinity College, Cambridge.
T. Wemyss Reid, The Life, Letters, and Friendships of Richard Monckton Milnes, 2 vols., 1890, i. 226–7 (—).
Mark L. Reed, 'Two Letters of Wordsworth to Richard Monckton Milnes', NQ ccix (Jan. 1964), 18–20.

Rydal Mount
Kendal
26th March [1838]

My dear Sir,

I am taking a step which I am all but persuaded is superfluous; by reminding you that the second reading of Sergeant

---

[1] For Horace Twiss see L. 1037 above. He replied on 28 Mar.: 'I will not fail to do "my little possible" on the subject of your note . . . The worst of it is, that in these times of party excitement, it is very difficult to get the calmer and higher interests of life attended to, even though they come with such a recommendation as yours.' (Cornell MSS.)

[2] Richard Monckton Milnes (see pt. ii, Ls. 714, 806), the Cambridge

Talfourd's Copyright Bill stands for April 11ᵗʰ. Wednesday. You will not I trust withhold from it your strenuous support. The Sergeant tells me the Book sellers threaten a very strong opposition, in which they rely upon the aid of the Doctrinaires; among which Party one of their most eminent, Mr Hume (lucus a non lucendo)[1] has as you know declared against it already in *his place*, a pretty place for such an Ignoramus!

I have read two pamphlets against this bill, both abounding in false statements as to facts, and the longer especially in monstrous opinions, and shallow reasoning. As to perishable literature the motion is obviously indifferent, the only argument against it, that I have seen, which is entitled to the least consideration; lies in the fear, or rather as some assume, the certainty that such an act would check the circulation of good Books: But the rapid encrease of Readers, is making it daily more and more the interest of Authors to send into the world cheap editions, while there cannot be doubt that with men of small means the hope of their children and grandchildren being in some degree benefited by their labours must act as an encouragement to their industry, and a support under present neglect. What we want is the production of Good Books; Authors as a body get as much as they deserve by the law standing as it now does, but how does it treat, confining myself to my own department, men like Burns, like Cowper, like Crabbe, Coleridge, Southey and many others?—But too much of this—

How came Sir R Inglis to say the other day in the house of P Thompson's motion[2] that Sir Walter Scott had set an example

'Apostle' and friend at Trinity of Tennyson, Hallam, and C. W. jnr., was now M.P. for Pontefract, and a prominent figure in London society by virtue of his famous breakfast parties. He failed to make much mark as a politician, either in the House of Commons, or in the Lords to which he was finally elevated as 1st Baron Houghton in 1863. He published several volumes of verse, and wrote in support of the Tractarian Movement, but is perhaps best remembered for his *Life and Letters of John Keats*, 2 vols., 1848.

[1] See particularly Quintilian, *Inst.*, 1. vi. 34. Joseph Hume was in alliance with Warburton and Grote in upholding the objections of the booksellers to the Bill. They wished to take no step which might impede the widest circulation of works of literature at the cheapest price.

[2] On 20 Mar. Poulett Thomson sought leave to bring in a Bill to establish a system of international copyright, giving to foreigners in this country the protection that was being sought by Talfourd's measure for English authors

of effectually providing against French piracy, by sending his life of Nap^n over in sheets to Paris; or P Thompson to think he had replyed to this inconsiderate observation, by saying that such a precaution could only avail for one Edition. Why, in America a book, which has been treated for with an English Author, has been reprinted in an inferior type, in 36 hours, and the first publisher being thus undersold, has found that his labour and money were thrown away. Gagliniani[1] told me that he wished English Copyright existed in France, to prevent these injurious Competitions; so that piracy is in some degree undermining itself.—

There are difficulties in this question but

Est quoddam prodire tenus etc[2]

I remain dear Sir
sincerely and respectfully yours
Wm Wordsworth

1219. W. W. to H. C. R.

Address: H. C. Robinson Esqre, 2 Plowdens Build^s, Temple.
Endorsed: 26 Mar: 1836 [i.e. 1838], Wordsworth, Squib agst Evans Opin^n of Univ^y College.
MS. Dr. Williams's Library.
K (—). Morley, i. 296.

March 26th [1838]

My dear Friend,
This will reach you through Mr Milnes, to whom I have written upon Sergeant Talfourd's Copyright Bill, which Stands

overseas. It aimed particularly to force the French and Americans to admit the principle of international copyright. In the discussion that followed, to which Milnes, Inglis and Lord Mahon on the one side, and Hume and Warburton on the other, contributed, the difficulties inherent in the whole proposal were ventilated. Charles Edward Poulett Thomson, 1st Baron Sydenham (1799–1841), was M.P. for Dover (1826) and Manchester (1832), and President of the Board of Trade in Melbourne's two administrations. In 1839 he became Governor-General of Canada, where he successfully implemented the reforms proposed by his predecessor Lord Durham.

[1] i.e. Galignani.
[2] Horace, *Epistles*, I. i. 32. Milnes replied on 31 Mar., promising to be present at the second reading of the bill and to give it his support. (*Cornell MSS.*)

for April 11th. Wednesday. Pray do *your* utmost in *every direction* to defeat the Rapacity of the Booksellers, and the stupidity of Hume, Grote, Warburton, and such like—

Thanks for your entertaining Letter; poor Mrs Dashwood![1] I am sorry, but not in the least surprized—she is of a queer Breed. Jones I knew, and all about him, he is a vain empty conceited Fellow, who would be mischievous if he were not such a fool.— We were glad to hear of Mr Trotter;[2] when you happen to see him, pray give our kind compliments.—

Your University and College[3] are humbugs; All these attempts to make men cooperate whose opinions are, or, were they conscientious men, ought to be, so widely different, are founded on false views of human Nature.—

Unless my Sonnets are to be sent forth in one Volume, I regret having ever consented to the publication. My view was to place them under the eye of the Reader at once; but I cannot have an objection to have two titles as Moxon proposes, so that they who prefer the work in two Volumes may be gratified. There will be half a dozen new ones—[4]

When I tell you that I have written these two or three days at least 40 Letters[5] in support of the Serjeant's

---

[1] A cousin of the Hares, according to H. C. R.'s letter to M. W. of 12 Mar., who was about to marry Col. Jones. '—He is an Ultra liberal both in politics and religion—A sort of evil genius even in our University College London . . . He is a very loud talker and takes the lead as an oppositionist to our most reasonable measures on all occasions—Has occasionally gained ephemeral reputation as a writer of party-letters in the Times . . . and is in short one of the extreme men in all party-disputes in this Metropolis.' (Morley, i. 357). Mrs. Dashwood was a descendant of Sir Francis Dashwood, 2nd Bart., Baron Le Despenser (1708–81), founder of the 'Hell Fire Club', which met for annual orgies in the deserted abbey of Medmenham on the banks of the Thames.

[2] Alexander Trotter, the companion of Goddard, who was drowned in the Lake of Geneva and commemorated in the *Elegiac Stanzas*. H. C. R. had met him again at the Athenaeum during a ballot of new members. See pt. i, L. 47, and Morley, i. 357–8.

[3] i.e. the new London University, and University College, with which H. C. R. was connected.

[4] 'It would be agreeable if a dozen *new* Sonnets could be framed in time for the new edition', H. C. R. had written, '—But the breed of such a delicate little animal must not be forced.'

[5] Most of these letters are untraced, but they must have followed the same pattern as the few that have survived. Replies are, however, preserved among

motion, you will not be surprized at this abrupt conclusion

ever most faithfully yours
W. Wordsworth

Thanks for the Bust[1]—it is an astonishing likeness and will be *much valued* in this house; all the Servants knew it at once.

When you see Mr Rogers tell him that the Printer of the Sonnets must proceed quickly and regularly, or I shall be utterly disgusted by the delay—it interferes with many of my engagements, and with my time.—

You know of old my partiality for Evans[2] the Squib below I let off immediately upon reading his modest self-defence speech the other day.

[There follows 'Said red-ribbon'd Evans', as in PW iv. 389]

One memorable stanza of the above is rather difficult to decypher, here you have it again—

> Sound flogging and fighting,
> No Chief, on my troth,
> Ere took such delight in
> As I in them both—

the *Cornell MSS.* from the following M.P.s, most of them favourable to the Bill:—Matthias Attwood (Whitehaven), Lord Adare (Glamorgan), Cresswell Cresswell (Liverpool), Sir Augustus Dalrymple (Brighton), John Ellis (Newry), Sir J. R. G. Graham (recently defeated in Cumberland, later elected for Pembroke), Edward Horsman (Cockermouth), Samuel Irton (Cumberland), William James (Cumberland), Hon. Henry T. Liddell (Durham), Sir Frederick Pollock (Huntingdon), Sir Robert Price, Bart. (Hereford), and Edward Stanley (Cumberland).

[1] Unidentified: presumably a bust of H. C. R.

[2] For Col. George de Lacy Evans, see L. 1085 above. He had just received the red ribbon of the K. C. B. for his services in Spain. Several questions were asked in the House of Commons on 23 Feb. about the procedure that had been adopted in making the award.

1220. W. W. to C. W. JNR.

Address: The Rev^d. The Master of Harrow, Harrow.
Postmark: 27 Mar. 1838.
MS. WL. Hitherto unpublished.

[26 Mar. 1838]
My dear Chris:
The second reading of Sergeant Talfourd's Copyright Bill stands for the 11th April, *Wednesday*. The Booksellers as the Sergeant tells me threaten a very strong opposition, in which they will be aided by the *Doctrinaires*. Pray bestir yourself or we poor Authors will be crushed. Write to Goulburn, and [? stir] other parliamentary friends to remind them of the day.—This is little short of the 40th Letter I have written on the subject. The Sergeant urged me to do my utmost, so pray do you, much engaged as I know you must be.

I rejoice to hear that your dear Father is so much better. Your Aunt Dorothy continues pretty much the same. Mary and I are well—

Your most affectionate Uncle
Wm Wordsworth

1221. W. W. to GEORGE BIDDELL AIRY[1]

MS. University of London Library. Hitherto unpublished.

[late Mar. 1838]
My dear Sir
I trust I do not take an unwarrantable liberty in requesting your vote as a member of the Senate of the London University in favor of Mr Graves[2] who is a Candidate for the office of Registrar.

This Gentleman you will most probably have heard of in the scientific world; and from my private knowledge of his character, general attainments, and abilities as a man of business

---

[1] The mathematician and astronomer (see pt. i, L. 8). He had been a Fellow of the new University since 1836.

[2] R. P. Graves's brother John Thomas Graves, F.R.S. (1806–70), jurist and mathematical colleague of W. R. Hamilton. He failed to get the Registrarship, but was elected Professor of Jurisprudence at University College, London, a year later. He was a poor-law inspector from 1847.

I have good reason for believing that such an office could not easily be better filled than by him. If you should be at liberty to give Mr Graves your Vote, and would do so, you would much oblige me.

Believe me to remain
faithfully yours
Wm Wordsworth

1222. W. W. to ROBERT PERCEVAL GRAVES

MS. Berg Collection, New York Public Library. Hitherto unpublished.

[late Mar. 1838]

My dear Mr Graves,

The second reading of Sergeant Talfourd's Copy right Bill stands for 11th April, Wednesday. The Booksellers threaten a strong opposition, in which They will be backed by the Doctrinaires. If either immediately or mediately, you have influence with members will you have the kindness to solicit their attendance in support of the matter, on that day—

I send Mr Empson's[1] Letter; I wrote also to Professor Airey from whom I have not yet received an answer and perhaps may not. Mr E—— is a Gentleman by breeding, Mr A——[2] scarcely so. farewell

W. W.

1223. W. W. to SAMUEL ROGERS

Endorsed: not to be published S. R.
MS. Berg Collection, New York Public Library. Hitherto unpublished.

[*In M. W.'s hand*]

[late Mar. 1838]

You my dear Rogers are placed by fortune above the necessity of considering your Works with reference to pecuniary

---

[1] William Empson (see L. 1017 above), an influential figure in the new London University, where Graves's brother was seeking the post of Registrar (see previous letter).

[2] Professor Airy's father lost his appointment in the excise and lapsed into poverty. His mother was a farmer's daughter from Suffolk.

profit now or hereafter. It is not so with most of your literary and personal friends, myself among the number—and therefore I take leave to mention that the 2^d reading of Sergeant Talfourd's Copy right bill stands for Wednesday the 11th of April—let me urge you to give it your Support among y^r Parliamentary friends of all Parties—as it is no party measure. Brooke's[1] is at hand, and you are every day and every hour seeing some influential Person. Need I say more—for you have probably heard that the rapacity of the Booksellers is putting them, under pretence of public good, upon what threatens to be a very strong opposition. They will be backed by the Doctrinaires (called so I suppose in the Spirit of the trite phrase, lucus a non lucendo). As the attendance is usually very thin upon a Wednesday the Sergeant tells me that it is desirable that the favourers of his motion should be in the house to prevent its being counted out.

Adieu, accept our affectionate regards and present them to y^r Sister.

Ever faithfully yours
[*signed*] Wm Wordsworth

1224. W. W. to FRANCIS LLOYD[2]

Address: Francis Lloyd Esqre, Bank, Birmingham. [*In M. W.'s hand*]
Postmark: 2 Apr. 1838. *Stamp*: Kendal.
MS. *Lilly Library, Indiana University. Hitherto unpublished.*

Rydal Mount
April 2nd 1838

My dear Sir,

Knowing the extent of your influence, and the value justly set upon your opinions, I take the liberty of soliciting your good offices among your parliamentary Friends, Tories or Liberals, in support of Sergeant Talfourd's Bill for the extension of the Term of Copyright, in case you yourself, which I can scarcely doubt, approve of the Measure. The second reading stands for Wednesday the 11th, but as that day of the week is always one of

---

[1] The London club founded in Pall Mall in 1764 and transferred to St. James's Street in 1778.
[2] The Birmingham banker (see L. 1090 above).

thin attendance, and as Lord John Russell has given notice that
he means to move the adjournment of the House, for the Easter
Recess, on that day, it is to be feared that the House may be
counted out; it is therefore desirable that all friends to the Bill
should attend *early*. You may perhaps be aware that the
Booksellers and Printers, in their rapacity, threaten a *very* strong
opposition, in which they will be supported by the Party, called
Doctrinaires.

Mr Attwood[1] member for Whitehaven is favorable to the
[measure], so as he tells me is Mr W. Attwood, and he engages
to communicate with your member of the same name;[2] who he
doubts not will give it his support.

Mrs Wordsworth joins me in very kind regards to yourself
and each member of your family. If our Nephew John
Wordsworth be still with you pray give our love to him.[3]

And believe me my dear Sir
faithfully yours
Wm Wordsworth

This letter ought to have been sent under Cover but time would
have been lost by its going first to London.

---

[1] For Matthias Attwood see pt. ii, L. 700. He replied on 30 Mar. (*Cornell
MSS.*): 'When I had the pleasure of meeting you at Lowther I had the
advantage of hearing you explain the character of the measure proposed by
Mr Sergeant Talfourd's Bill—I will make it a point to attend whenever the Bill
comes before the House of Commons and will give it my support. . . . I
consider the Bill as a measure of indispensible justice, and should be gratified in
contributing to its success.'

[2] Two of Matthias Attwood's brothers were also in the House: Thomas
Attwood (1783−1856) banker, led the local agitation for the Reform Bill,
and became the first M.P. for Birmingham, 1832−40. William, the other
brother, was M.P. for Greenwich.

[3] Lloyd replied on 4 Apr. (*Cornell MSS.*): 'Free Trade is all very plausible
when reciprocity is its basis. If Booksellers cannot produce "Excursions"
themselves they must pay a proportionate duty.' And he ended by referring to
John Wordsworth's candidature for the headmastership of King Edward's
Grammar School in Birmingham (see L. 1227 below): 'His location here
would afford us all much pleasure.'

MS. WL.
LY ii. 921.

[c. 5 Apr. 1838]

My dear Daughter,

Thanks for your letter. Your Mother left Rydal on Tuesday noon for Penrith that day, next for Carlisle, and will not return till Saturday. Mr H.[1] thought the journey too long for one day.—

Poor Mr Wilkinson[2] of Sedbergh died a few days ago, of inflammation in the chest, we believe, brought on by cold while he was overlooking his workmen.—I hope you will be able to see Tintern Abbey on your way to Brinsop, following up the Wye as far as Monmouth and Ross, in which case you would pass close by Mrs Elliot's[3] near Goodrich Castle. Could not you write to Thomas Hutchinson[4] to meet you either at Monmouth, or Mr Elliot's, in his Father's Carriage, at all events if you can see Tintern and Piercefield without injurious fatigue, do so.—I am sorry for the formidable opposition to the Copyright Bill; if other Persons to whom it would be far more beneficial than to me had done half as much as I have, it would be carried to a certainty. I grieve much for Miss Fenwick's distress—but am not in the least surprised at the turn the affair has taken. When Mr T[5] began to pay attention to the Lady she must have been a mere child, and relative to his age which I presume is between 35 and 40, what is she now? If Men or Women will form engagements so little in accordance with nature and reason, they have no *right* to expect better treatment; better *may* come, but the probabilities are much against it. Observe I do not mean that rejection such as Mr T. has met with

[1] Benson Harrison, as is clear from *MW*, pp. 204 ff., which describe M. W.'s visit to Carlisle to attend the Garrison ball with his wife and family.

[2] Henry Wilkinson, headmaster of Sedbergh.

[3] The Elliots were formerly tenants of Ivy Cottage.

[4] i.e. Thomas Hutchinson, jnr.

[5] Henry Taylor first saw Theodosia Spring Rice in 1834, and proposed to her in 1836, when she was seventeen and he was thirty-six. No immediate answer was given, and in June 1837 he was definitely refused on religious grounds. However, the marriage took place in Oct. 1839. The whole affair caused much anxiety to his cousin I. F. See *Autobiography of Henry Taylor*, i. 213–23, 286; and Una Taylor, *Guests and Memories*, 1924, pp. 69–120.

is a thing in regular course, and to be feared as such, but evils far worse to bear, evils without remedy occurring after marriage, or then first displaying themselves.—

We have not heard again from John, so I trust that neither he nor Isabella are worse—If you don't take care, one of these severe inflammatory colds will be carrying you out of this world, as poor Mr Wilkinson has been carried. You did well, very well, in not going to St Pauls.—To-day I have received three sheets of Sonnets; not having had one for nearly a month. I hope you will be able to take Mr Trench's Vol. of Poems[1] with you, and read them, as I am sure from his letter to me, and his former productions, they must be of no common merit. Don't on any account send your Box by coach; the last containing the Bonnet and gown cost half a guinea carriage. I bought a Brussels Carpet at Mrs Pritt's sale—it fits the hall exactly, it is very little worse for wear, and cost 4—11/—Owen's things were sold yesterday; I did not attend.—Your account of dear Southey rejoices me greatly.—As it will probably be long before we see the last Vol. of Sir Walter's life, tell us how you like it. The newspapers are, as they did in Sheridan's case, extolling his genius, that is his poetical genius, most ridiculously—these follies pass away and truth only remains.—I take no notice of the conclusion of your Letter; indeed part of it I could not make out. It turns upon a subject which I shall never touch more either by pen or voice. Whether I look back or forward it is depressing and distressing to me, and will for the remainder of my life, continue to be so.[2]

[1] R. C. Trench (see L. 949 above), *Sabbation; Honor Neale, and Other Poems*, 1838.

[2] Dora W. had now revealed to W. W. her wish to marry E. Q., which was to cause the poet such pain during the following years. Amid a good deal of harmless banter, their relationship had been deepening for some time, perhaps since 1832 when E. Q. asked Dora W. to act as guardian of his children in the event of his death, and certainly since his narrow escape from shipwreck in Nov. 1836 (see L. 1112 above), and their exchange of letters before and after his return to England (see Ls. 1172 and 1189 above). After E. Q. left Rydal Mount in Dec. 1837, he wrote to Dora W. again on the 27th (*WL MSS.*), admitting that he had toyed with her feelings in the past and played 'an idle butterfly part' in society, but deriving encouragement from the deeper tone of her replies. 'My love for you has certainly in one sense not been a happy one; but without it, I should have been dead long since; nothing else could have sustained me through what I have endured of evil: lighter affections might have buoyed my spirit up under common troubles; but I have had some

You appear to take delight in catching at anything derogatory to my judgment or discernment—I never said or thought anything more of the young Rice,[1] than that she was very pretty, and [as] far as general appearance went, an engaging Girl or rather Child, for being small of stature she looked younger than she is; but I never exchanged three words with her in my life; so that of her heart or head, as fitting her for a wife, I neither did, nor cared to form any judgment. With Miss Rice[2] I have conversed frequently, and deem myself competent to draw an inference, worthy of some regard, as to her character.

I can only add remember me most kindly to the Marshalls, Mrs M. in particular if you see her again. Sir Wm Gomm I wrote to upon the Copyright Bill, and received a kind and flattering answer. He told me Lady Gomm was exerting herself much in support of it; and that he himself would do his best. I enter my 69th year the day you will receive this. Aunty is going on as usual. Love to dear Miss Fenwick.

Ever faithfully your affectionate Father,
W. W.

1226. W. W. to DORA W.[3]

MS. WL. Hitherto unpublished.

[c. 6 Apr. 1838]

Dearest D,

I have sent you two of the sheets for the sake of the 4 new Sonnets, page 110—pray forward them as directed—

troubles so severe as nothing but a rational and thoughtful and downright and resolute, though *passionate*, love for a good and virtuous girl could have given me fortitude to bear.' According to E. Q.'s MS. Diaries (*WL MSS.*), he saw Dora W. frequently at I. F.'s at Dover , and at Mrs. Hoare's in Hampstead, in Jan. and Feb. 1838. But now that E. Q. had almost lost hope of benefiting from the Brydges estate, and his religion as a Roman Catholic made him an unwelcome suitor for Dora W.'s hand, the poet set himself firmly against the proposed alliance, and he was confirmed in his opposition by the precarious state of her health.

[1] Presumably Theodosia Spring Rice.

[2] Mary Spring Rice, Theodosia's eldest sister.

[3] A note written on the inside sheet of the previous letter, presumably shortly afterwards.

Aunty sends her love, saying that she will be glad to see you when you come, and hopes that she will be better—tell her[1] I have suffered sadly.

[unsigned]

1227. W. W. to THE GOVERNORS of KING EDWARD'S GRAMMAR SCHOOL, BIRMINGHAM

MS. Mr. Jonathan Wordsworth. Hitherto unpublished.

[9 Apr. 1838]

Gentlemen,

Having been informed by the Rev[nd] John Wordsworth Fellow of Trin: Coll: Cambridge, that he has offered himself as a Candidate for the Head-mastership of the Grammar School[2] of which you are Governors, and that he is desirous of Testimonials from me; I do not scruple to comply with his request. If accurate and profound Scholarship be among the leading qualifications for this office and it is reasonable to suppose they must be, few Persons who are competent to give an opinion, will be disposed to question his taking rank among the first Scholars of Great-Britain.

As my near relationship to Mr Wordsworth has given me opportunities for acquiring an intimate knowledge of his general character and conduct in daily life, I am enabled conscientiously to declare, that they are exemplary, and that the soundness of his opinions does honor to his judgement, and that in supporting them he never deviates from the manners of a Gentleman.

Being so nearly connected with Mr Wordsworth it would not become me to say more, though had . . .

[cetera desunt]

---

[1] W. W. is here quoting D. W.'s words.

[2] Granted a charter by Edward VI in 1552, and reformed by Act of Parliament in 1830. The successful candidate was James Prince Lee, whom W. W. was to meet a little later.

1228. W. W. to JOHN WORDSWORTH

Address: The Revd John Wordsworth, Trin: Coll: Cambridge [*In M. W.'s hand*]
Postmark: 9 Apr. 1838. *Stamp*: Kendal Penny Post.
Endorsed: From Wm Wordsworth.
MS. Mr. Jonathan Wordsworth. Hitherto unpublished.

April 9th 38

My dear John,
I wish the Enclosed were worthier of the occasion. As you think the Situation eligible and no doubt your Father, Brothers, and other Relations and Friends do the same, your two Aunts and I heartily wish you success. [*M. W. adds*: tho' I, *M. W.* think the Situation unworthy of you.]

Many thanks for your letter, and for your Remarks which will be remembered. I rejoiced to hear that my dear Brother was so much better, so did we all—excuse this brief Letter. Mary says, that we have three Grandsons, and that the three School-Masters must take them among them, as their poor Father is in a bad way as to this world's goods, and likely to be. He is much better in health, but the effects of the fever, Isabella tells us, hang much upon his nerves, and she herself has been very ill and continues feeble. Pray do your utmost to serve the cause of Authors versus Publishers and Printers, and Economists or Doctrinaires, in the matter of the Copy right Bill. They are now every way strong against it.

your affectionate Uncle
W. W.

I have written between forty and fifty Letters in support of the Sergeants Bill, with various success.

1229. W. W. to THOMAS NOON TALFOURD

Address: Mr Sergeant Talfourd M.P., Russell Square, London [*readdressed to*] Temple.
Postmark: (1) [? 14]. Apr. 1838 (2) 16 Apr. [   ]. *Stamp*: Kendal Penny Post.
MS. Cornell.
Broughton, p. 75.

[14 Apr. 1838]

My dear Sergeant Talfourd,

I have not been unmindful of your Copyright Bill, having written scarcely less than 50 notes or Letters, many of them to members of Parliament[1] in support of it. Among these is Mr P. Howard, Member for Carlisle, who has written me an obliging letter, from which it appears that he has had an interview with you, and that you have expressed a desire to have a Petition from Mr Southey and myself.[2] As such is your wish, I shall on that account, endeavour to get over every objection, which I feel to appearing publicly as a Suppliant, for what I consider cannot be denied without the most flagrant injustice to the best Authors of the Country, and a correspondent injury to its literature. But really I know not how to set about drawing up the petition, from utter inexperience in the wording of such things; I am not in health well enough to go over to Keswick to consell with Mr S—, and, so bad are the arrangements of the post office in this quarter, that it requires as long a time for Letters to pass to and fro between Ambleside and Keswick, (15 miles) as between those places and London. I shall forward Mr Howard's Letter to Mr S; and if he with his experience can draw up the Petition I will readily assist.—

I have directed the Editor of the Kendal Mercury to forward to you the last N° of his journal, in which you will see some comments[3] upon a petition against your Bill from certain

---

[1] See L. 1219 above.

[2] In his letter of 11 Apr., announcing the postponement of the Second Reading until the 25th, Howard had written that 'Mr Serjt Talfourd complains that whereas many of the publishers and the Trade have publickly taken steps to oppose his Bill Authors have taken no steps, by Petition at least. . . . Mr Serjt Talfourd stated to me between ourselves that if Mr Southey and yourself were to send him a petition to present in favor of his Bill it w^d have weight and be something to show.' (*Cornell MSS.*, quoted by Zall, op. cit., pp. 135–6.) See also L. 1231 below.

[3] W. W. published a long letter, signed A. B., in the *Kendal Mercury* for 14 Apr., commenting point by point on the petition against the proposed Bill

Persons of that Town. I thought the occasion a fair one for bringing forth the facts stated in my strictures, as they concern the men of Letters who live, or have lived in this neighbourhood—

Whatever be the fate of your Bill, it must always be gratifying to you to remember the effort which you have made in defense of so just a cause. And the knowledge that its distinguished advocate is one of my most valued Friends will to the close of my life, be to me a source of pride and pleasure.[1] Believe me ever Most faithfully

your much obliged
Wm Wordsworth

Mr Stephenson, the American Minister, tells by letter (now before me) my friend Mr Kenyon that he was assured by two of the Ministers that the Bill would pass.—In the Times of the 11th is an Article against your Bill, respecting which it is difficult to say whether its stupidity or its profligate impudence are more striking—

[*In M. W.'s hand*]
Mrs W. will be obliged to Mr Sergeant Talfourd to forward the enclosed letter at his perfect convenience—and to give the bit of a Note to our friend when he sees him.

drawn up by the local printers and published in the previous issue of the paper on the 7th. In rebutting the contention that the Bill would check the circulation of literature and be contrary to the public interest, he argued that those, like Coleridge, Southey, and himself, who aimed permanently to benefit the national literature, were entitled to protection and an equitable remuneration. The letter was reprinted by J. G. Lockhart in 'The Copyright Question', *Quarterly Review*, lxix (1841), 186–227, and is included in *Prose Works*, iii. 309–12.

[1] Talfourd struck a despondent note in his reply of the 16th: 'I am afraid we shall be beaten; but, for my own poor part, I shall be nobly overpaid by the recollection of having attempted to obtain some portion of justice for one to whom I owe as great a debt of gratitude as can be owed by one human being to another.' (*Cornell MSS.*)

1230. W. W. to THOMAS NOON TALFOURD

Address: Mr Sergeant Talfourd M.P., Russel Square, London [*In M. W.'s hand*]
Postmark: (1) 18 Apr. 1838 (2) 20 Apr. *Stamp:* Kendal.
MS. Cornell and Berg Collection, New York Public Library.[1] *Hitherto unpublished.*

[18 Apr. 1838]

My dear Sir,

Your's reached me while I was preparing rather a long Letter to you on the subject. But I shall not proceed, and am contented to send you the introduction,[2] of which pray make what use you like; if you think it would at all serve the cause or it would be on any account grateful to you to publish it pray do.

I am rather surprized and withal a little mortified by learning that you fear we shall be beaten. Adieu with a thousand thanks your sincere friend   [W. W.][3]

By way of mixing a little pleasure with the disagreeable, I send you a Sonnet which I threw off last Sunday evening almost extempore——[4] I shall write to Sir R. Peel today.

[*There follows 'Hark! 'tis the Thrush', as in PW iii. 56, except that in l.9 read 'face' for 'front'*]

W. W. Easter Sunday.

Pray shew the above, with my best regards, to Mrs Talfourd. It will be printed in the Volume now going through the press, consisting of all the sonnets I have written. And Mrs W. will thank you to forward the enclosed at your early convenience.

---

[1] The two parts of this MS. have become separated. The first half, which was quoted by Zall, op. cit., p. 137, is at Cornell: the second half, from the sonnet onwards, together with the address sheet, is in the Berg Collection.

[2] See next letter, which Talfourd published in the *Morning Post*. The rest of this 'rather long letter' was never published, but fragments have survived among the Cornell MSS., and were published by Paul M. Zall in the *TLS*, 16 Oct. 1953. See *Prose Works*, iii. 308, 315–17.

[3] *MS. torn.* Talfourd replied on 23 Apr. (*Cornell MSS.*), thanking him for his encouraging letter and promising to publish it in the *Morning Post*. 'I am also most grateful for your delicious Sonnet—may you have very many returns of the season which inspired it!'

[4] 'Some of the expressions he softened', M. W. wrote to Thomas and Mary Hutchinson, 'otherwise, it was not the labour of more than an hour,' if so much—A proof, I think, that age is not making the havoc with him as he seems to apprehend.' (*MW, p 209.*)

1231. W. W. to THOMAS NOON TALFOURD

MS. untraced.
Morning Post, 23 Apr. 1838. LY ii. 924. Prose Works, iii. 313.

Rydal Mount, April 18th 1838.

My dear Sir,

A strong opposition, which has manifested itself by public meetings and petitions to the House of Commons, having started up among printers, publishers, and others to your Bill for amending the law of copyrights, and no other like counter-movement being made by authors on their part, it has been suggested to me,[1] from quarters entitled to great respect, that it might be of service if, along with a most distinguished literary friend,[2] I should present a petition to Parliament, praying that the Bill may pass, or at least one in favour of its principle. This compliment has no doubt been paid me as one among the oldest of living writers, and of one therefore whose heirs must, in course of nature, be injured sooner than those of younger men, if the proposed measure be rejected. You will not be surprised if I feel some scruple in taking a step, though so well recommended, on account of an aversion to appear prominently in any public question, and because I am loth to think so unfavourably of Parliament as to deem that it requires petitions from authors as a ground for granting them a privilege, the justice of which is so obvious. I cannot bring myself to suppose that the mere shadows of argument advanced by printers and publishers against the claims of a class to whom they owe the respectability of their condition, if not their very existence, should avail with any intelligent and disinterested Assembly. Yet further am I averse thus to petition Parliament, because I would not ask as an individual suppliant, or with a single associate, what in equity I consider to be the *right* of a class, and for a much longer period than that defined in your Bill—for ever. Such right, as you have stated in your admirable speech,[3] was acknowledged by the common law of England; and let them who have cried out so loudly against the extension of the term as is now proposed show cause why that original right should not be restored. The onus clearly rests with them to do

---

[1] By Philip H. Howard. See L. 1229 above.

[2] Southey.

[3] Talfourd's speech on 18 May 1837, introducing his first Bill.

so; but they have not attempted it, and are glad to take shelter under the statute law as it now stands, which is a composition or compromise between two opinions; the extreme point of one being, that, by giving his thoughts to the world, an author abandons all right to consider the vehicle as private property; and of the other, that he has the right in perpetuity, that descends to his heirs, and is transferable to those to whom he or they may assign it.

This right I hold to be more deeply inherent in that species of property than in any other, though I am aware that many persons, perceiving wherein it differs from acquisitions made in trade and commerce, etc, have contended that the law in respect to literature ought to remain upon the same footing as that which regards the profits of mechanical inventions and chemical discoveries; but that this is an utter fallacy might easily be proved.

From the considerations above stated I decline to petition, as suggested, and content myself, in the silence of others better entitled to speak, with this public declaration of my judgment, so that at least, my dear Sir, you may not be liable to be treated as a volunteer intruding without wish or sanction openly expressed by any one of the class whose rights and interests you have so much to your honour stepped forward to maintain. Here this letter shall close, its purpose being answered, for no general arguments from me, and no statements of fact belonging to my own case, and which have come to my knowledge with respect to my illustrious friends Coleridge, Scott, Southey, and others, would avail to produce conviction where that has not been effected by your unrivalled speech made upon your first introduction of the Bill into the House of Commons, and by reasonings which have lately been set forth with great ability by writers[1] in the public journals, who were more at liberty to enter into details than you could be while treating the subject before Parliament.

Should your Bill be overborne, which I cannot allow myself to fear, by the interested opposition now at work, justice, nevertheless, sooner or later, must triumph; and at all events the respect and gratitude which authors feel towards you and your

[1] W. W. is thinking particularly of William Johnston, a journalist on the *Morning Post*, as is clear from a first draft in M. W.'s hand of part of the penultimate paragraph of this letter (*Cornell MSS.*). See also L. 1234 below.

coadjutors upon this occasion will be cherished by them to the last hour of their lives.

I have the honour to be,

My dear Sir,

Faithfully yours,

William Wordsworth

1232. W. W. to SIR ROBERT PEEL

MS. untraced.
K. LY ii. 923.

Rydal Mount, Kendal, April 18th, 1838.

Dear Sir,

The consideration of your eminence as a statesman may, to a man of letters, be a sufficient apology for writing to you upon the subject of Serjeant Talfourd's copyright bill;[1] and I am further encouraged to take this step by remembrance of the interest you kindly expressed (some time ago) in a concern of mine, by letter to Lord Lonsdale; and also in what you did me the honour of writing to myself upon the same occasion.[2]

Allow me then to state the fact that if the bill do not pass, or a comprehensive one grounded upon its principle, I shall be aggrieved in the most tender points; and in respect to almost every individual eminent in Literature whom I have intimately known, I can of themselves or their heirs affirm the same.

The *justice* of the principle of the bill must be too obvious to so comprehensive a mind as yours to allow of my saying a word upon the subject; but there can be no presumption in declaring my opinion that, as a remedial measure, it is urgently called for. The literary talent of the country is in a great measure wasted upon productions of light character and transitory interest, and upon periodicals. Surely the extension of copyright, as contemplated in this bill, could not but avail greatly in putting

---

[1] Peel was known to have misgivings about the Bill. In a letter to W. W. on 5 Apr., H. C. R. had written: 'If you keep but Sir Robert Inglis and get Peel—Your bill is in no danger.' (*Cornell MSS.*) In the event, however, Peel took no part in the Parliamentary proceedings on the 25th, and by the 30th Talfourd was forced to admit to W. W., 'I fear Sir Robert Peel is not with us.' (*Cornell MSS.*) See also L. 1237 below for Peel's reply to this letter.

[2] See L. 866 above.

authors upon exertions of a nobler kind, and in justifying and encouraging them to proceed.

I have the honour to be, with the highest respect,

Faithfully, your obedient servant,
Wm Wordsworth

1233. W. W. to JOHN GIBSON LOCKHART

MS. National Library of Scotland.
LY ii. 926.

[In M. W.'s hand]

Rydal Mount Ap. 27 [1838]

My dear Mr Lockhart,

The time is come to which I thought it right to defer thanking you for your valuable present of the Life of Sir Walter Scott, as I have just received the last volume. I congratulate you sincerely upon having brought to a conclusion so arduous an under- taking: three of the volumes fell at different times into my hands while I was travelling abroad last summer. I need not say that I read them with lively interest—the other four I have since perused, as they reached me, and with still deeper concern. A day or two before our Friend's last departure to the South, he told me that upon reviewing his life, he could not but reckon it a favored, and upon the whole, a very happy one; nor do I think that your Narrative, melancholy as in many respects it is, proves the contrary: the most painful part of his trials, and that which in my mind causes the strongest regret, is the burthen of Secrecy, for a burthen it must have been to one of his open and genial nature, under which so great a portion of it was spent. If, as I suspect, his admirable Works would not, at least many of them, have been produced, but for the spur of worldly ambition, the world at large will, for the sake of those Works, be little disposed to blame what you yourself must have reckoned weaknesses, as is evident from the mode in which you account for, and with no inconsiderable success, palliate them. Again, in the misfortunes of the latter part of his life there is to be found much consolation both for those who loved him, and for Persons comparatively indifferent to his fate. How nobly does his character rise under his calamities, what integrity, what

559

fortitude, what perseverance under pain both of body and mind—qualities which he himself would not have known he possessed to that degree, but for the very infirmities that were the origin and leading cause of his reverses of fortune—so that balancing one thing with another, and above all looking at his immortal Works, I feel at liberty after perusing your Memoir to accede to his own view that his was a favored and a happy life. For yourself, my dear Sir, and your friends it must be matter of sincere pleasure to have your name thus associated with that of your Father-in-law. So much of Sir Walter's affairs having become objects of public investigation, nothing remained for you but to act as openly and sincerely as you have done in writing his Life. Whatever complaints may have been made upon this point will pass away, and ere long your mode of treating the delicate and difficult subject will meet with universal approbation. In your P.S. you allude to the length of the work as having been objected to, and I hope you will not be hurt when I say, that I have been somewhat of the same opinion. The Diary of his northern voyage[1] ought, I think, to have been printed apart from the life; and some of the letters also would have been more in their place, if separated from the narrative. But all this is of little consequence.

You notice some incorrect statements and express a wish that others may be pointed out for amendment in a future Edition.There are a few trifling inaccuracies relating to Mr Southey and myself. Mr Southey was not at Storrs when Sir W. S. and you were entertained there along with Mr Canning, Prof. Wilson, and myself;[2] nor did I accompany your Party to Lowther as you state—but only to Mr Marshall's at Hallsteads. The anecdote of Crabbe and the candle smoke[3] was often *told me* by Sir George Beaumont, and in the conclusion drawn from it by *him* I concurred, not so much as set down by Sir Walter that it was a proof of the Poet's *want of imagination* as of a sense of *beauty*, but I was not present when the thing occurred—whether at Murray's or elsewhere I do not recollect. 'And can you see any beauty in that?' was the exclamation of Crabbe when Sir G. having in vain attempted to stop his hand, gave vent to his

---

[1] With the Commissioners of the Northern Lights, July–Sept. 1814. Scott's Diary of the voyage was printed in Lockhart's third volume.

[2] In Aug. 1825. See pt. i, L. 187.

[3] See the entry in *The Journal of Sir Walter Scott* for 3 Jan. 1827, quoted by Lockhart, *Life of Scott*, vii. 5–6.

regret for what had been done. Sir George's perception of beauty and grace in Art, and still more in Nature, was most exquisite—and broke forth from him perpetually, both when speaking of his remembrances, and when any thing met his eyes in which those qualities were apparent—and frequently where scarcely any one but himself would have been conscious of their existence. One word more on the story of the Bust. I have a crow to pick with 'honest Allan',[1] he has misled Sir W. by misrepresenting me. I had not a single wrinkle on my *forehead* at the time when this bust was executed, and therefore none could be represented by the Artist (a fact I should have barely been able to speak to, but that it was noticed by a Painter while drawing a Portrait of me a little while before) but deep wrinkles I had in my cheeks and the side of my mouth even from my boyhood—and my Wife, who was present while the Bust was in progress, and remembered them, from the days of her youth, was naturally wishful to have those peculiarities preserved for the sake of likeness, in all their force. Chauntry objected, saying those lines if given with shut mouth, would sacrifice the spirit to the letter, and by attracting undue attention, would greatly injure instead of strengthen the resemblances to the living Man. My own knowledge of Art led me to the same conclusion. I supported the Sculptor's judgment in opposition to my Wife's desire: this is the plain story, and it is told merely that I may not pass down to posterity as a Man, whose personal vanity urged him to importune a first-rate Artist to tell a lie in marble, without good reason; but in reality the sacrifice of truth would have been much greater, if the principles of legitimate art had been departed from. Excuse so many words upon what may be thought, but I hope not by yourself, an insignificant subject.—

And now, my dear Sir, let me condole with you on your sad bereavement;[2] the tidings reached me in Italy—they cast a

---

[1] Allan Cunningham, Chantrey's clerk of works. In a letter to Cunningham, quoted by Lockhart, *Life of Scott*, v. 40–1, Scott had written: 'I am happy my effigy is to go with that of Wordsworth [to the Royal Academy Exhibition in 1821], for (differing from him in very many points of taste) I do not know a man more to be venerated for uprightness of heart and loftiness of genius. Why he will sometimes choose to crawl upon all fours when God has given him so noble a countenance to lift to heaven I am as little able to account for as for his quarrelling (as you tell me) with the wrinkles which time and meditation have stamped his brow withal.'

[2] The death of Lockhart's wife the previous year. See L. 1141 above.

gloom over my mind, amid the splendours of that Country, for I knew the virtues of the departed and was an early admirer of the many attractions with which she was graced. Never shall I forget her light figure, her bounding step, her bright eyes, her animated tones when with a confiding simplicity that was quite enchanting she led my wife and her deceased Sister (our fellow traveller) and myself round the precincts of Abbotsford, then a small Cottage, to every object in which for antiquarian or other reasons,her Father who was then absent took an interest. This was in 1814 when he was on his voyage to the Shetlands. The last time I saw Mrs Lockhart was on a day when she took us in her carriage to the recitations at Harrow. She sate by me at the collation given at the Master, my nephew's house: these little particulars will not be without interest to you, as affording proof of my sympathy with your sorrow from the loss of one who was beloved wherever she was known.

I cannot conclude without expressing a hope that your Children are well—Mrs W. joins me in kind remembrances to yourself and begs me to say that she sincerely sympathizes in all I have said concerning your heavy loss.

With the best of good wishes I am faithfully yours

[signed] Wm Wordsworth

1234. W. W. to THOMAS NOON TALFOURD

MS. Harvard University Library. Hitherto unpublished.

[*In M. W.'s hand*]

[c. 27 Apr. 1838]

My dear Mr Talfourd,

In consequence of a bad head-ache I am obliged to employ Mrs W's pen. I cannot let a Post-day go by without thanking you for your noble exertions.[1] The thin attendance places the

---

[1] During the debate on the Second Reading of the Copyright Bill on 25 Apr. It was carried by 39 votes to 34. John Ellis, M.P., wrote to W. W. on the 28th: 'At one time of the evening I confess I had no hope of our being able to pass the 2nd Reading—The House, I regret to say, was very meagre in its attendance, and the opposition offered to the measure of a very determined character. Had the Division taken place earlier, it must have been fatal. Feeling

House in no favorable light; and I much fear so indifferent are most of its members, that without greater exertions than appear to have been made by Authors themselves in your Support, the matter cannot be brought to so successful an issue as you and I could wish. Pray be so kind as to point out to me any way in which you think I could be of further Service. My zeal is inextinguishable, but tho' my bodily health is upon the whole very good, years have in one respect brought a sad change. Intellectual and bodily labour both jade me much sooner than they used to do—by bringing on head-ache, and a *jarring* (but I scarcely know what to call it) in the nerves.

I have not seen the Morning Post of today. Your Speech[1] in the Standard I *have read*, it seems copied from the Times which I have *glanced* at—could not you spare time to have it printed separately:—its circulation would do good, and I should like to bind it up with your former Speech for a sort of heir-loom in my family.

The other day I was most agreeably surprized, by the receipt of a letter from the Gentleman who wrote those Articles in the Morning Post which we approved of; in some parts I think they were excellent—his name is Johnson,[2] and in consequence of his acting as private Secretary to Lord Lowther, I have seen him more than once in West^d, and we have had intercourse both by letter, and in London. He had, he says, often thought of writing to me but he feared it might be an intrusion, as tho' he had learned from Lord L. that I was interested in your bill, he did not know to what extent, until he read my letter to you in the M^g Post.[3] He tells me that he is in the habit of writing for that journal, and could procure immediate insertion, for any thing I might wish to say, in it, either with or without my Name. He is a Person of retired habits, as he expresses it a *home-staying man,*

an anxiety for the success of the Bill, and that it wo^d be a disgrace to the House to have thrown it out, at the instigation of Sir R. Inglis and D'Israeli I took a cab during the debate and went to the Carlton Club where I was fortunate enough to persuade one or two to relinquish their claret and go down for the division.' (*Cornell MSS.*)

[1] Reprinted in *Three Speeches . . . In Favour of a Measure for An Extension of Copyright,* 1840.

[2] William Johnston had written to W. W. on 24 Apr., offering to publish anything he might care to contribute to the *Morning Post* on the Copyright issue (*Cornell MSS.*).

[3] See L. 1231 above.

and tells me he has not the honor of knowing you. I therefore took the liberty of saying, knowing him to be quite a Gentleman in his habits, and in all points a most respectable Man, that if it were *mutually* agreeable, tho' he must be well aware how much you were engaged, I should be happy in being the medium of introducing you to each other.

Pray, if you can find a spare moment, tell me how you are disposed upon this point. I was much pleased that you did not send the letter to the Times, that journal has behaved infamously upon this occasion, as upon many others. I hardly ventured to think that you would deem my letter worthy of publication, or I should have written it with more care, both. . . .

[*cetera desunt*]

1235. W. W. to ROBERT SOUTHEY

MS. Harvard University Library.
LY ii. 930.

[*In M. W.'s hand*]

Monday Mornᵍ [30 Apr. 1838]

My dear Southey,

Thank you for clearing away my apprehensions—You will have [s]een¹ from my letter to Sergeant T.² that [p]etitioning was not to my taste, and why. But I think that the frequent recurrence [of] your name in the debate³ is no [ex]cuse why you should not write and send [th]e letter as approved of by Sir J. G.⁴—not being mentioned at yʳ own request.

¹ *MS. torn.*
² L. 1231 above.
³ On the Second Reading of Talfourd's Copyright Bill on 25 Apr. In the course of the debate, Southey was often mentioned along with Coleridge, Scott, and W. W. himself.
⁴ In his letter of 29 Apr. to W. W. (Curry, ii. 473), Southey had explained that on the advice of Henry Taylor and Sir James Graham, he had determined to write a letter that might be read out during the debate, rather than submit a petition; but he had changed his mind on seeing how often his name was introduced into the discussion. But his interest in the matter could not be called in doubt: 'Having said what I had to say, first in the *Q. R.* for May 1819, and

30 April 1838

[Y]ou perhaps have seen that a Mr Walker[1] has given notice—'that upon the motion being made for the Copy-right bill going into Committee, he should move, for its being considered in Committee that day six months'. Which in other words is putting an extinguisher upon it. This Mr W.—whoever he may be, is a new enemy, for his name does not appear in the division. I have no doubt that stupidity and cupidity will cause more Mr Walkers to rise up and therefore it is incumbent upon us all to do the utmost we can—*speedily*—consistent with our other duties and engagements. As far as *we* are personally concerned, and *I* especially, it is little comfort to say the thing *will* be carried some day or other—My Excursion was printed in the same year as your Roderic and 4/5^{ths} or more of my writings would therefore fall a prey to Mr Tegg[2] like your own, instantly on my death, or 4 years after were I to die tomorrow.

But to return to your letter—it would be read I am very sure with great effect on the day when Mr Walker means to make his hostile motion.—You question its prudence—I cannot see how a Statement of facts from your self can do aught but good—As to the question as[3] one of natural right, or as a right in

afterwards repeated it in the Colloquies, my opinion was thus put upon record, and my protest entered against the injustice of the existing law.' Sir James Graham, who was one of the Members to whom W. W. had written in late March, had supported the Second Reading of the Bill. He had replied to W. W. on 30 Mar.: 'I am disposed on every account to pay the utmost attention to a request made by you. My respect for your private worth and literary fame is sincere; and your authority and deep Interest in the subject, to which you direct my attention, would command the favorable notice even of a Stranger.' (*Cornell MSS.*)

[1] W. W. means Wakley (see L. 1201 above), who brought forward his motion on 9 May, after Serjeant Talfourd had moved the Committee Stage of the Bill. Wakley's motion was rejected, but Talfourd's triumph was short-lived, for the further progress of the Bill was delayed by the presssure of other business, and he finally withdrew his measure and reintroduced it in Feb. 1839. See Ls. 1251, 1255, and 1257 below.

[2] Thomas Tegg (1776–1845) opened a bookshop in Cheapside in 1805, and rapidly became a successful publisher of cheap reprints of English classics and abridgements. A stout opponent of Talfourd's Bill, he had published in 1837 *Remarks on the Speech of Serjeant Talfourd on the Laws relating to Copyright*, and he followed this up in 1840 with a pamphlet *Extension of Copyright proposed by Serjeant Talfourd*. See also L. 1251 below.

[3] *Written of.*

perpetuity established by common law, the less those points are dwelt upon at this crisis, the better, but I can see no harm in barely stating y[r] opinion as I have done in my letter to Sergeant T. By the bye that letter before publication was sent by me to him to determine whether or not it s[d] be publ[d], and he thanked me for it warmly—as being sure that it would be of service.

The facts you thought of stating, and any others bearing upon the Subject would I repeat be of great weight. Nor perhaps would it be amiss to glance at the injury which to y[r] knowledge would accrue, to the Heirs of Coleridge and to y[r] other friends, myself included. Coleridge['s] earlier poems including the Ancient Mariner *have* been published as you foresee our own would be, exactly as they first appeared, but in all probability much deteriorat[ed] by reckless printing.

As to the Att[y] Gen's proposal[1] I could not relish it—I should both dislike and dread such a tribunal.—Besides, such a distinction would put those Authors on whom it was conferred in an invidious position. Let the remuneration come from [the] public who would chearfully bestow it—We want no pensions and reversions for our heirs, and no monuments by public or private Subscription—We shall have a monument in our works if they survive and if they do not we should not deserve it. So with regard to a lease from the dictum of the Privy Council, if our works cease to be called for, the privilege would be but a mockery and an occasion of malignant sarcasm from the evil disposed.

I have found applications to Ladies of use in spurring Members to do their duty—Your old friend Mrs Hughes[2] is a person of wide acquaintance and indefatigable zeal—You recollect how she stirred in getting Kenyon into the Atheneum—a word to her from you—might keep many a man

[1] He had suggested in the debate that the extention of Copyright might be vested in the Judicial Committee of the Privy Council, and in his letter to W. W. Southey had commended this proposal. The Attorney General was Sir John Campbell, later 1st Baron Campbell (1779–1861), M.P. for Stafford (1830), and then Edinburgh (1834–41), Lord Chief Justice (1850), and Lord Chancellor (1859) in Palmerston's second cabinet.

[2] She was Mary Anne Watts, a cousin of the hymn-writer, and widow of Dr. Thomas Hughes (1757–1833), Canon of St. Paul's, 1807–33. She was an early friend of Scott, who referred to her as 'my clever, active, bustling friend', and was the author of *Letters and Recollections of Sir Walter Scott* (ed. G. H. Hutchinson, 1904). See also Curry, ii. 324–5. She had visited W. W. at Rydal Mount in 1823.

from his claret or his evening Party, and the battle be won by an attendance so gained.

Ever aff ^{ly} yours

[*signed*] Wm Wordsworth

I wish you had mentioned y^r health.

1236. W. W. to VISCOUNT MAHON [1]

Endorsed: May 1. 1838
MS. Stanhope MSS., Chevening. Hitherto unpublished.

[30 Apr. 1838]

My dear Lord,

Do not deem it an intrusion if I thank you for your speech upon the copyright Bill. I present my acknowledgements for your flattering introduction of my name and writings.[2] I was assured you would support us, or I should have taken the liberty of writing to you some time since, as I did to several members of whose opinions or zeal I could not be confident.

I see that a Mr Walker[3] has given notice of a motion to oppose the Bill being considered in a Committee, and no doubt the enemies to it, will do their worst. But let us not slacken but rather quicken our exertions and a cause so just must triumph.

Perhaps you may be able to find a leisure moment for looking over the accompanying paper, in which a few facts are stated. It explains itself—only I ought to say that it is from my own pen.

I have the honor to be faithfully

my dear Lord

your obliged Ser^{vnt}

Wm Wordsworth

[1] See L. 1047 above. He replied on 2 May (*Cornell MSS.*), promising continued support for the Bill.

[2] Lord Mahon does not appear to have mentioned W. W. by name in the debate, but several other speakers did. For example, Sir Robert Inglis asked, 'Was it just that the families of such men as Wordsworth, and Scott, and Coleridge, and Southey, were to be deprived of the property created by the minds of their illustrious progenitors, in order to enrich the families of John Murray and Thomas Longman?' Inglis wrote to W. W. on 26 Apr. that, 'The reception given to the mention of your name was very gratifying.' (*Cornell MSS.*)

[3] i.e. Thomas Wakley. See previous letter.

1237. W. W. to THOMAS NOON TALFOURD

Address: Mr Sergeant Talfourd, M.P., Russel Square, London. [*readdressed to*] Temple.
Postmark: (1) 3 May 1838 (2) 5 May 1838. *Stamp*: Kendal Penny Post.
MS. Amherst College Library.
Amherst Wordsworth Collection, p. 63 (—). *LY ii. 932*.

Private

[2 May 1838]

My dear Mr Talfourd

Don't let your hopes down, or relax—True it is, we have cause to fear about Sir R. Peel.[1] He declined voting, because he had not made up his mind. I will give you his difficulties in his own words, in a Letter I have just had from him—

'I confess to you that I do not see my way clearly. If the rights of the author to such extended protection be admitted, can we refuse it in the case of Patents? and of every discovery mainly owing to the ingenuity or skill of the discoverers. There are also the difficulties of determining what constitutes an original work, as distinguished from plagiarism, difficulties incident indeed to any degree of protection, but increasing with the protraction of it. And there are too the difficulties of effectually preventing piracy in Countries not subject to our jurisdiction.'—Sir R. concludes with obligingly assuring me that he will consider maturely the arguments in favor of the Bill, and that his regret will on my account be encreased if he should not be convinced by them—These are his last words and not very encouraging—

On the other hand Mr Horseman,[2] member for Cockermouth, who takes great interest in the success of the measure,

---

[1] See L. 1232 above.

[2] Edward Horsman, an advocate at the Scottish Bar, was elected M.P. for Cockermouth on the retirement of F. L. B. Dykes in 1836 and continued to represent it until 1852, when he was defeated. He thereafter represented Stroud. He was a Lord of the Treasury in 1841, and Chief Secretary for Ireland, 1855—7, under Palmerston. He had replied cordially on 19 Apr. to W. W.'s letter of late March, offering his support in the Copyright struggle, 'though we do differ, as you remind me, in polity. . . . When the author of "The Excursion" apologises as being unknown to one who has most of what he has given to the world by heart, he must not be surprized that the latter should in return avail himself of the only opportunity he may ever have of thanking him for all he has owed him, and more than he can ever repay.' He

568

and is very sorry that, though he endeavored to attend, he was not able, tells me that he has little or no doubt you will succeed, and that the more numerous the attendance the more sure you are to do so; for, says he, 'There is a general and strong feeling in all [? ranks] and parties, in favor of the claims of Authors'—Mr H. must know a great deal about the mind of his Party at least; for is he not what is commonly called 'Whipper'?

I do not know Mr H. personally, but he has written me two long and interesting Letters upon the subject, and you may depend upon his Cooperation.—Mr Attwood[1] member for Whitehaven is also very zealous, and will stir up the other Cumberland Members—

I shall write to Sir R. Peel today, and will cut out of the newspaper that part, so eloquently expressed, of your speech upon the little analogy between Patents and copyright[2]—I shall also touch briefly his other objections.

Ever faithfully and gratefully yours W. Wordsworth.

I am glad you are printing your speech.

P.S. This day I have heard from Mr Lockhart who tells me that unless your Bill be carried he considers the emancipation of Abbotsford all but hopeless. He then enters into the particulars. How beautifully you touched, or rather hinted, poor dear Sir Walter in his last struggles! Alas for the heart of the Solicitor-General![3] I shall write to Mr Johnson, and mention your wish to see him.

wrote again on 30 Apr., more warmly still: 'I am no politician except when "on duty"—and if you can forgive my being a follower of the *Whigs* in consideration of my being a still more ardent wooer of the *Poets*, I shall only feel myself too much honored by your kindly offering me the opportunity of making your acquaintance.' (*Cornell MSS.*)

[1] Matthias Attwood had written again on 29 Apr.: 'I have heard nothing which weakens the strong ground in which when I had the pleasure of seeing you at Lowther you explained the necessity of this Bill, which is the right of the Scholar to his Labour, or Genius—and their produce:—as great as that of the Lawyer or the Merchant—or as is the right of the Landowner to his Land. If this be the right of the author—he is entitled to be protected by the law in its Enjoyment.' (*Cornell MSS.*)

[2] This analogy was pressed by Joseph Hume in his speech opposing the Second Reading.

[3] Sir Robert Monsey Rolfe (see pt. i, L. 279), H. C. R.'s friend. He had argued in the debate on 25 Apr. that extension of Copyright amounted to a tax on knowledge: 'the illustrious Wordsworth', as Talfourd had shown, was

[*M. W. writes*]

[Please direct and forward the enclosed at y^r perfect leisure][1]
I crossed out the above request, fearing I might not
accomplish my purpose of writing the enclosed, excuse the
liberty I take, I pray you,   M. W.

1238. W. W. to EDWARD MOXON

Address: Edward Moxon Esqre, 44 Dover Street. [*In M. W.'s hand*]
MS. Henry E. Huntington Library.
LY ii. 951.

[early May 1838]
My dear Mr Moxon,
Cast your eye at your leisure over the two enclosed Letters:
they in a great measure explain themselves.—I have only to add
that Southey discouraged any hope of the Poems spoken of
being published by you, or indeed any one else, and simply told
Mr Shand[2] how sorry I was that he had been thrown on so unpromising a way of gaining his bread. I was a good deal pleased
with the modesty and humility of his manner, when I exhorted
him to discard all notion of distinction, for the present at least;
and to controul his inclinations, and write or labour merely for
his bread, till he should find himself at ease; and that *then* it
would be time enough for his thinking about indulging his
Genius—I added that I was well aware of your kindness of
disposition and thought it possible, but barely so, that you
might be able to point out to him some line of exertion among
publishers, by which he might earn something towards his
frugal maintenance. This was all the hope I held out to him,
adding that with that view I would write to you and enclose his
Letter if he had no objection. On the contrary said he, I should
be thankful. It seemed to me possible that something might be
procured for his translations from the German, from some

careless of present benefit, satisfied that posterity would do him justice, and this
proved that an extention was not necessary to induce great authors to instruct
and amuse the public.
   [1] The sentence in brackets is erased.
   [2] Unidentified: the poems were probably not published. See also L. 1262
below.

Editor of a Magazine. There is also merit in his Poems; they are free from false ornaments, but not striking enough to attract attention in their presentation, where Poetry finds so little favor with the Publick. Mr Kenyon's[1] and Mr Milnes'[2] and Mr Trench's[3] Poems have all great merit, and not a little originality. They have pleased us much. I will write my acknowledgments to their respective Authors.

Pray send a Copy of my Sonnets[4] to Sergeant Talfourd for his exertions in the copyright way; and one to Mr Dyce, from whom I have received so many of his own Books and whom I can only repay in this way; and give one to Thomas Powell Esqr from me when he calls for it.—The rest of my Friends must patronize the Book which is a Book of Luxury, that I would not have taken the trouble of carrying through the Press but on their account. There will be 13 new Sonnets, one however of the number has been published in some of the provincial newspapers—

ever most faithfully yours
W W.

As the Vol: will amount, with notes, Contents etc, to above 480 pages I am inclined to think that your suggestion, or Mr Robinson's, of having a portion of the Copies with a 2nd title page (so as that they who preferred it in 2 volumes might have their wish) ought to be acted upon; but do in this matter as you may think best.

---

[1] *Poems for the most part occasional*, 1838, dedicated to the memory of Thomas Poole. See also Ls. 1243 and 1246 below.

[2] See L. 1242 below.

[3] See L. 1225 above.

[4] The forthcoming *Sonnets of William Wordsworth. Collected in One Volume, With a few additional ones, now first published*, 1838.

1239. W. W. to SIR ROBERT PEEL

Address: The Right Honble Sir Robert Peel Bart M.P. etc etc, Whitehall, London.
Postmark: (1) 3 May 1838 (2) 5 May 1838. *Stamp*: Kendal Penny Post.
MS. Cornell.[1]
K. LY ii. 934.

Rydal Mount
Ambleside
3 May —38

Dear Sir Robert,

I am unwilling to encroach so far upon the kind and flattering expressions of your letter and the assurance it gives me that you will maturely consider the important subject to which it relates; but pray allow me to do this, and yet something more.

As you may not have seen or heard what Serjeant Talfourd said upon Patents, and such cases of copyright as his bill mainly looked to, I have taken the liberty of annexing part of the passage from *The Times*, that it may be read with less trouble.

'It remains to be proved that the protection granted to patentees is sufficient; but supposing it to be so, although there are points of similarity between the cases, there are grounds of essential and obvious distinction. In cases of patent, the merits of the invention are palpable, the demand is usually immediate, and the recompense of the inventor, in proportion to the utility of his work, speedy and certain. In cases of patent, the subject is generally one to which many minds are at once applied; the invention is often not more than a step in a series of processes, the first of which being given, the consequence will almost certainly present itself sooner or later to some of these inquirers; and if it were not hit on this year by one, would probably be discovered the next by another; but who will suggest that if Shakespeare had not written *Lear*, or Richardson *Clarissa*, other poets or novelists would have invented them? In practical science every discovery is a step to something more perfect; and to give to the inventor of each a protracted monopoly would be to shut out all improvement by others. But who can improve or supersede (as is perpetually done in mechanical invention) these masterpieces of genius? They stand perfect, apart from all things else, self-sustained, the models for imitation, the source whence

---

[1] *MS. incomplete.*

rules of art take their origin. And if we apply the analogy of
mechanical invention to literature, we shall find that, in so far as
it stands, there is really in the latter no monopoly at all, however
brief. For example, historical or critical research bears a close
analogy to the process of mechanical discovery, and how does
the law of copyright apply to the treasures it may reveal? The
fact discovered, the truth ascertained, become at once the
property of mankind, to accept, to state, to reason on; and all
that remains to the author is the style in which it is expressed.'

Of the broad distinctions I may not, perhaps, be an impartial
judge, as I have had the honour of hearing them adopted from
suggestions of my own, and they appear to have made an
impression upon the public. The conclusion of the extract meets
in fact the difficulty stated by you of determining what
constitutes an original work, as distinguished from plagiarism.
Dr Arnold is now engaged in writing a *History of Rome*,[1] in
which I know that he will be greatly indebted to Niebuhr,[2] but
I have no doubt of the subject being treated by him in such a
manner that neither Niebuhr—had he been an Englishman, and
written in English—would be found, were he alive, to
complain, nor could any competent tribunal to which the case
might be referred condemn the subsequent writer for having
made an unfair or illegal use of his predecessor's labours. So
would it always be with the successful labours of men of honour
and great talent employed upon the same subjects; and it is only
upon the productions of such authors that the proposed
extension of term has any bearing. Mere drudges and dishonest
writers are sometimes protected by the law as it now exists; but
their works, if not cried down at once, soon die of themselves,
and the plundered author seldom thinks it worth while to
complain, or seek a remedy by law. For these reasons—though
suspecting my judgment when it differs from yours— I cannot
see a formidable difficulty here; nor can I agree with your
opinion that the difficulty incident to any degree of protection

[1] It was published in 3 vols., 1838–43 (the third volume edited by
J. C. Hare).

[2] Barthold Georg Niebuhr (1776–1831), the founder of the new
'scientific' history, was Bunsen's predecessor as Prussian Minister in Rome,
before he settled down to teach in the University of Bonn, where W. W. and
S. T. C. had met him in 1828 (see pt. i, L. 346). His *Römische Geschichte* was
published in 3 vols., 1811–12, and 1832 (English trans., 1828–42, the first 2
volumes being by J. C. Hare and Connop Thirlwall).

increases with the protection of it. I incline to think that the contrary would be the fact.

As to piracy, much wrong is done by it; but imperfect as protection must be in this case, is not that rather a reason for prolonging it at home, in order that there may be, in its duration, something of an equivalent for what is lost by foreign injustice?

The feeling is strong, however, among leading men in America in favour of international copyright. So it is, I believe, in France; and last year I was told in Paris, at Galignani's, that their trade of this kind was destroying itself by competition and underselling. But, if we cannot altogether succeed in this point, *est quodam prodire tenus*; and let us hope and trust that justice, gratitude, and generous feelings will gain ground among nations, in spite of Utilitarians and Economists who would banish such qualities from our heads and hearts, as they have done from their own; and to the discomfiture of overgrown publishers, who—to my knowledge—have instigated their misled dependents to oppose the measure.

Permit me to state a fact as throwing light upon the reasonableness of lengthening the term of copyright. My own poems, and I may add Mr Coleridge's, have been in demand since their first publication, but till lately only to that degree which confined both publisher and author, in common prudence, to small editions, the profits of which were accordingly small to the publisher, and the residue to the Author almost insignificant. I have gained much more from my long-published writings within the last five or six years than in the thirty preceding, and the Copy-right of much the greatest portion of them would die with me, or within the space of four years. And, if from small things we may ascend to great, how slowly did the poetry of Milton make its way to public favor; nor till very lately were the Works of Shakespeare himself justly appreciated even within his own Country.

Pardon me for writing at such length, and believe me, gratefully, and with the highest respect,

Your faithful Ser^{nt}
Wm Wordsworth

1240. W. W. to THOMAS WYSE[1]

MS. untraced.
LY ii. 937.

Rydal Mount, Kendal.
May 3ᵈ, 1838.

Sir,

On the suggestion of my friend and neighbour, Mrs Graves, I take the liberty of addressing a few lines to you on the subject of the Copyright Bill now before Parliament, and also of forwarding by her desire a short paper which, as you will see, I was indu[c]ed to write upon local considerations.

With the exception of a certain class of Theorists who by system think it at once expedient and right to get work as cheaply done as they can, tho' at whatever cost of health, comfort and life to the workmen, all disinterested Persons are of opinion that thoughtful genius and persevering industry do not derive sufficient reward and encouragement from the protection afforded by the law, as it now exists. Nor will it be denied, by men of comprehensive mind, that the character of our literature would be raised by the proposed extension; Gibbon could not have written his history with the law even as it now is, had he not been a man of fortune. The question as lying between Publishers and Authors is as easily disposed of, so that all that remains, is the objection, stated by you, 'that prolonged protection to Authors would kill all cheap Editions'. Conscientiously speaking, I do not believe anything of the kind, and for reasons glanced at in the paper I take the liberty to send you, and your perusal of which, as it is not long, I venture to request. You are no doubt aware that there has been and still continues a conventional arrangement among Publishers who have pur-

---

[1] Thomas, later Sir Thomas, Wyse (1791–1862), an Irish politician of wide culture and versatile talents, came of an ancient landowning Waterford family. He entered Lincoln's Inn in 1813, married in 1821 a niece of Napoleon, and thereafter lived for several years in Italy, returning to Ireland to support O'Connell in the emancipation campaign. He was M.P. for Co. Tipperary, 1830–2, and for Waterford, 1835–47; a Lord of the Treasury, 1839–41, and Secretary for the Board of Control under Lord John Russell, 1846–9. Thereafter he served with distinction as British Minister in Athens. He was particularly farsighted in his views on national education.

chased Copy-rights, not to interfere with each other's exclusive claims, after their rights by law have expired. This convention is breaking down under the force of the rapidly increasing demand for books, the consequence of extending education and an increase in the wealth of the community. Booksellers, while they enjoy exclusive right by law, are every year finding it more and more their interest to sell an increased number of Copies at a low price rather than a few at a high one. The same considerations would operate in the same way upon the heirs and descendants of Authors—as it is already doing among themselves—with a further motive in both cases of increased honour and distinction to the name and family. Besides, it would be of greater consequence to *them*, than to Publishers who have each the works of *many* to profit by, and they would naturally take more care to give to the public correct Editions. Nothing can be more detestable and injurious to knowledge and taste than the inaccuracies in the low priced Editions, that are thrown out upon the world by Tegg, and others of his stamp. After all, for the great body of the people *dirt-cheap* literature, excuse the term, is rather a disadvantage than a benefit; in America whole volumes of works produced in England are often as they come out to meet the appetite of novelty each sold in a newspaper form for three-halfpence or twopence a piece—but what good is done by them? They are as carelessly treated and as recklessly destroyed, as they were unthinkingly bought—and if you take a higher point in the scale, the effect is much the same. Libraries, even very small ones, are almost unknown in America, except among the upper ranks of their society. The books which really improve the human mind are those that tempt to repeated perusal, and are read till they sink into it—and are even treasured up in the very shape they bore, when the reader first felt grateful to the Author for the good he had done him. This observation applies in its degree to the poorest mechanic, or rural labourer. Do but look at the fate of tracts and books that are distributed gratis! or cast your eye upon the way in which education works, that is purely eleemosynary, and compare the results with those, where a sacrifice has been made, or more difficulty encountered. But I am tiring you, and must beg your excuse. Concluding with a hope that the examination you intend to give to the subject will lead you to support the Bill, both by your vote and influence among friends, and also by speaking in its favour (which could not but have great weight) when the motion is made for its going into Committee,[1]

I have the honour to be, Your obed[t] Servant,
Wm Wordsworth

The latter part of this letter is mainly a transcript from what I had prepared to send to some journal or other, in which perhaps it may appear.

1241. W. W. to JOHN GIBSON LOCKHART

Address: J. G. Lockhart Esq[re], 24 Sussex Place, Regent's Park. [*In M. W.'s hand*]
Postmark: 8 May 1838. *Stamp*: St. James's St.
MS. National Library of Scotland.
LY ii. 939.

Rydal Mount May 4th [1838]

My dear Mr Lockhart,
(I have made a mistake by beginning to write on the wrong page, pray excuse it)
I am much gratified by your having taken in good part all that sincerity urged me to say upon the subject of your Book; and rejoice to hear that the sale has been so large.[2] What you add concerning Abbotsford grieves me much, and will strengthen my desire to do more than I have done, and that I assure you is not a little, in support of Serg[nt] Talfourd's Bill. If we should be defeated this Session, there ought to be a combined effort among Authors for the purpose of overcoming the opposition. The indifference among Members of the H. C. for the most part, to any thing but party measures, is after all the great difficulty in our way. If we all bestirred ourselves among our several Friends, to induce them to consider the measure, and if convinced of its justice and expediency give it their support, they would take the requests as a compliment and not a few would with pleasure range themselves on our side. This I write from *experience*, for I am pretty sure, that without my own

---

[1] Wyse supported Talfourd's motion on 9 May that the Copyright Bill should go into Committee.

[2] Lockhard had written on 1 May about the success of his biography of Scott.'But still I regret to say that unless Talfourd's bill be carried I consider the Emancipation of Abbotsford as all but hopeless.' (*WL MSS.*)

endeavour in this way the Bill would not have proceeded so far. Among the intelligent who consider the principle of the Bill (the Utilitarians do not deserve the name) dispassionately, and who, admitting the injustice done to Authors, are desirous of a remedy, the difficulties seem to be chiefly in giving extended protection to Authors, yet at the same time witholding it from those whose mechanical inventions give them claim to apply for Patents. There comes with this class the difficulty of determining what constitutes an original work, as contradistinguished from Plagiarism; and lastly the impossibility of preventing publication in countries not subject to our jurisdiction; this is incidental to the law as it now stands. And the objection with these Reasoners strengthens as the privilege is protracted. Though there are difficulties undoubtedly in all these points, they will not, I think, be found insurmountable, by those who distinctly perceive the delusions so industriously spread in respect to other bearings of the measure.—Being sure that both from general and particular, not to say *personal* motives, you will do your utmost, I drop the subject. But what leads you [to] attribute the opposition to *small* Publishers? Longman presided at the public meeting and Murray countenanced it.

Mrs Wordsworth rejoiced with me to hear that your children have got through a trying disease, that took one of our's, a fine Boy of six years and a half, away from us.[1] Be assured that our best good wishes attend them, and we should like to know how your Brother, Mr Charles Scott, is, for we heard with much concern an ill report of the general state of his health. I have no objection to my notes upon the Diary being given in my own words but should like first to see the passages again, as the whole Letter was written without any such view. Therefore be so kind as to send it me at your leisure and I will return it. But it is time to subscribe myself, as I do sincerely, and with great respect, your obliged Friend

Wm Wordsworth

I feel ashamed not to have noticed your wish to see me at your Brother's[2] in Lanarkshire; my travelling engagements for next summer, if I leave home at all, lie unluckily in quite a different direction. But cannot we see you and yours in passing or repassing? pray offer my best remembrances to your Brother.

[1] Thomas had died of measles in 1812.
[2] The Revd. Lawrence Lockhart of Milton Lockhart.

1242. W. W. to RICHARD MONCKTON MILNES

Address: R. M. Milnes Esqre M.P., London.
MS. *Trinity College, Cambridge.*
  Mark L. Reed, 'Two Letters of Wordsworth to Richard Monckton Milnes',
  NQ ccix (Jan. 1964), 18—20.

[*In M. W.'s hand*]

Rydal Mount
May 4th [1838]

My Dear Sir

I have just received your valuable Volume,[1] for which pray accept my thanks—which I regret to say is all I can say in respect to it at present—my thoughts and pen being so much occupied by the business now before the House of Commons, in which we Authors are so much interested for our own Sakes, but more especially for the honor of literature—that I confess I must defer the perusal of your Poems to a time of less excitement—One piece beginning 'They tell me I have won thy love' is the only one I have read, and it has given me a foretaste of the pleasure I have to expect.

I was truly glad to see your name among the list of our small majority—and trust that, out of the House and in it, you will continue to exert yourself, in its favor

Believe me d^r Sir to be
sincerely and faithfully y^rs
[*signed*] Wm Wordsworth

---

[1] *Poems of Many Years,* 1838.

1243. W. W. to H. C. R.

Address: H. C. Robinson Esqre, 2 Plowdens Build^s, Temple.
Postmark: 9 May 1838. *Stamp*: Old Broad St.
Endorsed: May 1838: Wordsworth, opinion of Clarkson and Wilberforce.
   Copyright Bill.
MS. Dr. Williams's Library.
Morley, i. 360.

[*In M. W.'s hand*]

[*c.* 5 May 1838]

My dear Friend

I should have written to you some time since, but I expected a
few words from you on the prospects of the Copy-right bill,
about which I have taken much pains, having written (which
perhaps I told you before) scarcely less than 50 letters and notes
in aid of it. It gives me pleasure that you approve of my letter to
Sergeant Talfourd. From modesty I sent it to him with little
hope that he would think it worth while to publish it, which I
gave him leave to do. He tells me, as you do, that it was of great
service. If I had been assured that he would have given it to the
world, that letter would have been written with more care, and
with the addition of a very few words upon the *policy* of the bill
as a measure for raising the character of our literature,—a
benefit which, heaven knows, it stands much in need of. I should
also have declared my firm belief that the apprehensions of its
injurious effect in checking the circulation of books, have been
entertained without due knowledge of the subject. The gentlemen of your quondam Profession, with their fictitious rights,
their public rights, their sneers at sentiment and so forth, and the
Sugdenian[1] allowance of 7 years, after the death of the Authors,

---

[1] Sir Edward Burtenshaw Sugden, later 1st Baron St. Leonards (1781–
1875), was Tory M.P. for Weymouth and Melcombe Regis (1828–30),
St. Mawes (1831–2), and Ripon (1837), Solicitor General in 1829–30, and
Irish Chancellor under Peel in 1834–5 and 1841–6. He was briefly Lord
Chancellor in 1852 in Lord Derby's first cabinet. He had spoken against
Talfourd's Bill in the debate on 25 Apr., but stated that he would not oppose
an extension of copyright for five or seven years after an author's death, to
'soothe his dying moments by the reflection that, for some time at least, his
wife and children would have some little provision'. He took the extreme
view that there was no common-law copyright residing in the author, beyond
the manuscript when it was written, or while it remained in his possession.

have indelibly disgraced themselves, and confirmed my belief that in many matters of prime interest, whether with reference to justice or expediency, laws would be better made by any bodies of Men than by Lawyers.

But enough of this. My mind is full of the subject in all its bearings and if I had had any practice in public speaking, I would have grasped at the first good opportunity that offered, to put down one and all its opponents—not that I think any thing can come up to the judgment and the eloquence with which the Sergeant has treated it.

What you say of the Wilberforces and Mr C.[1] I thoroughly sympathize with—there is nothing in my judgment in the slightest degree discreditable to Mr C. in what you report. We all know how his health was shattered by his labours—his private fortune, I heard either from himself or Mrs C. long ago never exceeded £8000, of which full one half was spent in the service. He gave all his time to it, thro the course of many years—till he came into West^d a complete wreck of what had been a most robust Man. Whether religious scruples prevented him from taking duty in the Church to which he was ordained Deacon, I do not know for a certainty, but I rather think so, at all events, had the state of his health allowed him to follow any other profession or calling—his previous ordination was an insuperable bar. If ever any man was entitled to a subscription for public services that man was Mr Clarkson. Then as to his Brother,[2] if he were really a Man of desert, as I never heard

---

[1] In his letter of 4 May, H. C. R. had drawn W. W.'s attention to *The Life of William Wilberforce*, just published by his sons Robert and Samuel (see *MY* ii. 482), which depreciated Clarkson's part in the abolition movement and cast doubt on the accuracy of his *History of the Rise, Progress and Accomplishment of the Abolition of the African Slave-Trade by the British Parliament* (see *MY* i. 152, 160). To vindicate himself, Clarkson published *Strictures on a Life of William Wilberforce*, 1838, to which H. C. R. contributed a preface and a supplement; and when this was answered by the Wilberforces in their edition of *The Correspondence of William Wilberforce*, 1840, H. C. R. put out an *Exposure of Misrepresentations contained in the Preface to the Correspondence of William Wilberforce*. The controversy dragged on till 1843, when the Wilberforces made some belated amends in the new abridged edition of the *Life*, and withdrew the offending passages. See Earl Leslie Griggs, *Thomas Clarkson, the Friend of Slaves*, 1936, pp. 169 ff.

[2] Lieut. John Clarkson (see *EY*, p. 527). Thomas Clarkson had sought to procure his brother's promotion to the rank of captain through the influence of Wilberforce. See *Life of William Wilberforce*, ii. 39.

anything to the contrary, What harm was there in his applying to M[r] W. to have his Brother's claims attended to in high quarters—Could it have been proved, that he made any sacrifice of truth or principle with these views? Or that he laid claim to more credit than he was fairly entitled to in respect to his motives; even then the publication of such letters could have answered no good purpose but as the matter stands, the conduct of the Wilberforces admits of no palliation, and M[r] C. either by himself or others will be vindicated at their cost. We have neither seen the review,[1] nor the books nor any extracts from them that at all interested us—except a droll story told to W. by M[r] Pitt, of a Frenchman's ever ready cure for his distress, in his dancing Dog.

Now may I presume upon your friendship so far as to beg you to serve me if possible in a little matter of business— M[r] Courtney writes me word, that there are a few hundred pounds of mine lying dead in his hands—and asks to know what he is to do with it. I have not answered his letter which came some time since—Will you be so good as to see him and consult with him what is best and safest to do with it. M[r] Strickland Cookson (6 Lincoln's Inn) has lodged some money for me which pays 5 per C. with what he believes to be good security— but I am not so anxious for high interest, as for *reasonable* interest—say not under 4 p[r] C[t] with entire safety. He M[r] Cookson might be of use in the matter and would be so I know cheerfully if it be in his power.

If the Railway from London to Preston only had been complete I would have set off before this to see you and my other friends in Town for a fortnight.

We have received volumes of Poems etc from M[r] Milnes, M[r] Kenyon and M[r] Trench—the[2] other day *only*—all of them if we may judge from what we have read, of great merit—but my head has been so full of this C. R[t][3] and other matters, that I have only thought myself authorized to write to M[r] Milnes to *thank* him for his attention—hereafter I shall write again—the others are unacknowledged—If you see K. pray report what I have written.

---

[1] James Stephen, 'The Life of William Wilberforce', *Edinburgh Review*, lxvii (1838), 142–80: repr. in *Essays in Ecclesiastical Biography*. In his letter of 4 May H. C. R. had mentioned the article, which cited W. W.'s sonnet on Thomas Clarkson, but was uncertain who had written it.

[2] the *written twice*. [3] Copyright.

My poor Sister is much the same—of Dora the acc^{ts} are pretty good, tho' she has had a severe cold—We expect her at home the beginning of next Month—Dear Mrs Clarkson's letter, tho' written last Aug. was gratefully received—and it was a satisfaction to think that good Mr C. is now so much better in health than when that letter was written.

We expect a call from the Ticknors[1] next Wednesday—they have written from Dumfries to that effect—they are steering their course *homeward*. Next week I mean to go over to see Lord Lonsdale for a few days at Lowther near Penrith where if you should be disposed to favor me with a [letter yo]u[2] might write under cover to his Lordship:

faithfully yours,

with M^{rs} W^s and my sister's affectionate regards.

[*signed*]   Wm Wordsworth

---

[1] The Ticknors had spent the winter in Paris, and were now on their way back to America. According to *The Life, Letters, and Journals of George Ticknor*, ii. 167, the visit to Rydal took place on 9 May, which helps to establish the date of this letter. Ticknor recorded in his Diary: 'Mrs. Wordsworth asked me to talk to him about finishing the Excursion, or the Recluse; saying, that she could not bear to have him occupied constantly in writing sonnets and other trifles, while this great work lay by him untouched, but that she had ceased to urge him on the subject, because she had done it so much in vain. . . . He said that the Introduction, which is a sort of autobiography, is completed. This I knew, for he read me large portions of it twenty years ago. The rest is divided into three parts, the first of which is partly written in fragments, which Mr. Wordsworth says would be useless and unintelligible in other hands than his own; the second is the Excursion; and the third is untouched. On my asking him why he does not finish it, he turned to me very decidedly, and said, "Why did not Gray finish the long poem he began on a similar subject? Because he found he had undertaken something beyond his powers to accomplish. And that is my case." '

[2] *MS. torn.*

1244. M. W. and W. W. to CATHERINE CLARKSON[1]

MS. Cornell. Hitherto unpublished.

Rydal Mount May 9th. [1838]

My very dear Friend,

I am most grateful to you for the letter received two days since; the more grateful, from its having been written by you so long ago—proving to me how your affectionate tenderness towards your friends broke thro' sorrow, then comparatively recent—besides, we read your letter with less of anxiety than we *could* have done, had we not *since* heard, at various times, of your Husband's amended health—and what was comforting of yourself. Tho' more recently tidings of your late bereavements have reached us—yet dear friend, the mind and heart are made up, *at our time of life*, to support such trials with greater composure; in large families like yours and ours, scarcely a week passes that we do not hear of some member of it—or of some cherished friend, that is removed, and the dispensation is merciful—leading our affections from this, towards that quiet rest, whither those, deeply loved *here*, may we trust *there* receive[2] us.

Mr Robinson, who kindly enclosed your letter, mentioned a subject which we apprehend may cause you and dear Mr Clarkson some trouble, if not annoyance—The Book put forth by the Wilberforces,[3]—we have neither seen it, or any review of it—but what he said referred me, my dear friend, to an admirably clear statement of certain facts written by you to my late beloved Sister, connected with the commencement of *that* book. If, to help your memory, or to save trouble by hunting out documents, any portion of that letter, or the whole of it, could be of use to you, I shall have pleasure in transcribing it. What a world of book-making, money-grasping, heart-disturbing age this is!

William, as you may have heard, has been busying himself by endeavours to aid the Bill which is before Parliament, for the extention of Copy-right to Authors—Yet these matters do not stifle the Muse—which still remains his Comforter, as I will give

---

[1] W. W.'s section of this letter is missing.
[2] *Written* receives.
[3] See previous letter.

you some *little* proof of (rather than dwell upon anxious cases, and sorrowful retrospection) before I close my letter—but not till I have briefly satisfied your wishes, so thoughtfully, at *such* a time, expressed, to hear of the well-doing of ourselves and those dear to us. To begin then with my Husband (tho' he shall in his own character, in part, speak for himself) You will be glad to hear that, tho' he had a sad and a long attack of inflammation after his return from the Continent—the eyes have since been unusually well thro' the long winter—and now, tho' somewhat affected by the extreme hot weather, they are not to complain of—In all other respects thank God! I may say few persons of 68 years of age are so free from infirmity—yet he would persuade himself that he feels old age fast advancing—*You* would not perceive this if you could witness his active habits—and the youthful spring of his mind. Our poor Sister alas! continues in the same state you have heard her described to be in—except that her memory is certainly improved—and for some *short* intervals, to hear her speak without looking at her—you are tempted to forget *how* she is afflicted.—She talks more of distant friends than she once did—and especially of those who are dead, or suffering—Mr Cl: and you are often in her thoughts—and her Attendant sometimes calls upon her to write to those upon whom her conversation is turning—I will enclose one letter addressed to you, which has lain some weeks in my portfolio. She will join in affectionate remembrances to you both, when I tell her I am writing—her feelings have been much alive to your sorrow—in which she has *for her* deeply partaken.

Dora, whose return home (after 15 months absence except for a 6 weeks interval when she conducted her Father to Rydal) we are looking for at the beginning of next month, and we hope to see her in tolerable health—from all we hear of her and her doings, she must have become much stronger during her southern sojourn—She is now at Brinsop and the account she writes of my dear Brother is very encouraging—tho' alas he is still a helpless Being—yet she says compared to what he was last Autumn the change is marvellous—On fine days, he can walk without support—and at all times is able to use his fists—can take off his Cap and Gloves—and can sign his name legibly— were his hands sufficiently strong to enable him to use crutches, he, poor man would feel himself more independent—but he has no power to grasp any thing. However, so much having been gained, we should be ungrateful not to look forward with hope—that having the summer before him further progress will be made. His poor Wife has been in only a very weak state—but she too, I am thankful to say, is rallying—they will all be happy to know I have heard from you—truly did they sympathise in your great affliction, which took place while I was one of their sorrowing household.

We have lately been under much alarm in connection with our Brigham family, John—after a long escape from the Typhus fever, which visited his Parish—at last was siezed, and was a severe sufferer for many weeks—for it is a lingering enemy, after its dangerous symptoms are passed—he came to Rydal at the end of six weeks, and the change was very serviceable by removing his nervous debility—and since his return home—laborious working in his grounds has quite reestablished his health—This house is at present enlivened by his two eldest boys—I wish you could see them, *Henry Curwen* the elder, is a marvellously stout and strong fellow—a Curwen in the face, but with a frame much like what his Father's was—when you dear Mrs Clarkson provided him with his first *manly* dress—how different from those elaborate braidings and cumbrous want of simplicity with which innocent children are now decked!—The younger one, *Willy* has been delicate from teething, and is now a *reduced* edition, in head and face, of what all my boys were—with his Grandfather's broad scull: and a sharp little fellow he is—the 3^d Son, John is a fine thriving Babe never having had I believe an hours illness—he will be a year old in June. The Mother and their eldest-born Jane are at home and well—By all accounts this last spoken-of Grandchild is we are told for quickness of intellect and facility in learning, quite a prodigy—so that I, who have never been used to *young* geniuses, do not like to enter upon the subject—besides I am tiring you with my egotism. Yet I must mention the *Willy*, who *is* a strong man, a treasure to us all—but poor fellow! in no situation to lay up this world's treasures for himself—being still his Father's Agent at Carlisle—with nothing more lucrative in prospect— he maintains himself however—and has a trifle to gratify his charitable inclinations withall—but nothing to lay up for a rainy day.

Our Keswick friends are now in a narrow compass. Southey, his daughter Bertha and Mrs Lovell, being the only ones at home—Cuthbert is at Oxford—and Kate visiting in, or about London and pining after the Mountains—she does not relish her newly tried life—being a home-loving useful little creature, with one of the sweetest, softest, most beautiful faces I ever saw—*to my mind*—Edith, with her two children, a daughter and a Son, are I believe well—and to be visited by all the family bye and bye.

Of Mrs Luff I have a pretty good report to give, but you will be surprised to learn that she has migrated from the dear old Cottage,[1] to the

[*cetera desunt*]

1245. W. W. to DANIEL STUART[2]

Endorsed: 1838 May 9—Wordsworth.
MS. British Library.
Grosart. LY ii. 940.

Rydal Mount Ambleside
May 9th, [1838].

My dear Mr Stuart,

I have just received your communication. I grieve much for the necessity of the disclosure,[3] which does more, much more, than justify yourself.

There is a question before Parliament in which, as an Author both upon personal and higher motives, I am much interested. Among your friends and acquaintances is there no member of the H.C.[4] whom you could interest in doing justice to men of Letters in this matter? Pray do your utmost; for the opposition is strong and persevering.

[1] Mrs. Luff moved to a house in Clappersgate.

[2] Daniel Stuart had sold his interest in the *Courier* in 1822, and now divided his time between Wykeham Park, nr. Banbury, and his London house in Upper Harley Street, where W. W. had probably seen him from time to time.

[3] Stuart had complained that errors of fact in the *Biographia Literaria* concerning his relations with Coleridge were now being perpetuated by Coleridge's relatives and friends, both in Henry Nelson Coleridge's volumes and in the first part of James Gillman's *Life of Samuel Taylor Coleridge*, which had just appeared. In two articles in the *Gentleman's Magazine*, May—June 1838 (ix. n.s., 485—92, 577—90), he set out his own version of the facts. H. N. Coleridge published a reply in the July issue (x. n. s., 22—3). See also L. 1247 below.

[4] House of Commons.

I know not where to address you. Believe me to be, very
faithfully yours,

Wm Wordsworth

1246. W. W. to JOHN KENYON

Address: John Kenyon Esqre, 4 Harley Place.
MS. Harvard University Library.
LY ii. 950.

[May 1838]

. . . I understand that you, Mr Robinson, and Southey and
his Son propose taking a trip on the Continent, this summer. It is
a promising scheme, and I am heartily glad of it for all your
sakes, especially for Southey and Robinson; who is getting too
old for the lonely and distant ramble that he talked of in
Norway and Sweden.—I took too much out of myself in my
Italian tour; the diet did not agree with me; and the exertion in
the heat was too much for a man of 67. Nothing however should
I like better than going again, (with my wife and family) and
two years of leisure: *then* I could accommodate myself to all the
novelties of climate, diet, exercise etc.

By the bye Mrs W. begs me to say that some passages of your
Vol.,[1] the moonlight especially, remind her of Parts of my own
Work (still in MSS) upon my early life. This is not the first
instance where our Wits have *jumped*, as great wits are apt to do.
Ever with Mrs W's best remembrances

faithfully your obliged
W Wordsworth

[1] *Poems, for the most part occasional*, 1838. The first poem is entitled
Moonlight. The *argument* reads: 'Moon—suggestive of poetic feeling, as
observed in Childhood, in Boyhood, in Manhood, etc.'

Address: Daniel Stuart Esq., 9 Upper Harley Street, London.
Franked: Penrith May Seventeen 1838 Lonsdale.
Postmark: 17 May 1838. *Stamp*: Penrith.
MS. British Library.
Grosart. K (—). *LY ii. 941*

[*In M. W.'s hand*]   [Lowther]
                                                    May 17, 1838.
Dear Mr Stuart,
   In Mr Gillman's life of Coleridge just published, I find these
words:—'The Proprietor of the Morng Post, who was also the
Editor, engaged Coleridge to undertake the Literary
department. As Contributors to this Paper, the Editor had the
assistance of Mr Wordsworth, Mr Southey, and Mr Lamb.
Mr S., from his extreme activity, and with a rapidity and
punctuality which made him invaluable to the Proprietor, etc.
The others were not of the same value to the Proprietor.'
   In the extracts from the Gent's. Mag:[1] you sent me the other
day, speaking, I imagine, of the Morng Post, *you* say, 'At this
time, I do not think Wordsworth sent any thing.' You have here
been speaking of a Salary being given to Mr C. and Mr L., as
contributors to the Morng Post, and the passage, coupled with
that of Mr G.s, would lead any one to infer that I was a *paid
Writer* of that Paper. Now, for my own part, I am quite certain,
that nothing of mine ever appeared in the Morng Post, except a
very, very, few sonnets upon Political subjects, and one Poem
called the 'Farmer of Tillsbury Vale,'[2] but whether this appeared
in the Morng Post or the Courier, I do not remember. In the
Courier were printed 2 articles in continuation, amounting
together to 25 pages, of the pamphlet I afterwards published on
the Convention of Cintra.[3] The Sonnets and the Pamphlet were
written by me without the slightest view to any emolument
whatever; nor have I, nor my Wife or Sister, any recollection of
any money being received for them, either directly from

---

[1] See L. 1245 above.
[2] *The Farmer of Tilsbury Vale* (*PW* iv. 240) had appeared in the *Morning
Post* for 21 July 1800. W. W. seems to have forgotten that *The Convict* (*PW*
i. 312) was published in the same paper (on 14 Dec. 1797), before it appeared
in *Lyrical Ballads*, 1798, but as he never reprinted the poem thereafter, he
probably did not regard it as part of his permanent *œuvre*.
[3] See *Prose Works*, i. 198–200.

yourself (as E. and P. [1] of those Papers), or mediately through C. [2]; and I wish to know from you, if you have any remembrance or evidence to the contrary. But certain I am, that the last thing that could have found its way into my thoughts would have been to enter into an engagement to write for any newspaper—and that I never did so. In short, with the exception of the things already mentioned, a very few articles sent to a West[d] Journal, during the first West[d] contest [3] one article which I was induced to publish in a London newspaper, when Southey and Byron were at war, [4] and a letter, the other week, to the Kendal Mercury upon the Copyright question, and a letter to Sergeant Talfourd on the same subject, published in the Morng Post, not a word of mine ever appeared, sent by myself at least, or as far as I know, by any other Persons, in any Newspaper, Review, Magazine, or Public Journal whatsoever. By the bye, I ought to except two sonnets and a light Poem, not connected with my works, which were printed in some Provincial Journal. [5]

I will be obliged to you if you will answer at your early convenience the question put above; as I wish to write to Mr G., whose book, I am sorry to say, is full of all kinds of mistakes. Coleridge is a subject which no Biographer ought to touch beyond what he himself was eye witness of. [6]

[1] Editor and Proprietor. [2] Coleridge.

[3] See *MY* ii. 420, 425, 434, 440, 470−1, 574; *Prose Works*, iii. 194 ff.

[4] In spite of diligent search by several scholars, this article is still untraced.

[5] W. W.'s recollections are a little vague here. He is probably referring to the sonnets published in the *Westmorland Gazette* in 1819 (see *MY* ii. 522), and the election squibs he offered for the *Cambridge Chronicle* in 1832 (see pt. ii, L. 730). He appears to have forgotten that the *Extempore Effusion upon the Death of James Hogg* first appeared in the *Newcastle Journal* (see L. 947 above).

[6] Gillman's *Life*, written with the approval of the Coleridge family, seems to have aroused as many misgivings as Allsop's and Cottle's earlier volumes. H. C. R. noted that it contained 'A deal too much that is old and very little new, and unworthy omissions both of Coleridge's letter on his opium-eating, and of De Quincey's early generosity to Coleridge; a palpable preference of the hero to truth. Too uniformly eulogistic and too anxious to make a good Church of England Trinitarian of him.' (*HCR* ii. 549.) Hartley Coleridge admired Gillman's self-effacement as a biographer and the overall tone of the work, but complained of the style: 'It is a good hearted, noble minded book, but it is not a well-written or well constructed book.' (*Letters of Hartley Coleridge*, ed. Griggs, p. 230.) Gillman died on 1 June 1839, and no further volumes of his biography were published.

When you write pray tell me how Mrs Stuart, yourself, and your family, are. Mrs W. unites with me in kind regards to Mrs S. and yourself, and believe me to remain, faithfully yours,

[*signed*] Wm Wordsworth

1248. W. W. to EDWARD MOXON

Address: Edward Moxon Esqre, 44 Dover Street.
MS. Henry E. Huntington Library.
K (—). *LY ii. 942.*

[*In M. W.'s hand*]

May 21 [1838]

My dear Mr Moxon,

A few days delay has been caused by a visit I have been paying to Lord Lonsdale at Lowther—but by this day's Post I send all the Notes and a short Advertisement and table of Contents—The volume will contain twelve[1] New Sonnets. So that when I get the proofs back from the Printer—with the remainder of *clean Sheets* in order to see that the notes are referred properly to their respective pages—my part of the work will be over.

I cannot form a conjecture whether this Publication is a well advised one or no—if it should at all interfere with the sale of your Six vols, I shall exceedingly regret our having been persuaded to undertake it. I should wish to have a few vols of the Sonnets sent down here—and at the same time a doz. copies of the six vols, which you will charge me with, as heretofore. The Poems will be placed in the hands of the Bookseller at Ambleside who sells a Copy now and then—with no add^l charge from me—by which means, she, being in a small way, and having no connection with London, gets a better profit than were she to procure them from a Country Bookseller, who has such connection.

The extension of term in Copy-right, whatsoever becomes of the principle during this Session, being both just and expedient

---

[1] There were six new sonnets included in the body of the volume, and six added in an appendix while the sheets were going through the press. Confusion arose over the exact number of new sonnets because an asterisk was omitted before the sonnet *At Dover* (*PW* iii. 198) on p. 212.

is sure of being carried sooner or later. In the mean while, by being the single exception among Publishers who have united to oppose it, you have done yourself great honor—and acted to y^r advantage also—depend upon it. Many thanks for your parcel rec^d thro' the hands of Mr Graves.

If you have remaining on hand some copies of Serg^t Talfourd's 1st Speech,[1] pray send me at least three, when you send the books—I have already mentioned this wish to the Sergeant—

What success has attended his Tragedy[2]—he is an astonishing man—for talents, Genius, and energy of mind. Mention Miss Lamb to us when you write—and with our Love to her, and give our kindest regards to your household. We expect our daughter home in about 10 days.

Ever faithfully y^r much obliged
[*signed*] Wm Wordsworth

1249. W. W. to JULIUS CHARLES HARE

Address: The Revd J. C. Hare, Herstmonceux, Sussex [*In M. W.'s hand*]
Postmark: (1) 29 May 1838 (2) 31 May 1838. *Stamp*: Kendal Penny Post.
MS. Mr. R. L. Bayne—Powell. Hitherto unpublished.

Rydal Mount, May 28 [1838]

My dear Mr Hare,

Books are mostly long in reaching me, and so it was with your's,[3] but I might have thanked you sooner both for the Volume and the honor you have done me by the Dedication.[4]

---

[1] Introducing his Copyright Bill on 18 May 1837. It was subsequently published by Moxon, and later included in *Three Speeches . . . In Favour of a Measure for An Extension of Copyright*, 1840.

[2] *The Athenian Captive*, 1838.

[3] A new, enlarged, edition of *Guesses at Truth*.

[4] In the Dedication to W. W., Hare wrote: 'For more than twenty years I have cherisht the wish of offering some testimony of my gratitude to him by whom my eyes were opened to see and enjoy the world of poetry in nature and in books. In this feeling, he, who shared all my feelings, fully partook. You knew my brother; and though he was less fortunate than I have been, in having fewer opportunities of learning from your living discourse, you could not deny him that esteem and affection with which all delighted to regard

That I have not sent you my acknowledgments sooner I am in fact to blame, but only for some want of resolution; I have been anxious to write but felt that I would not do justice to my feelings, especially in regard to your lamented Brother.—I cannot exactly recall the time when I received his sermons,[1] but it was not long before I went abroad, and Mrs Wordsworth tells me she fears I never returned thanks for them. If so, I have to request your indulgence, the reason must have been that I had not read them all, and the cause of that, the frequent irritations and inflammations to which my eyes are subject, an infirmity which has brought my knowledge of new books into very narrow compass and also taken from my familiarity with old ones. Nor have I any one near me who can read *much* aloud, so that we are a disabled Household even when my Daughter, who has long been about, is at home [*M. W. adds in the margin*: This is not quite the fact—Mrs W *can* read but listening sends her husband to sleep. M W] Your excellent Brother's death[2] was much lamented by me and mine, and what a loss he was to the world and to his sacred calling his sermons prove. The Copy you were so kind as to send me, I have lent to my Son, as my Daughter possesses another. He much values the work for its own sake, and as a memorial of one to whom he was so greatly obliged. My own judgement is perhaps not entitled to high

him. . . . Then too would another name have been associated with yours,—the name of one to whom we felt an equal and like obligation, a name which, I trust, will ever be coupled with yours in the admiration and love of Englishmen,—the name of Coleridge. You and he came forward in a shallow, hard, worldly age,—an age alien and almost averse from the higher and more strenuous exercises of imagination and thought,—as the purifiers and regenerators of poetry and philosophy. It was a great aim; and greatly have you both wrought for its accomplishment. Many, among those who are now England's best hope and stay, will respond to my thankful acknowledgement of the benefit my heart and mind have received from you both. Many will echo my wish, for the benefit of my country, that your influence and his may be more and more widely diffused. Many will join in my prayer, that health and strength of body and mind may be granted to you, to complete the noble works which you have still in store, so that men may learn more worthily to understand and appreciate what a glorious gift God bestows on a nation when He gives them a poet.'

[1] *Sermons to a Country Congregation* (See L. 1181 above). For some account of Augustus Hare's ministry at Alton, Wilts., see Augustus J. C. Hare, *Memorials of a Quiet Life*, 3 vols., 1872–6, i. 284 ff.

[2] At Rome, on 18 Feb. 1834.

respect, for I do not profess to be much of a Theologian or Divine, but there can be no presumption in stating that the sermons appeared to me models of simplicity in laying down the truths, and of unbounded earnestness in enforcing it. Some of the illustrations however though quite suited, I have no doubt, to a congregation so illiterate as your brother's, would be found a little too homely for the taste of our Yeomanry, who have all more or less of a school education. They would think that their attainments were rated too low, and that they were treated a little too much like Children, or at least more as inferiors in Culture and exercise of mind, than they ought to be.

I have contrived to read a great part of the Guesses of Truth, and with great pleasure and profit; though I have not yet compared the present edition with the former.—I know little of Hazlitt's writings, but judging from my recollections of his conversation, I should be inclined to say you treat him with more respect than for any originality of mind that was in him [which] he could lay claim to.[1] He was an acute analyst, but he had little imagination, and no wholesome or well regulated feeling. But for what he learned from Coleridge and Lamb, he never would have been listened to as a critic. Something also, he learned from myself, but I never took to him, and therefore that

[1] In *Guesses at Truth*, Hazlitt's Shakespearian criticism had been contrasted with Francis Horn's, in Germany: 'Nobody can doubt that Hazlitt by nature had the acuter and stronger understanding of the two; he had cultivated it by metaphysical studies; he had a passionate love for poetry, and yielded to no man in his admiration for Shakspeare. By his early intercourse with Coleridge too he had been led to perceive more clearly than most Englishmen, that poetry is not an arbitrary and chanceful thing, that it has a reason of its own, and that, when genuine, it springs from a vital idea, which is at once constitutive and regulative, and which manifests itself not in a technical apparatus, but in the free symmetry of a living form. Yet, from the want of a proper intellectual discipline and method, his perception of this truth never became an intuition, nor coalesced with the rest of his knowledge: and owing to this want, and no doubt to that woful deficiency of moral discipline and principle, through which his talents went to rack, Hazlitt's work on Shakspeare, though often clever and sparkling, and sometimes ingenious in pointing out latent beauties in particular passages, is vastly inferior to Horn's as an analytical exposition of the principles and structure of Shakspeare's plays, tracing and elucidating the hidden, labyrinthine workings of his all-vivifying, all-unifying genius.' In his reply to this letter, on 4 June, Hare wrote of Hazlitt's powers: 'Perhaps, as I have had reason to suspect, though I never met him, he was more brilliant a writer than in conversation.' (*WL MSS.*)

perhaps was not much. As you most justly observe, the wreck of his morals was the ruin of him, as it must be of every one else—

I am anxious to hear of your Brother Francis; he was very kind to us at Rome, and we saw him again at Florence, where he was seized with an illness which I did not hear of, till between nine and ten at night, our horses being ordered for Bologna early next morning. I wrote to Mrs Hare from Bologna to make inquiries and learned from her that he was convalescent, though she was still somewhat anxious about him.—Pray give me a line, were it only to let me know how he and his family are going on. I am really anxious about this for before that seizure, I had an apprehension that his liveliness of nature was wearing him out before his time. Give my best regards to him and Mrs Hare when you write and believe me dear Sir faithfully your much obliged Friend W. Wordsworth

My Continental Tour was very agreeable but too fatiguing and taken too late in life to turn to much profit. My allowance of time was too short for the work I had to do.

[*M. W. adds*]

Mrs W. begs her respectful remembrance, and thanks for the pleasure and instruction she has derived from your Books.

1250. W. W. to [?] THOMAS POWELL

MS. Harvard University Library.
K (—). *LY ii. 943.*

Rydal Mount
June 9th [1838]

My dear Sir

Never had a book, a reprint especially, such a tedious and long journey through the Press as my Vol. of Sonnets. It is however on the point of being finished, and pray when you hear of its being advertized go or send to Moxon's where I have directed a Copy to be laid aside for you, as a small return for your many attentions to me and mine.

Mr Gillman's Book [1] is not better than I feared I should find it. It is full of mistakes as to facts, and misrepresentations

---

[1] See L. 1247 above.

concerning facts. Poor dear Coleridge from a hundred causes many of them unhappy ones was not to be trusted in his account either of particular occurrences, or the general tenor of his engagements and occupations. Mr G. may be more fortunate when he shall come to what he himself had an opportunity of observing, but there again I have my fears. Of idolatrous Biography I think very lightly: we have had too many examples of it lately; take Mr Wilberforce's life by his Sons[1] as a specimen; and Coleridge I am afraid will not be dealt more wisely with. Observe in what I have said above I do not mean to impeach poor C.'s veraciousness, far from it, but his credibility. He deceived himself in a hundred ways; relating things according to the humor of the moment, as his spirits were up or down, or as they furnished employment for his fancy, or for his theories.—

As you do not mention your health I hope it is quite restored. The Copyright Bill goes on but unpromisingly.[2]

> Ever my dear Sir
> most faithfully yours
> Wm Wordsworth

1251. W. W. to THOMAS NOON TALFOURD

Address: Mr Sergeant Talfourd M.P., Russell Square, London [*In M. W.'s hand*]
Postmark: (1) 17 June 1838 (2) 19 June 1838. *Stamp*: Kendal.
MS. Lilly Library, Indiana University.[3]
Russell Noyes, '*Wordsworth and the Copyright Act of 1842: Addendum*', *PMLA* lxxvi (1961), 380—3.

[*c.* 14 June 1838]

[*First sheet missing*]

> 'A Book time-cherished and an honor[ed name]
> Are high rewards; but bound they Nature's cla[im]
> Or Reason's? No—hopes spun in timid line

---

[1] See L. 1243 above.
[2] See L. 1255 below.
[3] *MS. extensively damaged*. This letter, of which the opening section is missing, seems to have been written several days before posting.

From out the bosom of a modest home,
Extend through unambitious years to come,
My careless Little one, for thee and thine!'[1]

Such is the conclusion of a Sonnet, which I was urged to write the other day on this subject, while I was playing with my little Grandchild upon the front of our Abode. This is the nature, and being the Nature, it is the wisdom, of this truly important question. But the sorrow of this and a thousand other matters of legislation is, that men of the World, and Legislators alas! are too exclusively so, can never screw up their minds to sufficient confidence in the principles of justice as touching any kinds of claim or rights whatsoever. Let justice but proceed in the case before us, and that expediency which, from the blind and narrow views of certain minds, obstruct the course of it, would then be sure to follow in its train. Not only would better Books be produced which is what we want, but they would be circulated in the shape which the last hand of their respective Authors gave them, which if the law be suffered [to s]tand as it now is, will not in a great [many] instances [?].

Tilt,[2] and Tegg[3] and scores of others, [upon the] decease of an eminent Author, are ready [to sei]ze upon the last Edition of his book or wor[k] which without violation of law may be at their Mercy, [? and] they impudently foist upon the world their publication [as] genuine. In consequence of its being open to them to [do] so, and to republish immediately upon the death of an author what he himself has rejected, Mr Southey, as he tells us in the preface to his Poems, now going through the Press, felt himself obliged to reprint many things which he would gladly have thrown overboard; for if he had not done so, these Harpies would have an advantage over his Heirs; by advertizing their publication as the only complete Edition of his Works. Again; the law, as it now stands, holds out a temptation for an author in the decline of life, to attach to his long-published works gossiping novelties, in the shape of notes or explanations, which only add to the bulk of the things, without any encrease of their

---

[1] See *A Poet to his Grandchild* (*PW* iii. 410), dated 23 May 1838, and described as 'a sequel' to *A Plea for Authors* (*PW* iii. 58). Both were among the new sonnets included in W. W.'s new volume, but the sequel later dropped out of the collected poems.

[2] A publisher of popular almanacks.

[3] For Thomas Tegg see L. 1235 above.

Value, but as the law would protect *these* new portions he is disposed to turn to account the protection of those parts for the sake of the rest the protection of which has ceased. *But* the main consideration is, and it cannot be too [much] insisted upon; that by the principles of your bill, a great Author's conscience [? would] be likely to be set at rest when he was labouring [? upon a wo]rk of which the pecuniary return must [?]. [A mar]ried Man with children who is what a [?] to be, must feel it to be his first [duty to] provide for the Woman who has entrusted her fate to him, and for the children which they have brought into the world. How can he go on with hope and heart in his labour, if his means be not sufficient to leave them at ease upon this point. He can not, and he ought not; it is on the contrary his duty to turn to some meaner employment and persist in it till that point shall be secured. Again, as I have hinted before, how unworthy how injurious to a people is it to take an advantage of the enthusiasm and self devotion of such Men of Letters as cannot resist the impulses of their Genius, and toil and toil heedless of what becomes either of themselves, their wives or those whom Nature and Law require that they should take care of. But injustice and the setting at naught of the most sacred feelings of nature, of generosity, of gratitude, all stare one in the face when one thinks of the course pursued by the opponents of your Bill. Never heed—'Sed contra [audentior]ita.'[1] You must prevail at last. If you are defeated this Session, we will have in the next an organization wh[ich no] feeble-minded Russels,[2] and no [?] thick-headed Lawyers, or hard [? hearted] Economists will be able to resist [?].

Look but a moment at the stupidity of [? these] last, even in their own department. Grant [that] at present certain Productions of Scott and other popular authors which have passed into common right are to be had at very low prices, does it follow that the same cheapness will continue. No, assuredly, the rule will apply here as it does to all other commodities. Underselling will go on, till it answers no longer, and then it will be found

[1] See Virgil, *Aen.* vi. 95.

[2] Lord John Russell, the Home Secretary, had considerable influence over the conduct of business in the House, and therefore over the time that could be made available for private members' Bills. He had also developed misgivings about the Copyright Bill. When the Committee stage opened on 1 June he raised many fresh difficulties about it, which he thought should be properly ventilated, and very little progress was made in the discussion.

that the best way of having comparatively new books at a low rate is for some one to have an exclusive right of Publishing them. That will secure him from being undersold, while the number of readers daily encreasing through the spread of education, and the improved condition of the people, will make it his interest, upon which he will be sure of acting, to furnish cheap editions for those who cannot afford to buy others; and so all ranks will be provided according to their means and tastes; and let us add, as far from insignificant, Readers according to their ages. Publishers, to meet the rage for low priced Books, are sending forth Voluminous Authors, in one Volume, double columns; but by necessity [in too] small a Type, that men past the middle [years] who are yet unwilling to be driven to [the] use of spectacles cannot read the[m] and others, still older throw them aside, because they must either read, with injured sight, or have recourse to glasses only required by still older people.

A Word or two more upon cheap Books and you shall be released. I have seen a large Volume printed in America for general circulation, within the compass, and in the shape of a newspaper and sold as such, for a penny or three half-pence. Should we gain any thing if our best works in divinity, history, or any other department of solid literature, could be, and were circulated in that shape or way. No, what was lightly procured would be as thoughtlessly destroyed. Accordingly it is a rare thing in most parts of America to discover among people of substance any thing like a library such as we have in almost every house belonging to persons in tolerably good circumstances. Now surely it is the very Books which we are attached to, in the very shape in which we have often read them, that do us the most good; that sink into our hearts, fix our opinions, direct our views, and rectify our [judgement.] Pray forgive this long scrawl, which ho[lds] [? together] I scarcely know how. I have [purposely left] unattempted any thing like eloquence [even] if it had been within my reach, [though] writing to one of the most eloquent of [? men].

God speed you well, my dear M[r. Talfourd.]

W W[ordsworth]

[*In M. W.'s hand*]

Upon glancing over this letter I find I have not touched upon two or three points which were present to my mind when I began to write. The one is the hardships which the Children of

Authors labour under as contrasted with those of most other
Men—the Lawyer, the Clergyman even who gains the top of
his profession—the eminent Physician—the Great Manufacturer or Merchant all either obtain large fortunes, or by
patronage which they command, or establishments which they
leave behind can provide independence for most of them—or
put them in the way of gaining it. But Authors however
meritorious—have no situations at their disposal, no patronage—and no means of realizing a fortune—unless possessed of
talents like Sir W. Scott, or two or three more—and do not
think it beneath them to apply those versatile talents as they did.
It is true that many excellent Clergymen and admirable Officers
in the Army and Navy, give their time, their abilities their
health, their strength and their lives—to the public Service—
without obtaining independence, for any portion perhaps of
their families. This is a hard very hard case—but cannot be
prevented—whereas in the case of deserving Authors extension
of [? copyright provides] an opening for the prevention of the
evil without any enforced tax [?] whatsoever—and in real
truth—no tax at all in the end. [?] [con]clusion point to the fact,
that the two most valuable works in these [fields] produced in
Europe during the last Century, were Gibbon's Decline and Fall
[? and Boswell's] Johnson—neither of which could have been
written, had not both [? authors attained] to more than easy
circumstances—yet it seems to be the [?] business of a large
portion of the Ho: of C. to resist doing away with [?] [whi]ch as
much perhaps as any other, hinders the production of [? works
of] merit in the same, or other departments of Literature.

—W. W.

Pray keep this letter—it may be useful to me as memoranda
hereafter—if we do not succeed at present.[1]

[1] On 20 June Talfourd, with the agreement of Gladstone, Mahon and
Inglis, agreed to withdraw his Bill until the next session rather than take the
risk of having it voted out, and the following day he wrote W. W. a long
explanation of their action, concluding, 'I had great pleasure in reading the
admirable and triumphant remarks of your long letter. I am almost ashamed
to think I have enjoyed the honour of such communications as this, and have
done so little to deserve them. I shall preserve it carefully and reverently
against the time when its reasonings will again be needed. Assuring you that I
can never forsake a cause which has been graced and (to my mind at least)
consecrated by the support of your genius . . .' (Noyes, op. cit., p. 382.)

1252. W. W. to THOMAS NOON TALFOURD

MS. Harvard University Library. Hitherto unpublished.

[mid-June 1838]

. . . at least, to be attempted towards them with less excuse—
I mean men of genius and great talent, if their views be so
limited. In my former letter I alluded to Boswell's life of
Johnson, and Gibbon's decline and Fall, as being in their several
Kinds works entitled to the highest respect. How little prospect
have we of seeing any thing of equal merit attempted in any
department. Encyclopedias by the prices which their Editors are
enabled to pay, seem to engross almost all the talent from which
works, in any degree to be compared with those of Boswell and
Gibbon, might be expected. Yet it is utterly impossible that such
a tree should bear such fruit. The Authors in such Collections
are limited both as to time and Space—they must go thro' their
several works, however scanty their materials, however jaded
their Spirits, however disordered their health, however distracted their affairs—how conscious soever they may be of the
unworthiness of what they are about to present to the public.
Boswell and Gibbon were Men of fortune—or, as I have
observed before, they could not have executed their works; and
what can be more obvious than that an extension of Copyright
would tend to place men of [   ] position [   ] to that
in which accidents . . .

[*cetera desunt*]

1253. W. W. to THOMAS NOON TALFOURD

MS. Cornell. Hitherto unpublished.

June 17th [1838]

My dear Mr Talfourd,
I cannot forbear telling you that my thoughts have often been
turned towards next Wednesday and the uphill work you will
have then to undertake. But I am sure you will not be
disheartened; whatever be the issue on that day, the course of
justice will triumph erelong; nothing can prevent it.—
So indignant was I at Lord John Russell's disingenuousness
and foolish behaviour that I resolved to write a Letter for

publication upon the general question; and accordingly I turned
it over and over in my mind, examining it in all its parts. But
really (and this above every thing makes me feel for your
situation) I could not find an argument against the extension
which deserved to be combated. I wished, like young Ascanius,
for Boars or Lions to contend with,[1] and found nothing but
asses kicking up their heels, or yelping curs—so that my spirit
sank and I left the field. You know Dr Arnold, at least by
reputation, as every one does. He sent a letter to a provincial
newspaper[2] from which I will trouble you with an Extract or
two.—Having stated that the existing law has fixed the right of
literary property upon a principle of Compromise, he goes on
to say, 'It is one thing to admit that an Author's right is not
absolutely indefensible, and another to insist that it shall expire
at the end of 30 or 40 years at the outside. There is no proportion
between the perpetuity of all other property, and the mere brief
occup[   ]³ tenure of this.[4] . . . The common feeling of all
mankind in allowing them to dispose of their property after
their own death, shews that our own welfare is supposed to be
inseparably connected with that of our own children, that
wealth must lose half its value if we cannot secure it to them
after we ourselves are taken away from them. This seems a clear,
an intelligible ground for the extension given by Mr T's Bill. It
will now in ordinary cases be insured to an Author and his
children. (If the D^r had been as I hope erelong he will be a
Grandfather, as I am, with a sweet little Fellow rising 3 years,
now under my roof, and the delight of his Grandmother's eyes,
and mine, He would have looked a little further) This seems to
be the very least that can be granted to him consistent with
justice. . . . As for the mere Consideration of benefit to the
Purchaser by restricting the term, this cannot be allowed to
determine the question, so long as there is any regard paid to
common honesty. It might be very convenient to the
purchasers, at least for a time, to be able to get bread and meat
for half the market prices; but few would probably be found,
who would therefore recommend a law for a maximum. Now
the argument about the public benefit in getting Books cheap,

[1] See Virgil, *Aen.* iv. 156−9.
[2] The *Hertford Reformer,* 5 May, 1838, repr. in *Miscellaneous Works,* 1845,
pp. 445−9.
[3] *MS. torn.*
[4] The passage omitted referred briefly to W. W.'s own case.

even if true, in fact which it is not, in any calculable degree, is precisely imposing a maximum upon Authors. It says, you all sell your property at, such a price, for if you do not, you cannot afford to wait for a better market; because, after a certain time we will take your property from you for nothing.' Thus far the Doctor; in an article well adapted to make impression upon a numerous class of Readers. But I am far from concurring with him in the degree of weight which in other parts of his letter he assigns, in the conflict of claims, to that of the Public. My own opinion is, but upon this it would be impolitic to insist, in the present state of general opinion, the only right of the Public is to require, (as your Bill provides) that a Work shall be republished within a certain reasonable time, if it be out of print and called for, or the exclusive right fall to the ground.—Dr Arnold in the ex[tract] says, *wealth* would lose half its value if we could not secure it for our children. But the question here is not one of *wealth*; but whether it be not unfeeling and unjust, to rob laborious authors who are content to sacrifice present reward, of the hope that some thing might proceed in future from their labours, which would contribute to prevent their children or more remote descendants from sinking in society, even to the point perhaps, that, for want of education they should be unable to understand the least recondite of their own ancestor's works. Hume[1] and that class Cry out, the law would be [? altered] for the advantage of one or two, but for the injury of the people. Now the object of the law in the first instance, is not to take advantage, in the common selfish sense of the word, of any Author, but to prevent the violation of justice, to hinder the sanctioning of a great wrong by the Legislature, which it never can [   ], without debasing the moral sentiments of the community, which is the greatest injury that can befall it. What were Sir E. Sugden's[2] heart and head about, when his tongue found leave to talk of 7 years being a sufficient additional allowance after the death of an Author whose Copyright expired with him. Sir E. may be an Elephant in Law, strong and heavy as a Castle, but his proboscis is paralysed, and he exhibits himself as attempting to [? pluck] with his feet, that are only fit to pound and to Crush, the sweet flowers of the meadow, or the green twigs and beautiful blossoms of the trees of the forest. But

---

[1] Joseph Hume, M.P.
[2] See L. 1243 above.

to return to the Economists and Doctrinaires. Their Conduct in this question is strictly *preposterous*.

Common sense would say, let us in the first place omit nothing that will tend to improve the article we wish to circulate, and then let . . .

[*cetera desunt*]

1254. W. W. to H. C. R.

Address: H. C. Robinson Esqre, 2 Plowdens Build^gs, Temple.
Endorsed: June 1838. Wordsworth. Printing Letters. The Clarkson and Wilberforce Affair.
MS. Dr. Williams's Library.
K (—). Morley, i. 364.

[18 June 1838]

My dear Friend,

There is only one drawback from the pleasure your Letters give, namely this, that we cannot send you any entertainment in return. Our way of life is wholly without interest or variety. We see few strangers, though they are beginning to make their appearance; and no new books not even periodicals, nothing in fact beyond what we value much, certain Vols of Poems that have been sent us, by Mr Kenyon, Mr Milnes and Mr Trench.—I dont know when Mr Moxon will send forth my Sonnets; I have done with them; perhaps he may think that they would fall still-born from the Press, if published till the ferment of the coronation[1] is over, and then will come the dead time of the long vacation. But these considerations may be of no importance in a Book of which the materials are old.—You will find however 13 new sonnets, some of which I hope will please you.

Your view of Mr Clarkson's case[2] seems quite correct, except that I cannot concur in blaming his two applications to Mr Wilberforce; I mean in the substance, for as to the *manner* I cannot speak, not having seen the Letters. Had Mr Clarkson been a boastful Person, who set himself off as a pure and absolute devotee and Martyr, it would have been different. If he had rejected all admixture of inferior considerations, in the course of

[1] On 28 June.
[2] See L. 1243 above.

his life, all pecuniary help or interference to prevent his being left perhaps a pennyless man, and closed his eyes to all opportunities of serving his connections or Friends I do not see that he would have stood at all upon higher ground; on the contrary such conduct I think would have been irrational. I may be mistaken, but I cannot censure M[r] C. as I am perfectly convinced that no sordid idea of gain from such a source or from any other, could enter his mind.—I had written before I got your letter to M[r] Stephen,[1] letting him know that I did not think I was in error, notwithstanding what had been said in the Life and Review, when I ascribed to M[r] C the honor of having 'first led forth that enterprize sublime';[2] and that, if M[r] Clarkson should not reckon it worth while to maintain his own claim, I should take some opportunity of attaching to that Sonnet the evidence upon which I make the assertion. I have also expressed myself to the same effect in a note which you will find at the end of the collection now about to be published.[3]

Pray send the enclosed back to me at your leisure; you will see by it what personal, in addition to general, grounds I am likely to have for regretting breaches of confidence in the publication of private Letters without the consent of the Writers or their Representatives. Is this Gentleman of Sir Charles Bunbury's[4] family; I can scarcely believe that a person of that rank in society would take so unwarrantable a liberty, and furnish so vile a precedent. Of my letter I recollect nothing distinctly, for it must have been written thirty-five years ago—

We never see the Edinburgh Review, except which is not once in 5 years I put myself out of the way to get it for some particular purpose; as the other day I procured it from a Book Club at Ambleside to which I am not a subscriber, for the sake of

---

[1] James Stephen, author of the review of *The Life of William Wilberforce* in the *Edinburgh Review*.

[2] See *To Thomas Clarkson* (*PW* iii. 126), l. 5.

[3] See *The Sonnets of William Wordsworth*, 1838, p. 452 (*PW* iii. 457). Writing to W. W. some months later, on 10 Nov., C. C. regretted that W. W. was not going to publish a defence of her husband: 'The Sonnet however will remain as long [as] the english Language' (*WL MSS.*).

[4] Sir Thomas Charles Bunbury, 6th Bart. (1740–1821), the 'beau-ideal of an English sportsman', according to H. C. R., was Whig M. P. for Suffolk for 43 years. His nephew, Sir Henry Bunbury, 7th Bart., had recently published W. W.'s letter to C. J. Fox of 14 Jan. 1801 (*EY*, p. 312) without his permission. See L. 1268 below.

a hasty glance at the Review of Wilberforce's Life. We shall however contrive to borrow the life if we can. Have you seen the Letters of poor dear Coleridge which the indiscretion of his Friends have compelled Stuart[1] to publish in his own vindication. They appeared in two late numbers of the Gentleman's Magazine and have been reprinted by the Morning Post; a journal which by the bye has done itself great honour lately by its zealous and able and praiseworthy defence of the rights of authors in the Copy right question. For my own part it is my earnest wish that every Letter I have written may be restored to me or my Heirs or destroyed. My mind never took pleasure in showing itself off after that manner; and to say the truth I think that the importance of Letters in modern times is much overrated. If they be good and natural as Letters, they will seldom be found interesting to solid minds beyond the persons or the circle to which they are immediately addressed. I was struck the other day with an observation of the Poet Gray upon Pope's Epistles. As Letters, says he, 'they are not good but they are something better than Letters'. How far this may be true in respect to Pope I do not know, for it is long since I read his Letters, but the remark as of general application is far from being unimportant—I am glad you have given up your Norway travels. You are getting too old to expose yourself to so much fatigue as such a journey would impose. Whatever becomes of the Sergeants Bill, this Session; if we organize our efforts, and throw ourselves fairly upon the justice, the gratitude and generous feeling of the British People, the principle of extension is sure of being carried and shortly too. Love from Mrs W and my sister.[2] We expect Dora tomorrow. ever most faithfully yours

W W.

I find I have said nothing about money;[3] I hate the subject; and know not what to do with the little we have to dispose of. I grieve that you have had so much trouble in looking after Courtenay, who lately stirred my wrath by telling me he could

---

[1] Daniel Stuart. See L. 1245 above.

[2] Just before this, M. W. had sent a long account of D. W. to Mary Hutchinson at Brinsop. See *MW*, p. 214.

[3] H. C. R. had written on 11 May that he and Courtenay did not see eye to eye on matters of investment. H. C. R. strongly recommended W. W. to invest in American stocks.

not sacrifice his Conscience to vote for such a JOB as the Sergents Copyright Bill.[1]

Yesterday Dr Kennedy[2] of Shrewsbury School called on me; he had with him a Vol. of W's: life I had a moment's glance at it and saw a few words that made me fear Mr Clarkson may have been somewhat indelicately importunate in urging his suit to Wilberforce on behalf of his B^r.

Our Friends have judged rightly in putting off the Copyright Bill, We must exert ourselves and the principle is sure of being carried.

18 June—24th I have kept this seven days. The Bunbury is no doubt Sir Charles or of his family. I have seen Wilberforce's Book; entirely concur with you as to regret that Clarkson should ever have written *such* a letter as *one* of them is particularly. ——

1255. W. W. to THOMAS NOON TALFOURD

MS. Berg Collection, New York Public Library. Hitherto unpublished.

June 24th [1838]

My dear Mr Talfourd,

Many and cordial thanks for your exertions.[3] I cannot say that I am much disappointed, fearing worse from the slackness of our Friends in attendance, and knowing that our opponents are zealous in the exact ratio of their ignorance, and stupidity.— You decided most judiciously in not pressing the Bill under such circumstances: The statement which your second letter (accept my thanks for both) mentions, as appearing in The [? Times][4] I had not seen; but from the bad conduct of that newspaper through the whole of this affair, I much fear it has been a woeful misrepresentation.

---

[1] Philip Courtenay had voted against the Second Reading of the Copyright Bill on 25 Apr.

[2] Benjamin Hall Kennedy (1804–89), Fellow of St. John's College, Cambridge (1828–30), assistant master at Harrow (1830–6), headmaster of Shrewsbury (1836–66), and thereafter Regius Professor of Greek at Cambridge: author of the celebrated *Latin Primer*.

[3] See L. 1251 above.

[4] *Word dropped out.*

We must be prepared in force for the next Session. I will do any thing that your superior knowledge may point [? out]. At present I presume it would be best to say little or nothing, but to reserve ourselves for the time when the Subject shall be about to be introduced to Parliament.

I am afraid that no review of the question, and no further illustration of its details, I mean of the minor arguements in support of the principal would much avail, unless every friend to it exerts his private influence, among Members both directly and in Society. What you tell me of Holmes[1] pleases me much; I wrote to him before the first Introduction of the Bill, and though he did not reply to my Letter, I was pretty sure of his services. He is a thoroughly good natured Fellow, whom I have long known having frequently met him at Lowther (and Appleby and elsewhere)—

If you can point out any way in which I can be useful, pray do; and believe me my dear Mr Talfourd most sincerely your much obliged Friend

W Wordsworth

1256. W. W. to WILLIAM STRICKLAND COOKSON

Address: Wm Strickland Cookson Esqre, 6 Lincoln's Inn. [*In M. W.'s hand*]
Postmark: 28 June 1838. *Stamp*: Pall Mall.
Endorsed: Wordsworth W^m. 25th June 1838.
MS. Yale University Library.
LY ii. 945.

Rydal Mount
25th June [1838]

My dear Mr Cookson,

Many thanks for your Letter and all the trouble you take about my little affairs.

I feel much obliged by your undertaking to place the 400£ as you did on the 12th of May last.—

The proposal of your Letter of yesterday is not so satisfactory. I will state my objections and doubts.

---

[1] William Holmes, the Tory Whip (see pt. i, L. 240).

The proposed security is so and so; but the party will not be in *possession* till after the death of another person.—Am I to understand that in the case the borrower should die before the present owner of the property, I should have a lien upon it; and if so, how could that be turned to the benefit of my estate? not at all I suppose during the life of the Lady, so that the security would resolve itself into the sufficiency and integrity of the two Persons who are to be Sureties for the regular payment of the interest.—Am I right in this view of the case? if so, with due submission to your superior Knowledge and experience, I should deem the transaction wholly inadviseable.—

Even if such security could be given as would attach to the Estate, in case of the Borrower dying before the Lady, I submit whether there might not be difficulties in ultimately recovering the principal after her death; But of this you must be a much better judge than I am.—

I have as usual consulted with Mr Carter.[1] He is no Lawyer any more than my self—and is more decidedly against the thing even than I am, adding another consideration, that he is afraid of our little property being so much scattered as it is. And he is quite against selling the India Bonds for what appears to him so questionable an investment.—

Could you find a moment to answer these questions—

Would there be a lien upon the Estate in case the Borrower should die before the Lady who is now in possession?—I suppose so.

Have you the means of being satisfied of the respectability of the Sureties who might be offered?

The lender with a power of sale to be exercised in case the interest be not punctually paid, is proposed. Could this be of any avail during the life of the Lady?—

—I have nearly 400£ lying in the Kendal Bank at 2 and a half per cent which is tangible for this, or any other investment that should be quite satisfactory, and the requisite Sum could be made up by money in Mr Courtenay's hands.

After all I have so much confidence in your caution and judgement, and am so sensible of my own inexperience, that I have not been quite at ease in writing the above; which is too indec[is]ive for my own taste and feeling.—You say the *only* objection is, the party not being in possession. Briefly, in what

---

[1] So MS., *but W. W. means* Carr, as L. 1259 below makes clear.

way and to what degree does this, with your experience in business, strike you as an objection.—If I had confined myself to putting at first this simple question I might have spared you the trouble of reading this long and perhaps confused Letter, and myself that of writing it.—Pray let me hear from you once more, and I will then decide absolutely.

We are glad to hear that you and Mrs C. mean shortly to visit West[nd].

ever my dear Sir
faithfully your much obliged
Wm Wordsworth

The family at Nook End[1] are all well. Dora came home two or three days ago. She does not complain, but looks much thinner than when she left us in the Autumn.—

1257. W. W. to WILLIAM EWART GLADSTONE

Endorsed: June. W. Wordsworth.
MS. British Library.
K (—). LY ii. 949.

Rydal Mount
Monday [25 June 1838]

My dear Mr Gladstone,

Your decision was most judicious, and I thank you sincerely and cordially both for your exertions on this occasion and through the whole business, and for your kind letter.[2]

The cause is at once so just, and the measure so expedient, that I have not a doubt of the principle being carried, provided those who understand the question (which they cannot do, without

---

[1] A house in Ambleside, which had been taken by Strickland Cookson's mother and sisters.

[2] Gladstone had written on the 21st, at the same time as Talfourd, to announce the withdrawal of the Copyright Bill for the present session (see L. 1251 above). But he was optimistic about getting the Bill through eventually: ' . . . You have at present from the divisions which have taken place an admirable parliamentary position from which to commence operations when we next meet . . . ' (*British Library MSS.*)

being sensible of its importance) support it with due zeal, in, and out of Parliament. If you can point out any way in which I can be useful, I should be happy to do my best. You are perhaps aware of the reasons why Sir R. Peel withholds his support; he was so obliging as to state them in a letter to me. Perhaps it would be as well, however, if I should briefly give them. His difficulties are three.

First, if we grant extension of right to authors, says he, how can it be withheld from applicants for Patents? 2nd, how can the originality of a work be defined so as to discriminate it from a Plagiarism? and lastly, how can we prevent works being reprinted in countries over which we have no jurisdiction?

I answered these several objections as well as I could, and satisfactorily as I thought; but not, I fear, to Sir R.'s conviction. All these hesitations arise out of that want of due confidence in the principles of justice, which is the bane of all practised Politicians.

Thanks for your animated stanzas from Manzoni.[1] I have often heard of the Ode, but it never fell in my way. You have puzzled me about a new sonnet of mine in the Quarterly,[2] I presume the last number; what could it be, and how could it get there? I have lately written 13 new ones, which will appear in the edition of the whole of my sonnets in *one* volume which Moxon is about to publish; but none of these were ever given by me to any writer in that Review or any other.

I hope that your attendance in Parliament is not too much for your health. Many urgent applications are made to me to sign the Petition that went from Kendal and the neighbourhood, in favour of immediate abolition of negro apprenticeship—I refused to do so, and am sure I shall never regret that resolution.

[1] Alessandro Manzoni (1785–1873), author of *I Promessi Sposi*, 1825–7, and *Gli Inni Sacri*, 1812–22, a series of hymns for the festivals of the Christian year. But the reference here is almost certainly not to one of these, but to *Il Cinque Maggio*, Manzoni's Ode on the death of Napoleon, a favourite poem of Gladstone's which he translated into English.

[2] An article in the *Quarterly Review*, lxii (June 1838), 131–61, on 'Art and Artists in England' has the following note: 'The following Sonnet on Napoleon at St. Helena in Sir R. Peel's Collection is not in our copy of Wordsworth's poems, and may be new to many of our readers: "Haydon! let worthier judges"' (etc., as in *PW* iii. 51). The sonnet was written in 1831 and published in 1832. The author of the article was Lord Francis Egerton, 1st Earl of Ellesmere (see pt. ii, L. 459).

Your own speech [1] was masterly. Ever yours with high respect and gratefully,

W. Wordsworth

1258. W. W. to BENJAMIN ROBERT HAYDON

Address: B. R. Haydon Esq., 4 Barwood Place, Edgware Road, London.
MS. untraced.
LY ii. 944.

Rydal Mount, 25th June, 1838.

My dear Haydon,

I lose no time in replying to your letter. [2] It gives me much pleasure to see you writing in such high spirits, as I conclude that you are prospering. It would ill become me not to say that I must deem the dedication to me of your Lectures[3] an honorable distinction, and the more gratifying as it comes from the feelings to which you have given utterance in your letter.

I have not seen any extracts from your Lectures, but I have somewhere heard that you speak of Michel Angelo in terms of disparagement to which I cannot accede, and therefore I should like that, in the terms of your dedication, you would contrive as briefly as you can to give it to be understood that I am not

---

[1] When slavery was abolished in 1833, a system of Negro apprenticeship had been set up in its place (see pt. ii, L..755), which it was now proving increasingly difficult to uphold. In the debate on 30 Mar. 1838 on the Second Reading of a Bill to abolish the system altogether, Gladstone spoke for 50 minutes in defence of the original arrangement made with the planters, arguing that the system had on the whole worked well, and that it would be disastrous for the Negroes themselves if it was suddenly brought to an end without adequate preliminary preparation of West Indian society for the change. He compared the lot of the Negro apprentices favourably with that of British factory children, and accused supporters of the Bill of turning a blind eye on slavery at home, when economic considerations led them to do so.

[2] Of 23 June. Haydon wrote: 'What a glorious creature you are!'— remember I did not wait for the cheers of the House to be convinced of your aweful Genius any more than you waited for the sanction of the People to hail mine!' (*WL MSS.*)

[3] Haydon had been lecturing in the north of England, but does not seem to have published his lectures at this time. Perhaps he was referring to materials that were later incorporated into *Lectures on Painting and Design*, 2 vols., 1844–6, which were dedicated to W. W.

pledged to the whole of your opinions in reference to an Art in which you are so distinguished.[1]

Pray present my kind regards to Mrs Haydon, and

Believe me to be faithfully yours,
William Wordsworth

1259. W. W. to WILLIAM STRICKLAND COOKSON

Address: W. S. Cookson Esqre, 6 Lincoln's Inn, London. [*In M. W.'s hand*]
Postmark: 28 June 1838. *Stamp*: Kendal Penny Post.
Endorsed: Wordsworth W^m. 26th June 1838.
MS. Yale University Library.
LY ii. 947.

Tuesday 26th June [1838]

My dear Mr Cookson,

I am so much dissatisfied with the confused, wordy, and indecisive Letter I wrote you yesterday, that you must excuse my returning to the subject:

I have carefully reperused your Letter, and reconsidered the subject:

The only objection, you say, is that the Party will not be in possession, till after the death of a Lady 77 years of age.—

I ask is there in this fact any further objection than[2] what is involved in the contingency of the Lady surviving the person who wishes to borrow the money, and the contingency of the insufficiency of the proposed sureties?—For I presume *now* with confidence, that the Lady has only a life's interest in the Estate, and that the Borrower has power at present to mortgage the Estate, in other words, make it responsible for the money, independent altogether of his outliving the Lady or not.—If this view be correct, and you have satisfactory means of ascertaining

---

[1] Haydon wrote again on 29 June in defence of his view of Michelangelo: 'I bow to his vast Genius . . . and great grasp of mind, in the intellectual comprehension of a whole to illustrate a principle, like the Sistina—but my dear Friend he was an Etruscan and had all the . . . fury of that savage and incomprehensible people, what was good in them was Greek—and what was gigantic and savage was their own.' (*WL MSS.*)

[2] *Written that.*

the sufficiency of the two proposed Sureties, I now think that I am justified in closing with the proposal, the lender being armed, as is proposed, with a power of sale.—

I am of the same mind as to not disturbing the India Bonds. What is wanting to complete the £600 beyond the Sum which may be in Mr Courtenay's hands, shall instantly be supplied through Wakefield's Bank,—

I have talked the matter over with Mr Carr, and he confirms me in my resolution to place the money as you propose.

On Mr Carr's suggestion also I mention that he has 3,500£ [three thousand five hundred][1] now in his hands, which he is desirous of placing upon un[e]xceptionable security at as good a rate of interest as could be procured.—If he could effect this he would go abroad immediately, and he would be very glad if you could assist him, through your professional aid, in carrying his wish into effect.—

I remain
My dear Sir
faithfully your much obliged
Wm Wordsworth

1260. W. W. to THOMAS POWELL

MS. University of Virginia Library.
LY ii. 948.

[28 June 1838]

My dear Sir,

As you will see by your own Book which I return I have misunderstood your wishes; I must now request you to accept on the part of your Son[2] a copy of my Poems from myself. The Parcel will go to Kendal today to be forwarded by the Mail.

Your Volume would have returned immediately, but I was hoping for some opportunity to return it, free of expense.

---

[1] *Written over the line.*

[2] On 24 June Powell had sent W. W. the first volume of his poems with the request that W. W. would inscribe them to his son Arthur Wordsworth Powell (d. 1839). 'I really feel ashamed at so frequently troubling you, but alas! how inconsiderate is human nature in pursuit of a cherished wish' (*WL MSS.*).

Be so kind as to present my sincere acknowledgements to
Dr Smith for his valuable Work, Divine Government, [1] both for
its own sake and the Compliment paid in sending it to me as a
Stranger.—The subject has been in part and shall be, maturely,
considered by me when more at leisure than this present season
allows me to be. Thanks for your lines. They are pleasing; but is
there not an error in the word 'lay' for 'lie'?

Your Godchild [2] is still more interesting to me as being the
Daughter of a distinguished Person who was so infamously
traduced for having done his duty to his Country, and to
mankind, by his bearing towards one of the worst Enemies of
the human race that ever existed; one who had the noblest
opportunities of doing good that ever fell to the lot of Man, and
who to selfishness and vulgar ambition sacrificed every thing—

Your Parcel came as you wished free of expense—

The Copyright Bill, at least the principle of it is, I think, sure
of being carried next Session, it must be so if justice have any
weight with the Legislature. [3]

Pray excuse this Letter written in great hurry on the morning
of the coronation

[*signature cut away*]

I have just received the amended Bill; be so good as to thank
Mr Chapman. [4]

1261. W. W. to JOHN KENYON

MS. Lilly Library, Indiana University.
Russell Noyes, 'Wordsworth: An Unpublished Letter to John Kenyon', MLR
liii (1958), 546–7.

[Summer 1838]

My dear Mr Kenyon,

We are sad slow readers in this house, I from infirmity of
eyesight and Mrs W. from lack of voice and numerous

---

[1] See L. 1199 above.

[2] Unidentified.

[3] 'Those worthies', Powell had written, 'seem to think that poets, like
Canary Birds, sing the better for being starved!'

[4] Aaron Chapman, M.P. (see L. 1199 above).

engagements. We have gone through the whole of your Vol:[1] however, and can honestly repeat what we may have told you before, that you are very smart and pungent in Couplet and can now add that you make a capital figure in blank verse and lyric also. To speak more gravely we have been entertained by parts of your volume and instructed also, and not a little moved and pleased by others—I fall in exactly with your train of thinking and feeling in your Moonlight, and Silchester, and Dorchester Amphitheatre. Stonehenge[2] has given you at your *advanced* years just such a feeling as he gave me when in my 23^d year,[3] I passed a couple of days rambling about Salisbury Plain, the solitude and solemnities of which prompted me to write a Poem of some length in the Spenserian Stanza.[4] I have it still in Mss and parts may be perhaps be thought worth publishing after my death among the 'juvenilia'. Overcome with heat and fatigue I took my Siesta among the Pillars of Stonehenge; but was not visited by the Muse in my Slumbers. I am therefore half-tempted to think that Milton was a little of a Fibber, when he talks of his nightly visitations 'or when the sun purples the east'.

Mrs W. is just come in, and begs me to say that she frequently returns with great pleasure to your volume; never having suspected that you have so very much of the *genuine* Poet in you.

You advert to what it is possible Italy may have done for me. I wrote one blank verse piece about 80 lines; suggested at Laverna; and was then strongly impelled to add another, (in which I made some little progress),[5] upon the Life and character of St Francis; but I sought in vain for Cardinal Bonaventura's Life of him,[6] both at Florence Venice Munich and elsewhere. Had I found the Book when the heat was upon me, I should

---

[1] *Poems, for the most part occasional*, 1838. See L. 1246 above.

[2] The blank-verse poem *Moonlight* contained some 60 lines on the mystery of Stonehenge.

[3] Actually W. W.'s 24th year: his wandering on Salisbury Plain belongs to the summer of 1793. See *EY*, p. 109.

[4] Eventually published in 1842 as *Guilt and Sorrow (PW* i. 94 ff,). For a full account of the various stages of this poem, see *The Salisbury Plain Poems (The Cornell Wordsworth*, vol. I), ed. Stephen Gill, 1975.

[5] *The Cuckoo at Laverna* (see L. 1145 above) consisted in its final form of 112 lines.

[6] St. Bonaventura (1221–74), sometimes considered as the second founder of the Franciscan Order, was the author of the Life of St. Francis, which was accepted as the official biography by his Order in 1263.

probably have done the work; but I am still without the Volume and the inclination has died away.—I went too late into Italy not for poetic feeling, but for clothing those feelings in words; and I also travelled through the delightful region much too fast. It is remarkable that my tour of nearly 5 weeks through Ireland, which was performed in a chariot with 4 Horses, never produced a verse; whereas three several tours through Scotland, in an Irish car, a fourwheeled Carriage with one horse, and very much pedestrianizing, were productive of many poetic exertions, and some of them I trust successful.

[*cetera desunt*]

1262. W. W. to EDWARD MOXON

Address: Edward Moxon Esqr, 44 Dover Street.
Postmark: 10 July 1838. *Stamp*: Charles St.
MS. Henry E. Huntington Library.
LY ii. 952.

July 4th [1838]

My dear Sir,

Thanks for your last Letter, announcing the despatch of the parcel, and telling me that you would endeavour to serve Mr Shand.[1] It gives me some pain to have to let you know, that yesterday, when I was passing through Keswick, Mr Southey shewed me a Letter from the Landlord of the Head Inn Carlisle, the Bush,[2] in which he stated that Mr Shand after staying some days in his House went off leaving a Bill of £7 6s. 0d. or thereabouts unpaid. I hasten to tell this to you, in order that if he should call you may be prepared to act as you think proper. I feel much obliged by your meeting my wish by an assurance that you will make an attempt to serve him, but dismiss that promise entirely from your thoughts. The worst part of the transaction, bad enough in all respects, is that being poor and needy, as he probably is, he should have gone to the most expensive Inn in the Place. This admits neither of excuse nor apology; had he been pennyless or nearly so and gone to a public house suitable

---

[1] See L. 1238 above.
[2] The Posting House in English Street.

to his condition, and even left his bill unpaid, from sheer necessity, that would have been an action much to be blamed, but still pity and compassion might have qualified one's censure, and would have done so. But in this case I cannot find an excuse. To save you the disagreeableness of any explanation, or even interview with him, unless you think proper to see him, I have enclosed a note which may be given to him. How long he may have continued such practices cannot be learned, and could one be sure this is his first performance one might still with *caution* try to serve him.

I shall be absent three weeks upon a Tour in the Counties of Northumberland and Durham.[1] I write from a Lady's house three miles from Carlisle. I am accompanying Miss Fenwick. Tomorrow we start by the rail way from Carlisle to Newcastle, we have most beautiful weather.—

I am afraid what with the Coronation and the long Vacation, our Vol: of Sonnets will have a poor chance of attracting the least notice.—

With kind regards to Mrs Moxon and your Sister and remembrance also to your Brother believe me faithfully yours

Wm Wordsworth

---

[1] On 2 July Dora W. had written to Rotha Quillinan: 'Today Father and Miss Fenwick are on the Railway between Carlisle and Newcastle, at Newcastle they remain a day then proceed to Alnwick and to the extreme north of Northumberland hoping to visit Holy Island etc. and they then go to Durham—then to Witton where Father leaves Miss F. and proceeds alone to visit our relatives at Stockton. This will employ about a week and Thursday 24th if all be well, will see them back at Rydal via Alston Moor Penrith and Patterdale.' (*WL MSS.*) In the event, this programme was somewhat modified. W. W. spent 5–6 July in Newcastle, where he met John Hernaman (see L. 947 above), and visited Tynemouth (see *Newcastle Journal* for 7 July 1838), and then moved into Northumberland, perhaps visiting relatives or connections of I. F. In the middle of the month he stayed for a few days with George Taylor at Witton-le-Wear (see *Newcastle Journal* for 28 July), and went on to Durham on the 20th in order to receive an honorary degree at the new University the following day (see *Durham Advertiser* for 27 July). By 27 July he was back at Rydal Mount.

1263. W. W. to UNKNOWN CORRESPONDENT

Endorsed: Wordsworth, July 18, 1838.
MS. E. L. McAdam, Jnr. Hitherto unpublished.

[18 July 1838]

. . . faithfully yours
Wᵐ Wordsworth

The [? *Dean*] of Castle-Eden[1] I have seen some years ago; and a very interesting spot it is, wanting only water.

1264. W. W. to BENJAMIN ROBERT HAYDON

Address: B. R. Haydon Esq., 4 Burwood Place, Connaught Terrace.
MS. untraced.
Haydon (—). *LY ii. 954.*

Rydal Mount July 28 [1838]

My dear Haydon,

I received your 2ⁿᵈ Letter more than a month ago when I was upon the point of setting off for Northumberland and Durham where I have been detained till yesterday. In the course of this tour I wrote to you at some length; but upon consulting your Letter when I had written my own I find no date but the general one of London and though you are a distinguished Person I thought that the Post office might nevertheless be ignorant of your habitat. I therefore did not send my Letter. Since it was written I have had an opportunity of reading your Essay in the Encyclopaedia, and neither in that, nor in your Letter, do I find any thing said concerning Michael Angelo, to which I object.[2] I acknowle[d]ged him to be liable to all the charges you bring against him; it would only be a question between us of the *degree* in which he is so. Therefore do not take the trouble of sending your essay for my inspection before hand. I need only add, that through Messrs Whitaker Booksellers Ave Mary Lane, I can receive any parcel addressed to me under cover to Messrs

---

[1] Castle Eden Dene, a rocky and wooded valley between Durham and Hartlepool through which a small river winds down to the sea.

[2] Haydon's article on Painting in the 7th edition of the *Encyclopaedia Britannica* was reprinted, with Hazlitt's contributions, in *Painting and the Fine Arts*, 1838. See Haydon's *Diary* (ed. Pope), iv. 454.

Hudson and Nicholson, Booksellers, Kendal, to be forwarded by Mr W. in his first Parcel to Messrs Hudson and Nicholson, with an under cover for me—

There are some opinions in your essay about which I should like to talk with you; as for example when you say that Raphael learned *nothing* from Perugino but what he had to unlearn. Surely this is far from the truth; undoubtedly there is in him, as in all the elder Masters, a hardness and a stiffness, and a want of skill in composition, but in simplicity, and in depth of expression he deserved to be looked up to by Raphael to the last of [his] days. The transfiguration[1] would have been a much finer picture than it is if Raphael had not at that period of his life lost sight of Perugino and others of his predecessors more than he ought to have done.[2]—Whoever goes into Italy, if Pictures be much of an object with him, ought to begin where I ended, at Venice. Not as I did, with the pure and admirable productions of Fra Bartolomeo at Lucca and with Raphael at Rome, so on to Florence, Bologna and Parma and Milan: and Venice by way of conclusion. Italian Pictures ought to be taken in the following order or as nearly as may be so, Milan, Padua, Venice, Bologna, Parma, Florence, Rome.—Your essay does you *great credit*; and your practise, I trust still more. I had a sad account of the French Academy at Rome; the students appear to be doing little or nothing and spend their time in dissipation.—Believe me with kind regards to Mrs Haydon

ever faithfully yours
W Wordsworth

[1] In the Vatican.

[2] Haydon replied on 31 July: 'Your approbation of my treatise is a great pleasure to me. I fear it is thoughtless to speak of Perrugino as I did—which I will correct, for you are certainly right. I have the highest opinion of all that simple race, the more we can revert to their simplicity, without their childishness, the better.' (*WL MSS.*)

1265. W. W. to EDWARD MOXON

MS. Henry E. Huntington Library.
K (—). LY ii. 953.

Rydal Mount
July 28th [1838]

My dear Mr Moxon,

I have been wandering for more than a month in the Counties of Durham and Northumberland, and am now fixed at home for I trust, a long time.—

The parcel of Books arrived during my absence, and I have not yet had time to do more than glance at it.—Mrs W. begs me to thank you which I do also, on my own part, for your kindness to my Son, [1] who, we are most happy to learn, is shaking off the sad effects of his Fever.

He tells me you say the Sonnets and poems are doing well. I have not heard a word about them from any other quarter.—It was well that a few new Sonnets were added, as I find them serve well as an advertisement in the provincial papers, which extract some one or other of these or more as may suit the Editor's fancy. The Examiner drolly enough says that a Sonnet on the Ballot, his favorite Hobby, damns the Volume. By the Bye, pray procure from Mr Bradbury the clean sheets that succeed page 432; otherwise those we have up to that Page will be useless; and I should be sorry to lose the Copy. They can be sent with any Parcel which you may have to forward in future, only let them be procured and kept for that Purpose. Is it true that you are going as far as Italy. Mr Robinson will give you all the directions you can possibly want.

With kindest regards to Mrs Moxon, yourself, and Sister and Brother, I remain dear Mr Moxon
faithfully yours
Wm Wordsworth

[*M. W. writes*]

Pray fill up the address to Haydon and send it to the 2^d P. Office. This shocking paper Mr W. always lay[s] hold of, when left to himself, does not at all suit *his* penmanship. Many many thanks for your Kindness to my Son. Be so good as send a

---

[1] John W., who had been in London.

copy of the sonnets to 'Master Herbert Coleridge[1] from Dora Wordsworth' and put another copy inside for Mr Quillinan when he calls for it. Kind regards to Mrs M. and loving hopes and wishes to y[r] children. Y[r] copies of the poems will be returned properly inscribed by the first safe opportunity.

1266. W. W. to H. C. R.

Address: H. C. Robinson Esq[re], Temple.
Endorsed: July 1838. W. Wordsworth (Autogr).
MS. Dr. Williams's Library.
Morley, i. 367.

Rydal 28th July [1838]

My dear Friend,

Having, by mere chance a cover from this Place I throw in a word to tell you that your Letter was duly received and forwarded to me while I was on a Tour in the Counties of Northumberland and Durham from which I am just returned after a month's absence—It pleased me much to hear of M[r] C's pamphlet.[2] There are a 100 things in Ws life which require sharper a remonstrance than they are ever likely to receive.

Thanks for your account of American investments; the little money I had is disposed of. M[r] S. Cookson is now in this neighbourhood, but I have not seen him.

I shall write to you again in a few days—

Ever faithfully yours
W[m] Wordsworth

I forgot to mention that the University of Durham the other day by especial convocation conferred upon me the honorary degree of

L.L.D.

Therefore, you will not scruple when a difficult point of Law occurs, to consult me. M[rs] W. and Dora join in Love, my poor Sister is no worse.

[1] The eight-year-old son of Sara and Henry Nelson Coleridge.
[2] Thomas Clarkson's *Strictures on a Life of William Wilberforce* (see L. 1243 above).

1267. W. W. to EDWARD MOXON

MS. *Henry E. Huntington Library.*
K (—). *LY ii. 956.*

[29 July 1838]

My dear Mr Moxon,

In my Letter of yesterday I omitted to request you would send a Copy of the Sonnets to Mr Stephen, and this happened exactly because his claim on my remembrance in this way was so much stronger than any other.[1] Pray let the Book be sent before publication.

What a queer Creature Lord John Russell is! Only think of his coming out against the Copy-right Bill at this late hour.[2] It is like all his other proceedings. Pray tell Mr Rogers with my kindest remembrance (how is he by the bye?) that I wish he could put a little sense into the head of his noble Friend upon this subject. Ever with kindest regards to you and yours

most faithfully
Wm Wordsworth

How are your Children? I have now with [me] a Grandson two years and a half old,[3] who is the delight of his Grandmother and myself and indeed the whole House. Our Daughter will return in ten days at the latest.—[4]

It won't be long till we have a railway as far as Preston, from London; when that is done if alive I shall insist upon a whole Party of you coming down to see us; and be assured that if I retain life health and strength every successive spring I will pass not less than one fortnight in London.

[1] Because he had forwarded W. W.'s proofs for him. See L. 1208 above.

[2] See also L. 1251 above.

[3] John W.'s son William.

[4] Dora W. had been on holiday with Kate Southey at Kent's Bank (see *MW*, p. 214).

623

1268. W. W. to SIR HENRY BUNBURY[1]

Address: Sir Henry Bunbury, Bart, London. Try Warrens Hotel.[2]
Postmark: 1 Aug. 1838. *Stamp*: Kendal Penny Post.
Endorsed: From Willm: Wordsworth July 30th: 1838.
MS. Henry E. Huntington Library.
LY ii. 957.

Rydal Mount Kendal
July 30th [1838]

Sir

On returning home after a month's absence I have had the pleasure of receiving the Correspondence, and Memoir, of Sir Thomas Hanmer, for which you will accept my sincere thanks. My acknowledgements also are due to you for a Letter which reached me some time before I left home; but I deferred making them till the Book you announced, should arrive.

In respect to the Letter which I took the great liberty of addressing to Mr Fox long ago and which you have given to the world I own that I feel some difficulty in expressing myself, in writing, as I could wish, though I should find none in doing so viva voce. It is, no doubt, gratifying to me to be told that the sentiments and opinions there expressed are so much in accordance with your own, and that in your judgement they are of sufficient importance to interest the world at large. Nor am I aware upon reperusing the Letter of which I had but a vague recollection that any reason exists why I should particularly regret that it has seen the light—But I will not conceal from you that I never set any value upon my Letters; and that it has ever

---

[1] General Sir Henry Edward Bunbury, 7th Bart. (1778–1860), of Barton, nr. Bury St. Edmunds, who was Under Secretary for War from 1809 to 1816, and the emissary chosen to convey to Napoleon his sentence of deportation to St. Helena, had represented Suffolk as a Whig, 1830–4, but had since devoted himself to military history and book-collecting. He had recently published the *Correspondence of Sir Thomas Hanmer, Bart., Speaker of the House of Commons, . . . to which are added other relicks of a Gentleman's* [i.e. Bunbury's] *Family* (*R. M. Cat.*, no. 123), and had written to W. W. on 8 June apologizing for including W. W.'s letter to C. J. Fox of 14 Jan. 1801 (*EY*, p. 312). He explained that his first wife was Fox's niece, and that the letter had been given to him by the statesman's widow: 'I have been proud to believe that my sentiments, with regard to the condition of our labouring classes, are in unison with yours.' (*WL MSS.*)

[2] The address is in M. W.'s hand. This last sentence was apparently added by the Post Office, who had difficulty delivering the letter.

been my wish that they should be destroyed as soon as read, and that I have frequently requested this should be done. Allow me further to say that publishing the Letters of a living Person without his consent previously obtained furnishes a precedent the effect of which, as far as it acts, cannot but be to check the free communication of thought between Man and Man. This is surely an evil; nor can I at all approve for this same and many other reasons the practice, now so prevalent, of publishing the Letters of distinguished persons, recently dead, without the consent of their representatives.—

As the openness and sincerity which pervade my Letter to Mr Fox are qualities by which no doubt it was recommended to you, I have had less scruple in speaking upon the present occasion without reserve. I have only to add that promising myself much pleasure from the Contents of your Volume

I have the honor to be
with thanks
sincerely yours
Wm Wordsworth

1269. W. W. to DAVID LAING

Address: D. Laing Esqr, Bookseller, Edinburgh.
Franked: Kendal August one 1838. E. Stanley.[1]
Postmark: 2 Aug. 1838. *Stamp*: Kendal Penny Post.
MS. Edinburgh University Library.
The Wordsworth—Laing Letters (—).

Rydal Mount
Kendal
August 1st [18]38

My dear Sir,

I have just had the pleasure of receiving from you more contributions to my little stock of first and early editions of Poetry, for which I return you sincere thanks. The Essay on Man is valuable though it be only a 2nd Edit:[2] as it proves upon

---

[1] Edward Stanley, M.P. for West Cumberland.
[2] Pope's *Essay on Man* appeared in four parts in 1733—4. The 2nd edition was 1734.

comparison with the Poem as it now stands how much it was altered, and if I may judge from a hasty inspection without reference except in Memory to the Work as we have it now, how much it has been improved.

I set a great value upon the Collins also; poor fellow! he was too much discouraged by the little notice his Poems attracted, to undertake the task of correcting them, which otherwise no doubt he would have done.

The [? gem] of Ossian is very curious. I am indebted to you also for the pleasure of having The rape of the Lock as it first appeared both without and with the machinery.[1] There seems to be a little disingenuousness in the advertisement to the second Poem for so it may be called, where it is said that the 1st was published in consequence of copies being multiplied in MSS before the Machinery was added. I am inclined to think that the machinery was altogether an after thought.

If you could pick up the first Edit. of Falconer's Shipwreck I should like it. The poem as we now have it is spoiled, for all good judges, by the Story of Arion, etc,[2] an after thought.

With many thanks
I remain truly
Your much obliged
Wm Wordsworth

1270. W. W. to H. C. R.

Endorsed: July or Augt 1838. Mr Wordsworth, Copyright bill.
MS. Dr. Williams's Library.
Morley, i. 368.

[early Aug. 1838]

My dear Friend,

I sit down to write a little more at leisure, though I have nothing to say that will interest you.—My ramble in Northumberland and Durham was agreeable in many respects; though if

---

[1] *The Rape of the Lock* appeared in 2 cantos in Lintot's *Miscellany* in 1712, and was enlarged to 5 cantos two years later, when the machinery of the Sylphs was added, as Pope explained in his Dedication to Mrs. Arabella Fermor.

[2] In the third canto.

it had not been an undertaking of duty I would rather have remained at Home.—I am now fixed I hope till late next spring. Heartily do I wish your expedition[1] may prove pleasant—your Party however will prove too numerous for bye plans unless you divide—

I see Brougham has brought into the house the Lords a New Copy-right Bill[2]—what are its merits? I fear it will prove a milk and water business. He talks about the privy-council—what the deuce can those Stupes know about the merit of works of Imagination—are the judges likely to be better than Jeffrey or B— himself, and yet one of them so late as 22—had the folly to write in the E. Review, that my productions were despicable without thought, without feeling taste or judgement etc etc See Edin. Review. No[vr] 1822—[3]

Now for a little business—pray see M[r] Turner about our Carriage[4]—What can be the reason that no Purchaser offers, the season being already so far advanced. It must be eating its head off—Can the gentleman of whom we bought it do nothing for us among his Friends; or would it not be better to take anything

[1] H. C. R. was to set out on a tour of Normandy and Brittany on 28 Aug. in the company of Southey, his son Cuthbert, Humphrey Senhouse, John Kenyon, and his friend Captain Jones, R. N. The party broke up in Paris on 9 Oct., when the Southeys returned to England: H. C. R. remained there with Kenyon until the end of the month (see *HCR* ii. 552–7). For Southey's journal of this tour, see *Journals of a Residence in Portugal 1800–1 and a Visit to France 1838*, ed. Adolfo Cabral, 1961.

[2] Introduced on 27 July, it proposed that arrangements similar to those for patents should be adopted. Brougham's object was to enable authors, or their assignees, by application to the Judicial Committee of the Privy Council, to obtain an extension of time when their terms of copyright were about to expire. But the proposal was bound to lapse with the end of the Parliamentary session, as Talfourd explained in a letter to W. W. on 19 Aug.: 'I believe it to be intended by Lord Brougham for the purpose—1st to secure to himself any credit there may be in legislating upon the question; 2[ndly] To secure to himself a power of deciding on the claims of Authors, as a member of the body he purposes to empower; 3[rdly] To disarm the advocates of the larger measure of their most efficient, though not their best arguments . . . by representing that his proposition would meet them.' And he promised to frustrate Brougham's scheme by reintroducing his own measure on the first day of the next session. (*Cornell MSS.*)

[3] See pt. i, L. 89.

[4] The carriage used during their Continental tour the previous year was still unsold. They had bought it from Mr. Turner of Long Acre.

we can get? But I submit the affair to your judgement altogether.

You would find the breaking up of the miscellaneous sonnets into classes, I think, impra[c]ticable. I thought a good deal about upon[1] your suggestion, but gave up the Idea. for example there are some 5 or 6 of a political character—these could not be incorporated with the political series; which begins in 1802; when Bonaparte was made Consul for life and ends with his over throw. Others are local sonnets, yet too few for a separate class; nor could they be intermixed with Itinerary ones, others religious, yet could not go among the Ec[c]lesiastical, nor are they numerous enough for a separate class—and so on (what an abominable pen! I have tried 50 times to mend it and only made it worse and worse.—

The Chapelets[2] have been received by my friends in France; and given them great pleasure; many thanks for the trouble you took upon the occasion. My son John is now at Havre; gone thither to join his Brother-in-Law Mr Stanley Curwen, being driven from home by the derangement of his nerves, consequent upon the Typhus fever that attacked him last Winter. These are injuries which Clergymen are exposed to, and which the Country never thinks about—he caught the Malady while visiting one of his Parishioners who was suffering under it.— We have had a sad summer for cold and rain, but at present the weather is fine. Pray write before you go abroad—With a thousand good wishes I remain very affectionately your friend

W Wordsworth

Love from all. My poor dear Sister much alone. Our House is enlivened by a charming little fellow my grandson.

---

[1] *Written thus.*
[2] Presents for the Baudouins.

1271. W. W. to THOMAS POWELL

Address: Thoˢ Powell, Leadenhall St.
MS. Wellesley College. Hitherto unpublished.

August 8ᵗʰ —38
Rydal Mount Kendal.

My dear Mr Powell,

We have been for a considerable time made uneasy by your silence apprehending that you may be ill again; and we fear this the more because [the parcel] we despatched several weeks ago, contained your first volume and a copy of my Poems for your Boy. We are not anxious about the parcel, because we apprized you by letter under cover to Mr Chapman[1] that it had been sent, and pointed out by what conveyance. Pray do let me hear from or of you as soon as you are [? well]—

ever most faithfully yours
Wᵐ Wordsworth

1272. W. W. to C. W. JNR.[2]

Address: Christopher Wordsworth Esqʳᵉ [   ] Bishop Stortford.
[*readdressed to*] Harrow, by London.
Postmark: (1) 20 Aug. 1838 (2) [   ] Aug. 1838. *Stamp*: Kendal.
MS. WL. Hitherto unpublished.

[Rydal Mount]
[16 Aug. 1838]

My dear nephew,

Excuse my stepping before Dora (for it is done at her own request) to congratulate you upon the prospect of happiness which your Letter lays before us,[3] and to add the united prayers of us all that through the grace of God it may be realized as far as human events will allow. I did indeed rejoice that such a matter was so far settled, as I had wished ever since you became Master of Harrow that you should be provided with a suitable Companion for life [   ] It made [   ] also to hear

---

[1] The City merchant whom Powell worked for (see L. 1199 above).

[2] This letter, with the note from Dora W. which follows, has been extensively damaged by damp.

[3] C. W. jnr.'s impending marriage to Susanna Frere. See L. 1284 below.

that your Father was so much better [   ] along with you.

One of the Durham papers had a transcript which [   ] into the London ones of the Speech of professor Jenkins,[1] exactly as it was spoken. There is as you observe some thing very awkward in constraining a Man to hear his own praises, before many listeners, in his Mother tongue.—I object to the practice also as lowering the University; nor could I learn any satisfactory reason why the old usage had been abandoned. I cannot conclude without begging [you] to present my affectionate regards, and [   ] wishes to my [   ] niece. Ever my dear Chris. your affectionate Uncle.

Wm Wordsworth

1273. W. W. and M. W. to JOHN KENYON

Postmark: 18 Aug. 1838.
Endorsed: Letter of Wordsworth about Miss Barrett's Poems, and wishing to see her Translation of Eschylus.
MS. Berg Collection, New York Public Library.
K. LY ii. 958.

[*In M. W.'s hand*]

Rydal 17th Aug. [1838]
My dear Friend,
    I have been so much pleased with the power and knowledge displayed in Miss Barret's vol of Poems[2] which you were so

---

[1] The Revd. Henry Jenkyns, D.D. (1796–1878), Fellow of Oriel College, Oxford, 1818-35, Professor of Greek at Durham University from 1835, and Canon of Durham from 1839. He had presented W. W. for his honorary degree on 21 July (see L. 1262 above): '. . . Without that shewiness of style which captivates the multitude he has yet by the mere simplicity of truth, by the depth of his thoughts, and the purity of his feelings, commanded that admiration during his life time, which has been with-held from some other great poets until after their decease.' (*Durham Advertiser*, 27 July 1838.)

[2] Elizabeth Barrett's *The Seraphim, and other poems*, 1838; her translation of the *Prometheus Bound* had appeared in 1833. W. W. had met her two years before (see L. 1027 above) at the house of John Kenyon, who also introduced her to Robert Browning. For W. W.'s view of her poems see *HCR* ii. 562: 'Her poems are too ideal for me. I want flesh and blood; even coarse nature and truth, where there is a want of refinement and beauty, is better than the other extreme.'

kind as to send Mr W. some time ago, that I am desirous to see her translation of Eschylus. C^d you send me a Copy thro' Mr Moxon, and tell me also where it is to be bought, as two of my acquaintances wish to purchase it.

We hear of you thro' that kindest of creatures H. Robinson, but not a word about your coming down, as you had given us leave to hope you might have done—but on the contrary that you are going off with your Brother. A thousand good wishes attend you both and pray remember us to him most kindly.

Ever aff^{ly} yours,
W^m and M. Wordsworth

1274. M. W. to H. C. R.

Address: H. C. Robinson Esqre, 2 Plowdens Buildings, Temple.
Postmark: 21 Aug. 1838. *Stamp*: Cornhill.
Endorsed: Augt 18. 38. Wordsworth.
MS. Dr. Williams's Library.
Morley, i. 370.

Rydal Aug 19th [1838]

My dear Friend

As I hear from Keswick that your departure for the continent is deferred for a few days—I venture to hope that the enclosed may be in time to give John a chance to have the pleasure of receiving it at your hands—or if not, as probably some of your Party at least, may visit Mr Curwen's family[1]—you can send it to him—otherwise pray put it into any Post office on the other side of the water. I have yet another request to make from William—that is, if you should see John, that you will give him from his Father £10—and it will be refunded to you by Mr Cookson[2] (who by the bye, with his wife is now at Ambleside) on your return. This little sum is a present sent in consequence of John's saying, in a letter rec^d yesterday, that he must, on this occasion, defer seeing Paris—for prudential

---

[1] Edward Stanley Curwen, John W.'s brother-in-law (see pt. ii, L. 748) was at this time living near Honfleur. H. C. R. and his fellow travellers visited him there on 8 Sept.

[2] Strickland Cookson.

considerations. Poor fellow, you have heard of his long illness—and that his present visit to the Continent was taken with a view to get rid of the depressing effects of it.

You will be sorry to hear that my Husband is now laid upon the Sofa, suffering from a rheumatic attack which suddenly seized him last Monday—his sufferings for a *short time* were extreme—and now I regret to add, he is very far from being so well as I had hoped he would have been by this time—indeed his general health seems to be affected, and you know he takes very ill with confinement, as most Persons do who have thro life been blessed with good health. He is now listening to the conversation of Proff: Sir Wm Hamilton—who has turned aside on his way to the Grand Meeting at Newcastle[1]—Proff. Buckland[2] passed too, by way of the Lakes, the other day. A little troublesome Grandson is at my elbow making it necessary that I should lay aside my pen—so with our united good wishes that you may all enjoy a pleasant journey, and that you will give us the pleasure of a letter from you in the course of it, believe me ever to be, my dear Sir your affec and obliged friend

M. Wordsworth.

W thanks you for y^r last letter.

1275. W. W. to UNKNOWN CORRESPONDENT

MS. Harvard University Library. Hitherto unpublished.

Ambleside, Wednesday
August 22. 1838.

My dear Sir,

I return Mr Serg^t Talfourd's letter with many thanks for the perusal. If he has any acquaintance with the Judges who usually compose the Judicial committee of the privy Council,

---

[1] The meeting of the British Association. See *Hamilton*, ii. 266—7. On his return from Newcastle, he called again at Rydal Mount on 30 Aug., after visits to Lowther and Hallsteads.

[2] See pt. ii, L. 710. Other visitors around this time included Whewell and Professor James MacCullagh (d. 1847), one of Hamilton's Dublin colleagues (*RMVB*).

Bosanquet,[1] Parke,[2] Erskine[3] etc I think he can have no difficulty in obtaining from them an expression of opinion unfavorable to Lord Brougham's measure,[4] on the ground that the proper duty of Judges is to declare the law of the land—not to decide on the merits of authors. I know nothing of Lord Brougham's bill but I concluded he had not attempted to lay down any rules for the guidance of the Judicial Committee in determining on the claim of an author's family to the retension of the privilege of copyright. Is the question to be decided with regard to the circumstances of the author's family, or to the talent displayed in the work, or the time devoted to it, or the probable or ascertained usefulness of the work?

I hope you approve of the History proposed to be published by the Serg[t]. I think the subject requires to be more generally understood and that the history will materially assist this object.

I did not see your servant when he called but understand he will call again when I hope to hear from him that you are . . .

[*cetera desunt*]

1276. W. W. to JAMES MARSHALL[5]

Address: James Marshall Esq., Coniston Water-head.
Postmark: 11 Oct. 1838. *Stamp*:. Kendal Penny Post.
MS. Cornell.[6]
LY ii. 958.

Rydal Mount
Thursday [11 Oct. 1838]

My dear Sir,

I am sorry I cannot have the pleasure of seeing you at Coniston to morrow, as I had hoped. My old Horse I find on my

[1] Sir John Bernard Bosanquet (1773–1847), a Judge from 1830, and a Privy Councillor from 1833.

[2] Sir James Parke, 1st Baron Wensleydale (1782–1868), Fellow of Trinity College, Cambridge (1804), a Judge (1828), and a Privy Councillor (1833). He visited W. W. in 1844 (*RMVB*).

[3] Thomas, 2nd Baron Erskine (1788–1864), son of the Lord Chancellor, and the chief judge in bankruptcy, 1831–42.

[4] His new Copyright Bill. See L. 1270 above.

[5] Third son of John Marshall of Hallsteads.

[6] Photostat of original in the Preussischen Staatsbibliothek, destroyed during the Second World War.

return has to go to Patterdale on Saturday, if a pair of broken knees will permit him, and he is quite unequal to two successive days travelling. Besides, the fine weather seems quite gone. I am truly, sorry[1] for this disappointment—My eyes are far from well but no worse, I think, for my late excursion.[2] ever faithfully you[rs]

Wm Wordsworth

1277. W. W. to THOMAS NOON TALFOURD

Address: Mr Sergeant Talfourd MP, Russel Square, London.
Postmark: (1) 25 Oct. 1838 (2) 27 Oct. 1838. *Stamp*: Kendal Penny Post.
MS. Harvard University Library. Hitherto unpublished.

[*In M. W.'s hand*]

Rydal Mt Octr 25th [1838]

My dear Sergeant Talfourd,

As we had almost given up our hopes of seeing you here on y^r return from Scotland your letter dated London, was much more welcome than it would otherwise have been—and I shall look forward, tho' not with as much confidence as I could wish, to our meeting in London. The unlucky accident which has interfered so much with Mrs T'^s liberty of enjoyment, and of course cast a damp upon your own pleasure, is so common among Persons not accustomed to mountainous Countries, that I have long made a point of exhorting all my friends, who are new to this Country, to take especial care that they are not disabled in the same way. But I am taking for granted the cause of this misfortune, the effects of which I wish may speedily disappear altogether.

I have been discouraged from writing to you as I had hoped to do, by a Succession of disabilities; and by many anxieties. No sooner had I got the better of my attack of Rheumatism, than I

---

[1] *Written* sorrow.

[2] On 8 Oct., W. W., Dora W., John Wordsworth (son of C. W.), and the Misses Ricketts, the four daughters of a friend of I. F.'s (see *MW*, p. 218), had set out on a three-day excursion to the Duddon Valley. Ellen Ricketts's recollections of the tour (*St. John's College, Cambridge, MSS.*) are printed in the Appendix.

was siezed with an inflammation in one of my eyes—perhaps caused by too sudden a recurrance to my ordinary diet and habits, after living for a month very sparely, and not venturing beyond our own grounds. I am now much recovered, tho' still unable to read or write—and what is worse, not thinking myself justified in engaging my mind to any close employment—So that my days, tho' not without much enjoyment, pass most unprofitably.

I have spoken, and with truth of enjoyment, tho' we have had, and still have much anxiety to undergo. My elder Son has been obliged to place himself under the care of D[r] Jephson[1] at Leamington on account of a disease in the throat, of that kind which is so common to Clergymen; and a general disorder in the System left by the Typhus fever with which he was siezed last Winter. My daughter also has been very unwell, and is at present too weak to expose herself out of doors. These particulars will, I know cause you no little concern. I have mentioned them however mainly, as shewing too much reason for my not being disposed to communicate readily with my friends.

As to acting or not, upon your first thought of a previous publication upon the Copy-right question, I admit the general force of the objections made by those in Scotland whose opinions you have had—but really this case seems to make an exception, if I may trust my own experience for I have never heard an argument against the extension, which appears to me of any force. I am nevertheless of opinion that there is no demand for a previous publication, in case, but *only* in case, of your Suggestion of a joint petition from the Body of Authors or petitions severally presented, can be acted upon with vigour.[2] This would undoubtedly be of very great weight, and an argument to which no answer could be made: for it is absurd to

---

[1] Henry Jephson, M.D. (1798–1878), had by this period built up a lucrative practice at Leamington, attracting patients from all over Europe.

[2] W. W.'s sentence is a little confused. Talfourd had written on 22 Oct. that he intended to reintroduce his Copyright measure as soon as the new session opened, and that petitions should be prepared for the Second Reading. 'We might certainly thus present a formidable array of the greatest names which our age has produced—and if each Author in petitioning would state his own individual case the force of all combined would be the greater.' He suggested that petitioners should not be confined to men of letters, but should include theologians, scientists, and publishers as well. (*Cornell MSS.*)

say, that men are not to be listened to, because they are pleading in behalf of their real, or supposed interests.

Since I rec^d. your former letter, I have conversed little upon the subject, but when Ld Northampton was here,[1] on his return from the Newcastle meeting; it was introduced, and he appeared to me not so favorable to the measure as I expected, but the only argument he advanced against it, was that the privilege would stand in the way of portions being selected from the less exceptionable Works of Authors (he instanced Ld Byron) whose writings in a body might be objectionable— Many, said he, might not object to Childe Harold, who would not admit Don Juan into their houses. By the bye I should say, if a cautious Parent or Teacher could tolerate the whole of Ch: Harold it would be scarcely worth while to make a Scruple about Don Juan. To Ld N'ˢ observation I made the obvious answers—that the holders of the Copy-right, be they who they might, would listen to any applications made by a considerable portion of the public, or even by influential Individuals, and would permit separately the Supposed unexceptionable part of an Author's writings, both for their own interest and credit's Sake. It is now I suppose actually an easy thing to procure most of Ld B'ˢ writings in separate forms—as most of Mr Southey's (and every other Author of distinction) may be had in the same way.

I must own I am deeply interested in the Success of your undertaking, far less from any personal benefit for myself, or my friends living or dead or their families—than from its bearing upon the justice of the legislature, and from a strong persuasion, which I cannot but entertain, that the establishment of justice would here, as in all other points carry along with it its own expediency. The apprehensions of evil would be proved to have been vain, and the character of the literature of the Country would I trust be considerably improved. Authors as a Class could not but be in some degree put upon exertions that would raise them in public estimation—And say what you will, the possession of Property tends to make any body of men more respectable, however high may be their claims to respect upon other considerations. And as to the real independent Authorship of the Country, I mean that in which men act from higher

---

[1] The Marquess of Northampton (see L. 1017 above) had called at Rydal Mount on 30 Aug. (*RMVB*).

motives than instant impressions, and immediate gains,—is it not in a deplorable State? And ought not something [   ]¹ from views of this kind that I am chiefly anxious for the Success of a measure which whatever be the issue can never be thought of hereafter by the just, the right-minded, the clear-sighted, and those properly endued with natural affection, without respectful admiration of your labors, and with gratitude flowing freely, as some slight reward for your deserts. As to natural [   ]²

Mrs W. will be obliged to Mr Talfourd to for[ward] the enclosed at his convenience.

1278. W. W. to C. W. JNR.

Address: The Revᵈ Dʳ Wordsworth, Harrow.
Franked: Whitehaven November Six 1838 Lonsdale.
Postmark: 8 Nov. 1838. *Stamp*: Whitehaven.
MS. British Library. Hitherto unpublished.

Whitehaven Novᵇʳ 6th [1838]

My dear Nephew,

I am now on a visit to Lord Lonsdale at this place, and being able to procure a Frank, I have taken up the pen to express a hope that your expectation expressed through Mrs Hoare's Letter that most of your books would be saved has been fulfilled. I am also anxious to learn that this disaster ³ will not have prevented your marriage taking place at the time previously fixed, and that we may look forward to seeing you with your Bride at Christmas. Pray let me know whether your furniture was insured to nearly the amount of its pecuniary value.

Your Brother John would tell you all about us. Dora has been very poorly and much weakened with a severe cold, but we trust she is recovering her strength though slowly. Your poor Aunt goes on much in the same way, neither better nor worse, except that upon the whole I think her mind is somewhat more like what it used to be.

¹ *Several lines cut away.*

² *Rest of sentence and signature cut away.*

³ The fire at Harrow on 22 Oct. (see *Christopher Wordsworth, Bishop of Lincoln*, pp. 93—5).

There will be a Letter at Rydal to day giving an account of your Cousin John's health,[1] I hope earnestly a more favourable one than the last, which however did speak of some improvement.

I must now conclude on account of my eyes which have troubled me sadly for some time past, indeed have prevented my writing or reading all together.

Believe me my dear Chris: Your affectionate Uncle and faithful friend

Wm Wordsworth—

Lord Lonsdale is wonderfully well to all appearance. When you come bring your 2nd Edit. of *Athens*[2] and also Charles's [? Memorabilia][3] of Horace, I have never seen it—

I forgot to mention that the other day I had a Letter from a Committee of the University of Glasgow proposing to put me in nomination as a Candidate for the Lord Rectorship.[4] I declined.

1279. W. W. to W. W. JNR.

Address: Wm Wordsworth Esqr, Carlisle.
Franked: Whitehaven November six 1838 Lonsdale.
Postmark: 6 Nov. 1838. *Stamp*: Whitehaven.
MS. Cornell. Hitherto unpublished.

6th Nov^{br} [1838]

My dear Wm,

I shall be happy to take the Horse, the price being so much below *that* first named.

I have delivered your message to Lady F. B.[5]—and shall do so to Lord Lonsdale, who is surprizingly well.

I came hither last Tuesday, and think of returning tomorrow Wednesday.—

[1] R. W.'s son, 'Keswick John', had been seriously ill the previous month (see *MW*, p. 218).

[2] C. W. jnr.'s *Athens and Attica* had gone into a second edition in 1837.

[3] *Notes on the Life of Horace*, compiled for use at Winchester.

[4] The retiring Rector was Sir Robert Peel. In the ensuing contest Sir J. R. G. Graham was elected against Augustus Frederick, Duke of Sussex (1773–1843), President of the Royal Society. W. W. was nominated for the office again in 1846.

[5] Lady Frederick Bentinck.

How are we to get the Horse sent, and where can we house him? As we shall only want him to make calls in the neighbourhood, our old one might do for a while, so that you need not be perhaps in any great hurry about sending or bringing him over.

Be so kind as to get the harness made, as you talked of, at Dumfries.

My dear Wm ever your affectionate Father

W Wordsworth

My eyes are a good deal better.

1280. W. W. to MRS. JOHN THELWALL[1]

Adress: Mrs Thelwall.
MS. Berg Collection, New York Public Library.
K (—). *LY ii. 959* (—).

[*In M. W.'s hand*]

Rydal Mount Nov[r] 16 [1838]

Madam,

It would have given me great pleasure if my reply to your letter would in any way have fulfilled the expectations which you entertain. Circumstances were not favorable to much intercourse between your late Husband and myself: I became acquainted with him during a visit which he made to Mr Coleridge, who was then residing at Nether-Stowey;[2] and I

---

[1] John Thelwall's second wife, formerly Cecil Boyle (d. 1863), had published the first volume of the *Life* of her husband the previous year, and had written to W. W. on 12 Nov. seeking material for a projected second volume (which never in fact appeared). 'In the 2nd vol: . . . I have to speak of my husband's sojourn in what he always in after time, termed "his exile", that is to say, the interregnum between his political and scientific careers, from 1796–1801. . . . Of course I do not wish to have any political reference to the acquaintance which then subsisted between you; but merely of that communion of kindred minds, which poetry and literature linked in the bonds of Friendship.' (*WL MSS.*)

[2] Thelwall spent ten days between Nether Stowey and Alfoxden at the end of July 1797. See Mrs. Henry Sandford, *Thomas Poole and His Friends*, 2 vols., 1888, i. 232–3, and Griggs, i. 339.

a little pleased with the natural eloquence of his
̷tion, and his enthusiastic attachment to Poetry. He was
̷ very sensible to the beauty of Rural Nature; one
̷e of this in particular I remember. Having led him and
̷ to a favorite Spot, near the house in the grounds of
A̷ ̷̷den—(where I then lived, in the neighbourhood of
Nether Stowey) a little Hollow in a wood down which the
brook ran making a Waterfall, finely overarched with trees,—
Mr C. observed that it was a place to soften one's remembrances
of the strife and turmoil of the world—'Nay' said Mr Thilwall
'to make one forget the world altogether.' Your impression is
correct that I, in company with my Sister and Mr Coleridge,
visited him at his pleasant abode on the banks of the Wye.[1] Mr
Southey was not of the party, as you suppose.

After the year 1798 I do not recollect having had any
intercourse with Mr Thelwall, till he called upon me at
Grasmere on his way to Edinburgh, whither he was going to
give Lectures upon Elocution. This must have been some time
between 1801 and 1807,[2] and I once called upon *him* in London.
After that time I think I never saw him, and I am not aware of
there ever having been any communication between us by
letter: if there was, it must have been upon some trivial occasion,
or I scarcely should have forgotten it. You will see therefore,
that it is not in my power to add any thing to your intended
publication. Had Mr Coleridge been living, he probably could
have thrown light upon that portion of your Husband's life, of
which you have no personal knowledge. All I can say is, that I
retained towards Mr T. a very friendly feeling, grounded upon
what I had seen of him, and particularly upon a vivid
recollection of some pleasant days which I passed in his
company—during the visit to him above mentioned, when
with the assistance of his Brother-in-law, and the wife to whom
he was first united,[3] and who was a truly aimiable woman, he
lived as a Farmer (not I believe a very successful one) in South
Wales.

[1] In early Aug. 1798. See *EY*, pp. 222, 232. In her letter Mrs. Thewall
recalled that, 'Thelwall often spoke of the friendly intercourse, which at one
time subsisted between you with much pleasure: and always spoke of you with
great admiration and friendship.'

[2] It was in Nov. 1803. See *EY*, p. 431.

[3] Susan Vellum (d. 1816) of Rutland, whom Thelwall had married in
1791: 'her husband's good angel', according to H. C. R. (Sadler, ii. 42).

Whether Mr Thelwall wrote much Poetry, or not, I am ignorant; but I possess a small printed volume of his,[1] containing specimens of an Epic Poem and several miscellaneous Pieces, in some of which he laments the death of a Daughter in strains that shew how grievously he suffered by that event,—Mr Coleridge and I were of opinion that the modulations of his blank verse were superior to those of most writers in that metre. I have lent the volume to a distant friend or I would have recurred to it upon this occasion with very little fear of finding my opinion changed upon this point.

If you are in correspondence with the Rev.d Sidney Thelwall,[2] whom I have occasionally had the pleasure of meeting, pray present my Kind regards to him.

My daughter returns thanks to Mrs Gaskell[3] for her kind remembrance of her, and allow me, thro' you, to acknowledge my sense of that Lady's obliging invitation to myself and family.—

With best wishes I remain, Madam

Sincerely yours,

[*signed*] W.m Wordsworth

---

[1] *Poems Chiefly Written in Retirement.* See *EY*, pp. 349, 431; *MY* ii. 361.

[2] Thelwall's eldest son, the Revd. Algernon Sydney Thelwall (1795–1863), had graduated at Trinity College, Cambridge, in 1818, and was curate of Blackford, Somerset (1828), minister of Bedford Chapel, Bloomsbury (1842–3), curate of St. Matthew's, Pell Street (1848–50), and a lecturer on elocution at King's College, London, from 1850. He published religious tracts and works on elocution, and a 'scriptural refutation' of Edward Irving (1834).

[3] See L. 1174 above.

1281. W. W. to H. C. R.

Address: 2ᵈ post. H. C. Robinson Esqʳᵉ, 2 Plowdens Buildings, London.
Postmark: 6 Dec. 1838.
Endorsed: Decʳ 1838. Wordsworth. Clarksons Strictures. Southeys Marriage
   intended.
MS. Dr. Williams's Library.
K (—). *Morley, i. 372.*

[*In M. W.'s hand*]

[*c.* 5 Dec. 1838]

My dear Friend

It was very good in you to write so long a letter from abroad—we found it not a little interesting, and it was the more so to me, because even with those parts of your tour which I had not seen I was previously pretty well acquainted by drawings, prints, books and conversation. You hint at the possibility of my taking some such a Tour, but I have no inclination that way; my *wishes* even, are bounded to getting to Chalons-sur-Soane and floating down that river to Lyons, and downward by the Rhone, to take the Steam boat from Marseilles to Naples; and thus complete our tour in Italy, so unfortunately cut short. If money were no object, and circumstances allowed, I would endeavour to do this; tho' I could not offer myself as a Companion to any one so vigorous and animated as you are. Rogers[1] is a wonderful Man—his life is worthy of being written with care, and *copiously*—but I fear so valuable a work as that would be, will never be produced—

Nothing has happened that gave me so much pleasure, joy I might say, as Mʳ Clarkson's triumph over his enemies—to which you, my good friend, have not a little contributed. Your part of the pamphlet,[2] exclusive of the extracts from the minutes which are so important, does you in every respect much honour. Mʳ Clarkson's performance, for a man of his years and infirmities, is scarcely less than wonderful; and the candour with which he admits the imperfections and deficiencies of his book, must endear him still more to his friends, and to the sound-hearted portion of the community who have taken an interest in the great cause.

[1] Samuel Rogers had been staying in Paris when H. C. R. was there in October.

[2] Clarkson's *Strictures on a Life of William Wilberforce* (see L. 1243 above), to which H. C. R. had contributed.

We had learnt the intended marriage of Southey[1] from his daughters, who were upon a visit to Miss Fenwick at Ambleside,[2] when their Father announced his intentions to them. It was naturally a great shock to them both—and nothing could have been more fortunate than that the tidings reached them when they were here; as we all contributed greatly to reconcile them to the step, much sooner and with less pain, than they could have effected a thing so difficult, of themselves. For our parts, we were all of one mind, that M[r] S. has acted wisely, provided he has taken the pains dispassionately to ascertain as far as he could, whether the state of Miss Bowles' health is such as to give him just ground to hope that he will find in her a help-mate, and a comforter, rather than a source of perpetual anxiety. Sorry am I to say, that from what I know, I cannot get rid of the fear that for this cause, things may not turn out satisfactorily—to his friends at least. M[r] Kenyon's information to you, that *both* the girls are about to be married is not correct—it is true of Bertha,[3] but not of Kate—tho' so amiable a Person is not likely long to remain single.

As to my employments, I have from my unfortunate attacks, in succession, been wholly without any thing of the kind—till within this last fortnight, when my eye, tho' still alas weak, was so far improved as to authorize my putting my brain to some little work—Accordingly timid as I was I undertook to write a few Sonnets,[4] upon taking leave of Italy—these gave rise to some more; and the whole amount to 9 which I shall read to you

---

[1] On his return from France in October, Southey had gone immediately to visit Caroline Bowles (see L. 1072 above) at Buckland, nr. Lymington, and it was from there on 15 Oct. that he wrote to his family of his impending marriage to her. See Curry, ii. 477–80. The wedding took place in June of the following year. The progress of their friendship, from the first exchange of letters in 1818, is chronicled in *The Correspondence of Robert Southey with Caroline Bowles*, ed. Edward Dowden, 1881.

[2] I. F. had taken the Lutwidges' cottage at Ambleside for a year in order to be near the Wordsworths and to help reconcile them to the proposed marriage of their daughter with E. Q.

[3] The following year Bertha Southey married Herbert Hill, jnr. (1810–92), second son of Southey's maternal uncle (see pt. i, L. 302), Fellow of New College, Oxford, 1829–39: at this time an assistant master at Rugby, and headmaster of the King's School, Warwick, 1842–76: editor of Southey's posthumous 'New-England Tale', *Oliver Newman* (1845).

[4] W. W. was now adding to what became the *Memorials of a Tour in Italy, 1837*, published in *Poems, Chiefly of Early and Late Years*, 1842.

when you come, as you kindly promised before you went away, that you would do, soon after your return. If however you prefer it, the 4 upon Italy shall be sent you, upon the one condition that you do not read them to *verse-writers*. We are all in spite of ourselves a parcel of thieves. I had a droll instance of it this morning—for while Mary was writing down for me one of these Sonnets, on coming to a certain line, she cried out somewhat uncourteously 'that's a plagiarism'—from whom? 'from yourself' was the answer. I believe she is right tho' she could not point out the passage, neither can I.

Pray remember me aff^{ly} to Sergeant Talfourd—I fear he will have a hard battle to fight for us in Feb^{ry} and it will be still proved that the Legislature of Britain prefer Stealing to buying—for themselves and the People.

Say all that is kind from me to Kenyon Moxon and other enquiring friends—Tell us something about dear Mary Lamb—and give her our love if she is in a state to receive it.

Have you heard that a proposal was made to me from a Committee in the University of Glasgow—to consent to become a Candidate for the Lord Rectorship[1] on a late occasion, which I declined—I think you must be aware that the University of Durham conferred upon [me] the Degree of DC.L—last summer—it was the first time that the honor had been received there by anyone in Person. These things are not worth adverting to, but as signs that imaginative Literature notwithstanding the homage now paid to Science is not wholly without esteem. But it is time to release my Wife, this being the second long letter she has written for me this mor^g

With best love from all ever faithfully
Yours
[*signed*] Wm Wordsworth

I have said nothing about public affairs—I am sick of them—for we are deluged with newspapers—tho' we do not pay for one.—Ld Durham[2] as I have had recent proof from a private source is a miserably weak Man.

[1] See L. 1278 above.

[2] John George Lambton, Ist Earl of Durham (1792–1840), a liberal of advanced views, had been sent out as Governor General to settle the Canadian question, following the rebellion earlier in the year (see L. 1203 above). His high-handed actions caused dismay in Britain, and he resigned and returned home in November. But his *Report on the Affairs of British North America*, published in Jan. 1839, had a decisive effect on British policy thereafter.

1282. W. W. to ANDREW FLEMING HUDLESTON[1]

Address: A. Huddlestone Esq, Hutton John, Penrith [*readdressed to*] Nether Hall. [*readdressed to*] Ponsynby Hall.
Postmark: 12 Dec. 1838.
Stamp: (1)Ambleside Penny Post (2) Kendal (3) Nether Hall Penny Post.
MS. Hudleston family archives. Hitherto unpublished.

Rydal Mount
Dec[r] 11th [1838]

My dear Sir,

When you were here I engaged to communicate with my nephew the Master of Harrow upon the subject of our Conversation but I thought it best to defer doing so, till he should come to Rydal Mount, as he had promised to do this Christmas holidays. In a letter received from him since I saw you he still expresses a hope of being able to visit us—but lest he should be prevented, I think it right, before I do any thing else to suggest to you, the advantage which probably would arise out of your speaking to Mr Crackanthorpe[2] upon the subject. Many years ago[3] having a desire to place my Younger Son in some foundation School, I received more information from Mr C. upon that question, than from any other Person. My interest was great, and in very high quarters, but I did not succeed, and for this reason—the Votes of all the Governors to whom we applied were preengaged, some years deep: and I much fear you will find this obstacle very difficult to get over, wherever you wish the Party to be placed. Even things of an inferior kind are for the same reason very difficult to procure as Mrs W is experiencing, in respect to a Relative of her own.[4] I am the more encouraged to mention Mr Crackanthorpe as a

---

[1] Andrew Fleming Hudleston (1796–1861), of Hutton John, nr. Penrith, was educated at Haileybury, and spent many years in the Indian Civil Service at Madras. He was High Sheriff of Cumberland, 1849, and in 1860 inherited the Fleming estates, including Rydal, through his mother, eldest daughter of Sir William Fleming, 3rd Bart.

[2] William Crackanthorpe, W. W.'s cousin. He had called on W. W. the previous August (*RMVB*).

[3] In 1821.

[4] One of the two sons of M. W.'s brother George Hutchinson (see *MW*, p. 217).

Cousin of his and mine[1] died a few years ago leaving several Sons uneducated—these have all been placed in different foundation Schools—in consequence no doubt of the exertion of Friends, among whom, and not the least efficient was Mr Crackanthorpe who was deeply interested in the welfare of the widow and her family. This circumstance (being much more recent than when enquiries were made for my own Son) affords me reason to think that Mr C. must be better able to give you information how to proceed, in this matter, than I am, or I apprehend my Nephew. But do not understand from this, that *I* shall not make every enquiry according to my engagement. Yet after all it would not surprize me, unless the Boy could wait some time, a measure much to be deprecated on many accounts, if you should be disappointed as to placing him on any foundation: in which case it would be still open to you to fix him in some public School, where at no very great expence he might be well instructed, at a distance from home—and upon terms that might prevent his having intercourse, except rarely and for a short time, with those connections which are so seriously objectionable.

I shall be glad to hear from you farther on the subject—if any thing arises out of your conversation with Mr C. or indeed under any circumstances.

I remain my dear S, faithfully
yours
Wm Wordsworth

1283. W. W. to EDWARD MOXON

MS. Henry E. Huntington Library.
Mem. (—). *K* (—). *LY ii. 960.*

[In M. W.'s hand]

Rydal Mount Decr 11th. [1838]

Dear Mr Moxon,

Very many thanks for your valuable present of Shakespeare and Jonson, they are handsome books and I hope will repay you.

---

[1] Probably Christopher (see also L. 1185 above), eldest son of Dr. William Cookson, who married Jane (d. 1871), daughter of John Strother Ancrum, and left behind six sons and a daughter on his death in 1834.

You must have had a very pleasant tour—all the cities and places you speak of as having seen in the North of Italy, were included in my late tour with Mr Robinson. You mention Lago di Garda; I hope you went to the head of it—if not, you missed some of the most striking Scenery to be found any where among the Alps. I wish you may be able to realize your plan of going to Rome next summer. I will talk with you about it when I come to Town in Spring—as Mrs W. and I mean to do, if all be well with us, and around us.

As to the Ed: in one Volume, I wait for your proposals.[1] In the mean while I have to observe upon the Specimen sent me of the type etc, I think so little is gained by having the lines wider apart, that I would chuse the 36 sheets in preference to the 40, but on account of the overflowing lines, I could myself have no pleasure in looking at either the one page or the other. In the American Ed:,[2] which you saw, not a single 10-syllable verse overflows, whereas in the pages sent me as specimens there are nine in one and 11 in the other; which both disfigures the book very much, and occupies so much space. The enclosed paper gives the length and width of the American page, within the marginal line, being within a hair-breadth *short*. Could not the book be printed on paper sufficiently wide to allow of a ten-syllable verse being uniformly included in one line, as something very considerable would be saved in space. This would lessen the cost which wider paper would require. I repeat that I have an insurmountable aversion to overflowing lines, except where they cannot be avoided. On this subject however, as a mere suggestion for Printers, I would ask, whether the overflowing word would not be better placed, as formerly, near the end of the verse it belongs to, than so near the beginning of that line and of the next.

I am in hopes that my nephew Mr John Wordsworth of Cambridge will correct the proofs for me,—he promised to do so, when he was here a few weeks ago, but I grieve to say he has

[1] On 19 Dec. Moxon sent his proposals for a stereotyped edition in one volume to be sold at £1. He offered £332 in instalments for the first printing of 2,000 copies, and £250 for every further 1,000 copies. Writing again on 11 Jan. 1839, he admitted that the proposed volume would be bound to reduce sales of the six-volume edition, and that is presumably why the project lapsed. (*WL MSS.*)

[2] Henry Reed's Philadelphia edition of 1837 was printed in double column. A 2nd edition followed in 1839

been very unwell since, and may not be equal to the task; but I shall write to him on the Subject—he is the most accurate Man I know, and if a revise of each sheet could be sent to him the Ed: would be *immaculate*. Unless he can undertake this office, such has been the State of my eyes that I dare not venture upon it, and I should little like trusting to another, as I could scarcely call upon Mr Carter so soon again—besides if it came *here*, it could not but take up time of mine which I can not spare.

If Sergeant Talfourd's bill should not pass I know not what will come of poor Authors and their Works. The American example will be followed here to the letter, as far as it can; and what do you as a Publisher say to an Ed: of *the whole* of my Poems being now sold in America for 1 fr., 25 cents, or something less than 13*d* of our money? This is a fact, as I learned the other day by a letter from that country. And in India, as I have just learned from a like authority, a Calcutta Ed: is sold for 6 rupees—so that we are cut off from the Indian market, unless the International Copyright touches that quarter. The respectable Publishers there are anxious about a remedy for this evil.

Excuse this long letter, and believe me, with Mrs W's. and Dora's kind regards to y[r] self, Mrs M. and your Sister, to be very faithfully y[rs]

[*signed*] Wm Wordsworth

Has Mrs M. received a couple of Hares forwarded some weeks ago?

1284. W. W. to C. W. JNR.

Address: The Rev[d] C. Wordsworth, D.D., Harrow, London.
Postmark: (1) 18 Dec. 1838 (2) 19 Dec. 1838.
Stamp: Ambleside Penny Post.
MS. British Library. Hitherto unpublished.

[*In M. W.'s hand*]

Dec[r] 18th [1838]

My dear Nephew,
    Thro' the kind attention of more than one friend who sent us newspapers we were duly informed of your marriage[1] and two

---

[1] C. W. jnr. had married Susanna Frere at Thorley, nr. Bishops Stortford, on 6 Dec. The bride, C. W. confided to Dr. Walton on 7 Dec., was 'a very

days ago we had the pleasure of receiving from yourself and your Bride, the good old-fashioned wedding token—with which our little Grandson—my namesake—was *especially* gratified. We should have written immediately upon hearing of the event, to offer our hearty congratulations but we were quite at a loss as to the direction of your movements—and even now, fearing this letter may have to dance after you, with a great expense of postage, we write somewhat reluctantly for we know that you would not doubt of our taking the liveliest interest in your happiness, which, if our good wishes could promote it, would be great indeed. Give our very kind love to our Niece, and say how much we wish to see her—and the sooner, and oftener the better.

Your last letter did not wholly take away our hope of seeing you this Christmas but it somewhat diminished it, to our regret: the rail-way offer[s] such facility for travelling, that our excellent Neighbour Miss Fenwick[1] is looking for friends of hers'—a Mr and Mrs Elliott from Town, to pass with her merely a few days, and back again. So that we will not give up an expectation that has been so grateful to us.

We were truly glad to hear that the fire had dealt so mercifully with your books, when I enquired after them I did not mention your papers because these things being easily removeable I took for granted they would be saved, and as you say nothing to the contrary, I trust it is so.

It grieved me much to hear of John's illness. When with us he was troubled with severe head-aches, not unfrequently—but we did not learn that they were worse than ordinary, so that we had no apprehension of so serious an attack as he has since had. If you have an opportunity give our love to him, and say how glad we should be to hear from himself of his amended health. Say also to him that I have been reminded by a letter from Moxon, of his most kind and valuable offer to superintend the correction of the Press in the next new Edition of my Poems—which M. tells me he wishes to set about speedily, as the 3,000 of the last are reduced to 450 Copies. The proposed new one is to be in

amiable and excellent person; not eminently handsome, nor of any great fortune; but very much beloved by her Family, and the Friends of her own sex; and likely I verily believe, to make a most excellent wife.' (*WL MSS.*). She was sister of C. W. jnr.'s friend John Frere (see pt. i, L. 376) and niece of John Hookham Frere, the translator of Aristophanes (see also pt. ii, L. 622).

[1] I. F. was spending the winter in Ambleside. See L. 1281 above.

double Column. What do you think of the whole of my Works being sold in America for 1 fr-25 cents? and in India, for 6 rupees—by the bye I am abused in the Journals of Delhi.[1] This, the greatest honor I have yet received. I forgot to thank you for your Miltonic speech in defence of the extention of Copy-right. I was not aware of its being yours' till John told me—it is eloquently and feelingly written, the latter part especially. Dora has suffered much lately from inflammatory tooth-ache—the rest of us are as usual—and unite in every kind wish—and believe me to be your affectionate

[signed] W. W.

Pray say how are Charles and his Wife—of her health we heard rather an alarming account. Give our love to them. I hope it is needless to say how glad we should be to see them at any time! Your father I trust continues well—

1285. W. W. to H. C. R.

Endorsed: 1838. Wordsworth.
MS. Dr. Williams's Library.
Morley, i. 375.

[*In Dora W.'s hand*]

Rydal Mount
Saturday Night ½ past 6—
Decr 22^d [1838]

My dear Friend,

I received y^r letter about a ¼ of an hour since And Mrs W. has just been down the hill to enquire about lodgings the rooms you occupied at Agnes' are now filled by our Curate Mr Fleming but you can have in the adjoining house a couple of apartments much more pleasantly situated and tho' no bargain was absolutely concluded as to price M^{rs} W came away with the impression upon her mind that you w^d not have to pay more than[2] 12/ or 14/ a week—exclusive of fire you not requiring more attendance then you did at Agnes'—

We shall be delighted to see you—there is a coach from Kendal Monday—Wednesday and Friday w^h passes the foot of our hill about ½ past 10 A.M. on the intermediate days you may

---

[1] See L. 1297 below.   [2] *Written* that.

have a gig or a car from Kendal for w^h I am never charged more than 9^d a mile—If you have time without causing any delay as to y^r setting off to send y^r servant to Mr Moxon's to ask if there is any letter or parcel for us so much the better—Dr Arnold and all his family arrived at Fox How last night—

Ever most aff^{ly} yours
William Wordsworth
read
Wm Wordsworth
[*signed by W. W.*]

We regret that you cant be here by Xmas day but you will be in time for our Grand sons birthday w^h we fear will be no festival for you as all the Family are engaged to dine with him at his hour *one* o'clock on that day—our hour is 5.

1286. W. W. to JOHN GIBSON LOCKHART

Address: J. G. Lockhart Esqre, 24 Sussex Place, Regents Park.
Postmark: 28 Dec. 1838. *Stamp*: Charles St. West^r.
MS. National Library of Scotland.
LY ii. 961.

[*In M. W.'s hand*]

Rydal Mount, Decr 24th [1838]

My dear Sir,

I am sorry that it did not suit you to give us a call on your return from Scotland, where I have no doubt you must have passed your time much more agreeably than one can well do in London, in the summer season at least. Your Brother was I hope well; my daughter and I remember with much pleasure the couple of days we passed under his roof.[1]

The occasion of my writing to you at present will appear if you will be so kind as take the trouble to read the enclosed. I know nothing of the young Man, the Author of the Work, upon which the letter turns—and I have only to say that the letter was forwarded to me, by a near Relative of Mrs Wordsworth with a request that if I could take the liberty to mention the subject to you I would do so. My reply was, that I could certainly venture to send the letter, but I would not

---

[1] During the Scottish tour in the autumn of 1831.

undertake anything more; feeling that I could not even guess how far it would suit you as Editor of the Qu^{rly} Review to notice the work either direct or indirect.

Mrs W. and my Daughter unite with me in kind regards and best wishes for yourself and your Children, who we earnestly hope are well—

believe me my dear Sir,
faithfully yours
[*signed*] Wm Wordsworth

1287. W. W. to SARAH COLES STEVENSON [1]

MS. Library of Congress. Hitherto unpublished.

Rydal Mount
24 Dec^{br} 1838

There are to whom the garden, grove and field,
Perpetual lessons of forbearance yield;
Who would not lightly violate the grace
The lowliest Flower professes in its place;
Nor shorten the sweet life, too fugitive,
Which nothing less than infinite Power could give. [2]

Wm Wordsworth

Mr Wordsworth hopes that the Autograph is not sent too late for Mrs Stephenson's purpose.—

1288. M. W. to JANE MARSHALL

Address: Mrs Marshall, Headingly, near Leeds.
Postmark: 27 Dec. 1838. *Stamp*: (1) Ambleside Penny Post (2) Kendal.
Endorsed: Rydal Mt Dec 26th.
MS. WL.
LY ii. 962 (—).

Rydal Mount, Decr 26th [1838]

My dear Friend,

Our dear Sister talks of writing to you herself, but as her *intentions* are not to be depended upon, I must at once

---

[1] Second wife of Andrew Stevenson, the American ambassador, whom W. W. had met in Aug. 1837 (see L. 1152 above).

[2] The closing lines of *Humanity* (*PW* iv. 102).

acknowledge the safe arrival of your friendly Birth-day offering—I wish you could have been present to see the exultation which sate upon the changed countenance when I was summoned to her room, and saw the contents of the basket spread at her feet—it having been opened in her presence by Dorothy; who, pulling out in triumph, one bird after another, and eagerly going on *still* searching for *more*—your old friend (in her *waggish* way) observed to her—'You're sure to find the eggs they have laid by the way.' This habit of bantering, which now is not unfrequent with her—so different to her character in former days—shews a great change, yet a wonderful acuteness and quickness of mind. And indeed, we all think that in other respects her mind is less feeble that it was, and certainly her memory is improved—and for a much longer space we can keep her interested by conversation, tho' her uncomfortable *habits* are still as bad as ever. Her bodily health has been remarkably good—except that within the last two days—owing to her having eaten some trifle, in which she is not generally allowed to indulge—her stomach has been a little disordered—so that we find it is quite necessary to be careful to confine her to such food as *we know* to be suitable to her. The Turkey *at her request*, was not dressed on Christmas day but reserved till tomorrow, that it may honour the board upon our Grandson's birthday, when he will be 3 years old—the family with his good Godmother, Miss Fenwick, are to dine at 1 oc., his own, as well as 'Old Aunty's' dinner hour—and in the midst of our festivity the chief Provider for our Feast will not be forgotten—as I am sure your old friend would be in your thoughts and heart, upon *her* own birthday—at Headingly.

It was a pleasure to us to hear of you all being so well at home, and tho' the report of your dear Sister Ellen was less favorable I trust from what you say nothing serious was threatened—and the news from Brighton[1] too we were glad to hear—tho' sorry for the anxieties that await dear Mrs Temple[2]—but on her Husband's account, I think with you, that *employment* is the best thing that could befal him.—

We were very much pleased by the friendly tho' transient visit, from your Son James a short time ago—and the kind interest, which in the course of conversation he seemed to take

[1] i.e. of Mrs. Marshall's daughter Julia, now married to the Revd. Henry Venn Elliott.

[2] Her daughter Jane.

ın the welfare of my dear William (who you know has long been wishful for a situation of more full employment) was very gratifying *to me*. Poor W. came over from Carlisle to pass a few holidays with us on Saturday. You will be sorry to hear that he neither looks, nor is quite well. Some stomach derangement, which he cannot correct, has hung about him for some time;— and bearing in mind what his constitution has gone thro', I cannot but be anxious about him—as I am for his Sister who neither gains strength, nor good looks. Yet as she does not consider herself much of an invalid, and takes her place, and does as the rest of the family do, I ought to feel thankful.—For Mr W. and myself, we are perfectly well in bodily health, and powers, beyond I think what most people of our age are blest with—and you will think that my husband's *Spirits* too, are more than usually buoyant when I tell you that at this early time, he talks of our going *together* for a short visit to Town in the Spring. And of this I would say a few words to you my dear Friend—You must know then, that we have many invitations from both old and new friends, who wish especially for our, at least for my husband's Company. Among the first of these, I know we shall find our oldest friends in Gros: St[1]— and for my own part I should not feel comfortable in taking up our abode in any other friend's house in London, till *after* we had visited your's; *provided* your wishes, the *time*, and circumstances suited your convenience to receive us on our *first arrival*. So that if you will, *when your own arrangements are made*, be kind enough to express what will be agreeable to you—*we* can settle our *own*— when the important determination as to leaving home or not can be settled.—All this however depends upon the health, and so many other considerations connected with others as well as ourselves, that we do not with any *confidence* speak of the journey—So that I only mention it as a possibility. We have good accounts from John, who is now in London in attendance upon his poor wife, who is at present under the Dentist's hands—The variety and amusement he meets with has, his wife tells us, been as Dr Jephson expected, *beneficial*, by diverting his mind from his own uncomfortable feelings. We can only hope that these may not recur, when the present excitement is removed, but we encourage the expectation that this may be so, from hearing that the state of *nervous* debility from which John has suffered, is such a common occurrence after Typhus.

[1] Grosvenor Street.

My Brinsop B^r keeps improving—but you will be sorry to hear that neither my B^r nor Sister at Douglas are well—poor Joanna confined by Lumbago, unable to visit Henry who is more seriously afflicted—and I fear declining.[1] God bless you and yours—with a thousand thanks—my d^r Friend aff^{ly} y^{rs}

M W[ordswor]th.

1289. W. W. to SIR WILLIAM ROWAN HAMILTON

MS. untraced.
Hamilton. K (—). LY ii. 963.

Rydal Mount, January 20, 1839.

Your letters and the verses under Lord Northampton's covers were received towards the end of September. In the few words of prose annexed, you tell me you do not expect an answer 'till it should be easy and pleasant to me to write'; you will not, I trust, deem that I have abused this friendly privilege when I tell you that I have been prevented from writing by a succession of indispositions, one of which disabled me from either reading or writing, such was the state of my eyes, for upwards of two months. Although I am still suffering from the effects of a severe cold, I cannot let slip the opportunity of sending you, by my friend and neighbour Mr Graves, a few words to thank you for your poem on the *Elysian Fields*,[2] and that[3] in which you have done me so much honour by the affectionate manner in which you speak of me. Be assured, my dear Sir William, that without the help of these interesting lines I should retain a most lively remembrance of our first meeting, and of the hours so pleasantly and profitably spent in your Society, both in Ireland and at Rydal.

My daughter avails herself of the same opportunity to write to your sister Eliza, of whom we all think with a thousand good wishes and a sincere affection; we know not what favour her

[1] Henry Hutchinson died the following year.
[2] Composed at Lowther the previous August. See *Hamilton*, ii. 268.
[3] The poem *Recollections* (*Hamilton*, ii. 275).

volume of poems[1] may have met with from the public, but we are convinced that they merit a degree of approbation far beyond what it is too probable they will receive, poetry being so little to the taste of these times. I am strongly persuaded that in my own case, should I have first appeared before the public at this late day, my endeavours would have attracted little attention; forty years have been required to give my name the station (such as it is) which it now occupies.

Alas for your unhappy country! I know not when I have been more affected by a public occurrence than when I read Lord Charleville's[2] account of his interview with Lord Norbury,[3] within so few hours of that nobleman's horrible assassination, and then to see that event followed by such a speech as O'Connell made upon the mode in which it had been treated by the Lord Lieutenant[4] and Lord Charleville. How long is the reign of this monster over the British Islands to endure?

Your godson is still with us, his father and mother being in London. Yesterday he asked where Dublin was, and what it was. I was surprised how the word came upon his lips, or the place into his thoughts; but he solved the difficulty by letting us know immediately that his 'godfather Hamilton lived there'. The day before he had seen his godfather Southey for the first time, who had come for a few days on a visit to your co-sponsor, Miss Fenwick, who has taken a house at Ambleside for a year. Southey, you will be sorry to hear, did not seem in good spirits. His depression was owing, we think, to the rather alarming state of health in which his youngest daughter has been for some time. I wish I could have written you a more

---

[1] *Poems by Eliza M. Hamilton*, Dublin, 1838.

[2] Charles William Bury, 2nd Earl of Charleville (1801–51), Irish peer: M.P. for Penryn and Falmouth, 1832–5.

[3] Hector John Graham Toler, 2nd Earl of Norbury (1781–1839), was shot in broad daylight on 1 Jan. in the grounds of his house Durrow Abbey, nr. Kilbeggan, and died two days later. Lord Norbury had been universally popular, and there appeared to be no religious or political motive for the crime. O'Connell suggested that the murderer was one bound to him by the nearest of natural ties, who had a material interest in his removal; but suspicion naturally fell on the association of Ribbonmen.

[4] Constantine Henry Phipps, 2nd Earl of Mulgrave (1797–1863), Lord Lieutenant of Ireland from 1835 until 1839, had been created 1st Marquess of Normanby the previous June. He was Home Secretary, 1839–41. W. W. had already met his brother, the Hon. Edmund Phipps (1808–57), in 1836 (see *R MV B*).

interesting letter, but I am obliged to employ the pen of Mrs Wordsworth, who herself is not quite so well as I could wish. Little William is at this moment leaning upon the table on which his grandmother writes; upon being asked what we should say to you, his reply was—'A kiss!' which he gave to be transmitted. With a thousand kind wishes to you and yours, in which my amanuensis cordially joins, I remain your affectionate friend . . .

[*cetera desunt*]

1290. W. W. to THOMAS NOON TALFOURD

MS. Harvard University Library. Hitherto unpublished.

[*In M. W.'s hand*]

[26 Jan. 1839]

My dear Mr Talfourd

I lose no time in replying to your letter for which I feel much obliged. I shall confine myself in this note merely to say that I am quite ready to Petition,[1] and shall prepare one to place in your hands as soon as possible. I can add with pleasure that Dr Arnold,—who is now our neighbour and to whom I took the liberty this morn^g of shewing your letter and the copy of the one addressed to Mr Southey,—will also forward you a Petition with a request that you will present it in his behalf.

I shall write more at length when I send the Petition.

Mr Robinson is still here but not returned from a visit which took him from Rydal yesterday morn^g[2]—so that I have not had an opportunity of seeing your note to him. He means to leave us next Thursday—to pay a visit or two on his way to Preston,

---

[1] Talfourd had written on 24 Jan. (*Cornell MSS.*) that he planned to submit petitions from authors in support of the Copyright measure which he proposed to reintroduce as soon as the new session of Parliament opened on 5 Feb., and he set out the form that such a petition from W. W. should take.

[2] H. C. R. had been at Rydal since 28 Dec., seeing much of the Wordsworth circle, I. F., the Arnolds and Southey. He spent the night of 25 Jan. at Field Head with John Harden, 'that good old man with the sunny face, as Wordsworth happily characterised him',—which helps to establish the date of this letter. See *HCR*. ii. 566

where Dr A. and his family are to join him and travel forward by rail-way together, to London about the middle of the following week, Mr R. being bent upon reaching town ag^t the open[in]g of Parl^t.

All our Household have had . . .
[cetera desunt]

1291. W. W. to MARY FRANCES HOWLEY

Address: Mrs Howley.
MS. Lambeth Palace Library transcript.
   Russell Noyes, 'Wordsworth and Sir George Beaumont's Family', TLS, 10 Aug. 1962 (—).

[*In M. W.'s hand*]

[early Feb. 1839]

My dear Mrs Howley,

   On the other side of this sheet I have taken the liberty of having transcribed for your perusal and the Archbishop's, a Sonnet which I wrote a few months ago, and in which, for the sake of the subject, you will, I trust, have some interest; it perhaps explains itself sufficiently—but lest that sh^d not be so, it may as well be premised, that the tree[1] was purchased of the proprietor by Sir G. Beaumont, to be left standing for the sake of its beauty. I should scarcely have had the courage to send you this effusion, but that it gives me an opportunity of enquiring after your own health and that of the Archbishop—and also concerning the dear Beaumonts, about whom we have heard nothing for a very long time. How is Sir George, and where? and pray tell us whether your little Grandaughter[2] be with you, and how her Brothers and herself are going on.

   We condole with you sincerely upon the death of Mr Rose[3]—he was a man of sweet dispositions, and a truly Christian character—by his friends he will be universally and deeply lamented, and his departure causes a gap in society that will not easily be made up.

---

   [1] See L. 1137 above.

   [2] Sir George Beaumont's daughter Constance.

   [3] Hugh James Rose had died at Florence on 22 Dec. 1838. He had been Archbishop Howley's chaplain.

The Archbishop has I hope taken some interest in the Bill for amending the law of Copy-right, which Sergeant Talfourd has again introduced to the House. Partly on my own account, but *infinitely* more for the general benefit of literature I am anxious that this bill should pass, and I have taken no little trouble about it; it will be opposed by the cold-hearted, and narrow-minded economists who abound in the house, and we have some fear, such is the general remissness, on what are called the open days, that the friends of the measure may not attend; allow me then to beg that if among your Acquaintance there be any inclined to support it, you would be so kind as to press upon them their being at their Post, early on the 27th, as the 2^d reading of the bill stands *first* on the list for that day.

My family is generally well. I have however myself had lately an attack of Rheumatism, which disabled and annoyed me a good deal, but it is going off.

Believe me, my d^r Madam, with respectful regards to yourself and the Archbishop, in which Mrs. W. unites,

faithfully your obliged
[*signed*] Wm Wordsworth

The Pine-tree upon the Summit of
Monte Mario

(Suggested at Rome.)

[*The sonnet follows, as in PW iii. 212, except that in l. 4 read 'clouds' for 'hues' and in l. 5 'as seem'd' for 'in peace'.*]

1292. W. W. to EDWARD QUILLINAN

MS. WL.
LY ii. 965 (—).

[*In M. W.'s hand*]

[early Feb. 1839]

My Dear Mr Quillinan

(I hold the pen for Mr W. who, you will be sorry to hear, is very unwell)

You are quite right in supposing that you have not forfeited my friendship, and as Dora has fully explained to you the state of my feelings I certainly do not consider it any 'intrusion' your accepting Miss Fenwick's invitation—and shall be pleased to see you at Rydal Mount.[1]

I remain, dear Mr Q., faithfully and aff^{ly} yours

[*signed*] Wm Wordsworth

[*M. W. adds*]

I hope d^r Mr Q. you may bring us better weather—the present is sadly against Rheumatic Subjects—and tho' the *acuteness* of W^{m's} attack is removed, a sad nervous derangement, attended with a cough keeps us very anxious. I trust he may be better before we see you, or you will come to a gloomy house: Dora is looking ill, and has lately been losing her appetite which you know was never [anything] to boast of.

Aff^{ly} yours, and looking with pleasure to the hope of seeing you I remain

M Wordsworth

1293. W. W. to THOMAS NOON TALFOURD

MS. Cornell. Hitherto unpublished.

[*In M. W.'s hand*]

13th Feb: [1839]

My dear Sergeant Talfourd

Things have proved very untoward, I have been confined to my room or bed by the rheumatism ever since I received your letter. Other awkward accidents have occurred and this morn^g,

---

[1] I. F. was now endeavouring to persuade W. W. to accept the mutual attachment of Dora W. and E. Q. on the understanding that there could be no question of their marrying unless some adequate provision could be found for her; and it was in order to effect this compromise and reconcile all parties to it that she invited E. Q. to spend a few days with her at Ambleside. According to his MS. Diary (*WL MSS.*), this visit took place 11–18 Feb., and though it did not bring the prospect of his marriage any nearer, it seems to have taken the heat out of the situation, to judge from his letter to Dora W. on the 20th from Dublin, where he had gone on some business assignment for his brother: 'I wish I could say what would be quite satisfactory to Miss Fenwick, for then you and I would be happier than we are as yet, though my visit has, I trust, removed the ill-omened gloom that darkened your house to me. How very kind Miss Fenwick has been! God will, I trust, favour an attachment which has excited the benevolence of a being so excellent.' (*WL MSS.*)

when I sent down to my Clerk the amended Copy of the Petition[1] to be transcribed, I find him in bed with the rheumatism also—so that it is doubtful whether I shall be able to send it off by tomorrow morn^{g's} post, which will convey this to London.

If my petition be thought not too long, you will deem it I hope considerably improved. Farewell with a thousand good wishes

Y^r sincere f^d
W Wordsworth[2]

1294. W. W. to HENRY AUSTEN DRIVER[3]

MS. untraced.
Bookseller's Catalogue.

[*In M. W.'s hand*]

Ambleside
18 February [1839]

. . . I must frankly tell you, that eminent Writers, whether in verse or in prose, are of all Men in my judgment, those who stand the least in need of such local testimonials of public

---

[1] For W. W.'s Petition in favour of Copyright reform, see *Prose Works*, iii. 317. H. C. R. had helped him to draft it before he returned to London on 2 Feb.

[2] Not signed by W. W.

[3] Henry Austen Driver (b. 1790), minor poet and admirer of Byron and Moore, published *The Arabs: a tale, in four Cantos*, in 1825, and *Harold de Burun, a semi-dramatic poem, in six scenes,* (*R.M. Cat.*, no. 600), in 1835. A native of Cambridge, he moved later to Islington, where he gave lectures; but his last years are shrouded in obscurity. In 1838 Driver published *Byron and 'The Abbey'*, 'a few remarks upon the poet, elicited by the rejection of his statue by the Dean of Westminster, with suggestions for the erection of a national edifice to contain the monuments of our great men'. He drew attention to the double rebuff Byron had suffered at the hands of the Abbey authorities, first when his body was refused burial there when it was brought back from Missolonghi, and later when Thorwaldsen's statue was rejected; and he proposed that a national pantheon should be erected, in which Byron should occupy the first place. 'What have such men as Southey and Wordsworth to fear? Byron and *they* are too secure of their fame to be prejudiced by each other. They, also, are too high-minded, too generous, not

admiration and gratitude as you are anxious to obtain for them; their books, if they survive, are their living, moving, and speaking monument—and if they do not, the cause must lie in their want of the vital principle of genius or truth . . .

1295. W. W. to ROBERT SOUTHEY

Address: Robt Southey Esqre, Keswick.
Postmark: 19 Feb. 1839. *Stamp*: (1) Ambleside Penny Post (2) Keswick.
MS. Harvard University Library.
K (—). *LY ii. 966.*

[*In M. W.'s hand*]

Ambleside, Feb. 18 [1839]

My dear Southey,

I had yesterday a letter from Sergeant Talfourd, acknowledging the receipt of a Petition which at his desire I had prepared, and expressing his satisfaction with it. He tells me that Sir Robt Inglis[1] holds one from Dr Arnold, which he means to present.—But as he does not say that he has either received or heard of one from you, I have some little fear that you may not have made up your mind to take that step. I write to beg that you will do so, from a *strong* conviction that if your name be not

to assist in raising a memorial to that genius, whose lustre, mingling with their own, has helped to characterize an era as one of peculiar splendour.' (p. 30). Thorwaldsen's statue of Byron had been commissioned in 1829 by a committee presided over by John Cam Hobhouse, but was refused for the Abbey by Dean Ireland when it was completed in 1834, and it lay in the Custom house vaults until 1842, when it was again rejected, by Ireland's successor, Dean Turton. In 1843, soon after Whewell had suceeded C. W. as Master of Trinity, a move was made to present it to the College, and Whewell accepted it on condition that it was placed in the Library, and not in the antechapel as was first proposed. But W. W. remained opposed to any such mark of approval for Byron. See his letter to C. W. jnr., 29 Aug. 1843 (in next volume). A memorial to Byron was not dedicated in Westminster Abbey until 8 May 1969. See John Cam Hobhouse, Lord Broughton, *Recollections of a Long Life*, 6 vols., 1910–11, iii, 277, 279–80; iv. 2; vi. 93, 125, 127, 186: A. P. Stanley, *Historical Memorials of Westminster Abbey*, 1868, p. 300: Mrs. Stair Douglas, *Life of William Whewell, D.D.*, pp. 292–3; and *NQ*, 6th series, iv (1881), 421–3.

[1] Sir Robert Inglis was actively promoting Talfourd's new Copyright Bill.

found in the list of Petitioners the effect upon the measure will be very injurious.[1] Excuse the anxiety which has put me upon troubling you in this way, which however I have had less scruple in doing, as we have, I know, been so long in sympathy upon this important subject—in which, as a public man, you yourself led the way. You will have seen that the 2nd reading stands first on the list for the 27th.

A severe cold in the head which seized me about 6 weeks ago ended in an attack of Lumbago, by which I have been a good deal annoyed—I am now (at Miss Fenwick's) in a steady course of recovery and, barring a relapse, hope to be quite well in 3 or 4 days—Miss F. we think has not been quite so well—but seems pretty well to day. Quillinan left this house at 6 oc this morng—having been here since last Monday[2]—on his way to Ireland. I had no private conversation with him—but thro' Dora he understands what my judgments and feelings are—and we all seemed at ease with each other.

I rejoice that we are likely to have dear Bertha and her Husband[3] as our Neighbours—We hope earnestly that Kate continues to amend. Pray give our kind love and best wishes to them both—they will be concerned to hear that Miss Althea North[4] is no more, she died at the house of her married Sister in Dublin 3 days ago—She left home for the benefit of better medical advice—but has sunk thro' weakness.

Ever affecly yours
[*signed*] Wm Wordsworth

---

1 Southey did not in the end submit a Petition, thinking that a statement of his case by Talfourd would be more effective. The final list of petitioners included Thomas Campbell, Robert Browning, Thomas Hood, Leigh Hunt, Carlyle, Dickens, Rogers, and a group of Scottish authors. The petitions were all reprinted in an Appendix to Talfourd's *Three Speeches* . . . , 1840.

2 See L. 1292 above.

3 The Revd. Herbert Hill.

4 A connection, probably a daughter, of Ford North of Ambleside.

1296. W. W. to H. C. R.

Address: H. C. Robinson Esqre, 2 Plowdens Build^gs, Temple.
Postmark: 21 Feb. 1839. *Stamp*: Charles St.
Endorsed: 19 Feb: 1839. Wordsworth health Copyright bill.
MS. Dr. Williams's Library.
Morley, i. 378.

[*In M. W.'s hand*]

19 Feb. [1839]

My dear Friend,

After having tired both myself and my Wife by dictating this long letter to Miss M.,[1] which you will fill up—having read it first—(if you think worth while, in order to prevent repetition—) we feel unable to write any thing at present to yourself, worthy your perusal. You must however accept our best thanks for your very interesting letter.—Finding that I did not throw off the muscular pain by the violent attack of Lumbago which I had ere you left us—I submitted to a course of *Invalidism*, under the management of Mr Fell[2]—that is, I kept my room a few days—my bed one, in order to encourage perspiration. We are now staying a few days at Miss Fenwick's for the sake of her society and change of air—and above all because it may not be prudent for me to walk to see her so often as I could wish.—We have had no card-playing since your departure and we hope the Kitchen Party have recovered from their fit of dissipation—John[3] and his family, stayed one day with us, on their passage home, last week—they took our Darling along with them—To our great regret the Magic Lantern was packed up—so that they could not get at it, that we might have witnessed the impression it made upon the Child— He well remembered not only the 'Peacock with the fairy tail'—but also your manner of repeating it—and made no bad attempt at an immitation. Mr Quillinan has paid us a visit of a week—lodging at Miss Fenwicks he took us on his way to Ireland, whither business calld him.

I sent up, as you know, a draft of the Petition adding in a letter to the Sergeant that my fear of being lengthy had prevented my inserting two or three clauses—which I mentioned, and as he

---

[1] Probably Miss Frances Mackenzie (see L. 1137 above).
[2] The Ambleside surgeon.
[3] John W. was now returning with his family to Brigham.

rather recommended the incorporating these I did so—He expressed his satisfaction of the whole, when it was returned to him upon parchment—I still regret however the omission of one clause, which did not strike me at the time—viz—

That the amended Bill would take away from venal Publishers the liberty of re-publishing such things as the Author might have discarded—whereas, as the law now is, when an Author who has begun early and lived to a good age dies—they can reprint those Pieces and pass off *their* injurious editions as the only complete collection of the Writers Works—The fear of this, absolutely prevented Southey from throwing overboard in his last Ed: several minor pieces that were written merely for the newspapers when he wanted money.

My Sister mourns and even weeps over the loss of her little Nephew[1]—she is well in health—but we cannot see Doras appetite make any improvement which hurts us much. Miss F. is, for her, well—She unites with us in every good wish—

Ever aff[ly] your faithful Friend—
[*signed*] W[m] Wordsworth

Pray stir about getting friends to attend at the House *early* on the 27th as Talfourds bill stands first upon the list for that day. Do you take in the *New York Review* at the Athenaeum? If so, and you think it worth while you may see a long and encomiastic notice of my volumes in the No: for Jan[y] last[2]—Do, in a New York Mag: called, I think, *Biblical Repository*,[3] but I have not seen it—tho' heard of it from the Editor of that work. Having had so many letters to write since you went—we have alas! read little—M[r] Taylor[4] and

---

[1] i.e. John W.'s son William, who had been staying at Rydal Mount.

[2] See next letter.

[3] The *American Biblical Repository* was published at Andover, Massachusetts. From 1835 until 1837 it was edited by Bela Bates Edwards (1802–52), Professor of Hebrew at Andover Theological Seminary from 1837, and a leading advocate of Classical studies in the U.S.A., who visited W. W. in 1846 (*RMVB*). It was edited from 1838 by Absalom Peters (1793–1869), one of the founders of the Union Theological Seminary in New York.

[4] Isaac Taylor (1787–1865), author of *The Natural History of Enthusiasm* (1830), *Fanaticism* (1833), and *Spiritual Despotism* (1835), wrote much about the problems presented by the corruptions of the Christian Church, particularly in *Ancient Christianity and the Oxford Tracts*, 2 vols., 1839–40. The work referred to here is *The Physical Theory of Another Life* (1836), which the Misses Ricketts, friends of the author, had presented to W. W. The poet had

Carlisle[1] being both untouched. I ought to have said that I am now convalescent. Nothing remains but a slight muscular pain at one side of the back—Dora has not forgotten the Sonnets[2] she promised to transcribe for you.

1297. W. W. to HENRY REED

Address: Henry Reed Esqre, Philadelphia, via Montreal.
Postmark: 2 Apr. *Stamp*: New York Ship.
Endorsed: W. Wordsworth Rydal Mount. February 22, 1839. Rec. April 3.
MS. Cornell.
K (—). *Wordsworth and Reed, p. 7* (—). *LY* ii. 967.

[In M. W.'s hand]

Rydal Mount Feb 22^d —39

My dear Sir

Your letter of the 3^d of Jan^ry accompanying your reviewal[3] of my Poems, reached me about 10 days ago. I sincerely thank you

been impressed by the extracts H. C. R. had read to him during his recent visit: 'Wordsworth was not tolerant of novelities, but he praised the imaginative power of Taylor's picture of heaven, remarking only that it ought to be in verse.' (*HCR* ii. 564.)

[1] Thomas Carlyle (1795–1881), Scottish essayist and historian, had achieved celebrity with his *French Revolution* (1837), which had become a firm favourite with I. F. and H. C. R., but not with W. W. 'It is not only his style he condemns, but his *inhumanity*. He says there is a want of due sympathy with mankind. Scorn and irony are the feeling and tone throughout.' (*HCR* ii. 566.) Carlyle had been settled in London since 1834 and W. W. had met him at Henry Taylor's in 1836 (see L. 1004 above). For Carlyle's recollections of W. W., see his *Reminiscences*, ed. J. A. Froude, 2 vols., 1881, ii. 330 ff. See also L. 1305 below.

[2] These contributions to the *Memorials of a Tour in Italy, 1837* included *The Pine of Monte Mario at Rome* and *At Florence* (*PW* iii. 212, 225), which were acknowledged by H. C. R. in March (see Morley, i. 382); but W. W. had composed about 12 new sonnets recently (*HCR* ii. 567), and the additional ones now to be sent probably included the sequence *At Rome* (*PW* iii. 213–5), which may well belong to this time. H. C. R. had been reading the first volume of Arnold's *History of Rome* during his recent visit to Rydal, and the sonnets seem to reflect his discussions of Arnold's and Niebuhr's methods with the poet.

[3] In his article in the *New York Review*, iv (1839), 1–70, Henry Reed set out to establish W. W. as the successor of Shakespeare, Spenser, and Milton in the great tradition of English poetry, and to uphold the essential rightness and

for both, but I had received and read the article before—the 'New York Review' having been sent me from London [by a friend],[1] to whom I have been obliged in the same way, occasionally. In respect to one particular both in your letter and critique, I can speak without diffidence or hesitation; I mean the affectionate tone in which you give vent to your feelings of admiration and gratitude—'Grant me thy love, I crave no other fee' is the concluding line of a valedictory Sonnet[2] at the close of a Volume (lately published by Mr Moxon) consisting of my Sonnets only. This sentiment is, I assure you predominant in my mind and heart; and I know no test more to be relied upon than acknowledgments such as yours, provided the like have been received from Persons of both sexes, of all ages and who have lived in different latitudes, in widely different states of society, and in conditions little resembling each other. Beyond what I have now said, I feel scrupulous in expressing the gratification with which I read your critique, being so highly encomiastic as it is—all that I can say with confidence is, that I endeavoured to do, what much and long reflection on your part justifies you to your own mind, in saying, I *have* done. It may amuse you to hear an odd proof that those Poems for whose fate you entertain no doubt, are yet sub judice elsewhere, in the 'Delhi Gazette',— mark the place—a vituperative article appeared not long ago upon the Subject, which was answered by another writer with great zeal and ardour, to the entertainment no doubt of the Palankeen critics of that enervating climate.

This letter is I feel very unworthy of being sent so far, but I have at present so many engagements, that it would be inconvenient to me to write at greater length—besides I am far from sure that I could satisfy you or myself if I were to attempt it. Let me add however that if the recently created facilities for crossing the Atlantic should tempt you to visit this Country [? I shall be glad][3] to see you, and pay you all the attention in my power.

consistency of his vision. 'There is a symmetry in the productions of Wordsworth's Youth, his manhood, and more advanced years. In the essential properties of his writings at different periods, we perceive no fluctuations, no recantation or backward movement.' In his letter of 3 Jan. (*Wordsworth and Reed*, pp. 5—7), Henry Reed described the spirit in which he undertook the article: '. . . in discussing the subject, I have deemed it high time to treat it as at length removed from the atmosphere of mere controversial criticism.'

[1] *Words apparently dropped out.*   [2] *See PW* iii. 38.   [3] *Words dropped out.*

The state of my eyes obliges me to employ an amanuensis, which I hope you will excuse and believe me to remain (these words are in my own handwriting)

affectionately your's
[*signed*] Wm Wordsworth

1298. W. W. to JOHN KENYON

MS. Lilly Library, Indiana University.
K (—). LY ii. 968 (—).

Rydal Mount, Febr^y 26th, —39.

My dear Mr Kenyon,

So far from having any objection, I was gratified by learning that you had made use of my name in the way you mention. Heartily do I wish that the Publication may succeed, beyond the limits of the Subscription.

How sorry I am that your Brother still continues to suffer from the Gout; perhaps you may have heard his near relation the Rheumatism, for the first time in my life paid me a visit last summer, and was so attentive as to repeat it about a month ago. I am however convalescent, and think of looking in upon you in London about two months hence; I hope my dear friend you will be there.

Mrs Wordsworth begs me to thank you cordially for your Lady-friend, Miss Barrett's Poems[1] which you sent her some time ago. Miss B. appears to be a very interesting person, both for Genius and attainments. My pen is execrable, and I must release you—Very kind remembrances to your Brother; accept them also yourself from us all, including my Sister, and believe me dear Mr Kenyon

faithfully yours
W. Wordsworth

---

[1] See L. 1273 above. The reference is probably to the volume containing her translation of the *Prometheus Bound*, in which W. W. had expressed interest.

1299. W. W. to UNKNOWN CORRESPONDENT

MS. Cornell. Hitherto unpublished.

[*In M. W.'s hand*]

Rydal Mount
March 11th [1839]

My dear Sir,

You have done me a Kindness by forwarding the Petitions upon Serg^t Talfourd's Copy-right Bill. Several of them place the matter in a strong light—and I have been particularly pleased with the one from Mr Smith[1] the *Publisher* of Lanark and Glasgow. He speaks in a way that does him great honour. Let me express also the pleasure I felt in seeing your name in the majority upon the 2^d reading.[2] Notwithstanding that decision, such is the slackness of attendance on open days, and the obstinate zeal of the opponents (Mr Warburton in particular) that some friends of the measure are, I understand, not without fear of its being defeated. I trust however, that it will not be so—for Sergent Talfourd tells me, that there is in the House a strong feeling in its favour. Let me beg the continuance of your Support. The extension of term is in the first place *just*—and next it could not fail to encourage greatly the production of good books—a benefit which the nation stands in great need of, our literature becoming every year more and more fugitive.

With many thanks, believe me to remain faithfully yours

[*signed*] Wm Wordsworth

P.S. May I trouble you to direct and forward the enclosed, at your perfect convenience—and pray excuse this liberty.

---

[1] John Smith III (1784–1849), of Crutherland, nr. East Kilbride, director of the publishing firm of John Smith and Son, Glasgow, founded by his grandfather in 1751. He had been a college friend at Glasgow of John Wilson, 'Christopher North', and published his *Isle of Palms* jointly with Longman and Ballantyne: he was also friendly with Scott and Campbell. From 1832 he was Secretary of the Maitland Club. In his petition John Smith contrasted his position as a publisher with that of those by whose creations he had been enriched. The profits he had accumulated could be handed down to his heirs; whereas the authors who had produced the works had no such opportunities under the existing law of copyright.

[2] On 27 Feb. See next letter.

1300. W. W. to THOMAS NOON TALFOURD

MS. Harvard University Library. Hitherto unpublished.

[*In M. W.'s hand*]

Rydal Mount Mar. 22ᵈ [1839]

My dear Mr Talfourd,

Your letter was very welcome, and in your judicious and eloquent Speech,[1] you did ample justice to the Subject. I should have thanked you before but you were on the Circuit, as I presume you still are, and I know you would give me credit for all the feelings that were due to you on this occasion. The interest which I took, in this bill on my own account at first, I have now almost lost sight of, so much do I feel that the character of Parliament is implicated in the Question—It is painful to observe the inattention, and even indifference of the great body of our Representatives in a matter so important.

Having had occasion to write to Sir Robᵗ Inglis, I asked him if he could point out any thing I could do to promote the passing of the Bill; he writes in reply, that after my petition, I can do nothing with the H. of C. as a Body, but he urges me 'to request the attention of every friend whose opinion is not already recorded.' This has puzzled me for as far as I can call to mind, all those M.P.s (to whom I had any ground for application) have voted on one or other or both of the *readings* with the exception of a very few, who either did not answer to my application, or explained to me by letter, why they had not been able to attend—In this latter number, was Lord Adair.[2] Had I been on the Spot I could not have resisted the temptation of commenting in the Morning Post upon the absurdities, ignorance and misrepresentations in that impudent Fellow, Tegg's[3] letter and petition. He sneers at us Authors of the present day, as contrasted with Goldsmith and Johnson who notwithstanding their poverty, and the much worse state of the law at that time,

---

[1] Moving the Second Reading of his Copyright Bill on 27 Feb. (repr. in Talfourd's *Three Speeches. . . . ,* 1840). The Bill was carried by 73 votes to 37, a majority of 36, but when the Committee stage finally came round on 1 May, it ran into serious difficulties.

[2] Viscount Adare, Sir William Rowan Hamilton's friend, M.P. for Glamorgan (see pt. ii, L. 619). He had written twice to W. W. in the spring of 1838 offering his support (*Cornell MSS.*).

[3] The bookseller. See L. 1235 above.

were above making a complaint. Poor Devils—what was the State of the law to them! who were obliged for bread, to part with their writings fast as they dropped from their pen. It is however remarkable that Thomson, and where you would least expect it, viz in verse, and in his Castle of Indolence, has given vent to a lamentation on this very point, which might have stayed the pens and tongues of all such selfish Creatures, if they had known it.

> Is there no Patron to protect the Muse
> And *fence* for her Parnassus' barren Soil,
> To every labour its reward accrues,
> And they are sure of bread who Swink and moil;
> But a fell Tribe the Aonian hive despoil,
> As *ruthless Wasps* oft rob the painful Bee,
> And while the laws not guard this noblest toil
> Nor for the Muses other Meed decree
> They praised are alone, and *starve* right merrily. [1]

On Easter Monday [2] we start for Bath with a view to keep out the Rheumatism—at present I am quite well, and about the beginning of the 2^d week in May, I hope to see you in London—but our time will necessarily be short.

If you wish me to do any thing before the 10th of April (when Sir R. I. tells me the Bill comes again before the house) let me . . .

[*cetera desunt*]

[1] *The Castle of Indolence*, II. ii.
[2] 1 Apr.

Address: Miss Wordswoth, Rydal Mount, Kendal [*readdressed to*] Mrs J. Wordsworth, Vicarage, Brigham, Cockermouth. *Single*.
Postmark: 3 Apr. 1839 *Stamp*: Ambleside Penny Post.
MS. WL. Hitherto unpublished.

Bath, 10 George Street 4 oc. Wed:
[3 Apr. 1839]

Dearest Dora,

Without preface farther than saying all well, I start with facts beginning at the beginning—and will try as much as possible to save your eyes. Willy had driven down Kendal Street as we approached the Commercial[2]—and the Landlord exclaimed on seeing us 'Mr W. W has just driven off in the mud'. A very little rain after Kendal, and since quite fair, but intensely cold. We reached Preston about 6. Isa[3] and the maids about 3. They had been well attended to tho' the disappointment to their fellow-travellers at starting was great. The luggage bearing our direction, the Poet had been expected. Crowded boat after Lancaster. Willy had reached the Inn and had had dinner before we arrived, looking better than I expected. A horrid dirty house—had tea and hard toast. The maids said, had we seen all they saw we never could have slept in the house. The two W[s] visited Mrs St. C.[4] and Sam H.[5] Father came home full of a recipe for the Gout, an infallible cure, which had made S. H. quite a new man. He gave Father the very Dr'[s] own prescription, and he means to abide by it, by way of prevention. They went to see about the Trains, to which we all repaired at a little past 8. Next morning Mrs St. C. and her husband met us there, and so much for Preston. The rail way is charming travelling, but neither *apparently* so rapid, so smooth or like flying as I expected, and I could see the prospects just as well as in

---

[1] Written over a letter from Mary Hutchinson to M. W., and sent on by Dora W. (who remained behind in Rydal with D. W.) to her sister-in-law Isabella.

[2] The Posting House in Highgate.

[3] I. F.'s niece Isabella Fenwick, who had been staying in Ambleside, was accompanying her aunt and the Wordsworths to Bath, where they were going to take the waters. She later married the Revd. Henry Preston Elrington, D.D., rector of Templeshambo and Precentor of Ferns.

[4] Mrs. St. Clare, formerly Sarah Horrocks (see pt. i, L. 199).

[5] Her father Samuel Horrocks, the Preston manufacturer.

any other carriage. At Park Side we were detained above 20 minutes, and there parted with our 6ᵗʰ in the [? carriage] a Mr Farish,[1] who is incumbent of one of the Preston Churches, and gave a most favorable report of the movement that has taken place among the Inhabitants, since the erection of the addˡ Churches.[2] In the Coach to which we were here transferred we found the Rector of Richmond and his Lady, as afterwards appeared upon their smoking the Poet. Willy was in the next Coach dose-a-dose with Isabella so that we could give him a tap when we wanted to speak from the windows, so that we were nicely placed. But rail-way travelling is not cheap, the Carriage £4−5, and first places £1−6−6 *each*. Servants (altho' in our own Carriage) second price 17/−. At the Bmg[3] Station we were long detained till the carriage was got off, and Willy and the Maids were obliged to leave us to catch the B. coach, but had delaid too long. It was off before their omnibus left the Hen and Chickens. So they had to wait two hours for a Worcester Coach. This gave W. an opportunity of seeing not only his Birmᵍ friends but Coz: John who, in cap and Gown was holding an examination at the School, into which Ed: H.[4] took him. But W. finding it not a *public* exam. as he had expected, was annoyed at the thought of disturbing John, retired without a greeting, tho his Coz recognized him, from his bench—To return to ourselves, upon halting at the Hop-pole came the disappointment this letter will explain. Father and I however alighted, and had cozy tea, and some alterations in the last passage he was working at before he left Rydal,[5] written down ere the coach party arrived, at 8 oc. We had been settled 2 hours before. After, they were all refreshed by tea, and warmed, for they had had an intensely cold drive (as well they might, we *having felt* the cold *bitterly* especially poor Isa on the box)

[1] The Revd. William Milner Farish (1803−63), perpetual curate of St. Peter's, Preston, 1837−63: son of William Farish (1759−1837), Jacksonian Professor of Natural Philosophy at Cambridge from 1813.

[2] The additional Churches. Two Commissioners' churches, St. Paul's and St. Peter's, had been completed in 1825: Christ Church on the west side and St. Mary's on the east had been added ten years later. The population of Preston had trebled since the beginning of the century.

[3] Birmingham.

[4] A Birmingham friend, but otherwise unidentified.

[5] For W. W.'s recent revision of *The Prelude*, see I. 1316 below.

Hannah[1] went to her mistress, and returned to tell us of *their* disappointment, Mrs D[2] having gone off in the morn[g] on acc[t] of her mother's danger. But Miss Charlton[3] hoped we would breakfast with them. Accordingly clean Shirts etc were put on and all ready at 9 oc. to start the Breakfast when a message came that Mrs Thorpe[4] was dead and Miss C. could not see us, and that we were to meet the Miss F's[5] at the Cathedral at 10. We therefore ordered our breakfasts, and repaired *all hands* (as the Bath coach did not start till 12 oc). Service being over, Willy, who was now to take James' place went to see the 3 Servants off and order the Carriage to take us up at Mrs Davidsons, where we waited, and saw Miss C. and the 3 nice youngest children. We had no adventures that I can stop to record. We have got nice lodgings at 10 George St. Miss F's are gone to Mrs Popham's,[6] we to follow to dine at 6 oc. It is now 5, and we are going to call meanwhile at Miss Pollard's,[7] so that further particulars I must leave till next time unless Willy can take the pen. While we were at the Cathedral Mr Field[8] called at the Hoppole to say that he had left all well at B. but as nothing was said of Ebba, I suppose she was not with him—I have returned from Miss Pollards, and Willy not come down. However I must go to dress so God bless you   M W—

Miss F is come for us, and Willy is not come from his *toilet* yet, so I must close. It is 6 oc. Post departs at ½ past 7. Dear Aunty how are you, and how does poor [?] tell us all about you. Jane[9] is young as a lark and as quick as a Lamplighter.

[*W. W. writes*]

Dearest D.—tell dear Aunty that Mrs Sinclair[10] was much gratified by being remembered by her, and begged to be

[1] I. F.'s maid.

[2] Presumably the Mrs. Davidson of Worcester, mentioned further on, a friend of I. F.'s.

[3] Another friend of I. F.'s.

[4] Presumably Mrs. Davidson's mother.

[5] i.e. I. F. and her niece.

[6] I. F.'s sister Susan had in 1809 married Francis Popham (b. 1780), of Bagborough, nr. Taunton. The Wordsworths visited them there on their return to Bath in 1841 (see *MW* p. 244).

[7] Jane Marshall's sister.

[8] A Brinsop acquaintance (see pt. i, L. 248).

[9] The Wordsworths' maid.

[10] i.e. Mrs. St. Clare.

remembered to her most kindly in return. I like railway travelling much. We have just seen the Miss Pollards. Miss Pollard is well but keeps to the House on account of the severe cold. I have not time to read Mother's letter and therefore do not know if she has told you how mortified we were in passing through Gloucester without knowing that the assizes were holding there, till we were driving through the Town with fresh Horses; otherwise I might have had a glimpse of Sergeant Talfourd, and a few words with him. I cannot write more than love to you and Sister, and kind remembrances to each and all of the Servants and say to Dorothy that I hope her health is improving—ever your most affectionate Father

W Wordsworth

[*Dora W. adds*]

Dearest Isabella, I have only time to say how are you. We [are] quite well here [?]¹ excepted who does not get on as I wᵈ wish— thanks for yʳ note—

Ever yours
D. W—

1302. W. W. to JOHN WORDSWORTH²

MS. British Library. Hitherto unpublished.

[Bath]
[early Apr. 1839]

My dear Nephew,

Your Aunt and I were much mortified upon learning from Wᵐ that you were in Birmingham the other day when we were obliged to pass through it without stopping a minute.

I now trouble you with this, to mention that Moxon wishes to put to Press immediately a new Edition of the Excursion,³ and he requests, knowing how much more accurate you are than I could be were my eyes as good as they ever were, that if your health and leisure allow, you would be so kind as to correct this Edition in its progress through the Press. I could contrive that the Sheets should pass and repass, between You and the Printer, free of Postage. As soon as I shall have communicated

---

¹ *MS. obscure.* ² C. W.'s son.

³ The new edition of the *Excursion* did not appear until 1841.

with Dora, in order that I may ascertain if there be any emendations in my copy at Rydal, and I have told you the Result, the Printing might begin. Mr Moxon would send you a copy of the last Edition from London.

Pray thank your Father for his kind Letter to me some time since,—and say that we accept with pleasure his invitation to visit him at Cambridge, provided it would be convenient for him to receive us, upon our journey towards Westmorland, which will not take place till about the beginning of June. We find that less than a month from our first arrival will not suffice for this place, which must curtail our visit to London a good deal.

They are going on well at Rydal, where Dora is Housekeeper, and she tells us that her health is improved—Your Aunt is much the same.

[*cetera desunt*]

1303. W. W. to EDWARD MOXON

Address: Edward Moxon Esqre, 44 Dover Street [*In M. W.'s hand*]
Postmark: 8 Apr. 1839. *Stamp*: [? Bath]
MS. Yale University Library.
LY ii. 968.

[Bath]
[8 Apr. 1839]

My dear Mr Moxon,

Will you be so kind as to pay the Amount of the enclosed to Messrs Longman and Co. We are here for a month, and about the end of the fifth week hence, I hope for the pleasure of seeing you and yours. Will you be so kind as to fill up the enclosed Address for Mr Stone[1] the artist—Pray remember me kindly to all inquiring Friends, especially Mr Rogers and Mr Kenyon. Mrs W. wrote to Mr Robinson yesterday.—

ever faithfully your much obliged Friend
Wm Wordsworth

Affectionate remembrances to Mrs Moxon and your Sister, if with you, not forgetting little Emma.[2]

[1] For Frank Stone see L. 1025 above.
[2] Moxon's daughter.

1304. W. W. to THOMAS NOON TALFOURD

Address: Mr Sergeant Talfourd M.P., Russell Square, London [*In M. W.'s hand*]
Postmark: (1) 9 Apr. 1839 (2) 10 Apr. 1839. *Stamp*: Bath.
MS. Cornell. Hitherto unpublished.

8th April [1839]
My address post off.

My dear Sergeant Talfourd,

Thanks for your Letter, which was duly received; and I now write to you on the day when the question is to be decided.[1] Be assured that whatever comes of the Motion, I shall retain and cherish the same feelings of gratitude towards you for the noble perseverance which you have shewn on the occasion; and the admirable talent with which you have conducted the whole *case* it will ever be a delight to me to think of.

Judge of my mortification upon finding last Wednesday afternoon at Gloucester that the Assizes were then holding. I was not aware of the fact till having changed Horses, we were driving on through the street towards Rothborough.[2] It would have given me so much pleasure to have had even a peep at you in Court, though we might not have been able to exchange a Word.

In answer to your most kind invitation of which Mrs W. is as duly sensible as myself, I have to say that circumstances, it is to be feared, will not allow us to profit by it as much as we could wish. We shall not be able we apprehend to reach London before the second week in May. Our stay in Bath which we are told must be little less than a month if we would benefit from the Baths and Waters leaves us but little time for London. Be it however less or more I look forward with the greatest pleasure to spending two or three days under your roof; Mrs Wordsworth is not so much at liberty, having engagements to fulfil of long standing, some of which she will be obliged to give up though to very old Friends. She is however not the less obliged to Mrs Talfourd and yourself for thinking of her in this friendly way. I will take care as you request to let you know as

---

[1] Further progress on the Copyright Bill was in fact delayed through lack of a quorum of members when it came up in the House for discussion, and the Committee stage was not opened until 1 May.

[2] W. W. probably means Rodborough, nr. Stroud.

soon as our plans are settled so that in receiving me neither Mrs Talfourd nor you may be put to inconvenience. At present I cannot speak more positively as our Movements are partly dependant upon our Friend and Companion in whose carriage we are travelling.[1] I like Bath very well, were it not for the bitter east Winds, far more severe than we have them at Rydal; the Mountains shelter us from them. I am quite well in health, so, God be thanked is Mrs Wordsworth. Mr Robinson has kindly sent us the *Examiner* on account of a Spirited Article it contains upon the Copyright. Carlyle's petition is like all he does and is, quite *racy*. Hartley Coleridge sent me a petition of his own on behalf of his father, which I hope you have received.

I have left only this awkward place to say how affectionately and faithfully I am your

much obliged friend
Wm Wordsworth

[*M. W. adds*]

Mrs W. will thank Sergeant Talfourd to direct and forward the enclosed at his perfect convenience

1305. W. W. to H. C. R.

Address: H. C. Robinson Esqre, 2 Plowden's Buildings, Temple. [*In M. W.'s hand*]
Postmark: 11 Apr. *Stamp*: Charles St. West^r.
Endorsed: 10 Apl 1839. Wordsworth. Carlyles Style.
MS. Dr. Williams's Library.
Morley, i. 382.

Bath 10th April 1839
10 George Street

My dear Friend—

The enclosed was put into my hands by Dr Sinclare of Preston; and as he knew, I believe, that I was not going direct to London, I hope no inconvenience will arise from my not having sent it to you earlier—Many thanks for the Examiner; it is well that the Copyright Question should be looked at from different points of view. Carlyle's petition and the extract from Landor's are both characteristic—Carlyle racy and may startle certain dull persons into attention to the subject—but the expression

[1] i.e. I. F.

678

has often too much the air of burlesque, for my taste. I looked at¹ some other Articles in the same paper, particularly an Extract from the Westminster Review on the duty and Policy of redressing the grievances of the working Classes. I cannot see how any good purpose can be answered by such writing— which *indirectly* holds out Universal Suffrage, for the redress of grievances most of which from the nature of things can never be eradicated. ²—We shall stay here full three weeks; if there were a rail-road to this place as to Birmingham I should venture, as we can table you, to ask you to come down for a week—At present I scarcely feel justified in even suggesting the thing. Ever your faithful and affectionate Friend

Wm Wordsworth

Please get the enclosed franked at your *perfect* convenience *haste* is not needed.

1306. W. W. to THOMAS NOON TALFOURD

Postmark: 11 Apr. 1839. *Stamp*: Bath.
MS. untraced.
K (—). *LY ii. 969.*

[Bath]
[c. 10 Apr. 1839]

My dear Serjeant Talfourd,
    Your letter just received has mortified me, not a little, that you should have had so much trouble and made such a sacrifice, to meet so unworthy a House of Commons. The consideration of the heartlessness and injustice of that Assembly is what vexes me most in the whole business. I entirely approve of the publication you meditate. Only, by selecting two or three petitions you might offend some of those authors to whom the

---

¹ at *written twice.*

² In his reply (Morley, i. 383), H. C. R. agreed that universal suffrage offered no final remedy for the sufferings of the poor. But it was valuable to call the attention of the rich to their plight. 'Even the thought you express as to the inevitability of certain evils, tho true, has the effect of falsehood if it be sufferd to engross the whole mind. —It serves as a cushion on which the privileged few can repose. Their consciences are lulled and they acquiesce in a continuance of much remediable evil—*You* personally do not need such a monitor, but those whose cause you now so exclusively espouse, do . . .'

like distinction was not paid. I therefore submit whether it would be advisable to print any of them.

As a fact connected with my own case I will mention that, in the year 1805, I concluded a long poem upon the formation of my own mind, a small part of which you saw in manuscript, when I had the pleasure of a visit from you at Rydal.[1] That book still exists in manuscript. Its publication has been prevented merely by the personal character of the subject. Had it been published as soon as it was finished, the copyright would long ago have expired in the case of my decease. Now I do honestly believe that that poem, if given to the world before twenty-eight years had elapsed after the composition, would scarcely have paid its own expenses. If published now, with the aid of such reputation as I have acquired, I have reason to believe that the profit from it would be respectable; and my heirs, even as the law now is, would benefit by the delay; but in the other case neither they nor I would have got a farthing from it, if my life had not been prolonged; the profit, such as it might be, would all have gone to printers and publishers, and would, of course, continue to do so. What could be more——?[2]

I wish my arrangements would allow me to be in Town before the bill comes on again. With best wishes I ever am

Much obliged, and affectionately yours,
W. Wordsworth

1307. W. W. to CHARLES HENRY PARRY[3]

MS. untraced.
LY ii. 972

12 North Parade
Thursday evening [? 11 Apr. 1839]

My dear Sir,

I should have been up with you this morning to breakfast but one of my eyes being a little affected yesterday, I was afraid of

[1] In Sept. 1834.

[2] De Selincourt points out that the dash is more likely to represent Knight's discretion than W. W.'s.

[3] Charles Henry Parry, F.R.S. (1779–1860), a physician practising in Bath, studied medicine at Göttingen, and was one of Coleridge's companions in his German tour of 1799. He was the eldest brother of Sir William Parry, the Arctic explorer, and a friend of Thomas Poole.

encountering the cold wind at so early an hour, being engaged
tomorrow morning I can say no more at present than that I will
do my best to be with you at ½ past 9 oC. on Saturday morning,
to breakfast; we all regret much having been from home when
you and the ladies called. On Saturday we will talk over your
kind invitation for which in the mean while accept our united
thanks.

Believe me to be
faithfully yours
Wm Wordsworth

1308. W. W. to EDWARD QUILLINAN

MS. WL.[1]
LY ii. 970.

[*In M. W.'s hand*]

Sat: 13th April [1839]

My dear Mr Quillinan,

By yesterday's post I rec[d] a letter from Dora, containing a
long extract from one of yours to her.[2] Upon the subject of this
extract I cannot enter without premising, that calling upon her

---

[1] A copy of the letter sent, written on the back of M. W.'s letter to
Dora W. (*MW*, p. 224).

[2] E. Q. had now renewed his appeals to Dora W.—which she had evaded
during their meetings at Rydal in February —that they should take the risk of
marrying without further delay; and he had thus broken the spirit of the
compromise agreed to by all parties (see L. 1292 above). Nevertheless he was
deeply offended by this letter of W. W.'s and returned an angry reply which
even his advocate I. F. condemned, writing to Dora W. on 17 Apr.: 'I can feel
with and for you all, and for Mr. Quillinan too, but I do most exceedingly
regret the tone of his letter, for it has disturbed feelings which certainly were
very kindly disposed towards him, and which in time would have been all that
he could have required, and which may still be, tho' not so soon. He ought to
have taken the rebuke implied in your father's letter more patiently; had he
done so I cannot but think that what he said of his expectations would have
made your father feel justified in dispensing with any absolute security—as it is
we must look for gentler movements in his mind, and Mr Quillinan's, or some
circumstance that will put all into a better train again. . . . Your father will
not answer Mr. Quillinan's letter, what more must come through you—
cannot you prompt a more conciliatory letter from him? I think it is due.' And

in so peremptory a manner to act on so important an occasion *during the absence of her parents*, is, to say the least of it, an ill-judged proceeding. And this I must, notwithstanding my present knowledge that the proposal you have made to her, and thro' her to me, was agitated between you when you were at Rydal; and notwithstanding any thing that appears in your letter, in justification of its being made now.—As sincerity required this declaration from me, I make no apology for it, nor do I, dear Sir, think you will require one.[1]—I will now come to the point at once. Your Letter contains these sentences, which are the only ones I shall touch upon.

'If hereafter I should have an opportunity of making a provision for you, I certainly will do so, and I could not ask you to run the risk if I thought it possible that my death would leave you destitute of resources as from *my* side, I have not any fear as to that. The thing is will you *dare* to run the rough chance?'—Before I enter upon the former sentence, I must direct your attention to the fact, that you must have overlooked the state of health in which Dora has long been, or you cannot have been fully aware of it; or you could not have called upon her Parents, thro' her, circumstanced as they are, as to age, to give their Daughter up to '*a rough chance*'.

But from the former part of what I have copied, I must infer, that, tho' you can settle nothing upon her at present, you are not without hope of being able to do so etc etc. Now it is *my duty* to request of you, my dear Sir, to state as specifically as you can, upon what the hopes and expectations implied or expressed in the above Quotation from your Letter, rest. I mean in respect of a provision in case of your death.

There is no call for my saying more till I have received your answer upon this point, which I beg may be, on all our accounts, as definite and explicit as possible.

Wm is here and in a state of health that causes us much anxiety—the Bath waters do not seem to agree with him, and

she went on to summarize the results of her consultations with W. W.: 'What he says seems to come to this conclusion—Why cannot this attachment be put on the footing it seemed to be [in] when Mr Q. left Ambleside?—a patient waiting for happier circumstances, your father reconciling himself to all objections and willing to consent when there could be any reasonable security of your being provided for, and there being no hindrance to your attachment in the mean time?' (*WL MSS.*) See also L. 1312 below.

[1] This last phrase added by W. W.

his stomach and bowels are much deranged. Miss F. owing, we hope, solely to the severity of the weather, is not quite so well as she was at Ambleside. We all unite in affectionate remembrances to yourself and Children, and believe me, my dear Mr Q., faithfully yours,

Wm Wordsworth.

1309. W. W. to THOMAS SPRING RICE

MS. WL transcript. Hitherto unpublished.

10 George St Bath
April 19—1839

Confidential

Copy

My dear Mr Spring Rice,

Be assured, I am truly sensible of the great kindness shown towards me by y^r letter, [1] and not a little gratified by the terms in which you express y^r favorable opinion of my literary endeavours.

In answer to y^r obliging proposal I have to say with regret, that I have reason to believe the thing is impracticable. A few years ago, that is, when Sir R^t Peel was last in power, I applied to him through my friend Ld Lonsdale, to have the office I hold transferred to my Son, with w^h request Sir R^t w^d have been happy to comply, as he told Ld Lonsdale in his answer. But a few posts after, I myself was honored by a letter from Sir R^t, stating that upon inquiry he learned there was a minute of the Treasury, to the effect that in the event of my office becoming vacant, it sh^d be united with that of Lancaster, and here the matter ended.

If the objection stated by Sir R^t continues to exist, I fear nothing can be done. There are many reasons why I sh^d desire the proposed transfer, but there are also (except under certain modifications and arrangements) others against it upon which I need not *now* enter. If the supposed obstacle does not continue to

---

[1] Spring Rice, the Chancellor of the Exchequer, had written from Downing Street on 18 Apr. (*WL MSS.*) inviting W. W. to London to discuss the feasibility of transferring his Distributorship to his son Willy. This was a change which W. W. had unsuccessfully tried to bring about in 1835 (see Ls. 862, 864, and 866 above), and he was now anxious to raise it again with the Government.

exist, or can with propriety be got over, I sh^d then embrace the opportunity which your kindness, I know, w^d readily grant of laying the particulars before you, either by going myself immediately upon the receipt of y^r answer to London (it is my intention at all events to be there on the 4th of May) or through my Son (who is now here in search of health) and who will be in London on Monday the 22nd instant, and w^d be happy to wait upon you at any time or place you may appoint. His address will be Mr Moxon's 44 Dover Street.

Repeating my cordial and sincere thanks for the offer of y^r services so kindly made, in a matter w^h you rightly suppose interesting to me.

I remain my dear Mr Spring Rice
faithfully your much obliged
W. W.

1310. W. W. to THOMAS SPRING RICE

MS. WL transcript. Hitherto unpublished.

April 21st [1839]
Bath, 10 George S^t.

Copy

My dear Mr S. Rice,

I am glad to learn from Mr Bourke's[1] note rec^d this morn^g, that you believe the obstacle alluded to in my letter no longer exists.[2] My Son will be in Town tomorrow even^g. He will be able to make you acquainted with all the particulars relating to the emoluments and duties of my office, as well as those which belong to my own personal circumstances as they w^d be affected by the change which you so kindly propose. After you are in possession of the facts, w^h my Son will be able to communicate, [if] you shall deem it expedient, I will hasten my journey to Town.

I have the honor to be my dear Mr S. R.

faithfully y^r much obliged
W. W.

[1] A Treasury official.
[2] See previous letter.

P.S. If you w^d be so kind as to favor my Son W^m with a line addressed to 44 Dover S^t, he w^d be most happy to wait upon you, any day and hour that you may be pleased to appoint.

1311. W. W. to WILLIAM LISLE BOWLES[1]

Address: The Revd W. L. Bowles, Bremhill, nr. Chippenham.
MS. untraced.
LY ii. 971.

Apr 23^d [1839]

My dear Mr Bowles

It is very mortifying that this Concert should happen on Friday, as I am engaged to be at Bristol[2] on that very day. Mr Moore I may, I hope see in London, otherwise I should regret still more than I do this disappointment. It would have given much pleasure to see Mrs Moore, and her son. Mrs M. I well remember, as she was when I had the pleasure of breakfasting with her in her own Garden Cottage at Paris;[3] and it is most unlucky that I must miss this opportunity of renewing my acquaintance with her—I need not add how happy I should have been to see you again; and to talk with you and think in your presence, of old times, and departed Friends—I shall return to Bath on Friday Evening. On the Wednesday following I go

---

[1] Bowles had written on 15 Apr. regretting that W. W. could not visit him at Bremhill: 'Connected by so many and affecting reminiscences, and so much of more higher reason for veneration, it would have been of great satisfaction and gratification if you could have look'd on me in my old Parsonage domain. . . . But I shall come to Bath, and shake you by the hand, not having seen you, I think, since you and I, and Rogers, were in a boat together on the Thames, and I *got out* and *ran away*, and I heard you pronounc'd . . . the boldest man, in England. Whether this be true or not, I shall face all dangers of two Post horses, to come and see you, Thursday next . . . I am much alter'd in Phiz., but not, I hope, much, either in heart or head . . . I am truly glad to find your outward machine is only a little worse for wear! I am as wizen as a witch, and as deaf as a Post!' (*WL MSS.*) Bowles called at the Wordsworths' lodgings on the 18th (see *MW*, p. 229), but apparently missed seeing W. W.; and he wrote again on the 22nd to announce he was coming over to a concert at Bath on Friday, 26th, with Thomas Moore and his wife, and hoped to see W. W. then.

[2] With John Peace (see L. 1313 below).

[3] In Oct. 1820. See *MY* ii. 641 and Moore's *Memoirs*, iii. 161.

to Salisbury[1] returning next day to Bath, and on Friday the 2nd of May, depart for London.——

I am just going to write a Note to your Friend Mr Wiltshire proposing to call upon him to morrow, with Miss Fenwick and Mrs Wordsworth, to see his fine pictures—He has kindly called twice upon me.——

Mrs Wordsworth leaves Bath on friday first for Hereford— She unites with me in kindest regards to Mrs Bowles and your self, and believe me my dear Mr Bowles

faithfully and affectionately yours
Wm Wordsworth

1312. W. W. to DORA W.

Address: Miss Wordsworth, Rydal Mount, Kendal.
Franked: *Down Post* Woburn April twenty seven 1839 R. H. Inglis.
Stamp: Woburn.
MS. British Library.
    'Some Unpublished Letters of William Wordsworth', Cornhill Magazine, xx (1893), 257—76 (—). K (—). LY ii. 973.

[*c.* 24 Apr. 1839]

My dear Daughter,
    The Letter which you must have received from W[m][2] has placed before you my judgement and feelings; how far you are reconciled to them I am unable to divine;[3] I have only to add,

---

[1] To visit his cousins the Fishers. But as next letters make clear, his plans were changed, and he left Bath for London on 29 Apr.

[2] E. Q. had taken offence at W. W.'s letter of 13 Apr., and in writing to Dora W. on the 17th (*WL MSS.*), he took no notice of her father's questions about his financial position, and launched instead into a lengthy justification of his own conduct in the course of the whole affair: 'I have been mortified enough already, and you have suffered the torments of suspense too long; you have had too painful a conflict between your love for your father and your kindness for me, and now that the hopelessness of the case is manifest I believe in my soul and conscience that you will be the less unhappy for having arrived at the conviction of its hopelessness.' W. W. jnr. had subsequently intervened to try and ease E. Q.'s resentment by explaining his father's point of view.

[3] Dora W. had reproached W. W. with overemphasizing the financial problem. ' . . . I must say that neither you nor Mr. Q. do your Father's feelings justice or shew him proper *respect even*, by such expressions retorted

that I believe Mr Q. to be a most honorable and upright man, and further that he is most strongly and faithfully attached to you—this I must solemnly declare in justice to you both; and to this I add *my blessing upon you and him*; more I cannot do and if this does not content you with what your Br has said, we must all abide by God's decision upon our respective fates. Mr Q. is, I trust, aware how slender my means are; the state of W's health will undoubtedly entail upon us considerable expense, and how John is to get on without our aid I cannot foresee. No more at present, my time is out; I am going to join Miss Fenwick at Miss Pollard's.

ever your most tender hearted and affectionate Father

Wm Wordsworth

In a beautiful churchyard[1] near Bath I saw the other day this inscription:

Thomas Carrol Esq[r]
Barrister at Law
Born—so—died, so—
Rest in peace, dear Father—
There was not another word.

Thursday—Y[r] letter to me just rec[d]—thanks, I will write from Brinsop. M. W.[2]

upon him as "L-s-d" and "the business of the matter". All the feelings for your sake, that he has extinguished—should not indeed my Dearest have been met in this spirit—by either of you.' (*MW*, p. 229).

[1] Whitcomb, where H. C. R.'s mother was buried (see Morley, i. 383).
[2] Added by M. W. at the top of the letter.

1313. W. W. to JOSEPH COTTLE

Address: Joseph Cottle Esq.
MS. Cornell.
LY ii. 973.

April 26th —39
Farfield House[1]

My dear Friend
I am truly sorry not to have found you here, as Mr Peace[2] and I expected. My allowance of time is so short, that I must take an early coach for Bath, and can do no more than beg you to accept the best wishes of your old and true Friend.

Wm Wordsworth

Pray let your sister Mrs Hare know how much I regret missing her——

1314. W. W. to CHARLES HENRY PARRY

Address: Dr Parry, Bath.
MS. Cornell. Hitherto unpublished.

Sunday Morn —
28th April [1839]

My dear Sir,
I should have been truly happy to see you tomorrow as you kindly propose, but I have received a Letter[3] this morning which summons me to London by tomorrow morning's Coach—

---

[1] Residence of Cottle's sister. See pt. i, L. 347.

[2] W. W.'s 'devoted admirer', John Peace (1785–1861), City Librarian at Bristol, who had called at Rydal Mount the previous October (see *R MVB* and *MW*, p. 219) and now sought him out in Bath (see *MW*, pp. 227–8). Peace had gone to Christ's College, Cambridge, intending to take Holy Orders, but was prevented from doing so by a chronic weakness of voice; but he remained a champion of the Church of England and its music, publishing *An Apology for Cathedral Service*, 1839, dedicated to W. W. See memoir prefixed to *Axiomata Pacis*, 1862.

[3] From Willy W. See L. 1316 below.

Pray accept my cordial thanks for your very valuable Volume,[1] from which advanced in life as I am, and often interrupted by inflamed or weak eyes, I hope to derive great benefit.

Do not trouble yourself to make the Oxford inquiry,[2] I can easily learn all I wish to know, in London—

With kind regards to M[rs] Parry, yourself, and your truly interesting young family;[3]

I remain—
My dear D[r] Parry
faithfully your
much obliged
W[m] Wordsworth

1315. W. W. to THOMAS SPRING RICE

MS. untraced.
LY. ii. 974.

Bath April 28th [1839]

Private

My dear Mr Spring Rice,

This morning I have received a Letter from my Son in which he speaks of himself as truly grateful for the manner in which you received him, and the interest you so kindly take in a matter that nearly concerns me, and which I would gladly hope may have a successful issue. That nothing may be wanting on my part, I have resolved to set off for London to morrow morning.

---

[1] Parry's edition of *A Memoir of Peregrine Bertie, eleventh Lord Willoughby de Eresby*, 1838 (*R.M. Cat.*, no. 123), the distinguished Elizabethan general and friend of Sir Philip Sidney.

[2] W. W. had been invited to Oxford to receive an honorary degree (see L. 1328 below), but was undecided whether to accept the offer on account of the expense (see *MW*, p. 232). The initiative came from Francis Atkinson Faber (1805–76), Fellow of Magdalen, who wrote on 17 Apr. to inquire on behalf of 'some of the leading members of the University' whether W. W. was willing to accept a D.C.L. (*WL MSS.*); but he had no doubt been prompted in this by his younger brother, Frederick (see L. 1195 above). See also L. 1320 below.

[3] W. W. called on the Parrys at Summer Hill later in the day, as recorded in Ellen Parry's journal (C. H. Parry, *Ellen Parry*, [1842], pp. 187, 237). See also L. 1408 (in next volume)

A note or message addressed to me at 44 Dover street will be sure to reach me, and I should be happy to wait upon you at any time you may appoint—. On second thoughts, however, it seems best that to save you the trouble of writing or sending,—I should call in Downing street on Tuesday morning, in the assured belief that if it be not *perfectly* convenient for you to give me a minute or two of your time, you will frankly let me know—

I grieve to hear so sad an account of Lady Theodosia's state,

> Believe me to be
> my dear Mr Spring Rice
> faithfully your
> much obliged
> Wm Wordsworth

1316. W. W. to DORA W.

Address: Miss Wordsworth, Rydal Mount, nr Kendal.
Franked: London May one 1839 T. N. Talfourd.
MS. WL.
LY ii. 975.

56 Russell Square May 1st [1839]

My dearest Dora,

Private. Maugre this tender beginning this will be only a Letter of matter of fact and business.—I left Bath on Monday, on account of a Letter from Wm—Have you been told that the Chancellor of the Exchequer addressed a Letter to me at Bath proposing to transfer my office to Wm? W. went up immediately to Town, and after a week I followed him to be upon the spot; and do what I could to place the matter upon an advantageous footing—We wait the result of Mr S. Rice's endeavours, but I fear the thing will prove impracticable. Dont say a word upon this subject to any one but Mr Carter.—

Now for business, pray read what follows to Mr C— first I should like to know what have been the net profits of my office to me for the last few years, after deducting his salary, and what he has annually had.

Next I should like to be instructed as to what I can do, while I am here, to have such statements made of our general money concerns, as may be intelligible and regular: next, I should like to know from him what we possess as far as he can make it out.—

By the bye, I saw Mr Courtenay last night, he gives a most flattering account of the Provincials,[1] in which he has 18,000 pounds of his own money—he attends every day, so that nothing can go wrong without his knowledge.

Wm is in health better a good deal than at Bath, but far from well: when Miss Fenwick arrives I shall take him to Dr Ferguson.[2]—

On Saturday your Mother and I shall meet at Miss Rogers to stay till Thursday, then we go to the Marshalls, afterwards to the Ricketts; then I hope to Cambridge and then home—I shall keep this Letter open till the afternoon—that you may know what becomes of the Copy-right.[3]—

Pray do not work *hard*, I cannot bear you should—at copying the Poem,[4] nor let Eliz. Cookson do so—Give my love to her— and kind remembrances to the Servants, one and all; with a thousand loving regards and remembrances to my dear Sister— How is she, how are you yourself, and how is Dorothy[5]— address under cover to Sergeant Talfourd, Temple.—

I say nothing of your affairs, as you have had all I can say; except that my best wishes and prayers for you are perpetually repeated.

My own health is good—except that my feet fail, especially about the ancles, which makes me afraid of walking much upon the flagged streets.

[1] i.e. National Provincial Bank shares.

[2] For Dr. Robert Ferguson see L. 1030 above.

[3] The Committee stage of Talfourd's Bill opened on 1 May, but its further progress was checked by a flood of amendments.

[4] W. W. had been preoccupied with revising *The Prelude* before he left Rydal, and Dora W. and Elizabeth Cookson were now producing a fair copy of the poem (see *Prel.*, pp. xxiii–xxiv). I. F. had written to Henry Taylor on 28 Mar.: 'Our journey was postponed for a week, that the beloved old poet might accomplish the work that he had in hand, the revising of his grand autobiographical poem, and leaving it in a state fit for publication. At this he has been labouring for the last month, seldom less than six or seven hours a day, or rather one ought to say the whole day, for it seems always in his mind—quite a possession, and much, I believe, he has done to it, expanding it in some parts, and perfecting it in all. I could not have imagined the labour that he has bestowed on all his works, had I not been so much with him at this time.' (*Correspondence of Henry Taylor*, p. 87.)

[5] Mrs. Benson Harrison.

Tell me how many copies of the Poems 6 vols you have at the Mount.

[unsigned]

1317. W. W. to DORA W. and D. W.

MS. WL.
LY ii. 977.

[c. 9 May 1839]¹

My dearest Dora,

I cannot let the frank go without a word or two from myself. Your Mother has no doubt told you of all our movements, some of which have been too fatiguing on account of our missing *Cabs* where we wished to find them: and of Omnibuses we have yet made no use.—

Our project as to the Transfer has been baffled—so that we are, as we have been, among the unlucky—I mean baffled by the resignation of Ministry:² what Sir R. Peel may think himself able to do for us I know not.— By Saturday at the latest (indeed it cannot be done earlier) I will call with Wm upon Dr Ferguson whom I prepared for the visit yesterday, having accidentally met him in Portland Place. Wm's case is a strange one, he was very much better on coming to London. The excitement, I suppose, did it and he had fallen off much when he left us on Monday for Chatham;³ so that one knows not what to think of

---

¹ Probably written from Mrs. Ricketts's house in Gloucester Place. M. W. had joined W. W. in London on 4 May, and thereafter they had divided their time between I. F., the Rogers, and Mrs. Ricketts, meeting (among others) Lord Northampton, Jeffrey, Empson, Henry Taylor, R. C. Trench, the Clarksons, and Milman, and dining with John Kenyon and Sara and Henry Coleridge. (See *Rogers*, ii. 180; *HCR* ii. 570; and *MW*, pp. 234–6.)

² Lord Melbourne had resigned on 7 May. Sir Robert Peel was invited to form a ministry, but declined, and Melbourne took office again; but Spring Rice left the Cabinet in August, being elevated to the peerage as Lord Monteagle, and thus W. W.'s hopes of transferring his Distributorship to his son were again frustrated. Melbourne's resignation also had the effect of further postponing consideration of the Copyright Bill.

³ Probably to stay with W. W.'s cousin, Mrs. Proctor Smith.

it—I scarcely venture to hope that he will be improved in health when he returns.

Now let me thank you and Elizabeth C. for the labours you have gone through in transcribing that long Poem;[1] pray, when it is done, let it be sealed, and deposited with Mr Carter, to provide against any unlucky accident befalling the other.—

My eyes continue in almost their very best way, notwithstanding lamp light, candle light, late Dinners, late hours, for the night I was at Miss Watts's[2] Ball, going to oblige that good and kind Lady, Mrs Ricketts, I was not in bed till half after one.—

I cannot my dear child but wish that your mind were put at rest by Mr Q. on this under all circumstances harrassing and trying affair. I wait for your report of his answer with anxiety;[3] so does your Mother, no doubt, though we do not talk about the subject.—

Your delightful description of the beauty that Spring has poured around you makes me wish to be present as Spectator and Listener—God Bless you, my dear Daughter, for ever and ever. Love to Elizabeth and kind regards to all the Household, and all enquiring Friends. Jane[4] has seen little or nothing of London yet, but she *has seen* the *Queen*. To day she goes to the Zoological Gardens. Once more farewell, my dear Dora—ever your affectionate Father, W. Wordsworth.

I have purposely deferred sending love to you, my dear Sister, that I might address you in particular. I am glad to hear that you have been out among the Birds and Flowers, and in the sweet sunshine, and I expect to find you in all things marvellously improved when I return. A thousand remembrances and love to you: were you here, you would delight in the prospect we

---

[1] *The Prelude*. See previous letter.

[2] Probably Amelia Watts (1780–1862), who was related to Mrs. Ricketts, and also to W. W.'s friend Lord Liverpool. She was the daughter of Edward Watts of Hanslope Park, Bucks.; a niece of George Ricketts, Governor of Barbados, 1794–1800, and a niece of the 1st Earl of Liverpool.

[3] W. W. was still hoping for some indication from E. Q. of his financial prospects, and this he seemed reluctant to give. Writing to Dora W. on 12 May, he seemed to admit the justice of her father's objections: 'I do not pretend to think that our prospects are such as will not make many people call our marriage madness . . . My great dread as to our union has always been lest you should find yourself removed from a comfortable to a comfortless home . . .' (*WL MSS.*)

[4] The Wordsworths' maid.

have from the windows of Regents park—and its trees so green and its bright flowers. Ever your W. W.

The world says Mr Rogers is going to be married to a girl of 20 named Jane Clerk—but I am sure it must be all nonsense.

1318. W. W. to THOMAS SPRING RICE

Endorsed: W. Wordsworth. May 11. 1839. For an Interview.
MS. Cornell.
LY ii. 976.

May 11th —39
41 Upper Grosvenor Street[1]

My dear Mr Spring Rice,

I write merely to acknowledge with thanks the receipt of your Note and the accompanying document.

As soon as a more settled state of public affairs shall allow you to give attention to what I have to observe upon your kind communication, I shall be glad of an interview at any time or place which you may do me the honor to appoint.

> Believe me
> my dear Mr Spring Rice
> faithfully
> your much obliged
> Wm Wordsworth

[1] W. W. and M. W. had now moved on to stay with the Marshalls. The following week W. W. had engagements with, among others, Talfourd, Lord Lonsdale, Lockhart, and Sir John Taylor Coleridge (to meet Bunsen), as recorded in a Diary preserved at Cornell. He also planned to attend one of Carlyle's lectures on 'The Revolutions of Modern Europe'. See *Wordsworth's Pocket Notebook*, ed. George Harris Healey, Cornell University Press, 1942, pp. 10, 20.

1319. W. W. to WILLIAM S. ORR[1]

Address: W. S. Orr Esq[r], Amen Court, Paternoster Row.
MS. Mary Couts Burnet Library, Texas Christian University. Hitherto un-published.

41 Upper Grosvenor Street
15th May [1839]

Mr Wordsworth presents his Compts to Mr Orr, and thanks him for the beautiful Copy upon India Paper of the Pictorial Greece.

He would have returned thanks earlier for this valuable Present, but it was only yesterday that he learned from his Nephew the Master of Harrow, that he was indebted for it to Mr Orr's attention.

1320. W. W. to CHARLES WORDSWORTH

MS. Mr. Jonathan Wordsworth. Hitherto unpublished.

41 Upper Grosvenor
Street
Thursday [16 May 1839]

My dear Nephew,

Your Aunt and I had heard the tidings of your heavy affliction,[2] before I received your Letter which had been detained some days in its way to us. We were much stricken and troubled by the sad intelligence, and do most sincerely condole with you, hoping and praying that the Almighty will in due Season voutchsafe to you that peace of mind which his mercy only can bestow.

The infant—whose life we are happy to hear has been preserved, will erelong prove to you a source of calmer consolation than at present it can possibly be.

—The manner in which you express yourself upon this deplorable event shews that you are prepared to bear it as a Christian ought; and makes me feel that there is no call for many

---

[1] Director of Messrs. Orr and Co., publishers of C. W. jnr.'s *Greece: Pictorial, Descriptive, and Historical*, which had just appeared.

[2] Charles Wordsworth's wife Charlotte had died on 10 May while giving birth to a daughter.

words from me. I cannot however refrain from saying, that it is to us an aggravation of sorrow that though we had heard so much of the amiable qualities of our departed Niece we never had the pleasure of seeing her, which we looked forward to with hope: but God's Will be done!—

Thanks for the information you gave me; I shall if possible attend at Oxford,[1] and allow me to thank, through you, at your leisure, Mr Hamilton,[2] and to say that I shall be happy to accept his hospitable offer. Your Letter was forwarded to Dora, so that I have not Mr H's address; nor am I indeed sure that you mentioned it; but I shall learn it from Christopher; and will then write to Mr H. myself.

If Mrs Hoare returns to Hampstead[3] on or before, Monday next, on that day your Aunt and I mean if convenient to her, to visit her. Your Cousin W^m who is here begs me to offer his sincere condolence: he will accompany us—as Ch^r specially wishes to see him. And now my dear Charles farewell; and believe me with a thousand good wishes

your affectionate Uncle
W Wordsworth

I need not say how happy we shall be to see you at Rydal, when your family may allow you to take such a journey.

[1] To receive his honorary degree. See L. 1328 below.

[2] Walter Kerr Hamilton (see pt. i, L. 362), was one of W. W.'s most fervent admirers at Oxford. According to Charles Wordsworth, he valued the *Excursion* 'next to the Bible' (*Annals of My Early Life*, p. 156).

[3] Mrs. Hoare had hastened to Winchester at the first news of the tragedy.

1321. W. W. to DODSHON FOSTER

Address: Dodshon Foster Esqre, 40 Charlotte Street, Portland Place.
Postmark: 20 May 1839. *Stamp*: Park Lane.
MS. Mrs..Spence Clepham.[1] *Hitherto unpublished.*

Upper Grosvenor Street
May 20th 1839

You are not mistaken in supposing that I remember your excellent Grandfather.[2] I can assure you I not unfrequently recall him to my mind and with much pleasure—

Sincerely yours
Wm Wordsworth

1322. W. W. to WALTER KERR HAMILTON

Address: Revd W. K. Hamilton, Merton College.
MS. Mr. W. Hugh Peal. Hitherto unpublished.

Harrow Tuesday
22nd May [1839]

My dear Sir,

My Nephew, Charles Wordsworth, having made me acquainted with the offer of your hospitalities at Merton College, during the approaching Oxford Commemoration,[3] I write to return you my sincere thanks and to say that I shall be happy to avail myself of your kindness.—

According to directions from Lady Davy, I address this under cover to the B^p of Salisbury.[4] Lady D. I am sorry to say was suffering from a severe cold when I saw her the other day.

Pray mention to Mrs W. Fisher,[5] if you happen to see her, that I have received her Letter; and nothing but a faint hope which I cherished that I might be able to run down from London to Salisbury, has prevented my answering it. She shall hear from me before I go into London from the Country.—

---

[1] Since sold (1971).

[2] Robert Foster of Hebblethwaite Hall, nr. Sedbergh (see *MY* ii. 84).

[3] See L. 1320 above.

[4] Edward Denison, formerly Fellow of Merton. See L. 983 above.

[5] W. W.'s cousin.

My Nephew Christopher and his wife are both well; poor dear Charles, what a blow has he had—

Believe me my dear Mr Hamilton faithfully your much obliged

Wm Wordswworth

P.S. Chris. is just come in and begs his kind regards.—

May I ask the favor of your procuring a Cover for the Enclosed from the Bishop at his leisure?

1323. W. W. to C. W.

MS. Mr. Jonathan Wordsworth. Hitherto unpublished.

41 Upper Grosvenor Street
Sunday Morning[1] [26 May 1839]

My dear B^r,

Here we arrived last night. I write this note to say how we should grieve were you to pass through London without a meeting. If you cannot call here, pray tell us where we may have a glimpse of you in passing through, and we will punctually repair to the spot.—

Dear Charles is well, but certainly requires the restoration of holiday quiet. His Child[2] is a most delightful little creature. We were two days with him[3] and two days at Salisbury—the Fishers[4] well. From Southampton we drove to see poor Mary[5] for a few minutes. Her most interesting Daughter is dying; the Mother never quits her room but for a few minutes. She knows there is no hope of recovery, and submits to the will of God. It was an affecting visit—The dear Sufferer begged to see me and I

---

[1] Written just before, or just after, the breakfast party at H. C. R.'s at which W. W. met Layard the explorer (see L. 1331 below).

[2] Charlotte.

[3] At Winchester. If W. W. was out of London for four days the previous week, he probably had to postpone or cancel his dinner engagement with Henry Hallam, the historian, a noted opponent of the Copyright Bill (see *Wordsworth's Pocket Notebook*, p. 11).

[4] Canon William Fisher and his wife Elizabeth, W. W.'s cousin (see L. 1185 above).

[5] Her elder sister, now a widow, had been left in straitened circumstances, and was living outside Southampton with her daughter Emma (b. 1818).

went into her room, staying not more than three minutes. She was in the last stage of debility and emaciation.

Ever with Mary's kindest love, your affectionate Brother

Wm Wordsworth

Mrs Marshall would be delighted if you could make it convenient to dine here.

1324. W. W. to WALTER KERR HAMILTON

Address: The Rev.—Hamilton, Merton Coll, Oxford.
Franked: London May thirty one 1839 W. Marshall.
Postmark: 31 May 1839.
MS. WL.
LY ii. 978.

May 30^{th1} [1839]
41 Upper Grosvenor Street

My dear Sir,

Thanks for your letter. My intention is to leave London for Oxford, Monday 10th June. Having received an invitation from the Master of University College[2] to dine with him that day, I have written to him to say that I shall be happy to do so, and on that night I hope to be received as your Guest.

Believe me to be
truly your obliged
Wm Wordsworth

[1] W. W. had arranged to breakfast with Sir Robert Inglis on the 27th and dine at Lambeth Palace with the Archbishop of Canterbury. On the 28th he breakfasted with Moxon, and visited Dr. Ferguson on the 29th, viewing Robert Vernon's celebrated collection of pictures in Pall Mall. On the 30th he breakfasted at Hampstead, and in the afternoon saw Lord Richard Grosvenor, later 2nd Marquess of Westminster (1795–1869), at this time M.P. for Chester, doubtless in connection with the Copyright Bill. (See *Wordsworth's Pocket Notebook*, p. 11.)

[2] The Revd. Frederick Charles Plumptre, D.D. (1796–1870), Fellow of University College, Oxford, 1817–36, and thereafter Master: Vice-Chancellor, 1848–51.

1325. W. W. to WALTER FARQUHAR HOOK[1]

Address: The Revd Dr Hook, 10 Dean's Yard, Westminster.
MS. Carl H. Pforzheimer Library. Hitherto unpublished.

41 Upper Grosvenor Street
Friday morning [31 May 1839]
9 oclock

My dear Sir,

Last night I found your Card, and truly sorry I am that I cannot return your obliging call. (I say *obliging*, for much engaged as you must be I deem it a great favor). Unluckily I must be off for Cambridge[2] within an hour, so that I cannot look for the pleasure of our meeting unless your stay in Town should be prolonged beyond next Wednesday; if so pray let me know, and when you would be within so that I might see. On Monday the 10th I go to Oxford to the Commemoration.

Believe me faithfully yours,
Wm Wordsworth

1326. W. W. to M. W.

MS. WL.
LY ii. 979.

Sat. morn. June 8 [1839]

My dearest Mary

Having nothing particular to say I should not have written now but for the Frank.—I long to know that you found Dora pretty well and that you both reached home in good plight. Pray tell dear Miss Fenwick that I met Mr and Mrs Villiers[3] at

---

[1] See pt. ii, L. 726.

[2] For this visit to Cambridge, see *Correspondence of Henry Taylor*, pp. 122–4. W. W. took I. F. to St. John's to see his old rooms, where (as he said) he had been 'as joyous as a lark', and he stayed in Trinity Lodge with C. W., 'a gentle yet dignified old Abbot', according to I. F., 'and learned in all the learning of the olden time'.

[3] Edward Villiers (1806–43), younger brother of Henry Taylor's close friend Thomas Hyde Villiers (1801–32), of the Colonial Office: barrister, Fellow of Merton College, Oxford (1831–6), clerk to the Privy Council, and a commissioner for the colonisation of S. Australia. In 1835 he had married Elizabeth (1808–90), younger sister of Henry Thomas Liddell, 1st Earl of Ravensworth (see L. 875 above). The couple had called at Rydal Mount the

H. Taylor's breakfast—Mrs V. wonderfully better, and both looking well.—Yesterday I was only able to go to Mr Taylor's breakfast, being disabled by the pain returning to my Ancle, so bad that I could not walk; and Determined last night to consult Sir B. Brodie—but it is so much easier today that I shall hardly trouble him; but should the pain return, I shall not go to Coleorton but proceed from Oxford, either on Friday or Saturday at the latest; if Saturday I shall stay over Sunday with the Arnolds. I do not mean to walk at all today for fear of bringing back the pain. This morning I went with Susan[1] to breakfast at Mr Rogers, thence to make a farewell call at Lambeth. I did not see the Archbishop; called also on Mr Spring Rice but found him engaged—he will communicate with me this afternoon by letter. Today we dine at home and go to the Opera, tomorrow have breakfast at Mr Kenyon's to meet Mr Webster,[2] reckoned the first man in America, and then a lunch and dinner with Mr Powell,[3] and in the morning start for Oxford. How I wish I were with you and long that the Oxford business was over. I shall have done all my calls, except Lady Coleridge,[4] Mr Haydon and poor George Dyer;[5] all of which would have been got over yesterday but for this plaguy lameness; whether a mere overworking of the tendons of the ancle or rheumatism or gout I know [not]; and if I can would like to consult Dr Ferguson tomorrow.—

previous autumn in the company of James Spedding and Henry Taylor (*RMVB*).

[1] C. W. jnr.'s wife.

[2] Daniel Webster (1782–1852), friend of Ticknor and Congressman for Massachusetts: the leading American lawyer on constitutional questions, a brilliant orator with influential views on public finance and slavery, and at this time a serious contender for the Presidency; Secretary of State, 1840–3. The party at Kenyon's also included Rogers, Monckton Milnes, and Henry Nelson Coleridge, and later they were joined by H. C. R., Talfourd, and Count Montalembert (see G. T. Curtis, *Life of Daniel Webster*, 2 vols., 1870, ii. 7 ff). Webster subsequently called at Rydal Mount c. 1 Aug. (*RMVB*), but W. W. was not at home, and the poet was unable to go over to see him at Lowther owing to eye trouble.

[3] Thomas Powell was continuing to ingratiate himself with W. W. On 30 Mar. he had sent a further present of Stilton cheese and a letter in which he deplored De Quincey's recent articles on the Lake Poets in *Tait's Magazine* (*WL MSS.*).

[4] Sir John Coleridge's wife (see L. 1077 above).

[5] Lamb's friend, who died two years later.

Yesterday I had a long interview with Mr Quillinan;[1] tell
dearest Dora.—I fear it was not satisfactory to either party. He
seems wretched at the thought of the marriage being put off;
and, as I told him, I could not look at [it] with that chearfulness
and complacency and hopefulness, which ought to accompany
such a transaction. As the event is inevitable, I told him I felt it
my duty to try to make the best of it; but how I should succeed I
could not tell. But said I blame no-one; I only do regret that the
affair should have pressed on this way in my absence, this was
[? sad] of all, only I must add that I felt easier for having seen him
and that our interview was perfectly friendly.—Now my
dearest Mary read as much of this to Dora as you like.—Unless I
go to Coleorton I perhaps shall not write again; if I do I will
however briefly—

Dearest Child how came you to say I never sent love to
you—I love you incessantly, how could I have suffered what I
have done were it not so. A thousand loves to you, and all tender
thoughts for my dear sister. My kindest love to Miss Fenwick.

Farewell dearest Mary
W. W.

1327. W. W. to DORA W.

MS. WL.
'*Some Unpublished Letters of William Wordsworth*', *Cornhill Magazine*, xx
(1893), 257–76. K (—). LY ii. 980 (—).

Sunday morning, nine o'clock [9 June 1839]

My dearest Dora,

I am looking for Mr Quillinan, every moment. I hope to
revive the conversation of yesterday.[2] The sum is: I make no

[1] This meeting at the Marshalls' is recorded in E. Q.'s MS. Diary (*WL
MSS.*). See also next letter.

[2] The following day E. Q. was able to report to Dora W. that his old
relationship with the Wordsworths had been restored: 'How delighted you
will be, if you are really my own Dora, at what I have to tell you! Your Father
and I are right good real friends. After that weary first interview of which I
gave a doleful and yet half hopeful account, I never was so thoroughly
subdued in my life. . . . On Sunday Morning I went again to Mr Marshall's
by Mr W.'s appointment. I was shewn in to all the family at breakfast, he
among them, that being his breakfast-breakfast, the one to follow at Kenyon's

opposition to this marriage. I have no resentment connected
with it toward any one: you know how much friendship I have
always felt towards Mr Q, and how much I respect him. I do not
doubt the strength of his love and affection towards you; this, as
far as I am concerned, is the fair side of the case. On the other
hand, I cannot think of parting with you with that
complacency, that satisfaction, that hopefulness which I could
wish to feel;[1] there is too much of necessity in the case for my
wishes. But I must submit, and do submit; and God Almighty
bless you, my dear child, and him who is the object of your long
and long-tried preference and choice.

Ever your affectionate father,
Wm Wordsworth

I have said little above of your dear mother, the best of
women. O how my heart is yearning towards her, and you, and
my poor dear Sister.—

My ancle is rather worse this morning than yesterday at this
time. Would that the next week were fairly over.—I enjoyed
the Ballet and the Opera last night.

was to be his talking breakfast. Presently he went with me into the library and
there read me that most kind letter which he had written to you. From that
moment all was right. I dismounted from my high horse, never more to get on
its back, by my fault at least, to him. Willy kindly gave me his seat in the
Cabriolet and walked to Kenyon's, that I might ride with his father to Harley
Street. In the Cab. he spoke to me with all the affection of a friend and a father,
and if he holds to that, it must be my delight as well as my duty to shew that
that *is the right course*.' (*WL MSS.*)

[1] E. Q. was still hoping that he would eventually benefit from the
settlement of the Brydges estate; but he was also at this time exploring the
possibility of becoming secretary of a new joint stock bank (see *HCR* ii. 573).

1328. W. W. to THOMAS GAISFORD [1]

Address: The very Rev^d the Dean, Ch. Ch.—[*delivered by hand*]
Endorsed: June 1839.
MS. Alan G. Hill. Hitherto unpublished.

Wednesday Evening—[2] [12 June 1839]
The Vice chancellor's—[3]

Mr Wordsworth presents his respects to the Dean of Christ church, and regrets that he cannot have the pleasure of dining with the Dean and Mrs Gaisford to-morrow, owing to a previous engagement—[4]

---

[1] Thomas Gaisford, D.D. (1779–1855), Classical scholar: Regius Professor of Greek at Oxford from 1811, and Dean of Christ Church from 1831. His invitation to 'Dr. Wordsworth' is among the *WL MSS*.

[2] W. W. was greeted with an extraordinary demonstration of public acclaim from the assembled University when he came forward to receive his honorary degree at the Commemoration on the 12th. 'His reception', according to G. V. Cox, the Esquire Bedel, 'was overpowering to others, though he stood it firm, and *apparently* unmoved as one of his Westmoreland mountains.' (*Recollections of Oxford*, 1868, p. 291.) The ovation he received seemed to set the seal finally on a reputation that had been growing for two decades, and to show that the younger generation had taken him to their heart. 'It was,' Mrs. Arnold confided later to Emily Trevenen, 'the public voice for once harmoniously joining to pay homage to goodness, and to talent, consistently employed in promoting the real happiness of his fellow creatures.' (*WL MSS.*) The Arnolds came specially from Rugby to attend, and Mrs. Arnold's MS. Diary (*WL MSS.*) gives a very full account of the proceedings. John Keble, Professor of Poetry, delivered the Creweian Oration, adding his own compliments (see L. 1330 below) to those of the Public Orator, Professor Joseph Phillimore. Other recipients of honorary degrees included Lord Ripon, Sir John Herschel, Chevalier Bunsen (see L. 1063 above), and Capt. W. H. Smyth (see next letter); and among University prizewinners present in the theatre to recite their compositions were Arthur Penrhyn Stanley, the future Dean of Westminster (see L. 1027 above), and John Ruskin of Christ Church, winner of the Newdigate. The ceremony was followed by lunch with the Provost of Oriel, Edward Hawkins (1789–1882), and Thomas Arnold. See *Gentleman's Magazine*, xii, new series (July 1839), 69–70; Frances Baroness Bunsen, *Memoir of Baron Bunsen*, i. 534–5: and Prothero and Bradley, *Life and Correspondence of Arthur Penrhyn Stanley*, i. 217.

[3] The Revd. Ashurst Turner Gilbert, D.D. (1786–1870), Principal of Brasenose College, 1822–42, and thereafter Bishop of Chichester.

[4] W. W. was to dine at Oriel to meet Bunsen.

704

1329. W. W. to WILLIAM HENRY SMYTH[1]

Endorsed: June 13th 1839.
MS. Harvard University Library. Hitherto unpublished.

The Vice chancellor's
Thursday noon [13 June 1839]

My dear Sir,

With much pleasure I snatch a moment to thank you for the very gratifying token of esteem, which I have just received at your hands, in your valuable Catalogue of Roman Imperial Medals.[2] The Book will be prized by me for its own sake, and as a memorial of one of the most interesting days of a pretty long life, in which I found myself associated in public honor with yourself, and so many other eminent Persons.

That Gentlemen of your laborious, perilous and noble profession, should also devote themselves to science and literature as far as their opportunities will allow, and with such distinguished success is a characteristic of our Country and times, which every Englishman ought to be proud of and rejoices in.

Believe me to be with every good wish, and a due sense of your favorable opinion,

faithfully yours
Wm Wordsworth

---

[1] Capt. William Henry Smyth, F.R.S. (1788–1865) served in the navy throughout the Napoleonic Wars, retiring from active service in 1824 to devote himself to science and literature. He wrote extensively on astronomy, geography, and nautical matters. In 1830 he had joined in founding the Royal Geographical Society, of which he became President in 1849: in 1845 he was President of the Royal Astronomical Society.

[2] *Descriptive Catalogue of a Cabinet of Roman Imperial large-brass Medals*, Bedford, 1834 (*R.M. Cat.*, no. 431).

1330. W. W. to JOHN KEBLE

MS. Keble College, Oxford. Hitherto unpublished.

University College
Friday Morning
[14 June 1839]

My dear Sir,

Pray excuse a bold request. Will you be so kind as to transcribe for me the passage in your admirable Oration in which you did me the honor of speaking of my Poetry.[1]—I should like to possess it.

Mr Faber,[2] of University College, will charge himself with forwarding it to me, if you send it to him.

faithfully
with sincere respect
yours W Wordsworth

---

[1] This section of Keble's Creweian Oration on the Church, the University, and the poor, in which he paid tribute to W. W. as 'one who alone among poets has set the manners, the pursuits, and the feelings, religious and traditional, of the poor not merely in a good but I might say even in a celestial light', is printed in *Mem.* ii. 355—6. See also Sir J. T. Coleridge, *Memoir of the Rev. John Keble*, 2 vols., 1869, i. 257—8. Replying to this letter the same day Keble wrote: 'You will observe that it was really part of my argument, and was not brought in merely by way of compliment. I have many thoughts in my mind of the desirableness of engaging all ranks of people more immediately in the service of the Church than has of late been customary in this country, and it seems to me nothing would tend more surely to such a purpose than inducing them to feel rightly about Poverty, and I feel, I doubt not in common with thousands besides, that we have in your writings a treasure of instruction on that subject, for which we cannot be too grateful.' (*WL MSS.*) W. W. had met Keble in person for the first time on the 13th, when they were both guests at a breakfast party given by Francis Faber at Magdalen College. W. W. had the opportunity of meeting many other prominent members of the high-church or Tractarian party there, including John Henry Newman, Isaac Williams, John Brande Morris, J. R. Bloxam, and J. B. Mozley. 'The Poet talked and we all listened.' See R. D. Middleton, *Newman and Bloxam, An Oxford Friendship*, 1947, pp. 52—4; *Letters of the Rev. J. B. Mozley, D.D.*, edited by his Sister, 1885, p. 92.

[2] Frederick Faber (see L. 1314 above) had now come under the influence of Newman and the high-church party, and was contributing to the *Library of the Fathers*. W. W. breakfasted with him (together with W. K. Hamilton and Bunsen) the next morning, before his departure from Oxford.

1331. W. W. to H. C. R.

Address: H. C. Robinson Esq, Plowdens Buildings, Temple.
Postmark: 26 June 1839. *Stamp*: Cornhill.
Endorsed: 22 June 1839. Wordsworth.
MS. Dr. Williams's Library.
Morley, i. 384.

Sat. Rydal Mount
June 22nd [1839]

My dear Friend,

It is a week today since I reached home; having[1] passed a few hours at Rugby on my [way?] from Oxford, where my reception was most enthusiastic; and of which the Morning Post gave the best account I have seen though *that* fell far short of the reality.[2] If you should see Mr Mayer[3] who was present pray thank him in my name for the very elegant Italian Sonnet which

---

[1] having *written twice*.

[2] 'The mail dropped him at my door' [in Ambleside], I. F. wrote to Henry Taylor, 'and I had a full history of all he had seen, heard, and thought since we parted . . . He was much touched with his reception at Oxford, which seemed to have been *heartfelt*; no such acclamations had been heard excepting on the appearance of the Duke of Wellington. These, however, did not much move him, but when the public orator spoke of him as the poet of humanity, and as having through the power of love and genius made us feel as nothing the artificial distinctions which separate the different classes of society, and that "we have all one common heart," then he felt he was understood, and thankful. Nothing seemed to have escaped him in the scene—the place itself, the people, the light and shade, the expression of everything, the impression it all made.' (*Correspondence of Henry Taylor*, pp. 124–5.)

[3] Enrico Mayer (1802–77), son of a German father and French mother, grew up at Livorno when he came to know Byron. He entered Italian revolutionary politics to further the cause of national independence and unification and fought in the war of 1848, becoming the friend and correspondent of Mazzini. Thereafter he was active in the spread of popular education in Tuscany, writing on educational questions and editing the works of Foscolo (1850, etc.). See A. Linaker, *La Vita e i tempi di Enrico Mayer*, Florence, 1898. H. C. R. had met him on his first visit to Italy, when Mayer was acting as secretary to Robert Finch (1783–1830), the antiquary, in Rome. W. W. had seen him in Florence in 1837, and more recently in London (see *HCR* ii. 571), and Mayer called at Rydal Mount late in July of this year (*RMVB*). Shortly afterwards, Mrs. Fletcher records a discussion of the Italian question and the character of Mazzini with the poet: 'Wordsworth spoke with strong and deep feeling of the present state of Italy and the crushing despotism of Austria . . .' (*Autobiography of Mrs. Fletcher*, p. 244).

he left at the Vice chancellor's for me immediately after the Ceremony. When I had taken my seat among the Doctors, I saw him standing in the dense crowd of the Area below; and tell him that I was much mortified by not falling in with him afterwards. Indeed there was such a throng that one got little more than a glimpse of anybody. A gentleman[1] came from Bristol for the sole purpose of *joining in the shout*, as he expressed it, on the Card he left for me and immediately after took his way home, so that I had no means of seeing him, though he has often times shown me much kindness before and in various ways.

Do you recollect when I breakfasted with you that one of the party[2] who had lived much in Italy pointed out and transcribed for me a sonnet of Michael Angelo; and seemed to regret that I had not translated it. This I have done today, and send it with my comp[ts] for his gratification; or to show at least my good will. It is as literal as two languages so different will allow, without more pains than I felt inclined to bestow; and probably had I endeavoured to give it word for word I should have succeeded no better with the spirit. The Arnolds are arrived and Bunsen and his Wife and Son.[3] We have seen them at the Mount, and shall call on them to day if the weather which has become unsettled will permit. The season during our long absence has been here (though cold) uncommonly fine; scarcely any rain, and the crops in our garden and the grass in our fields are most abundant; then as to the beauty of the place, nothing can exceed it.—I have the promise of a Letter from the Chancellor of the Exchequer[4] which will give the result of his endeavours to serve me. As my hopes are not very high the disappointment, if I am to be disappointed, will be less accordingly. W[m], my Son, I grieve to say was scarcely any better, when I parted with him at Oxford, thursday week past. We hope to hear from him to day—By the Bye D[r] Arnold only means to stay three weeks in Westmorland, and thence post off with his eldest daughter[5] for Switzerland and the North of Italy. What a Velocipede he is—

---

[1] John Peace. See L. 1341 below.

[2] Henry, later Sir Henry, Layard (1817—94), the excavator of Nineveh, spent most of his youth in Italy. W. W. had met him at H. C. R.'s breakfast party on 26 May (*HCR* ii. 571). In July he set out on the first of his journeys to Persia and the Middle East.

[3] See A. J. C. Hare, *Life and Letters of Frances Baroness Bunsen*, 2 vols., 1879, i. 510—11.

[4] Thomas Spring Rice.   [5] Jane.

Yesterday I went over to Kendal to support the Diocesan plan of Education in connection with and under the superintendance of the Church of England. This I did, being convinced that the extension of the education that may be so effected is the best and safest way of promoting instruction and training through the whole Country: The Church is and ought to be ascendant, and for reasons that I have often expressed in your hearing.—

Dora is as thin as a Ghost and almost as sallow as an autumnal leaf; my Sister much as usual—M^rs W— pretty well, and I should have been quite so I trust, but that I was imprudent in walking too far the day after I got Home. Miss Fenwick, dear and good Creature, is recovering her looks. All unite in love: pray let us hear from you soon.

Affectionately yours.   W W

[*In M. W.'s hand*]

By power incited of a lovely face,
Hers in whose sway alone my heart delights,
I climb, nor fail to win Those heavenly heights
Where Mortal Creature rarely finds a place.
With him who made the Work that Work accords
So well—that by its help and thro' his grace
I raise my thoughts, inform my deeds and words;
Clasping her beauty in my Souls embrace.
Thus if from two fair eyes I cannot turn
I feel that in those eyes there doth abide
Sight that to God is both a Way and Guide;
And, kindling at their lustre if I burn,
My noble fire emits the joyous ray
That thro' the realms of Glory shines for aye.[1]

Wm Wordsworth

Rydal Mount
    June 22^d —39

Pray let Mr Mayer copy this translation if he should think it worth the trouble.

---

[1] '*At Florence—From Michael Angelo* (*PW* iii. 226), published in *Memorials of a Tour in Italy, 1837*. This early version of the sonnet was subsequently corrected by H. C. R. in the light of the alterations sent in the next letter.

1332. W. W. to H. C. R.[1]

Address: H. C. Robinson Esq., Plowden's Buildings, Temple—
Endorsed: 1839. Wordsworth. Autograph. Corrections of Sonnet from
   Michael Angelo.
MS. Dr. Williams's Library.
Morley, i. 387.

[22 June 1839, *or shortly after*]

My dear Friend,
   Correct the translation as follows,

   Rapt above earth by power of one fair face,
   Hers in whose sway alone my heart delights
   I mingle with the blest on those pure heights
   Where Man, yet mortal, rarely finds a place.
   With Him who made the Work that Work accords
   So aptly that I thence inform
   Thus if from two fair eyes these cannot turn
   I feel that in their presence doth abide

[*overleaf*]

My dear Friend,
   Pray correct the Translation from Michael Angelo, as follows

   Rapt above earth by power of one fair face
   Hers in whose sway alone my heart delights
   I mingle with the blest on those pure heights
   Where man, yet mortal, rarely finds a place.
   With him who made the Work, that Work accords[2]
   So aptly that I thence inform (through grace
   Shower'd down upon me all my thoughts and words

[*unsigned*]

---

[1] This item appears to be a separate letter, but it may possibly have been sent with the previous one.

[2] H. C. R. incorporated these corrections in ll. 1—5 into the text sent by W. W. with the previous letter, and they were unaltered thereafter in the published version. The rest of the sonnet underwent further revision before publication (see *PW* iii. 226, *app. crit.*), and H. C. R. seems to have added further corrections to the earlier draft, which are not noted in this letter, and which must have been sent subsequently.

1333. W. W. to EDWARD MOXON

MS. *Mitchell Library, Sydney.*
G. L. Little, 'Two Unpublished Wordsworth Letters', NQ ccvii (May 1962), 178—9.

[late June 1839]

My dear Mr Moxon,

I enclose all the Corrections, which I mean to make in the 1st Vol:[1]—those for the other Volumes shall follow speedily. I should like to know, for my guidance in future, what will be the cost of making the changes now sent—

You are anxious about Hartley Coleridge's book;[2] I am told by a common Friend who has seen it that it is far advanced. He speaks in the very highest terms of the execution of what Hartley read to him. But I grieve to say that H. cannot be relied on as punctual to time. Mrs Wordsworth let him have three pounds unfortunately the other day and he broke out into a fit of rambling and drinking that continued several days. What a pity—for he is a man of inimitable Power—

ever faithfully yours
W. Wordsworth

1334. W. W. to EDWARD MOXON

MS. *Henry E. Huntington Library.*
LY ii. 981.

[*In the hand of C. W.'s son, John*]

Rydal Mount
July 6th 1839

My dear Mr Moxon,

I sent you some days ago under cover to Mr St Talfourd a sheet of corrections being all that are required for the first vol of the Stereotype Editn of my Poems. I now write by my nephew

---

[1] Of the new stereotype edition.

[2] The edition of Massinger and Ford which Moxon had commissioned at the beginning of this year. See *Letters of Hartley Coleridge* (ed. Griggs), pp. 230—3.

to say that in the Parcel of Books wh you sent was a vol printed
for the Camden Society entitled Plumpton Correspondence:[1]
as the same parcel cont^d three vols printed by the same Society
for wh I am indebted to Mr Robinson I think it not improbable
that he in his kindness designed a copy of this book also for me;
but the one which has reached me contains on a fly leaf the
words 'To Sir N H Nicolas B^{t2} with the Editor's reg^{ds}' from wh
I fear this Copy has been forwarded to me by mistake. Was I
sure of this I would at once return the book by my nephew, but
it would save trouble if the copy (not improbably) intended for
me by Mr Robinson could be transfer^d to Sir N H Nicolas in lieu
of the one wh I retain—for the present at least: Should there be
no copy of this Plumpton Corresp^{dn} intended for me by
Mr Robinson I will return the copy I have by the first opportunity: the objects of the Camden Society are praiseworthy
and the specimens they have given not a little interesting.

Pray let me know when you go abroad if you do go, and take
care to charge the printer to be careful in executing the
alterations in the Stereotype and as I said before I should like to
have the expense upon those already sent. With kindest reg^{ds} to
Mrs Moxon and your Sister and Brothers

Believe me my dear Mr Moxon

faithfully yours.

[*signed*] Wm Wordsworth

[1] *Plumpton Correspondence, A Series of Letters, chiefly domestic, written in the reigns of Edward IV, Richard III, Henry VII, and Henry VIII*, ed. Thomas Stapleton, 1839. The Camden Society was founded in 1838 for the publication of early historical texts: some 60 volumes of their productions, presumably presented by H. C. R. who was closely involved with its activities (see *HCR* ii. 548), were in the poet's library at his death. See *R.M. Cat.*, no. 15.

[2] Sir Nicholas Harris Nicolas (1799–1848), antiquarian and editor of numerous historical works, including *Despatches and Letters of Lord Nelson*, 7 vols., 1844–6.

1335. W. W. to H. C. R.

Address: H. C. Robinson Esq.
Endorsed: 7 July 1839. Wordsworth on Church Estab[t] and Education.
MS. Dr. Williams's Library.
K (—). *Morley, i. 389.*

[*In Dora W.'s hand*]

Rydal Mount
Sunday even[g] [7 July 1839]

My dear Friend

As my nephew John Wordsworth means to set off tomorrow for London, I write, not to enter into particulars of your letter just received;[1] which he will be able to do vivâ voce—but to thank you for it and to tell you that the two pictures[2] answer perfectly well their intended purpose—They were received several days ago along with many books, among which were three of the Camden Society, for which I thank you cordially— The same parcel also contained a fourth volume of the same Society, viz the Plumpton correspondence; but in this on the fly leaf, as I mentioned a few days ago to M[r] Moxon[3] for your information, is written 'to Sir N. H Nicholas from the Editor'— I therefore apprehend some mistake, and that possibly this copy may be substituted for one which your kindness designed for me—If not, I will return the copy I have by the first opportunity. The Plumpton Correspondence being of such an old date cannot but prove extremely interesting.

I have this moment had read to me in the newspaper the news of the death of Lady Flora Hastings.[4] The sorrow which I feel

---

[1] H. C. R. had written on 5 July forwarding a parcel from Henry Reed containing the Philadelphia edition (1802) of *Lyrical Ballads*. See Morley, i. 388.

[2] See *HCR* ii. 572.

[3] See previous letter.

[4] Lady Flora Hastings (1806–39), daughter of the 1st Marquess of Hastings, Governor General of India, and a Maid of Honour to the Duchess of Kent, had been the central figure in the Bedchamber crisis earlier in the year, which had brought the Crown into disrepute, and cast doubt on the judgment of Lord Melbourne. Her tragic death, to which the unfounded rumours of immoral conduct probably contributed, took place at Buckingham Palace on 5 July. Her *Poems* were published posthumously in 1841. W. W. also knew her sister Sophia (1809–59) who in 1845 married the 2nd Marquess of Bute (1793–1848).

on this melancholy occasion is mixed with regret that I missed seeing her in London. Upon two occasions we were to have had an interview by express appointment. But upon one, our meeting was prevented by an unexpected engagement on her part with the Duchess of Kent,[1] and afterwards by my being engaged when she was at liberty—I have a letter from her addressed to myself which does her great credit.

I do not see that any misconduct on the part of churchmen at this time affects the general question of the reasonableness of the Church of England being at the head of the general religious education of the country. As long as we shall retain a Church Establishment, if there be any consistency in our proceedings, the education of the young in matters of religion, as far as the state is concerned, ought to be in the hands of those whom the state entrusts with the religious instruction of adults—and there is no more injustice to the rest of the religious community in that, than is implied in the mere existence of a Church Establishment.[2] But in the proceedings of Government at this time what I detest most is the practice of Metropolitan organization—Upon this subject D'Israeli[3] spoke in parliament like a philosopher—Relieve the *people* of the burden of their duties, and you will soon make them indifferent about their rights. There is no more certain way of preparing a people for slavery, than the practice of central organization, which our

[1] Victoria Mary Louisa, Duchess of Kent (1786–1861), mother of Queen Victoria.

[2] Up till now, state aid for popular education had been channelled through the National Society and the British and Foreign Bible Society, and the Established Church had thereby maintained its influence in the schools. But the Cabinet was now prepared to modify this system in order to meet the legitimate grievances of Dissenters, and move in the direction of a national system of education. On Lord John Russell's initiative, a special committee of the Privy Council was set up early in 1839 to administer the grant made by the House of Commons. It proposed to establish a training college for teachers, and to adopt the principle that general religious teaching should be given in schools under state authority and open to state inspection, while denominational teaching was left to ministers of religion. The aims of the scheme were largely frustrated by the opposition of both Churchmen and Dissenters, but the committee survived under its energetic Secretary, Dr. Kay, later Sir James Kay-Shuttleworth. See also L. 1412 (in next volume).

[3] Benjamin Disraeli (1804–81), the celebrated statesman and novelist, had been M.P. for Maidstone since 1837. He would already have come to W. W.'s notice for his support of the Copyright Bill.

philosophists with Lord Brougham at their head are so bent upon importing from the Continent—I should have thought that in matters of Government, we Englishmen had more to teach those nations than to learn from them.

I forget how the first line of the translated sonnet[1] stood; I know however it is much improved in the correction so is the third; and upon the whole I think the translation is not now inferior to the original. The eighth line I cannot but think greatly superior—If M[r] Maier's[2] curiosity should lead him down to the Lakes in his way to Edinburgh and Scotland, which he ought to see if possible, pray tell him I shall be glad to receive him here. I was sadly mortified that I had not an opportunity of thanking him personally for the elegant sonnet which he addressed to me at Oxford, two lines of it were especially beautiful. I have not yet received the second parcel of books which I suppose contains the poem of Ernest.[3] With M[rs] Wordsworth and Dora's kindest remembrances

ever affectionately y[rs]
[*signed*] W[m] Wordsworth

1336. W. W. to JOHN LIGHTFOOT[4]

MS. Mrs. M. J. Roberts. Hitherto unpublished.

Rydal Mount
Monday morn. [Summer 1839]

Dear Sir,

There is a paper in circulation from the trustees of Keswick School[5] soliciting subscriptions for the increase of the stipends

---

[1] See L. 1332 above. [2] i.e. Enrico Mayer (see L. 1331 above).

[3] An epic poem in 12 books by Capel Lofft, jnr. (1806—73), privately printed and issued anonymously in 1839, and again in 1868. It was dedicated to the memory of Milton, and recounted the growth, struggles, and trimph of Chartism. Harriet Martineau found it 'a poem of prodigious power, but too seditious for publication' (see *Autobiography*, i. 416—17), but H. C. R.'s verdict was that it was 'a declamation with few facts or characters' (*HCR* ii. 572).

[4] The Keswick attorney who had married R. W.'s widow.

[5] The ancient Grammar School, which at this time adjoined Crosthwaite Church, had about 80 pupils and was administered by a board of 18 trustees. The landed endowments produced about £100 a year, £80 of which was paid to the headmaster.

or salaries of the masters, the application of the sum raised to be under the management of the trustees. Pray could you let me know what the amount of this stipend at present is and whence it proceeds and how it happens that funds whether coming from a fixed salary or quarter pence or both which appears by the circulated papers to have been formerly adequate to the support of an able master or masters, now no longer serves. These particulars and any others which you might think useful for the guardians or any one disposed to listen to such an application I should be glad to learn, information having been asked from me upon the subject. I hope you will be so kind to excuse my addressing myself to you upon this occasion as I know no one to whom I could apply with a like prospect of success.

You may have heard lately from dear John.[1] When I was in London I called upon Sir James Macgregor[2] on John's account but unluckily he was out of town and not to return for a month—so I may send to him. With kind remembrances to Mrs Lightfoot,

W Wordsworth

[1] R. W.'s son had now qualified as a doctor and was practising at Fort Pitt, Chatham, pending an appointment abroad with the Army Medical Service.

[2] Sir James McGrigor, Bart., F.R.S. (1771—1858) served as an army surgeon and became an inspector of hospitals and chief of Wellington's medical staff in the Peninsula. He was Director-General of the army medical department, 1815—51, and W. W. had written to him on 11 Jan. in support of his nephew's application. W. W.'s letter is untraced, but McGrigor replied on 30 Jan. (*MS. Mrs. M. J. Roberts*), promising to do what he could 'out of my respect for the character of Mr. Wordsworth', though there were many others who had more pressing claims. While in London, W. W. had also planned to approach another distinguished medical man, Sir John McNeill (1795—1853) (see *Wordsworth's Pocket Notebook*, p. 17). In the event, an appointment in the Ionian Islands was secured for 'Keswick John' shortly after this, with the help of Dr. John Davy and Sir William Gomm (see Ls. 1339 and 1347 below).

1337. W. W. to W. P. HAVANAUGH[1]

Address: W. P. Havanaugh Esq, 147 New Bond Street.
Postmark: 10 July 1839.
MS. *University of Pennsylvania Library. Hitherto unpublished.*

[*In M. W.'s hand*]

Rydal Mount
July 8th —39

Dear Sir,

I have to thank you for a Copy of your Poem of the Reign of Lockrin and the obliging letter with which it was accompanied. The work reached me the other day in a parcel containing several other presentation Copies, but being troubled with an inflammation in one of my eyes—a Complaint to which I have been too often subject, I have not been able to read any of these works, except one short pamphlet in prose. I can do no more than thank you for this mark of your attention, Promising myself much pleasure from the perusal of your Work hereafter,

I remain dear Sir
Sincerely yours
[*signed*] Wm Wordsworth

1338. W. W. to BENJAMIN ROBERT HAYDON

MS. untraced.
LY ii. 982.

Rydal Mt July 8th 39.

My dear Haydon

I wished to have called upon you again before I left London— but during the last few days of my residence there I was disabled by a sprain in my ancle—which put a stop to many attentions of the same kind, I had intended to pay to my friends. Since my return, I have received from you a letter of warm congratulation upon my reception at Oxford.[2] The tribute of applause was far beyond any thing of which the Papers gave account—

---

[1] *The Reign of Locrin* was published in 1839 and is listed among other items in *R. M. Cat.*, no. 524; but nothing has been traced about the author.

[2] See L. 1328 above.

not excepting that of the Mng Post, which came nearest the truth.

Your Picture of the Duke of Wellington[1] I thought very promising but excuse my saying—that as you had given that of Buonaparte[2] with his back to the Spectator, I could not help wishing that you had not repeated so much of the same position in that of his Conqueror. I do not know that I am right in this remark but such was my impression.

You are a much better judge of Exhibitions than I am, but I did think that in choice of subjects and the Manner of treating them, tho' that was far short of what one would wish, there was a good deal of promising Talent—The genius of our times in your art is ruined by painting to Commission that is under the controul of those who order the Pictures.—Landseer[3] if he does not take care will be killed by this. In y[r] Lectures, pray dwell upon this mischief—and point out as you may do, without giving just offence, instances of its deplorable effect—Take for example that picture in L[d] Westminster's[4] Gallery, a family piece—Is it possible a Man of his genius and skill could have painted such a thing except under the like baneful influence?

Ever faithfully y[rs]
Wm Wordsworth

[1] 'Wellington Musing on the Field of Waterloo, or A Hero and the Horse which Carried him in his Greatest Battle, Imagined to be on the Field again Twenty Years After.' The picture was begun in Dec. 1838, and after a visit to the Field of Waterloo in August of this year and sittings by the Duke in October, it was finally completed in November. It now hangs in St. George's Hall, Liverpool.

[2] 'Napoleon on the Island of St. Helena.' See pt. ii, L. 605 and 618.

[3] Edwin, later Sir Edwin, Landseer, R. A. (1802–73), the popular artist whose 'Monarch of the Glen' and other sentimental studies of animals won him wide acclaim from the Victorian public. Haydon had for a time supervised his early training and advised him to dissect and make anatomical studies of animals and to study the Raphael cartoons and the Elgin marbles. W. W. had met him a few years before this (see L. 1149 above), and would have been familiar with his 'Fighting Dogs getting Wind' which hung at Coleorton, having been purchased by Sir George Beaumont in 1818.

[4] Robert Grosvenor, 1st Marquess of Westminster (1767–1845).

1339. W. W. to JOHN DAVY

MS. *Yale University Library.*
LY iii. 1380.

[*In M. W.'s hand*]

Rydal Mt
Aug. 21st [1839]

My dear Sir,

By this time my Nephew[1] will have presented himself to you—and upon this occasion I cannot but repeat my acknowledgements for the great service you have rendered him. His principles are sound, his conduct as far as I know has been exemplary, and his dispositions are truly amiable. If there should be, as I fear there may, some deficiency in his attainments, it may partly be imputed to a cause which his constitutional modesty may prevent his mentioning to you—I mean a severe and dangerous illness which attacked him about this time last Autumn, and left him in a state that made relaxation for the recovery of his health, the necessary object of his almost exclusive consideration—throughout the winter and Spring. He seems now perfectly recovered—and encouraged by your exhortations and advice, which I venture to request you to bestow upon him, I trust he will do no discredit to those who have befriended him, or may do so in future.

An inflammation in one of my eyes prevented me from seeing so much of Miss Fletcher[2] and her friend Mrs Arnold, as I wished to do, while they were in our neighbourhood.—I am now recovering gradually from that attack, and beg that Mrs Davy, when she writes to her Sister, will let her know that I have not been inattentive to her request about the small Estate,[3] in this neighbourhood, in which she took an interest. I should have written to Miss F. myself—but she left me no address—the Land has been separately valued by two judicious friends of mine whose estimate agreed within £30—I mean the value of it as a Farm: £720 and £750 were the respective valuations. The extent something less than 20 Acres—the timber, which is but

---

[1] 'Keswick John'.

[2] Mary, Mrs. Fletcher's youngest daughter (see L. 1157 above), was staying at Fox How.

[3] Lancrigg, in Easedale, which Mrs. Fletcher purchased with W. W.'s help later this year. See *Autobiography of Mrs. Fletcher*, pp. 242–5.

719

little, was not included—nor any allowance for the house and out-buildings. If Miss F. and her Mother should be inclined to proceed in this business—let me beg, as their friend, that the negociation may be entrusted to me, and I will do justice between both parties—which I say with an apprehension that their good nature and generosity might subject them, to say the least of it, to rather a hard bargain. I learned from my Clerk— one of the valuers, that a small coppice wood in front of the house Miss F. did not wish for—allow me to say this is a great mistake. The wood is now of 17 years' growth, and the felling of it would much disfigure the Spot—indeed, I reckon the command of that coppice indispensable for the beauty of the Situation.

With kindest remembrances to yourself and Mrs Davy, in which Mrs W. cordially unites, I remain my dear Sir faithfully your much obliged

[*signed*] Wm Wordsworth

1340. W. W. to EDWARD MOXON

Address: Edward Moxon Esqre, 44 Dover Street, London.
Postmark: (1) 30 Aug. 1839 (2) 31 Aug. 1839.
Stamp: (1) Ambleside Penny Post (2) Kendal.
MS. Henry E. Huntington Library.
LY ii. 983.

[*In M. W.'s hand*]

Rydal Mount August 30th [1839]

My dear Moxon,

In respect to the Yarrow,[1] I only mentioned it for this reason—we had just, at the time when I saw it prettily got up and charged 3/6 in the Shop, received from you at our request half a doz copies charged to us 3/7, these copies being got up in the ordinary way. They were ordered to favour a worthy person in Ambleside, who sells books supplied to her by her Son, a Stationer in Kendal—Therefore she cannot sell them at this price for any profit, as so much nicer copies being to be had at the other Shop at a lower rate. I thought proper to mention

---

[1] The 3rd edition of *Yarrow Revisited; and Other Poems*, 1839.

this to you, not with any view of objecting to your selling them so neatly got up, at a lower price, or at any price you think proper, but to prevent the unpleasantness which I have mentioned, in future. To conclude the subject, if I may judge from the demand in this neighbourhood for this Vol: of Yarrow, so got up—the sale of it may be expected to be considerable.

I grieve exceedingly to hear of your situation in respect to the Editions of Fletcher and Massinger. Hartley keeps out of our way, I would have called on him this very mornᵍ but it is stormy weather, and I dare not go out.—no exertions however shall be spared to spur him on to bring the work[1] to a conclusion. As to poor dear Mr S.'s[2] case I am certain that whatever he can do he will do to fulfil his engagement, and that your loss will meet with every just consideration on his part, for a more conscientious and upright Man no where breathes.

The 2 remaining Vols of corrections will be sent in the course of a fortnight or three weeks. I cannot make them without the assistance of Mr Carter and he is going to Liverpool for that time.

I am pleased you liked the slight corrections in your Sonnets.

Now for your trip to Florence—would not you contrive to make a little circuit in going from Lyons, down the Rhone by steam as far as you can go towards Marseilles, and thence by Toulon and Nice, and along the Cornice road to Genoa, and so on to Massa, and turn off to Lucca and Pisa, and so to Florence. Or if straitened by time, go by Steam from Marseilles to Genoa at once. But nothing can be more beautiful than the whole land road from Nice by Genoa to Massa.

Farewell with best wishes from all to yourself and your family I remain my dear Mr M.

faithfully yours
[*signed*] Wᵐ Wordsworth

---

[1] See L. 1333 above. Hartley Coleridge was editing Ford, not Fletcher.

[2] Southey had married Caroline Bowles on 4 June, and returned to Keswick for his daughter Bertha's marriage at the end of August, much impaired in health. He had recently agreed to edit for Moxon a volume of ballads, songs, and carols, but the work was never completed. See Merriam, *Edward Moxon, Publisher of Poets*, pp. 97–8.

1341. W. W. to JOHN PEACE

MS. WL transcript. [1]
Mem (—). *Grosart* (—). *K* (—). *LY ii. 984* (—).

Rydal Mount, Aug. 30, 1839.

My dear Sir,

. . . It was not a little provoking that I had not the pleasure of shaking you by the hand at Oxford when you did me the honour of coming so far to 'join in the shout'. [2] I was told by a Fellow of University College [3] that he never witnessed such an outburst of enthusiasm in that place, except upon the occasions of the visits of the Duke of Wellington,—one unexpected. My nephew, [4] Fellow of Trinity College, Cambridge, was present, as well as my son William, who, I am happy to say, is much better in health than when you saw him in Oxford. He is here, and desires to be kindly remembered to you.

Now for a word about [? the portrait] of Coleridge. [5] I told his Nephew and Son-in-law M[r] H. N. Coleridge, what I had seen, and how very highly the picture must be valued by all judicious persons who remembered what the original was at the time of life when it was taken: I said further that I had recommended to the Possessor, M[r] Wade, either to leave it

---

[1] One of a number of copies made by Susan Wordsworth for C. W. jnr. when he was gathering materials for *Mem.*

[2] Peace had written on 12 Aug.: 'Indulge me my dear Sir by permitting me to thank you once more for those heart-mending volumes from which I have for many years drawn less benefit than I ought, but enough to make me your perpetual debtor.' And he added his own recollections of the Oxford Commemoration for M. W. 's benefit: 'It was overpowering . . . That which he received, thundering as it was, had not to my ear an uproarious character; it had a beautiful tone about it; just such as one would expect to characterize or burst from the central heart of the best men of England at the best period of their lives. . . . It was a blessed thing my dear Madam that it fell to the lot of the congenial and heavenly-minded John Keble to avouch before that audience, not few, that the highest praise which Christian life may utter belonged to the Christian Poet who stood before them.' (*WL MSS.*)

[3] Frederick Faber.

[4] C. W. 's son, John.

[5] Washington Allston's portrait of Coleridge (see Griggs, vi. 1029–30), painted at Bristol in 1814 for Josiah Wade (see *EY*, pp. 230–1; *MY* i. 80, ii.. 133), acquired by the National Portrait Gallery in 1864, and now on permanent loan to Dove Cottage, Grasmere. A replica is at Jesus College, Cambridge.

directly to some public Body, say Jesus Coll. Cambridge, or the
Library at Bristol, the place with which C. has been a good deal
connected, and in which it was actually painted—either to do
this at once, or to bequeath it to anyone of M[r] C's nearest
connexions, for his, or her, lifetime, upon condition that it
should afterwards pass to some repository where it might be
publickly seen, and preserved from the changes of fortune to
which all private families are subject. With this opinion so
expressed to M[r] Wade, M[r] H. N. Coleridge did not seem
displeased; and this is all that I have done in the matter, having to
regret that during my short and hurried visit to Cambridge,
since I saw you, it did not occur to me to inquire at Jesus College
whether it might be placed there with advantage, as I cannot but
think the Master and Fellows would be proud to possess it. It is
true that Coleridge did not remain long enough at Cambridge
to take a degree; but he distinguished himself there by gaining a
University Prize for a Greek Ode,[1] and was known as a man of
great genius, and extraordinary attainments. You would
naturally wish the Portrait to remain at Bristol, a city in which it
has so long been, and I justly appreciate your feeling, but all
things considered, *I* cannot but incline to Jesus College in
preference to any other, and this leaning I am sure you will
excuse . . .

faithfully yours,
W[m] Wordsworth

[1] See Griggs, i. 34. The text of Coleridge's *Greek Prize Ode on the Slave Trade*, which won the Browne Gold Medal in 1792, is given in J. D. Campbell, *The Poetical Works of Coleridge*, 1893, p. 476.

1342. W. W. to MONTAGU MONTAGU[1]

Address: M. Montagu Esqre, James Street, Golden Square, London. [*re-addressed to*] at Mr Helliwells, 22 Arundel St.
Postmark: 2 Sept. 1839. *Stamp*: Charles St West^r.
MS. Cornell. Hitherto unpublished.

[*In M. W.'s hand*]

Rydal Mount
Aug 31st [1839]

Dear Sir

You must not be hurt if in reply to your obliging letter dated 15th July, but only received the day before yesterday, I am compelled to say that the interview to which you refer has escaped my remembrance—unless you be the Gentleman, who several years ago was resident for a short time at Fox Ghyll, Miss Blackett being of the Party, whom I had the pleasure of accompanying to the top of Helvellyn.[2] If I am mistaken in this supposition, you will excuse me, if you be aware of the very great number of Visitors, whom the beauty of this Country tempts to Rydal every year.

Pray accept my thanks for your Translation of Schiller's Song of the Bell, which I shall read, I doubt not with pleasure, when the state of my eyes, which are now much disordered, will permit.

I remain Sir,
sincerely yours
[*signed*] Wm Wordsworth

---

[1] Capt. Montagu Montagu (b. 1786) translated Casti's sonnets (1826), and published metrical versions of the psalms, and two volumes of his own sonnets (1860–1). His translation of Schiller's *Das Lied von der Glocke* appeared in 1839.

[2] See *PW* ii. 286 and the I. F. note, p. 521.

1343. W. W. to LORD MONTEAGLE[1]

Endorsed: Wm Wordsworth 6 Sepr 1839 Congratulations on Peerage. Ans^d.
12 Sept/39.
MS. Yale University Library.
LY ii. 985.

[*In M. W.'s hand*]

Rydal Mount
Septr 6th 1839

My dear Lord

'It is only a congratulatory letter'—Such I was once told was the observation of the private Secretary of a certain eminent Lawyer who had just been raised to a high office and a Peerage—upon which the new Peer had the letter thrown into the fire, as had been the fate of a Score or two others received upon the same occasion, the Signatures, most of them perhaps, not looked at.

Fearing that the like might be the doom of the few words, which when I first heard of your elevation to the Peerage, I felt prompted to write to you, I have been induced to defer the expression of my own friendly interest in this event till the press of congratulation was over, and I now trust that a favorable acceptance will be given to my best wishes that you may have health and happiness long to enjoy the honor and privileges which have been conferred upon you, as the reward of severe and anxious Service.

We have lately had a very pleasant visit from Cordelia Marshall, and from her, as from other quarters, we have heard with much pleasure, that Lady Monteagle's health was greatly improved; the state of comparative repose in which you now are placed will allow you to see much more of each other, and that no relapse may occur to disturb or sadden your domestic Circle, is the sincere prayer, my dear Lord, of your

faithful and much obliged
[*signed*] Wm Wordsworth

---

[1] W. W.'s friend Thomas Spring Rice, now elevated to the peerage and appointed Comptroller-General of the Exchequer.

1344. W. W. to JOHN PEACE

MS. WL transcript (—). *Hitherto unpublished.*

19 Sept. 1839

My dear M[r] Peace,

Do not think ill of me because my letters are always written to request favours or to thank you for them. The cover for this note is from M[r] Milnes,[1] as you will see, who having expressed to me a strong wish to procure M[r] Gilbert's[2] Poem of the Hurricane 'Published in the year 1796. Printed and Sold for the author by R. Edwards, Sold also by Martin and Bain, and by B. Crosby, London, Eddowes, Salop; and Haywood and Barratt, Bath.' it immediately struck me that you might perhaps be able to fall in with the Book. M[r] Cottle will perfectly remember both the Author and the Publication, and you I think must assuredly have heard of him: he was a Barrister and had practised in the West Indies, and lived some time at Bristol, between the year −95 and −98, at which time I often conversed with him, and admired his genius though he was in fact insane. If you should light upon the Book, you would oblige me by directing it to R. M. Milnes Esq[re] under cover to M[r] Moxon, 44 Dover Street London. With M[r] Milnes yesterday I talked about M[r] Wade's Portrait of Coleridge,[3] he is of opinion, in which I entirely concur, though with regret on your account, that the Fitzwilliam Museum[4] Cambridge, would be the most proper place for the reception of this valuable Picture. Pray mention this, with my kind regards, to the owner, he will probably be aware that they are erecting at Cambridge, a superb Museum for the fine collection of Pictures, Prints, etc etc left them by Earl Fitzwilliam. I know that the

[1] Richard Monckton Milnes, who called at Rydal Mount this month (*RMVB*).

[2] For William Gilbert (?1760−?1825), see Cottle, i. 62−9, and *PW* v. 422−3.

[3] See L. 1341 above.

[4] Richard, Viscount Fitzwilliam (1745−1816) bequeathed to the University of Cambridge his pictures and books and his South Sea Stock, the income from which was to be used for the building of a museum to house his collections. A site in Trumpington Street was acquired in 1821, and an open competition for the design was won by George Basevi, but the building was still uncompleted on his death in 1845, and was not ready to receive the pictures until three years later.

Heads of the University would be glad to receive any valuable addition, as such a Portrait of so eminent a man would be. . . .

your faithful friend,
Wm Wordsworth

1345. W. W. to THOMAS POWELL

MS. Lilly Library, Indiana University, Hitherto unpublished.

Lowther Castle [13 Oct. 1839]

My dear Mr Powell,

I am embarrassed by your Letter just received, partly on account of the uncertainty of all that relates to the state of my eyes and partly upon conditional engagements.—Nevertheless if Miss Gillies[1] could find compensation in the beauty of our Country, in case she should be disappointed in her main object, I would say that I should be glad to see her early in the week after next. Today is Sunday, the 13th I believe; so that it would be about the 21st when I hope I may be in a condition to sit; and I trust that no engagement will interfere at that time. I rejoice in the account you give of Mrs Powell and your little Boy. Trusting you are yourself well

I remain my dear Mr Powell
faithfully yours
W Wordsworth

Should any thing contrary to my wish occur before the end of the coming week I shall take care to write. I return home on Wednesday next, I hope.

---

[1] Margaret Gillies (1803–87), an artist who specialized in water-colour miniatures on ivory, had requested a sitting from the poet through their mutual friend Thomas Powell, who wrote a letter of introduction on her behalf on 20 July (*WL MSS.*). She stayed at Rydal Mount for several weeks, painting M. W., Dora W., and I. F. as well as the poet. Her miniatures are now in Dove Cottage. See Blanchard, *Portraits of Wordsworth*, pp. 85–7, 163–5.

1346. W. W. to SUSANNA WORDSWORTH[1]

Address: Mrs Chris: Wordsworth, Harrow, London.
Postmark: 21 Oct. 1839.
Stamp: Ambleside.
MS. British Library. Hitherto unpublished.

[In Dora W.'s hand]

Rydal Mount
Octo^r 21st 1839

My dear Niece,

Dora is so good as to hold the pen for me tho' my eyes are so much improved I could write myself—as I did in the cases which my good brother doubted about: I thank you sincerely for your letter which followed me to Lowther where I have been staying a week with my excellent Friend Lord Lonsdale. Having little or nothing particular to mention except that your aunt and Miss Fenwick leave us tomorrow for an absence of three weeks[2] I should have put off writing till I had seen my Grand Children at Brigham about whom I might have told you some interesting particulars, at least I hope so, tho' I am aware that nothing is generally more irksome than stories of children told to those who don't know them, but I write to you *now* on account of a little business of my own, The Excursion, as the last Vol: of the 6 is now called for by the Printer. My Nephew, your brother John, who as you know is a most careful reader, told me he had noticed some incorrectnesses and these I am in need of. I am ignorant of his present address and therefore beg you would be so kind as to write and request him to forward me those corrections of his, with as little delay as possible.

We have received thro' Moxon the numbers of 'Greece' for which Dora and myself return our best thanks. We are both only just come home from the other side of Kirkstone and have scarcely had time yet to do more than look over the prints[3]

---

[1] Wife of C. W. jnr.

[2] M. W. was about to visit her relatives at Stockton-on-Tees: I. F. was going to Whitton to meet Henry Taylor and his bride, formerly Theodosia Spring Rice.

[3] C. W. jnr.'s *Greece* was embellished with engravings by Copley Fielding and many other artists of the day. Haydon was full of praise for the volume, writing to C. W. jnr. on 19 Dec.: ' . . . it is the very best book on the subject for a Classical artist, for it brings the leading Poetical points of that exquisite

which we find very interesting. During your Aunt's absence we shall read the text which will happily help on the time while I am sitting to a Female Portrait Painter, a Miss Gillies,[1] such an Enthusiast that she is coming down from London on purpose, at her own earnest request communicated to me by a common Friend. She is to be with us on Tuesday.

John Wordsworth of Sockbridge has thro' Sir James MacGregor's[2] kindness received orders to prepare for service in the Ionian Isles, much to his satisfaction; he naturally wishes for introductions and it has struck me that Chris: might be able to furnish him with some letters that would prove of use; if he can, pray let them be enclosed to him at 'Fort Pitt Chatham' and if C. would add any cautions respecting climate, diet or anything else that would be servicable, I am sure he will have pleasure in doing so. Poor John is just now recovering from the Small Pox caught from his Patients in the Hospital at Fort Pitt. If the newspaper report be right your Cousin[3] has missed his Fellowship at Trinity and we were all very sorry to think it was so, and I had not philosophy enough to find adequate consolation for the disappointment in the fact that seemed implied that five candidates had surpassed him. He is certainly a most amiable young man: perhaps his modesty stood in the way of the full display of his attainments. Owen Lloyd we think on the whole not quite so wretched as when you saw him. We do not hear of any improvement in Mr Southey's state. We have not yet been able to call upon him and pay our respects to his Wife.

We were grieved to hear of Charles' illness and the more so because he has always been so liable to attacks of indisposition. When you write to him Dora would be obliged if you would mention to him that one of the Winchester boys (a little fellow she believes lately gone) by name Pigott[4] is a great nephew of

Country with all its associations at once to his Imagination. In fact you are a Painter and Poet and Classic combined . . . ' (*MS. Mr. Jonathan Wordsworth*).

[1] See previous letter.   [2] For Sir James McGrigor see L. 1336 above.

[3] Probably James Alexander Frere (1814—77), who was elected to a fellowship at Trinity the following year. He was Christian Advocate of the University, 1848—50, and vicar of Shillington, Beds., from 1853. His father was Susan Wordsworth's uncle James Hatley Frere (1779—1866), the writer on prophesy and inventor of an alphabet for the blind.

[4] Probably James Piggot (1827—47), who went up to University College, Oxford, in 1845, but died soon afterwards.

her old and good friend Mrs Gee and if Charles could without inconvenience to himself or impingment of general rules give him a kind word now and then she would feel much obliged. It is high time to conclude only let us add 'Aunty' begs her love (we think her improving)—in which we all join—Love to *one* includes of course *both*

Your affect^{e}
Uncle
[*signed*] Wm Wordsworth

[*Dora W. writes*]

When you see our friends at Hampstead pray remember us most kindly. Miss Fenwick keeps quite well, and is enjoying this glorious season. How we wish you could see our country in this its autumnal splendour.

Dora W.

William met his Father at Lowther—he is not worse but we fear not much better. The last accounts from Brigham very satisfactory.

We were truly glad to hear about y^{r} Chapel[1] and House—may they both prosper.

1347. W. W. to SIR WILLIAM MAYNARD GOMM[2]

Address: Lieutenant General Sir William Gomm etc etc etc Ryde, Isle of *Wight*. [*readdressed to*] No. 6 Grosvenor St. London
Postmark: (1) 29 Oct. 1839 (2) 30 Oct. 1839 (3) 31 Oct. 1839.
Stamp: (1) Ambleside (2) Ryde.
Endorsed: Mr Wordsworth Oct: 29th/39. Written to him from Kingston, Feby 26th/40.
MS. Henry E. Huntington Library.
LY ii. 985.

Rydal Mount
Ambleside Oct^{b} 29th [1839]

I deem myself fortunate, dear Sir William, in being at home when your Letter arrived, as I can thank you for it as I do most

[1] See L. 1175 above.

[2] By a curious error of W. W.'s, this and all succeeding letters to Sir William Gomm are addressed to *Gordon* instead of Gomm. There is no question as to the identity of the addressee, and the error has been silently corrected in all cases. Gomm was about to assume command of the forces in Jamaica.

sincerely by return of Post, and with good hopes that my Letter will reach you before you leave Spithead. You have obliged me greatly by the service you have render[ed] my Nephew,[1] and I feel happy in the opportunity of offering my very best good wishes for Lady Gomm and yourself upon leaving your own Country. May health prosperity and happiness attend you both, and may you return to England without any cause whatsoever to regret the sacrifices which cannot but be made upon yielding to the calls of duty upon such occasions!—

Sir James MacGregor[2] has been very kind in offering my Nephew so agreeable a Station and I thank you for enclosing his Letter. The Young Man is in high spirits, though just recovering from the Small Pox, which he caught in the Hospital of Fort Pitt. As he had had the Cow-pox before, the Disease was nothing like so severe as it would probably otherwise have been, so that I trust he is already fit for his departure.—

The Papers speak of the probability of Sergeant Talfourd being raised to the Bench.[3] I wish he may be so, notwithstanding the loss the Copyright Bill would suffer by the event; for I am sure he would be much happier and I trust still more useful in that calm and dignified station, than as a Representative obliged to fashion his proceedings, and to a certain degree his opinions to the standard of a popular assembly.—

I will take care that his publication upon the Copy Right Bill[4] shall be duly sent you.

Repeating my good wishes for yourself and Lady Gomm, in which Mrs Wordsworth were she here, would most cordially join I remain my dear Sir Wm

faithfully your much
obliged Wm Wordsworth

[1] R. W.'s son.

[2] See L. 1336 above.

[3] Talfourd was not made a Judge until ten years later.

[4] Talfourd had written on 10 July to report very little progress on the Copyright Bill, and he wrote again on 18 Aug. that he was proposing to publish his *Three Speeches* on the Copyright question, 'closed by your two exquisite Sonnets which you gave me leave to publish when I contemplated such a publication last year.' (*Cornell MSS.*)

Address: 2ᵈ post Edward Moxon Esqʳ, 44 Dover Sᵗ.
Postmark: 4 Nov. 1839. *Stamp*: Charing Cross.
MS. Henry E. Huntington Library.
LY ii. 987.

[*In Dora W.'s hand*]

Novᵇʳ 1ˢᵗ [1839] Rydal Mount

My dear Mʳ Moxon,

I have sent the corrections of the Excursion which tho' appearing formidable relate to little more than the punctuation.

I have now done with the six Vols: which may be put into circulation as soon as they are complete, only I think it right to add the 12 Sonnets wʰ are already published in the Vol: of sonnets[1] and wʰ were written since the 6 Vols: were published, and these must take their place as an appendix at the end of the 5ᵗʰ Vol: with a small notice that shall be sent in about *10* days at the latest; in the mean while the Excursion may be corrected and struck off.

I have not ceased to stimulate Hartley Coleridge in every possible way to finish his notice[2] and I have done all that was possible in the still more difficult case of Mʳ Southey[3] but I am most happy to say that I heard two days ago that things looked brighter in that quarter. Mʳ S. has resumed the labour of selecting and transcribing tho' I have not learnt yet that he has ventured upon original composition; before I was aware of this improvement in his health I recommended in consequence of the melancholy account his son gave of it that you sᵈ be written to—this was last Monday mᵍ and perhaps you may have received a letter on the subject.

My daughter thanks you for the Vols: of Shelley[4] wʰ she values much. I am not aware that I have anything more to add—

---

[1] *The Sonnets of William Wordsworth*, 1838.

[2] i.e. his introduction to the edition of Massinger and Ford (see L. 1333 above).

[3] For his proposed collection of old ballads and songs, see L. 1340 above.

[4] In 1839 Moxon published the first collected edition of Shelley's *Poetical Works*, ed. Mary Shelley (2nd edition, 1840). See Merriam, *Edward Moxon, Publisher of Poets*, pp. 115 ff. In June 1841 proceedings were instituted against him for blasphemy: he was defended by Talfourd and the judge summed up in his favour, but the jury convicted. Moxon was ordered to come up for judgment when called for, but he received no punishment.

I leave home on Tuesday for a week but before I go I will endeavour to see H. C. again and if I do not succeed will set upon him one of his friends, a neighbour of mine, as I have done before, he having great influence over him. Miss Gillies[1] an artist who paints in miniature of whom you may have heard has come down from London on purpose to take my portrait and it is thought she has succeeded admirably. She will carry the picture with her to London where you may see it if you think it worth while.

Ever faithfully yours
[*signed*] Wm Wordsworth

Might it not be well if it could be done without expense or disfiguring the Title Page to add 'second stereotype* impression' or something to that effect if the Title Page of the 1st Vol be not already struck off.

By the bye I have received this day from India a translation of one of my *Sonnets* into the Hindu tongue by 'Mane Chunda Metter.'

*Have I spelt the word right?

1349. W. W. to EDWARD MOXON

MS. untraced.
Esther C. Dunn, 'Notes on Wordsworth', MLN xxxviii (1923), 246-7.

Dear Mr. Moxon,— [early Nov. 1839]

When you write to Mr. Reed, if you do so soon—pray tell him that I have adopted his substitution of *our child* for *your child* and think it a decided improvement.[2] Mr. H. C.[3] has not come near us for a long time, but Mrs. W. called and delivered your message some days since, when he promised that you should hear from him soon.

You shall have a sheet of correction from me in a day or two.

Yours Sincerely,
W. W.

[1] Margaret Gillies.
[2] See *Vaudracour and Julia*, l. 192 (*Prel.*, pp. 358–9). The poem, which originally formed part of the early text of *The Prelude*, was published separately in 1820 (see *MY* ii. 562, 592, 594). The date of this letter is established by Moxon's reply to Henry Reed of 7 Nov., quoted by Dunn.
[3] Hartley Coleridge.

Address: Miss Fenwick, G. Taylor's Esqᶜ, Whitton, Bishop Auckland, Durham.
Postmark: 4 Nov. 1839. *Stamp*: Ambleside.
MS. WL. Hitherto unpublished.

[*In Dora W.'s hand*]

Rydal Mount
Sunday Ev^{ng} [3 Nov. 1839]

Father speaks

My dearest Friends,

I do not mean to employ much time in noticing the contents Mary of y^r letter. I must however say that we were glad to hear so good an account of our relations[1] and that y^r extract from Miss Fenwick's letter rejoices us much. The impression made by Mrs Henry Taylor[2] is all that c^d be wished and we trust that there is a firm ground for hope to build upon in this marriage and can rationally be looked for. But dear Miss Fenwick I was a little mortified to learn from y^r not writing to us on account of the expence of postage how much I must have spoken to you of trivial matters; if you were but aware how continually I had expected to hear from you every day, you w^d be sorry that you had not made an exception and in [my][3] own case. My intention for this week, is to go to Whitehaven by mail on Tuesday to remain there if Ld L.[4] stays so long till Friday, to pass Sat. and Sunday at Brigham and to meet you at Keswick on Monday or Tuesday as may suit y^r convenience. Only you must take care to let me know for a certainty *which* of these days by a letter addressed to me at Brigham. If John has the command of a carriage and the weather pretty good and the children well I trust I shall prevail upon the mother to let two of them accompany her husband and me to Keswick. Of this place we think with much more pleasure than we could do a few days since.[5] Bertha who returned yesterday brings a much more

---

[1] M. W. had been visiting her relatives at Stockton-on-Tees.

[2] Formerly Theodosia Spring Rice.

[3] *Word dropped out.*

[4] Lord Lonsdale.

[5] The Southey family quarrel had now broken out. Soon after her arrival at Greta Hall, Southey's second wife Caroline found herself involved in

favorable report of her Father's state both of body and mind. Her visit did much more good than c^d have been expected. She soothed and quieted the parties and reconciled Kate, Betty and Cuthbert to the thought of no other change than that Betty s^d be housekeeper under Mrs Southey. It is settled also that Kate is to have an allowance w^h will place her at liberty to move about among her friends w^h happily for herself she is strongly inclined to, and accordingly she will be at Rydal on Saturday next on a visit to her sister in the first instance and is prepared after to visit you Miss Fenwick and us. What the poor creature has endured in mind is terrible to think of—the particulars you will hear from Dora when you return. I do not like to enter upon them and will dismiss the distressing subject by saying that Bertha has been taught by this visit to think much more highly of Mrs Southey and her maid than she did before. Betty also behaved perfectly well and it seems that the main root of the pain and discomfort w^h has spread thro' the whole house (Mr Southey not excluded) was in the wrong view w^h Kate had taken of persons and things thro' her understanding being affected by serious irritability amounting at times to derangement of mind. Mrs Southey it appears is very hot tempered, this her maid acknowledges. She speaks of her as a most excellent person, kind, aff^te, and with qualities that have made her beloved and respected wherever she becomes intimately known. Nevertheless it is but justice to poor Kate to say that Mrs S has uttered things during their derangements w^h any one w^d have found hard to bear and something not to be excused by mere defects of temper. As to poor dear Mr Southey he has returned to his employments, even to composition, but it still subject to bewilderment, for example he asked B when she had seen Mr Rickman. [1]

acrimonious disputes with her stepdaughters Kate and Bertha, and with her stepson Cuthbert who excluded virtually all reference to Southey's life after his second marriage from *the Life and Correspondence*. Other relatives and friends of the family were obliged to take sides. Caroline found support from the Warters, but the Wordsworths sided with Southey's other children in opposing her. On 26 Feb. 1841 Kate Southey drew up at W. W.'s suggestion 'an account concerning the sad occurrences that had taken place in my Father's house since his marriage', which is now preserved in the Victoria University Library, Toronto.

[1] Southey's friend John Rickman, the census official.

Now for ourselves. Miss Ricketts and Anna[1] took Miss Taylor's[2] place on Monday and remained with us till Friday noon. The dry weather, for we have scarcely had a drop of rain for *11* days, allowed us to move about a good deal and we past our time pleasantly. Yesterday Miss Gillies and I had a very long walk on the other side of Rydal Water round by Loughrigg tarn and went over the Fell where we encountered a tremendous wind from the east w[h] as the twilight was come and I was obliged to use both glasses and gauze shade to protect my eyes made the journey, for such it seemed, to be rather hazardous. Nevertheless we enjoyed ourselves much and the objects and the novelty of the situation greatly interested my companion; we were in motion three hours and 20 minutes. Miss G a little tired today but I scarcely felt the walk notwithstanding the violence of the wind. Today the wind is almost gone but for at least 4 days during the last week it blew what the sailors call great guns and throughout the woods has turned autumn into winter. But the fields are still beautifully green; our Dahlias in front of the window are still blooming—so are those, and other flowers at Elleray, but at M[r] Roughsedge's[3] they have been long destroyed by the frost which is another proof of what I have long observed, that blossoms, flowers, and leaves, in high situations, often escape the mischief to w[h] they are subject in low ones where the moister air and vapours being acted upon by frost are apt to destroy them. The dry weather we have had by making so much walking exercise agreeable has made me feel finally how much our muscular strength depends upon exercise, three hours walking tire me now less than one did a few weeks back. But I ought to have talked to you long ago about the miniature. Every one says that the bust[4] only excepted it is much the best thing that has been done of me and if you dearest Mary do not like it we shall be mortified indeed; Miss Fenwick I am pretty confident will be pleased, we hope and trust you will both be so if it were only for Miss Gillies' sake. She has worked so carefully and been so anxious and is really for this charming art a person of genius. She is to paint M[rs] Harrison,[5] her son

---

[1] For the Ricketts sisters see L. 1276 above.

[2] A friend of Mrs. Ricketts: apparently a niece of Mrs. Lutwidge of Ambleside (see L. 1369 in next volume).

[3] A neighbour and friend of the Wordsworths.

[4] Chantrey's bust of W. W.

[5] Mrs. Benson Harrison.

Richard in the same piece, and on Tuesday she goes to Elleray to make a likeness of Lady Farquhar.

William writes in a cheerful strain, but does not mention his own health. Hannah Cookson[1] writes that he is *much* better and generally looks so and looks much younger, a report w^h Mr Wilkinson[2] confirmed to M^r and Mrs Harrison who met him at Keswick yesterday. This is the best news, and I have kept it to the last but we have also heard today from Brinsop. Elizabeth is much better but her father suffers severely from the nipping cold. Mr Carr and the Miss Dowlings are to be there on Thursday. I hope Thomas[3] will benefit from this visit. Remember me most kindly to M^r and Mrs Taylor. God grant us a happy meeting at Keswick and believe me my beloved friends

faithfully yours
W W.

I am going up stairs to Sister who is much as usual. She has gone today to her own room, a change w^h she greatly enjoys.
I have heard nothing more from Mr Jackson about the house he [? wants] for Mr Huddleston.[4]
John Wordsworth[5] sails from Gibraltar on the 7th inst. He has just sold £1500 worth of his little estate to Mr Cowper[6] and feels himself quite at ease.
Anne is come home looking thin but not at all lame. She had made us good bread out of flour w^h we were on the point of sending away as bad. Jane saw Mr Fell who comforted her and is all much [?][7] about her leg and she is in good spirits again. I am very anxious about the house and as soon as I return will see what can prudently be done to push the matter forward. Mrs Luff is hot again upon Mr Partridge's[8] house. She has thrown off her severe cold in a surprising manner.

---

[1] Sister of Elizabeth Cookson.

[2] Perhaps the Revd. George Wilkinson (see pt. i, L. 393).

[3] Thomas Hutchinson was presumably to benefit from Mr. Carr's professional ministrations.

[4] The MS. is obscure at this point. The reference is possibly to Thomas Jackson of Waterhead, Lady le Fleming's agent, and Andrew Fleming Hudleston, the heir to the Fleming estates (see L. 1282 above).

[5] R. W.'s son.

[6] Perhaps a farmer in Ambleside, as I. F. is presumed to have heard of him.

[7] *MS. obscure.*

[8] Probably Mr. Partridge of Ambleside.

By the by I have had a translation sent me by Mʳ Richardson[1] of one of my Sonnets, the one composed on Westminster bridge, into the Bengalese tongue; it is by a native Indian gentleman of Consideration who is said to be thoroughly master of the English language. Again farewell

W W.[2]

1351. JOHN W. and W. W. to EDWARD MOXON

MS. Henry E. Huntington Library.
K (—). LY iii. 1145 (—).

Brigham
Cockermouth
Novʳ 8ᵗʰ [1839][3]

My dear Moxon,

Many thanks for Shelley entire,[4] whom I now possess or enjoy through yʳ kindness. I hope your continental trip was a pleasant one, and that you found all well on yʳ return. I will accept yʳ invitation of last Xtmas, and give you a week or 10 days of my compʸ sometime during the Spring unless I am prevented by necessary engagements. My Father who is here, and begs his kind regards, wishes that the 12 Sonᵗˢ composed while the vol. of Sonᵗˢ was going through the press[5] should be added at the end of the 5ᵗʰ vol. together with a Latin translation of mine of the two Odes to May and the Somnambulist[6] (Latin Title 'Somnivaga') to conclude with the enclosed Latin verses— all in small print (viz the Latin) and not stereotyped, the advertisment on the other side being prefixed. I sent the translations a fortnight ago to my Cousin at Harrow telling him you were in no immediate want of them I thought, and asking him both to correct my blunders as well as those of your printers, which friendly office I told Him I should tell you when I wrote to you *He* would do for me, if I heard not from Him to

---

[1] Later Sir John Richardson.
[2] Dora W. adds a brief note: ' . . . Father is wonderfully well. He really astonishes me with what he goes thro' in the way of walking and talking . . . '
[3] Incorrectly assigned to 1842 by Knight and de Selincourt.
[4] See L. 1348 above.
[5] See L. 1248 above.
[6] *PW* iv. 116, 118, 49.

the contrary. I have not heard from him, therefore I am pretty sure he assents to my proposal, especially as he had already, when at Rydal, seen two of my three trans[ns] and liked them. I wish them to be published in this way thinking they may be partly helps to me in getting Pupils, answering as testimonials. I am not quite certain about the french name in the note to be enclosed 'Isle Bonne' 20 miles up the Seine. Perhaps you can find out for me whether it is rightly spelt. It is not down in my map. After the verses are struck off and corrected, *mind*, by the Master of Harrow, for even if *I* have made no blunders, I should be too nervous to see those of the Printers, let me, please, have a few copies of them. If you have not yet got the trans[ns] and have the 5th vol in hand, you must be so good as to write, or send for them. Let me have a few lines from you soon. My wife joins me in kind regards.

Believe me to remain,

dear Moxon, y[r] very sincere Friend

J. Wordsworth

[*W. W. writes*]

Rydal Mount Friday

My dear Mr Moxon,

Before the sheet is struck off containing the Sonnets and the Latin translations I wish it to be sent down to me, for revision—it shall be sent back immediately and the work may then be published and the sooner the better.—I have been from here some time. Has H. C.[1] sent the remaind[er] of his work. I hope so as I have had promising assurances from his Friend. [The] day before yesterday I saw Mr Southey: he is better but still sadly shaken. I have recommended to Mrs Southey that D[r] Southey should have an interview with you to consult as to what is best to be done, for your joint interests and welfare. In my judgement it would be ruinous to Mr Southey's health for him to undertake any task work whatsoever, as nothing but absolute rest can bring him about. I am sorry, very sorry for your entanglement, as I see no probability of his being able to finish the work[2] in time for your purpose, and I expect Southey will indeed have to give it up; you will then be obliged to look out for some one else—a most unfortunate necessity but a necessity I

---

[1] Hartley Coleridge.

[2] The volume of ballads which he was editing (see L. 1340 above), or possibly the forthcoming edition of Beaumont and Fletcher (see L. 1370 in next volume).

am sure it is. Mrs Southey was convinced it would be very injurious to her Husband to propose to him to put what he had already done into other hands; I think the same for he has partly unfounded hopes of being able soon to resume his Labours; but what is the fact—he sits down to write a common Letter, proceeds in the old way for a few lines, and then his nerves fall into disorder, and his head becomes quite confused. Common humanity therefore requires that he should be kept from work as much as possible. If Charles Lamb, dear Man, had been [? concerned][1] how gladly would he have done the work for you. I would also have done it to the best of my power, but my eyes will not allow it.

ever faithfully and affectionately yours
W Wordsworth—

[*In John W.'s hand*]

The Sonnets are

p 110	Forth rushing	443	If with old
111	Blest Statesman	444	Life with yon
112	What strong	445	Hark 'tis
113	From the Pier's	446	Tis He
*144	Serving no haughty	447	Failing
		448	Son of my

* Let this sonnet be placed last[2]

Advertisement

Since the first impression of this stereotyped Edition was taken, a collection of the Son^ts was published separately, which contained also twelve Sonnets composed while that vol. was going through the Press. It has been thought proper to annex them here; and for my own satisfaction, [*W. W. writes*] and in the hope, I acknowledge, of gratifying some Readers, I have added Latin translations, by a near Relative of mine, of the two Odes to May, and also of the Somnambulist, with an account, by the Translator, in an elegiac Epistle to a Friend, of the circumstances under which the translations were made.[3]

[1] MS. illegible.

[2] John W. omits to list the twelfth sonnet, 'Oh what a wreck'.

[3] Most of the last sentence has been erased by W. W., including the words 'Such occupation served to beguile some tedious hours during a recovery from a long and oppressive illness.'

Address: Mrs S. T. Coleridge, 10 Chester Place, Regents Park.
MS. Victoria University Library, Toronto.
LY ii. 988.

Nov. 21ˢᵗ [1839]

My dear Mrs Coleridge,

Your letter was given to me on my return from a visit to my Durham Relations a week ago, but since that time I have been confined partly to my bed consequent upon a bad cold, taken in the course of our homeward journey; which was prolonged by paying visits by the way. Our friend Miss Fenwick was my fellow-traveller—indeed it was my *inducement* to leave home, that she was going to visit the Taylors who live in the same neighbourhood as my friends, and that I had an opportunity of travelling with her. We were absent three weeks, and took Keswick on our way home, for the purpose of seeing dear Southey, and paying my respects to his wife. We found S., I am happy to say, better than I expected from all the melancholy accounts I had had; but alas, alas there is a sad change; yet his being better than he had been tends to give hope that perfect rest, time, and mild weather (for he is very sensitive to cold) may restore him to something like his former self. The earnest prayer of all—especially of *us* who know of what important consequence his invaluable life is universally—as well as in his own family. It is truly an awful thing to think of such a mind being prematurely so weakened, but these decrees are from a Power who knows what is best—and our duty is to submit, but not without hope. Mrs Southey was very kind, and seemed much in her place, was exceedingly glad to see us (Miss F. and I met Wm there who had returned from a visit to Brigham) as was your Sister Lovell, who was looking as well, and as comfortable as I ever saw her, and the two ladies seemed to be very cordially united in their feelings, and care of the Invalid. Kate had left Keswick for Rydal a day or two before our arrival there, and Cuthbert was expected at home that day from Carlisle where he had been paying a visit of a week to my son William. You will be glad to hear that *dear Willy* reports himself as being less annoyed by his complaint of late. Poor fellow, I have had much anxiety about his health.

I have seen Kate several times since my return, and think her looks and spirits much improved—she drank tea with us last evening, and returned home with Miss Fenwick to Ambleside afterwards, where she means to spend a few days, with that dear good woman who is a treasure to us all. Bertha I have not seen, she is not quite well and did not come up, and I have not been able, as yet, to go to her. Nothing unusual to her situation is the matter with her, and she has been remarkably well; and I never saw any one's looks so much improved as hers, since she became a resident in Rydal. Dear Creature, I trust she may do well—she will make a nice Mother, and she need not be a more happy one, than she is a Wife. Herbert[1] looks delicate, but I hear no complaints of his health.

I have not seen, nor heard *particularly* of Hartley since my return, but I hope Moxon's work, if not done, is nearly so, as he told Mr Quillinan[2] (who arrived here on Tuesday) and who called upon him with a message from Moxon, that he should not dine out till he had finished. As soon as this is accomplished, I know we shall see him with his packet, to be sent off from this house.

I will enclose you his bills, which have been paid, and tell you the amount of monies remaining in his purse. But my head is not clear enough (indeed it is never clear *enough*, for nothing in the course of my life ever bothers me like accounts) to see whether I am right or wrong in my calculations,—only knowing my intentions are honest I am easy on that point, as I am sure, dear friend, you will be. I must however tell you— what you may have forgotten—that Moxon gave Hartley, when he was here, £3,—all he c^d spare out of the provision he had made for his journey, but promised to send him £7 in addition, to make up £10 which Hartley begged to have: the £7 was sent by Willy from M., we kept this whole sum back for some time, till poor H. asked for a part of it, and got £3, and at the same time he mentioned the Keswick Tailor's bill, which you will see, and we propose to pay it from the remaining sum—he willingly consented so that so much, at any rate, of his earnings has been turned to a good account—as you will find, a trifle of this fund still rests with me. We cannot say, poor fellow, that his expenses are great—but how well would it be for himself if his great talents were applied as they ought to be to his entire maintenance. We must however congratulate ourselves

---

[1] Herbert Hill, Bertha's husband.

[2] According to his MS. Diary (*WL MSS.*), E. Q. arrived at Rydal Mount on 17 Nov. and left on 3 Dec.

that he is going on as well as he now seems to be doing, and hope for the best for the future.

My Sister Joanna is now with us—she and I were among our friends in Durham. She was then looking well—but like myself has since had a bad cold from which she is still suffering, and she has lost her good looks. She begs her affec. remembrances to you and Sara, and was very glad, as we all are, to hear a tolerable account of you. She was very little upon the Island,[1] where she has now two nieces,[2] last summer, and I rather think did not see your Sisters; she means to pass the winter with us, and return in the spring to her favourite Island, to which she is as much attached as ever, notwithstanding the sorrow she has undergone.[3] But her pure and happy spirit binds her to the point where she feels she can be of most use, and find most leisure to fit herself for the change which at no distant day awaits us all.

William, I am glad to say, is quite well, Dora tolerably so, and all the Brigham family flourishing. Grandfather is come home delighted with his youngest grandchild Charles,[4] and with all the rest in degree. With love believe me d[r] Mrs C. ever affect[ly]

M. Wordsworth.

The purse contains £27.10 and I hold balance of Moxon's £10, £1. 18. 4. So we are rich enough.

[1] The Isle of Man.
[2] Probably two of the daughters of M. W.'s brother George Hutchinson, of Brinsop (see *MW* p. 189).
[3] The death of their brother Henry.
[4] John W.'s fifth child, born this year.

1353. W. W. to H. C. R.

Address: H. C. Robinson Esq., No. 30 Russel Square.
Endorsed: Dec^b 7th 1839. Wordsworth. Investments.
MS. Dr. Williams's Library.
Morley, i. 394.

Rydal Mount
Ambleside
(not Kendal)
Dec^b 7th [1839]

My dear Friend,

We had been looking long for a letter from you. It gives us pleasure to hear of your new arrangement[1] and we all join in good wishes that your happiness may be promoted by it.—I need not say that it would delight me to be under your roof.— As our wish to see you here at Christmas was far from being selfish, we resign it in a manner which is neither unworthy of ourselves nor you. Should your plan alter we shall be still more happy to receive you after this disappointment.—

Your account of the United States Bank[2] is appalling. We are truly sorry for your loss; several of our Friends are far more deeply concerned. Can you tell us anything about Missisippi Bonds? Dear Miss Hutchinson's little fortune was all there; and Dora, by bequest of her's has an interest in them—to the amount of 40£ per ann:—I hope, as I have expressed to Courtenay, the fall in our *Provincial*[3] is nothing more than the consequence of the general monetary depression, and that that Bank is not involved in direct dealings with any foreign securities. Courtenay I know sets his face against anything of that kind, and his advice it was that preserved me from such engagements. Perhaps you could learn from your Friend M^r

---

[1] H. C. R. moved from Plowden's Buildings to 30 Russell Street on 25 Sept. 1839. 'I am to pay for this, my new domicile, £ 100 per annum. It gives me no vote, subjects me to no service. I have no reason to complain of my surroundings.' (Sadler iii. 179—80.) As Morley notes, he remained there for the rest of his life.

[2] The Second Bank of the United States was chartered in 1816, but owing to the increasing political opposition it incurred the charter was not renewed in 1836; it ceased to be a national institution and found a new role as the State Bank of Pennsylvania. In the financial crisis of 1839 it suspended payments on 9 Oct., and was finally closed down just over a year later, in Jan. 1841.

[3] i.e. National Provincial stock.

Jaffery[1] as [to] how far I am right in the notion I have expressed of the National Provincial.

If you see Mr Moxon pray tell him I would be obliged if he could write a note to the Master of Harrow, begging, if it be not already done, that he would cast his eye over my Son's Latin translations of my Poem[s];[2] as soon as he can. The republication of the six Volumes is detained by the want of them. And pray add to M^r M— that I wish before the sheet is struck off to have it sent down to me for correction.—

I have a kind letter from Miss Mackenzie,[3] dated Rome— She speaks of you as one Friend should of Another

ever faithfully yours
W. W.

Can you learn whether the Philadelphia Bank is in better plight than the United States. You were right as to poor dear Southey. He continues very feeble.—

1354. W. W. to EDWARD MOXON

Address: Edward Moxon Esq, 44 Dover Street, London.
Postmark: (1) 12 Dec. 1839 (2) 15 Dec. 1839. *Stamp*: Ambleside.
MS. National Library of Scotland. Hitherto unpublished.

[In John Carter's hand]

Rydal Mount. 12 Decr. 1839

Dear Moxon,

Don't you think it would answer to strike off an additional hundred or more of the Appendix[4] to accomodate certain purchasers of the former Edition and for the pleasure of presenting copies to particular friends?

[1] Robert Jaffray, a business friend of H. C. R.'s, whose name occurs frequently in his diary. He helped particularly in the negotiations H. C. R. conducted on W. W.'s behalf with the Baudouins.

[2] See next letter.

[3] Miss Frances Mackenzie.

[4] The Appendix to Vol. v of the new edition, dated Rydal Mount 20 Nov. 1839, which was to contain the 12 sonnets published in 1838 and John W.'s Latin translations (see L. 1351 above). One of the unbound copies, a present from John W. to his former tutor at Oxford, Dr. John Anthony Cramer (1793–1848), Dean of Carlisle, is preserved at the *WL*.

If you don't like this proposal I should wish to have for myself and my Son at least thirty Copies.

Be so good as to get the Book [1] out as speedily as you can, as perhaps a few persons might wish to make Xmas presents of it. I will thank you to send at least a dozen copies down.

I am, dear Sir
Y^{rs} faithfully
[*signed*] Wm Wordsworth

1355. W. W. to EDWARD MOXON

MS. untraced.
K (—). LY iii. 1149.

Rydal Mount, Dec. 13th, [1839][2]

. . . Pray send us down a dozen copies of the new edition, and, if you have them, the like number of the *Yarrow* done up as those last sent, there being a great demand for them in this neighbourhood. I received from Mr Quillinan your message this morning; the last part of the proofs was sent off before it arrived. . . . I have done all that can be done for you in Hartley's case, both directly, and through the medium of a common friend; but he now avoids us both, and tells every one who speaks on the subject to him that 'he is going to send off the last remainder of the copy next day', and this has been the case for the last month or six weeks. It is, therefore, evident that you must trust nothing to him in future. He cannot be relied on for unperformed work that is to be done in a limited time. This is a great pity, for both his genius and talents are admirable. As to poor dear Southey, there is [as] yet no improvement in him to warrant a confident hope that he ever will be able to complete any of his unfinished works. He is prepared, I understand, to give up the continuation of the Admirals,[3] and I trust will do the same in respect to his engagement with you. In this distressing

---

[1] *Yarrow Revisited, and other poems*, 3rd edition, 1839.

[2] Incorrectly assigned to 1842 by Knight and de Selincourt.

[3] Southey wrote *The Lives of the Admirals, with an Introductory View of the Naval History of England*, in five volumes, 1833—40, for Lardner's *Cabinet Cyclopaedia*. The fifth volume was completed by Robert Bell. See Jack Simmons, *Southey*, 1945, pp. 193—4.

affair I can do no more than I have done. When you see
Mr Rogers, do not fail to remember us affectionately to him.
And if dear Miss Lamb be well enough, let her be reminded of us
when you see her. . . .

1356. W. W. to THOMAS KIBBLE HERVEY

MS. Mr W. Hugh Peal. Hitherto unpublished.

[*In M. W.'s hand*]

Rydal Mount
Decr 22^d [1839]

My dear Sir,

Having an opportunity of sending a letter free of Postage to
London I avail myself of it to thank you for your elegant present
of the Amaranth,[1] which came to my hands two or three days
ago. It is a very splendid book; and no doubt will be much
admired as it deserves to be. I have not yet had it in my power to
peruse more than a few of the pieces in the volume—but as far as
I can judge they appear to be of great merit—and the very
names of most of the Authors are a sufficient guarantee for the
value of their contributions. Heartily wishing you every success
the work deserves, I remain

sincerely yours
[*signed*] Wm Wordsworth

[1] *The Amaranth; a miscellany of original prose and verse. Contributed by
distinguished writers, and edited by T. K. Hervey,* 1839. Among the contributors
to this imposing quarto volume were Allan Cunningham, Mary Howitt,
Caroline Bowles, 'Barry Cornwall', Thomas Hood, James Montgomery, and
Elizabeth Barrett.

MS. British Library. Hitherto unpublished.

Decr 22^d [1839]

My dear Nephew,

The contents of your letter have distressed us much. Poor dear John![1] Though it had been mentioned to me the other day by Mr Dobson[2] that he was very unwell, as I knew that he was often so, I felt no alarm whatever. We are thankful that you have written, painful as the duty must have been to you; for should this disease terminate fatally, we shall be spared something of the shock which must attend the tidings. When I reflect however, how ill William was in confirmed dropsy soon after he came to us from the Charterhouse[3] and that his Life was despaired of by the most experienced of his Medical Attendants, I cannot but entertain hope that John may recover. Your poor Father too, I fear he may break down under his anxiety and fatigue! You have every one of you our tender sympathy and our prayers. Dora does not yet know of this illness; she is staying at Ambleside with Miss Fenwick, and her own health is so much deranged that we hesitate about telling her what her Cousin is suffering; but it must be done; and I shall walk over today for the purpose. If any marked change either for better or worse takes place pray do write immediately; We shall be very anxious till we hear from you again.

I am gratified that you thought so well of John's Verses[4]—I am no critic in these matters; there might be many small faults in Latinity which I shall not be aware of, and therefore I could not have consented to the publication of these translations, unless some scholar like yourself, who had an interest in the Translator had looked them over. They appeared to me to be well executed, and as you say so, I cannot doubt it.

John you know is anxious to add to his small income by one or more pupils. Though he has not been tried, he is competent,

---

[1] C. W.'s son John was now in the last stages of his terminal illness. See also L. 1362 (in next volume).

[2] The Revd. William Dobson (1809–67), Fellow of Trinity College, Cambridge, 1834–41, and Principal of Cheltenham College, 1845–59: author of *Schleiermacher's Introductions to the Dialogues of Plato, translated*, 1834. His wife was Benson Harrison's daughter by his first marriage. He visited W. W. twice this year, in June and December (*RMVB*).

[3] See pt. i, L. 71. [4] See L. 1351 above.

and I trust would do his duty: *Do* be so good as to keep it in mind: for, as appears from a late Letter it is of serious importance to him.

The situation I think most favorable but unless he were well paid, as you will understand, his purpose would not be answered; in fact he would be better as he is, though so much straitened.

William has also been very unwell, but is a good deal better; we hope to see him to spend his Christmas-day with us. Kind love to all, to your Father, to Charles and his Baby, and to yourself and Susan, whose visit[1] we remember with gratitude and much pleasure. Say to John whatever you think proper, ever your affectionate

Uncle
W Wordsworth

1358. W. W. to LORD MONTEAGLE

Address: Lord Monteagle, Mansfield St, London.
MS. untraced.
LY ii. 991.

Rydal Mount 23^d Dec^{br} —39

My dear Lord

Let me hope that I am justified in offering you my condolence upon the grievous loss which you have sustained—[2]

I should have scarcely ventured to break in upon your Sorrow, had I not heard, through Miss Fenwick, from Mr Taylor in what an admirable manner the affliction was borne by yourself and the children of the departed. Having thought much and often upon you all during this trial I trust that this expression of sympathy, in which Mrs Wordsworth sincerely joins, will carry with it some sense of comfort, as I am sure it will be kindly received. To Mr and Mrs Taylor, and to your Daughter Mary, more particularly, for of her I have seen more, I beg to be affectionately remembered upon this mournful occasion.

Pray accept my thanks for the Letter which I received from you some time ago. Nothing but the importance of the points

[1] The previous August (*RMVB*).
[2] The death of Lady Monteagle earlier this month.

upon which it turned prevented my replying to it at the time. I felt I could not by Letter treat them to my own satisfaction and far less to your's; and therefore I was silent in the hope that an opportunity would at some time or other be offered when the difficulties that stood in my way might be removed by conversation

I remain—
My dear Lord
faithfully your obliged
Wm Wordsworth

1359. W. W. to HENRY REED

Address: Henry Reed Esqre, Philadelphia.
Postmark: (1) 24 Dec. 1839 (2) 25 Dec. 1839.
Stamp: (1) Ambleside (2) Boston Ship.
Endorsed: Rec. March 30.
MS. Cornell.
Mem. (—). *K* (—). *Wordsworth and Reed, p. 13.*

[*In M. W.'s hand*]

Rydal Mount Decr 23, 1839

My dear Sir

The year is upon the point of expiring, and a letter of yours dated May 7th tho' not rec^d till late in June, for I was moving about all last spring and part of the summer, remains unacknowledged. I have also to thank you for the acceptable present of the two Volumes[1] which reached me some time afterwards. In the month of July I was again seized with an inflammation in my eyes, which cut me off for several months from reading, writing, and also from consecutive or laborious thinking—during this time I was little in the mood of even dictating letters to any one, where it was in my power to defer the undertaking. This you must be kind enough to accept as my apology for my silence—I might add much more, particularly that Mrs W. and my daughter, who write for me, are severally under many engagements, and occasional incapacities. To prevent any unfavourable inference for similar omissions in

[1] *Lyrical Ballads*, 2 vols., Philadelphia, 1802: the first American edition.

future if they should occur, let me at once assure you of my affectionate regard and sincere esteem.

Your letters are naturally turned upon the impression which my Poems, have made, and the estimation they are held, or likely to be held in, thro' the vast country to which you belong;[1] I wish I could feel as livelily as you do upon this subject—or even upon the general destiny of those works— pray do not be long surprized at this declaration. There is a difference of more than the length of your life, I believe, between our ages. I am standing on the brink of that vast ocean I must sail so soon—I must speedily lose sight of the shore and I could not once have conceived how little I now am troubled by the thought of how long or short a time they who remain upon that shore may have sight of me. The other day I chanced to be looking over a MS. poem belonging to the year 1803—tho' not actually composed till many years afterwards. It was suggested by visiting the neighbourhood of Dumfries, in which Burns had resided and where he died; it concluded thus.

> Sweet mercy to the gates of heaven
> This Minstrel lead, his sins forgiven,
> The rueful conflict, the heart riven
>   With vain endeavour,
> And memory of earth's bitter leaven
>   Effaced for ever.

[1] In his letter of 7 May (*Wordsworth and Reed*, p. 8), Reed had adverted again to his recent article on W. W. (see L. 1297 above): 'When after mature reflection I ventured to class your name with those most illustrious in the history of English Poetry, I was quite uncertain whether the general study of your works was such as to sustain such an opinion in criticism. . . . Indeed the strong spoken expression of my admiration and affection, in the Review, was not only prompted by a confidence in its truth, but to provoke (as it were) public literary opinion on the subject. . . . I am enabled to say to you, that a careful observation of popular sentiment, as manifested both in the press and in private communications, has assured me of a much greater appreciation of the poetry in question than, with all my predilections, I had imagined. It has been in my power to observe the hold your writings have gained upon the minds and hearts of persons of both sexes and in different conditions both as to cultivation and to modes of life. Thinking as I do of the spirit of that poetry, there is something, my Dear Sir, of nationality in the gratification I have in making this statement respecting my countrymen and countrywomen.'

Here the verses closed, but I instantly added the other day

> But why to Him confine the prayer,
> When kindred thoughts and yearnings bear
> On the frail heart the purest share
> With all that live?
> The best of what we do and are,
> Just God, forgive![1]

The more I reflect upon this last exclamation, the more I feel and perhaps it may in some degree be the same with you, justified in attaching comparatively small importance to any literary monument that I may be enabled to leave behind. It is well however, I am convinced, that men think otherwise in the earlier part of their lives, and and why it is so is a point I need not touch upon in writing to you. Before I dismiss this subject let me thank you for the extract from your intelligent friend's letter,[2] and allow me to tell you, that I could not but smile at your Boston Critic, placing my name by the side of Cowley.[3] I suppose he cannot be such a simpleton as to mean any thing more, than that the same measure of reputation, or fame, if that be not too presumptuous a word, is due to us both.

German transcendentalism which you say this Critic is infected by, would be a woeful visitation for the world were it not sure to be as transitory as it is pernicious.

[1] See *PW* iii. 69 and L. 954 above.

[2] Reed had enclosed a letter from John Sergeant (1779–1852), in whose office he had studied law, praising his article, rejecting Jeffrey's pretensions as a critic, and recalling the early reception of *Lyrical Ballads* in America. 'They were so simple in their dress, so humble in their topics, so opposite to the pomp and strut of what had been the poetry of the times *immediately* preceding, that they were a good deal of a puzzle. Yet, it was manifest, even then, that they touched a kindred chord in the heart, and I remember a conversation about them in the first four or five years of the present century, in which their power was acknowledged.' (*Wordsworth and Reed*, p. 11). As Broughton notes, Sergeant served over a long period as a Congressman. He was the leading champion of the Northern States in procuring the passage of the Missouri Compromise in 1820, and was the Whig candidate for Vice-President of the United States in 1832.

[3] Reed had referred to a recent discussion of W. W. in a Boston periodical, '— in which after an abundant outpouring of Gallo-German Metaphysics—transcendentalism and pantheism—the closing judgment pronounces you "the *Cowley* (!) of the 19th Century" '. For W. W.'s attitude to New England Transcendentalism, see Alan G. Hill, 'Wordsworth and His American Friends', *Bulletin of Research in the Humanities*, lxxxi (1978), 146–60.

The way in which you speak of me in connection with your possible visit to Eng^d was most gratifying,[1] and I here repeat that I should be truly glad to see you, in the delightful spot where I have long dwelt—and I have the more pleasure in saying this to you, because, in spite of my old infirmity, my strength exceeds that of most men of my years, and my general health continues to be, as it always has been, remarkably good. A page of blank paper stares me in the face, and I am not sure that it is worth while to fill it with a sonnet, which broke from me not long ago on reading an account of misdoings in many parts of your Republic—Mrs W. will however transcribe it

> Men of the Western World! in Fate's dark book,
> Whence this opprobrious leaf of dire portent?
> Think ye your British ancestors forsook
> Their narrow Isle, for outrage provident?
> Think ye they fled restraints they ill could brook
> To give, in their descendants, freer vent
> And wider range to passions turbulent,
> To mutual tyranny a deadlier look?
> "Nay" said a voice more soft than Zephyrs breath,
> "Dive thro' the stormy surface of the flood
> To the great current flowing underneath;
> Think on the countless Springs of silent good;
> So shall the truth be known and understood
> And thy grieved Spirit brighten, strong in faith.[2]

To turn to another subject. You will be sorry to learn that several of my most valued Friends are likely to suffer from the monetary derangements in America. My *family* however is no way directly entangled in them unless the Mississipi bonds prove invalid. There is an opinion pretty current among discerning Persons in England that Republics are not to be

---

[1] Reed wrote, 'I cherish the anticipation more earnestly, because I know it is not in your nature to make an offer inconsiderately of your friendship, and because of the hope that personal intercourse would not lessen the kindly feelings which seem to have sprung from our casual correspondence.' Reed never visited England in the poet's lifetime. He came to Rydal Mount five years after W. W.'s death.

[2] See *PW* iv. 131. The text here differs in some particulars from the published version. W. W. is thinking particularly of the recent Bank failures in America and the financial uncertainty which followed,—which affected members of his own family (see L. 1353 above).

trusted in money concerns;—I suppose because the sense of honor is more obtuse, the responsibility being divided among so many. For my own part I have as little or less faith in absolute despotisms, except that they are more easily convinced that it is politic to keep up their credit by holding to their engagements. What power is maintained by this practice was shewn by Great Britain in her struggle with Buonaparte. This lesson has not been lost on the leading Monarchical states of Europe. But too much of this—Believe me to remain

faithfully yours

[*signed*] Wm Wordsworth

1360. W. W. to LORD MONTEAGLE

MS. Cornell.
LY ii. 991.

Dec[r] 30th —39

My dear Lord

Your Letter, and the Enclosure, gave me, and let me add my family, great pleasure. I hope you will also excuse my having shewn both to Miss Fenwick. We were all made happy by this additional proof that your affliction[1] was borne by yourself and those most dear to you, with christian resignation and with the best solace of Christian hope. We congratulate you upon having a Son[2] on whose youthful mind piety has made so deep an impression, and in whom good principles have taken such firm root.

I was gratified by the touching allusion you make to a passage in the Excursion[3] and I am accordingly encouraged to present to your notice a stanza in one of my minor Poems which you may not be acquainted with. As it often recurs to my memory, in the

[1] The death of Lady Monteagle (see L. 1358 above).

[2] Stephen Edmund Spring Rice (1814–65), Deputy Chairman of the Board of Customs, who had recently married Ellen Mary, eldest daughter of William Frere, Master of Downing College, Cambridge, and uncle of C. W. jnr.'s wife, Susanna. He eventually predeceased his father, and the title passed to his son Thomas.

[3] Lord Monteagle had written warmly on 26 Dec. about his loss, describing how it was in his wife's company that he had first come to know and appreciate *The Excursion* (*WL MSS.*).

trials to which grief has subjected me, it will be taken by you, (by which I mean understood and felt,) in its true degree and meaning.

Thou takest not away O Death!
Thou strikest—absence perisheth
Indifference is no more;
The future brightens on our sight;
For on the past hath fallen a light
That tempts us to adore. [1]

Your notice of Mr and Mrs Taylor was delightful to us all.—His solid virtues have, through Mrs Southey and Miss Fenwick, been long known to me. To the happy pair, to yourself, and yours, we present our best wishes.

ever my dear Lord faithfully your's
W Wordsworth

1361. W. W. to THOMAS POWELL

Address: Tho⁵ Powell Esqʳᵉ , Leadenhall St.
MS. Pierpont Morgan Library.
MLN xlv (1930), 216—7. LY ii. 992 (—).

[*In M. W.'s hand*]

[late 1839]

My dear Mr Powell

Excuse my not writing earlier as I wished to do—From a letter of mine to Dʳ Smith,[2] which I enclose you will learn every thing respecting the Sanatorium to which your last letter referred,—so that I need not here dwell upon the subject.—I am glad that you enter so warmly into the Chaucerian project,[3] and

---

[1] See *PW* iv. 270.

[2] For Dr. Thomas Southwood Smith see L. 1199 above, and for his projected sanatorium L. 1382 (in next volume).

[3] The proposal for a volume of modern versions of Chaucer which was being planned by Powell, R. H. Horne, Leigh Hunt, Elizabeth Barrett, and others. It appeared as *Chaucer's Poems Modernized*, 1841, to which W. W. contributed *The Cuckoo and the Nightingale* (then attributed to Chaucer), and a passage from *Troilus and Cresida*. See *PW* iv. 217—33. These versions, together with *The Prioress' Tale* (published in 1820) and the unpublished

that Mr L. Hunt is disposed to give his valuable aid to it. For myself I cannot do more than I offered, to place at your disposal the Prioresses Tale, already published, the Cuckoo and the Nightingale, the Manciples Tale, and I rather think, but I cannot just now find it, a small portion of the Troilus and Cressida— You ask my opinion about that Poem—Speaking from a recollection only of many years past, I should say that it would be found too long—and probably tedious. The Knights Tale is also very long, but tho' Dryden[1] has executed it, in his own way observe, with great spirit and harmony, he has suffered so much of the simplicity, and with that of the beauty, and occasional pathos of the original to escape, that I should be pleased to hear that a new version should be attempted upon my principle by some competent Person. It would delight me to read every part of Chaucer over again, for I reverence and admire him above measure, with a view to your work, but my eyes will not permit me to do so—who will undertake the Prologue, to the C. Tales? For your publication that is indispensible, and I fear it will prove very difficult. It is written, as you know, in the couplet measure, and therefore I have nothing to say upon its metre—but in respect to the Poems in stanza, neither in the Prioresses Tale, nor in the Cuckoo and Nightingale have I kept to the rule of the original as to the form and number and position of the *rhymes*, thinking it enough if I kept the same number of lines in each stanza, and this I think is all that is necessary—and all that can be done without sacrificing the substance of sense, too often, to the mere form of sound.

I feel much obliged by y[r] offer of the 1st Ed: of the Paradise Lost,[2] and I apprehend from what you say that you are already aware of my possessing a Copy—otherwise I should not have felt justified in accepting the one you so kindly intend for me— The copy I possess was given me by Mr Rogers—and your's shall take its place on my shelves by its side. Mr Moxon is about to send down a parcel of books in which your valuable present might be included, with a certainty that it would arrive safe.

It is thought by every one that Mrs W.'s Portrait[3] (who

Maunciple's Tale (*PW* iv. 209–17, 358–65), both of which W. W. at first offered for the volume, were composed in Dec. 1801 (see *DWJ* i. 86 ff.).

[1] In his *Fables*, 1700.

[2] The copy given by Thomas Powell to W. W. is now in the New York Public Library.

[3] By Margaret Gillies (see L. 1345 above).

appears, as now engaged writing for me) is an excellent likeness
—The chalk drawing has yet a good deal to do at it. Dora has
been *attempted,* but not yet, as we think, with much success. I
think you will be delighted, with a profile Picture on ivory of
me, with which Miss G. is at this moment engaged, Mrs W.
seems to prefer it as a likeness to any thing she has yet done. We
all rejoice as you and Mrs P. will in her general success in this
neighbourhood.

Thanks for your kind enquiries after Mrs W's health—She is I
am glad to say quite well again, and joins with Miss G., my
Daughter, and myself in affec regards to you and Mrs P.—and
believe me

ever faithfully and aff ^{ly} yours
[*signed*] Wm Wordsworth

[*M. W. adds*]

Will you tell Dr S. that I am *quite well.*   M. W.

1361a. W. W. to JOHN WORDSWORTH[1]

MS. Mrs. M. J. Roberts. Hitherto unpublished.

Carlisle Mon. Nov. 13th [? 1835−9]

My dear John,

I am vexed above measure about your letter. It was put into
my hands on Thursday evening by Wm, at a house where I was
dining four miles off; as I could not read it in so much company I
put it into my side pocket and forgot until this morning that I
had received such a letter. Be assured I am exceedingly mortified
at your disappointment at this apparent neglect. It is possible,
however, you may not have set off upon your tour; and
therefore I write. First for Inns I must observe that it is too early
in the season to be as sure as one would wish that beds might not
prove damp. I will begin at Keswick—The House at Scale Hill is

[1] R. W.'s son. This letter seems to belong to the later 1830s, before the
breakdown of John's health, but the exact year cannot be established with
certainty. In early Nov. 1837 W. W. was in the Carlisle area for some days (see
Ls. 1179 and 1180 above), and in that year 13 Nov. fell on a Monday, but
according to L. 1175, John had left the Lake District to return to London at the
beginning of October and it seems unlikely that he would return to make a
tour so soon afterwards. It remains possible that W. W. himself simply
miswrote the day or the month.

in every respect good, that at Buttermere far from bad, at Calder Bridge are two very good inns and as they lie in the main road you might lodge well at Wastdale foot. But I rather fear for their beds at this time. No doubt you might lodge safely either at Ravenglass or Bootle if it should happen to suit. Mr Gulliver[1] said he was comfortable at Ulpha Plough Inn, and very much so at the King's Head Inn Broughton. At Dalton you may be accommodated well enough and your way would be to drive your carriage down to the Abbey[2] and thence to Rampside where no doubt you could lodge as it is a Bathing place. The road thence to Ulverston near the coast and by Bardsey is pleasing. At Ulverston of course you could lodge and you might proceed either by Newby Bridge where there is an excellent Inn or at Conniston waterside to Rydal Mount. I have said nothing about distances for I do not know them and very much the greatest part of your tour is without turnpikes or milestones—Though Mr Green[3] in his official book gives the distances . . .

[*cetera desunt*]

[1] Unidentified: probably a summer visitor.
[2] Furness Abbey.
[3] William Green (see *MY* i. 195).

APPENDIX

Recollections of our 3 Days Excursion at the Lakes with Mr Wordsworth, 1838

(see L. 1276)

I do not remember any pleasure that I looked forward to with greater delight than I did to this little Excursion and certainly none that more *completely* answered my most ardent expectations; for in general I am inclined to think that my anticipated and even my retrospective *enjoyments*, are often greater than *present* ones, for my expectations are usually very bright and sanguine and my retrospections are coloured with a *tinge* of Romance just sufficient to make them very delightful to *myself*; the present therefore has *often* (I will not say *always*) appeared to me vapid and disappointing. In this instance however *all* was delightful, all that was expected, all that was present, and all that has past, and never to be forgotten!

We all were prepared to be pleased and to please as far as we could hope to do so, and certainly the dear Poet's magic touch seemed to turn even our disasters into amusements, and to render each 'Scene of enchantment, *more* dear'.[1]

We started precisely at 8 oclock on Monday morning Oct 8th from our house, the Poet, his Daughter and myself inside the carriage (a britcha), his nephew Mr John Wordsworth and A[2] on the box, and Letitia for the sake of *propriety* with Melfort[3] in a car, came in tow. It was a mild autumnal day, not sunny, but clear, 'a sweet *pensive* day' to use the Poet's own words, with occasional beautiful gleams. We passed through Clappersgate and its lovely stream the Brathay to Coniston, where according to Mr Wordsworth's directions, a pr. of strong horses had been sent on, which were to accompany us for the remainder of our tour.

---

[1] Perhaps an echo of *The Reverie of Poor Susan* (*PW* ii. 217), l. 5.

[2] Anna Ricketts.   [3] Mrs. Ricketts's maid.

We were delayed here longer than our dear *Guide* liked, as he said we had a long day's work before us, and time was precious, but in spite of all his wishes, our movements could not be expedited, the landlord was gone for change, the drivers to refresh themselves, and there we were left to our fate.

The beauty of our situation however amply reconciled us to the delay: the Lake of Coniston reminds me more than any other I have yet seen of one of the small Italian Lakes, this day it was looking peculiarly lovely, there was a mellowness of colouring, the reflections on the Water were very clear and there was a perfect look of tranquillity in which all Nature animate, as well as inanimate, seemed to participate, for we remarked that not a living object was to be seen, not even an insect, not a leaf appeared to stir; except the clatter of *our* tongues, and an occasional splash in the Water by the jumping up of a little fish, not a murmur was heard in the air. At length appeared our landlord with change in hand, upon which our dear Poet produced a little shabby brown leather purse, the *once* smart embroidered flower on it faded, and the tassels on one side off. 'Here (he said) you see we are quite *classical*. This little purse to be sure rather the worse for wear you will say, *I* prize particularly, and shall never part with, for I brought it from Rome.'

Off we went at last, as we were drawing away Mr Wordsworth turned round to his daughter and said, 'My dear Dora, I hope you will forgive my little irritability just now to hasten our departure from Coniston, knowing better than any of you could do, what a long and fatiguing day we have before us, I felt we had no time to lose, but pardon me if I appeared *too* hasty.' As our driver had never been on the road we were now pursuing, and as Mr Wordsworth had not for many years been over it, we were obliged to make some enquiries as to our direct route.

The first place we stopt at was a small Ale-House. There were several idle-looking men standing at the Door. Mr W. addressed them in a tone of extreme civility and urbanity as particularly struck us, and which is *peculiar* to him, for his manner is strikingly courteous and gracious to all in every rank of life, yet mixed with this refinement of manner there is a simplicity of character that one rarely sees. In this instance all his politeness was thrown away upon his hearers, they all with open mouths and stupid gaze turned to him, and muttered some confused directions, which our dear *Guide* was endeavouring to render intelligible, but was much pained on discovering that it was perfectly useless, for they were all in a besotted state of drunkenness. 'Oh shocking, shocking', he exclaimed, 'at this early hour too in the morning, poor human Nature.' We could not resist here repeating two lines of his that naturally suggested themselves to us:

> 'And much it grieved my heart to think
> What man had made of man!'[1]

We had a repetition of the same distressing sight at 5 or 6 cottages that we stopt at, and at length we obtained the information we required from an old man working in a field many miles further on. We observed to Mr Wordsworth that this gave us a bad opinion of his *North country* people, however he disclaimed them being of this part of England, he said they were all miners, and that they were chiefly Cornish and Devonshire people, they had been paid their quarterly or monthly wages on the previous Saturday and from that day to this (Monday) had been in a perfect state of intoxication. Mr W. was much distressed by it, and he took an opportunity (as we found out) later in the day to speak his mind on the subject very openly to our drivers.

I do not think I shall ever forget our dear old Poet's *Quixotic* appearance on this eventful little tour, or rather I should say he resembled more the representations of one [of] the Weird Sisters in Macbeth than any thing else I can think of. He had been lately recovered from a very severe attack of Sciatica, he had suffered so much, and 'felt for himself (as he said) so much', this being almost the only serious illness he had ever had, that he was determined to take every precaution against cold. He had a little cloth cap on his head with a piece of fur falling from the back of it, and serving occasionally as a Collar. He had one of those Sheppard Scotch Plaids, used in the Highlands, and the gift of one of his many fair admirers, this plaid being sewn up one side and end, he threw over his head; it formed a conical peak at the top of it and them hung down shapeless and lank straight down his back, and being too long for him the remainder generally trailed on the ground like a train. It is true he suddenly recollected (when he stumbled over it every now and then) to hold it up on one arm, but this never lasted *long* for

---

[1] See *Lines Written in Early Spring* (*PW* iv, 58), ll. 7–8.

in his eagerness in talking and walking, away went the poor train again, sweeping the ground. He had on a pr. of dark glass spectacles, as he was suffering from inflammation in his Eyes, and as a further protection to them whenever there was the least wind, up went an old weather-beaten faded green Umbrella with some of the points coming out, but from the flexible state to which it was altogether reduced by constant usage, it accommodated itself most agreeably to its owner's wishes and suited itself to every point of the compass. This completed our Hero's *turn out*, and a fund of amusement did it occasion us, for we were saucy enough to laugh at him repeatedly, which seemed much to divert him.

We had a great deal of interesting communication in the course of our drive, I only wish my memory could enable me to write down more accurately many of Mr Wordsworth's remarks; what he said on the state of Ireland I particularly wish I could have noted down, but from my ignorance of the subject I think I had better not attempt it, I might mistake and certainly should mar what was so beautiful; his eloquence was remarkable, for he became quite animated with his subject, and his language appeared to me so elegant and choice, that I could have listened to him for hours, it seemed to flow like the most melodious harmony on the Ear, it was at the same time very energetic and forcible. Major C[1] [was] equally struck by his Eloquence, and remarked that for the brilliancy of his language and the refinement of his taste he reminded him more of Ld Wellesley than any one he had ever seen, and though he had heard the opinion of many able and learned statesmen on the affairs of Ireland he had never heard the matter more ably treated, for Mr Wordsworth (he said) appeared thoroughly to have investigated the subject, and to have obtained a very *just* opinion of the character of the nation. This Major C was the better able to judge of from his long residence among them. He regretted that Mr Wordsworth could not take an active part in the adjustment of affairs in that unhappy country.

Mr W. told us he had ever taken a lively interest in her situation and had for many years profoundly studied her politics[2]

[1] Probably Major Campbell, a friend of the Ricketts family (see *MW*, p. 259).

[2] For W. W.'s long-standing views on the Irish problem, see Alan G. Hill, 'Wordsworth and the Two Faces of Machiavelli', *RES* xxxi (1980), pp. 285–304.

and therefore felt authorized to speak as decidedly as he did. In a conversation Mr Wordsworth had many years ago with Mr Tennant[1] on the Catholic Emancipation Question, the latter was so much struck by the force of Mr W.'s remarks, that he made notes at the time of them. He had quite lately called on Mr W. and told him that the words he had uttered at that time seemed to have been delivered in a prophetic spirit, so exactly has the result of that measure proved as Mr W. foretold it wd do. Our conversation shortly afterwards turned upon *Jealousy*. Mr Wordsworth defined my own feeling on this subject so completely and we agreed so well upon it, that we gradually unburthened our hearts to each other and became the best of friends, and *I* felt proud to think I should now have such high authority to bring forward when I am next attacked on this point. He confessed it to be a weakness that poor human nature was heir to, for he believed no strong affection existed without a tinge of it. '*I* speak feelingly (he said) for I certainly plead guilty to this weakness, not that I have ever felt it to that degree as to cause any real uneasiness, but I have felt sensitive when I have even been overlooked by those around me in perhaps a trifle, having lived all my life so much in the society of *ladies* perhaps I have been spoilt on this subject and am the more alive to any little oversight on their part.' Yet he said although he was pleading guilty to this weakness, he was by no means excusing Jealousy, for it was a fearful passion and one that required a constant and vigilant watchfulness of heart to be kept under control. In another conversation on the same subject he observed that he never could *doubt* the affection of those he loved, as he had heard some people do, this was suggested to his mind [by] those lines of his own

> 'A well of love—it may be deep,
> I trust it is,—and never dry,'[2]

---

[1] Sir James Emerson Tennent, 1st Bart. (1804−69): author of *A Picture of Greece in 1825*, based on his own travels, 1824−5, when he met Byron; *Letters from the Aegean*, 2 vols., 1829; and *A History of Modern Greece, from its conquest by the Romans . . . to the present time*, 2 vols., 1830. He was M. P. for Belfast from 1832, supporting the policy of Grey, and then Peel, and resolutely opposing the repeal of the Union: later (1841−3) he was Secretary to the India Board, See Henry Thomas Ryall, *Portraits of Eminent Conservatives and Statesmen* [1836, etc.].

[2] *A Complaint* (*PW* ii. 34), ll. 13−14.

from 'the Complaint' which he repeated to us with much feeling. These doubts he said he could not enter into, but at the same time he certainly did like a demonstrative affection, a living principle of action. He could not he said express it better than he had done in that same poem

> 'Now, for that consecrated fount
> Of *murmuring, sparkling living* love.'

This was what he liked to see, for (he said) I may compare it to the Sun. We should not be satisfied if it remained continually under a Cloud, we could feel assured it *was* there, but we should sadly want its cheering rays, its glowing beams, to brighten our path and give life and animation to our hopes; and thus with affection, he liked to see it glowing and 'sparkling' testifying itself in the every day *nothings* of life. I cannot attempt to recollect his exact words on the subject but this was the general meaning of it.

We parted with one of our party, Mr John Wordsworth, shortly after leaving Coniston. He was advised by his Uncle to walk over one of the mountains which would furnish him with a beautiful View of the surrounding country, and we were to meet him at Seathwaite, *our* object being to trace the course of the Duddon,

> 'For Duddon, long-loved Duddon (was our) theme,'[1]

and could ever people have been more happy than we were to have visited these interesting scenes under the guidance of him who had immortalized them?

We soon had a splendid view of the Sea, stretching out in the horizon. The tower of Broughton lay before us, its picturesque Castle in the foreground, the Broughton Sands extended some miles out into the Sea; and here we first beheld Duddon emptying itself into the mighty main. This view was magnificent, on leaving it and following the course of the river, the character of the country varied extremely, all was retired and peaceful, the rich and extensive Vale of Donnerdale was before us, with beautiful hills on each side covered with rich verdure. The river became in parts much narrower and at times we lost sight of it, then it would appear again wending silently and peacefully along.

---

[1] See *The River Duddon* (*PW* iii. 246), Sonnet I, l. 14.

'The old inventive Poets, had they seen
Or rather felt, the entrancement that detains
Thy waters, Duddon! mid these flowery plains;
The still repose, the liquid lapse serene,
Transferred to bowers imperishably green,
Had beautified Elysium!' Son. 20.

We reached Ulpha I think about 2 oclock, and here we
determined to halt and recruit exhausted nature. We left the
carriage, at a little Inn, and transported our [selves] to a little
sunny bank in Ulpha Kirk Yard. . . .[*Here the Journal breaks off*]

INDEX

Abbotsford, 270, 562, 569, 577.

Abbeville, 379.

Abercromby, Ralph, 408 and n.

Adare, Viscount, *see* Quin, Edward Richard Wyndham.

Acland, Sir Peregrine, Bart., 205 and n., 286 and n.

Addington Park (Surrey), 452, 453, 459, 466, 478, 479.

Addison, Richard (of Gray's Inn), 248, 251, 252, 263, 266, 268.

Aders, Charles, 262, 315.

— Mrs. Elizabeth, 315.

Aglionby, Major Francis, *Letter to*: 535; 8 and n.

Ainsworth, Harrison, 255n.

Airy, Professor George Biddell, *Letter to*: 544; 545.

Aix-en-Provence, 390, 391.

Akenside, Mark, Dyce's edition, 28 and n., 31, 502 and n.; *On Recovering from a Fit of Sickness*, 43 and n.

Albano, 394; lake of, 403; 405, 410.

Alford, Revd. Henry, *Letter to*: 94; *The School of the Heart*, 94 and n.

Alfoxden (Som.), 287, 640.

Allonby (Cumb.), 277.

Allsop, Thomas, *Letters, Conversations, and Recollections of S. T. Coleridge*, 134 and n., 148 and n.

Ambleside, 181, 204, 283; Book Club, 605.

American Biblical Repository, 665 and n.

Amsterdam, 419.

Anderson, Dr. Robert, 136 and n.

Anne (servant at Rydal Mount), 67, 69, 73, 74, 82, 83, 87, 373.

Anster, John, *Letter to*: 80; his translation of *Faust*, 80 and n.

Antibes, 391.

Antwerp, 432, 436.

Appleby, 102.

Armathwaite (Cumb.), 182.

Armstrong, John (poet), 136 and n.

Arnold, Dr. Thomas, his political views, 14–15; *Principles of Church Reform*, 175 and n.; a member of London University Senate, 523 and n.; *History of Rome*, 573; 284, 331, 344, 355, 367, 369, 518, 526, 602–3, 651, 657, 658, 662, 708.

— Mrs., 175, 299, 355, 370, 719.

Arnolds, the, 341 and n., 701, 708.

Arno (river), 405, 406, 408.

Askew, Eleonora ('Bella'), Mrs. Washington, 244 and n.

Athenaeum (Club), 437, 665.

Athenaeum, The, 162.

Atherley, Mr., 226 and n.

Atkinson, Agnes, 144.

Attwood, Matthias, M.P., 547 and n., 569 and n.

— William, M.P., 547 and n.

Augsburg, 429, 432, 436.

Augustus Caesar, 390.

Ausonius, 334 and n.

Avignon, 355, 389, 390.

B., Mr., *Letter to*: 40 and n.

Baden, 60.

Baillie, Joanna, 272 and n., 434.

Bangor, 281.

Bathurst, Dr. Henry, Bishop of Norwich, 179 and n.

Baudouins, the, 42n., 385 and n., 534, 628n.

Bavaria, Queen Dowager of, 167 and n.

Beattie, James, Dyce's edition, 28 and n.; *Judgment of Paris*, 136 and n.; *The Minstrel*, 137.

Index

Beaumont, Constance, 460 and n., 479, 658.
— Sir George, 7th Bart., 98; his picture, 306; 396, 398, 560−1, 658.
— Sir George, 8th Bart., *Letters to*: 211, 459; 232, 319, 330, 333, 370, 371, 658.
— William Francis (brother), death of, 370 and n., 371.
— William (W. W.'s godson), 460, 478.
Beauvais (Cathedral), 379.
Beckett, Sir John, Bart., M.P., 29 and n., 376.
— Lady Ann, 98 and n., 376.
Bedingfield, Mrs. Mary, 255 and n., 256, 296, 300.
Bell, Sir Charles, *Letter to*: 310; 308, at Rydal 310.
— Lady, 311.
— George, *Descriptive and Other Miscellaneous Pieces*, 128 and n.
Bell Brothers and Co. (stock-brokers), *Letter to*: 46; 54, 260, 264, 448, 452, 458.
Benn, Joseph (land agent), *Letter to*: 101.
Benson, Revd. Christopher, 248 and n.
Bentinck, Lady Frederick, *Letters to*: 79, 475; 98, 113, 173, 230, 315, 323, 363−4, 375, 530, 638.
Bentley, Dr. Richard, *Dissertation on the Epistles of Phalaris*, 503.
Beresford, William Carr, Viscount Beresford, 247 and n.
Bergamo, 409, 416, 435, 438.
Betty (servant at Greta Hall), 75.
Birmingham, 47, 290, 315, 324, 469, 496, 673, 675, 679.
Blackwood, William, *Letters to*: 255, 296; 517.
Blackwood's Magazine, 52, 296, 297, 517.
Blakesley, Revd. Joseph William, 241 and n.

Blamire, Thomas, 161 and n.
Blessington, Marguerite, Countess of, 233 and n.
Bligh, John, 6th Earl of Darnley, 448 and n.
Blomfield, Dr. Charles James, Bishop of London, 18, 62.
Bologna, 409, 415, 416, 435, 595, 620.
Bolton, John (of Storrs), 36, 86, 188, 197, 198, 329, 361; his death 368; legacy to W. W., 433n.
— Mrs., 197, 198, 433.
Bonaventura, St., 616 and n.
Bootle (Cumb.), new church, 181 and n., 186.
Bosanquet, Sir John Bernard, 633 and n.
Bossuet, Jacques Bénigne, 383.
Boswell, James, *Life of Johnson*, 149 and n., 176.
Boulogne, 284, 370.
Bowles, Caroline (later Mrs. Southey), her poems, 296 and n.; marries Southey, 643 and n.; 729, 735, 739−40, 741, 755.
— William Lisle, *Letter to*: 685.
Bowness, 12, 175; new school, 188; 278, 303, 476.
Boxall, William (later Sir William), R.A., 262, 280 and n.
Bradbury and Evans (printers), 367, 621.
Brathay, new church, 181 and n., 204, 294.
— (river), 294.
Bremen, 30.
Brentano, Clemens, 427 and n.
Brescia, 409, 416.
Brigham, parish, 103, 104, 171; new rectory for John W., 290, 341; dissenters in, 340; typhus in, 586; 109, 477, 728, 730, 734.
Brinsop Court (Herefordshire), 280, 364, 367, 396, 398, 408, 416, 451, 468, 497, 521, 548, 585, 737.
Bristol, 290, 312, 395, 443, 723.

768

Index

Compton, Spencer, 2nd Marquess of Northampton, 223 and n., 251, 501; at Rydal Mount 636; 655.

Coniston, 90, 759, 760, 764.

Connelly, Pierce, 250 and n.

Constable, John, R.A., *English Landscape*, 254, 262–3 and n., 270; subscription to buy *The Cornfield*, 458 and n.

Conway (Caern.), 281.

Cookson, Elizabeth, 183, 277; copying *The Prelude*, 691 and n., 693.

— Hannah, 737.

— Henry, 469 and n.

— William Strickland, *Letters to*: 231, 375, 608, 613; 148, 184, 227, 244, 248, 252, 260, 268, 315, 338, 370, 371, 377–8, 434, 460, 582, 622, 631.

Copyright Bills, 498n., 517, 520, 535, 536–46, 548, 550, 552, 553, 554, 557–8, 565, 567, 569, 572, 575, 577, 580, 584, 596, 600n., 602, 606, 607, 615, 623, 648, 659, 663, 665, 669, 671, 680, 731 and n.

Cornwall, 324.

Cottesmore, 80, 375.

Cottle, Joseph, *Letters to*: 442, 688; *Early Recollections*, 313 and n., 443; 726.

Courier, The, 589.

Courtenay, Francis Foljambe, *Letter to*: 363.

— Philip, *Letter to*: 131; 29, 46, 53, 54, 78, 118, 122, 202, 207, 212, 215, 217, 224, 226, 227, 229, 231, 232, 239, 240, 244, 245, 248, 251, 254, 260, 264, 265, 268, 273, 370, 371, 389, 434, 440, 441, 458, 582, 606, 609, 614, 691, 744.

— Miss, her album, 241.

Coventry, 43.

Cowley, Abraham, 752.

Cowper, William, Southey's edition, 99, 100 and n., 434, 463; 126, 483, 510

Crabbe, George (poet), Murray's edition, 149 and n.; 348, 540, 560.

— George (jnr.), 222, 226.

Crackanthorpe, Sara (W. W.'s cousin), 261 and n., 485, 507.

— William (W. W.'s cousin), 261 and n., 645, 646.

Cumberland, election, 8n., 14.

Cunningham, Allan, *Letter to*: 32; his edition of Burns, 32; 561 and n.

— Revd. John William, 271 and n.

Curwen, Charles, 151 and n.

— Edward Stanley, 628, 631.

— Mrs., 141.

— Henry (of Bellisle and Workington Hall), 51, 324, 433, 448, 469, 511.

— Mrs. Henry, 89, 141, 146, 151, 341, 433, 505.

— Revd. Henry, 141, 342 and n.

— Mrs., 141 and n.

— Jane, 141.

Darley, George, 224 and n.,

Dashwood, Mrs., 542 and n.

Davidson, Mrs. (of Worcester), 674.

Davy, Sir Humphry, 270 and n.

— Lady, 284, 697.

— Dr. John, *Letters to*: 89, 252, 719; 267, 270, 271, 311, 447, 448.

— Mrs. 719.

Delaroche, Paul, *The Earl of Strafford on his Way to Execution*, 381 and n.

Delhi Gazette, 667.

Denison, Dr. Edward, Bishop of Salisbury, 179n., 697.

De Quincey, Thomas, 201.

Derby, 274.

Derbyshire Guide, 527.

Derwent, river (Cumb.), 37, 193, 342, 469.

Devil's Bridge (Card.), 281.

Dieppe, 359, 369.

Disraeli, Benjamin, M. P., 174 and n.

D'Israeli, Isaac, *Curiosities of Literature*, 504 and n.

Distington (Cumb.), 186.

771

779

Index

Mayer, Enrico, 412 and n., 707 and n., 708, 709, 715.

Melbourne, Lord (Prime Minister), 62; trial of, 260 and n.

Merewether, Revd. Francis, *Letter to*: 180; *Popery, a new religion*, 180 and n.; 211, 215, 220; at Rydal Mount, 470, 476, 478; his pamphlet, 533 and n.

— Mrs., 211, 220, 470, 476, 478.

— Henry Alworth, 220 and n.

Michelangelo, 612, 619; his sonnet, 708.

Middleham Hall (nr. Durham), 72 and n.

Middleton, Thomas, 503.

Milan, 284, 404, 409, 410, 416–18, 421, 435, 620.

Mildert, William Van, Bishop of Durham, death of, 179 and n.

Milnes, Richard Monckton, *Letters to*: 539, 579; *Poems of Many Years*, 571 and n., 579, 582, 604; at Rydal Mount, 726; 541.

Milnthorpe, new church at, 181 and n.

Milton, John, his sonnets, 49; 54, 98, 126; *Paradise Lost*, quoted 150, 616, cited 411, W. W.'s copy 756; in Italy, 470–1; 486, 574.

Mitford, John, his edition of Gray, 31 and n.

Modena, 409, 416.

Molière, 383.

Monkhouse, John (of the Stow, M. W.'s cousin), 169, 176, 280, 299, 457, 462, 496.

— Mary, 169 and n., 457.

Monmouth, 280, 548.

Montagu, Basil, *Letters to*: 1, 133, 237; his edition of Bacon, 1; 227, 273.

— Montagu, *Letter to*: 724; his translation of Schiller, 724 and n.

Monteagle, Lord, *see* Spring Rice, Thomas.

Monte Cavo, 402, 405.

Montgomery, James, *Letter to*: 326; *Wanderer of Switzerland*, 326; 308.

— Robert, *Letter to*: 23; *Selections from*, 23 and n.; *Omnipresence of the Deity*, 23 and n., 24 and n.

Montreuil, 379.

Moore, Thomas, 685 and n.

— Mrs. 685 and n.

Morning Chronicle, 261 and n.

Morning Post, 29, 563, 589, 590, 606, 670, 707, 718.

Morvonnais, Hippolyte de la, his translations of W. W., 246n., 348 n.

Moxon, Edward, *Letters to*: 6, 49, 81, 93, 113, 119, 120, 130, 133, 143, 147, 162, 163, 164, 210, 279, 281, 300, 304, 317, 336, 338, 346, 352, 420, 430, 462, 505, 518, 531, 570, 591, 617, 621, 623, 646, 676, 711, 720, 732, 733, 738, 745, 746; his sonnets, 49, 81, 150; offers terms for new edition, 231, 232, 233, 239, 240; terms accepted, 241, 242, 296; in France with W. W., 378–387; 3, 48, 86, 117, 121, 122, 143, 144, 173, 184, 191, 200, 208, 210, 215, 216, 221, 225, 227, 243, 246, 247, 248, 251, 253, 260, 263, 269, 271, 273, 274, 296, 321, 335, 354, 359, 367, 370, 371, 393, 413, 439, 448, 449, 451, 452, 458, 460, 497, 521, 530, 542, 595, 604, 611, 644, 649, 651, 675, 728, 732, 742.

— Mrs., 7, 82, 113, 120, 123, 126, 676.

— Emma, 279, 676.

Muleen, Mrs. J. M., *Letter to*: 527.

Munich, 409, 414, 418, 421, 425, 431, 432, 435, 436, 437, 616.

Murray, John (publisher), editions of Crabbe and Boswell's *Johnson*, 149 and n; 560, 578.

— Miss, *Letter to*: 147.

Naples 280, 387, 394, 398, 402, 419, 423, 466, 488, 642.

780

Wordsworth, Charles (*cont.*):
chester and marriage, 95, 156;
candidate for Harrow, 193 and n.;
Notes on Horace, 638 and n.; 51,
108, 187, 189, 209, 262, 336, 341,
448, 451, 456, 471, 472, 492, 650,
697, 698, 729, 730.
— Mrs. Charles, 344, 471, 487, 650;
death of, 695 and n.
— Charles (W.W.'s grandson), 743
and n.
— Dr. Christopher (W. W.'s brother), *Letters to*: 67, 95, 323, 698;
Christian Institutes, 341 and n.,
346; *The Ecclesiastical Commission
and the Universities*, 468 and n.,
471; health, 471, 472; 9, 21, 29,
34, 171, 187, 207, 214, 220, 232,
262, 320, 327, 336, 370, 371, 487,
492, 495, 504, 507, 552, 748.
— Christopher (C.W.'s son), *Letters
to*: 50, 107, 165, 188, 340, 376,
468, 544, 629, 637, 648, 748; his
Ode, 95 and n.; public orator at
Cambridge, 165, 177, 179; appointed headmaster of Harrow,
196 and n., 203; *Athens and Attica*,
262 and n., 341, 638; marriage,
629, 637, 648 and n., 649; defends
extension of copyright, 650;
*Greece:Pictorial, Descriptive, and
Historical*, 695 and n., 728—9; 108,
220, 223, 224, 233, 236, 262, 267,
272, 273, 274, 336, 376, 384, 395,
401, 408, 411, 419, 471, 472, 532,
563, 645, 698, 722, 738—9, 745.
— Mrs. Christopher, *Letter to*: 728;
649, 701.
— Dorothy (W.W.'s sister), *Letters
to*: 373, 385, 389.
Writings and interests: her
verses, 101, 299, 455—6, 473; *Recollections of a Tour Made in
Scotland, 1803*, 206 and n., 245 and
n., 495 and n., 505—6; on the
present of a picture, 50; her
memory for poetry, 79, 98; her

faculties of mind, 83, 96—7, 98,
653; asks for Norfolk beefins, 123;
receives present of poultry, 140—
1; hopes to go to Cambridge, 189;
her own view of her illness, 189,
472; writes to W. W., 224; reading newspapers, 300; writes letter
of condolence, 331; receives
legacy, 520; visit to Thelwall with
W. W. (1798), 640.
Health: bilious fever, 2; 6, 11,
35, 42, 47, 49, 51, 53; declining,
57, 58, 59, 60, 61, 62, 63, 65, 67,
68, 69, 72, 73, 74; symptoms, 78;
81, 82, 83, 85, 87; opium reduced,
89, 100, 110; 112, 115, 121, 131,
133; long term effects, 140, 144,
147, 152, 155, 158, 159, 161, 166,
172; walking again, 181, 183, 187,
189, 190; in the garden, 199, 202;
205, 226; in merlin chair in the
garden, 276; 281, 286, 290, 316,
343, 487, 501, 507, 544, 585, 637,
665, 693, 730, 737.
— Dorothy ('Dora', W. W.'s
daughter). *Letters to*: 235, 371,
372, 386, 404, 409, 415, 431, 441,
450, 452, 476, 480, 488, 524, 528,
548, 550, 672, 686, 690, 692, 702;
health, 2, 11, 35, 38, 42, 44—5, 47,
49, 50, 53, 58, 59, 60, 61, 62, 63,
66, 67, 68, 69, 72, 73, 74, 78, 81,
82, 83, 85, 87, 89, 96, 100, 107,
112, 115, 118, 133, 141, 147, 152,
155, 158, 159, 161, 166, 172, 185,
199, 205, 222, 230—1, 235, 239,
242—3, 247, 249, 252—3, 260—1,
268, 271, 276—7, 284, 286, 290,
299, 310, 312, 316, 319, 330, 341,
343, 360, 363—4, 368, 370, 397,
399, 421, 434, 439, 440, 441, 447,
448, 449, 610, 635, 637, 654, 660,
665, 709, 748; new carriage, 226;
at Leamington, 355, 361, 362,
363, 376; at Rugby, 371, 375,
376; acts as trustee, 377—8; at
Chatham, 446—53; at Brinsop,

Wordsworth, William (*cont.*):
episcopacy, 179; on popular election to benefices, 200; on religion in Cockermouth, 357; on the proper ascendancy of the Church in education, 709, 714 and n., 715.

Views on literature: on Robert Montgomery's poems, 24; on the verdict of posterity, 25; on his own writings, 44; praises verses by Simms, 46; on Moxon's sonnets, 49, 81; his aversion to annuals, 55; on Alford's *School of the Heart*, 94; on Southey's *Life of Wesley*, 100; sends Lamb's letter with omissions, 113; on Chiabrera's epitaphs, 114–15; on Talfourd's *Ion*,125–6; on the achievements of poets in old age, 126; admires Trench's poems, 129; on Mrs. Hemans, 139 and n., 491; on publishing Lamb's, and his own, letters, 133; on the letters of S.T.C., 134 and n., 148 and n. 443; on the letters of deceased authors, 144, 624–5; praises Lamb's poems, 148; on the sonnet, 150; on Keble's style, 192; on imitating the Classics, 192; commends Mrs. Bedingfield's tale, 255; on James Montgomery's poems, 326; on Shenstone's *Schoolmistress*, 348; on Crabbe, 348; praises Reed's edition, 445; on authors' influence, 446; on Gray, 464; on E. Q.'s poetry, 464–5; on Emmeline Fisher's poems, 485–6, 490–2; on writing criticism, 509; on the memoirs of himself by Hall and Chorley, 504, 516; on Sir Walter Scott, 559–60; on Hazlitt, 594; on cheap books, 599; on writers and posterity, 661–2; on Chaucer, 756.

Works, General: on Hine's *Selections*, 8, 163; on French 'piracies', 93, 541; plans to change

publisher, 178, 191; Longman's proposals, 226, 230, 236, 240; Moxon's terms, 231, 232, 233, 240, accepted 241, 242; poems translated into French, 246 and n., illustrated 383; revises poems for 1836 edition, 282 and n., 292–3, 297, 299, 300, 315, 337, 338, 344, 355; growing reputation, 293; illustrations for poems, 318; engraving of Chantrey's bust as frontispiece, 319, 330, 333; attempt at new national anthem, 474, 490; on Johnson's influence on himself, 492; projects one-volume edition, 506, 514, 518, 520, 647 and n., 650; his early imitations of Juvenal, 516; contributions to *Morning Post*, 589; translates sonnet by Michelangelo, 708–10; Hindu translation of a sonnet, 733; attaches little importance to his own works, 751–2; contributes to *Chaucer's Poems Modernized*, 755 and n., 756.

POETRY:

Ecclesiastical Sketches, proposed republication, 337; 344, 352.

Excursion, The, 91, 148, 190, 191, 244, 266, 282, 309; revised 318, 350; 352, 509, 565, 583n.; new edition proposed, 675 and n.; 728, 732, 754.

Lyrical Ballads (Philadelphia edition), 750.

Memorials of a Tour in Italy, 1837, 643 and n., 644, 666 and n.

Poetical Works (Boston edition), 321 and n.

— (1827), 239, 246.

— (1832), 91, 122, 190.

— (New Haven edition), 351 and n.

— (Philadelphia edition), 444 and n., 445, 474, 647 and n.

— (1836), 226, 241, 248, 262, 266, 284, 296, 307, 309, 311,